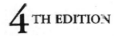

4TH EDITION

THEORY AND PRACTICE OF COUNSELING AND PSYCHOTHERAPY

GERALD COREY is Professor and Coordinator of the Human Services Program and Professor of Counseling at California State University at Fullerton. He received his doctorate in counseling from the University of Southern California. He is a licensed psychologist; is a Diplomate in Counseling Psychology, American Board of Professional Psychology; is registered as a National Health Service Provider in Psychology; is a National Certified Counselor; and is a licensed marriage, child, and family counselor. He is a Fellow of the American Psychological Association (Counseling Psychology). In addition to coordinating an undergraduate program in human services, Jerry teaches courses each semester in theories and techniques of counseling, professional ethics, the counseling profession, and group counseling, and he trains and supervises students in group work. With his colleagues he has conducted workshops in the United States, Germany, Belgium, Mexico, and China, with a special focus on training in group counseling. He regularly presents lectures and workshops for professional organizations, state and national conventions, and universities. Along with his wife, Marianne Schneider Corey, and other colleagues, he offers weeklong residential personal-growth groups as well as training and supervision workshops each summer in Idyllwild, California. In his leisure time Jerry enjoys traveling, bicycle riding, and hiking in the mountains.

Other recent books he has authored or co-authored (all published by Brooks/Cole Publishing Company) are:

- *Case Approach to Counseling and Psychotherapy,* Third Edition (1991)
- *I Never Knew I Had a Choice,* Fourth Edition (1990)
- *Theory and Practice of Group Counseling,* Third Edition (and *Manual*) (1990)
- *Becoming a Helper* (1989)
- *Group Techniques,* Revised Edition (1988)
- *Issues and Ethics in the Helping Professions,* Third Edition (1988)
- *Groups: Process and Practice,* Third Edition (1987)

4 TH EDITION

THEORY AND PRACTICE OF COUNSELING AND PSYCHOTHERAPY

GERALD COREY

California State University, Fullerton

*Diplomate in Counseling Psychology,
American Board of Professional Psychology*

Brooks/Cole Publishing Company
Pacific Grove, California

Brooks/Cole Publishing Company
A Division of Wadsworth, Inc.

Printed in the United States of America
10   9   8   7   6   5

Library of Congress Cataloging-in-Publication Data

Corey, Gerald.
    Theory and practice of counseling and psychotherapy / Gerald
Corey. — 4th ed.
        p.   cm.
    Includes bibliographical references.
    ISBN 0534133142
    1. Counseling.   2. Psychotherapy.   I. Title.
BF637.C6C574   1990
158′.3—dc20   90-33124
                                                                  CIP

Sponsoring Editor: *Claire Verduin*
Editorial Assistant: *Gay C. Bond*
Production Editor: *Fiorella Ljunggren*
Manuscript Editor: *William Waller*
Permissions Editor: *Marie DuBois*
Interior and Cover Design: *E. Kelly Shoemaker*
Interior Illustrations: *John Foster*
Photo Editor: *Ruth Minerva*
Typesetting: *Progressive Typographers*
Cover Printing: *Phoenix Color Corporation*
Printing and Binding: *Arcata Graphics/Fairfield*
(Credits continue on p. 477.)

TO FOUR SIGNIFICANT WOMEN IN MY LIFE:

*To my mother, Josephine, who retains her wit and vitality
and who knows how to grow old gracefully*

*To my wife and best friend, Marianne
who radiates presence, compassion, and honesty*

*To my daughter Heidi, whose creativity and charisma
are expressed in the field of drama*

*To my daughter Cindy, whose warm and engaging manner
is a delight to the elderly with whom she works*

PREFACE

This book is intended for counseling courses for undergraduate and graduate students in psychology, counselor education, social work, and the human-services and mental-health professions. It surveys the major concepts and practices of the contemporary therapeutic systems and addresses some ethical and professional issues in counseling practice. The book aims at teaching students how to select wisely from various theories and techniques, which will help them develop a personal style of counseling.

I have found that students appreciate an overview of the divergent contemporary approaches to counseling and psychotherapy. They also consistently say that the first course in counseling means more to them when it deals with them as persons. Therefore, I stress the practical application of the material and encourage reflection, so that using this book can be both a personal and an academic growth experience.

In this new fourth edition every effort has been made to retain the major qualities that students and professors have found helpful in the previous editions: the succinct overview of the key concepts of each theory and their implications for practice, the straightforward and personal style, and the book's comprehensive scope. Care has been taken to present the theories in an accurate and fair way. I have also attempted to be simple, clear, and concise. Because many students want suggestions for supplementary reading as they study each therapy approach, I have included a reading list for each chapter.

The aim of this edition is to update the material and refine existing discussions. There is a change in the chapter order from earlier editions. After the initial chapter, which puts the book into perspective, students are introduced to the topic of the counselor as a person and as a professional in Chapter 2. It seemed fitting that this material be dealt with before introducing theoretical concepts and counseling techniques, because the role of the counselor as a person is highlighted throughout the text. Chapter 3 offers an overview of current ethical and professional issues facing counseling professionals. It has been updated and largely rewritten to focus on key controversies in counseling practice. I have selected those ethical issues that tend to generate the most interesting discussions in my classes. This new organization of chapters encourages students to think about basic issues in the counseling profession early, and it also provides a mental set for their active and personal involvement in the book and the course.

New to this edition is a brief discussion of the contributions and limitations of each of the nine theories from a multicultural perspective. Both the client's and the counselor's cultural backgrounds are significant factors that influence the therapeutic relationship, and this edition takes increased note of cultural factors. As readers review the theories, they are challenged to think of ways of adapting the techniques from the various approaches to the unique needs of the person in the environment.

There are other new features in some of the theory chapters: (1) More attention has been given to a clear presentation of the techniques of *psycho-analytic* therapy; coverage of contemporary psychoanalytic thinking has been increased, and a discussion of borderline and narcissistic personality disorders has been added. (2) The *Adlerian* chapter has been rewritten to give more attention to the phases of the counseling process and the application of techniques to various areas of counseling. (3) Considerable rewriting of the *person-centered approach* has been done, with increased attention to the influence of Carl Rogers, recent developments and applications, research issues, international perspectives, and implications of the approach for working with cultural diversity. (4) In the chapter on *behavior therapy* there is an updating of recent research findings, more coverage of specific behavioral techniques, and an expanded section describing Arnold Lazarus's multimodal therapy. (5) The chapter on *rational-emotive therapy* has been retitled to include other *cognitive-behavioral approaches,* reflecting the expanded and updated sections on Aaron Beck's cognitive therapy and Donald Meichenbaum's cognitive behavior modification. (6) The *reality-therapy* chapter has been virtually rewritten to bring readers up to date with the implications of control theory for this approach. The revision also provides a detailed description of the counseling environment and procedures of reality therapy, including special techniques such as paradoxical intervention.

The chapters on exististential therapy, Gestalt therapy, and transactional analysis have fewer changes, but they have been updated as deemed appropriate. The "Case of Stan" has been retained in Chapter 13, because it helps readers see the application of a variety of techniques at various stages in the counseling process with the same client. There is expanded coverage of the ways in which the nine different therapies could be applied to counseling Stan. Because I describe a basis for working with him by integrating the therapies, this chapter offers a good review of the various theories as applied to a case example.

The final chapter provides charts and other integrating material to help the student compare and contrast the nine approaches. There is more emphasis in this edition on providing a framework for a creative synthesis among the therapeutic models. More space has been given to the trend toward eclecticism. Students are given guidelines for beginning to formulate their own integration and personal philosophy of counseling that will incorporate the *thinking, feeling,* and *behaving* dimensions of human experience.

This text can be used in a flexible way. Some instructors will follow the new sequencing of chapters, as many have told me that they would prefer this revised organization. Other instructors will prefer to begin with the theory chapters and then deal later with the student's personal characteristics and ethical issues. They think that students are better able to look at their own impact on clients once they have been exposed to the theories. The topics can be covered in whatever order makes most sense for the way a course is taught. Readers are offered some suggestions for using this book at the end of Chapter 1.

In this edition I have made every effort to incorporate those aspects that have worked best in the courses on counseling theory and practice that I regularly teach. To help readers apply theory to practice, I have also revised the student manual, which is designed for experiential work. The *Manual for Theory and Practice of Counseling and Psychotherapy* still contains openended questions and cases, structured exercises, self-inventories, reading suggestions, and a variety of activities that can be done both in class and out of class. The fourth edition of the manual contains a structured overview and a glossary for each of the theories, chapter quizzes for assessing the level of student mastery of basic concepts, and suggestions for working with a single case (Stan) using each theory. The manual also contains both the 1988 AACD Ethical Standards and the 1989 APA Ethical Principles. Of course, a revised and updated *Instructor's Resource Manual* is available, which includes suggestions for teaching the course, class activities to stimulate interest, and a variety of test questions and final examinations. To complete this learning package, there is a newly revised and enlarged *Case Approach to Counseling and Psychotherapy* (Third Edition), which features several cases for each of the nine therapeutic approaches. Readers are provided with practical illustrations of the application of various techniques to these diverse cases. The casebook can either be used as a supplement to this book or stand alone for use in certain courses.

Some professors have found the textbook and the student manual to be ideal companions and realistic texts for a single course. Others like to use the textbook and the casebook as companions. And some use all three books as a package in their courses. The casebook can also be used in a case-management practicum or in fieldwork courses, because the cases include information extending from intake to termination. The integrated package affords instructors a great deal of versatility to adapt the materials to their particular style of teaching and to the special needs of their students.

ACKNOWLEDGMENTS

The suggestions I received from many of the readers of prior editions who had taken the time to complete the survey at the end of the book have been most helpful and are reflected in the fine-tuning of the present edition. Many people contributed ideas that have found their way into this fourth edition, all of whom are not possible to mention. I especially appreciate the time and efforts of the manuscript reviewers, who provided constructive criticism and supportive commentaries, as well as the feedback offered by those professors who have used the book. Those who reviewed the manuscript of this edition are Michael Dougherty of Western Carolina University; Roy D. McDonald of San Diego State University; Eileen S. Nelson of James Madison University; Jorja Manos Prover of

California State University at Fullerton; and Howard B. Smith of South Dakota State University.

The new material on multicultural counseling was reviewed by four of my colleagues at California State University at Fullerton: Mikel Garcia, Dolores Jenerson, George Williams, and Jerome Wright, and also by Paul Pedersen of Syracuse University, Noreen Mokuau of the University of Hawaii, and Man Ping Lam of Chinese University in Hong Kong.

Special thanks are extended to the following chapter reviewers for their insightful and valuable comments, most of which have been incorporated into this edition: William H. Blau of Patton State Hospital in California and J. Michael Russell of California State University at Fullerton (Chapter 4); Jim Bitter and Monford Sonstegard, both of California State University at Fullerton, and Don Dinkmeyer of the Communication and Motivation Training Institute in Coral Springs, Florida (Chapter 5); James L. Jarrett of the University of California at Berkeley and J. Michael Russell (Chapter 6); David J. Cain, editor of *Person-Centered Review* and a private practitioner in Carlsbad, California (Chapter 7); Joseph Zinker of the Gestalt Institute of Cleveland (Chapter 8); John Dusay, a private practitioner in San Francisco (Chapter 9); L. Sherilyn Cormier of the University of West Virginia, Alan E. Kazdin of Yale University, and Arnold A. Lazarus of Rutgers University (Chapter 10); Albert Ellis of the Institute for Rational-Emotive Therapy in New York and Linda Gilbert of the Institute for Rational-Emotive Therapy in Irvine, California (Chapter 11); and William Glasser of the Institute for Reality Therapy in Canoga Park, California, Ronald Harshman (formerly of the institute), and Robert Wubbolding of the Center for Reality Therapy in Cincinnati (Chapter 12).

Student reviewers who provided insightful comments are Michael Safko, Christine Heacox, Becky Mueller, Karen Cladis, and Katie Dutro, who also prepared the indexes. Their input helps keep the book practical and readable. I'd like to acknowledge Debbie DeBue, who painstakingly typed and checked the references and much of the manuscript.

This book is the result of a team effort, which includes the combined talents of several people in the Brooks/Cole family. Over the many years I appreciate the opportunity to continue to work with Claire Verduin, managing editor and psychology editor; with Fiorella Ljunggren, production services manager; and with William Waller, manuscript editor, who gives careful attention to the clarity, conciseness, and readability of my books. Their efforts, dedication, and extra time have certainly contributed to the quality of this book. With the professional assistance of these people the ongoing task of revising this book continues to bring more joy than pain.

Gerald Corey

CONTENTS

1

INTRODUCTION
AND OVERVIEW

INTRODUCTION

This book surveys nine approaches to counseling and psychotherapy. Instead of emphasizing the theoretical foundations of these models, it presents the basic concepts of each and discusses features such as the therapeutic process (including goals), the client/therapist relationship, and specific procedures used in the practice of counseling. The book will help you develop a balanced view of the major ideas of various therapists and the practical techniques they employ.

I encourage you to keep an open mind and to seriously consider both the unique contributions and the particular limitations of each therapeutic system presented in this book. From my perspective no single model is comprehensive enough to explain all facets of human experience. Although attempts have been made to integrate various approaches, those practitioners who align themselves with one theoretical viewpoint still tend to view their system as complete in itself. Some proponents operate on the assumption that their approach is the best available theory to guide practice. A psychoanalytic practitioner, for instance, may view behavior therapy as a technique-oriented, superficial therapy that cannot produce long-term changes in clients. Some behavior therapists, in turn, are convinced that psychoanalysis is based on unfounded premises and simply does not work. And some existential psychologists criticize both psychoanalytic therapy and behavior therapy on the ground that they are mechanistic, reductionistic, and deterministic and therefore are very limited in dealing with human struggles.

This book assumes that beginning students of counseling can start to acquire a counseling style tailored to their own personality if they familiarize themselves with the major approaches to therapeutic practice. I always emphasize to my students that they will not gain the knowledge and experience needed to synthesize various approaches merely by completing an introductory course in counseling theory. This process will take many years, with extensive study, training, and practical counseling experience. Nevertheless, I still recommend a personal synthesis as a framework for the professional education of counselors. The danger in presenting one model that all students are expected to advocate to the exclusion of other fruitful approaches is that beginning counselors will unduly limit their effectiveness with different clients. Valuable dimensions of human behavior can be overlooked if the counselor is restricted to a single theory.

On the other hand, an undisciplined eclectic approach can be an excuse for failing to develop a sound rationale for systematically adhering to certain concepts and to the techniques that are extensions of them. It is easy to pick and choose fragments from the various therapies that merely support one's biases and preconceptions. Nevertheless, a study of the various models presented in this book will show that a genuine integration of many of the approaches is possible. The last chapter presents a framework for developing such an integrative perspective.

As I continue to develop the material for this book, I become increasingly aware that each therapeutic approach has useful dimensions and that accepting the validity of one model does not necessarily imply a rejection of seemingly divergent models. It is not a matter of a theory's being "right" or "wrong," for each theory offers a unique contribution to understanding human behavior and has unique implications for counseling practice. It is clear that there is a place for theoretical pluralism.

WHERE I STAND

My own philosophical orientation is strongly influenced by the existential approach. Because techniques and procedures are not specified by this approach, I feel the freedom to draw techniques from the other models of therapy. I particularly like using role-playing techniques. I find that when people can reenact scenes from their lives, they become far more involved than when they merely report details or anecdotes about themselves. In addition, many techniques in my approach are derived from cognitive-behavioral therapy assertiveness training and social-skills training, behavior rehearsal, modeling, and a variety of coaching techniques.

I respect the psychoanalytic emphasis on early psychosexual and psychosocial development. I believe that one's past plays a crucial role in shaping one's current personality and behavior. Although I reject the deterministic notion that humans are the product of their early conditioning and, thus, a victim of their past, I think that an exploration of the past is essential, particularly to the degree that the past is related to present emotional or behavioral difficulties.

From the cognitive and behavioral therapies I value the focus on ways in which our thinking affects how we feel and how we behave. These therapies also give weight to current behavior. Although thinking and feeling are important dimensions, it can be a mistake to overemphasize them and not explore how clients are behaving. What people are doing often gives us a good clue to what they really want. I also value the emphasis on specific goals and on encouraging clients to formulate concrete aims for their own therapy sessions and in life. I find that "contracts" developed by clients are extremely useful, and I frequently either suggest specific "homework assignments" or ask my clients to devise their own. These devices extend the counseling sessions into their outside life. Although I accept the value of increasing clients' insight and awareness, I consider it essential that they put into practice what they are learning in therapy.

A related assumption of mine is that clients can exercise increasing freedom to choose their future. Although we are surely shaped by our social environment and although much of our behavior is a product of learning and conditioning, an increased awareness of these forces that have molded us allows us to transcend these influences. Most of the contemporary models of counseling and therapy operate on the basic assumption that clients are able to accept personal responsibility and that their failure to do so has largely resulted in their present emotional and behavioral difficulties.

This focus on acceptance of personal responsibility does not imply that we can be anything that we want. There are social, environmental, cultural, and biological realities that we need to accept. Admittedly, a restricted environmental background limits the range of our choices. What seems crucial is learning how to cope with the external and internal forces that limit our decisions and behavior. Thus, a comprehensive approach to counseling goes beyond focusing on our internal dynamics by addressing those environmental realities that influence us.

My philosophy of counseling does not include the assumption that therapy is exclusively for the "sick" and is aimed at "curing" psychological "ailments." I find that such a focus on psychopathology severely restricts therapeutic practice, mainly because it stresses one's deficits rather than one's strengths. Counselors with an Adlerian orientation contend that people are not emotionally sick and in dire need of curing; rather, people become discouraged and need encouragement. This is a positive and growth-oriented model that is focused on the future, on the goals that provide direction in life, and on the ability of clients to create their destiny. Counseling, then, is viewed as a vehicle for helping "normal" people get more from life. The clients with whom I work in group situations are, for the most part, healthy people who see counseling as a self-exploratory and personal-growth experience. With this population I find that the Adlerian, existential, person-centered, Gestalt, and rational-emotive and cognitive-behavioral perspectives offer valuable tools for helping people change.

The existential approach and person-centered therapy both emphasize the client/therapist relationship as the major factor that leads to constructive personal change. My experience continues to show me how important the therapeutic relationship is. The kind of person a therapist is, or the ways of being that he or she models, is the most critical factor that affects the client and promotes change. If practitioners possess wide knowledge, both theoretical and practical, yet lack human qualities of compassion, caring, good faith, honesty, realness, and sensitivity, they are merely technicians. In my judgment those who function exclusively as technicians do not make a significant difference in the life of their clients. Thus, it seems essential to me that counselors explore their own values, attitudes, and beliefs in depth and that they work to increase their own awareness. Throughout the book I encourage you to find ways of personally relating to each of the therapies. Unless you study and apply these therapeutic approaches to yourself personally, a superficial understanding is the best that you can hope for.

I see the process of psychotherapy as a dialogue and engagement between two persons. Therapists must be willing to remain open to their own growth and be willing to struggle in their life if they are to be believed by their clients. Why should clients seek therapists who are "finished products" and who do not do in their own life what they expect their clients to do in theirs? In short, counselors teach clients by the behavior they model.

Although I emphasize that the human qualities of a therapist are of primary importance, I do not think it is sufficient to be merely a good person with good intentions. To be effective, the therapist also requires supervised experiences in counseling and a knowledge of counseling theory and techniques. Further, it is essential to be well grounded in the various *theories of personality* and to learn how they are related to theories of counseling. Your conception of the person affects the interventions that you are likely to make. Because of psychoanalysts' view of human nature, they focus on techniques designed to tap the unconscious, for therapy is aimed at making unconscious material available to the person. These practitioners use interpretations as a way of fostering insight, which is seen as an essential part of therapeutic progress. The person-centered therapist, in contrast, holds that people can move forward in a constructive direction without interpretation or any other active intervention from the therapist. Thus, those who subscribe to this view of human nature tend not to rely on directive techniques, for they have faith in their clients' capacities for self-direction. Still another example of how therapists' conceptions of the person affect their interventions is provided by rational-emotive therapy. This approach, grounded in the assumption that people by nature tend to uncritically incorporate a host of irrational ideas about themselves and about life, emphasizes a therapeutic style characterized by forceful persuasion, active and directive teaching techniques designed to help clients attack these stubborn irrational notions, and a high degree of therapist confrontation to undermine the client's tendencies toward self-sabotage.

Depending on your view of personality and the theory of personality from which you are operating, you will select different forms of intervention. Another factor, of course, is the individual characteristics of the client. Some practitioners make the mistake of relying on one type of intervention (supportive, confrontational, information-giving, or some other) for most of the clients with whom they work. It is extremely important to be aware that different clients may respond to various types of intervention. Thus, practitioners must have a broad base of counseling techniques from which to draw what is best for an individual client, rather than forcing the client to fit their specialized form of intervention. Flexibility in adapting techniques is particularly important in working with clients who have diverse cultural backgrounds.

It is essential for counselors to develop sensitivity to cultural differences if they hope to make interventions that are congruent with the values of their clients. Counselors bring their own heritage with them to their work, so they must know how cultural conditioning has influenced the directions they take with their clients. Moreover, unless the social and cultural context of clients is taken into consideration, it is most difficult to appreciate the nature of their struggles. For instance, many counseling students have come to value characteristics such as making their own choices, expressing what they are feeling, being open and self-revealing, and striving for independence. Yet these characteristics may not be the goals of some of their clients. Certain cultures emphasize being emotionally reserved or being very selective about sharing personal concerns. Thus, counselors need to examine the assumptions they have made about the nature and functioning of therapy to determine if these assumptions are appropriate for culturally diverse populations. We will look at the various theories presented in this book in light of their applications in a multicultural society.

The principles of cultural sensitivity also have relevance for other special groups. Effective counseling takes into account differences in areas such as gender, class, age, and disability. All of these elements separate people into different groups with unique concerns.

SUGGESTIONS FOR USING THE BOOK

Here are some specific recommendations on how to get the fullest value from this book as you read. The personal tone of the book invites you to relate what you are reading to your own experiences. As you read Chapter 2, "The Counselor as a Person and as a Professional," begin the process of reflecting on your needs, motivations, values, and life experiences, considering how you are likely to bring the person you are becoming into your professional work. You will assimilate much more knowledge about the various therapies if you remain open as you read about them *and* if you make a conscious attempt to relate the key concepts of each model to your own life. You can make this material come alive for you if you apply the techniques you are studying to your personal growth. Chapter 2 can also help you think about how to use *yourself as a person* as your single most important therapeutic instrument. Merely memorizing the ideas and procedures of the models is of little value. What *will* make a difference is your ability to incorporate selected concepts and procedures into a personalized style of counseling that expresses your own uniqueness. This topic is worth considering in depth again after you have studied the therapy models in the later chapters. Chapter 3 deals with significant ethical issues in counseling practice, and it is useful to begin considering them early in the course. These issues include the rights and responsibilities of clients, the ethics of the client/therapist relationship, multicultural issues in counseling, and legal aspects of practice. You will be in a position to explore these issues in greater depth after you have been exposed to the counseling models, and thus a second reading of Chapter 3 will help you integrate theory with practice.

Students learn a lot by seeing a theory in action, preferably in a live demonstration or as part of experiential activities in which they function in the alternating roles of client and counselor. Many students find the case history of one client, "Stan" (Chapter 13), helpful to read *before* they study each therapy, because it gives an overview of how various therapists might view Stan and how they might proceed during the course of the sessions. I also present how I would work with Stan, suggesting concepts and techniques that I would draw on from each of the models. *This case should also be reread carefully after you have studied each of the therapies* and then again after you have completed studying all of them.

Next, and also before you study each therapy in depth in Chapters 4–12, I suggest that you at least skim Chapter 14, which is a comprehensive review of basic issues that cut across all nine of the theories you will study. I have attempted to show how an integration of these perspectives can form the basis for creating your own personal synthesis to counseling.

To provide you with a consistent framework for comparing and contrasting the various therapies, the nine theory chapters share a common format. This format includes a few notes on the personal history of the founder or another key figure; a brief historical sketch showing how and why each theory developed at the time it did; a discussion of the approach's key concepts; an overview of the therapeutic process (including the therapist's role and client's work); therapeutic techniques and procedures; a summary and evaluation; questions for reflection and discussion; suggestions of how to continue your learning about each approach; and suggestions for further reading.

OVERVIEW OF THE THEORY CHAPTERS

This section explains why I have selected the nine therapeutic approaches discussed in this book. Table 1–1 presents an overview of these approaches,

TABLE 1–1

Overview of Contemporary Counseling Models

Psychoanalytic psychotherapy	Key figure: Sigmund Freud. A theory of personality development, a philosophy of human nature, and a method of psychotherapy. Focus is on unconscious factors that motivate behavior. Attention is given to the events of first six years of life as determinants of the later development of personality.
Adlerian therapy	Key figure: Alfred Adler. Following Adler, Rudolf Dreikurs is credited with popularizing the approach in the United States. A growth model, it stresses taking responsibility, creating one's own destiny, and finding meaning and goals to give Lfe direction. Key concepts are used in most other current therapies.
Existential therapy	Key figures: Viktor Frankl, Rollo May, and Irvin Yalom. Reacts against the tendency to view therapy as a system of well-defined techniques. Stresses building therapy on the basic conditions of human existence, such as choice, freedom and responsibility to shape one's life, and self-determination. Focus is on the quality of the person-to-person therapeutic relationship.
Person-centered therapy	Founder: Carl Rogers. Originally a nondirective approach developed during the 1940s as a reaction against psychoanalysis. Based on a subjective view of human experiencing, it places more faith in and gives more responsibility to the client in dealing with problems.
Gestalt therapy	Founder: Fritz Perls. An experiential therapy stressing awareness and integration. Grew as a reaction against analytic therapy. Integrates functioning of body and mind.
Transactional analysis	Founder: Eric Berne. A model that leans toward cognitive and behavioral aspects. Designed to help people evaluate past decisions in light of their present appropriateness.
Behavior therapy	Key figures: Arnold Lazarus, Albert Bandura, Joseph Wolpe, Alan Kazdin. Application of the principles of learning to the resolution of specific behavioral disorders. Results are subject to continual experimentation. This technique is always in the process of refinement.
Rational-emotive therapy	Founder: Albert Ellis. A highly didactic, cognitive, action-oriented model of therapy that stresses the role of thinking and belief systems as the root of personal problems.
Reality therapy	Founder: William Glasser. Short-term, with focus on the present. Stresses a person's strengths. Basically, a way clients can learn more realistic behavior and thus achieve success.

which are explored in Chapters 4–12. I have classified them into three general categories.

First is the psychodynamic approach, based largely on insight, unconscious motivation, and reconstruction of the personality; it is the approach used in *psychoanalytic therapy*. The reason for including the psychoanalytic model (and placing it first) is its major influence on all of the other formal systems of psychotherapy. Some of the therapeutic models are basically extensions of psychoanalysis, others are modifications of analytic concepts and procedures, and still others are positions that emerged as a reaction against psychoanalysis. Many of the theories of counseling and psychotherapy have borrowed and integrated principles and techniques from the analytic approach. Thus, from a practical as well as a historical vantage point, this model continues to play an important role in contemporary psychotherapy.

The second category comprises the experiential and relationship-oriented therapies: the *existential approach,* the *person-centered approach,* and *Gestalt therapy*. The existential approach stresses a concern for what it means to be fully human. It suggests certain themes that are a part of the "human condition," such as freedom and responsibility, anxiety, guilt, awareness of being finite, creating a meaning in the world, and shaping one's future by making active choices. This approach is not a unified school of therapy with a clear theory and a systematic set of techniques. Rather, it is a philosophy of counseling that stresses the divergent methods of understanding the subjective world of the person. The person-centered approach, which is rooted in a humanistic philosophy, places emphasis on the basic attitudes of the therapist. It maintains that the quality of the client/therapist relationship is the prime determinant of the outcomes of the therapeutic process. Philosophically, this model assumes that clients have the capacity for self-direction without active intervention and direction on the therapist's part. It is in the context of a living and authentic relationship with the therapist that this growth force within the client is released. Another experiential approach is Gestalt therapy. It offers a range of techniques for helping clients focus on what they are experiencing now and become aware of the diversity of feelings within them at any moment.

Third are the cognitively oriented and behaviorally oriented "action therapies," which include *Adlerian therapy, transactional analysis, behavior therapy, rational-emotive and cognitive-behavioral therapy,* and *reality therapy*. There has been a reawakening of interest in Alfred Adler's ideas, and greater credit is being given to his contributions to all of the contemporary therapies. In the 1920s and 1930s Adler was truly a pioneering genius, and his approach was a precursor of many of the cognitive therapies that thrived in the 1980s. Transactional analysis, in turn, has contributed to the understanding of how people make early decisions in response to parental messages they receive. It stresses the "life script," or life plan, of individuals, and it focuses on their capacity to make new decisions that are more appropriate to their current level of maturity. The behavior therapies put a premium on *doing* and on taking steps to make concrete changes. A current trend in behavior therapy is toward paying increased attention to cognitive factors as an important determinant of behavior.

Rational-emotive therapy and cognitive therapy highlight the necessity of learning how to challenge irrational beliefs and automatic thoughts that lead to human misery. These systems are closely related to other cognitive-behavioral therapies and share many of the same concepts and techniques. These approaches are used to help people undermine their faulty and self-defeating assumptions and form a rational philosophy of life. Reality therapy also focuses on clients' current behavior. It stresses their personal responsibility for changing themselves by developing clear plans for new behaviors.

In my view practitioners need to pay attention to what their clients are *thinking, feeling,* and *doing*. Thus, a complete therapy system must address all three of these facets. Some of the therapies included in this book highlight the role that *cognitive factors* and *thinking* play in counseling; others place emphasis on the *experiential* aspects of counseling and the role of *feelings;* and others emphasize putting plans into *action* and learning by *doing*. Combining all of these dimensions provides the basis for a powerful and comprehensive therapy. If any of these dimensions is excluded, the therapy approach is incomplete.

RECOMMENDED SUPPLEMENTARY READINGS

A list of suggested readings follows the text of each chapter, so that you can deepen your knowledge of areas of special interest. Supplementary reading is encouraged, because the scope of this book necessitates focusing on only the highlights of each approach. Reading of primary sources will be especially valuable in rounding out your knowledge of those therapies that you find most meaningful. Following are a few books that are very useful as supplementary reading throughout the course.

Current Psychotherapies, edited by Raymond Corsini and Danny Wedding (F. E. Peacock, 1989), contains a comprehensive discussion of the nine major systems (plus some others), each written by either the founder or a key spokesperson. This collection of articles will give you another perspective on these therapies.

Case Studies in Psychotherapy, edited by Danny Wedding and Raymond Corsini (F. E. Peacock, 1989), is a collection of case histories that provides a cross section of contemporary therapeutic approaches. Each of the 12 cases presented is written by a key spokesperson of that approach.

Theories of Counseling and Psychotherapy by C. H. Patterson (Harper & Row, 1986), is a scholarly, in-depth treatment of most of the contemporary theoretical models. He also has useful chapters on eclectic psychotherapy and he does an excellent job of presenting the areas of convergence and divergence among current therapeutic models.

Manual for Theory and Practice of Counseling and Psychotherapy, by Gerald Corey (Brooks/Cole, 1991), is designed to help you integrate theory with practice and to make the concepts covered in this book come alive. It consists of self-inventories, overview summaries of the theories, a glossary of key concepts, study questions, issues and questions for personal application, activities and exercises, comprehension checks and quizzes, case examples, a code of professional ethics, and a list of professional organizations to contact for resources. The manual is fully coordinated with the textbook to make it a personal study guide.

Case Approach to Counseling and Psychotherapy, by Gerald Corey (Brooks/Cole,

1991), is structured along the same chapter lines as this textbook. Thus, if you want to focus more on case applications and see how each of the theories works in action, this casebook will be a handy supplement to the course. It follows one client, Ruth, as she experiences counseling from all of the therapeutic vantage points. Other cases are presented for each theory, and you are invited to test your thinking in applying techniques from the theories to a variety of cases.

2

THE COUNSELOR AS A PERSON AND AS A PROFESSIONAL

INTRODUCTION

In this chapter I ask you to examine my assumption that one of the most important instruments you have to work with as a counselor is *yourself as a person*. In preparing for counseling, you can acquire a knowledge of the theories of personality and psychotherapy, you can learn diagnostic and intervention techniques, and you can learn about the dynamics of human behavior. Although such knowledge and skills are essential, I do not believe that they are, by themselves, sufficient for establishing and maintaining effective therapeutic relationships. To every therapy session we bring our human qualities and the experiences that have influenced us. In my judgment this human dimension is one of the most powerful determinants of the therapeutic encounter that we have with clients. If we hope as counselors to promote growth and change in our clients, we must be willing to promote growth in our own life. Our most powerful source of influencing clients in a positive direction is our living example of who we are and how willing we are to continually struggle to live up to our potential.

A good way to begin your study of contemporary counseling theories is by reflecting on the personal issues that are raised in this chapter. Then, after you have studied the nine theories of counseling, this chapter deserves another reading. I suggest that you reevaluate ways in which you can work on your development as a person, considering especially your needs, motivations, values, and personality traits that could either enhance or interfere with your effectiveness as a counselor. By remaining open to self-evaluation, you not only expand your awareness of self but also build the foundation for developing your abilities as a professional. The theme of this chapter is that the *person* and the *professional* are intertwined entities that cannot be separated in reality.

PERSONAL CHARACTERISTICS OF THE EFFECTIVE COUNSELOR

The trend today is toward stressing the beliefs and behavior of the counselor. Much of the literature on counselor education emphasizes therapists' ability to look at, understand, and accept their own self as well as the self of the other person. It is the quality of the client/counselor relationship that seems to best facilitate growth in both parties in the relationship.

In summarizing 13 studies in five helping professions, Combs (1986) found clear distinctions between the characteristics of effective and ineffective helpers. What appears to make the difference is what helpers believe about empathy, self, human nature, and their own purposes. According to Combs, the studies suggest that the following beliefs are associated with success: Effective counselors are primarily concerned about how the world appears from the subjective vantage point of their clients. They hold positive beliefs about people, seeing them as trustworthy, capable, dependable, and friendly. They have a positive view of themselves and a confidence in their abilities. The interventions they make as counselors are based on their values.

THE AUTHENTICITY OF THE COUNSELOR

Therapy, because it is an intimate form of learning, demands a practitioner who is willing to shed stereotyped roles and be a real person in a relationship. It is precisely within the context of such a person-to-person relationship that the client experiences growth. If as counselors we hide behind the safety of our professional role, our clients will keep themselves hidden from us. If we become merely technical experts and leave our own reactions, values, and self cut of our work, the result will be sterile counseling. It is through our own genuineness and our aliveness that we can significantly touch our clients. If we make life-oriented choices, radiate a zest for life, are real in our relationships with our clients, and let ourselves be known to them, we can inspire and teach them in the best sense of the words. This does not mean that we are self-actualized persons who have "made it" or that we are without our problems. Rather, it implies that we are willing to look at our lives and do what is necessary to make the changes we want. Because we have a sense of hope that changing is worth the risks and the efforts, we can hold out hope to our clients that they have the capacity to become their own person and to like the person they are becoming.

In short, as therapists we serve as models for our clients. If we model incongruent behavior, low-risk activity, and deceit by remaining hidden and vague, we can expect our clients to imitate this behavior and to be untrusting. If we model realness by engaging in appropriate self-disclosure, our clients will tend to acquire this quality and thus will be honest in interacting with us in the therapeutic relationship. To be sure, counseling can be for better or for worse. Clients can become more of what they are capable of becoming, or they can become less than they might be. In my judgment the degree of aliveness and psychological health of the counselor is the crucial variable that determines the outcome. As will become clear in the next chapter, of course, an alive counselor also needs to have knowledge, technical competence in using skills, and an ethical sense. Merely "being a good person" does not make one an effective counselor.

THE COUNSELOR AS A THERAPEUTIC PERSON

How can counselors *be* therapeutic persons and model awareness and growth for their clients? I continue to raise this question for myself as a counseling psychologist and educator. In thinking about counselors who are therapeutic, I have isolated a cluster of personal qualities and characteristics. I do not expect any therapist to fully exemplify all these traits, and I am not proposing a fixed model of perfection. Rather, for me the willingness to struggle to become a more therapeutic person is the crucial quality. The following list is not a dogmatic itemizing of the "right" ways to be a therapist. It is intended to stimulate you to examine your ideas of what kind of person can make a significant difference in the lives of others.

- *Effective counselors have an identity.* They know who they are, what they are capable of becoming, what they want out of life, and what is essential. Although they have a clear sense of their priorities, they are willing to reexamine their values and goals. They are not mere reflections of what others expect or want them to be but strive to live by internal standards.

• *They respect and appreciate themselves.* They can give help and love out of their own sense of self-worth and strength. They are also able to ask, to be needed, and to receive from others, and they do not isolate themselves from others as a false demonstration of strength.

• *They are able to recognize and accept their own power.* They feel adequate with others and allow others to feel powerful with them. They do not diminish others so that they can feel a relative sense of power. They use their power and model its healthy uses for clients, but they avoid abusing it.

• *They are open to change.* Rather than settling for less, they extend themselves to become more. They exhibit a willingness and courage to leave the security of the known if they are not satisfied with what they have.

• *They are expanding their awareness of self and others.* They realize that if they have limited awareness, they also have limited freedom. Instead of investing energy in defensive behavior designed to block out experiences, they focus on reality-oriented tasks.

• *They are willing and able to tolerate ambiguity.* Most of us have a low threshold for coping with a lack of clarity. Because growth depends on leaving the familiar and entering unknown territory, people who are committed to personal development are willing to accept some degree of ambiguity in their lives. As they build their ego strength, they develop more self-trust—that is, trust in their intuitive processes and judgments and willingness to experiment with novel behavior. They eventually come to realize that they are trustworthy.

• *They are developing their own counseling style.* It is an expression of their philosophy of life and an outgrowth of their life experiences. Although they may freely borrow ideas and techniques from many other therapists, they do not mechanically imitate another's style.

• *They can experience and know the world of the client, yet their empathy is nonpossessive.* They are aware of their own struggles and pain, and they have a frame of reference for identifying with others while at the same time not losing their own identity by overidentifying with others.

• *They feel alive, and their choices are life-oriented.* They are committed to living fully rather than settling for mere existence. They do not allow events to passively shape them, for they take an active stance toward life.

• *They are authentic, sincere, and honest.* They do not live by pretenses but attempt to *be* what they think and feel. They are willing to appropriately disclose themselves to selected others. They do not hide behind masks, defenses, sterile roles, and facades.

• *They have a sense of humor.* They are able to put the events of life in perspective. They have not forgotten how to laugh, especially at their own foibles and contradictions. Their sense of humor enables them to put their problems and imperfections in perspective.

• *They make mistakes and are willing to admit them.* Although they are not overburdened with guilt over how they could or should have acted, they learn from mistakes. They do not dismiss their errors lightly, yet they do not choose to dwell on misery.

- *They generally live in the present.* They are not riveted to the past, nor are they fixated on the future. They are able to experience the "now," live in the now, and be present with others in the now. They can be with others in their pain or their joy, for they are open to their own emotional experience.
- *They appreciate the influence of culture.* They are aware of the ways in which their own culture affects them, and they have a respect for the diversity of values espoused by other cultures. They are also sensitive to the unique differences arising out of social class, race, and gender.
- *They are able to reinvent themselves.* They can revitalize and recreate significant relationships in their life. They make decisions about how they would like to change, and they work toward becoming the person they would like to become.
- *They are making choices that shape their life.* They are aware of early decisions they made about themselves, others, and the world. They are not the victims of these early decisions, for they are willing to revise them if necessary. Because they are continually evaluating themselves, they are not restrained by limited self-definitions.
- *They have a sincere interest in the welfare of others.* This concern is based on respect, care, trust, and a real valuing of others. It implies that they are willing to challenge people who are significant in their lives to also remain open to growth.
- *They become deeply involved in their work and derive meaning from it.* They can accept the rewards flowing from their work, and they can honestly admit the ego needs that are gratified by it. Yet they are not slaves to their work, and they do not depend on it exclusively to live a full life. They have other interests that provide them with a sense of purpose and fulfillment.

This picture of the characteristics of the therapeutic person might appear monumental and unrealistic. Who could ever be all those things? Certainly I do not fit this bill! Do not think of these personal characteristics from an all-or-nothing perspective; rather, consider them on a continuum. A given trait may be very characteristic of you, at one extreme, or it may be very uncharacteristic of you, at the other extreme. For example, it is not a question of either being emotionally present for others or being completely detached and distant. To some extent you can learn to become more present when you are with others. I have presented this picture of the therapeutic person with the hope that you will examine it and develop your own concept of what personality traits you deem it essential to strive for in order to promote personal growth.

PERSONAL COUNSELING FOR THE COUNSELOR

Discussion of the counselor as a therapeutic person raises another issue debated in counselor education: whether people should participate in counseling or therapy before they become practitioners. My view is that counselors should have the experience of being a client at some time, because such self-exploration can increase their level of self-awareness. This experience can be obtained before their training, during it, or both, but I strongly endorse some form of personal exploration as a prerequisite to counseling others.

Such counseling should be viewed not as an end in itself but as a means to help a potential counselor become a more therapeutic person who will have a greater chance of positively influencing clients. Opportunities for self-exploration can be instrumental in helping counselors-in-training assess their motivations for pursuing this profession. Examining our values, needs, attitudes, and life experiences can illuminate what we are getting from helping others. It is important that we know why we want to intervene in the lives of others, so that we can avoid the pitfalls of continually giving to others yet finding little personal satisfaction from our efforts. There is value in continuing individual or group counseling as we begin to practice as professionals. At this time we often feel a sense of professional impotence, and we frequently feel like quitting. Student counselors would do well to recognize their helplessness and despair but to avoid deciding too soon that they are unsuited to be a counselor. Personal counseling is an ideal place for beginning counselors to express and explore their concerns over whether they are able to help anyone. Issues such as the hazards of the counseling profession, as well as those related to the therapist's personal life, can be profitably explored in a counselor's personal therapy as the need arises (Guy, 1987).

When I began counseling others, I found that old wounds were opened and that feelings I had not explored in depth came to the surface. It was difficult for me to encounter a client's depression, because I had failed to come to terms with the way I had escaped from my own depression. Being therapists forces us to confront our unexplored blocks related to loneliness, power, death, sexuality, our parents, and so on. This does not mean that we need to be free of conflicts before we can counsel others, but it does mean that we should be aware of what these conflicts are and how they are likely to affect us as counselors. For example, if we have great difficulty in dealing with anger and guilt in our personal life, the chances are that we will do something to dilute these emotions when they occur in our clients. How can we be present for our clients and encourage them to openly express feelings that we are so intent on denying in ourselves?

As counselors we can take our clients no further than we have been willing to go in our own life. If we are not committed personally to the value of struggling, we will not convince clients that they should pay the price of their struggle. Through being a client ourselves, we know what it is like to look at ourselves as we really are. It gives us a basis for compassion for our clients, for we will be able to draw on our own memories of reaching impasses in our therapy, of both wanting to go further and at the same time wanting to stay where we are. We learn what it feels like to deal with anxieties that are aroused by self-disclosure and self-exploration. We experience transference and thus know firsthand how it is to view our therapist as a parent figure. Being willing to participate in a process of self-exploration can reduce the chances of assuming an attitude of arrogance or of being convinced that we have "arrived" as a person.

The main reason for having students receive some form of psychotherapy is to help them learn to deal with countertransference (the process of seeing themselves in their clients, of overidentifying with their clients, or of meeting their needs through their clients). Recognizing the manifestations of their countertransference reactions is one of the most essential abilities of effective counselors. Unless counselors are aware of their own conflicts, needs, assets, and liabilities, they can use the therapy hour more for their own purposes than for being available for their clients. For example, therapists who become sexually involved with their clients are taking advantage of the client's transference and misusing their power to satisfy their needs. A descriptive account of this type of "professional incest" is given by Carolyn Bates, who describes in *Sex in the Therapy Hour* the impact of a therapist who used the therapeutic relationship to take care of his needs, at a high cost to his client. Her story illustrates a dramatic way that therapists can harm clients (see Bates & Brodsky, 1989). This topic will be explored further in Chapter 3.

Personal therapy can be instrumental, then, in healing the healer. If student counselors have not healed their own psychological wounds and to some extent resolved their own conflicts, it is very likely that they will experience considerable difficulty in entering the world of their clients. Unaware counselors are in danger of being carried away on the client's emotional tidal wave, which is of no help to themselves or the client. It is unrealistic to think that counselors can completely rid themselves of any traces of countertransference. But they can acquire the means to become aware of the signs of these reactions and can deal with these feelings in their own therapy and supervision sessions.

Personal counseling may be most opportune as students start their academic program, before they begin to see clients (Wise, Lowery, & Silverglade, 1989). Later in their training program, as they become more comfortable with their counseling skills, is another good time. Once they become aware of problems in their relationships with their clients (such as countertransference issues and value conflicts), personal therapy can again be useful.

Ideally, I would like to see some individual counseling combined with group-oriented growth experiences. My preference is for personal-growth groups, for here counselor candidates can benefit from the reactions of other members. A useful focus of the group experience can be on helping the participants clarify their motivations for wanting to become counselors. Some questions for exploration are "Why do I want to pursue a career in the helping professions? What are my own needs and motivations? What rewards do I receive from being a counselor? How can I differentiate between satisfaction of client needs and satisfaction of my own needs?" Some other questions that might profitably be asked in a personal-growth experience include "What are some of my problems, and what am I doing to resolve them? How might my own problems get in the way of effectively working as a counselor? What are my values, where did they originate, and how will they affect my counseling style? How courageous and willing to take risks am I? Am I willing to do what I encourage my clients to do? What are some ways in which I avoid using my own strengths, and how can I more fully utilize my potential power? What keeps me from being as open, honest, and real as I might be? How do others experience me? What impact do I have on others? How sensitive am I to the reactions of others?"

Those questions reflect but a few of the possible areas to explore in a personal-growth experience. The aim of the experience is to provide a situation in which counselors can come to greater self-understanding. I never cease to be

surprised by the amount of resistance I encounter from the ranks of professionals on this issue. I hear this argument: "Requiring the therapist to be a client
in personal counseling is based on a medical model of sickness. It's like saying
that a surgeon cannot perform an operation that he or she has not also undergone." I simply cannot accept this analogy. I am left with the strong conviction
that therapists cannot hope to open doors for clients that they have not opened
for themselves. If we are fearful of facing ourselves, how can we help others
look at their lives? If we have limited vision, how can we help our clients expand
their vision of what they might become? However, although I deem a therapeutic experience necessary for prospective counselors, I do not believe it to be a
sufficient and complete experience in itself. A formal therapy experience is but
one way in which counselors can actively do something about becoming more
therapeutic in their relationships with people.

What does the empirical research say about personal therapy for practicing
counselors and therapists? A national survey examined psychotherapists' use of
personal therapy before and after they entered professional practice (Guy,
Stark, & Poelstra, 1988). The researchers noted that 18% of the practicing
therapists involved in the study had never received any form of psychotherapy.
Also, 23% had not received any individual therapy, the form of counseling
commonly regarded as most useful for resolving the therapist's own conflicts
and blind spots.

Apparently, many practitioners view themselves as beyond making personal use of the kind of help they offer to others, which makes me wonder about
their beliefs regarding the true value of therapy. It is as though some counselors
believe that they should be able to work out all of their problems by themselves
and that seeking professional help is a sign of personal and professional weakness. It is clear that a major problem facing psychotherapy is the impaired or
distressed practitioner (see Kilburg, Nathan, & Thoreson, 1986). It is obvious
that, at times, experienced practitioners go through a crisis or an impairment.
People do not have total control over their lives. Unexpected events must be
faced, such as illness and death. Thus, anyone may need counseling at a given
time to successfully work through a crisis. Periodic self-review with the help of
another professional can help us acquire a new perspective on a problem.

THE COUNSELOR'S VALUES AND PHILOSOPHY OF LIFE

The discussion of the importance of self-exploration for counselors also pertains to the values and beliefs they hold. My experience in teaching and supervising students of counseling shows me how crucial it is that they be aware of
their values, of where and how they acquired them, and of how their values
influence their interventions with clients. An excellent focus for the process of
self-searching is examining how one's values are likely to affect one's work as a
counselor.

Counseling or therapy is not a form of indoctrination whereby practitioners
persuade clients to act or feel in the "right way." Unfortunately, many well-in-

tentioned counselors are overzealous in their mission of helping to "straighten people out." The implication is that by virtue of their greater wisdom, they will provide answers for the troubled client. But counseling is not synonymous with preaching or teaching. This is not to say that counselors should maintain an indifferent, neutral, or passive role, silently listening to and accepting everything the client reports. Counselors can challenge the values of their clients and, when they sense that certain behaviors are destructive, can confront them on the importance of examining the consequences of their actions.

Counselors are sometimes taught that it is ideal for them to remain "value neutral." They receive the injunctions that they should avoid passing value judgments on to their clients and that they should keep their own value system and philosophy of life separate from the therapeutic relationship. Yet others, such as Patterson (1989), take the position that the therapist's values cannot be kept out of the therapeutic process, which makes it imperative that practitioners be clearly aware of their values. For Patterson, the awareness that the therapist is a person who is participating in a personal relationship with the client brings the importance of the therapist's values into focus.

Along with Patterson, I maintain that we cannot exclude our values and beliefs from the relationships we establish with clients unless we do routine and mechanical "counseling" and thereby limit ourselves to being merely skilled technicians. It seems sensible that we make our values known to our clients and openly discuss the issue of values in counseling. We also have an ethical obligation to refrain from imposing our values on clients.

THE ROLE OF VALUES IN COUNSELING

A core issue is the degree to which the counselor's values should enter a therapeutic relationship. A counselor cannot have goals for clients and yet be devoid of value judgments, for goals are based on our values. Let me pose a series of questions designed to help you search for your own tentative answers about the role of values in counseling:

- Is it desirable that counselors hold back value judgments about their clients' choices? Is it possible for therapists to make value judgments only about events that affect their own personal life and pass no judgments on to clients?
- Is it possible for counselors to disagree with a client's values and still accept him or her as a person?
- Can counselors remain "neutral" and still challenge their clients to make an honest assessment of whether their behavior is getting them what they want? Is there a difference between neutrality and objectivity?
- How can helping professionals retain their own sense of values and remain true to themselves yet at the same time allow their clients the freedom to select values and behavior that differ sharply from theirs?
- What is the essential difference between counselors who honestly expose their core values, when appropriate, and those who in subtle ways

"guide" their clients to accept the values that they deem to be good for them?

- Is it possible to separate a discussion of values from the therapeutic process?
- What is the best course of action when counselors become aware of sharp value conflicts with certain clients?
- What is the role of counselors when the institution they work for takes a definite position regarding certain values and behaviors?
- Is it ever justifiable for counselors to impose their values on clients? What about those situations in which the counselor is convinced that a client's values result in self-destructive behavior?

One national survey revealed a consensus among a representative group of mental-health professionals that certain basic values are important for healthy lifestyles and for guiding and evaluating psychotherapy (Jensen & Bergin, 1988). The following ten values were thought by these professionals to contribute to a positive, mentally healthy lifestyle: (1) competent perception and expression of feelings, (2) a sense of being a free and responsible agent, (3) management of stress, (4) self-awareness and growth, (5) commitment to marriage, family, and other relationships, (6) self-maintenance and physical fitness, (7) having orienting goals and meaningful purpose, (8) forgiveness, (9) regulated sexual fulfillment, and (10) spirituality/religiosity. This study implies that the value systems of practitioners are an integral part of therapeutic theory and practice, challenging the view that therapists should be neutral with respect to values.

The question of the influence of the counselor's values on the client has ethical implications when we consider that the goals and therapeutic methods of the counselor are expressions of his or her philosophy of life. Even though therapists should not directly teach the client or impose specific values, they do put into practice a philosophy of counseling, which is, in effect, a philosophy of life. Counselors communicate their values by the type of therapeutic goals they subscribe to and through the therapeutic procedures they employ to reach these goals (Patterson, 1989). Counselors' view of what they want their clients to be like, or their view of a healthy and optimally functioning person, *does* reveal their values. As reflected in the Jensen and Bergin study, practitioners' ideas of what constitutes a mentally healthy lifestyle do indeed influence the interventions they make with their clients. Because they respect their clients' self-determination, ethically sensitive therapists are aware of their own values and are careful not to make decisions for their clients. As counselors they confront and challenge clients about their values and help them decide whether they are truly living by them or merely incorporating parental and societal values without evaluating them. Helping professionals need to be alert to the possibility that they are manipulating a client to accept values wholesale, for to do so would mean that they were simply becoming another parent substitute.

As an example of the influence that a counselor's philosophy of life can have on a client and of possible clashes over values between the client and the counselor, consider this case: The client is a married woman in her late 30s, with three children who are approaching their teen years. She has been in weekly individual therapy for six months. She is struggling to decide whether she wishes to remain with her husband, whom she perceives as boring, uninvolved with her children, complacent, and overly wrapped up in his work. Although she has urged him to join her in marriage counseling or to try some form of therapy for himself, he has consistently refused. He maintains that he is fine and that she is the one with the problems. She tells the therapist that she would divorce him immediately "if it weren't for the kids" and that when the children finish high school, she will surely leave him. She is presently ambivalent, however; she cannot decide whether she wants to accept the security that she now has (along with the deadness of her relationship with her husband) or whether she is willing to give up this security and risk making a better life for herself (as well as risk being stuck with even less than she has now). She has been contemplating having an affair so that someone other than her husband can meet her physical and emotional needs. She is also exploring the possibility of finding a job so that she will be less dependent on her husband. By getting a job, she could have outside opportunities for personal satisfaction and still remain in her marriage by deciding to accept what she has with him.

Consider the following questions and decide what value judgments can be made, both by this client and her therapist:

- One of her reasons for staying married is "for the sake of the children." What if you, as her therapist, accept this value and believe that she should not challenge her marriage, because children need both parents? Might she be using the children as an excuse? What if your judgment is that she would be better off by divorcing? What do your beliefs about divorce, marriage, and children have to do with her possible decisions?
- She is talking about an affair. What are your values concerning monogamy and extramarital sex? Do you believe that having an affair would be helpful or destructive for your client? What influence might your views have on her?
- There is the value question of security versus possible growth. If you are conservative and place primary value on security, what effects might your view have on your client? What are some of your own life experiences that might have some bearing on her decisions?

VALUE-LADEN ISSUES

I think that we deceive ourselves when we contend that our own experiences, values, and beliefs do not enter into our therapeutic relationships and that they do not have an influence on a client's decision making and behavior. It behooves us to clarify our positions on such controversial issues as the following:

- *Religion.* If therapists call themselves "Christian counselors" and have definite beliefs about life, salvation, sin, and the person's relationship with Christ and if they see these beliefs as a central part of the therapeutic process, how does their view influence clients who are not religious, are non-Christian, or are Christian but do not accept the therapist's religious beliefs? What potential impact does an atheist therapist have on a client with a definite religious persuasion? Can the therapist allow the client to maintain his or her religious values, or will the therapist confront these values as forms of "immature defenses"? What are your views on religion, and how do you see them as influencing your work as a counselor?

• *Abortion.* When a client who is pregnant enters counseling and wants to explore alternatives to having the child, how might you work if you fully believed that she should have an abortion? How might you work differently if you were morally opposed to abortion? Would you tell her about your view? How would your values affect the range of the client's exploring for herself possible alternatives? When might you refer such a client?

• *Alternative lifestyles.* In working with clients with a gay or lesbian lifestyle, how might your values influence what you say or do? If you see a gay lifestyle as immoral or as a form of psychopathology, would you be genuinely able to encourage such clients to retain their behavior and values? Could you encourage them to define their own goals, or would you be inclined to direct them toward the goals you think they should have? If a gay client did not want to change, would you still be able to work with him on meeting his personal goals for therapy? When would you be inclined to refer such a client? What would be your reasons for making a referral?

• *Extramarital sex.* What are your values with respect to adultery? Could you objectively counsel clients with values that differed from yours in this area? Might you be inclined to attempt to convince your clients to change to your way of thinking? Do you view it as your role as a counselor to persuade clients who are having affairs to change their behavior? Might you encourage certain clients to have affairs? Would you be able to allow a client who was having an affair to determine the goals of his or her own therapy?

• *Divergence of cultural values.* As you work with culturally mixed populations, are you able to recognize that clients' values may be working for them? For instance, a client may put great emphasis on guiding her life by not letting her parents down. One of her cultural values is that she owes her parents respect and should gear her decisions toward the expectations that her family has for her. If you value independence and autonomy, might you be inclined to encourage her to do what *she* wants as opposed to living up to parental expectations?

• *Drugs.* Many of your clients may use various drugs. What are your values relating to drugs, and how might they influence your capacity to work with drug users? Assume that your client is a habitual user and that whereas your perception is that he is escaping through drugs, he disagrees and sees no harm in "getting loaded." What might you do when there is a clash of values and perceptions in a case like this? Would you react any differently if the client wanted to smoke a joint on Saturday night for relaxation? Do you react differently to people who use drugs or alcohol on occasion for social purposes than you do to habitual users?

• *Right to die.* You may be involved with a client who is in the advanced stages of AIDS and who has been given no hope. Assume that he wants to talk about ways of ending his misery rather than going through what seems to be an expensive and futile treatment. What are your values pertaining to a person's right to die, and how do you think they would come into play in this situation? How would legal mandates influence you in following what you believed to be an ethical course?

SOME RECOMMENDATIONS

In his discussion of the role of values in counseling and psychotherapy, Patterson (1989) presents several reasons why it is inappropriate for a therapist to indoctrinate clients or attempt to inculcate a system of values in them. Nevertheless, he allows room for therapists to discuss values and ethics. When therapists express their values openly, they are not attempting to coerce clients, and there is less likelihood of imposing these values on clients.

On this issue my colleagues and I take the position that it is neither possible nor desirable for counselors to be scrupulously neutral with respect to values in the counseling relationship (Corey, Corey, & Callanan, 1988). We contend that counselors should be willing to express their values openly when they are relevant to the questions that come up in their sessions with clients. My colleagues and I caution counselors against the tendency to assume either of two extreme positions. At one extreme are counselors who hold definite and absolute beliefs and see it as their job to exert influence on clients to adopt their values. These counselors tend to direct their clients toward the attitudes and values *they* judge as being "right." At the other extreme are counselors who maintain that the ideal is to strive for "value-free" counseling. Because these counselors are so intent on remaining "objective" and because they are so anxious not to influence their clients, they run the risk of immobilizing themselves.

Furthermore, we take the position that clients often want and need to know where their therapist stands in order to test their own thinking. Thus, clients deserve an honest involvement on the part of their counselor. We also believe that it seems arrogant to make the assumption that counselors know what is best for others. Therefore, counselors would do well to avoid equating counseling with pushing people to conform to certain "acceptable" standards to live by. Counseling is a process whereby clients are challenged to honestly evaluate their values and then decide for themselves in what ways they will modify these values and their behavior.

BECOMING A MULTICULTURALLY SKILLED COUNSELOR

In the previous section we explored the influence of the counselor's values on the therapeutic process. Effective counseling must also take into account the impact of culture. Culture is, quite simply, the values and behavior shared by a group of individuals. It is important to remember that culture does not refer just to an ethnic or racial heritage. It can also be determined by age, gender, lifestyle, or socioeconomic status. Cultural diversity is a fact of life in today's international "global village." Counselors cannot afford to ignore the issue of culture. Pedersen (1988, 1990) maintains that counselors have two choices: to ignore the influence of culture or to attend to it. Whatever choice is made, culture will continue to influence both the client's and the counselor's behavior, with or without the counselor's awareness. This section focuses on the need for counselors to develop an increased awareness of their own cultural values and personal assumptions so that they can work sensitively with differences in age, gender, race, religion, ethnic background, and lifestyle.

FACING UP TO CULTURAL DIVERSITY

Until recently the counseling profession had not addressed the special issues involved in working with people of various cultures. Now there is an increasing tendency in the helping professions to face the reality of cultural diversity. This multicultural perspective respects the needs and strengths of diverse client and counselor populations (Pedersen, 1990). Pedersen believes that the focus on cultural diversity is the most important development in the counseling profession in the past decade.

Some counselors are culturally "encapsulated," living in a cultural cocoon in which they escape reality by depending entirely on their own internalized value assumptions about what is good for people. Encapsulation is a process in which counselors (1) rely on stereotypes in making decisions about people from different cultural groups, (2) ignore cultural differences among clients, and (3) define reality according to one set of cultural assumptions (Pedersen, 1988). To avoid this narrowness, it is necessary for counselors to challenge their beliefs and reorganize old knowledge when it no longer fits. Through increasing one's personal awareness and through training, it is possible to avoid being culturally encapsulated. A multicultural perspective recognizes a client's culturally based beliefs, values, and behaviors and emphasizes sensitivity to the client's cultural environment (Pedersen, 1988, 1990).

If you are not aware of how your own culture influences you or of the cultural dimensions that your clients bring to therapy, you may practice culturally biased counseling, and your clients are likely to feel dissatisfied. Avoiding cultural tunnel vision involves examining your expectations, attitudes, and assumptions about working with various groups as well as understanding and accepting clients who have a different set of assumptions about life. The key to effectiveness rests with the attitudes and beliefs of counselors. If therapists recognize their limitations and their cultural bias and are willing to change their perceptions, they will probably become more culturally sensitive over a period of time.

Counselors have the task of helping their clients clearly identify why they are seeking counseling. They can help by focusing clients on where they are now and where they want to go. Clients should be informed of the likelihood that the counseling process will result in some attitudinal and behavioral changes on their part. They should be made aware of the possible consequences of change, not only for themselves but also for others in their lives. For example, some clients may be shunned by members of their family (or by their own self-image) if they become too outspoken or too highly individualistic.

Ethnic-minority clients and people of color may display behavior that counselors interpret as resistance. It is important to make a distinction between uncooperative behavior and a sense of reluctance to participate fully in the counseling process. Often, these clients are not so much *resistant* as they are *reluctant* or, in some cases, simply politely respectful. Clients adopt behaviors that are consistent with the values of their cultural framework. There may be many meanings for behaviors that could wrongly be labeled as resistance. For example, silence during a counseling session should not always be interpreted as resistance. Some clients may be responding to their cultural conditioning and waiting for the counselor to ask them questions, or they may perceive the counselor as an authority figure who is to be listened to respectfully. Simply put, they may lack familiarity with the counseling process and may not be clear about what is expected of them. Some clients may be very hesitant to talk about members of their family. This hesitation should not necessarily be interpreted as a stubborn refusal to be open and transparent. Instead, such clients may be influenced by cultural taboos against openly discussing family matters. Counselors who are able to understand and accept the world of their clients are in a better position to patiently help these clients begin to speak. If these clients feel that they are respected, there is a greater chance that they will begin to challenge their hesitation. As their trust builds, along with an understanding of how counseling can be used to their benefit, they are much more likely to share themselves freely with the counselor.

Sue (1981a) calls for burying the assumption that the same therapeutic approaches will be effective with all clients regardless of their cultural background. For example, many clients prefer active and directive counseling to an approach that leaves many decisions to them. Because of their cultural background, such clients may place value on the authority of a professional counselor. These clients may be very uncomfortable with a counselor who too quickly expects them to challenge his or her authority or who expects them to function in an informal atmosphere.

In recent years the roster of people of color has grown because of an influx of refugees seeking asylum in the United States. Although some have come from countries where there are established social-service agencies, many have come with no prior knowledge of service providers. Despite their serious need of assistance, they are often reluctant to use formal helping institutions. In order to work effectively with these new groups, counselors need multicultural training that emphasizes differences in the behavior of those seeking help, including differences in perceptions of mental health (Wright, Coley, & Corey, 1989). Counselors hoping to reach clients who are culturally different from them must develop a basic respect for these clients' experiential world. In the process of becoming more open to the client's world, the counselor is also enabled to reach a higher level of self-awareness.

ACQUIRING COMPETENCIES IN MULTICULTURAL COUNSELING

Graduate programs have been accused of dealing inadequately with the mental-health issues of certain ethnic and other cultural groups. Too often, minority-group issues have been studied from a White, male, middle-class perspective. Casas (1986) contends that traditional counseling programs have ignored the existence of ethnic minorities and have ethnocentrically assumed that the education and training provided could be applied to all groups. It is his view that most counseling students and instructors are not aware of their culturally biased values and attitudes. He recommends that counselor-education programs devote more attention to addressing directly ethnic and cultural variables. Counselors cannot afford to be deficient in multicultural knowledge and skills. The profession has an obligation to provide services to clients that meet their cultural preferences, and counselors have an obligation to be sensitive to the ways in which clients' cultural background influences how they receive services.

Sue and his associates proposed a number of minimum cross-cultural counseling competencies to be incorporated into counselor-education programs. The characteristics listed below are considered to be essential components of multicultural counseling (Sue 1981a, 1981b; Sue et al., 1982).

1. *Beliefs and attitudes of multiculturally effective counselors.*
   - They are aware of their own values, attitudes, and biases and of how these are likely to affect minority clients. As a check on this process, they monitor their functioning through consultation, supervision, and continuing education.
   - They can appreciate diverse cultures; they feel comfortable with differences between themselves and their clients in race and beliefs.
   - They believe that an integration of different value systems can contribute to both therapist and client growth.
   - They have the capacity to share a client's world view without critically judging this view.
   - They are sensitive to circumstances (such as personal biases and stage of ethnic identity) that call for referral of the minority client to a member of his or her own race or culture.

2. *Knowledge of multiculturally effective counselors.*
   - They understand the impact of oppression and racist concepts on the mental-health professions and on their personal and professional lives.
   - They are aware of institutional barriers that prevent minorities from making full use of psychological services in the community.
   - They understand how the value assumptions of the major theories of counseling may interact with the values of different cultural groups.
   - They are aware of basic characteristics of counseling that cut across classes and cultures and influence the counseling process.
   - They are aware of culture-specific (or indigenous) methods of helping.
   - They possess specific knowledge about the historical background, traditions, and values of the group they are working with.

3. *Skills of multiculturally effective counselors.*
   - They are able to use a wide range of counseling styles that are congruent with the value systems of different minority groups.

- They can modify and adapt conventional approaches to counseling and psychotherapy in order to accommodate cultural differences.
- They are able to send and receive both verbal and nonverbal messages accurately and appropriately.
- They are able to make out-of-office interventions when necessary by assuming the role of consultant and agent for change.

In working with culturally diverse clients, it helps to assess the degree of acculturation that has taken place. This is especially true for clients who have the experience of living in two or more cultures. They often have allegiance to their own culture, and yet they also find certain characteristics of their new culture attractive. They may experience conflicts in integrating the two or more cultures in which they live. These conflicts can be explored very productively in the counseling sessions if the practitioner respects this cultural conflict.

Multicultural counseling is by its very nature diverse No one therapeutic approach fits well all ethnic clients. Instead, different theories have distinct features that have appeal for different cultural groups. Some approaches also have distinct limitations, both in their concepts and in their techniques, when they are applied to certain populations. Effective multicultural practice demands an open stance on the part of the practitioner, a flexibility, and a willingness to modify strategies to fit the needs and the situations of the individual client. Practitioners who truly respect their clients will demonstrate a willingness to learn from them. They will be aware of hesitation on the client's part and will not be too quick to misinterpret it. Instead, they will patiently attempt to enter the client's world as much as they can. This is called the *emic* approach. It is not necessary for practitioners to have the same experiences or perceptions as their clients; what is more important is that they attempt to be open to clients' feelings and struggles. Understanding universal human themes (such as loneliness, fear, and psychological pain) is as important as understanding cultural themes. It is not always by similarity, but rather by differences, that we are challenged to look at what we are doing.

Even though counselors can acquire general knowledge and skills that will enable them to function effectively with culturally diverse client populations, it is not realistic to expect that they will know everything about the cultural backgrounds of their clients. There is much to be said for letting clients teach the counselor about relevant aspects of their culture. This practice also empowers clients, for they are taking a more active role in their counseling. Counselors need to assess what is a reasonable amount of information to ask clients about their culture. They would do well to ask questions not merely to satisfy their own curiosity but, rather, to deepen an understanding of the client's world that will facilitate the counseling process.

As you study the contemporary theories of counseling, strive to think about the cultural implications of the techniques that grow out of the various approaches. Evaluate the cultural appropriateness of your interventions. Perhaps most important of all, reflect on ways in which you can acquire the personal characteristics required for becoming an effective counselor in a multicultural society.

ISSUES FACED BY BEGINNING THERAPISTS

This section is based on my observation and work with counselors-in-training and on my own struggles when I began practicing. It identifies some of the major issues that most of us typically face, particularly during the beginning stages of learning how to be therapists. I have become aware of a recurring pattern of questions, conflicts, and issues that provide the substance of seminars and practicum experiences in counseling. When counselor interns complete their formal course work and begin facing clients, they are put to the test of integrating and applying what they have learned. They soon realize that all they really have to work with is themselves — their own life experiences, values, and humanity. At that point some real concerns arise about their adequacies as a counselor and as a person and about what they can bring of themselves to the counseling relationship. In what follows I attempt to formulate some useful guidelines for beginning counselors.

DEALING WITH OUR ANXIETIES

Most beginning counselors, regardless of their academic and experiential backgrounds, anticipate meeting their initial clients with ambivalent feelings. As beginners, if we have enough sense, we are probably anxiety ridden and ask ourselves such questions as "What will I say? How will I say it? Will I be able to help? What if I make mistakes? Will my clients return, and if they do, what will I do next?" In my view a certain level of anxiety demonstrates that we are aware of the uncertainties of the future with our clients and of our abilities to really be there and stay with them. Because therapy is serious business and can have a strong impact on the clients, we can accept our anxieties as normal. Whereas too much anxiety can torpedo any confidence we might have and cause us to be frozen, we have every right to experience some anxiety. We may also fear that our peers know far more than we do, that they are much more skilled and perceptive, and that they will see us as incompetent.

The willingness to recognize and deal with these anxieties, as opposed to denying them by pretenses, is a mark of courage. That we have self-doubts seems perfectly normal; it is how we deal with them that counts. One way is to openly discuss them with a supervisor and peers. The possibilities are rich for meaningful exchanges and for gaining support from fellow interns, who probably have many of the same concerns, fears, and anxieties.

BEING AND DISCLOSING OURSELVES

Because we are typically self-conscious and anxious when we begin counseling, we tend to be overconcerned with what the books say and with the mechanics of how we should proceed. Inexperienced therapists too often fail to appreciate the values inherent in simply being themselves. I have suggested to many of my students that they attempt to put their theories and academic learning into the background and follow their intuitions, even though they do not fully trust their hunches. Ideally, their course work, readings, fieldwork, and other training experiences have been integrated, and they can call on their acquired knowledge and skill as it is appropriate I frequently encourage counselors-in-training to follow through with some of their hunches and later to confirm their intuitive directions with a fellow student, the client, a supervisor, or their own internal reactions.

A common tendency is for counselors to become passive. They listen. They reflect. They have insights and hunches but mull over them so long that even if they decide to act on a hunch, the appropriate time for action has already passed. So they sit back, passively wondering whether their internal reactions are correct. Thus, I tend to encourage an active stance for the student counselor, because I believe that it is generally better to risk being inappropriate than to almost ensure bland results by adopting passive, nondirective stances.

Let me push further with the issue of being oneself. I do not believe that we should be either of two extremes: at one end are counselors who lose themselves in their fixed role and who hide behind a professional facade; at the other end are therapists who strive too hard to prove that they, too, are human. If we are at either of these poles, we are not being ourselves.

Take the first extreme. Here counselors are so bound up in maintaining stereotyped role expectations that little of them as a person shows through. Although we do have role functions, it is possible for us to responsibly perform them without blurring our identity and becoming lost in our role. I believe that the more insecure, frightened, and uncertain we are in our professional work, the more we will cling to the defense afforded by a role. The unrealistic expectation that we must be superhuman leads to becoming ossified in fixed roles. Consider some unrealistic expectations that a beginning counselor often becomes ensnared in: "I should always care; I need always to demonstrate warmth (whether I feel it or not); I should like and enjoy all my clients; I must be all-understanding and fully empathic; I should know what is going on at all times; I can't be acceptable as a counselor unless I'm fully put together myself, and any indication of personal problems rules against my effectiveness; I am expected to have answers for clients, answers that they say they cannot find within themselves." If we accept these unrealistic notions, we can fall victim to presenting a role to clients instead of presenting ourselves. By accepting these lofty standards, we deceive ourselves into being what we are not, because we indoctrinate ourselves with the idea that we should be a certain way. The role we play is not always congruent with the way we deeply feel. Thus, finding ourselves bored, we deny our boredom and force attention; or discovering negative feelings toward clients, we deny our feelings by stressing the positive qualities we see in clients; or becoming aware that we are uncaring in a particular moment, we trick ourselves into caring instead of letting the feeling stand.

At this extreme of too little self-disclosure, counselors are unwilling to discuss the reactions they are having toward clients or what has been going on with them during the session. They focus too much on the clients, often by questioning or probing, which is a subtle demand for them to be open and revealing. At the same time they are modeling closed behavior. They expect their clients to do what they are not doing themselves in the therapy relationship. Their clients are left guessing about what the counselor is experiencing during the session; thus, a valuable basis for an honest dialogue is lost.

At the other extreme counselors actively work at demonstrating their humanness. Instead of getting lost in a professionally aloof and nondisclosing role, such counselors overreact and blur any distinction between helper and one who is helped. They would rather be seen as a buddy with similar hang-ups than as a therapist. Their approach is one of sharing their own problems, past and present, and of using the relationship to work on their own needs. A pseudorealness develops out of their need to be seen as human, and in a desperate attempt to be themselves, they fail. At this extreme we tell clients too much about ourselves, and thus we take the focus off of them and put it on ourselves as therapists. We might make the mistake of inappropriately burdening them with fleeting reactions or impressions we are having toward them; our disclosures in these cases have the effect of closing them up. The key point is that disclosure should have the effect of encouraging clients to deepen their level of self-exploration or to enhance the therapeutic relationship. Excessive counselor disclosure often originates from the counselor's own needs, and in these cases the client's needs are secondary.

I have found the following guidelines useful in determining when self-disclosure is facilitative. First, disclosing my persistent feelings that are directly related to the present transaction can be useful. If I am consistently bored or irritated in a session, it becomes essential to reveal my feeling. On the other hand, I think it is unwise to share every fleeting fantasy or feeling that I experience. Timing is important. Second, I find it helpful to distinguish between disclosure that is history telling and disclosure that is an unrehearsed expression of my present experiencing. For me to mechanically report events of my past might be pseudodisclosure. If it is easy to relate or if it sounds rehearsed and mechanical to me, I have a clue that I am trying too hard to be authentic. However, if my disclosure is an outgrowth of something I am feeling in the moment and if, as I share this feeling, it has some freshness of expression, I can be more sure that my self-disclosure is facilitative. Last, I often ask myself why I am revealing myself and to what degree it is appropriate to the task of helping the client.

AVOIDING PERFECTIONISM

Both undergraduate students in human services and graduate students in counseling are prone to putting themselves under tremendous pressure. They tell themselves things such as "I have to be the perfect counselor, and if I'm not, I could do severe damage"; "I should know everything there is to know about my profession, and if I show that there is something I don't know, others will see me as incompetent"; "I ought to be able to help everybody who seeks my help. If there is someone I can't help, that just proves my incompetence"; "If a client doesn't get better, it must be my fault"; "Making a mistake is horrible, and failure is always fatal. If I were really professional, I wouldn't make mistakes"; "I should always radiate confidence; there is no room for self-doubt."

Perhaps one of the most common self-defeating beliefs that we burden ourselves with is that we must be perfect. Although we might well know intellectually that humans are not perfect, emotionally we often feel that there is little room for error. I attempt to teach counseling interns and students that they need not burden themselves with the idea that they must be perfect. They do not have to know everything, and there is no disgrace in revealing their lack of knowledge. Rather than trying to impress others and bluffing their way through difficult situations, they can always admit the truth and then set out to find information or answers (if indeed there is an answer). It takes courage for them to admit their imperfections, but there is a value in being open about them. In their book *The Imperfect Therapist,* Kottler and Blau (1989) develop the thesis that counselor educators need to encourage an open and frank discussion about errors. They invite their readers to open themselves up to studying their misjudgments and to celebrate their mistakes as opportunities for increased personal and professional development.

To be sure, we *will* make mistakes, whether we are beginning or seasoned therapists. If our energies are tied up with presenting an image of perfection, we will have little energy left to be present for our clients. What is more important than our mistakes is the lesson that we learn from each mistake. In working with students, I tell them to challenge their notion that they should know everything and should be perfectly skilled. I encourage them to share their mistakes or what they perceive as errors. If they are willing to risk making mistakes in supervised learning situations and are willing to reveal their self-doubts, they will find a direction that leads to growth.

BEING HONEST ABOUT OUR LIMITATIONS

A related fear that most of us have is of facing our limitations as counselors. We fear losing the client's respect if we say "I really feel that I can't help you on this point" or "I just don't have the kind of information or skill to help you with this problem." Clients' responses overwhelmingly confirm the value of honesty as opposed to an attempt to fake competence. Not only will we perhaps not lose our clients' respect, but we may gain their respect by frankly admitting our limitations. An illustration comes to mind. A counselor in-training had intake duty in a college counseling center. Her first client came in wanting to discuss the possibilities of an abortion for his girlfriend. Many questions raced through her mind: "Should I admit to him my lack of awareness and skill in dealing with this problem, or should I somehow bluff my way through to avoid looking like a neophyte? Should I know how to help him? Will he get a negative impression of the counseling center if I tell him I don't have the skill for this case? What about the girl in this situation? Is it really enough to work only with him? Is all that he really needs at this point simply information? Will information resolve the issue?" Fortunately, the counselor-in-training let the client know directly that the matter was too complicated for her to tackle, and she got another counselor on duty to help him. A point of this illustration is that we sometimes burden ourselves with the expectation that we should be all-knowing and skillful, even without experience. The counselor-in-training's willingness to be realistic helped her avoid the pitfalls of trying to look good for the client and of presenting a false image.

We cannot realistically expect to succeed with every client. Even experienced counselors at times become glum and begin to doubt their value when they are forced to admit that there are clients whom they are not able to touch, much less reach in a significant way. Be honest enough with yourself and with your client to admit that you cannot work successfully with everyone.

There is a delicate balance between learning our realistic limits and challenging what we sometimes think of as being "limits." For example, we may tell ourselves that we could never work with the elderly because we cannot identify with them, because they would not trust us, because we might find it depressing, and so forth. In this case, however, it might be good to test what we see as limits and open ourselves to this population. If we do, we may find that there are more grounds for identification than we thought. The same holds true for other populations (the handicapped, young children, mentally ill people, alcoholics, adolescents). Before deciding that we do not have the life experiences or the personal qualities to successfully work with a given population, we might do well to attempt working in a setting with a population we do not intend to specialize in. This can be done through diversified field placements or visits to agencies.

UNDERSTANDING SILENCE

Those silent moments during a therapeutic session may seem like silent hours to a beginning therapist. It is not uncommon to be threatened by silences to the point that we frequently do something counterproductive to break the silence and thus relieve our anxiety. I recall a time when I was a counselor intern and was tape-recording an individual session with a highly verbal high school girl. Toward the end of the session she became silent for a moment, and my anxiety level rose to the degree that I felt compelled to rush in and give several interpretations to what she had been saying earlier. When my supervisor heard the tape he exclaimed: "Hell, your talk really got in her way. You didn't hear what she was saying! I'll bet she doesn't come back for her session next week." Well, she came back, and by that time I was determined not to intervene and talk my anxiety away. So, rather than taking the initiative of beginning the session, I waited for her to begin. We waited for about half an hour. We played a game of "you first." Each of us sat and stared at the other. Finally, we began exploring what this silence felt like for each of us.

Silence can have many meanings, and I believe that it is essential to learn how to effectively understand these meanings. Some of the possible meanings of silence, during either an individual session or a group session, are the following: the client may be quietly thinking about some things that were discussed earlier or evaluating some insight just acquired; the client may be waiting for the therapist to take the lead and decide what to say next, or the therapist may be waiting for the client to do this; either the client or the therapist may be bored, distracted, or preoccupied or may just not have anything to say for the moment; the client may be feeling hostile toward the therapist and thus be playing the game of "I'll just sit here like a stone and see if he (she) can get to me"; the client and the therapist may be communicating without words, the silence may be refreshing, or the silence may say much more than words; and perhaps the interaction has been on a surface level, and both persons have some fear or hesitancy about getting to a deeper level.

I suggest that you explore alternative meanings of silence and that when silences occur, you explore with your client what they mean. You could first acknowledge the silence and your feelings about it and then, rather than pretending it does not exist and making noisy talk simply to make each other comfortable, pursue its meaning.

DEALING WITH DEMANDING CLIENTS

A major issue that puzzles many beginning counselors is how to deal with the overdemanding client. Typically, because therapists feel that they should extend themselves in being helpful, they often burden themselves with the unrealistic standard that they should give unselfishly regardless of how great the demands on them are. The demands may manifest themselves in a variety of ways. Clients may call you frequently at home and expect you to talk at length; demand that they see you more often or for a longer period than you can provide; want to see you socially; want you to adopt or in some other way take care of them and assume their responsibilities; expect you to manipulate another person (spouse, child, parent) to see and accept their point of view; demand that you not leave them and that you continually demonstrate how much you care; or demand that you tell them what to do and how to solve a problem. One way of heading off these problems is to make your expectations clear during the initial counseling session.

It could be useful for you to review some of your encounters with clients to assess the ways you feel that you have been the victim of excessive demands. What are some demands that were placed on you? How did you handle those situations? Can you say no to clients when you want to? Are you able to value yourself enough that you can make demands for yourself? Do you confront demanding clients, or do you allow them to manipulate you in the same way that they have manipulated others? If you let them manipulate you, are you doing them a favor?

DEALING WITH UNCOMMITTED CLIENTS

Related to the problem of demanding clients is that of clients who really have very little investment in their own counseling. Their lack of motivation may be evidenced by their frequent "forgetting" or canceling of appointments, stated indifference, or unwillingness to assume any of their own responsibility in the counseling process.

It is easy for beginning counselors to get drawn into unproductive games with these clients, to the extent that far more investment is being shown by the counselor than by the client. It is possible for counselors to try too hard to be understanding and accepting and therefore not to make any demands on their clients. I see it as a mistake to fail to confront clients who seem to lack personal investment. This is true even of the involuntary client.

I have seen too many instances in which the issue of the uncommitted client was used as a reason to justify the lack of progress in counseling. It is especially difficult for beginning counselors to confront a client who is not committed to working, for they fear that if they do so, the client will surely not return. Perhaps this direct confrontation is the very factor that can lead to a level of commitment from clients. If they persistently seem to forget appointments or fail to do any work during or outside of the therapy session, they can be asked if they want to continue coming for counseling. At least a clear decision not to continue if they are not willing to get involved is some step. In the case of clients who are sent to counseling by the court, the therapist can still tell them that although they are required to attend sessions, it is up to them to decide how they will use this time. They can eventually be shown that even though they are involuntary clients, they can use this time well.

ACCEPTING SLOW RESULTS

Do not expect instant results. You will not "cure" clients in a few sessions. So many beginning therapists experience the anxiety of not seeing the fruits of their labor. They ask themselves: "Am I really doing my client any good? Is the client perhaps getting worse? Is anything really occurring as a result of our sessions, or am I just deceiving myself into believing we're making progress?" I hope that you will learn to tolerate the ambiguity of not knowing for sure whether your client is improving, at least during the initial sessions. Understand that clients may apparently "get worse" before they show therapeutic gains. After clients have decided to work toward self-honesty and drop their defenses and facades, they can be expected to experience an increase of personal pain and disorganization, which might result in a depression or a panic reaction. Many a client has uttered: "My God, I was better off before I started therapy. Now I feel more vulnerable than before. Maybe I was better off when I was ignorant." Also, realize that the fruitful effects of the joint efforts of the therapist and the client may not be manifest for months (or even years) after the conclusion of therapy.

The year I began doing full-time individual and group counseling in a college counseling center was, professionally, the most trying year for me. Up until that time I was teaching a variety of psychology courses, and I could sense relatively quick results or the lack of them. I found teaching gratifying, reinforcing, and many times exciting; by contrast, counseling seemed like a laborious and thankless task. The students who came to the counseling center did not evidence any miraculous cures, and some would come each week with the same complaints. They saw little progress, sought answers, wanted some formula for feeling better, or wanted a shot of motivation. I was plagued with self-doubts and skepticism. My needs for reinforcement were so great that I was antitherapeutic for some. I needed them to need me, to tell me that I was effective, to assure me that they were noticing positive changes, and so on. I became aware that I had attempted to refer the depressed male students to other counselors, whereas I had put effort into encouraging a bright, attractive young woman to continue in counseling. Learning the dynamics of my motivation did not come easily, and I appreciated the confrontation that several of my colleagues provided in helping me become more honest about whose needs were really being met. Eventually I discovered that growth and change did occur in a number of my clients as a result of our joint efforts. They were willing to assume their responsibilities for taking risks, and I became more willing to stay with them, even though I was not at all sure of the results.

My beginning experiences taught me that I needed to be able to tolerate not knowing whether a client was progressing or whether I was being instrumental in that person's growth or change. I learned that the only way to acquire self-trust as a therapist was to allow myself to feel my self-doubts, uncertainty about my effectiveness, and ambivalence over whether I wanted to continue as a counseling psychologist. As I became less anxious over my performance, I was able to pay increasing attention both to the client and to myself in the therapeutic relationship.

AVOIDING SELF-DECEPTION

No discussion of guidelines for beginning counselors could be complete without mentioning the phenomenon of self-deception as it occurs in the counseling process — both by the counselor and by the client. Self-deception is not necessarily conscious lying, for it can be subtle and unconscious. For both parties the motivation for deception may be based on the need to make the relationship worthwhile and productive; both have invested in seeing positive results. Our need to witness personal changes may blur reality and cause us to be less skeptical than we should be.

Our need to feel that we are instrumental in assisting another to enjoy life more fully and our need to feel a sense that we do make significant differences can at times lead to self-deception. We look for evidence of progress, and we rationalize away elements of failure. Or we give ourselves credit for our clients' growth when it may be due largely to another variable, perhaps to something unrelated to the therapeutic relationship. My point is that being aware of a tendency toward self-deception in a counseling relationship can lead to an exploration of the phenomenon and thus lessen the chances of its occurring.

AVOIDING LOSING OURSELVES IN OUR CLIENTS

A common mistake for beginners is to worry too much about clients. There is a danger of incorporating clients' neuroses into our own personality. We lose sleep wondering what decisions they are making. We sometimes identify so closely with clients that we lose our own sense of identity and assume their identity. Empathy becomes distorted and militates against a therapeutic intervention. We need to learn how to "let clients go" and not carry around their problems until we see them again. The most therapeutic thing is to be as fully present as we are able to be (feeling with our clients and experiencing their struggles with them) but to let them assume the responsibility of their living and choosing outside of the session. If we become lost in clients' struggles and confusion, we cease being an effective agent in helping them find their way out of the darkness. If we take on ourselves the responsibility our clients need to learn to direct their lives, we are blocking rather than fostering their growth.

This discussion relates to an issue that we all need to recognize and face in our work as counselors—namely, *countertransference,* which occurs when a counselor's own needs or unresolved personal conflicts become entangled in the therapeutic relationship. Because countertransference that is not recognized and not successfully dealt with has the effect of blurring therapist objectivity (and actually intruding in the counseling process), it is essential that counselor trainees focus on *themselves* in supervision sessions. By dealing with the reactions that are stirred up in them in their relationship with a particular client, they can learn a lot about how their needs and unfinished business in their own life can bog down the progress of a client. Here are a few illustrations of common forms of countertransference:

- the need to be liked, appreciated, and approved of by clients
- the therapist's fear of challenging clients lest they leave and think poorly of the therapist
- sexual feelings and sexually seductive behavior on the therapist's part toward clients (to the extent that the therapist becomes preoccupied with sexual fantasies or deliberately focuses clients' attention on sexual feelings toward the therapist)
- extreme reactions to certain clients who evoke old feelings in the therapist—for example, clients who are perceived by the therapist as judgmental, domineering, paternalistic, maternalistic, controlling, and the like
- the therapist's need to take away clients' pain or struggles because their experience is opening up old wounds or unrecognized conflicts in the therapist
- compulsive giving of advice, with the counselor assuming a superior position of wanting to dictate how clients should live and the choices they should make

This brief discussion is not a complete treatment of the issue of learning how to work through our feelings toward clients. Because it may not be appropriate for us to use clients' time to work through our reactions to them, it makes it all the more important that we be willing to work on ourselves in our own sessions with another therapist, supervisor, or colleague. Although recognizing how our needs can intrude in our work as counselors is one beginning step, we need to be willing to continually explore what we are seeing in ourselves. If we do not, we increase the danger of losing ourselves in our clients and using them to meet our unfilled needs.

DEVELOPING A SENSE OF HUMOR

Although therapy is a responsible matter, it need not be deadly serious. Both clients and counselors can enrich a relationship by laughing. I have found that humor and tragedy are closely linked and that after allowing ourselves to feel some experiences that are painfully tragic, we can also genuinely laugh at how seriously we have taken our situation. We secretly delude ourselves into believing that we are unique in that we are alone in our pain and we alone have experienced the tragic. What a welcome relief when we can admit that pain is not our exclusive domain. The important point is that therapists recognize that laughter or humor does not mean that work is not being accomplished. There are times, of course, when laughter is used to cover up anxiety or to escape from the experience of facing threatening material. The therapist needs to distinguish between humor that distracts and humor that enhances the situation.

ESTABLISHING REALISTIC GOALS

Realistic goals are essential for a potential relationship with a client. Assume that your client is truly in need of a major overhaul. He presents himself as a man who is intensely dissatisfied with life, rarely accomplishes what he begins, and feels inadequate and helpless. Now for the reality of the situation. He comes into a community crisis-counseling clinic where you work. Your agency has a policy of limiting a person to a series of six counseling sessions. There are long lines, waiting lists, and many people in need of crisis counseling. The man comes to you because of his personal inability to function; his wife has just abandoned him. Even though both of you might agree that he needs more than a minor tune-up, the limitations of the services at hand prevent exploring his problems in depth. Both counselor and client need to decide on realistic goals. This does not mean that the two need to settle on patch-up work. One possibility is to explore the underlying dynamics of the presenting problem, with attention to what alternatives are open beyond the six sessions. If our aims are realistic we may be sad that we could not accomplish more, but at least we will not be steeped in frustration for not accomplishing miracles.

DECLINING TO GIVE ADVICE

A mistaken notion of those who are unsophisticated about the nature of therapy is to equate giving advice with the counseling process. Quite often clients who are suffering come to a therapy session seeking and even demanding advice. They want more than direction; they want a wise counselor to make a decision or resolve a problem for them. Counseling should not be confused with the dispensing of information or advice. As I view it, a therapist's tasks are to help clients discover their own solutions and recognize their own freedom of action, not to deprive them of the opportunity to act freely. A common escape by many clients is not trusting themselves to find solutions, use their freedom, or discover their own direction. Even if we, as counselors or therapists, were able to effectively resolve their struggles for them, we would be fostering their dependence on us. They would continually need to seek our counsel for every new twist in their difficulties. Our job is to help them independently make choices and have the courage to accept the consequences of their choices. Giving advice (as a style) does not work toward this end.

I am not ruling out occasional use of the technique of giving advice. There are appropriate times for direct advice, particularly when clients are clearly in danger of harming themselves or others or when for the time being they are unable to make choices. Also, information can be used legitimately in therapy as a basis for helping clients make their own choices. Essential to decision making is having pertinent information.

My caution is against overusing the technique of giving information and advice and considering doing so as counseling. Far too many inexperienced counselors fall into the trap of believing that they are not doing their job unless they are being prescriptive and meeting the apparent demands for advice from clients. I recommend that instead of merely being advice givers, we ask our clients questions such as "What alternatives are open to you? What possibilities do you see? If I were able to solve this particular problem, how would this help you with future problems? Are you asking me to assume your responsibility for you? How have you avoided accepting the responsibility for directing your own life in the past? Can part of your present problem stem from listening to the advice of others earlier?"

DEVELOPING OUR OWN COUNSELING STYLE

Counselors-in-training need to be cautioned about the tendency to mimic the style of their supervisor, therapist, or some other model. It is important that we accept that there is no "right" way of therapy and that wide variations in approach can be effective. I believe that we inhibit our potential effectiveness in reaching others when we attempt to imitate another therapist's style or when we fit most of our behavior during the session into the Procrustean bed of some expert's theory. Although I am fully aware that one's style as a counselor will be influenced by teachers, therapists, and supervisors, I caution against blurring one's own potential uniqueness by trying to imitate them. At best one becomes a carbon copy, a poor imitation of the other. I do not have any formula for the way to develop a unique therapeutic style, but I do think that the awareness of our tendency to copy our teachers is critical in freeing ourselves and finding a direction that is compatible with our personality. I advocate borrowing from others but, at the same time, finding a way that is distinctive to oneself.

STAYING ALIVE AS A PERSON AND AS A PROFESSIONAL

If the thesis that I have presented in this chapter is valid—that ultimately our single most important instrument is the person who we are and that our most powerful technique is our ability to model aliveness and realness—then taking care of ourselves so that we remain fully alive is essential. We need to work at dealing with those factors that threaten to drain life from us and render us helpless. I am presenting a discussion of this issue early in the book because I encourage you to consider how you can apply the theories that you will be studying to enhancing your life from both a personal and a professional standpoint. My assumption is that if you are aware of those factors that contribute to sapping your vitality as a person, you are in a better position to prevent the condition that is known as *professional burnout.*

What is burnout? I have heard counselors complain that they are just going through the motions on their job. They feel that whatever they are doing makes no difference at all and that they have nothing left to give. Some of these practitioners have convinced themselves that this feeling of burnout is one of the inevitable hazards of the profession and that there is not much that they can do to revitalize themselves. This assumption is lethal, for it cements the feeling of impotence and leads to a giving up of hope. Equally bad are those practitioners who do not realize that they are burned out!

Burnout manifests itself in many ways. Those who experience this syndrome typically find that they are tired, drained, and without enthusiasm. They talk of feeling pulled by their many projects, most of which seem to have lost meaning. They feel that what they do have to offer is either not wanted or not received; they feel unappreciated, unrecognized, and unimportant, and they go about their jobs in a mechanical and routine way. They tend not to see any concrete results or fruits from their efforts. Often they feel oppressed by the "system" and by institutional demands, which, they contend, stifle any sense of personal initiative. A real danger is that the burnout syndrome can feed off of itself, so that practitioners feel more and more isolated. They may fail to reach out to one another and to develop a support system. Because burnout can rob us of the vitality we need personally and professionally, it is important to look at some of its causes, possible remedies, and ways of preventing it.

CAUSES OF BURNOUT

Rather than having a single cause, burnout is a condition that results from a combination of factors. It is best understood by considering the individual, interpersonal, and organizational factors that contribute to the condition. Recognizing the causes of burnout can itself be a step in dealing with it. A few of them are:

- doing the same type of work with little variation, especially if this work seems meaningless
- giving a great deal personally and not getting back much in the way of appreciation or other positive responses
- lacking a sense of accomplishment and meaning in work
- being under constant and strong pressure to produce, perform, and meet deadlines, many of which may be unrealistic
- working with a difficult population, such as those who are highly resistant, who are involuntary clients, or who show very little progress
- conflict and tension among a staff; an absence of support from colleagues and an abundance of criticism
- lack of trust between supervisors and mental-health workers, leading to a condition in which they are working against each other instead of toward commonly valued goals
- not having opportunities for personal expression or for taking the initiative in trying new approaches, a situation in which experimentation, change, and innovation are not only unrewarded but also actively discouraged
- facing unrealistic demands on your time and energy
- having a job that is both personally and professionally taxing without

much opportunity for supervision, continuing education, or other forms of in-service training
- unresolved personal conflicts beyond the job situation, such as marital tensions, chronic health problems, financial problems, and so on

Rather than looking at burnout as something that could afflict you, you may find it useful to consider your own role in increasing the risk of burnout. Certain personality traits and characteristics can increase the risk factor. For instance, a strong need for approval for all that you do or an inordinate desire to be needed can lead to burnout. As long as the source of your value lies outside of yourself, you are in a tentative position, because once this external validation ceases, you begin to starve emotionally.

REMEDIES FOR BURNOUT

Learning ways to take care of ourselves is a necessary step beyond this initial recognition of the problem of burnout. I see acceptance of *personal responsibility* as one of the most critical factors. In my experience in conducting training workshops, it has become almost standard to hear mental-health workers blame the system and other external factors for their condition; the more they look outside of themselves for the reasons that they feel dead, the greater becomes their sense of impotence and hopelessness. At these workshops I often hear statements such as these:

- "I'm failing as a counselor because my clients are highly resistive and don't really want to change. Besides, they're not capable of much change!"
- "The system here keeps us down. We're merely small cogs that need to keep functioning if this big machine is to continue working."
- "I have far too many clients, and I also have too many demands on my time. All these demands make me feel useless, because I know I'll never be able to meet them."

Notice that these professionals are placing responsibility *outside* of themselves and that someone else or some impersonal factor is *making* them ineffective. This is the passive stance that so often contributes to general feelings of hopelessness and powerlessness. To the degree that professionals continue to blame external factors, they also surrender their own personal power and assume the position of a victim. This very passive state lends itself to the development of cynicism that makes it very difficult to harness energy and apply it to meeting tasks. It is essential that counselors recognize that even though external realities do exert a toll on personal energy, they themselves are playing a role in remaining passive. Although bureaucratic obstacles can make it difficult to function effectively, it is possible to learn ways to survive with dignity within an institution and to engage in meaningful work. This means that counselors will have to become active and stop blaming the system for all that they *cannot do*. Instead, as a place to begin, they can focus on what they *can do* to bring about *some* changes and to create a climate in which they can do work that has meaning for them.

PREVENTING BURNOUT

Learning to look within yourself to determine what choices you are making (and not making) to keep yourself alive can go a long way in preventing what some people consider to be an inevitable condition associated with the helping professions. It is crucial to recognize that you have considerable control over whether you become burned out. Although you cannot always control stressful events, you do have a great deal of control over how you interpret and react to these events. What is so important to realize is that you cannot continue to give and give while getting little in return. There is a price to pay for always being available and for assuming that you are able to control the lives and destinies of others. Become attuned to the subtle signs of burnout, rather than waiting for a full-blown condition of emotional and physical exhaustion to set in. Develop your own strategy for keeping yourself alive personally and professionally. A few suggestions of some ways in which you can prevent burnout follow:

- Evaluate your goals, priorities, and expectations to see if they are realistic and if they are getting you what you want.
- Recognize that you can be an active agent in your life.
- Find other interests besides work, especially if your work is not meeting your most important needs.
- Think of ways to bring variety into work.
- Take the initiative to start new projects that have personal meaning, and do not wait for the system to sanction this initiative.
- Learn to monitor the impact of stress, on the job and at home.
- Attend to your health through adequate sleep, an exercise program, proper diet, and meditation or relaxation.
- Develop a few friendships that are characterized by a mutuality of giving *and* receiving.
- Learn how to ask for what you want, though don't expect always to get it
- Learn how to work for self-confirmation and for self-rewards, as opposed to looking externally for validation.
- Find meaning through play, travel, or new experiences.
- Take the time to evaluate the meaningfulness of your projects to determine where you should continue to invest time and energy.
- Avoid assuming burdens that are properly the responsibility of others. If you worry more about your clients than they do about themselves, for example, it would be well for you to reconsider this investment.
- Take classes and workshops, attend conferences, and read to gain new perspectives on old issues.
- Rearrange your schedule to reduce stress.
- Learn your limits, and learn to set limits with others.
- Learn to accept yourself with your imperfections, including being able to forgive yourself when you make a mistake or do not live up to your ideals.
- Exchange jobs with a colleague for a short period, or ask a colleague to join forces in a common work project.
- Form a support group with colleagues to share openly feelings of frustration and to find better ways of approaching the reality of difficult job situations.

- Cultivate some hobbies that bring pleasure.
- Make time for your spiritual growth.
- Become more active in your professional organization.
- Seek counseling as an avenue of personal development.

Although this is not an exhaustive list, it does provide some direction for thinking about ways in which to keep ourselves alive. Our attempts to keep ourselves professionally updated will not mean much if we feel dead personally. This is why we must make periodic assessments of the direction of our own life to determine if we are living the way we want. If we are not, we must decide what we are willing to actually do to *make* changes occur, rather than simply wait for new life to enter us. By being in tune with ourselves, by having the experience of centeredness and solidness, and by feeling a sense of personal power, we have the basis for integrating our life experiences with our professional experiences. Such a synthesis can provide the basis for being an effective professional.

SUMMARY

One of the most basic issues in the counseling profession concerns the significance of the counselor as a person in the therapeutic relationship. Since counselors are asking people to take an honest look at themselves and to make choices concerning how they want to change, it is critical that counselors themselves be searchers who hold their own lives open to the same kind of scrutiny. Counselors should repeatedly ask themselves such questions as "What do I personally have to offer others who are struggling to find their way? Am I doing in my own life what I urge others to do?"

Counselors can acquire an extensive theoretical and practical knowledge and can make that knowledge available to their clients. But to every therapeutic session they also bring themselves as persons. They bring their human qualities and the life experiences that have molded them. It is my belief that professionals can be well versed in psychological theory and can learn diagnostic and interviewing skills and still be ineffective as helpers. If counselors are to promote growth and change in their clients, they must be willing to promote growth in their own life by exploring their own choices and decisions and by striving to become aware of the ways in which they have ignored their own potential for growth. This willingness to attempt to live in accordance with what they teach and thus to be positive models for their clients is what makes counselors "therapeutic persons."

QUESTIONS FOR REFLECTION AND DISCUSSION

1. Assume that you are applying for a counseling position and are asked "What personal characteristics would make you an effective counselor?" How would you reply?
2. When you think about selecting counseling as a profession, what psycho-

logical needs are bound up with your choice? What are your main motivations for wanting to pursue a career in the helping professions?

3. What are your thoughts about personal counseling for those who are going into the counseling profession? Do you think it should be required (or recommended) for students in graduate programs? What about personal counseling for practicing counselors? What value do you place on some type of personal-growth experience for yourself?

4. Can you think of one value you hold that may make it difficult for you to be objective and helpful in counseling certain types of clients? Can you identify a potential area where you may expect a conflict between a client's values and your values?

5. As a counselor, do you see it as your role to teach values to your clients? Do you think that it is ever justified to impose your values on clients? What would you do if you were convinced that your client's values were leading him or her down a path of self-destruction?

6. Can you identify a few ways in which your cultural background and past experiences have a continuing impact on you today? How do you think these factors would influence your effectiveness as a counselor?

7. When you think of yourself working with culturally diverse client populations, how ready do you feel to meet this challenge? If you are not yet ready, what steps could you take to become a more effective counselor with these groups?

8. When you think of beginning to practice counseling, what issues and concerns are most prominent in your mind? How could you deal with the most pressing issues you expect to face as a practitioner?

9. What are some specific personal factors or traits that would probably contribute most to your burnout as a professional helper?

10. Given the fact that so many helpers experience burnout, what specific steps can you think of to lessen your chances of burning out? If you burn out, what will you do?

WHERE TO GO FROM HERE

In writing about the use of self in therapy, Virginia Satir (1987) emphasizes the person of the therapist as the central point around which successful therapy revolves. Although theories and techniques are important, in her view, they are merely tools to be used in a fully human context. The aim of this chapter has been to invite you to think about ways in which you may use your own self in the counseling endeavor.

When you study the nine therapeutic approaches, I encourage you to apply their key concepts and central themes to your life. If you read this book in a personal way, you will be able to get more from the experience than simple knowledge about theories and techniques of counseling. You can use this book and the course you are taking as an opportunity for personal growth. I hope that you will select one or more of the books listed in the "Recommended Supplementary Readings" of this chapter as material for personal reflection

RECOMMENDED SUPPLEMENTARY READINGS

Burnout: The Cost of Caring (Maslach, 1982) is my top recommendation for a comprehensive and readable discussion of how to recognize signs of burnout and strategies for remediation and prevention. I see this book as a classic in providing information about the scope of burnout. There is an excellent annotated bibliography.

I Never Knew I Had a Choice (G. Corey & Corey, 1990) is a good resource with which to continue a reading program on the counselor as a person. Topics include our struggle to achieve autonomy; the roles that work, love, sexuality, intimacy, and solitude play in our lives; the meaning of loneliness, death, and loss; and the ways in which we choose our values and philosophy of life. Readers are continually encouraged to apply what they read to their personal life and to examine the choices they have made and how these choices affect their present level of satisfaction. The central theme of the book can be summed up in these words: "As we recognize that we are not merely passive victims of our circumstances, we can consciously become the architects of our lives. Even though others may have drawn the blueprints, we can recognize the plan, take a stand, and change the design."

Becoming a Helper (M. Corey & Corey, 1989) has many chapters that expand on topics dealing with the personal and professional lives of helpers. Some of these topics include the motivations for becoming helpers, the helper in the helping process, value issues, common concerns facing counselors, self-exploration and personal growth, managing stress, and dealing with professional burnout.

Issues and Ethics in the Helping Professions (G. Corey, Corey, & Callanan, 1988) is also relevant to the issues in this chapter. Especially appropriate are the chapters on the counselor as a person and as a professional and on the counselor's values.

The Art of the Psychotherapist (Bugental, 1987) is designed to help therapists of various orientations give priority to the subjective world of the client as well as to their own subjective world. The author draws on a wide variety of clinical examples and personal reflections to describe the art of psychotherapy.

The Use of Self in Therapy (Baldwin & Satir, 1987) is a collection of articles that focuses on the therapist's role in the therapeutic process. This subject is dealt with from a historical, philosophical, clinical, and research perspective.

The Imperfect Therapist: Learning from Failure in Therapeutic Practice (Kottler & Blau, 1989) describes how unrealistic expectations and perfectionism can influence therapists' experience of failure. The authors write about the common mistakes of beginning therapists and show how they can learn from these experiences.

On Being a Therapist (Kottler, 1986) discusses how therapists' work directly affects their personal life. By becoming involved in the exploration of their clients' pain, therapists open up their own psychological wounds. Examples are given of the price that therapists pay for working with high levels of stress.

Professionals in Distress: Issues, Syndromes, and Solutions in Psychology (Kilburg, Nathan, & Thoreson, 1986) is an excellent compilation of articles dealing with stress, burnout, and the hazards of the profession.

Counseling the Culturally Different: Theory and Practice (Sue, 1981a) presents an integrated framework for viewing issues of cross-cultural counseling. The book identifies similarities and differences among the various ethnic groups as they relate to mental-health practices, and it provides a wider focus on how the social and political system affects minorities and counseling. The concept of the culturally skilled counselor is especially well described. Sue offers perspectives for understanding Asian Americans, Blacks, and Hispanics and provides recommendations for counseling them.

A Handbook for Developing Multicultural Awareness (Pedersen, 1988) is based on the assumption that all counseling is to some extent multicultural. The author contends that we can either choose to attend to the influence of culture or ignore it. This useful handbook deals with topics such as developing multicultural awareness, becoming aware of our culturally biased assumptions, acquiring knowledge for effective multicultural counseling, and learning skills to deal with cultural diversity.

Counseling American Minorities: A Cross-Cultural Perspective, 3rd Edition (Atkinson, Morten, & Sue, 1989) describes a minority-identity development model. This edited book has excellent sections dealing with counseling for Native Americans, Asian Americans, Blacks, and Latinos.

REFERENCES AND SUGGESTED READINGS*

AMERICAN ASSOCIATION FOR COUNSELING AND DEVELOPMENT. (1988). *Ethical standards* (rev. ed.). Alexandria, VA: Author.

AMERICAN PSYCHOLOGICAL ASSOCIATION. (1981). *Ethical principles of psychologists* (rev. ed.). Washington, DC: Author.

APONTE, H. J., & WINTER, J. E. (1987). The person and practice of the therapist: Treatment and training. In M. Baldwin & V. Satir (Eds.), *The use of self in therapy* (pp. 85–112). New York: Haworth Press.

*ATKINSON, D. R., MORTEN, G., & SUE, D. W. (Eds.). (1989). *Counseling American minorities: A cross-cultural perspective* (3rd ed.). Dubuque, IA: William C. Brown.

BALDWIN, D. C., JR. (1987). Some philosophical and psychological contributions to the use of self in therapy. In M. Baldwin & V. Satir (Eds.), *The use of self in therapy* (pp. 27–44). New York: Haworth Press.

*BALDWIN, M. (1987). An interview with Carl Rogers on the use of self in therapy. In M. Baldwin & V. Satir (Eds.), *The use of self in therapy* (pp. 45–52). New York: Haworth Press.

*BALDWIN, M., & SATIR, V. (Eds.). (1987). *The use of self in therapy.* New York: Haworth Press.

BARUTH, L. G., & ROBINSON, E. H., III. (1987). *An introduction to the counseling profession.* Englewood Cliffs, NJ: Prentice-Hall.

*BATES, C. M., & BRODSKY, A. M. (1989). *Sex in the therapy hour.* New York: Guilford Press.

BENESCH, K. F., & PONTEROTTO, J. G. (1989). East and West: Transpersonal psychology and cross-cultural counseling. *Counseling and Values, 33,* 121–131.

BERGIN, A. E. (1988). Three contributions of a spiritual perspective to counseling, psychotherapy, and behavior change. *Counseling and Values, 33,* 21–31.

BLOCHER, D. (1989). Invited commentary on Values in Counseling and Psychotherapy, by C. H. Patterson. *Counseling and Values, 33,* 178–181.

*BUGENTAL, J. F. T. (1987). *The art of the psychotherapist.* New York: Norton.

CASAS, J. M. (1986). *Falling short of meeting the counseling needs of racial/ethnic minorities: The status of ethical and accreditation guidelines.* Unpublished manuscript, University of California at Santa Barbara.

CLARK, M. M. (1986). Personal therapy: A review of empirical research. *Professional Psychology: Research and Practice, 17,* 541–543.

*COMBS, A. W. (1986). What makes a good helper? A person-centered approach. *Person-Centered Review, 1,* 51–61.

COREY, G. (1989). Invited commentary on Values in Counseling and Psychotherapy, by C. H. Patterson. *Counseling and Values, 33,* 177–178.

---

* Books and articles marked with an asterisk are suggested for further study.

*COREY, G., & COREY, M. (1990). *I never knew I had a choice* (4th ed.). Pacific Grove, CA: Brooks/Cole.

*COREY, G., COREY, M., & CALLANAN, P. (1988). *Issues and ethics in the helping professions* (3rd ed.). Pacific Grove, CA: Brooks/Cole.

*COREY, M., & COREY, G. (1989). *Becoming a helper.* Pacific Grove, CA: Brooks/Cole.

CORMIER, L. S., & HACKNEY, H. (1987). *The professional counselor: A process guide to helping.* Englewood Cliffs, NJ: Prentice-Hall.

DEUTSCH, C. J. (1984). Self-reported sources of stress among psychotherapists. *Professional Psychology: Research and Practice, 15,* 833–845.

DEUTSCH, C. J. (1985). A survey of therapists' personal problems and treatment. *Professional Psychology: Research and Practice, 16,* 305–315.

FARBER, B. A. (1983a). Psychotherapists' perceptions of stressful patient behavior. *Professional Psychology: Research and Practice, 14,* 697–705.

FARBER, B. A. (1983b). *Stress and burnout in the human service professions.* New York: Pergamon Press.

FARBER, B. A., & HEIFETZ, L. J. (1982). The process and dimensions of burnout in psychotherapists. *Professional Psychology, 13,* 293–301.

*GUY, J. D. (1987). *The personal life of the psychotherapist.* New York: Wiley.

*GUY, J. D., & LIABOE, G. P. (1986). The impact of conducting psychotherapy upon the interpersonal relationships of the psychotherapist. *Professional Psychology: Research and Practice, 17,* 111–114.

*GUY, J. D., STARK, M. J., & POELSTRA, P. L. (1988). Personal therapy for psychotherapists before and after entering professional practice. *Professional Psychology: Research and Practice, 19,* 474–476.

*HERR, E. L., & NILES, S. (1988). The values of counseling: Three domains. *Counseling and Values, 33,* 4–17.

*JENSEN, J. P., & BERGIN, A. E. (1988). Mental health values of professional therapists: A national interdisciplinary survey. *Professional Psychology: Research and Practice, 14,* 290–297.

*KILBURG, R. R. (1986). The distressed professional: The nature of the problem. In R. R. Kilburg, P. E. Nathan, & R. W. Thoreson (Eds.), *Professionals in distress: Issues, syndromes, and solutions in psychology* (pp. 13–26). Washington, DC: American Psychological Association.

*KILBURG, R. R., NATHAN, P. E., & THORESON, R. W. (Eds.). (1986). *Professionals in distress: Issues, syndromes, and solutions in psychology.* Washington, DC: American Psychological Association.

*KOTTLER, J. A. (1986). *On being a therapist.* San Francisco: Jossey-Bass.

*KOTTLER, J. A., & BLAU, D. (1989). *The imperfect therapist: Learning from failure in therapeutic practice.* San Francisco: Jossey-Bass.

*MASLACH, C. (1982). *Burnout: The cost of caring.* Englewood Cliffs, NJ: Prentice-Hall (Spectrum).

MILLER, G. D., & BALDWIN, D. C., JR. (1987). Implications of the wounded-healer paradigm for the use of the self in therapy. In M. Baldwin & V. Satir (Eds.), *The use of self in therapy* (pp. 139–152). New York: Haworth Press.

PATTERSON, C. H. (1978). Cross-cultural or intercultural counseling or psychotherapy. *International Journal for the Advancement of Counseling, 1,* 231–247.

*PATTERSON, C. H. (1989). Values in counseling and psychotherapy. *Counseling and Values, 33,* 164–176.

*PEDERSEN, P. (1988). *A handbook for developing multicultural awareness.* Alexandria, VA: American Association for Counseling and Development.

*PEDERSEN, P. (1990). The multicultural perspective as a fourth force in counseling. *Journal of Mental Health Counseling, 12,* 93–95.

REISMAN, J. M. (1986). Psychotherapy as a professional relationship. *Professional Psychology: Research and Practice, 17,* 565–569.

RICE, P. L. (1987). *Stress and health: Principles and practice for coping and wellness.* Pacific Grove, CA: Brooks/Cole.

RUSSO, T. J. (1984). A model for addressing spiritual issues in counseling. *Counseling and Values, 29,* 42–48.

*SAPER, B. (1987). Humor in psychotherapy: Is it good or bad for the client? *Professional Psychology: Research and Practice, 18,* 360–367.

*SATIR, V. (1987). The therapist story. In M. Baldwin & V. Satir (Eds.), *The use of self in therapy* (pp. 17–26). New York: Haworth Press.

*SCOTT, C. D., & HAWK, J. (Eds.). (1986). *Heal thyself: The health of health care professionals.* New York: Brunner/Mazel.

*SUE, D. W. (1981a). *Counseling the culturally different: Theory and practice.* New York: Wiley.

*SUE, D. W. (1981b). *Position paper on cross-cultural counseling competencies.* Education and Training Committee report delivered to Division 17, APA Executive Committee.

*SUE, D. W., BERNIER, J. E., DURRAN, A., FEINBERG, L., PEDERSEN, P., SMITH, E. J., & NUTTALL, E. V. (1982). Position paper: Cross-cultural counseling competencies. *The Counseling Psychologist, 10,* 45–52.

*SUE, S. (1988). Psychotherapeutic services for ethnic minorities: Two decades of research findings. *American Psychologist, 43,* 301–308.

*WISE, P. S., LOWERY, S., & SILVERGLADE, L. (1989). Personal counseling for counselors in training: Guidelines for supervisors. *Counselor Education and Supervision, 28,* 326–336.

*WRIGHT, J., COLEY, S., & COREY, G. (1989). Challenges facing human services education today. *Journal of Counseling and Human Service Professions, 3,* 3–11.

3

ETHICAL ISSUES IN COUNSELING PRACTICE

INTRODUCTION

This chapter introduces you to some of the ethical principles and issues that will be a basic part of your professional practice. Its purpose is to stimulate you to think further about these issues so that you can form a sound basis for ethical decision making. As a practitioner you will ultimately have to apply the ethical codes of your profession to the many practical problems you will face. You will not be able to rely on ready-made answers or prescriptions given by professional organizations, which typically provide only broad guidelines for responsible practice. These organizations include the American Association for Counseling and Development (AACD) (1988), the American Association for Marriage and Family Therapy (AAMFT) (1988), the American Mental Health Counselors Association (AMHCA) (1980), the American Psychiatric Association (1986), the American Psychoanalytic Association (1983), the American Psychological Association (APA) (1981, 1989), the National Association of Social Workers (NASW) (1979), the National Board for Certified Counselors (NBCC) (1987), and the National Federation of Societies for Clinical Social Work (1985). (The addresses of most of these organizations are found in the Appendix of the student manual of this textbook.) Additionally, many regional, state, and local professional organizations for social workers, psychologists, counselors, and other mental-health specialists have developed their own guidelines. You should be aware of the consequences of practicing in ways that are not sanctioned by organizations of which you are a member.

As you become involved in counseling, you may find that interpreting these guidelines demands the utmost ethical sensitivity. Even among responsible practitioners there are differences of opinion over the application of established ethical principles to specific situations. Consequently, a vital dimension of becoming a professional counselor or therapist is facing questions to which there are no obvious answers. You will have to struggle with yourself to decide how to act in ways that will further the best interests of your clients. To help you make such decisions, you should be willing to consult with colleagues, keep yourself informed about laws affecting your practice, keep up-to-date in your specialty field, stay abreast of developments in ethical practice, reflect on the impact that your values have on your practice, and be willing to engage in honest self-examination.

One practical way to keep yourself informed on ethical and professional matters is by reading about these issues and discussing them with fellow students and colleagues. Another good way is by joining one of the professional organizations, which provide members with current information. Within the past decade there has been a definite increase in the frequency of articles in the professional journals dealing with ethics, and the number of books on ethical issues has significantly increased. (See the "References and Suggested Readings" at the end of this chapter for a sampling of these books and articles.)

TRENDS IN THE TEACHING OF PROFESSIONAL ETHICS

The process of learning to become an ethical practitioner begins with counselor-education programs, which normally include seminars in ethical principles and practices. Students should, as a beginning, familiarize themselves thoroughly with established ethical standards. They need to be sensitive to any ethical problems that arise in their practicum experiences and then to discuss these problems in a seminar session or with their supervisor. Part of a counselor's education is developing a sense of sound judgment, and dealing with basic ethical issues can assist in that development.

Fortunately, there is a clear trend toward introducing counselors-in-training to the kinds of ethical and legal issues that they are likely to encounter. Lipsitz (1985) reports that the literature reveals a sevenfold increase in the availability of training experiences over the past 30 years. Ninety-two percent of the participants in his study had been exposed to some systematic attempt to incorporate professional ethics into their curriculum. Of this group 51% had had a formal course in ethics, and 41% had been exposed to ethical issues throughout several courses in their program. One study found that 87% of the master's programs in psychology had some format for teaching ethics, either through a formal course or by informal discussions of ethical issues during practicum and internship supervision sessions (Handelsman, 1986a). Even though many programs attempt to increase students' awareness by introducing ethical dilemmas into various courses, a case can be made for devoting a formal course to professional ethics as well. Handelsman (1986b) contends that there are problems with ethics training by "osmosis," and he argues for formal course work. He thinks that to rely exclusively on informal methods through the context of supervision is a dangerous practice.

From my perspective, students need both formal and informal opportunities to discuss ethical dilemmas throughout their training program. I have found that students are eager to exchange ideas and willing to think critically about cases involving ethical concerns. Through role-playing case vignettes, followed by discussion, students learn to identify issues and clarify their positions. Many students begin the course expecting to find definite answers for every problem they might encounter. However, they typically leave the course with an increased capacity to raise germane questions and to make ethical decisions. They also become aware of the complexity of most of these issues and come to appreciate that there are few simplistic solutions. By following up on my students, I have found that their ethical sense progresses as they gain practical experience in a variety of settings. Many of these students show a willingness to consult with their supervisors and colleagues, and they also get involved in continuing-education programs through their professional organizations.

The ethical issues raised in this chapter need to be periodically reexamined throughout your professional life. Even if you resolve some of these issues after completing a graduate program, there is no guarantee that everything will be settled once and for all. These issues are bound to take on new dimensions as you gain more experience. I have found that students often burden themselves unnecessarily with the expectation that they should resolve all difficult issues before they are ready to practice. Ethical decision making is an evolutionary process that requires you to be continually open and self-critical.

APPLYING ETHICS TO SOCIAL PROBLEMS

In recent years interest has increased in applying the ethical standards of counseling to alleviate human suffering on a broader scale. No longer can the practitioner be safely tucked away in the office; the trend is toward social action. Many mental-health professionals now emphasize this ethical responsibility by exerting their influence against such wrongs as discrimination against women and minority groups, the continuation of racism in society, the neglect of the aged, and inhumane practices against children. Seminars and workshops are conducted to awaken the dulled consciences of many professionals. Counselors need to be acquainted with these pressing social and political issues. In sum, counselors are discovering that, to bring about significant individual change, they cannot remain blind and deaf to the major social ills that often create and foster problems for individuals; they must become active agents of constructive social change. This social consciousness is an ethical mandate for effective counseling practice.

THERAPIST COMPETENCE, EDUCATION, AND TRAINING

As a basic ethical principle, therapists are expected to recognize their own personal and professional limitations. Ethical counselors do not employ diagnostic or treatment procedures that are beyond the scope of their training, nor do they accept clients whose personal functioning is seriously impaired unless they are qualified to work with those clients. Counselors who become aware of their lack of competence in a particular case have the responsibility to seek consultation with colleagues or a supervisor or to make a referral.

CRITERIA FOR DETERMINING COMPETENCE

What is the basis on which practitioners can decide whether they are qualified to offer specific professional services? According to the APA's *Ethical Principles of Psychologists* (1989), "Psychologists recognize the boundaries of their competence and the limitations of their techniques. They only provide services and only use techniques for which they are qualified by training and experience." The AACD's *Ethical Standards* (1988) state: "Members [counselors] recognize their boundaries of competence and provide only those services and use only those techniques for which they are qualified by training or experience. Members should only accept those positions for which they are professionally qualified." Such a guideline still leaves unanswered the question "How can I recognize the boundaries of my competence, and how can I know when I have exceeded them?" This issue is not solved by the mere possession of advanced degrees or of licenses and credentials. In reality, many people who complete master's and doctoral programs in a mental-health specialty still lack the skills training, practical experience, or personal characteristics needed to function effectively as practitioners with certain populations. Licenses and certifications are not necessarily better criteria of competence than degrees.

Licenses mainly reassure the public that the holders have completed some type of formal academic program, have been exposed to a certain number of hours of supervision, and have a *minimum* number of hours of professional experience (some of which has been supervised by a licensed person). The licensing of marriage and family therapists, mental-health counselors, clinical social workers, and psychologists is an issue of intense interest to practitioners' organizations, mainly because it has come to be associated with professionalism. In fact, practitioners who misrepresent themselves as being licensed are subject to legal penalties in most states. Yet licenses alone do not ensure that these practitioners can competently perform the permitted duties. Further, licenses typically do not specify the clients or problems that practitioners are competent to deal with or the specialized techniques they have mastered. A licensed psychologist may work very effectively with a certain population of adults, for example, yet not be qualified by virtue of training or experience to work with children or adolescents. Professional standards and most licensing regulations do specify that licensees are to engage only in those methods of intervention for which they have adequate training.

Arguments for and against professional licensing.   The argument for licensure is based on the assumption that the consumer is better protected with legal regulation than without it. The premise is that incompetent practitioners could cause harmful consequences. Those who challenge professional licensing, however, often maintain that it encourages self-serving interests of professional groups, such as financial advantage and status.

Professional disclosure as an alternative to licensing.   One alternative to the present licensing practices would be requiring practitioners to fully disclose information about themselves and their practice. Professional disclosure can take many forms, but it usually entails the following: informing prospective clients about one's qualifications; describing the counseling services offered, with an explanation of the therapeutic process; describing the rights and responsibilities of clients; clarifying the nature of confidentiality and the release of information; and outlining the administrative procedures relating to time and money (Lovett & Lovett, 1988). The rationale is that clients must have this information to make intelligent decisions about the use of a practitioner's services.

I think that professional disclosure has benefits for both clients and practitioners. It is useful even if practitioners are licensed, for it provides some basis for an assessment of how well services are being provided. Holding a license does not always mean that a professional is providing services that will benefit clients. Although therapists can legally practice by automatically renewing their licenses, ethical practice demands an approach that will keep their knowledge and skills up-to-date.

Consultation.   Practitioners must continually assess their competence to help particular clients. There will be times when even experienced therapists will need to consult colleagues or a specialist in a related field. It is possible that therapists who have worked with clients over a long period will lose their perspective with these clients. At times it is wise for therapists to confer with colleagues to share their perceptions of what is occurring with their clients, within themselves, and between them and their clients. If a client complains all the time of physical symptoms (such as headaches), it seems essential that any organic problem be ruled out by a physician before the assumption is made that the client's problem is psychologically caused. What if the client had a brain tumor and the psychological counselor failed to refer him or her to a physician for a physical examination? It is also a good practice for counselors to find a psychiatrist with whom they can consult, especially about their more seriously disturbed clients.

TRAINING AND SUPERVISION

Related to the issue of competence are the questions "What education, training, and supervision are necessary for ensuring competent practice?" and "What experiences are necessary for prospective counselors?" There are two points of view about the preparation necessary for counseling. On one side is the position that clinical work of any form, even under supervision, should not be undertaken until late in a candidate's doctoral program or even until the post-doctoral period. This view regards as dangerous any untrained and unseasoned "amateurs" who have not acquired a Ph.D. and considers it unwise (perhaps unethical) to allow a person to practice counseling below a doctoral level. On the other side are those who favor training in counseling and various practicum experiences at an early stage in the student's program. This viewpoint endorses the initiation of supervised practical experience as early in the course of prepa-ration as the maturity and responsibility of the individual student allow. My view is that a counseling program ought to incorporate both academic and experien-tial phases and that counselors can be effectively trained at the master's level.

If experienced practitioners need occasional consultation, it goes without saying that beginning therapists need supervision and continuing consultation. In working with undergraduate human-services students and with graduate students in counseling programs, I have found most of them eager for direction and supervision. They often ask for extra time and are quite willing to discuss openly their reactions, blockages, frustrations, and confusions. Realizing that they need skills in working effectively with the problems that clients bring, they tend to want to discuss their fieldwork experiences. It thus becomes an ethical and practical concern that appropriate supervision be given to the intern, for the sake of both the client's welfare and the intern's professional growth. A problem can arise when the counselor intern is placed in a community agency and the on-the-job supervisor is so busy with the duties of the agency that he or she has little time left for supervising interns. I encourage interns to seek actively and assertively the supervision they need to carry out the duties of their field place-ment. If the supervisor does not initiate close supervision, trainees need to persist in asking for what they need.

CONTINUING EDUCATION

Professional competence is not something that we attain once and for all, even by the earning of advanced degrees and licenses. Continuing professional education is essential for keeping up-to-date with new knowledge in your professional speciality as well as for sharpening your skills. Although most professions support efforts to make continuing education a mandatory condition of relicensing, it is still possible for some practitioners to stop the process of learning once they have earned an advanced degree. Some professional organizations have a voluntary program, even if the state does not mandate continuing education. For example, all clinical members of the AAMFT are encouraged to complete 150 hours of education every three years.

As another example, consider the recertification requirements for a National Certified Counselor (NCC). To become a National Certified Counselor, one must have at least a master's degree in counseling (or a related field), have a specified number of hours of supervised field experience and practicum, and pass an examination. The certification is designed to assess the counseling knowledge of candidates. Regardless of one's specialization, the examination samples eight areas deemed important for all professional counselors: the helping relationship; group dynamics, group process, and counseling; human growth and development; lifestyle and career development; professional orientation; appraisal of individuals; social and cultural foundations; and research and evaluation. The National Board for Certified Counselors operates on the assumption that NCCs should continually demonstrate their readiness to deliver quality services to the public. The certification is valid for five years, after which an NCC will be recertified if the following conditions are met: completion of 100 hours of continuing education, continuing professional practice, and adherence to the national board's code of ethics in professional practice. In summary, the objectives of this recertification process are to encourage NCCs to obtain current information on professional developments, explore new knowledge in specific content areas, master new skills and techniques, learn a variety of approaches for effective counseling, develop critical inquiry skills and professional judgment, and conduct their professional practice in an ethical and appropriate manner.

Those counselors who fail to keep abreast of developments are certainly vulnerable on both ethical and legal grounds. Personally, I would like to see practitioners decide for themselves the kind of in-service and continuing education that would be most meaningful. They might choose a combination of formal course work, attendance at professional workshops, participation in professional conferences where one can be challenged and stimulated, and some opportunities for having one's work observed and critiqued by colleagues. Continuing such personalized education and training seems better than merely complying with state regulations that stipulate completion of a minimum number of hours in a given area.

One area where continuing education is particularly important is in providing counseling in a multicultural society. Although graduate programs are giving increased emphasis to the cultural factors in counseling, too many counselors ignore the reality of ethnic diversity (Pedersen, 1989, 1990). Continuing education can provide practitioners with both the knowledge and the skills they need to work effectively with a culturally diverse clientele.

ETHICAL ISSUES IN A MULTICULTURAL PERSPECTIVE

In the previous chapter, as you will recall, we considered the importance of taking the client's cultural context into account in counseling. We now look at how it is possible that conscientious and well-intentioned practitioners who follow their professional code of ethics can still be practicing unethically if they do not address cultural differences. Pedersen (1986, 1989) contends that the APA's (1981) ethical principles are culturally encapsulated. That is, to the extent that these codes are based on stereotyped values from the dominant culture's perspective, they need to be revised so that the interests of minority groups are taken into account. Furthermore, if these codes are grounded on a single standard of normal and ethical behavior, they require revision to incorporate a variety of culturally defined alternatives.

Contending that the 1981 version of the AACD's ethical code was limited, Ibrahim and Arredondo (1986, 1990) recommended that it be extended to address multicultural perspectives. They proposed standards in the areas of preparing culturally effective counselors, providing ethical and effective counseling for diverse cultural and ethnic groups, selecting and using culturally appropriate assessment devices, and conducting culturally appropriate research.

After the AACD revised its *Ethical Standards* in 1988, Ibrahim and Arredondo (1990) took the position that these standards still fell short in addressing the needs of diverse cultural groups. They contend that although training programs give the appearance of recognizing the needs of minority groups, they all too frequently educate professionals to render services to a middle-class, mainstream population. Reaffirming their commitment to multiculturalism, they write that it is unethical for counselors to remain monocultural and practice in a multicultural society. As a minimum goal they propose that every professional become biculturally effective.

If counselors do not have a frame of reference for being sensitive to and understanding clients who are of a different gender, race, age, social class, or sexual orientation, they lessen the possibilities of establishing an effective client/counselor relationship. The failure to address these factors and to train to work with such groups constitutes unethical practice (Cayleff, 1986; Pedersen & Marsella, 1982). Traditional therapeutic practices for people of color, and other special populations such as the elderly, have been criticized by some counselors as irrelevant. Most techniques are derived from counseling approaches developed by and for White, male, middle-class, Western clients, and therefore they may not be applicable to clients from different racial, ethnic, and cultural backgrounds (Cormier & Hackney, 1987). The Western models of counseling have major limitations when they are applied to certain special populations and minority groups such as Asian and Pacific Islanders, Hispanics, Native Americans, and Blacks. Moreover, value assumptions made by culturally different counselors and clients have resulted in culturally biased counseling and have led to underuse of mental-health services (Pedersen, 1988). For a more detailed treatment of ethical issues in multicultural counseling see La-Fromboise and Foster (1989), Ibrahim and Arredondo (1990), and Corey, Corey, and Callanan (1988).

FOUNDATIONS OF ETHICAL PRACTICE

As a general definition ethical practices benefit the client; unethical practices are done for the practitioner's benefit. Some practices are clearly ethical, others are blatantly unethical, and still others do not lend themselves to clear categorization.

ASSESSING ETHICAL AND UNETHICAL PRACTICES

A national survey was conducted to identify what therapists considered to be good practices and poor practices in psychotherapy (Pope, Tabachnick, & Keith-Spiegel, 1988). The researchers found that a vast majority (80%) of the respondents judged several actions pertaining to sex, business activities, confidentiality, and providing services beyond one's competence to be poor practices. The following five practices involved sexual issues: "engaging in sexual contact with a client," "engaging in erotic activity with a client," "disrobing in the presence of a client," "allowing a client to disrobe," and "engaging in sex with a clinical supervisee." The three items pertaining to business issues were "getting paid to refer clients to someone," "going into business with a client," and "borrowing money from a client." The confidentiality issues included "unintentionally disclosing confidential data" and "discussing a client [by name] with friends." The other items included "signing for hours a supervisee has not earned" and "doing therapy while under the influence of alcohol."

Activities judged by at least 60% of the respondents to be poor practices involved dual relationships or a violation of the appropriate boundaries of the therapeutic relationship. Some examples of these practices are "becoming sexually involved with a former client," "providing therapy to one of your friends," "inviting clients to a party or social event," and "directly soliciting a person to be a client."

Separating good practices from poor ones is not always a clear matter. Some examples of areas involving difficult judgment include "terminating therapy if a client cannot pay," "engaging in sexual fantasy about a client," "being sexually attracted to a client," "accepting only male or female clients," and "accepting a gift worth less than $5 from a client."

This survey and another by Pope and his colleagues (1987) shed interesting light on the beliefs and behaviors of therapists pertaining to ethical practice. As you read about the other ethical issues discussed in this chapter, attempt to clarify your thinking on the degree to which you view certain practices as ethical or unethical and as good or bad. Remember that many of the ethical issues we are considering are subtle and need to be evaluated in context.

THE RIGHTS OF CLIENTS

Counselors who demonstrate that they respect the rights of their clients are building good will with them. A way to break through what appears to be stubborn resistance with involuntary clients is to discuss with them the rights they have and what they can expect from their counselor.

The right of informed consent.   One of the best ways of protecting the rights of clients is to develop procedures to help them make informed choices. This process of providing clients with the information they need to become active participants in the therapeutic relationship begins with the initial session and continues throughout counseling. The challenge of fulfilling the spirit of informed consent is to strike a balance between giving clients too much information and giving them too little. For example, it is too late to tell minors that you intend to consult with their parents after they have disclosed that they are considering an abortion. In such a case both the girlfriend and the boyfriend have a right to know about the limitations of confidentiality before they make such highly personal disclosures. On the other hand, clients can be over-whelmed if counselors go into too much detail initially about the interventions they are likely to make. It takes both intuition and skill for practitioners to strike a balance between providing too much information to clients and providing too little.

Providing for informed consent tends to promote the active cooperation of clients in their program. Clients often do not realize that they have any rights and do not think about their own responsibilities in solving their problems. Those who feel desperate for help may unquestioningly accept whatever their counselor says or does. They seek the expertise of a professional without realizing that the success of this relationship depends largely on their own investment in the process.

Most professional codes of ethics provide that clients have the right to be presented with enough data to make informed choices about entering and continuing the client/therapist relationship. Depending on the setting and the situation, this discussion can involve those issues that may affect the client's decision to enter the therapeutic relationship. Some of these factors are the general goals of counseling, the responsibilities of the counselor toward the client, the responsibilities of clients, limitations of and exceptions to confiden-tiality, legal and ethical parameters that could define the relationship, the qualifications and background of the practitioner, the fees involved and the services one can expect, and the approximate length of the therapeutic process. Further areas might include the benefits of counseling, the risks involved, and the possibility that one's case will be discussed with the therapist's colleagues or supervisors. Providing this kind of information in writing is a good method of helping clients understand what is involved in the counseling process. Clients can take this written information home and can then bring up questions at the following session. (A sample "informed-consent document" is reproduced in the student manual that accompanies this textbook.)

It is a good idea for counselors to become knowledgeable about commu-nity resources so that they can present alternatives or adjuncts to psychotherapy. Some of these alternatives are self-help methods, peer self-help groups or support groups, day-treatment programs, skill-building programs, and crisis-intervention systems such as shelters for battered wives or crisis pregnancy counseling.

Factors affecting the client's desire to enter counseling. The AACD (1988) provides the following general guideline on the issue of the client/counselor relationship: "The member [counselor] must inform the client of the purposes, goals, techniques, rules of procedure and limitations that may affect the relationship at or before the time that the counseling relationship is entered." Several factors are likely to affect the client's decision to enter the relationship. For example, the recording of an interview by videotape or by tape recorder might affect the client. Others besides the client and the therapist might listen to or view the tapes. Also, some agencies use observation through one-way glass, so that supervisors or trainees can monitor the sessions. Some school districts have a policy that if clients reveal that they use drugs, the counselor is obliged to report their names to the principal. And in some schools, if a girl tells a counselor that she is pregnant or wants information about contraceptives or abortion, the counselor is expected to report her to the school nurse, who must then inform her parents. In other cases people are required to seek counseling or psychiatric help; they do not voluntarily initiate a therapeutic relationship but are subjects of "mandatory counseling." It is clear that in each of these instances certain policies or conditions can affect the client's decision to enter a therapeutic relationship. Thus, it is ethical practice for the therapist to make known to the potential client the limitations of the relationship. Let us examine the issues underlying practices such as these that may affect the therapeutic relationship.

First, what are the ethics of taping an interview or of using one-way glass for observation? A clear guideline in using either procedure is to secure the client's permission in advance; it is considered unethical to record or observe without the client's awareness and consent. Making recordings (audio or visual) for supervision purposes is a common procedure in clinical training and supervision. It is important for the client as well as for the counselor. Clients may wish to listen to some earlier sessions as their therapy progresses. Their anxiety can be diminished by letting them know that supervisors who listen will be focusing on the therapist's movement in the session.

I typically find that practitioners (beginning or experienced) are hesitant to have their sessions recorded. Many times a counselor will build a case for not recording the interview based, supposedly, on the client's mistrust or discomfort. Where does the mistrust and anxiety lie — with the client or with the counselor? My hope is that supervisors can create a climate in which student counselors, even though they may be anxious, will voluntarily bring in tapes for consultation. The supervisor's attitude is important. If supervisors adopt a harsh, critical, domineering style, interns are likely to conceal any element of uncertainty in the sessions. If the supervisor instead takes the approach that the sessions are a learning experience and that the trainees are not expected to be polished therapists, the chances of interns' exposing themselves to opportunities for learning will be maximized. In a sense the supervisor/supervisee relationship becomes a partial model for the therapy relationship.

A second factor that might affect the client's decision to enter a counseling relationship is the existence in some school districts of policies that are geared more to the legal protection of the district than to helping students in crisis. For example, some school counselors are prohibited from exploring a pregnant girl's alternatives unless the parents are notified and brought into the conference. This practice may have merit at times, but what becomes of the terrified girl who either cannot or does not want to tell her parents that she is pregnant? Must the counselor refuse even to see her or to have a session in which she can at least express her feelings of panic? If the counselor follows school policy, how much "real counseling" will occur? A point of ethics is that at the very least the counselor is obligated to inform potential clients of the limitations of confidentiality. Then they are able to decide how much they want to disclose or whether they even want to begin a counseling relationship.

A third issue to be explored here is whether therapy can occur under mandatory conditions. What can a counselor do when clients are required to come in for counseling but are unwilling to get involved? The issue is the ethics of forcing counseling on a person who is clearly opposed to any form of therapeutic intervention.

In my opinion counseling can be effective only if the client is eventually willing to cooperate with the counselor in working toward mutually acceptable goals. The clients mentioned above may not be willing to cooperate, although we should not be too quick to decide that initial resistance necessarily implies insurmountable barriers to counseling. It is essential that counselors deal with this resistance from the outset. Although some clients may initially be highly resistant to seeing a counselor, this situation can eventually change to one of cooperation. This is especially true if the counselor respectfully, yet firmly, deals with the client's initial resistance. One avenue is to present the resistant client with some of the possibilities that counseling might offer. For example, the clinic counselor may agree to see the adolescent girl for three sessions simply to explore the possibilities of that relationship and then terminate therapy if the girl still does not want to continue. School counselors may see students once, explain what services are available, and then leave it up to them to decide whether they want to seek further counseling.

Minors' rights.   An issue related to clients' rights is a minor's right to treatment. What are some of the ethical and legal issues in counseling children and adolescents? Can minors agree to treatment without their parents' knowledge and consent? To what degree should minors be allowed to participate in setting the goals for counseling? What are the limits of confidentiality? In most states parental knowledge and consent are legally required for a minor to enter into a relationship with a health-care professional. There are some exceptions, however: some states have laws that grant adolescents the right to seek counseling about birth control, abortion, substance abuse, child abuse, and other crisis matters. The justification for allowing children and adolescents to seek a therapeutic relationship without parental consent is that they otherwise might not obtain this crucial treatment. This is particularly true in cases involving drug or alcohol abuse, family conflict, physical or psychological abuse, and pregnancy or abortion counseling. In such cases therapists who work with minors frequently find themselves in the role of an advocate. An ethical standard relevant to this matter is "When working with minors or persons who are unable to give consent, the member protects these clients' best interests" (AACD, 1988).

The right to a referral.   The APA guideline is that "psychologists terminate a clinical or consulting relationship when it is reasonably clear that the consumer is not benefiting from it" (1989). What should therapists do when they judge that a client should be referred, either because they feel unqualified to continue working with the client or because they believe that the type or duration of treatment at hand is too limited for what the client should receive? For example, Sherri has been seeing her high school counselor, Miss Romero, weekly for two months, and she feels that the sessions are extremely helpful. The counselor agrees that Sherri is making progress but is also aware of some other realities: her time is limited, because she has 450 counselees; the school has a policy that long-term counseling should not be provided and that a referral should be made when indicated; and Sherri's emotional problems are deep enough to indicate intensive psychotherapy. Because of these realities, Miss Romero suggests a referral to Sherri and gives her the reasons. Assume that Sherri responds in one of these two ways: One, she may agree to accept the referral and see a private therapist. In this case when does the counselor's responsibility to Sherri end? The guideline is that the responsibility for the client's welfare continues until she begins seeing the other therapist. Even after that some form of consultation with the other therapist may be in order. Two, Sherri may refuse to be referred and say that she does not want to see anyone else. Should the counselor terminate the relationship? Should she continue but still encourage Sherri to accept an eventual referral? What if the counselor feels that she is getting "in over her head" with Sherri? The following guideline from the AACD (1988) applies to Sherri:

> If the counselor determines an inability to be of professional assistance to the client, the counselor must either avoid initiating the counseling relationship or immediately terminate that relationship. In either event, the counselor must suggest appropriate alternatives. (The counselor must be knowledgeable about referral resources so that a satisfactory referral can be initiated.) In the event the client declines the suggested referral, the counselor is not obligated to continue the relationship.

The ethical guidelines of the APA and the AACD raise three questions for consideration: (1) What criteria can you use to determine whether your client is benefiting from a counseling relationship? (2) If clients believe they are profiting but you see no signs of progress, how do you handle this disagreement? (3) Are you justified in continuing to see clients who are seeking friendship more than self-exploration?

ISSUES IN THE CLIENT/THERAPIST RELATIONSHIP

Our professional relationships with our clients exist for their benefit. A useful question that we can frequently ask ourselves is "Whose needs are being met in this relationship, my client's or my own?" It takes considerable professional maturity to make an honest appraisal of our behavior and its impact on clients. I do not think it is unethical for us to meet our personal needs through our professional work, yet it is essential that these needs be kept in perspective. For me, the ethical issue exists when we meet our needs, in either obvious or subtle ways, at the expense of our clients.

THE COUNSELOR'S NEEDS VERSUS THOSE OF THE CLIENT

I do not think that counselors can keep their personal needs completely separate from their relationships with clients. Ethically sensitive counselors recognize the supreme importance of becoming aware of their own needs, areas of unfinished business, potential personal conflicts, and defenses and vulnerability. They realize how such factors could interfere with helping their clients. I am convinced that unless practitioners develop this self-awareness, they will obstruct clients' change or in various ways will use them for satisfying their own needs. Therapy then shifts from a matter of client satisfaction to one of therapist satisfaction. The crux of the matter is to avoid exploiting clients for the purpose of meeting the counselor's needs. The ethical guideline of the AACD on this issue is "In the counseling relationship, the counselor is aware of the intimacy of the relationship and maintains respect for the client and avoids engaging in activities that seek to meet the counselor's personal needs at the expense of that client" (1988).

What kind of awareness is crucial? We all have certain "blind spots" and distortions of reality. Therapists have responsibilities to themselves and to their clients to work actively toward expanding their own self-awareness and to learn to recognize their own areas of prejudice and vulnerability. They must develop a sensitivity to their unmet needs so that they do not use the therapeutic relationship as a main avenue of satisfying those needs. If they recognize and work through their own personality problems, there is less chance that they will project them onto clients. If certain areas of struggle surface and old conflicts become reactivated, therapists have an ethical obligation to seek their own therapy, so that they will be able to help clients explore these same struggles.

The APA offers guidelines on this issue of counselor self-awareness. One guideline states that therapists recognize that their effectiveness depends on their ability to maintain sound personal relationships and that their own personal problems may interfere with creating these relationships. It would surely seem that the mental health and level of self-integration and self-awareness of practitioners are vitally related to their ability to establish and maintain a therapeutic relationship, as opposed to a toxic one. The APA (1989) guideline recommends that therapists

> refrain from undertaking any activity in which their personal problems are likely to lead to inadequate performance or harm to a client, colleague, student, or research participant. If engaged in such activity when they become aware of their personal problems, they seek competent professional assistance to determine whether they should suspend, terminate, or limit the scope of their professional and/or scientific activities.

As counselors we must also examine other, less obviously harmful, personal needs that can get in the way of creating growth-producing relationships. These other aspects of our personality include the need for control and power; the need to be nurturing and helpful; the need to change others in the direction of our own values; the need to teach and preach and to persuade and suggest as well; the need for feeling adequate, particularly when it becomes overly important that the client confirm our competence; and the need to be respected and appreciated. I am not asserting that these needs are neurotic; on the contrary, it is essential that our needs be met if we are to be involved with helping others find satisfaction in their life. Nor do I think that there is anything amiss in our deriving deep personal satisfaction from our work. And surely many of our needs for feeling worthwhile, important, respected, and adequate may enhance the quality of our work with others.

Power is a quality that every effective helping person possesses. It is a vital component of good therapy, and many clients improve as a result of sharing in the power of their therapist. It has been suggested that therapists be models, and one aspect of modeling is for therapists to be powerful persons—that is, to have the sort of life they want or to know how to obtain it. People who genuinely feel powerful do not dominate the lives of others and do not encourage others to remain in a dwarfed state so that they can feel superior. They are able to appreciate other people's potency and their own at the same time. The impotent therapist uses clients in an attempt to achieve a sense of power. To a powerful therapist, the client's accomplishments and strengths are a source of joy.

Clearly, the fact that power can be used against the client is an ethical concern. For example, consider the therapist's use of control (both consciously and unconsciously) as a way of reducing personal threat and anxiety. If a counselor is unsure of his own sexuality, he may use power to keep his female clients from threatening him. For instance, he may distance a woman with abstract, intellectual interpretations or by assuming an aloof, "professional" stance. If she desires to become a mature and assertive woman and he feels uncomfortable in the presence of powerful women, he may subvert her attempts and encourage her to remain dependent.

Consider also the counselor's need to nurture, which certainly attracts some students to the helping professions. These are the people who may be inclined to "teach people how to live the good life," to "straighten people out," and to "solve others' problems," all with the intention of being nurturing. Others at one point recognized that they were miserable, or at least that they wanted to make basic changes in their life, and then embarked on a successful journey of self-exploration. Such people may now deeply desire to help others find their own way and, in so doing, provide for themselves a sense of meaningfulness and personal significance. One aspect of therapists' need to nurture is their need for others to nurture *them* through respect, admiration, approval, appreciation, affection, and caring. The helping person quickly learns that the rewards for nurturing others are abundant.

Again, I see nothing amiss in counselors' need to be nurtured. The ethical questions are these: What are the dangers to the client's well-being when the therapist has an exaggerated need for nurture from the client? Can counselors distinguish between counseling for the client's benefit and that for their own gains? Are therapists sufficiently aware of their needs for approval and appreciation? Do they base their perceptions of adequacy strictly on reactions from clients?

In summary, I believe that many are motivated to enter the counseling profession because of their needs for power, for feeling useful and significant, and for reinforcing their feelings of adequacy. If helpers depend inordinately on others for their psychological gratification, they are likely to keep others in a dependent position. Because of their own emotional hunger and their own need to be psychologically fed, they are unable to genuinely focus attention on the client's deprivations. At the extreme, the helper is in greater need of the "helpee" than the other way around. For these reasons ethical practice demands that counselors recognize the central importance of continuously evaluating in which direction their personality might influence clients—for progress or for stagnation.

SOCIAL AND PERSONAL RELATIONSHIPS WITH CLIENTS

A special issue is how social and personal relationships mix with therapeutic ones. In general, although friendships can be therapeutic, it is difficult to be primarily concerned with a counseling relationship and at the same time maintain a personal relationship with a client outside the sessions. Three questions that can be raised are "Will I confront and challenge a client with whom I am involved socially as much as or more than I do clients with whom I have a strictly professional relationship?" "Will my own needs for keeping the friendship interfere with my therapeutic activities and thus defeat the purposes of therapy?" and "How will my client react to combining a personal and a professional relationship?" One of the reasons that most counselors cannot counsel members of their own family is that they are too close to them, and their own needs interlock with the others' problems. The same dynamic, as I see it, operates in a social relationship. Another potential problem is that by the very nature of the therapeutic relationship counselors are in a more powerful and influential position than clients. Thus, there is the danger of subtle exploitation of clients when the relationship becomes other than a professional one (Kitchener, 1988; Kitchener & Harding, 1990).

On this point the APA (1989) has the following principle on "dual relationships" with clients:

> Psychologists are continually cognizant of their own needs and of their potentially influential position vis-à-vis persons such as clients, students, and subordinates. They avoid exploiting the trust and dependency of such persons. Psychologists make every effort to avoid dual relationships that could impair their professional judgment or increase the risk of exploitation.

The AACD (1988) guideline on this issue is "Dual relationships with clients that might impair the member's objectivity and professional judgment (e.g., as with close friends or relatives) must be avoided and/or the counseling relationship terminated through referral to another competent professional." The issue of combining social with professional relationships does not have a simple answer. For example, some peer counselors contend that the friendships they have with people before or during counseling are a positive factor in building trust that leads to productive therapeutic results. What is essential is that counselors develop an awareness of their own motivations as well as the motivations of their clients. They must honestly and accurately assess the impact that a social relationship might have on the client/therapist relationship. Further, counselors who as a matter of course tend to develop most of their friendships from their relationships with clients would do well to examine the degree to which they are using the power of their position to make social contacts.

In sum, it is necessary for counselors to keep their relationships with clients on a professional basis. When counselors engage in dual relationships, they tend to impair their professional judgment, the danger of exploiting the client increases, and clients are put in a vulnerable position by the power implicit in the therapist's role (Pope, 1985a). Some dealings with clients that might be considered dual relationships are forming social relationships, developing friendships, counseling family members, and bartering with a client for services.

TOUCHING AS A PART OF THE CLIENT/THERAPIST RELATIONSHIP

A topic that students inevitably raise is whether to touch their clients. They ask: "How can I tell when touching will be helpful or not? Is touching for the client or my own benefit? Do I have to hold myself back from expressing affection or compassion in a physical way? What if my touch is misinterpreted by the client? If I feel sexually drawn to certain clients, is it dangerous to express physical closeness?"

In one study approximately half of the therapists who responded took a position that nonerotic physical contact would be beneficial for clients, at least occasionally. The four general categories of appropriate nonerotic contact were (1) in counseling socially and emotionally immature clients, such as those with a history of maternal deprivation; (2) in counseling people in crisis, such as those suffering from grief or trauma; (3) in providing general emotional support; and (4) in greeting or at the end of a session (Holroyd & Brodsky, 1977). In a later study these authors conducted a survey to determine whether touching clients led to sexual intercourse. They came to the following conclusions:

- Touching that does not lead to intercourse is associated with older and more experienced therapists.
- It is the practice of restricting touching to opposite-sex clients, not touching itself, that is related to intercourse.

Holroyd and Brodsky observe that it is difficult to determine where "nonerotic hugging, kissing, and affectionate touching" leave off and "erotic contact" begins. They also suggest that any therapeutic technique that is reserved for one gender can be suspected of being sexist. They conclude: "The use of nonerotic touching as a mode of psychotherapeutic treatment requires further research. Moreover, the sexist implications of differential touching of male and female patients appear to be an important professional and ethical issue" (1980, p. 810).

Although I agree that erotic contact with clients is unethical, I think that nonerotic contact in the form of touching can be therapeutically valuable. What is important is that touching not be done as a technique or something that a counselor does not genuinely feel. Touches that are not authentic and not spontaneous are detected as such; if clients cannot believe your touch, why should they believe your words? Another important dimension of this issue is the client's readiness and need to be touched. In some cases victims of incest may be resistant to physical contact, and they may be offended and frightened by a counselor's well-intended touch. Other clients, because of their cultural background, may be very uncomfortable with any physical expressions of concern. Sometimes, counselors reach out too soon to comfort clients who are crying and expressing some pain. Clients do need at times to fully experience and express their pain, and touching them can cut off what they are feeling. Counselors may reach out physically, not to meet the needs of their clients but to comfort themselves, because they are uncomfortable with the pain their clients are expressing. However, not all touching is a sign that counselors are uncomfortable with pain. Once clients have an opportunity to express their struggle, they may welcome touching. Although this is a complex issue, therapists need to be honest with themselves and their clients, and they need to be aware of whose needs are primarily being met when they have physical contact. The question "Whose needs are being met, my client's or my own?" needs to be raised time and again.

EROTIC AND SEXUAL CONTACT WITH CLIENTS

The topic of sexual intimacy between counselor and client is receiving a great deal of attention in the professional literature. For example, the *Journal of Counseling and Development* featured this ethical issue as a major concern facing the counseling profession (see Hoteling, 1988; Kitchener, 1988; Pope, 1988; Schoener & Gonsiorek, 1988; Vasquez, 1988; Vasquez & Kitchener, 1988). All of the professional codes now have some specific statement declaring that sexual relationships with clients are unethical. Sexual intimacies in the client/therapist relationship are also illegal in several states. Nevertheless, during the last few years the greatest single category of complaints to the ethics committees of the APA involves sexual misconduct (Ethics Committee, American Psychological Association, 1987, 1988)

Research indicates that sexual misconduct is one of the major causes for malpractice actions against mental-health providers. Those who have written about sexual intimacy between therapists and clients report that the rate of these unethical practices is alarming and that reports of sexual intimacies and sexual harassment have been increasing (Brodsky, 1986; Gottlieb, Sell, & Schoenfeld, 1988; Holroyd & Bouhoutsos, 1985; Pope, 1988; Pope & Bouhoutsos, 1986; Vasquez & Kitchener, 1988). The findings of one study revealed that the number of complaints of sexual misconduct against psychologists increased 482% from 1982 to 1985 (Gottlieb et al., 1988). This increase may be due, in part, to a greater sense of awareness of the problem by the public, as well as to better reporting procedures.

What about the ethics of therapists who become intimately involved with their clients once the therapy relationship has ended? State licensing boards are deciding that psychotherapists may be held liable for their actions long after terminating a therapeutic relationship (Gottlieb et al., 1988). In the matter of sexual involvements the therapeutic relationship may be considered never to end. In another study Sell, Gottlieb, and Schoenfeld (1986) maintain that sexual relations with former clients are clearly unethical, regardless of the time elapsed or the practitioner's intent. They recommend that the ethical principles of the APA (1981) be amended to read (added portion in italics) "Sexual intimacies with clients *or former clients* are unethical."

A number of professional organizations have established subcommittees to investigate and deal with ethical violations involving sexual activities between therapists and both current and former clients. Furthermore, as noted, some state legislatures have taken steps to protect clients by outlawing therapist/ client sexual intimacies. For example, Wisconsin, Minnesota, and Colorado have enacted laws in which sexual intimacies with clients (and sometimes with former clients) can be considered a felony with prison terms of up to ten years and fines up to $20,000 (Ethics Committee, APA, 1988). Licensing boards have suspended or revoked the licenses of some practitioners. The APA professional liability policy now puts a $25,000 cap on coverage pertaining to sexual intimacies; the policy specifies sex with both current and former clients. The consent of the client is not a defense in malpractice litigation.

Views and actions of therapists.   In a questionnaire designed to assess the beliefs and behaviors of psychologists, Pope, Tabachnick, and Keith-Spiegel (1987) found the following:

- Ninety-seven percent of the therapists said that they had never engaged in erotic activity with a client (and 95% of them considered this behavior unethical).
- Seventy-one percent said that they had never kissed a client (and 48% considered this behavior unethical).
- Eighty-eight percent said that they had never become sexually involved with a former client (and 50% of them considered this behavior unethical).

In a national survey of attitudes and behaviors among practitioners regarding intimate relationships with former clients, Akamatsu (1988) found the following: 45% of the respondents believed that such relationships were "highly unethical," 24% viewed them as "somewhat unethical," and 23% saw them as "neither ethical nor unethical." His survey indicates that the crucial factor in determining the ethics of such relationships is the amount of time that has elapsed since the end of therapy. Other factors to take into account include transference issues, the length and nature of therapy, and the nature of termina-

tion. Gabbard and Pope (1988) outline seven major reasons why sexual intimacies with clients after termination are clinically, ethically, and professionally
unacceptable.

Most mental-health practitioners take the position that sexual intimacy
between counselors and clients is both unethical and professionally inappropriate (Gutheil, 1989). Vasquez and Kitchener (1988) maintain that "sexual
relationships between counselors and therapists and their clients are fundamentally and without question unethical. They violate the ethical codes of
human service professions as well as the more basic ethical principles" (p.
215). There are several reasons for judging sexual intimacies in therapy to be
unethical. The general argument typically involves the potential for abuse of
the power that therapists have by virtue of their function and role. Clients are
usually more vulnerable than the therapist. They are the ones who are revealing
themselves in deeply personal ways. They are sharing their fears, secrets, fantasies, hopes, sexual desires, and conflicts, and it could be easy to take advantage
of them. Counseling rests on the foundation of trust. When clients initiate
counseling, they trust that their well-being will be given primary consideration.
Counselors who enter into sexual alliances with clients violate this basic trust,
which can have a profound negative impact. Clients took the risk of trusting
their counselor, and they might well say "Look at what happened when I *did*
trust." Another reason for the negative view of sexual involvement is that it is
likely to foster dependence. Clients can very easily come to view therapists in
an idealized way, especially when they see them in the limited context of the
office. They may settle for this type of minimal contact instead of working on the
quality of their relationship with their spouse, or they may not look outside of
the therapy relationship for longer-term meaningful relationships with others.
The book *Sex in the Therapy Hour* (Bates & Brodsky, 1989) gives a moving
firsthand account of the psychological harm that results from sexualizing the
client/therapist relationship. Carolyn Bates recounts the vivid details of how
she felt manipulated by her therapist after he said "Trust me!" Such a powerful
betrayal of trust leaves the client with a legacy of unfinished business.

In his discussion of the research findings about the harmful consequences
to clients of sexual intimacies, Pope (1988) argues that these clients often suffer
long-term psychological scars similar to those of victims of sexual assault and of
incest. He discusses the "therapist-patient sex syndrome," which includes ambivalence, guilt, severe depression, sexual confusion, a sense of emptiness and
isolation, impairment of trust, suppressed rage, identity confusion, increased
risk of suicide, and cognitive dysfunctions. He indicates that counselors may be
aware that they are violating ethical, legal and professional standards when
they engage in sexual intimacies with clients. However, they are generally not
aware of the devastating ways in which they are violating the client's welfare and
potential for future development. Clients who feel used may discount the value
of anything they have learned in their therapy and may also be closed to any
further kind of psychological assistance out of their bitterness and resentment.

Learning to deal with sexual attractions.   Although most of my students
seem intellectually clear on their position against engaging in intercourse with

clients, they do struggle with matters such as their sexual attractions to clients and the attractions of their clients to them. It is clear that romantic involvements and sexual behavior that do not lead to intercourse can have a similar effect of interfering with therapy. Indeed, the majority of therapists apparently do experience sexual attraction to clients, and most are troubled by it (Pope, 1987). Many therapists (66%) reported feeling guilty, anxious, or confused about this attraction; only 9% reported that their training and supervision had been adequate in this regard (Pope, Keith-Spiegel, & Tabachnick, 1986).

Graduate training programs and counseling internships apparently leave trainees unprepared for dealing successfully with their sexual attractions to clients. I agree with Pope and his colleagues (1986) that the taboo must be lifted so that therapy trainees can recognize and accept their sexual attractions as human responses. Vasquez (1988) makes an excellent case for the need for training strategies to prevent counselor/client sexual contact. These strategies include imparting knowledge, providing activities that promote self-awareness, and creating a climate that enhances the development of moral values and behavior. She emphasizes that instructors and supervisors can best teach ethical behavior not by lecturing but by modeling sensitive and nonexploitive behavior with their students and supervisees. According to her, successful training programs provide a context for exploring issues such as sexual attraction, sexual socialization, and other relevant concerns.

Educational programs must provide a safe environment in which trainees can acknowledge and discuss feelings of sexual attraction. If counselors do not learn how to deal with these feelings, they are more likely to become involved in seductive interchanges. Ideally, practitioners will be able to accept their sexual feelings and desires toward certain clients and at the same time see the distinction between *having* these feelings and *acting on* them. This is an area in which beginning counselors can greatly benefit from consultation sessions with a supervisor. In this way they can explore how their own needs might negatively intrude into their work, and they can learn how to deal with their feelings in such a way that neither clients nor they themselves suffer.

ETHICAL AND LEGAL ASPECTS OF CONFIDENTIALITY

Besides the issues discussed above, confidentiality is central to developing a trusting and productive client/therapist relationship. Confidentiality is both a legal and an ethical issue. State laws now address confidentiality in therapy, as do the ethical codes of all the mental-health professions (Leslie, 1989). Every therapist must come to grips with this thorny issue. Surely no genuine therapy can occur unless clients trust the privacy of their revelations to their therapists. It is the counselor's responsibility to define the degree of confidentiality that can be promised. In making their determinations, therapists must consider the requirements of the institution in which they work and the clientele they serve. Although most counselors agree on the essential value of confidentiality, they realize that it cannot be considered an absolute. There are times when confidential information must be divulged, and there are many times when whether to keep or to break confidentiality becomes a cloudy issue.

Because these circumstances are frequently not clearly defined by accepted ethical standards, counselors must exercise professional judgment. In general, confidentiality must be broken when it becomes clear that clients might do serious harm to either themselves or others. There is a legal requirement to break confidentiality in cases involving child abuse, abuse of the elderly, and dangers to others. All mental-health practitioners and interns need to be aware of their duty to report such abuses (Leslie, 1989) The following ethical guideline is given by the AACD (1988): "When the client's condition indicates that there is clear and imminent danger to the client or others the member must take reasonable personal action or inform responsible authorities. Consultation with other professionals must be used where possible."

The crux of the matter often comes down to *when* therapists can feel sure that their clients are a "clear and imminent danger" to themselves or others. Are all threats by a client to be followed up with a report to the authorities? What if the client does not make a verbal threat, but the counselor has a strong hunch that the client could be homicidal or suicidal?

Other limitations to confidentiality also need to be considered. It is generally accepted that therapists will have no professional contact with the family or friends of a client without first securing the client's permission. It is accepted, in addition, that information obtained in therapeutic relationships should be discussed with others for professional purposes only and with persons who are clearly related to the case. It is good practice to inform the client early in counseling that you may be discussing certain details of the relationship with a supervisor or a colleague. This practice can also apply to the use of a tape recording or videotape. There are times when a therapist may want to share a recording of a particular session with a colleague simply to confirm his or her perspective by obtaining another viewpoint on the dynamics of the therapeutic relationship. A new guideline was added to the revised AACD (1988) ethical standards: "The member [counselor], at the onset of a counseling relationship, will inform the client of the member's intended use of supervisors regarding the disclosure of information concerning this case. The member will clearly inform the client of the limits of confidentiality in the relationship."

The issue of confidentiality takes on added dimensions for students who are involved in a fieldwork placement or internship as part of their program. In most cases these counselor interns are required to keep notes on their proceedings with their individual clients or the members of their group. Also, group-supervision sessions at a clinic or university typically entail open discussions about the clients with whom these counselor interns are working. These discussions should always be conducted in a professional manner. If a particular client is being discussed, it is important that this person's identity be protected. In my supervision classes I tend to focus on the intern's dynamics more than on a detailed presentation about a client. At my university all of the fieldwork instructors make it a practice to ask their interns to discuss this situation with their clients at the outset. With regard to safeguarding any information that is recorded about clients, there are many situations in which interns can actually show their clients what they are writing and discuss these notes with them. Again, it is a good practice not to use last names. This type of openness from counselors, I have found, prompts clients to respond with greater frankness, for they feel that information will be used *for* them, not *against* them.

GENERAL GUIDELINES

Given the reality that confidentiality is not an absolute, both counselors and clients need guidelines to determine its limits. Certain circumstances dictate when information *must* legally be reported by counselors:

- when clients pose a danger to others or themselves
- when the therapist believes that a client under the age of 16 has been the victim of incest, rape, child abuse, or some other crime
- when the therapist determines that the client needs hospitalization
- when information is made an issue in a court action

In general, however, it is a counselor's primary obligation to protect the client's disclosures as a vital part of the therapeutic relationship. It is a good practice to discuss the nature and purpose of confidentiality with clients early in the counseling process. When reassuring clients that what they reveal in sessions will generally be kept confidential, counselors should also tell them the major circumstances in which this will not be done. If clients know the conditions that limit confidentiality, they are in a better position to determine whether to enter a counseling relationship.

The limits to confidentiality do not necessarily inhibit successful counseling. One study indicates that most practitioners apparently do not believe that absolute confidentiality is necessary for therapeutic effectiveness. Pope and his colleagues (1988) found that many practitioners viewed breaking confidentiality as uniformly good practice in cases of homicidal risk, suicidal risk, and child abuse. However, there is a gap between what clients expect and what is commonly accepted as therapeutic practice. In a survey to assess the public's knowledge and beliefs about confidentiality, most of the respondents perceived confidentiality as an all-encompassing mandate for therapists (Miller & Thelen, 1986). For instance, the majority of the respondents (69%) believed that everything they discussed with a mental-health professional would be held strictly confidential. Most of them (74%) believed that there should not be *any* exceptions. Interestingly, the vast majority of them (96%) wanted more information about confidentiality. Another study was designed to explore the impact on clients of discussing the limits of confidentiality (Muehleman, Pickens, & Robinson, 1985). The authors found very little evidence that providing detailed information about the limits of confidentiality inhibited clients' disclosures. On the basis of their findings, the authors recommend that practitioners provide clients with accurate, impartial, and comprehensive information.

After another study designed to assess public attitudes toward confidentiality, Rubanowitz (1987) suggested that both practitioners and their professional organizations work to educate the public. He found that the general public tended to endorse the ideal that therapists should not reveal information about their clients without written authorization. However, the public did expect practitioners to consult with one another, and they clearly expected confidentiality to be breached in cases involving child abuse or physical harm to oneself or to others.

With these survey findings and general guidelines in mind, what would your position be if you were the counselor in the following five cases?

1. You have been seeing an adolescent girl in a community mental-health clinic for three months. Lately she has complained of severe depression and says that life seems hopeless. She is threatening suicide and even wants details from you about how to carry it out. Are you obliged to disclose this information to her guardians, because she is under legal age? What would you tell your client? What kind of consultation might you seek?

2. Your client reveals that he has stolen some expensive laboratory equipment from the college where you are a counselor. A week later the dean calls you into her office to talk with you about this client. What do you tell the dean? What don't you tell her?

3. You are working in a community agency that provides testing and counseling services for those suspected of being affected by AIDS. The legal and ethical question your staff is debating is the duty to protect others from HIV infection by a client. What would you advise your staff on the question "Must counselors violate confidentiality and perhaps take coercive action when a client known to be HIV-infected is believed to be sexually active or sharing needles?"

4. A youth tells you in a counseling session that he is planning to do serious physical harm to a fellow student. What would you tell your client? How would you proceed?

5. Your client is a 15-year-old girl sent to you by her parents. One day the parents request a session to discuss their daughter's progress and to see what they can do to help. What kind of information can you share with them, and what can you not disclose? What will you discuss with the girl before you see her parents? What will you do if she makes it clear that she does not want you to see her parents or tell them anything?

SOME TRENDS IN CONFIDENTIALITY

Legislators seem inclined to bind all mental-health practitioners to confidentiality while at the same time limiting its scope. They appear to believe that confidentiality is necessary for a counseling relationship to be effective but that it need not be absolute.

Another trend toward legislation that restricts confidentiality involves the regulations that require professionals to report a variety of suspected crimes against the person. For example, laws impose stiff penalties for failing to report instances of incest, child molestation, and child abuse. Such laws raise questions such as these: Is the reporting done for the client's ultimate benefit? Is the reporting done primarily to protect innocent people? Are counselors expected to monitor the legality of their clients' behavior?

As we have seen, counselors must become familiar with local and state laws and court decisions that govern their specialization. Yet this knowledge alone will not resolve difficult situations. There are various and sometimes conflicting ways to interpret a law, and professional judgment does play a critical role in most cases.

Duty to warn and protect.   As a result of a number of court decisions, mental-health practitioners have become increasingly aware of and concerned about their double duty: to protect other people from potentially dangerous clients and to protect clients from themselves. These court decisions have mandated that practitioners protect the public from potentially dangerous clients. This responsibility entails liability for civil damages when practitioners neglect this duty by failing to diagnose or predict dangerousness, failing to warn potential victims of violent behavior, failing to commit dangerous individuals, and prematurely discharging dangerous clients from the hospital (APA, 1985).

What is expected is that counselors use sound professional judgment and that they seek consultation when they are in doubt about a given individual or situation. Further, those practitioners who work in mental-health clinics or agencies should inform their supervisor or director and document in writing the nature of these consultations. If they determine that a client poses a serious danger of violence to others, they are obliged to use reasonable care to protect the potential victims. In addition to notifying the proper authorities, they should warn the intended victims and, in the case of a minor, notify the parents. In this regard counselors need to inform their clients of the actions they may have to take to protect a third party. Once again, because there are frequently no clear-cut answers, as these situations are often unique, it is a good policy for counselors to consult with colleagues to get other opinions concerning the gravity of a case as well as suggestions on how to proceed.

In the mental-health profession probably the best known and most influential legal case pertaining to confidentiality and the protection of potential victims is *Tarasoff* v. *Board of Regents of the University of California.* In August 1969 Prosenjit Poddar, who was a voluntary outpatient at the student-health service on the Berkeley campus of the university, informed the psychologist who was counseling him that he was planning to kill his girlfriend. The therapist later called the campus police and told them of this threat. He asked them to observe Poddar for possible hospitalization as a person who was dangerous. The campus officers did take Poddar into custody for questioning, but they later released him when he gave evidence of being "rational." The psychologist followed up his call with a formal letter requesting the assistance of the chief of the campus police. Later, the psychologist's supervisor asked that the letter be returned, ordered that the letter and the therapist's case notes be destroyed, and asked that no further action be taken in the case. It should be noted that no warning was given to the intended victim or to her parents.

Two months later, Poddar killed Tatiana Tarasoff. Her parents filed suit against the Board of Regents and employees of the university for having failed to notify her of the threat. A lower court dismissed the suit, but the parents appealed, and the California Supreme Court ruled in favor of them in 1976 and held that the failure to warn the intended victim had been irresponsible.

The most significant implication of this court decision for practitioners is that they can be held accountable for failing to warn a potential victim of violence. In its conclusion the court affirmed the guiding principle that was basic to its decision: "The public policy favoring protection of the confidential character of patient-psychotherapist communications must yield to the extent to which disclosure is essential to avert danger to others. The protective privilege ends where the public peril begins."

The *Tarasoff* decision implies that therapists must first accurately diagnose the client's propensity for behaving in dangerous ways toward others. Therapists may have to demonstrate that they were not professionally negligent in a given situation. In this case the therapist did not fail in this area and even went further, in requesting that the dangerous person be detained by the campus police. Yet the court ruled that simply notifying the police was not sufficient to protect the identifiable victim (Laughran & Bakken, 1984). The decision in this case also implies that when therapists determine that a client presents a serious danger of violence to another, they have the duty to use reasonable care to protect the potential victim against this danger. Protecting a third party consists of whatever steps are reasonably necessary in each particular case.

In "*Tarasoff*: Five Years Later," Knapp and VandeCreek (1982) make the point that variations in state laws make the procedures involved in the "duty to warn" a difficult matter. In the *Tarasoff* case the identity of the potential victim was known. However, therapists are often concerned about their legal responsibility when the identity of the potential victim is unknown. What are the therapist's obligations in cases of generalized statements of hostility? What is the responsibility of the therapist to predict future violence?

Knapp and VandeCreek (1982) suggest that therapists are bound only to follow reasonable standards in predicting violence. They add that therapists should not become intimidated by every idle fantasy, for every impulsive threat is not evidence of imminent danger. In their opinion recent behavioral acts can best predict future violence. In addition to warning potential victims, they suggest, practitioners should consider other alternatives that could diffuse the danger and, at the same time, satisfy their legal duty. They recommend seeking consultation with other professionals who have expertise in dealing with potentially violent people and also documenting the steps taken. Fulero (1988) also suggests that consultation provides evidence of professional consensus about a course of action taken by a professional. Therapists are not liable for negative outcomes unless their actions fall below the expected standard of care. They are responsible for keeping up-to-date with ways of dealing with violent clients (Roth, 1987) and of evaluating dangerousness (Simon, 1987). Furthermore, they must keep abreast of the current laws of their state, consulting attorneys if necessary (Fulero, 1988).

In "*Tarasoff*: 10 Years Later," Fulero (1988) concludes that the issues raised by the decision are very likely to continue to generate litigation, legislation, and controversy for many years to come. Because a number of state courts have not yet ruled on these types of cases, mental-health professionals remain uncertain about the nature of their duty to warn and to protect.

Confidentiality involving clients with AIDS.   AIDS is a reality that mental-health professionals cannot deny. They will be increasingly confronted with ethical issues involving clients who have the disease or are infected with its virus. The professional literature and the ethical codes of various professional organizations have not defined the limits of confidentiality raised by the life-threatening activities of clients who have the AIDS virus and who continue to be sexually active without informing their partners. To what degree do therapists have the duty to protect others from HIV infection by a client? For example, must counselors break confidentiality and even take coercive action in cases where an HIV-infected person is believed to be sexually active or to be sharing needles with partners who are not aware of the client's infection? There must be a balance between maintaining the confidentiality and privacy of the client and protecting others from potential infection. As part of the therapy process, counselors need to do what they can to reduce the risk of transmission to a sexual partner (Melton, 1988; Morin, 1988).

Gray and Harding (1988) take the position that sexually active clients who have the AIDS virus are placing an uninformed sexual partner at risk and that there are limits to confidentiality in such cases. They have developed guidelines for counselors who deal with such clients. On learning that a client has the AIDS virus, Gray and Harding suggest, counselors should ask the client to inform his or her current sexual partner(s). They endorse a process of helping these clients assume that responsibility. This process includes educating, consulting, and actively supporting clients in this situation. Gray and Harding emphasize that for this process to be effective and therapeutic for the client, it is first necessary to establish a supportive and trusting counseling relationship. If this process of education, consultation, and active support does not persuade AIDS clients to inform their sexual partner(s), however, Gray and Harding suggest that the following steps be taken:

- In order to protect the helping relationship, counselors should first inform the client of their intention to breach confidentiality.
- Counselors who work with clients who have identified sexual partners should directly inform the partners.
- Counselors who work with clients who have anonymous sexual partners should inform the state public-health officer.

Others in the field, however, have concerns about the mandatory breaching of confidentiality. Kain (1988) contends that the proposed guidelines of Gray and Harding might well cause more harm than good. If clients are not telling their sexual partners about their infection, Kain wonders, why aren't they? He recommends a working through of issues of rejection, abandonment, loneliness, homophobia, and infidelity.

The key challenge is how to protect others from serious harm. Melton (1988) asserts that a more prudent course than warning a potential victim is to alert public-health authorities to the danger. His concern is for third-party safety with minimal intrusion on the privacy of the client.

Confidentiality becomes a critical matter in support groups for people with AIDS and for those who test positive for its virus. Posey (1988) has worked with such groups, and she sees confidentiality as a matter of responsibility. She raises the question "Who is responsible for protecting whom?" For her, the goal of the counselor and of support groups is to help each person develop a style for dealing with AIDS by caring for oneself and for others. She adds further suggestions to those provided by Gray and Harding: (1) counselors can refer a client to a support group if one is available, (2) counselors can explore issues related to a reluctance to inform sexual partners or others at risk, and (3) counselors can offer to work with significant others, such as partners, family, and friends.

The issues surrounding clients who have the AIDS virus pose new challenges for counselors. Some questions are raised: Who is the client — the individual, the uninformed sexual partner(s), the family, or society? What are the responsibilities of helpers when education and appeals to reason fail with AIDS clients? Will the practice of reporting people with AIDS, especially those who have anonymous partners, to the authorities threaten those people who most need educating? Should informing public-health and mental-health personnel be mandatory, or should it be a last resort? How can the rights of the client with AIDS and the rights of others best be safeguarded? Although clear answers to these questions may be difficult to identify, reading, taking workshops, and holding discussions with colleagues can be helpful.

Consider the issues involved in this case: You are doing an intake interview with a male client who tells you that he is bisexual. He was referred to you because he is experiencing a crisis after receiving laboratory evidence of HIV infection, although he has no symptoms of AIDS. He lets you know that his wife is unaware of his occasional relationships with male friends, and under no circumstances does he intend to bring up this subject with her. Likewise, he sees no way that he can let her know about the discovery that he has been infected. He tells you: "Look, if she is going to be infected, the damage has already been done. What's the point of letting her know about my laboratory results? It would only cause her extreme agony. Besides, I just know that she could not handle knowing that I have had sexual relations with men over the past few years. It would mean the end of our marriage and the breakup of our entire family. I can't handle all that stress right now on top of what I just found out about my condition."

Does this man present a danger to his wife? Do you have a duty to warn and to protect? Would you be inclined to push him to inform his wife, even though he is very resistant to this idea? Would you tell him that you are obliged to break confidentiality because he poses a danger to others, especially to his wife? Would the fact that a warning might be too late to be effective influence your interventions? What do you see as being the central clinical, ethical, and legal issues in this case?

GUIDELINES FOR DEALING WITH SUICIDAL CLIENTS

Practitioners have an obligation not only to protect others from the acts of dangerous people but also to protect suicidal clients. There are definite limitations to confidentiality when the counselor determines that a client is a suicidal risk. The assessment and management of suicidal clients are typically stressful for counselors. The possibility of a client's suicide raises a number of difficult issues that practitioners must face, such as their influence, competence, and level of involvement with the client; their responsibility; and their legal obligations. Counselors need to demonstrate the ability to make appropriate interventions in critical situations. Suicides by clients represent an occupational hazard for therapists, not only because of their frequency but also because of their impact on the personal and professional lives of practitioners. One study found that 22% of a sample of psychologists had been faced with a client's suicide (Chemtob, Hamada, Bauer, & Torigoe, 1988). For such therapists the benefits of peer-group support and peer consultation were noted. These researchers suggested structuring training programs to prepare practitioners. In addition to producing stress, the failure to prevent suicide is one of the leading reasons for successful malpractice suits against mental-health professionals.

When practitioners are faced with suicidal threats by clients, what steps can they take to increase their chances of behaving ethically and legally? First, it is essential to make a decision about the seriousness of the threat. Second, if therapists judge that a foreseeable risk does exist, they are *required* to take action. They are expected to use direct intervention that is consistent with the standard of practice common to their profession. The client's right to confidentiality assumes secondary importance when his or her life is at risk.

Certain characteristics are associated with suicide-prone behavior, including chronic depression, hopelessness, a clear plan for taking one's life, and prior suicidal attempts. In the practice of assessing lethality, Wubbolding (1988a) suggests that therapists use direct questioning about the suicide threat to assess the kind of intervention necessary. He suggests asking clients questions such as the following: "Are you thinking about killing yourself?" "Have you tried to kill yourself before?" "Do you have a plan?" "Do you have the means to kill yourself?" "Will you make a unilateral contract not to kill yourself accidentally or on purpose? For how long?"

More detailed guidelines for assessing threats are described by Wubbolding (1988b). The following are some signs that a therapist is advised to look for:

- giving away prized possessions
- making and discussing suicidal plans, including methods of suicide
- previous suicide attempts or gestures
- expressions indicating hopelessness, helplessness, and anger at oneself and the world
- statements that family and friends would not miss them
- recent loss through suicide
- sudden positive behavior change following a period of depression

Once the therapist makes the assessment of foreseeable risk, what are some possible courses of action? What are some ethical and legal options to consider? How can counselors take appropriate steps to demonstrate that a reasonable attempt was made to control the suicidal client? Wubbolding (1988b) contends that the therapist should discuss signs of suicide characterized by change in behavior directly with the client. If there is a serious threat, appropriate and responsible intervention must be made. Consultation is most important, in both the assessment and the intervention phases The practice of consultation offers protection to the client as well as the counselor. The counselor's course of action should follow a predetermined, agreed-on, and flexible policy (Wubbolding, 1988a). Schutz (1982) maintains that the options for intervening are basically the same as those for the patient who may be dangerous to others. He indicates that failure to take action can result in the therapist's being held liable. Liability generally becomes an issue when counselors fail to intervene in ways that could have prevented the suicide or intervene in a way that might contribute to a suicide. The following list of possible courses of action and suggestions has been developed from the writings of Schutz (1982); Pope (1985b); Fujimura, Weis, and Cochran (1985); and Wubbolding (1988a, 1988b):

- If at all possible, have the client agree to call you or a local emergency service in time of crisis.
- If the client possesses any weapons, make sure that they are in the hands of a third party.
- Consider increasing the frequency of the counseling sessions.
- Arrange a method for the client to call you between sessions so that you can monitor his or her emotional state.
- Consider the use of medication as an adjunct to the therapy (with a psychiatrist's referral).
- Depending on the seriousness of the case, consider hospitalization as an option. First seek the patient's cooperation. If necessary, a commitment procedure may be called for as a way of protecting the client.

I find that other measures are important in preventing suicide:

- In cases in which you think you are exceeding the boundaries of your competence, consult with your supervisor or colleagues, bring in a consultant, or arrange for a referral.
- Be clear and firm with the client, and do not allow yourself to be manipulated by threats.
- Do not make yourself the only person responsible for the decisions and actions of your clients. It is essential that your clients share in the responsibility for their ultimate decisions. Bring significant others into the client's social network for support (with the client's knowledge and consent).
- Let the client know that you will be seeking consultation and discussing possible courses of action. It is a good idea to document in writing the steps that you take in crisis cases, to demonstrate that you did use sound professional judgment and acted within acceptable legal and ethical limits.
- Obtain training in suicide-prevention and crisis-intervention methods. Keep up-to-date with research, theory, and practice.

Fujimura and her colleagues (1985) maintain that counselors must take their clients' "cry for help" seriously and must also have the necessary knowledge and skills to intervene once they make the determination that a client is suicidal. They stress the importance of acquiring skill in suicide prevention and intervention. Many suicidal clients are facing a short-term crisis, and if they can be given help in coping with this crisis, they can be saved. These authors also stress the importance of knowing how, when, and where to appropriately refer clients whose concerns are beyond the counselor's boundary of competence.

Although this discussion has emphasized the legal and ethical obligations of therapists in assessing and intervening in cases where suicide is a real threat, a case has been made *against* suicide prevention. Szasz (1986) challenges the commonly accepted notion that therapists have an absolute professional obligation to attempt to prevent suicide. In his view clients are ultimately responsible for their actions. Thus, mental-health professionals who assume total responsibility for keeping clients alive are depriving them of their rightful share of accountability for their own actions. Szasz believes that therapists do have an ethical and legal obligation to offer help to those clients with suicidal tendencies who request it. However, for those clients who are not seeking this help or who actively reject it, the professional's duty is either to persuade them to accept help or to leave them alone. For Szasz, coercive methods of suicide prevention, such as forced hospitalization, deprive people of their liberty and responsibility.

At this point you might reflect on your own views about suicide and how you might react to suicidal threats in the counseling session. Therapists are bound by the law to make assessments and intervene in professionally appropriate ways. However, if you were not under this legal imperative, how might you handle suicidal threats? Do you think that ethical practice always involves taking those steps that are legally required? As you think about this issue, do you see any potential conflict between ethics and the law?

LEGAL LIABILITY AND MALPRACTICE

After the preceding discussion of unethical practices, the rights of clients, the abuses related to the client/therapist relationship, legal aspects of confidentiality, the duty to warn and protect, and assessing and managing cases involving suicidal risk, you may well be asking questions such as the following: "What are the consequences of not practicing within the established ethical guidelines? Is it possible to exercise reasonable care and still make mistakes? How vulnerable am I to malpractice suits? What are some practical safeguards against being involved in a lawsuit? What is the impact of malpractice litigation on professional practice?"

A review of the professional literature shows that mental-health practitioners face an increasing risk of being sued for malpractice. Malpractice-insurance premiums reflect this trend toward greater vulnerability. Psychologists' professional-liability-insurance premiums have increased 800% since 1984. Despite the rising threat of litigation, most psychologists who responded in one study were not significantly concerned about being sued (Wilbert & Fulero, 1988). However, over half of those surveyed said that they were taking specific steps to prevent a malpractice suit. Wilbert and Fulero conclude that the threat of litigation appears to act as an impetus for a variety of sound and ethical practices. They also offer a note of reassurance: "A careful practitioner who follows the prescribed guidelines for proper professional practice and who refrains from sexual improprieties appears to run a very small risk of malpractice litigation" (p.382).

GROUNDS FOR MALPRACTICE SUITS

For malpractice litigation to occur, four conditions must be present: (1) a client/counselor relationship must have been established, (2) the therapist must have acted in a negligent or improper manner, (3) an actual injury must have been sustained by the client, and (4) the counselor's conduct must have caused the injury (Lovett & Lovett, 1988).

Unless counselors take due care and act in good faith they are liable to a civil suit for failing to perform their duties as provided by law. When practitioners assume a professional role, they are expected to abide by legal standards and adhere to the ethical codes of their profession in providing care to their clients. Civil liability means that an individual can be sued for not doing right or for doing wrong to another. Malpractice can be seen as the opposite of acting in good faith. It is defined as the failure to render proper service, through ignorance or negligence, resulting in injury or loss to the client. Negligence consists of departing from usual practice; in other words, standards commonly accepted by the profession are not followed, and due care is not exercised. Examples of malpractice injuries include harm to clients caused by misuse or abuse of therapy techniques, exacerbation of presenting symptoms, and the appearance of new symptoms.

There are many general causes of malpractice, including the following: (1) the procedure followed was not within the realm of accepted professional practice, (2) the counselor was not trained in the use of the technique that was employed, (3) the possible consequences of the counseling process were not adequately explained to the client, and (4) the counselor failed to follow a procedure that might have been more helpful in the given situation (Lovett & Lovett, 1988).

Here are some specific examples of grounds for malpractice actions against therapists:

- failing to inform clients of the limits of confidentiality
- violating a client's confidentiality by unauthorized release of information
- sexual misconduct
- failure to make a referral
- dispensing drugs
- using improper methods to collect fees
- a countersuit for fee collection
- providing birth-control and abortion counseling to minors (as opposed to making appropriate referrals for such help)
- failing to recognize and treat an obvious symptom or failing to diagnose accurately
- libeling or slandering a client

- causing physical injuries to be sustained by members in a group experience
- striking or physically assaulting a client as part of the treatment
- failing to exercise reasonable care before a client's suicide
- failing to warn and protect the victim of a violent crime
- improper hospitalization of a client
- misrepresenting one's professional training
- abandoning a client
- failing to keep adequate records
- breaching a contract with a client
- failing to provide for informed consent
- failing to provide close supervision to trainees
- failing to adhere to a recognized professional code of ethics

Recent court decisions have held counselors liable for damages when poor advice was given. If clients rely on the advice given by a professional and suffer damages as a result, they can initiate civil action. Professional health-care providers would do well to avoid the temptation to try to work with all clients, regardless of their level of competence to render appropriate service.

LEGAL SAFEGUARDS FOR CLINICAL PRACTICE

The key to a counselor's avoiding a malpractice suit is maintaining *reasonable, ordinary,* and *prudent* practices. In *The Law and the Practice of Human Services* (1984), Woody and his associates outline the main responsibilities and liabilities of human-services professionals. According to them, the best defense against being charged with malpractice is obtaining informed consent. Clients should be adequately informed about the therapeutic process and should intelligently consent to such treatment. If they have a diminished capacity to consent, a guardian or advocate should consent to treatment. Practitioners are advised to develop written informed-consent procedures early in the course of therapy. A specific therapeutic contract signed by both the client and the therapist is an example of such a procedure. In a survey of the record-keeping practices of clinical and counseling psychologists, Fulero and Wilbert (1988) found substantial variability in policies and practices. The majority of respondents reported that their record keeping was influenced by the threat of a malpractice suit. Soisson, VandeCreek, and Knapp (1987) maintain that thorough record keeping is the best defense in a litigious era. They conclude that proper records, kept in anticipation of future litigation, are crucial for practitioners who become involved in a malpractice action. Inadequate records jeopardize a therapist's case in court, even if the therapist provided quality services consistent with professional standards. Although keeping good records serves as a self-protective strategy against malpractice claims, Soisson and her colleagues emphasize that records should serve the client, not the therapist. The primary purposes of keeping records are to facilitate the coordination and continuity of services to the client, to assist in evaluating the client's progress, and to evaluate the outcomes of therapy.

Woody (1984) makes a number of other helpful recommendations for legal safeguards for clinical practice:

- Have a clear standard of care that can be applied to your services, and communicate this standard to your clients.
- Be willing to consult with colleagues or supervisors in cases that involve difficult legal and ethical issues.
- Use some form of diagnostic system. Adopt assessment procedures to ensure that your services are reasonably tailored to the needs of clients and are consistent with accepted standards of care
- Base your therapeutic practice on a well-established theory that provides a rationale for the techniques you employ. Regardless of the system, however, there are minimum requirements of knowledge and skills. There is no legal refuge in simply practicing within the boundaries of a particular theoretical school.
- Serve strictly as a therapist to your clients, avoiding social relationships.
- Do not allow clients to accrue a deficit in payments.
- If a complaint arises, revert to a defensive posture.
- Learn to rely on an attorney in malpractice issues.
- Recognize those situations in which you legally *must* break confidentiality. Examples are cases of suspected child abuse, incest, abuse of the elderly, danger to the life of others, and suicidal threats.
- Carry malpractice insurance.
- If you work for an agency or institution, have a contract that specifies the employer's legal liability for your professional functioning.

From attending professional conventions and reading on the subject, I offer other suggestions for preventing a malpractice lawsuit:

- Evaluate the efficacy of your interventions with clients.
- Know and follow the code of ethics of your professional organization.
- Become aware of the state and local laws that limit your practice.
- Abide by the policies of the institution that employs you. If you disagree with certain policies, do what you can to change them.
- Keep up-to-date with the expanding knowledge in your area of specialization. Take steps to upgrade your counseling and assessment skills through a program of continuing education.
- Be aware of the quality of your relationship with clients. Develop openness and directness with them, demonstrating a sincere interest in their welfare.
- Create reasonable expectations about what counseling can and cannot do. Don't offer guarantees of magical cures.
- Keep accurate and current records of your clients' treatment plans. These might include notes on the presenting problems, initial assessment, goals of counseling, potential risks and why they are justified, the rationale for interventions, informed-consent documents, progress reports, and a copy of the therapeutic contract.

This discussion of legal liability and malpractice is not intended to increase your anxiety or make you so careful that you avoid taking any risks. Because counseling is probably more art than science, creativity is an important dimension of the profession. Practicing counseling is a risky venture, and you will undoubtedly make mistakes from time to time. I see it as a disservice to clients to treat them as though they were fragile. Although it is unrealistic to expect perfection of any professional, it does not seem unrealistic to hope that practitioners will think about what they are doing and why they are doing it. Professional practice implies that they be aware of the ethical guidelines established by their profession, as well as having the ability to apply these principles to specific situations. Remember that ethical decision making is a continuing process throughout your career rather than a cut-and-dried process of having ready-made answers for difficult situations.

SOME GUIDELINES FOR ETHICAL PRACTICE: A SUMMARY REVIEW

I would like to summarize this chapter by putting into focus some principles that I believe are important for counselors to review throughout their professional practice. My hope is that you will think about these as guidelines rather than absolute decrees. Apply them to yourself, and attempt to formulate your own views and positions on some of the topics raised in this chapter. The task of developing a sense of professional and ethical responsibility is never really finished. Because there are no final or universal answers to many of these ethical questions, new issues will constantly be surfacing. Ethical decisions demand periodic reflection and an openness to change as you gain more experience.

1. Counselors are aware of what their own needs are, what they are getting from their work, and how their needs and behaviors influence their clients. It is essential that the therapist's own needs not be met at the client's expense.
2. Counselors have the training and experience necessary for the assessments they make and the interventions they attempt.
3. Counselors become aware of the boundaries of their competence and seek qualified supervision or refer clients when they recognize that they have reached their limit. They become familiar with community resources so that they can make appropriate referrals.
4. Although practitioners know the ethical standards of their professional organizations, they exercise their own judgment in applying these principles to particular cases. They realize that many problems are without clear-cut answers, and they accept the responsibility of searching for appropriate answers.
5. It is important for counselors to have some theoretical framework of behavioral change to guide them in their practice.

6. Counselors update their knowledge and skills through various forms of continuing education.
7. Counselors avoid any relationships with clients that are clearly a threat to the therapeutic relationship.
8. Counselors inform clients of any circumstances that are likely to affect the confidentiality of their relationship and of any other matters that are likely to negatively influence the relationship.
9. Counselors are aware of their own values and attitudes, recognize the role that their belief system plays in the relationships with their clients, and avoid imposing these beliefs on their clients, in either a subtle or a direct manner.
10. Counselors inform their clients about matters such as the goals of counseling, techniques and procedures that will be employed, possible risks associated with entering the relationship, and any other factors that are likely to affect the client's decision to enter therapy.
11. Counselors realize that they are teaching their clients through a modeling process. Thus, they attempt to practice in their own life what they encourage in their clients.
12. Counselors realize that they are bringing their own cultural background to the counseling relationship and recognize the ways in which their clients' cultural values are operating in the counseling process.
13. Counselors learn a process for thinking about and dealing with ethical dilemmas, realizing that most ethical issues are complex and defy simple solutions. The willingness to seek consultation is a sign of professional maturity.

Resolving the ethical dilemmas that you will face requires a commitment to question your own behavior and motives. A sign of good faith on the part of counselors is their willingness to openly share struggles with colleagues. Such consultation can be of great help in clarifying issues by giving you another perspective on a situation. I want to emphasize that being a professional counselor does not imply that you are perfect or superhuman. If you are willing to risk doing anything worthwhile in your work, you are bound to make some mistakes. What seems crucial is your willingness to reflect on what you are doing and on whose needs are being given priority.

If there is one fundamental question that can serve to tie together all the issues discussed in this chapter, it is this: Who has the right to counsel another person? This question can be the focal point of your reflection of ethical and professional issues. It can also be the basis of your self-examination each day that you meet with clients. You can continue to ask yourself: "What makes me think I have a right to counsel others? What do I have to offer the people I'm counseling? Am I doing in my own life what I'm encouraging my clients to do?" If you answer these questions honestly, you may be troubled. At times you may feel that you have no ethical right to counsel others, perhaps because your own life isn't always the model you would like it to be for your clients. More important than resolving all of life's issues is knowing what kinds of questions to ask and then remaining open to reflection.

QUESTIONS FOR REFLECTION AND DISCUSSION

1. After reading this chapter, what problems do you see in defining and evaluating your own competence? How can you strike a balance between the extremes of thinking that you can work competently with any client and thinking that no matter how much training you have, you will never know enough?

2. Assume that you are meeting a new client. What matters would you most want to discuss before the two of you entered a therapeutic relationship?

3. You are working in a community clinic, and a 15-year-old girl seeks counseling because she is torn between her wish to have an abortion and her fear of it. She tells you that under no circumstances does she want her parents to know that she is talking with you. What might you ask her and tell her at this point? What are the legal and ethical issues involved?

4. An elementary school pupil is referred to you for counseling by her teacher. At the initial session Betty tells you that, because her father frequently beats her, she is afraid that he might kill her. She shows you welts on her back but pleads with you not to say anything to anyone, because she is afraid he will find out. What could you say to her? What actions would you take? What legal issues are involved?

5. As a counseling intern, you know a fellow intern who makes it a practice to initiate social relationships with his clients. He justifies his practice on the grounds that both he and his clients are adults and that these social relationships allow them to engage in more meaningful counseling. What might you want to say to him? Do you have an obligation to do something?

6. What ethical and legal issues would concern you if you worked with clients with AIDS? How might you explain the limits of confidentiality to them?

7. Court decisions make it clear that therapists have a duty to warn and protect. What guidelines can you think of to help you assess a situation in which you would feel responsible to warn and protect?

8. What ethical and legal issues do you see as being involved in counseling a suicidal client? How might you deal with a client who informed you that he was convinced that he did not want to live and that he did not want you to interfere with his right to make this choice?

9. Traditional therapeutic approaches to minority clients have been challenged as being irrelevant to them. As you read about the therapy systems in the remaining chapters, ask yourself how this particular approach can be adapted in working with culturally diverse populations.

10. If you were a counselor in a community clinic serving various ethnic and cultural groups, what specific knowledge and skills would you have to possess to counsel your clients effectively? How might you go about acquiring such knowledge and skills if you were lacking them?

WHERE TO GO FROM HERE

This chapter has introduced you to a wide range of ethical and legal issues that you are bound to face at some point in your counseling practice. One chapter cannot begin to give in-depth coverage of these topics. Now that your interest has been piqued, you can continue by getting a copy of either *Ethical Standards Casebook* (Herlihy & Golden, 1990) or *Casebook on Ethical Principles of Psychologists* (APA, 1987). Both of these books are listed in the "Recommended Supplementary Readings," which follow, as are several textbooks on ethics in counseling that will give you a broader perspective on these issues. Reading selected journal articles on professional ethics is another way to increase your awareness of the ethical dimensions of practice. There is a comprehensive and updated list of these journal articles in the "References and Suggested Readings" at the end of this chapter. In addition to reading, taking a separate course on ethical and professional issues in counseling would be most helpful in stimulating your thinking and giving you a framework for ethical decision making. As you read the rest of the chapters in this book, be alert for ethical issues as they relate to the various therapeutic approaches.

Recommended Supplementary Readings

Issues and Ethics in the Helping Professions (G. Corey, Corey, & Callanan, 1988) is devoted entirely to issues of the sort that were introduced briefly in this chapter. Some relevant chapters deal with the role of values in the client/counselor relationship, therapist responsibilities, therapist competence, factors influencing the client/therapist relationship, and ways of dealing with transference and countertransference. The book is designed to involve readers in a personal and active way, and many open-ended cases are presented to help them formulate their thoughts on various issues.

Ethical and Legal Issues in Counseling and Psychotherapy (Van Hoose & Kottler, 1985) is a helpful resource that deals with professional issues such as incompetent and unethical behavior, legal regulations on professional psychology, problems of diagnosis and assessment, and value problems in therapy.

Ethical Decisions for Social Work Practice (Loewenberg & Dolgoff, 1988) deals with values and standards in social work. Some of the topics are societal ethics and professional ethics, foundations for ethical decisions, specific dilemmas in practice, guidelines for making ethical decisions, and codes of ethics. The book contains many case examples helpful in applying ethical codes to a variety of problem situations.

Ethics in Psychology: Professional Standards and Cases (Keith-Spiegel & Koocher, 1985) is a comprehensive treatment of professional standards and cases, geared to the ethical principles of the American Psychological Association. Issues covered include ethical decision making, ethics committees, confidentiality and privacy, psychological testing, money matters, advertising, dual relationships with clients, relationships with colleagues, scholarly publishing and teaching, research issues, and ethical dilemmas in special work settings. The case studies described throughout the book are quite effective in stimulating thought and discussion.

Ethics and Values in Psychotherapy: A Guidebook (Rosenbaum, 1982) is a comprehensive volume that deals with a variety of ethical issues in practice. Some of these are ethics in the training of therapists, client rights, ethics in group therapy, ethics in family therapy, the ethical use of biofeedback, ethical problems in the use of videotape, and ethics and therapy research.

Legal Liability in Psychotherapy (Schutz, 1982) is a very useful practitioner's guide to risk management that should be of interest to those in the helping professions. The author provides clear definitions and discussions of such topics as informed consent, contracts, managing the therapeutic relationship, the dangerous patient, the suicidal patient, the effects of the malpractice crisis on therapeutic practice, and legal aspects of practice. Examples and cases make this a readable book on an important subject.

The Law and the Practice of Human Services (Woody & Associates, 1984) provides an excellent beginning for readers wanting a comprehensive, up-to-date source of basic legal information. Some of the topics discussed are understanding the legal system, criminal law, juvenile law, family law, personal-injury law, the rights of institutionalized patients, the rights of handicapped children to an education, and professional responsibilities and liabilities.

The Counselor and the Law (Hopkins & Anderson, 1985) is a useful reference dealing with topics such as the legal aspects of the counselor/client relationship, civil liability, malpractice, and legal issues in private practice.

Ethical Standards Casebook, 4th Edition (Herlihy & Golden, 1990), contains a variety of useful cases that are geared to the 1988 AACD *Ethical Standards*. The examples illustrate and clarify the meaning and intent of the standards. The Appendix contains the association's divisional codes of ethics and the ethical standards of the National Board for Certified Counselors. Also described are the specific steps to be followed in reporting and processing allegations of unethical behavior by members. (This book can be purchased from the AACD, 5999 Stevenson Avenue, Alexandria, VA 22304; telephone: 703-823-9800.)

Casebook on Ethical Principles of Psychologists (APA, 1987) contains a wide variety of cases involving ethical issues. These cases cover areas such as responsibility, competence, moral and legal standards, public statements, confidentiality, the welfare of the consumer, professional relationships, assessment techniques, research with human participants, and care and use of animals. This is excellent material for reflection and discussion, and each case includes an adjudication. (This book can be purchased from the APA, Order Department, P.O. Box 2710, Hyattsville, MD 20784.)

REFERENCES AND SUGGESTED READINGS*

*AKAMATSU, T. J. (1988). Intimate relationships with former clients: National survey of attitudes and behavior among practitioners. *Professional Psychology: Research and Practice, 19,* 454–458.

AMERICAN ASSOCIATION FOR COUNSELING AND DEVELOPMENT. (1988). *Ethical standards* (rev. ed.). Alexandria, VA: Author.

AMERICAN ASSOCIATION FOR COUNSELING AND DEVELOPMENT. (1989, January 12). Knowledge of cultural values helpful to counselors. *Guidepost,* p. 14.

AMERICAN ASSOCIATION FOR MARRIAGE AND FAMILY THERAPY (1988, August). *Code of ethical principles for marriage and family therapists* (rev. ed.). Washington, DC: Author.

AMERICAN MENTAL HEALTH COUNSELORS ASSOCIATION. (1980). *Code of ethics for certified clinical mental health counselors.* Falls Church, VA: Author.

AMERICAN PSYCHIATRIC ASSOCIATION. (1986). *Principles of medical ethics with annotations especially applicable to psychiatry.* Washington, DC: Author.

AMERICAN PSYCHOANALYTIC ASSOCIATION. (1983). *Principles of ethics for psychoanalysts and provisions for implementation of the principles of ethics for psychoanalysts.* New York: Author.

* Books and articles marked with an asterisk are suggested for further study.

AMERICAN PSYCHOLOGICAL ASSOCIATION. (1981). *Ethical principles of psychologists*. Washington, DC: Author.

AMERICAN PSYCHOLOGICAL ASSOCIATION. (1985). *White paper on duty to protect*. Washington, DC: Author.

*AMERICAN PSYCHOLOGICAL ASSOCIATION. (1987). *Casebook on ethical principles of psychologists*. Washington, DC: Author.

*AMERICAN PSYCHOLOGICAL ASSOCIATION. (1988). Special issue: Psychology and AIDS. *American Psychologist, 43*(11).

AMERICAN PSYCHOLOGICAL ASSOCIATION. (1989). *Ethical principles of psychologists* (rev. ed.). Washington, DC: Author.

AMERICAN PSYCHOLOGICAL ASSOCIATION, DIVISION OF COUNSELING PSYCHOLOGY. (1979). Principles concerning the counseling and therapy of women. *The Counseling Psychologist, 8,* 21.

ASSOCIATION FOR SPECIALISTS IN GROUP WORK. (1983). *Professional standards for training of group counselors*. Alexandria, VA: Author.

ASSOCIATION FOR SPECIALISTS IN GROUP WORK. (1990). *Ethical guidelines for group counselors*. Alexandria, VA: Author.

*ATKINSON, D. R., MORTEN, G., & SUE, D. W. (Eds.). (1989). *Counseling American minorities: A cross cultural perspective* (3rd ed.). Dubuque, IA: William C. Brown.

*AXELSON, J. A. (1985). *Counseling and development in a multicultural society*. Pacific Grove, CA: Brooks/Cole.

BACKER, T. E., BATCHELOR, W. F., JONES, J. M., & MAYS, V. M. (1988). Introduction to Special Issue: Psychology and AIDS. *American Psychologist, 43,* 835–836.

BAIRD, K. A., & RUPERT, P. A. (1987). Clinical management of confidentiality: A survey of psychologists in seven states. *Professional Psychology: Research and Practice, 18,* 347–352.

*BARROWS, P. A., & HALGIN, R. P. (1988). Current issues in psychotherapy with gay men: Impact of the AIDS phenomenon. *Professional Psychology: Research and Practice, 19,* 395–402.

*BATES, C. M., & BRODSKY, A. M. (1989). *Sex in the therapy hour: A case of professional incest*. New York: Guilford Press.

*BENESCH, K. F., & PONTEROTTO, J. G. (1989). East and West: Transpersonal psychology and cross-cultural counseling. *Counseling and Values, 33,* 121–131.

BERNSTEIN, B., & LECOMTE, C. (1981). Licensure in psychology: Alternative direction. *Professional Psychology, 12,* 200–208.

BOUHOUTSOS, J., HOLROYD, J., LERMAN, H., FORER, B. R., & GREENBERG, M. (1983). Sexual intimacy between psychotherapists and patients. *Professional Psychology: Research and Practice, 14,* 185–196.

*BRODSKY, A. M. (1986). The distressed psychologist: Sexual intimacies and exploitation. In R. R. Kilburg, P. E. Nathan, & R. W. Thoreson (Eds.), *Professionals in distress: Issues, syndromes, and solutions in psychology* (pp. 153–172). Washington, DC: American Psychological Association.

CARROLL, M. A., SCHNEIDER, H. G., & WESLEY, G. R. (1985). *Ethics in the practice of psychology*. Englewood Cliffs, NJ: Prentice-Hall.

CASAS, J. M. (1986). *Falling short of meeting the counseling needs of racial/ethnic minorities: The status of ethical and accreditation guidelines*. Unpublished manuscript, University of California at Santa Barbara.

CAYLEFF, S. E. (1986). Ethical issues in counseling gender, race, and culturally distinct groups. *Journal of Counseling and Development, 64,* 345–347.

CHEMTOB, C. M., HAMADA, R. S., BAUER, G., & TORIGOE, R. Y. (1988). Patient suicide: Frequency and impact on psychologists. *Professional Psychology: Research and Practice, 19,* 416–420.

CHRISTENSEN, C. P. (1989). Cross-cultural awareness development: A conceptual model. *Counselor Education and Supervision, 28,* 270–289.

*COLEMAN, E., & SCHAEFER, S. (1986). Boundaries of sex and intimacy between client and counselor. *Journal of Counseling and Development, 64,* 341–344.

*COMMITTEE ON WOMEN IN PSYCHOLOGY, AMERICAN PSYCHOLOGICAL ASSOCIATION. (1989). If sex enters into the psychotherapy relationship. *Professional Psychology: Research and Practice, 20,* 112–115.

*COREY G., COREY, M., & CALLANAN, P. (1988). *Issues and ethics in the helping professions* (3rd ed.). Pacific Grove, CA: Brooks/Cole.

COREY, M., & COREY, G. (1987). *Groups: Process and practice* (3rd ed.). Pacific Grove, CA: Brooks/Cole.

*COREY, M., & COREY, G. (1989). *Becoming a helper.* Pacific Grove, CA: Brooks/Cole.

CORMIER, S., & HACKNEY, H. (1987). *The professional counselor: A process guide to helping.* Englewood Cliffs, NJ: Prentice-Hall.

EBERLEIN, L. (1987). Introducing ethics to beginning psychologists: A problem-solving approach. *Professional Psychology: Research and Practice, 18,* 353–359.

EDELWICH, J., with BRODSKY, A. (1982). *Sexual dilemmas for the helping professional.* New York: Brunner/Mazel.

*ETHICS COMMITTEE, AMERICAN PSYCHOLOGICAL ASSOCIATION. (1987). Report of the Ethics Committee: 1986. *American Psychologist, 42,* 730–734.

*ETHICS COMMITTEE, AMERICAN PSYCHOLOGICAL ASSOCIATION. (1988). Trends in ethics cases, common pitfalls, and published resources. *American Psychologist, 43,* 564–572.

EVERSTINE, L., EVERSTINE, D. S., HEYMANN, G. M., TRUE, R. H., FREY, D. H., JOHNSON, H. G., & SEIDEN, R. H. (1980). Privacy and confidentiality in psychotherapy. *American Psychologist, 35,* 828–840.

FITZGERALD, L. F., & NUTT, R. (1986). The Division 17 principles concerning the counseling/psychotherapy of women: Rationale and implication. *The Counseling Psychologist, 14,* 180–216.

*FLORA, J. A., & THORESEN, C. E. (1988). Reducing the risk of AIDS in adolescents. *American Psychologist, 43,* 965–970.

*FRETZ, B. R., & MILLS, D. H. (1980). *Licensing and certification of psychologists and counselors.* San Francisco: Jossey-Bass.

*FUJIMURA, L. E., WEIS, D. M., & COCHRAN, J. R. (1985). Suicide: Dynamics and implications for counseling. *Journal of Counseling and Development, 63,* 612–615.

*FULERO, S. M. (1988). *Tarasoff:* 10 years later. *Professional Psychology: Research and Practice, 19,* 184–190.

*FULERO, S. M., & WILBERT, J. R. (1988). Record-keeping practices of clinical and counseling psychologists: A survey of practitioners. *Professional Psychology: Research and Practice, 19,* 658–660.

GABBARD, G., & POPE, K. (1988). Sexual intimacies after termination: Clinical, ethical, and legal aspects. *The Independent Practitioner, 8,* 21–26.

GARFIELD, S. L. (1987). Ethical issues in research on psychotherapy. *Counseling and Values, 31,* 115–125.

GLASER, R. D., & THORPE, J. S. (1986). Unethical intimacy: A survey of sexual contact and advances between psychology educators and female graduate students. *American Psychologist, 41,* 42–51.

GOTTLIEB, M. C., SELL, J. M., & SCHOENFELD, L. S. (1988). Social/romantic relationships with present and former clients: State licensing board actions. *Professional Psychology: Research and Practice, 19,* 459–462.

*GRAY, L. A., & HARDING, A. I. (1988). Confidentiality limits with clients who have the AIDS virus. *Journal of Counseling and Development, 56,* 219–223.

GROSS, S. J. (1977). Professional disclosure: An alternative to licensure. *Personnel and Guidance Journal, 55,* 586–588.

GUTHEIL, T. G. (1989, November/December). Patient-therapist sexual relations. *The California Therapist,* pp. 29–31.

*GUY, J. D., STARK, M. J., & POELSTRA, P. L. (1988) Personal therapy for psychothera- pists before and after entering professional practice. *Professional Psychology: Re- search and Practice, 19,* 474–476.

*HAAS, L. J., MALOUF, J. L., & MAYERSON, N. H. (1986). Ethical dilemmas in psycholog- ical practice: Results of a national survey. *Professional Psychology: Research and Practice, 17,* 316–321.

HANDELSMAN, M. M. (1986a). Ethics training at the master's level: A national survey. *Professional Psychology: Research and Practice, 17,* 24–26.

*HANDELSMAN, M. M. (1986b). Problems with ethics training by "osmosis." *Profes- sional Psychology: Research and Practice, 17,* 371–372.

HERLIHY, B., & GOLDEN, L. (1990). *Ethical standards casebook* (4th ed.). Alexandria, VA: AACD Press.

HERLIHY, B., HEALY, M., COOK, E. P., & HUDSON, P. (1987). Ethical practices of licensed counselors. A survey of state licensing boards. *Counselor Education and Supervision, 27,* 69–76.

HERLIHY, B., & SHEELEY, V. L. (1988). Counselor liability and the duty to warn: Selected cases, statutory trends, and implications for practice. *Counselor Education and Supervision, 27,* 203–215.

HILLERBRAND, E. T., & CLAIBORN, C. D. (1988). Ethical knowledge exhibited by clients and nonclients. *Professional Psychology: Research and Practice, 19,* 527– 531.

HILLERBRAND, E., & STONE, G. L. (1986). Ethics and clients: A challenging mixture for counselors. *Journal of Counseling and Development, 64,* 240–245.

HOGAN, D. B. (1979). *The regulation of psychotherapists: A handbook of state licensure laws* (4 vols.). Cambridge, MA: Ballinger.

HOLROYD, J. C., & BOUHOUTSOS, J. C. (1985). Sources of bias in reporting effects of sexual contact with patients. *Professional Psychology: Research and Practice 16,* 701–709.

HOLROYD, J. C., & BRODSKY, A. (1977). Psychologists' attitudes and practices regard- ing erotic and nonerotic physical contact with patients. *American Psychologist 32,* 843–849.

HOLROYD, J. C., & BRODSKY, A. (1980). Does touching patients lead to sexual inter- course? *Professional Psychology, 11,* 807–811.

*HOPKINS, B. R., & ANDERSON, B. S. (1985). *The counselor and the law* (2nd ed.). Alexandria, VA: AACD Press.

*HOTELLING, K. (1988). Ethical, legal, and administrative options to address sexual relationships between counselor and client. *Journal of Counseling and Develop- ment, 67,* 233–237.

HUDDLESTON, J. E., & ENGELS, D. W. (1986). Issues related to the use of paradoxical techniques in counseling. *Journal of Counseling and Human Service Professions, 1,* 127–133.

HUEY, W. C., & REMLEY, T. P., JR. (1989). *Ethical issues in school counseling.* Alexan- dria, VA: American Association for Counseling and Development.

*IBRAHIM, F. A. (1985). Effective cross-cultural counseling and psychotherapy: A frame-work. *The Counseling Psychologist, 13,* 625–638.

*IBRAHIM, F. A., & ARREDONDO, P. M. (1986). Ethical standards for cross-cultural counseling: Counselor preparation, practice, assessment, and research. *Journal of Counseling and Development, 64,* 349–352.

*IBRAHIM, F. A., & ARREDONDO, P. M. (1990) Ethical issues in multicultural counsel-ing. In B. Herlihy & L. Golden, *Ethical standards casebook* (4th ed.). Alexandria, VA: AACD Press.

*JENSEN, J. P., & BERGIN, A. E. (1988). Mental health values of professional therapists: A national interdisciplinary survey. *Professional Psychology: Research and Practice, 19,* 290–297.

*KAIN, C. D. (1988). To breach or not to breach: Is that the question? A response to Gray and Harding. *Journal of Counseling and Development, 66,* 224–225.

*KEITH-SPIEGEL, P., & KOOCHER, G. (1985). *Ethics in psychology: Professional stan-dards and cases.* New York: Random House.

*KITCHENER, K. S. (1988). Dual role relationships: What makes them so problematic? *Journal of Counseling and Development, 67,* 217–221.

KITCHENER, K. S., & HARDING, S. S. (1990). Dual relationships. In B. Herlihy & L. Golden, *Ethical standards casebook* (4th ed.). Alexandria, VA: AACD Press.

KNAPP, S., & VANDECREEK, L. (1982). *Tarasoff:* Five years later. *Professional Psychol-ogy, 13,* 511–516.

*LAFROMBOISE, T. D., & FOSTER, S. L. (1989). Ethics in multicultural counseling. In P. Pedersen, J. Draguns, W. Lonner, & J. Trimble (Eds.), *Counseling across cultures* (3rd ed.) (pp. 115–136). Honolulu: University of Hawaii Press.

LAUGHRAN, W., & BAKKEN, G. M. (1984). The psychotherapist's responsibility toward third parties under current California law. *Western State University Law Review, 12,* 1–33.

LEFLEY, H. P., & PEDERSEN, P. (Eds.). (1986). *Cross-cultural training for mental health professionals.* Springfield, IL: Charles C Thomas.

LESLIE, R. (1989, July/August). Confidentiality. *The California Therapist,* pp. 35–42.

*LEVENSON, J. L. (1986). When a colleague practices unethically: Guidelines for inter-vention. *Journal of Counseling and Development, 64,* 315–317.

LEVINE, C. (1987). *Taking sides: Clashing views on controversial bioethical issues* (2nd ed.). Guilford, CT: Dushkin Publishing Group.

LIPSITZ, N. E. (1985). *The relationship between ethics training and ethical discrimina-tion ability.* Paper presented at the annual meeting of the American Psychological Association, Los Angeles.

*LOEWENBERG, F., & DOLGOFF, R. (1988). *Ethical decisions for social work practice* (3rd ed.). Itasca, IL: F. E. Peacock.

LOVETT, T., & LOVETT, C. J. (1988). *Suggestions for continuing legal education units in counselor training.* Paper presented at the annual meeting of the American Association for Counseling and Development, Chicago.

MABE, A. R., & ROLLIN, S. A. (1986). The role of a code of ethical standards in counsel-ing. *Journal of Counseling and Development, 64,* 294–297.

*MAPPES, D. C., ROBB, G. P., & ENGELS, D. W. (1985). Conflicts between ethics and law in counseling and psychotherapy. *Journal of Counseling and Development, 64,* 246–252.

*MELTON, G. B. (1988). Ethical and legal issues in AIDS-related practice. *American Psychologist, 43,* 941–947.

*MILLER, D. J., & THELEN, M. H. (1986). Knowledge and beliefs about confidentiality in psychotherapy. *Professional Psychology: Research and Practice, 17,* 15–19.

*MORIN, S. F. (1988). AIDS: The challenge to psychology. *American Psychologist, 43,* 838–842.

*MUEHLEMAN, T., PICKENS, B. K., & ROBINSON, R. (1985) Informing clients about the limits to confidentiality, risks, and their rights: Is self-disclosure inhibited? *Professional Psychology: Research and Practice, 16,* 385–397.

NATIONAL ASSOCIATION OF SOCIAL WORKERS. (1979). *Code of ethics.* Silver Spring, MD: Author.

NATIONAL BOARD FOR CERTIFIED COUNSELORS. (1987). *Code of ethics.* Alexandria, VA: Author.

NATIONAL FEDERATION OF SOCIETIES FOR CLINICAL SOCIAL WORK. (1985). *Code of ethics.* Silver Spring, MD: Author

*PARKER, W. M., VALLEY, M. M., & GEARY, C. A. (1986). Acquiring cultural knowledge for counselors in training: A multifaceted approach. *Counselor Education and Supervision, 26,* 61–71.

PATRICK, K. D. (1989). Unique ethical dilemmas in counselor training. *Counselor Education and Supervision, 28,* 337–341.

*PEDERSEN, P. (Ed.). (1985a). *Handbook of cross-cultural counseling and therapy.* Westport, CT: Greenwood Press.

PEDERSEN, P. (1985b). Intercultural criteria for mental-health training. In P. Pedersen (Ed.), *Handbook of cross-cultural counseling and therapy* (pp. 315–321). Westport, CT: Greenwood Press.

PEDERSEN, P. (1986). *Are the APA ethical principles culturally encapsulated?* Unpublished manuscript, Syracuse University.

*PEDERSEN, P. (1988). *A handbook for developing multicultural awareness.* Alexandria, VA: American Association for Counseling and Development.

PEDERSEN, P. (1989). Developing multicultural ethical guidelines for psychology. *International Journal of Psychology, 24,* 643–652.

PEDERSEN, P. (1990). The multicultural perspective as a fourth force in counseling. *Journal of Mental Health Counseling, 12,* 93–95.

PEDERSEN, P. B., & MARSELLA, A. J. (1982). The ethical crisis for cross-cultural counseling and therapy. *Professional Psychology, 13,* 492–500

PELSMA, D. M., & BORGERS, S. G. (1986). Experience-based ethics: A developmental model of learning ethical reasoning. *Journal of Counseling and Development, 64,* 311–314.

POPE, K. S. (1985a). Dual relationships: A violation of ethical, legal, and clinical standards. *California State Psychologist, 20,* 3–5.

POPE, K. S. (1985b). The suicidal client: Guidelines for assessment and treatment. *California State Psychologist, 20,* 3–7.

*POPE, K. S. (1987). Preventing therapist-patient sexual intimacy: Therapy for a therapist at risk. *Professional Psychology: Research and Practice, 18,* 624–628.

*POPE, K. S. (1988). How clients are harmed by sexual contact with mental health professionals: The syndrome and its prevalence. *Journal of Counseling and Development, 67,* 222–226.

*POPE, K. S., & BOUHOUTSOS, J. C. (1986). *Sexual intimacy between therapists and patients.* New York: Praeger.

*POPE, K. S., KEITH-SPIEGEL, P., & TABACHNICK, B. G. (1986). Sexual attraction to clients: The human therapist and the (sometimes) inhuman training system. *American Psychologist, 41,* 147–158.

POPE, K. S., LEVENSON, H., & SCHOVER, L. R. (1979). Sexual intimacy in psychology training: Results and implications of a national survey. *American Psychologist, 34,* 682–689.

POPE, K. S., SCHOVER, L. R., & LEVENSON, H. (1980). Sexual behavior between clinical supervisors and trainees: Implications for professional standards. *Professional Psychology, 10,* 157–162.

*POPE, K. S., TABACHNICK, B. G., & KEITH-SPIEGEL, P. (1987). Ethics of practice: The beliefs and behaviors of psychologists as therapists. *American Psychologist, 42,* 993–1006.

*POPE, K. S., TABACHNICK, B. G., & KEITH-SPIEGEL, P. (1988). Good and poor practices in psychotherapy: National survey of beliefs of psychologists. *Professional Psychology: Research and Practice, 19,* 547–552.

POSEY, E. C. (1988). Confidentiality in an AIDS support group. *Journal of Counseling and Development, 66,* 226–227.

PRICE, A., OMIZO, M., & HAMMETT, V. (1986). Counseling clients with AIDS. *Journal of Counseling and Development, 65,* 96–97.

QUACKENBOS, S., PRIVETTE, G., & KLENTZ, B. (1986). Psychotherapy and religion: Rapprochement or antithesis? *Journal of Counseling and Development, 65,* 82–85.

REAVES, R. P. (1986). Legal liability and psychologists. In R. R. Kilburg, P. E. Nathan, & R. W. Thoreson (Eds.), *Professionals in distress: Issues, syndromes, and solutions in psychology* (pp. 173–184). Washington, DC: American Psychological Association.

ROBINSON, S. E., & GROSS, D. R. (1986). Counseling research: Ethics and issues. *Journal of Counseling and Development, 64,* 331–333.

ROBINSON, W. L., & REID, P. T. (1985). Sexual intimacies in psychology revisited. *Professional Psychology: Research and Practice, 16,* 512–520.

*ROSENBAUM, M. (Ed.). (1982). *Ethics and values in psychotherapy: A guidebook.* New York: Free Press.

ROTH, L. (1987). *Clinical treatment of the violent person.* New York: Guilford Press.

*RUBANOWITZ, D. E. (1987). Public attitudes toward psychotherapist-client confidentiality. *Professional Psychology: Research and Practice, 18,* 613–618.

*RUDOLPH, J. (1989). The impact of contemporary ideology and AIDS on the counseling of gay clients. *Counseling and Values, 33,* 96–108.

SCHOENER, G. R., & GONSIOREK, J. (1988). Assessment and development of rehabilitation plans for counselors who have sexually exploited their clients. *Journal of Counseling and Development, 67,* 227–232.

*SCHUTZ, B. (1982). *Legal liability in psychotherapy.* San Francisco: Jossey-Bass.

*SELL, J. M., GOTTLIEB, M. C., & SCHOENFELD, L. (1986). Ethical considerations of social/romantic relationships with present and former clients. *Professional Psychology: Research and Practice, 17,* 504–508.

*SHEELEY, V. L., & HERLIHY, B. (1986). The ethics of confidentiality and privileged communication. *Journal of Counseling and Human Service Professions, 1,* 141–148.

SIMON, R. (1987). *Clinical psychiatry and the law.* Washington, DC: American Psychiatric Press.

SLATER, B. R. (1988). Essential issues in working with lesbian and gay male youths. *Professional Psychology: Research and Practice, 19,* 226–235.

*SOISSON, E. L., VANDECREEK, L., & KNAPP, S. (1987). Thorough record keeping: A good defense in a litigious era. *Professional Psychology: Research and Practice, 18,* 498–502.

*STADLER, H. A. (1986). To counsel or not to counsel: The ethical dilemma of dual relationships. *Journal of Counseling and Human Service Professions, 1,* 134–140.

STANLEY, B., SIEBER, J. E., & MELTON, G. B. (1987). Empirical studies of ethical issues in research. *American Psychologist, 42,* 735–741.

*SUE, D. W. (1981a). *Counseling the culturally different: Theory and practice*. New York: Wiley.

SUE, D. W. (1981b). *Position paper on cross-cultural counseling competencies.* Education and Training Committee report delivered to Division 17, APA Executive Committee.

SUE, D. W., BERNIER, J. E., DURRAN, A., FEINBERG, L., PEDERSEN, P., SMITH, E. J., & NUTTALL, E. V. (1982). Position paper: Cross-cultural counseling competencies. *The Counseling Psychologist, 10,* 45–52.

*SUE, S. (1988). Psychotherapeutic services for ethnic minorities: Two decades of research findings. *American Psychologist, 43,* 301–308.

*SZASZ, T. (1986). The case against suicide prevention. *American Psychologist, 41,* 806–812.

*VAN HOOSE, W. H., & KOTTLER, J. A. (1985). *Ethical and legal issues in counseling and psychotherapy* (2nd ed.). San Francisco: Jossey-Bass.

*VASQUEZ, M. J. T. (1988). Counselor-client sexual contact: Implications for ethics training. *Journal of Counseling and Development, 67,* 238–241.

*VASQUEZ, M. J. T., & KITCHENER, K. S. (1988). Introduction to special feature. *Journal of Counseling and Development, 67,* 214–216.

VINSON, J. (1989, November/December). Reflecting on dual relationships: Therapist-patient sex. *The California Therapist,* p. 41.

WHISTON, S. C., & EMERSON, S. (1989). Ethical implications for supervisors in counseling of trainees. *Counselor Education and Supervision, 28,* 318–325.

*WILBERT, J. R., & FULERO, S. M. (1988). Impact of malpractice litigation on professional psychology: Survey of practitioners. *Professional Psychology: Research and Practice, 19,* 379–382.

*WILLISON, B. G., & MASSON, R. L. (1986). The role of touch in therapy: An adjunct to communication. *Journal of Counseling and Development, 64,* 497–500.

*WOODY, R. (1984). Professional responsibilities and liabilities. In R. H. Woody and Associates (Eds.). *The law and the practice of human services* (pp. 373–401). San Francisco: Jossey-Bass.

*WOODY, R. H., & ASSOCIATES. (Eds.). (1984). *The law and the practice of human services.* San Francisco: Jossey-Bass.

*WRIGHT, R. H. (1981). What to do until the malpractice lawyer comes: A survivor's manual. *American Psychologist, 36,* 1535–1541.

*WRIGHTSMAN, L. S. (1987). *Psychology and the legal system.* Pacific Grove, CA: Brooks/Cole.

WUBBOLDING, R. E. (1987). Professional ethics: Handling suicidal threats in the counseling session. *Journal of Reality Therapy, 7,* 12–15.

WUBBOLDING, R. E. (1988a). Intervention in suiciding behaviors. *Journal of Reality Therapy, 7,* 13–17.

WUBBOLDING, R. E. (1988b). Signs and myths surrounding suiciding behaviors. *Journal of Reality Therapy, 8,* 18–21.

4

PSYCHOANALYTIC THERAPY

SIGMUND FREUD

SIGMUND FREUD (1856–1939) was the firstborn in a Viennese family of three boys and five girls. His father, like many others of his time and place, was very authoritarian. Freud's family background is a factor to consider in understanding the development of his theory.

Even though Freud's family had limited finances and was forced to live in a crowded apartment, his parents made every effort to foster his obvious intellectual capacities. He had many interests, but his career choices were restricted because of his Jewish heritage. He finally settled on medicine. Only four years after earning his medical degree from the University of Vienna at the age of 26, he attained a prestigious position there as a lecturer.

Freud devoted most of the rest of his life to formulating and extending his theory of psychoanalysis. Interestingly, the most creative phase of his life corresponded to a period when he was experiencing severe emotional problems of his own. When he was in his early 40s, he had numerous psychosomatic disorders, as well as exaggerated fears of dying and other phobias. During this time he was involved in the difficult task of self-analysis. By exploring the meaning of his own dreams, he gained insights into the dynamics of personality development. He first examined his childhood memories and came to realize the intense hostility that he had felt for his father. He also recalled his childhood sexual feelings for his mother, who was attractive, loving, and protective. He then clinically formulated his theory as he observed his patients work through their own problems in analysis.

Freud had very little tolerance for colleagues who diverged from his psychoanalytic doctrines. He attempted to keep control over the movement by expelling those who dared to disagree. Carl Jung and Alfred Adler, for example, worked closely with Freud, but each founded his own therapeutic school after repeated disagreements with him on theoretical and clinical issues.

Freud was highly creative and productive, frequently putting in an 18-hour day. His collected works fill 24 volumes. Freud's productivity remained at this prolific level until late in his life, when he contracted cancer of the jaw. During his last two decades he underwent 33 operations and was in almost constant pain. He died in London in 1939.

As the originator of psychoanalysis, Freud distinguished himself as an intellectual giant. He pioneered new techniques for understanding human behavior, and his efforts resulted in the most comprehensive theory of personality and psychotherapy ever developed.

INTRODUCTION

Freud's views continue to influence contemporary practice. Many of his basic concepts are still part of the foundation on which other theorists build and develop. Indeed, most of the other theories of counseling and psychotherapy discussed later in this book have been influenced by psychoanalytic ideas. Some of these therapeutic approaches extended the psychoanalytic model, others modified its concepts and procedures, and others emerged as a reaction against it. Many borrowed and integrated its principles and techniques.

Freud's psychoanalytic system is a model of personality development, a philosophy of human nature, and a method of psychotherapy. Freud gave psychotherapy a new look and new horizons. He called attention to psychodynamic factors that motivate behavior, focused on the role of the unconscious, and developed the first therapeutic procedures for understanding and modifying the structure of one's basic character. His theory is a benchmark against which many other theories are measured.

In this relatively short chapter it is impossible to capture the diversity of the psychodynamic approaches that have arisen since Freud. The main focus of this chapter, rather, is on the basic psychoanalytic concepts and practices, many of which originated with him. The chapter sketches therapies that apply classical psychoanalytic concepts to practice less rigorously than Freud did. The chapter also summarizes Erik Erikson's theory of psychosocial development, which extends Freudian theory in several ways. Brief mention is also given to contemporary psychoanalytic theory and practice, including some of the concepts of an approach known as object-relations theory.*

KEY CONCEPTS

VIEW OF HUMAN NATURE

The Freudian view of human nature is basically deterministic. According to Freud, people's behavior is determined by irrational forces, unconscious motivations, biological and instinctual drives, and certain psychosexual events during the first six years of life. As Kovel notes, however: "Given the dialectic between conscious and unconscious, the strict determinism that has been ascribed to Freudianism . . . melts away. True, thoughts are determined, but not in a linear way. Psychoanalysis teaches a person that his behavior is far more complex than had been imagined" (1976, p. 77).

Instincts are central to the Freudian approach. Although Freud originally used the term *libido* to refer to sexual energy, he later broadened it to include the energy of all the *life instincts*. These instincts serve the purpose of the survival of the individual and the human race; they are oriented toward growth, development, and creativity. Libido, then, should be understood as a source of motivation that encompasses but goes beyond sexual energy. Freud included

* I want to acknowledge the contributions of William Blau and J. Michael Russell to the updating and refining of the ideas in this chapter, especially those dealing with contemporary trends in psychoanalytic practice.

all pleasurable acts in his concept of the life instincts; he saw the goal of much of life as gaining pleasure and avoiding pain.

Freud also postulated the concept *death instincts*, which accounted for the *aggressive drive*. At times, he asserted, people manifest through their behavior an unconscious wish to die or to hurt themselves or others. In his view both the sexual and aggressive drives are powerful determinants of why people act as they do.

Although there may be conflicts between the life instincts (known as Eros) and the death instincts (known as Thanatos), human beings are not condemned to be the victims of aggression and self-destruction. In his book *Civilization and Its Discontents* (1930/1962) Freud gave an indication that the major challenge facing the human race was how to manage the aggressive drive. For Freud, the unrest and anxiety of people was related to their knowledge that the human race could be exterminated. How much more true is this today than it was in Freud's time?

STRUCTURE OF PERSONALITY

According to the psychoanalytic view, the personality consists of three systems: the id, the ego, and the superego. These are names for psychological processes and should not be thought of as manikins that separately operate the personality; one's personality functions as a whole rather than as three discrete segments. The id is the biological component, the ego is the psychological component, and the superego is the social component.

From the orthodox Freudian perspective humans are viewed as energy systems. The dynamics of personality consist of the ways in which psychic energy is distributed to the id, ego, and superego. Because the amount of energy is limited, one system gains control over the available energy at the expense of the other two systems. Behavior is determined by this psychic energy.

The id.   The id is the original system of personality; at birth a person is all id. The id is the primary source of psychic energy and the seat of the instincts. It lacks organization, and it is blind, demanding, and insistent. A cauldron of seething excitement, the id cannot tolerate tension, and it functions to discharge tension immediately and return to a homeostatic condition. Ruled by the pleasure principle, which is aimed at reducing tension, avoiding pain, and gaining pleasure, the id is illogical, amoral, and driven by one consideration: to satisfy instinctual needs in accordance with the pleasure principle. The id never matures but remains the spoiled brat of personality. It does not think but only wishes or acts. The id is largely unconscious, or out of awareness.

The ego.   The ego has contact with the external world of reality. It is the "executive" that governs, controls, and regulates the personality. As the "traffic cop" for the id, superego, and external world it mediates between the instincts and the surrounding environment. The ego controls consciousness and exercises censorship. Ruled by the reality principle, the ego does realistic and logical thinking and formulates plans of action for satisfying needs. What is the relation of the ego to the id? The ego is the seat of intelligence and rationality that checks and controls the blind impulses of the id. Whereas the id knows only subjective reality, the ego distinguishes between mental images and things in the external world.

The superego.   The superego is the judicial branch of personality. It is a person's moral code, the main concern being whether action is good or bad, right or wrong. It represents the ideal, rather than the real, and strives not for pleasure but for perfection. It represents the traditional values and ideals of society as they are handed down from parents to children. It functions to inhibit the id impulses, to persuade the ego to substitute moralistic goals for realistic ones, and to strive for perfection. The superego, then, as the internalization of the standards of parents and society, is related to psychological rewards and punishments. The rewards are feelings of pride and self-love; the punishments are feelings of guilt and inferiority.

CONSCIOUSNESS AND THE UNCONSCIOUS

Perhaps Freud's greatest contributions are his concepts of the unconscious and of the levels of consciousness, which are the keys to understanding behavior and the problems of personality. The unconscious cannot be studied directly; it is inferred from behavior. Clinical evidence for postulating the unconscious includes the following: (1) dreams, which are symbolic representations of unconscious needs, wishes, and conflicts; (2) slips of the tongue and forgetting, for example, a familiar name; (3) posthypnotic suggestions; (4) material derived from free-association techniques; (5) material derived from projective techniques; and (6) the symbolic content of psychotic symptoms.

For Freud, consciousness is a thin slice of the total mind. Like the greater part of the iceberg that lies below the surface of the water, the larger part of the mind exists below the surface of awareness. The unconscious stores up all experiences, memories, and repressed material. Needs and motivations that are inaccessible — that is, out of awareness — are also outside the sphere of conscious control. Most psychological functioning exists in the out-of-awareness realm. The aim of psychoanalytic therapy, therefore, is to make the unconscious motives conscious, for only when one becomes conscious of motivations can one exercise choice. Understanding the role of the unconscious is central to grasping the essence of the psychoanalytic model of behavior. The unconscious, even though out of awareness, does influence behavior. Unconscious processes are the roots of all forms of neurotic symptoms and behaviors. From this perspective, a "cure" is based on uncovering the meaning of symptoms, the causes of behavior, and the repressed materials that interfere with healthy functioning. It is to be noted, however, that intellectual insight alone does not resolve the symptom. The client's need to cling to old patterns (repetition) must be confronted by the working through of transference distortions, which will be discussed later in this chapter.

ANXIETY

Also essential to the psychoanalytic approach is its concept of anxiety. Anxiety is a state of tension that motivates us to do something. It develops out of a conflict among the id, ego, and superego over control of the available psychic energy. Its function is to warn of impending danger.

There are three kinds of anxiety: reality, neurotic, and moral. Reality anxiety is the fear of danger from the external world, and the level of such anxiety is proportionate to the degree of real threat. Neurotic and moral anxiety are evoked by threats to the "balance of power" within the person. They signal to the ego that unless appropriate measures are taken, the danger may increase until the ego is overthrown. When the ego cannot control anxiety by rational and direct methods, it relies on unrealistic ones — namely, ego-defense behavior (which will be explained shortly). Neurotic anxiety is the fear that the instincts will get out of hand and cause one to do something for which one will be punished. Moral anxiety is the fear of one's own conscience. People with a well-developed conscience tend to feel guilty when they do something contrary to their moral code or to parental introjections.

EGO-DEFENSE MECHANISMS

Ego-defense mechanisms help the individual cope with anxiety and prevent the ego from being overwhelmed. These ego defenses, rather than being pathological, are normal behaviors. They can have adaptive value if they do not become a style of life to avoid facing reality. The defenses one uses depend on one's level of development and degree of anxiety. Defense mechanisms have two characteristics in common: they either deny or distort reality, and they operate on an unconscious level. Following are brief descriptions of some common ego defenses:

• *Repression.* The mechanism of repression is one of the most important Freudian processes, and it is the basis of many other ego defenses and of neurotic disorders. It is a means of defense through which threatening or painful thoughts and feelings are excluded from awareness. Freud explained repression as an involuntary removal of something from consciousness. It is assumed that most of the painful events of the first five years of life are so excluded, yet these events do influence later behavior.

• *Denial.* Denial plays a defensive role similar to that of repression, yet it generally operates at preconscious and conscious levels. Denial of reality is perhaps the simplest of all self-defense mechanisms; it is a way of distorting what the individual thinks, feels, or perceives in a traumatic situation. It consists of defending against anxiety by "closing one's eyes" to the existence of threatening reality. In tragic events such as wars and other disasters, people often tend to blind themselves to realities that would be too painful to accept.

• *Reaction formation.* One defense against a threatening impulse is to actively express the opposite impulse. By developing conscious attitudes and behaviors that are diametrically opposed to disturbing desires, people do not have to face the anxiety that would result if they were to recognize these dimensions of themselves. Individuals may conceal hate with a facade of love, be extremely nice when they harbor negative reactions, or mask cruelty with excessive kindness.

• *Projection.* Another mechanism of self-deception consists of attributing to others one's own unacceptable desires and impulses. Lustful, aggressive, or other impulses are seen as being possessed by "those people out there, but not by me." Thus, a man who is sexually attracted to his daughter may maintain that it is *she* who is behaving seductively with him. Thus, he does not have to recognize or deal with his own desires.

• *Displacement.* One way to cope with anxiety is to discharge impulses by shifting from a threatening object to a "safer target." Displacement consists of directing energy toward another object or person when the original object or person is inaccessible. For example, the meek man who feels intimidated by his boss comes home and unloads inappropriate hostility onto his children.

• *Rationalization.* Some people manufacture "good" reasons to explain away a bruised ego. Rationalization involves explaining away failures or losses. Thus, it helps justify specific behaviors, and it aids in softening the blow connected with disappointments. When people do not get positions they have applied for in their work, they think of logical reasons why they did not succeed, and they sometimes attempt to convince themselves that they really did not want the position anyway.

• *Sublimation.* From the Freudian perspective, many of the great artistic contributions resulted from a redirection of sexual or aggressive energy into creative behaviors. Sublimation involves diverting sexual energy into other channels, ones that are usually socially acceptable and sometimes even admirable. For example, aggressive impulses can be channeled into athletic activities, so that the person finds a way of expressing aggressive feelings and, as an added bonus, is often praised.

• *Regression.* Some people revert to a form of behavior that they have outgrown. In this regression to an earlier phase of development the demands are not so great. In the face of severe stress or extreme challenge, individuals may attempt to cope with the anxiety they feel by clinging to immature and inappropriate behaviors. For example, children who are frightened in school may indulge in infantile behavior such as weeping, excessive dependence, thumbsucking, hiding, or clinging to the teacher. They are seeking to return to a time in their life when there was security.

• *Introjection.* The mechanism of introjection consists of taking in and "swallowing" the values and standards of others. For example, in concentration camps some of the prisoners dealt with overwhelming anxiety by accepting the values of the enemy through an identification with the aggressor. Another example is the abused child, who assumes the abusing parent's way of handling stresses and thus continues the cycle of child beating. It should be noted that there are also positive forms of introjection, such as the incorporation of parental values or the attributes and values of the therapist (assuming that these are not merely uncritically accepted).

• *Identification.* Although identification is part of the developmental process by which children learn sex-role behaviors, it can also be a defensive reaction. It can enhance self-worth and protect one from a sense of being a failure. Thus, people who feel basically inferior may identify themselves with successful causes, organizations, or people in the hope that they will be perceived as worthwhile.

• *Compensation.* Compensation consists of masking perceived weaknesses or developing certain positive traits to make up for limitations. Thus, children who do not receive positive attention and recognition may develop behaviors designed to at least get negative attention. People who feel intellectually inferior may direct an inordinate degree of energy to building up their bodies; those who feel socially incompetent may become "loners" and develop their intellectual capacities. This mechanism can have direct adjustive value, and it can also be an attempt by the person to say 'Don't see the ways in which I am inferior, but see me in my accomplishments.''

• *Ritual and undoing.* At times people perform elaborate rituals as a way of undoing acts for which they feel guilty. Undoing is designed to negate some disapproved thought or behavior. Anxiety is sometimes lessened when a person uses methods to right a wrong or to take away the guilt he or she feels for some perceived misdeed. For example, a rejecting father may attempt to alleviate his guilt by showering his child with material goods; he also attempts to demonstrate his caring through this act.

DEVELOPMENT OF PERSONALITY

Importance of early development. A significant contribution of the psychoanalytic model is the delineation of the stages of psychosocial and psychosexual development from birth through adulthood. It provides the counselor with the conceptual tools for understanding trends in development, key developmental tasks characteristic of the various stages, normal and abnormal personal and social functioning, critical needs and their satisfaction or frustration, origins of faulty personality development that lead to later adjustment problems, and healthy and unhealthy uses of ego-defense mechanisms.

In my opinion, an understanding of the psychoanalytic view of development is essential if a counselor is to work in depth with clients. I have found that the most typical problems that people bring to either individual or group counseling are (1) the inability to trust oneself and others, the fear of loving and forming close relationships, and low self-esteem; (2) the inability to recognize and express feelings of hostility, anger, rage, and hate, the denial of one's own power as a person, and the lack of feelings of autonomy; and (3) the inability to fully accept one's own sexuality and sexual feelings, difficulty in accepting oneself as a man or woman, and fear of sexuality. According to the Freudian psychoanalytic view, these three areas of personal and social development (love and trust, dealing with negative feelings, and developing a positive acceptance of sexuality) are all grounded in the first six years of life. This period is the foundation on which later personality development is built.

Erikson's psychosocial perspective. Erikson (1963) built on Freud's ideas and extended his theory by stressing the *psychosocial* aspects of development beyond early childhood. His theory of development holds that psychosexual growth and psychosocial growth take place together, and that at each stage of life we face the task of establishing an equilibrium between ourselves and our social world. He describes development in terms of the entire life span, divided by specific crises to be resolved. According to Erikson, a *crisis* is equivalent to a turning point in life, when we have the potential to move forward or to regress. At these turning points in our development we can either achieve successful resolution of our conflicts or fail to resolve them. To a large extent our life is the result of the choices we make at these stages.

Erikson is often credited with bringing an emphasis on social factors to contemporary psychoanalysis. Classical psychoanalysis is grounded on *id psychology,* and it holds that instincts and intrapsychic conflicts are the basic factors shaping personality development (both normal and abnormal). Contemporary psychoanalytic thinking tends to be based on *ego psychology,* which does not deny the role of intrapsychic conflicts but does emphasize the striving of the ego for mastery and competence throughout the human life span. Erikson's focus is on the ego, which is seen as possessing strength and offering ways of dealing with life's tasks in competent and creative ways. Ego psychology deals with both the early and the later developmental stages, for the assumption is that current problems cannot simply be reduced to repetitions of unconscious conflicts from early childhood. The stages of adolescence, mid-adulthood, and later adulthood each involve particular crises that must be addressed. As one's past has meaning in terms of the future, there is a continuity in development, reflected by stages of growth; each stage is related to the other stages.

Because I believe in the value of viewing an individual's development from a combined perspective that includes both psychosexual and psychosocial factors, I have included both Freud's and Erikson's views of the development of personality. This integration is possible because Erikson's ideas are consistent with Freud's. Erikson would contend, however, that Freud did not go far enough in explaining the ego's place in development and did not give social influences throughout the life span enough attention (see Table 4-1).

The first year of life: The oral stage.   Freud postulated infantile sexuality. Society's failure to recognize this phenomenon can be explained by cultural taboos and the individual's repression of early experiences in this area.

The oral stage goes from birth to the end of the first year. Sucking the mother's breasts satisfies the infant's need for food and pleasure. As the mouth and lips are sensitive erogenous zones, sucking produces erotic pleasure. Two activities during this developmental period are oral-incorporative behavior and oral-aggressive behavior. These early behaviors are considered to be the prototypes of some of the character traits of adulthood.

First to appear is *oral-incorporative* behavior, which involves pleasurable stimulation of the mouth. Libidinal energy is at first focused on the mouth, and then with maturity other areas of the body develop and become the focal points of gratification. However, adults who exhibit excessive oral needs (such as excessive eating, chewing, talking, smoking, and drinking) may have an *oral fixation.* Deprivation of oral gratification during infancy is assumed to lead to problems in adulthood.

As the infant teethes, the *oral-aggressive* period begins. Biting is one activity at this time. Adult characteristics such as sarcasm, hostility, aggression, gossip, and making "biting" comments to others are related to events of this developmental period.

TABLE 4–1
Comparison of Freud's Psychosexual Stages and Erikson's Psychosocial Stages

PERIOD OF LIFE	FREUD	ERIKSON
First year of life	*Oral stage* Sucking at mother's breasts satisfies need for food and pleasure. Infant needs to get basic nurturing, or later feelings of greediness and acquisitiveness may develop. Oral fixations result from deprivation of oral gratification in infancy. Later personality problems can include mistrust of others, rejecting others' love, fear of and inability to form intimate relationships.	*Infancy: Trust versus mistrust* If significant others provide for basic physical and emotional needs, infant develops a sense of trust. If basic needs are not met, an attitude of mistrust toward the world, especially toward interpersonal relationships, is the result.
Ages 1–3	*Anal stage* Anal zone becomes of major significance in formation of personality. Main developmental tasks include learning independence, accepting personal power, and learning to express negative feelings such as rage and aggression. Parental discipline patterns and attitudes have significant consequences for child's later personality development.	*Early childhood: Autonomy versus shame and doubt* A time for developing autonomy. Basic struggle is between a sense of self-reliance and a sense of self-doubt. Child needs to explore and experiment, to make mistakes, and to test limits. If parents promote dependency, child's autonomy is inhibited, and capacity to deal with world successfully is hampered.
Ages 3–6	*Phallic stage* Basic conflict centers on unconscious incestuous desires that child develops for parent of opposite sex and that, because of their threatening nature, are repressed. *Male phallic stage,* known as *Oedipus complex,* involves mother as love object for boy. *Female phallic stage,* known as *Electra complex,* involves girl's strivings for father's love and approval. How parents respond, verbally and nonverbally, to child's emerging sexuality has an impact on sexual attitudes and feelings that child develops.	*Preschool age: Initiative versus guilt* Basic task is to achieve a sense of competence and initiative. If children are given freedom to select personally meaningful activities, they tend to develop a positive view of self and follow through with their projects. If they are not allowed to make own decisions, they tend to develop guilt over taking initiative. They then refrain from taking an active stance and allow others to choose for them.

(continued)

TABLE 4–1
Comparison of Freud's Psychosexual Stages and Erikson's Psychosocial Stages *(continued)*

PERIOD OF LIFE	FREUD	ERIKSON
Ages 6–12	*Latency stage* After the torment of sexual impulses of preceding years, this period is relatively quiescent. Sexual interests are replaced by interests in school, playmates, sports, and a range of new activities. This is a time of socialization as child turns outward and forms relationships with others.	*School age: Industry versus inferiority* Child needs to expand understanding of world, continue to develop appropriate sex-role identity, and learn the basic skills required for school success. Basic task is to achieve a sense of industry, which refers to setting and attaining personal goals. Failure to do so results in a sense of inadequacy.
Ages 12–18	*Genital stage* Old themes of phallic stage are revived. This stage begins with puberty and lasts until senility sets in. Even though there are societal restrictions and taboos, adolescents can deal with sexual energy by investing it in various socially acceptable activities such as forming friendships, engaging in art or in sports, and preparing for a career.	*Adolescence: Identity versus role confusion* A time of transition between childhood and adulthood. A time for testing limits, for breaking dependent ties, and for establishing a new identity. Major conflicts center on clarification of self-identity, life goals, and life's meaning. Failure to achieve a sense of identity results in role confusion.
Ages 18–35	*Genital stage continues.*	*Young adulthood: Intimacy versus isolation* Developmental task at this time is to form intimate relationships. Failure to achieve intimacy can lead to alienation and isolation.
Ages 35–60	*Genital stage continues.*	*Middle age: Generativity versus stagnation* There is a need to go beyond self and family and be involved in helping the next generation. This is a time of adjusting to the discrepancy between one's dreams and one's actual accomplishments. Failure to achieve a sense of productivity often leads to psychological stagnation.
Ages 60+	*Genital stage continues.*	*Later life: Integrity versus despair* If one looks back on life with few regrets and feels personally worthwhile, ego integrity results. Failure to achieve ego integrity can lead to feelings of despair, hopelessness, guilt, resentment, and self-rejection.

Greediness and acquisitiveness may develop as a result of not getting enough food or love during the early years of life. Material things that children seek become substitutes for what they really want — namely, food and love from the mother. Later personality problems that stem from the oral stage are the development of a view of the world based on mistrust, fear of reaching out to others, rejection of affection, fear of loving and trusting, low self-esteem, isolation and withdrawal, and inability to form or maintain intense relationships.

In Erikson's psychosocial view this stage of infancy is characterized by a struggle between *trust* and *mistrust.* An infant's basic task is to develop a sense of trust in self, others, and the world. Infancy is a time when the individual needs to count on others and to develop a sense of being wanted and secure; it is a time when the foundations of trust are being established. This sense of trust is learned by being caressed and cared for.

From Erikson's viewpoint if the significant others in an infant's life provide the necessary love, the infant develops a sense of trust. When love is absent, the result is a general sense of mistrust of others. Clearly, infants who feel accepted are in a more favorable position to successfully meet future developmental crises than are those who do not receive adequate nurturing.

Ages 1 – 3: The anal stage.   The anal stage marks another step in development. The tasks to be mastered during this stage are learning independence, personal power, and autonomy and learning how to recognize and deal with negative feelings.

Beginning in the second year and extending into the third year, the anal zone comes to be of major significance in the formation of personality. Now children continually face parental demands, experience frustrations when they handle objects and explore their environment, and are expected to master control of their bowels. When toilet training begins during the second year, children have their first major experience with discipline. The method of toilet training and the parents' feelings, attitudes, and reactions toward the child can have far-reaching effects on the formation of personality traits. Many of the attitudes children learn about their own bodily functions are the direct result of the attitudes of their parents. Later personality problems such as compulsivity have roots in the ways parents rear their children during this stage.

Children may attempt to control their parents by either withholding their feces or defecating at inappropriate times. If strict toilet-training methods are used, children may express their anger by expelling their feces at inappropriate places and times. This behavior can lay the foundation for later adult characteristics such as cruelty, inappropriate displays of anger, and extreme disorderliness. Freud described this as the *anal-aggressive* personality. In contrast, other parents might focus too much attention on their children's bowel movements by giving praise whenever they defecate, which can contribute to a child's exaggerated view of the importance of this activity. This focus might be associated with a person's need for being productive. Again, certain adults develop fixations revolving around extreme orderliness, hoarding, stubbornness, and stinginess. This is known as the *anal-retentive* personality. The important point is that later adult characteristics have their roots in the experiences of this period.

During the anal period of development, the child will surely experience so-called negative feelings such as hostility, destructiveness, anger, rage, hatred, and so on. It is important that children learn that these are acceptable feelings. Many clients in therapy have not yet learned to accept their anger and hatred toward those they love. Because they were either directly or indirectly taught that these feelings were bad and that parental acceptance would be withheld if they expressed them, they repressed them.

According to Erikson, early childhood is a time for developing *autonomy;* children who do not master the task of gaining some measure of self-control and ability to cope with the world develop a sense of *shame* and *doubt* about their abilities. Parents who do too much for their children hamper their independence. Children who are encouraged to stay dependent will doubt their capacities for successfully dealing with the world.

It is important at this stage that children begin to acquire a sense of their own power. If parents do too much for their children, the message transmitted is "Here, let me do thus-and-so for you, because you are too weak or helpless to do these things for yourself." During this time children need to experiment, to make mistakes and feel that they are still acceptable persons, and to recognize some of their own power as separate and distinct individuals. So many clients are in counseling precisely because they have lost touch with their potential for power; they are struggling to define who they are and what they are capable of doing.

Ages 3 – 6: The phallic stage.   We have seen that between the ages of 1 and 3 the child discards infantile ways and actively carves a distinctive niche in the world. This is the period when capacities for walking, talking, thinking, and controlling the sphincters develop rapidly. As increased motor and perceptual abilities develop, so also do interpersonal skills. The child's progression from a period of passive/receptive mastery to a period of active mastery sets the stage for the next psychosexual developmental period—the phallic stage. During this period sexual activity becomes more intense, and now the focus of attention is on the genitals—the boy's penis and the girl's clitoris.

According to the orthodox Freudian view, the basic conflict of the phallic stage centers on the unconscious incestuous desires that children develop for the parent of the opposite sex. Because these feelings are of such a threatening nature, they are typically repressed; yet they are powerful determinants of later sexual development and adjustment. Along with the wish to possess the parent of the opposite sex comes the unconscious wish of the child to "do away with" the competition—the parent of the same sex.

According to Freudian theory, boys and girls both experience sexual longings and conflicts, which they repress. In the *male phallic stage* the boy craves the attention of his mother, feels antagonistic toward his father, and develops fears that his father will punish him for his incestuous feelings toward his mother. This is known as the *Oedipus complex.* Thus, the mother becomes the love object for the boy. Both in his fantasy and his behavior, he exhibits sexual longings for her. He soon realizes that his more powerful father is a rival for the exclusive attention he desires from her. However, about the time when the mother becomes the object of love for the boy, repression is already operating, which prevents a conscious awareness of a part of his sexual aims

At this time the boy typically develops specific fears related to his penis. Freud described the condition of *castration anxiety,* which is said to play a central role in the boy's life at this time. His ultimate fear is that his father will retaliate by cutting off his offending organ. The reality of castration is empha- sized when the boy notices the absence of the penis in girls. As a result of this anxiety of losing his prized possession, the boy is said to repress his sexual desire for his mother. If the Oedipal conflict is properly resolved, the boy replaces his sexual longings for his mother with more acceptable forms of affection; he also develops strong identification with his father. In a sense, it is a matter of realizing that, if he cannot beat his father, then he might as well join him. Through this identification with his father, the boy experiences vicarious satisfaction. He becomes more like his father, and he may adopt many of his father's mannerisms.

The *female phallic stage* was not so clearly described by Freud as was the male stage. Also, the orthodox Freudian view of female development has stirred up considerable controversy and has met with negative reactions from many women. The *Electra complex* is the girl's counterpart to the Oedipus complex. The girl's first love object is her mother, but love is transferred to her father during this stage. She is said to develop negative feelings toward her mother when she discovers the absence of a penis, the condition known as *penis envy.* This is the girl's counterpart to the boy's castration anxiety. She is said to have a desire to compete with her mother for the father's attention, and when she realizes that she cannot replace her mother, she begins an identification pro- cess by taking on some of the characteristics of her mother's behavior.

The development of sexual attitudes assumes critical importance during this period of life. Perhaps one of the most frequently misunderstood terms in Freud's theory is *sexuality.* He uses it much more broadly than it is typically used. Sexuality refers to organ pleasure of any kind. The type of sexuality that becomes evident during the phallic stage does not necessarily refer to the child's desire for sexual intercourse with the opposite-sex parent. Although the boy's feelings toward his mother are erotically tinged, this kind of sexuality is more diffuse than sexual intercourse, and the child's concept of actual sexual intercourse is often undefined. It is during this period of psychosexual develop- ment that behaviors such as the following become increasingly evident: curios- ity about sexual matters, sexual fantasies, masturbation, sex-role-identification patterns, and sex play.

Masturbation, accompanied by sexual fantasies, is a normal accompani- ment of early childhood. In the phallic period its frequency increases. Children become curious about their bodies; they desire to explore them and to discover differences between the sexes. Childhood experimentation is common, and because many attitudes toward sexuality originate in the phallic period, the acceptance of sexuality and the management of sexual impulses are vital at this time. During this period the conscience develops, and children learn moral standards. One critical danger is the parental indoctrination of rigid and unrealistic moral standards, which can lead to overcontrol by the superego. If parents teach that all impulses are evil, children soon learn to feel guilty about their natural impulses and may carry these feeling of guilt into their adult life and be blocked from enjoying intimacy with others. This kind of parental indoctrination results in an infantile conscience. That is, children are afraid to question or to think for themselves but blindly accept the indoctrination without question; they can hardly be considered moral, but merely frightened. Other effects include rigidity, severe conflicts, guilt, remorse, low self-esteem, and self-condemnation.

During this period children are forming attitudes about physical pleasure and about what is "right" and "wrong," what is "masculine," and what is "feminine." They are getting a perspective of the way women and men relate to each other. They are deciding how they feel about themselves in their roles as boys and girls.

The phallic period has significant implications for the therapist who works with adults. Many clients have never fully resolved their feelings about their own sexuality. They may have very confused feelings about sex-role identification, and they may be struggling to accept their sexual feelings and behavior. In my judgment it is important that therapists give just recognition to early experiences when they are working with adult clients. I am not suggesting that therapists view people as condemned to a lack of sexual responsiveness or impotence if they have not successfully mastered the developmental tasks of the phallic period. What I do see as important, however, is that clients become aware of their childhood experiences in this area, perhaps even relive and reexperience them in fantasy. As they relive events and feel again many of their buried feelings, they become increasingly aware that they are capable of inventing new endings to dramas they experienced as children. Thus, they come to realize that, although their present attitudes and behavior are surely shaped by the past, they are not doomed to remain victims of the past.

From the psychosocial perspective the core struggle of the preschool phase is between *initiative* and *guilt*. Erikson contends that the basic task of the preschool years is to establish a sense of competence and initiative. He places more stress on social development than on concerns relating to sexuality. During this time children are psychologically ready to pursue activities of their own choosing. If they are allowed the freedom to select meaningful activities, they tend to develop a positive outlook characterized by the ability to initiate and follow through. If they are not allowed to make some of their own decisions, however, or if their choices are ridiculed, they develop a sense of guilt over taking the initiative. Typically, they withdraw from taking an active stance and permit others to make decisions for them.

Ages 6 – 12: The latency stage.   With the passing of the turbulence of the first expression of the Oedipus complex and the combined stresses of the oral, anal, and phallic stages of psychosexual development, the individual can enjoy a period of relative rest. The major structures of personality (id, ego, superego) are largely formed, as are the relationships between these subsystems.

During this latency period new interests replace infantile sexual impulses. Socialization takes place, and children direct their interests to the larger world. The sexual drive is sublimated, to some extent, to activities in school, hobbies, sports, and friendships with members of the same sex.

The oral, anal, and phallic stages taken together are known as the pregenital period. A major characteristic of this period is a *narcissistic* orientation, or an inward and self-centered preoccupation. During the middle-childhood years there is a turning outward toward relationships with others. Children of this age have an interest in the things of the external world as well as of their internal world. This period prevails until the onset of puberty; it is during adolescence that the individual begins to establish an adult identity, along with a genital orientation.

Corresponding to the latency stage is Erikson's school-age stage, marked by a need to resolve the conflict between *industry* and *inferiority*. Some of the unique psychosocial tasks that must be met if healthy development is to proceed are expanding one's understanding of the physical and social worlds; continuing to develop an appropriate sex-role identity; continuing to develop a sense of values; engaging in social tasks; learning how to accept people who are different; and learning basic skills needed for schooling.

According to Erikson, the central task of middle childhood is to achieve a sense of industry; failure to do so results in feelings of inadequacy and inferiority. A sense of industry is associated with creating goals that are personally meaningful and achieving them. If this is not done, it will be difficult to experience a sense of adequacy in later years, and future developmental stages will be negatively influenced.

Some of the following problems originate during middle childhood; they are often manifested in later problems that counselors deal with:

- a negative self-concept
- feelings of inadequacy relating to learning
- feelings of inferiority in establishing social relationships
- conflicts over values
- a confused sex-role identity
- unwillingness to face new challenges
- a lack of initiative
- dependency

Ages 12 – 18: The genital stage.   Young adults move into the genital stage unless they become fixated at an earlier period of psychosexual development. During adolescence Oedipal and Electra conflicts are among the old themes of the phallic stage that are revived and recapitulated. Adolescents typically develop interest in the opposite sex, engage in some sexual experimentation, and begin to assume adult responsibilities. As they move out of adolescence and into mature adulthood, they develop intimate relationships become free of parental influence, and develop the capacity to be interested in others. There is a trend away from narcissism and toward altruistic behavior and concern for others. According to Freud, the goals of *lieben und arbeiten* are core characteristics of the mature adult; that is, the freedom "to love and to work" and to derive satisfaction from loving and working are of paramount importance.

Freud was primarily concerned with the impact of resolving sexual issues during the first six years of life. He did not go into great detail in discussing the crises associated with adolescence or the stages of adulthood. Erikson's view of development, however, continues where Freud left off. It accounts for forces influencing adolescent development and various phases of adulthood. According to Erikson, the major developmental conflicts of the adolescent years are related to the development of a *personal identity*. Adolescents struggle to define who they are, where they are going, and how to get there. If they fail to achieve a sense of identity, *role confusion* is the result. Because they experience diverse pressures — from parents, peers, and society — they often find it difficult to gain a clear sense of identity.

Adolescents have the task of integrating a system of values that will give their life direction. In the formation of a personal philosophy of life, they must make key decisions relating to religious beliefs, sexual ethics, values, and so forth. In this search for identity, models are especially important.

Adulthood.   For Freud, the genital stage continues through adulthood. Erikson has delineated three stages that cover the adult period: young adulthood, middle age, and later life. He sets forth the psychosocial experiences, expectations, and developmental tasks typical of these stages:

1. *Young adulthood: intimacy versus isolation.* In Erikson's view we approach adulthood after we master the adolescent conflicts over identity and role confusion. During young adulthood our sense of identity is tested again by the challenge of *intimacy* versus *isolation*. One of the key characteristics of the psychologically mature person is the ability to form intimate relationships. A prerequisite to establishing this intimacy with others is a confidence in our own identity. Intimacy involves an ability to share with others and to give to others from our own centeredness.

2. *Middle age: generativity versus stagnation.* This is a time for learning how to live creatively with both ourselves and others. On the one hand, it can be one of the most productive periods of life. On the other hand, we may painfully experience the discrepancy between our dreams of young adulthood and the reality of what we have accomplished. Erikson sees the stimulus for continued growth in middle age as the crisis between *generativity* and *stagnation*. He considers generativity in the broad sense to include creating through a career, family, leisure-time activities, and so on. The main quality of productive adults is the ability to love well, to work well, and to play well. If adults fail to achieve a sense of productivity, they begin to stagnate and to die psychologically.

3. *Later life: integrity versus despair.* According to Erikson, the core crisis of the elderly is *integrity* versus *despair*. Ego integrity is achieved by those who feel few regrets; they have lived a productive and worthwhile life and have coped with their failures as well as their successes. They are not obsessed with what might have been, and they are able to derive satisfaction from what they have done. They are able to view death as a part of the life process, and they can

still find meaning in how they are now living. The failure to achieve ego integrity tends to lead to feelings of despair, hopelessness, guilt, resentment, and self-disgust. Such people think about all of the things they could have done, and they may yearn for "another chance." This realization that they have wasted their life leads to a sense of despair.

Counseling implications.   By taking a combined psychosexual and psychosocial perspective, counselors have a useful conceptual framework for understanding developmental issues as they appear in therapy. Regardless of a counselor's theoretical preference, relevant questions such as the following can give direction to the therapeutic process:

- What are some major developmental tasks at each stage in life, and how are these tasks related to counseling?
- What are some themes that give continuity to this individual's life?
- What are some universal concerns of people at various points in life? How can people be challenged to make life-giving choices at these points?
- What is the relationship between an individual's current problems and significant events from earlier years?
- What influential factors have shaped one's life?
- What choices were made at these critical periods, and how did the person deal with these various crises?

Counselors who work with a developmental perspective are able to see a continuity in life and to see certain directions their clients have taken. This perspective gives a broader picture of the individual's struggle, and clients are able to discover some significant connections among the various stages of their life.

CONTEMPORARY TRENDS:
SELF PSYCHOLOGY AND OBJECT-RELATIONS THEORY

Psychoanalytic theory, rather than being closed or static, is continually evolving. As we have seen, Freud emphasized intrapsychic conflicts pertaining to the gratification of basic needs. Later, writers in the neo-psychoanalytic school moved away from Freud's orthodox position and contributed to the growth and expansion of the psychoanalytic movement by incorporating the cultural and social influences on personality. Then ego psychology, with its stress on psychosocial development throughout the life span, was developed, largely by Erikson.

The evolution of psychoanalytic theory and practice did not cease with these developments. A new trend in psychoanalytic thinking characterized the 1970s and the 1980s. Hedges (1983) writes that this newer thinking emphasizes:

- the origins, transformations, and organizational functions of the self
- the contrasting experiences of others
- the differentiation between and integration of the self and others
- the influence of critical factors in early development on later development

These newer approaches are often classified under the label *self psychology* or *object-relations theory*. Object relations are interpersonal relationships as they are represented intrapsychically. The term *object* was used by Freud to refer to that which satisfies a need, or to the significant person or thing that is the object, or target, of one's feelings or drives. It is used interchangeably with the term *other* to refer to an important person to whom the child and, later, the adult become attached. Rather than being individuals with a separate identity, others are perceived by an infant as objects for gratifying needs. Thus, object relations are interpersonal relationships that shape the individual's current interactions with people, both in reality and in fantasy. Object-relations theories have diverged from orthodox psychoanalysis, although some theorists attempt to integrate the increasingly varied ideas that characterize this school of thought (St. Clair, 1986).

Summary of stages of development.   These recent psychoanalytic theories center on predictable developmental sequences in which the early experiences of the self shift in relation to an expanding awareness of others. Once self/other patterns are established, it is assumed, they influence later interpersonal relationships. Specifically, people search for relationships that match the patterns established by their earlier experiences. People who are either overly dependent or overly detached, for example, can be repeating patterns of relating that they established with their mother when they were toddlers (Hedges, 1983). These newer theories provide insight into how an individual's inner world can cause difficulties in living in the actual world of people and relationships (St. Clair, 1986).

Mahler (1968) is a key figure in the evolution of the object-relations approach. Her studies focus on the interactions between the child and the mother in the first three years of life. According to Mahler, the self develops through four broad stages, which she conceptualizes somewhat differently from the traditional Freudian psychosexual stages. Mahler's belief is that the individual begins in a state of psychological fusion with the mother and progresses gradually to separation. The unfinished crises and residues of the earlier state of fusion, as well as the process of separating and individuating, have a profound influence on later relationships. Object relations of later life build on the child's search for a reconnection with the mother (St. Clair, 1986). Psychological development can be thought of as the evolution of the way in which individuals separate from and differentiate themselves from others.

The first phase of development of the self, in the first three or four weeks of life, Mahler calls *normal infantile autism.* Here the infant is presumed to be responding more to states of physiological tension than to psychological processes. The infant is, in many respects, unable to differentiate itself from its mother, and, according to Melanie Klein (1975), the infant perceives parts — breasts, face, hands, and mouth — rather than a unified self. In this undifferentiated state there is no whole self and there are no whole objects. When adults show the most extreme forms of lack of psychological organization and sense of self, they may be thought of as revealing fixations at this most primitive infantile stage.

Mahler's second phase, called *symbiosis,* is recognizable by the third month and extends roughly through the eighth month. Here, as with the first stage, the infant has a pronounced dependency on the mother. She, or the primary care-giver, is clearly a partner and not just an interchangeable part. The infant seems to expect a very high degree of emotional attunement with the mother. Psy-choanalysts think that psychotic disorders are linked to the failure to pass beyond the symbiotic phase.

Mahler's third phase starts by the fourth or fifth month, thus overlapping the second stage. This third phase she calls the *separation/individuation* process. It involves the child's moving through several subphases, away from symbiotic forms of relating. During this time of differentiation the child experiences separation from significant others yet still turns to them for a sense of confirma-tion and comfort. The child may demonstrate ambivalence, torn between en-joying separate states of independence and dependence. The toddler who proudly steps away from the parents and then runs back to be swept up in approving arms can be said to illustrate some of the main issues of this period (Hedges, 1983, p. 109). Others are looked to as approving mirrors for the child's developing sense of self; optimally, these relationships can provide a healthy sort of self-esteem.

Children who do not experience the opportunity to differentiate, and also those who lack the opportunity to idealize others while also taking pride in themselves, may later suffer from forms of *narcissistic* character disorders and problems of self-esteem. The narcissistic personality is characterized by a gran-diose and exaggerated sense of self-importance and an exploitive attitude toward others, which serves the function of masking a frail self-concept. Such individuals are exhibitionistic and seek attention and admiration from others. They unrealistically exaggerate their accomplishments, and they have a ten-dency toward extreme self-absorption. Kernberg (1975) characterizes narcis-sistic people as focusing on themselves in their interactions with others, having a great need to be admired, possessing shallow affect, and being exploitive and, at times, parasitic in their relationships with others. Kohut (1971) characterizes such people as perceiving threats to their self-esteem and as having feelings of emptiness and deadness.

"Borderline" conditions are also rooted in the period of separation/indi-viduation. People with a *borderline personality disorder* have moved into the separation process but have been thwarted by maternal rejection of their indi-viduation. In other words, a crisis ensues when the child does develop beyond the stage of symbiosis but the mother (or the mothering figure) is unable to tolerate this beginning individuation. Borderline people are characterized by instability, irritability, self-destructive acts, impulsive anger, and extreme mood shifts. They typically experience extended periods of disillusionment, punc-tuated by occasional euphoria. Kernberg describes the syndrome as including a lack of clear identity, a lack of deep understanding of other people, poor impulse control, and the inability to tolerate anxiety (1975, pp. 161–162).

Mahler's fourth and final phase involves a move toward constancy of self and object. This development is typically pronounced by the 36th month (Hedges, 1983). By now others are more fully seen as separate from the self.

Ideally, children can begin to relate without being overwhelmed with fears of losing their sense of individuality, and they may enter into the fantasies of competition that Freud described as the Oedipal conflicts and that are one source of neuroses.

Treating of borderline and narcissistic disorders.   Borderline and narcissistic disorders seem to be rooted in traumas and developmental disturbances during the separation/individuation phase. However, the full manifestations of the personality and behavioral symptoms tend to develop in early adulthood. Borderline and narcissistic symptoms such as splitting (a defensive process of keeping incompatible feelings separate) and notions of grandiosity are behavioral manifestations of developmental tasks that were disturbed or not completed earlier (St. Clair, 1986).

A great deal of recent psychoanalytic writing deals with the nature and treatment of borderline and narcissistic personality disorders. Object-relations theory sheds new light on the understanding of these disorders. Among the most significant theorists in this area are Kernberg (1975, 1976), Kohut (1971, 1977, 1984), and Masterson (1976). Kohut has maintained that people are their healthiest and best when they can feel both independence and attachment, taking joy in themselves and also being able to idealize others. Since mature adults feel a basic security grounded in an identity that involves a sense of freedom, self-sufficiency, and self-esteem, they are not compulsively dependent on others, but neither do they have to fear closeness.

This chapter permits only a brief treatment of the newer formulations in psychoanalytic theory. If you would like to pursue this emerging approach, an overview of this vast and growing literature can be found in Hedges (1983), Kaplan (1978), and St. Clair (1986).

The Therapeutic Process

THERAPEUTIC GOALS

Two goals of Freudian psychoanalytic therapy are to make the unconscious conscious and to strengthen the ego so that behavior is based more on reality and less on instinctual cravings. Successful analysis is believed to result in significant modification of the individual's personality and character structure. The focus is on using therapeutic methods to bring out unconscious material that can be worked through. Childhood experiences are reconstructed, discussed, interpreted, and analyzed. It is clear that the process is not limited to solving problems and learning new behaviors. Rather, there is a deeper probing into the past in order to develop the level of self-understanding that is assumed to be necessary for a change in character. Analytic therapy is oriented toward achieving insight, but not just an intellectual understanding; it is essential that the feelings and memories associated with this self-understanding be experienced.

THERAPIST'S FUNCTION AND ROLE

Classical analysts typically assume an anonymous stance, which is sometimes called the "blank-screen" approach. They engage in very little self-disclosure and maintain a sense of neutrality, because they are attempting to foster a *transference relationship,* in which their clients will make *projections* onto them. Therapists believe that if they say little about themselves and rarely share their personal reactions, whatever the client feels toward them is largely the product of feelings associated with other significant figures from the past. These projections, which have their origins in unfinished and repressed situations, are considered "grist for the mill," and their analysis is the very essence of therapeutic work.

In classical psychoanalysis it is assumed that an *analysand,* or client, will eventually develop a "transference neurosis," in which the emotional conflicts that originated during the first six years of life will be recapitulated in the therapeutic relationship. Tarachow (1963) writes that "when the therapeutic relationship assumes rigidly irrational characteristics and is determined by fantasy and not the real interplay between the [analyst and analysand], we may speak of a *transference neurosis*" (p. 11). In classical analysis this transference is encouraged and fostered by the analyst's neutrality, objectivity, anonymity, and relative passivity. Although the analysand regresses and displays primitive, "neurotic" symptoms during the sessions, the transference neurosis is not intended to disrupt the client's functioning outside the analytic hour. If the analysand's transference neurosis leads to negative behavior outside the session, it is termed "acting out." Significant acting out is viewed as detrimental.

One of the central functions of analysis is to help the analysand acquire the freedom to love, work, and play. There are other functions. Analysts are concerned with assisting their analysands in achieving self-awareness, honesty, and more effective personal relationships, in dealing with anxiety in a realistic way, and in gaining control over impulsive and irrational behavior. Of course, these issues are problems to the degree that they impair one's capacity to fully love and work in the broad sense of the terms as used by Freud. The analyst must first establish a working relationship with the analysand and then do a lot of listening and interpreting. Particular attention is given to the client's resistances. While the analysand does most of the talking, the analyst listens, learns, and decides when to make appropriate interpretations. A major function of interpretation is to accelerate the process of uncovering unconscious material. The analyst listens for gaps and inconsistencies in the analysand's story, infers the meaning of reported dreams and free associations, carefully observes during the therapy session, and remains sensitive to clues concerning the analysand's feelings toward the analyst.

Organizing these therapeutic processes within the context of understanding personality structure and psychodynamics enables the analyst to formulate the nature of analysands' problems. One of the central functions of the analyst is to teach clients the meaning of these processes so that they are able to achieve insight into their problems, increase their awareness of ways to change, and thus gain more rational control over their lives.

As Saretsky (1978) notes, the process of psychoanalytic therapy does not neatly follow a direct path from an insight to a cure. It is more like putting the pieces of a puzzle together. Whether clients change depends considerably more on their readiness to change than on the accuracy of the therapist's interpretations. If the therapist pushes clients too rapidly or offers ill-timed interpretations, therapy is likely to become counterproductive.

CLIENT'S EXPERIENCE IN THERAPY

Clients interested in psychoanalysis must be willing to commit themselves to an intensive and long-term therapy process. Typically, they come to therapy several times weekly for three to five years. After some face-to-face sessions with the analyst, analysands lie on a couch and free-associate; that is, they say whatever comes to mind without self-censorship. This process of free association is known as the "fundamental rule." Clients report their feelings, experiences, associations, memories, and fantasies to the analyst. Lying on the couch encourages deep, uncensored reflections and reduces the stimuli that might interfere with their getting in touch with their internal conflicts and productions. It also reduces their ability to "read" their analyst's face for reactions and, hence, fosters the projections characteristic of a regressive transference. At the same time the analyst is freed from having to carefully monitor facial clues.

What has just been described is classical psychoanalysis. It should be noted that many psychoanalytically oriented practitioners (as distinct from analysts) do not use all these techniques. Yet they do remain alert to transference manifestations and work with dreams and with unconscious material.

Clients in psychoanalytic therapy make a commitment with the therapist to stick with the procedures of an intensive therapeutic process. They agree to talk, because their verbal productions are the heart of psychoanalytic therapy. They are typically asked not to make any radical changes in their lifestyle during the period of analysis, such as getting a divorce or quitting their job.

Psychoanalytic clients are ready to terminate their sessions when they and their analyst agree that they have clarified and accepted their emotional problems, have understood the historical roots of their difficulties, and can integrate their awareness of past problems with their present relationships. Successful analysis answers a client's "why" questions regarding his or her life. For example, a lawyer or a psychologist in psychoanalytic therapy should develop an understanding of why he or she chose law or psychology as a profession, as well as resolving conflicts associated with the choice. Clients who emerge successfully from analytic therapy report that they have achieved such things as an understanding of their symptoms and the functions they serve, an insight into the ways that the environment affects them and how they affect the environment, and a reduced defensiveness and increased awareness of when they are being defensive (Saretsky, 1978).

RELATIONSHIP BETWEEN THERAPIST AND CLIENT

The client's relationship with the analyst is conceptualized in the transference process, which is the core of the psychoanalytic approach. Transference is the unconscious shifting to the analyst by the client of feelings and fantasies, both positive and negative, that are displacements from reactions to significant others in the client's past. Transference allows clients to attribute to the therapist "unfinished business" from these past relationships. The treatment process involves their reconstruction and reliving of the past. As therapy progresses, childhood feelings and conflicts begin to surface from the depths of the unconscious. Clients regress emotionally. Some of their feelings arise from conflicts such as trust versus mistrust, love versus hate, dependence versus independence, and autonomy versus shame and guilt. Transference takes place when clients resurrect from their early years intense conflicts relating to love, sexuality, hostility, anxiety, and resentment; bring them into the present; reexperience them; and attach them to the analyst. Clients might see the analyst as an authority figure who punishes, demands, and controls. For example, they might transfer unresolved feelings toward a stern and unloving father to the analyst, who, in their eyes, becomes stern and unloving. Hostile feelings are the product of negative transference, but clients might also develop a positive transference and, for example, fall in love with the analyst, wish to be adopted, or in many other ways seek the love, acceptance, and approval of an all-powerful therapist. In short, the analyst becomes a current substitute for significant others.

If therapy is to produce change, the transference relationship must be worked through. The *working-through* process consists of an exploration of unconscious material and defenses, most of which originated in early childhood. Working through is achieved by the repetition of interpretations and by exploring forms of resistance. It results in a resolution of old patterns and allows clients to make new choices. In the process of working through there is a constant going back to the raw data of the session in an attempt to gain new understandings of present experience. Clients have many opportunities to see the variety of ways in which their core conflicts and core defenses are manifested in their daily life. It is assumed that for clients to become psychologically independent they must not only become aware of this unconscious material but also achieve some level of freedom from behavior motivated by infantile strivings, such as the need for total love and acceptance from parental figures. If this demanding phase of the therapeutic relationship is not properly worked through, clients simply transfer their infantile wishes for universal love and acceptance to other figures they deem powerful. It is precisely in the client/therapist relationship that the manifestation of these childhood motivations becomes apparent. Because the transference relationship takes time to build in intensity and additional time to understand and resolve, working through requires a lengthy period in the total therapeutic process.

Among modern psychoanalytic writers there is agreement that reconstructive therapy is a lengthy process, ranging from three to five years or more. There is also widespread awareness that short-term individual and group techniques (such as crisis and supportive interventions) can be of therapeutic value for clients with borderline personality disorders. Such briefer therapy strategies aim at increasing self-awareness and strengthening an individual's adaptive or coping skills (Hedges, 1983).

With respect to therapy with the narcissistic client, the focus is on the development of mirror and idealizing transferences to the therapist. Narcissistic disorders improve as the therapist repeatedly acknowledges ways in which the client has been emotionally wounded in the past as well as the client's present disappointments in relationship to the therapist. Therapy is seen as a process in which clients learn to provide themselves with reassurance, rather than seeking confirmation from others in the environment. The focus is on improving self-esteem and repairing original psychological wounds received at an early age (Kohut, 1971, 1977, 1984). Thus, with narcissistic personalities the course of therapy consists of establishing an emotional bond with the therapist. Earlier symbiotic relationships now become emotionally *replicated* with the therapist. As this replication of past emotional experiences occurs, a separation/individuation process begins in relation to the therapist. Through this therapeutic relationship, the client experiences changes.

It must be emphasized, however, that all traces of our childhood needs and traumas will never be completely erased. Thus, our infantile conflicts may not be fully resolved, even though many aspects of transference are worked through with a therapist. We may need to struggle at times throughout our life with irrational feelings that we project onto others as well as with unrealistic demands that we expect others to fulfill. In this sense we experience transference with many people, and our past is always a vital part of the person whom we are presently becoming.

This notion of never becoming completely free of past experiences has significant implications for therapists who become intimately involved in the unresolved conflicts of their clients. This intense relationship is bound to ignite some of the unconscious conflicts within therapists. Even if these conflicts have surfaced to awareness, and even if therapists have dealt with these personal issues in their own intensive therapy, this does not imply that they are now free of any distortions that they may project onto clients. *Countertransference* refers to the irrational reactions therapists have toward their clients that may interfere with their objectivity. For example, a client may become excessively dependent on his therapist. He may look to her to direct him and tell him how to live, and he may look to her for the love and acceptance that he felt he was unable to secure from his mother. The therapist herself may have unresolved needs to nurture, to foster a dependent relationship, and to be told that she is significant, and she may be meeting her own needs by in some way making her client infantile. Unless she is aware of her own needs as well as her own dynamics, it is very likely that her dynamics will interfere with the progress of therapy.

The analyst's own reactions and problems can stand in the way of dealing with the client's problems. Thus, therapists must be aware of how their conflicts can be triggered by certain clients, so that they can guard against disturbing effects. Therapists are expected to develop some level of objectivity and not to react irrationally and subjectively in the face of anger, love, adulation, criticism, and other intense feeling of their clients. Because therapists are human, however, they do have to be aware of their own areas of vulnerability as well as unresolved problems that may intrude from time to time. As a result countertransference is seen as an inevitable part of the therapeutic relationship. Most psychoanalytic training programs require that trainees undergo their own extensive analysis as a client. If analysts become aware of symptoms (such as strong aversion to certain types of clients, strong attraction to other types of clients, developing psychosomatic reactions at definite times in therapeutic relationships, and the like) it behooves them to seek professional consultation or enter their own therapy for a time to work out their unresolved personal issues that stand in the way of their being effective therapists.

It is a mistake to assume that all feelings that clients have toward their therapists are manifestations of transference. Many of these reactions may have a reality base, and clients' feelings may well be directed to the here-and-now style that the therapist exhibits. On the one hand, every positive response (such as liking of the therapist) should not be labeled "positive transference." On the other hand, a client's anger toward the therapist may be a function of the therapist's behavior; it is a mistake to label all negative reactions as signs of "negative transference." Likewise, therapists have feelings toward their clients, and they do not react uniformly to all clients. So it is not precise to contend that all positive and negative feelings of therapists toward their clients are merely countertransference. Countertransference is the phenomenon that occurs when there is an inappropriate affect, when therapists respond in irrational ways, or when they lose their objectivity in a relationship because their own conflicts are triggered—specifically, when they relate to the client as if this person were mother, father, or lover.

A reconceptualization of countertransference (Searles, 1979) suggests that there can be some positive outcomes to countertransference. A growing number of psychoanalysts are maintaining that countertransference reactions can provide an important means for understanding the world of the client. The analyst who notes a countertransference mood of irritability, for instance, may learn something about a client's pattern of being demanding. In this light countertransference can be seen as potentially useful, if it is explored in analysis. As the focus on the analytic process moves into material that is rooted in what Mahler calls symbiosis, issues emerge that deal with the early mother/infant partnership. Like this early relationship the therapist/client relationship requires an especially high degree of emotional attunement. Viewed in this more positive way, countertransference becomes a key means of potentially helping the client. For a more detailed discussion of countertransference, see Searles (1979), who has done pioneering work in this area.

It should be clear that the client/therapist relationship is of vital importance in psychoanalytic therapy. As a result of this relationship, particularly in working through the transference situation, clients acquire insights into their own unconscious psychodynamics. Awareness of and insights into repressed material are the bases of the analytic growth process. Clients are able to understand the association between their past experiences and their current behavior and character structure. The psychoanalytic approach assumes that without this dynamic self-understanding there can be no substantial personality change or resolution of present conflicts.

APPLICATION: THERAPEUTIC TECHNIQUES AND PROCEDURES

Because of the limited applicability and prohibitive cost of classical analysis and because most psychoanalytic clinicians do not use the classical approach, this section deals with the techniques most commonly used by psychoanalytically oriented therapists. Some features of psychoanalytic therapy (as opposed to traditional psychoanalysis) are:

- The therapy is geared more to limited objectives than to restructuring of one's personality.
- The therapist is less likely to use the couch.
- There are probably fewer sessions.
- There is more frequent use of supportive interventions — such as reassurance, expressions of empathy and support, and suggestions — and of self-disclosure by the therapist.
- There is more focus on pressing practical issues than on working with fantasy material.

The techniques of psychoanalytic therapy are aimed at increasing awareness, fostering intellectual insights into the client's behavior, and understanding the meanings of symptoms. The therapy proceeds from the client's talk to catharsis to insight to working through unconscious material. This work is done to attain the goals of intellectual and emotional understanding and reeducation, which, it is hoped, lead to personality change. The six basic techniques of psychoanalytic therapy are (1) maintaining the analytic framework, (2) free association, (3) interpretation, (4) dream analysis, (5) analysis of resistance, and (6) analysis of transference.

MAINTAINING THE ANALYTIC FRAMEWORK

The psychoanalytic process stresses maintaining a particular framework aimed at accomplishing the goals of this type of therapy. "Maintaining the analytic framework" refers to a whole range of procedural and stylistic factors, such as the analyst's relative anonymity, the regularity and consistency of meetings, and starting and ending the sessions on time. One of the most powerful features of psychoanalytically oriented therapy is that the consistent framework is itself a therapeutic factor, comparable on an emotional level to the regular feeding of an infant. Analysts attempt to minimize departures from this consistent pattern (such as vacations, changes in fees, or changes in the meeting environment).

FREE ASSOCIATION

Free association plays a central role in the process of maintaining the analytic framework. At the initial phase the analyst will explain the fundamental rule of psychoanalysis, which involves clients' saying whatever comes to mind, regardless of how painful, silly, trivial, illogical, or irrelevant it may be. Such *free association* is the central technique in psychoanalytic therapy. In essence, clients flow with any feelings or thoughts by reporting them immediately without censorship. As the analytic work progresses, most clients will occasionally depart from adhering to this basic rule, and these resistances will be interpreted by the therapist when it is timely to do so. In classical psychoanalysis clients typically lie on the couch while the analyst sits behind them so as not to distract them during the free flow of associations; in psychoanalytic therapy the couch is less regularly part of the usual procedure.

Free association is one of the basic tools used to open the doors to unconscious wishes, fantasies, conflicts, and motivations. This technique often leads to some recollection of past experiences and, at times, a releasing of intense feelings that have been blocked off. This release is not seen as crucial in itself, however. During the free-association process the therapist's task is to identify the repressed material that is locked in the unconscious. The sequence of associations guides the therapist in understanding the connections that clients make among events. Blockings or disruptions in associations serve as cues to anxiety-arousing material. The therapist interprets the material to clients, guiding them toward increased insight into the underlying dynamics, of which they were unaware.

As analytic therapists listen to their clients' free associations, they hear not only the surface content but also the hidden meaning. This awareness of the language of the unconscious has been termed ''listening with the third ear'' (Reik, 1948). Nothing the client says is taken at face value. For example, a slip of the tongue can suggest that an expressed affect is accompanied by a conflicting affect. Areas that clients do not talk about are as significant as the areas they do discuss. Although psychoanalytic theory offers guidelines, the individual client must determine the actual meanings of specific content through associations.

INTERPRETATION

Interpretation consists of the analyst's pointing out, explaining, and even teaching the client the meanings of behavior that is manifested in dreams, free association, resistances, and the therapeutic relationship itself. The functions of interpretations are to allow the ego to assimilate new material and to speed up the process of uncovering further unconscious material.

Interpretation is grounded in the therapist's assessment of the client's personality and of what factors in the client's past contributed to his or her difficulties. Under contemporary definitions interpretation includes identifying, clarifying, and translating the client's material.

In making an appropriate interpretation, the therapist must be guided by a sense of the client's readiness to consider it (Saretsky, 1978). The therapist uses the client's reactions as a gauge. It is important that interpretations be well timed, because clients will reject ones that are inappropriately timed. A general rule is that interpretation should be presented when the phenomenon to be interpreted is close to conscious awareness. In other words the analyst should interpret material that clients have not yet seen for themselves but are capable of tolerating and incorporating as their own. Another general rule is that interpretation should always start from the surface and go only as deep as clients are able to go. A third general rule is that it is best to point out a resistance or defense before interpreting the emotion or conflict that lies beneath it.

DREAM ANALYSIS

Dream analysis is an important procedure for uncovering unconscious material and giving the client insight into some areas of unresolved problems. During sleep, defenses are lowered, and repressed feelings surface. Freud saw dreams as the "royal road to the unconscious," for in them one's unconscious wishes, needs, and fears are expressed. Some motivations are so unacceptable to the person that they are expressed in disguised or symbolic form rather than being revealed directly.

Dreams have two levels of content: the latent content and the manifest content. The *latent content* consists of hidden, symbolic, and unconscious motives, wishes, and fears. Because they are so painful and threatening, the unconscious sexual and aggressive impulses that make up the latent content are transformed into the more acceptable *manifest content,* which is the dream as it appears to the dreamer. The process by which the latent content of a dream is transformed into the less threatening manifest content is called *dream work.* The therapist's task is to uncover disguised meanings by studying the symbols in the manifest content of the dream. During the session the therapist might ask the client to free-associate to some aspect of the manifest content of a dream for the purpose of uncovering the latent meanings.

According to Caligor and Caligor (1978), the trend in clinical practice has been to move from Freud's emphasis on latent content to a major focus on the manifest content and the experience in the dream, including looking at dreams as reflections of the client's personality. Rather than simply serving as a pathway to repressed material, dreams can provide an understanding of the client's current functioning.

In therapy clients report their dreams and are encouraged to free-associate to the elements in the dream, recalling the feelings that were evoked. Gradually, they are able to uncover the meaning of their dream. Therapists participate in the process by exploring the clients' associations with them. Interpreting the meanings of the dream elements helps clients unlock the repression that has kept the material from consciousness and relate the new insight to their present struggles.

ANALYSIS AND INTERPRETATION OF RESISTANCE

Resistance, a concept fundamental to the practice of psychoanalysis, is anything that works against the progress of therapy and prevents the client from producing previously unconscious material. Specifically, in analytic therapy resistance is the client's reluctance to bring to the surface of awareness unconscious material that has been repressed. Resistance refers to any idea, attitude, feeling, or action (conscious or unconscious) that fosters the status quo and gets in the way of change. During free association or association to dreams, the client may evidence an unwillingness to relate certain thoughts, feelings, and experiences. Freud viewed resistance as an unconscious dynamic that people use to defend against the intolerable anxiety that would arise if they were to become aware of their repressed impulses and feelings.

As a defense against anxiety, resistance operates specifically in psychoanalytic therapy by preventing the client and therapist from succeeding in their joint effort to gain insights into the dynamics of the unconscious. Because resistance prevents threatening material from entering awareness, the analytic therapist points it out, and clients must confront it if they hope to deal with conflicts realistically. The therapist's interpretation of the resistance is aimed at helping clients become aware of reasons for the resistance so that they can deal with them. As a general rule the therapist points out and interprets the most obvious resistances in order to lessen the possibility of clients' rejecting the interpretation and to increase the chance that they will begin to look at their resistive behavior.

Resistances are not just something to be overcome. Because they are representative of usual defensive approaches in daily life, they need to be recognized as devices that defend against anxiety but that interfere with the ability to accept changes that could lead to a more gratifying life.

ANALYSIS AND INTERPRETATION OF TRANSFERENCE

Transference manifests itself in the therapeutic process at the point where clients' earlier relationships contribute to their distorting of the present. Clients react to their therapist as they did to some significant person. The transference situation is considered valuable in therapy because its manifestations provide clients with the opportunity to reexperience a variety of feelings that would otherwise be inaccessible. Through the relationship with the therapist, clients express feelings, beliefs, and desires that they have buried in their unconscious. They repeat aspects of their past experiences, unconsciously, in the therapeutic relationship. Through appropriate interpretations and working through of these new editions of early feelings, clients are able to change some of their long-standing patterns of behavior.

The analysis of transference is a central technique in psychoanalysis and psychoanalytically oriented therapy, for it allows clients to achieve here-and-now insight into the influence of the past on their present functioning. Interpretation of the transference relationship enables clients to work through old conflicts that are keeping them fixated and retarding their emotional growth. In essence the effects of early relationships are counteracted by working through a similar emotional conflict in the therapeutic relationship with the analytic therapist.

These last remarks about basic techniques can be brought together by a brief illustration. A client enters the office, saying to the therapist: "Sorry, I forgot my checkbook again. I'll get you next week." He lies down and starts in with, "Well, I had a dream, but I don't think here's much to learn from it. All I remember was that there was some elderly woman who got run over by a bus, and I couldn't decide whether I wanted to help her." He says that he does not have any ideas about the dream. As the session progresses, this client talks about how he is going to need to miss the next few sessions, because he wants to go out of town for a few days on a spur-of-the-moment vacation. Later, he mentions how much he enjoyed watching the football game the night before. The home team soundly defeated the opposition, whom he describes as "a bunch of old ladies."

The therapist notes at the outset of the session that she feels a bit of irritation at this client's habit of "forgetting" to pay regularly. She then notes her surprise at the rather sudden announcement that the next sessions are going to be missed. Prompted by her own associations rooted in her knowledge of this client's previous work on his feelings about his passive mother, she says "I wonder whether there is anything going on between you and me that comes out in your forgetting your checkbook and then announcing that you won't be coming for a few days?" The client's subsequent remarks suggest that other matters have higher priority than bringing along his checkbook. "I just assumed it would be OK whether or not I paid you for a week or so." The analyst suggests: "Were you hoping this old lady would be flattened by the bus?"

In this vignette the therapist made use of her own reactions as well as her knowledge of the client's past. Her interpretations highlighted the departures from the analytic framework, represented by irregularity in payment and attendance. She treated the dream as a reference to the transference, with the associations expressing ambivalence about the weakness and passivity that the client attributes to his mother and his therapist.

SUMMARY AND EVALUATION

SUMMARY

The major concepts of Freudian psychoanalytic theory include the struggle between the life and death instincts at the heart of human nature; the tripartite structure of personality, with its systems of the id, the ego, and the superego; the dynamics of the unconscious and its influence on behavior; the role of anxiety; and the development of personality at various life periods, including the oral, anal, phallic, latency, and genital stages.

Building on many of Freud's basic ideas, Erikson broadened the developmental perspective by including psychosocial trends. Under his model each of the eight stages of human development is characterized by a crisis, or turning point. We can either master the developmental task or fail to resolve the core struggle. These eight stages of the life span are infancy, early childhood, preschool age, school age, adolescence, young adulthood, middle age, and later life. (For a succinct review of these developmental turning points, Table 4-1 compares Freud's and Erikson's views of growth and development.)

The contemporary trend in psychoanalytic theory is reflected in self psychology and object-relations theory. These approaches are based on the notion that at birth there is no differentiation between others and the self and that others represent objects of need gratification for the infant. Through the process of attachment the child enters the second stage, symbiosis, during which there is still a lack of clarity between what is self and what is object. In the third stage children begin to draw away from this symbiosis and to individuate, differentiating themselves from the parents to whom they are attached. The fourth stage is one of integration. Others are perceived as both separate and related. In normal development children are able to relate to their parents without the fear of losing their sense of autonomy.

Psychoanalytic therapy consists largely of using methods to bring out unconscious material that can be worked through. Its focus is primarily on childhood experiences, which are discussed, reconstructed, interpreted, and analyzed. The assumption is that this exploration of the past, which is typically accomplished by working through the transference relationship with the therapist, is necessary for character change. The most important techniques typically employed in psychoanalytic practice are maintaining the analytic framework, free association, interpretation, dream analysis, analysis of resistance, and analysis of transference.

CONTRIBUTIONS OF THE PSYCHOANALYTIC APPROACH

I believe that counselors can broaden their understanding of clients' struggles by appreciating the many significant contributions of Freud. It must be emphasized that competent use of psychoanalytic techniques requires training beyond the scope of most counselors. Regardless of their theoretical orientation, however, it is well for counselors to be trained so that they will understand such psychoanalytic phenomena as transference, countertransference, resistance, and the use of ego-defense mechanisms as reactions to anxiety. The psychoanalytic approach provides counselors with a conceptual framework for looking at behavior and for understanding the origins and functions of symptoms. If counselors ignore the early history of the client, they are limiting their vision of the causes of the client's present suffering and the nature of the client's present functioning. Although there is little to be gained from blaming the past for the way a client is now or from dwelling on the past, it is very useful to understand and work with the past as it pertains to the client's current situation.

For therapeutic practice the psychoanalytic point of view is particularly useful in (1) understanding resistances that take the form of canceling appointments, fleeing from therapy prematurely, and refusing to look at oneself; (2) understanding that unfinished business can be worked through, so that clients can provide a new ending to some of the events that have crippled them emotionally; (3) understanding the value and role of transference; and (4) understanding how the overuse of ego defenses, both in the counseling relationship and in daily life, can keep clients from functioning effectively.

My teaching experience has demonstrated that students sometimes have a difficult time understanding and accepting some of the Freudian notions about the stages of development. The Oedipus complex, penis envy, castration anxiety, incestuous feelings, and connections between past situations and current character may seem rather obscure on initial presentation. Personally, I recall that I had many doubts about the validity of these concepts when I first studied them in my undergraduate days. However, my observations of the development and behavior of my own children and other children and my work in both individual and group therapy have given me a wider perspective on the Freudian view of psychosexual development. It is essential to keep in mind that this view must be understood from the vantage point of the time in which Freud wrote, during the Victorian era of the authoritarian father. Much of what he described makes sense when it is seen in historical and cultural perspective.

Moreover, it is a mistake to dismiss these concepts in totality or to see them as merely historically interesting. Considered more broadly, many of these developmental themes still have relevance for practicing counselors and therapists. Without taking penis envy and castration anxiety literally in the narrow context in which they were originally presented by Freud, practitioners can learn much about the dynamics of their clients' behaviors by appreciating some of his insights into psychosexual development. These concepts have current relevance if seen as metaphors rather than as based in biology. For example, women often experience "castration anxiety" when asserting themselves. Especially in my work with intensive therapeutic groups, I have time and again observed what appear to be universal struggles. A few of these are incestuous feelings toward parents of the opposite sex, competition with the parent of the same sex and intense feelings of jealousy, guilt over sexual feelings and actions, fears relating to sexual intimacy and loving, fears of abandonment, struggles in defining one's own sexual identity, anger and even rage over not getting what one wanted as a child, and love/hate conflicts. The psychoanalytic approach provides a framework for a dynamic understanding of the role of these early childhood events and the impact of these experiences on the contemporary struggles faced by clients. Without completely accepting the orthodox Freudian position, we can still draw on many of these analytic concepts as a framework for understanding clients and for helping them achieve a deeper understanding of the roots of their conflicts.

Students of counseling can learn a great deal about the therapeutic process by becoming familiar with the concepts and techniques of the analytic approach. Although many counselors will have neither the training for nor any interest in conducting psychoanalytic therapy per se, they can gain much by adding the analytic perspective to their practice. Even if they do not possess the skills to work toward personality reconstruction, the concepts can give depth to their counseling. Knowledge of the dynamics of behavior, ego defenses, the workings of the unconscious, and the development of personality will help them gain this depth.

If the psychoanalytic approach is considered in a broader context than its initial Freudian perspective, it becomes a more powerful model for understanding human behavior. Although I find Freud's *psychosexual* concepts of great value, I think that adding Erikson's stress on *psychosocial* factors gives a more complete picture of the critical turning points at each stage of development. Integrating these two perspectives is, in my view, most useful for understanding key themes in the development of personality. Erikson's developmental schema does not avoid the psychosexual issues and stages postulated by Freud; rather, Erikson extended the stages of psychosexual development throughout life. His perspective integrates psychosexual and psychosocial concepts without diminishing the import of either.

Sociocultural factors provide practitioners with a framework for understanding the major tasks and crises of each stage of development. According to

Hamachek (1988), the principal strength of psychosocial theory is that it acknowledges that humans are biological, psychological. and social beings and that an interactive mix of these inner and outer forces shapes humans. The key needs and developmental tasks, along with the challenges inherent at each stage of life, provide a model for understanding some of the core conflicts that clients explore in their therapy sessions. This approach gives special weight to childhood and adolescent factors that are significant in later stages of development while recognizing that the later stages also have their significant crises. In this sense we can find themes and threads running through a client's life.

Contributions of recent theorists.   The contemporary trends in psychoanalytic thinking have contributed to the understanding of how our current behavior in the world is largely a repetition of the patterns set during one of the early phases of development. Object-relations theory helps us see the ways in which clients interacted with significant others in the past and how they are superimposing these early experiences on present relationships. For the many clients in therapy who are struggling with issues such as separation and individuation, intimacy, dependence versus independence, and identity, these newer formulations can provide a framework for understanding how and where aspects of development have been fixated. They have significant implications for many areas of human interaction such as intimate relationships, the family and child rearing, and the therapeutic relationship.

In my opinion it is possible to have an analytic framework that gives structure and direction to a counseling practice and at the same time to draw on other therapeutic techniques. I find value in the contributions of those writers who have built on the basic ideas of Freud and have added an emphasis on the social forces affecting personality development. In contemporary psychoanalytic practice more latitude is given to the therapist in using techniques and in developing the therapeutic relationship. The newer psychoanalytic theorists have gone far beyond classical analytic techniques and the emphasis on intellectual insight. They are focusing on the development of the ego and are paying attention to the social factors that influence the differentiation of an individual from others.

Contributions to multicultural counseling.   Psychoanalytically oriented therapy, if modified, can be appropriate for culturally diverse populations. Comas-Diaz and Minrath (1985) recommend that the diffused sense of identity prevalent among borderline clients from ethnic minorities be examined from both a sociocultural and a developmental perspective. They also suggest that exploring the meaning of ethnicity and race within the therapeutic relationship is essential for the working through of the clients' diffused sense of identity. One aid to helping minority clients rebuild their identity is to emphasize their assets rather than their deficiencies (Comas-Diaz & Minrath, 1985). Erikson's psychosocial approach, with its emphasis on critical developmental issues, has particular application to people of color. Counselors can help these clients review environmental situations at the various critical turning points in their lives to determine how certain events have affected them either positively or negatively.

A strength of the psychoanalytic approach is its emphasis on the value of intensive psychotherapy as part of the training of therapists, which helps them become aware of their own sources of countertransference. Although some nonpsychoanalytic approaches also encourage trainees to participate in their own therapy, psychoanalytic training gives special emphasis to the role of therapy as a way for therapists to recognize and work through their counter-transference.

Therapists of all ethnic and racial backgrounds need to recognize and confront their own biases and prejudices. The process of therapy for the thera-pist has crucial implications for multicultural counseling, because therapists can become more effective by gaining access to their unconscious reactions to clients. Comas-Diaz and Minrath (1985) point out that issues of prejudice and discrimination and feelings of guilt occur in cross-cultural counseling (a situa-tion in which the counselor has a different cultural, ethnic, or racial background from the client's). They emphasize that the conflicts of ethnically different clients result from the interplay of intrapsychic and sociocultural forces and that therapists may at times feel overwhelmed by the myriad of problems presented by these clients. These authors suggest that is the therapist's role to address the pervasiveness of these factors in the client's daily life. If these sociocultural forces are not acknowledged, many ethnic clients are likely to feel alienated from both the therapist and the therapy process.

Psychoanalytic concepts have also been applied to the practice of brief therapies. The Institute for Psychoanalysis in Chicago, for example, is playing an expanding role in maintaining the mental health of the city. This low-fee public clinic is finding new ways to use the vast body of theory developed by psychoanalysts. During the last 20 years, for example, it has established special programs to meet community needs. The institute has established a special center offering therapy for children who have suffered the loss of a parent. It also provides psychoanalytic training for inner-city teachers and for profes-sionals who work with emotionally disturbed children. Over 2000 teachers have taken courses through the program, and in one year 1300 people received about 30,000 hours of diagnosis, therapy, and referral (see Desruisseaux, 1983). As far away as France, Lacan and his followers have applied psychoanalytic theory innovatively among a variety of populations.

LIMITATIONS AND CRITICISMS OF THE PSYCHOANALYTIC APPROACH

What are the limitations of the psychoanalytic approach for counselors (as a view of human nature, as a model for understanding behavior, and as a method of therapy)? How applicable is this approach to counseling in a mental-health clinic? in a school? in other public and private human-services agencies? In general, considering factors such as time, expense, and availability of trained psychoanalytic therapists, I think the practical applications of many analytic techniques are very limited. This is true especially of techniques such as free association on the couch, dream analysis, and analysis of the transference relationship. A major limitation of psychoanalysis as a practical technique is that the majority of clients with symptoms of mental disturbance lack the level of ego strength needed for "transference-neurosis" treatment. Some psychoanalytic techniques, however, can be used widely in counseling. Examples are interpretation and working with client resistance. A deeper understanding of psychoanalytic theory and technique might help counselors understand why some interpretations and other interventions work and why many are utter failures.

A theoretical notion that I find limiting is the anonymous role of the therapist. Although the analyst's anonymity can be justified on theoretical grounds, I think that in therapy situations other than classical psychoanalysis this stance is unduly restrictive. The classical technique of nondisclosure can be misused in nonclassical situations such as short-term individual therapy and assessment. Therapists in these situations who adopt blank-screen aloofness may actually be keeping themselves hidden as persons in the guise of "being professional." Whereas the analyst who practices classical analysis is intentionally frustrating the client's relationship needs in the service of inducing regression and a transference neurosis, the nonclassical psychoanalytical practitioner has more freedom to interact with clients. The variation in technique results from different intents rather than from different styles.

Not all analytically oriented therapists subscribe to the notion of neutrality and anonymity. Psychoanalytically oriented therapists may engage in appropriate self-disclosure with their clients. Harry Stack Sullivan's interpersonal theory of therapy is an example of an approach derived from psychoanalysis that does not subscribe to therapist anonymity. Sullivan (1956), who is identified with the social-psychological theories, used the interview as the primary therapeutic procedure for gathering data from clients. He saw the therapist as a *participant/observer* and an expert in interpersonal relations. In the dual role of participant and observer, therapists must be alert not only to the client's behavior but also to their own reactions and behavior. Sullivan cautioned against therapists' assuming a strictly objective observational role. He stressed the importance of personal involvement and the impact of the therapist's personality.

Sullivan viewed the therapeutic process as a unique interpersonal relationship, differing from other intimate relationships in its basic purpose. Clients have a right to expect that they will benefit from the interview, that they will learn something about themselves and the way they live, and that they will be able to apply this knowledge to living more effectively. In short, the ultimate goal of the psychiatric interview is that clients leave with a greater degree of clarity about themselves and how they are living with others.

Limitations for multicultural counseling.   One practical limitation in applying psychoanalytic techniques in multicultural situations is that most clients do not want or cannot afford to devote five years to intensive treatment. Few people have the motivation, time, and money for a therapy involving that degree of commitment. Psychoanalytic therapy is generally perceived as being based on upper-class and middle-class values, and surely the financial commitment rules out most people who are not wealthy.

Another particular difficulty in working from a perspective of intrapsychic analysis is that this focus may be in direct conflict with some clients' social framework and environmental perspective. The concerns of clients in the lower socioeconomic classes typically center on basic issues of survival and security. These clients are not inclined to see value in a long-term process of personality restructuring. They tend to want help in getting information and finding resources to solve immediate and pressing problems. Furthermore, the number of clients who can be seen by a therapist is small in comparison with other approaches. Also, the goals of analytic therapy—that is, probing the unconscious and working toward reconstruction of personality—are frequently not as appropriate in helping clients deal with the practical concerns in their social environment. This does not imply that ethnic-minority clients are unable to profit from analytic therapy but, rather, that this particular orientation could be more beneficial *after* more pressing issues and concerns have been resolved. A systems perspective, including the role of the family, one's network of friends and extended family, and social and environmental factors, may be more often suitable for the concerns that ethnic clients bring to therapy.

QUESTIONS FOR REFLECTION AND DISCUSSION

1. Psychoanalytic psychotherapy is not a creed handed down by Freud never to be changed; it is a dynamic, continually developing method of helping people solve psychological problems. As you think about this chapter, look for evidence to support the above contention. What aspects of the Freudian revisionists and the contemporary psychoanalytic writers do you find of most value to you personally?

2. The psychoanalytic approach underscores the importance of early psychosexual development. Do you see evidence that one's current problems are rooted in the significant events of one's first six years of life? When you apply this concept specifically to yourself, what connections between your childhood experiences and your present personality are you aware of? What additions has Erik Erikson made to this view of development?

3. Review the case of Stan in Chapter 13. From what you have learned about psychoanalytic therapy, what are some of the major themes that would be explored in applying this therapeutic approach to Stan? How applicable is this type of therapy to the problems Stan presents?

4. In your work as a counselor, many psychoanalytic techniques such as free association, dream interpretation, probing the unconscious, and interpretation and analysis of resistance and transference may not be appropriate, or they may be beyond your level of training. What are some concepts of the psychoanalytic approach that can nevertheless provide you with a useful framework in deepening your understanding of human behavior? How do you see psychoanalytic views as being potentially related to your work as a counselor?

5. As you study the other therapies described in this book, compare them with the psychoanalytic approach. To what degree are other approaches based on psychoanalytic concepts or on a reaction against supposed limitations of psychoanalysis?

6. What were some of your stereotypes or misconceptions of psychoanalysis before you read about this theory? Is it possible that some of your misconceptions might prevent you from seeing valid concepts that are related to your work as a counselor?

7. How might Freud's concept of the unconscious be important for you to understand, even though in your work as a counselor you might not deal directly with your clients' unconscious motives and conflicts?

8. The psychoanalytic view of anxiety is that it is largely the result of keeping unconscious conflicts buried and that the ego defenses develop to help the person curb anxiety. What implications does this view have for your work with people? Do you think defenses are necessary? What are the possible values of defense mechanisms? What do you think might happen if you were able to successfully strip away a client's defenses?

9. What is your evaluation of the psychoanalytic view of personality development? Consider the stages of early development, particularly with respect to how fully a person's basic needs were met at each stage. Do you think it is necessary or important to explore with clients areas of conflict and unmet needs of the early years? Do you believe people can resolve their adult problems that stem from childhood experiences without exploring past events? How much emphasis would you place on a person's past?

10. Can you apply any aspects of the psychoanalytic theory to your own personal growth? Does this approach help you in any way to deepen your self-understanding? If so, how and in what ways?

WHERE TO GO FROM HERE

If this chapter has provided the impetus for you to learn more about the psychoanalytic approach or the contemporary offshoots of psychoanalysis, select a few books from the "Recommended Supplementary Readings" and "References and Suggested Readings." Various colleges and universities offer special workshops or short courses through continuing education on topics such as therapeutic considerations in working with borderline and narcissistic personalities. Such workshops could give you a new perspective on the range of applications of contemporary psychoanalytic therapy. An organization to contact for further information about training programs, workshops, and graduate programs in various states is:

American Psychoanalytic Association
309 East 49th Street
New York, NY 10017

This organization has a code of ethics, revised in 1983, that deals with many aspects of the practice of psychoanalytic therapy.

RECOMMENDED SUPPLEMENTARY READINGS

If you are interested in expanding your knowledge of the Freudian approach, a good place to begin is *A Primer of Freudian Psychology* (Hall, 1954), a concise overview. The next step would be to consult *An Elementary Textbook of Psychoanalysis* (Brenner,

1974), an excellent orientation text for those who want to acquaint themselves with psychoanalytic theory. Chapter topics include basic hypotheses, drives, the psychic apparatus, dreams, psychopathology, and conflict.

I highly recommend two textbooks, with identical titles. *Theories of Personality* (Schultz, 1990) is a concise overview of the major personality theories; it would be a good place to begin. Theories are clearly presented, as well as techniques of inquiry and therapeutic implications. *Theories of Personality* (Hall & Lindzey, 1978) is an advanced treatment of the major contemporary theories of personality. It has excellent overviews of the social-psychological theories of Adler, Erich Fromm, Karen Horney, and Sullivan. The chapter on Jung's analytic theory is also excellent. This book is a superb resource.

References and Suggested Readings*

AMERICAN PSYCHIATRIC ASSOCIATION. (1987). *Diagnostic and statistical manual of mental disorders* (4th ed.). Washington, DC: Author.

*ARLOW, J. A. (1989). Psychoanalysis. In R. J. Corsini & D. Wedding (Eds.), *Current psychotherapies* (4th ed.) (pp. 19–62). Itasca, IL: F. E. Peacock.

BALINT, M. (1968). *The basic fault.* London: Tavistock.

*BARUCH, D. (1964). *One little boy.* New York: Dell (Delta).

BETTELHEIM, B. (1987). The therapeutic milieu. In J. K. Zeig (Ed.), *The evolution of psychotherapy* (pp. 223–231). New York: Brunner/Mazel.

BLUM, H. P. (1986). Psychoanalysis. In I. L. Kutash & A. Wolf (Eds.), *Psychotherapist's casebook.* San Francisco: Jossey-Bass.

*BOYER, L. B. (1989). Working with a borderline patient. In D. Wedding & R. J. Corsini (Eds.), *Case studies in psychotherapy* (pp. 3–21). Itasca, IL: F. E. Peacock.

*BRENNER, C. (1974). *An elementary textbook of psychoanalysis* (rev. ed.). Garden City, NY: Doubleday (Anchor).

CALIGOR, L., & CALIGOR, J. (1978). The dream in psychoanalytic therapy. In G. D. Goldman & D. S. Milman (Eds.), *Psychoanalytic psychotherapy.* Reading, MA: Addison-Wesley.

*COMAS-DIAZ, L., & MINRATH, M. (1985). Psychotherapy with ethnic minority borderline clients. *Psychotherapy, 22,* 418–426.

COREY, G. (1990). *Theory and practice of group counseling* (3rd ed.). Pacific Grove, CA: Brooks/Cole.

COREY, G. (1991). *Case approach to counseling and psychotherapy* (3rd ed.). Pacific Grove, CA: Brooks/Cole.

COREY, G., & COREY, M. S. (1990). *I never knew I had a choice* (4th ed.). Pacific Grove, CA: Brooks/Cole.

DESRUISSEAUX, P. (1983, January 12). "Psychoanalysis: Off the couch and into the streets of Chicago." *Chronicle of Higher Education.*

*ERIKSON, E. H. (1963). *Childhood and society* (2nd ed.). New York: Norton.

ERIKSON, E. H. (1968). *Identity: Youth and crisis.* New York: Norton.

*ERIKSON, E. H. (1982). *The life cycle completed.* New York: Norton.

✓ FAIRBAIRN, W. R. D. (1954). *An object-relations theory of the personality.* New York: Basic Books.

FREUD, A. (1966). *The writings of Anna Freud: Vol. 2. The ego and the mechanisms of defense.* New York: International Universities Press. (Original work published 1936)

* Books and articles marked with an asterisk are suggested for further study.

FREUD, S. (1949). *An outline of psychoanalysis.* New York: Norton.

*FREUD, S. (1955). *The interpretation of dreams.* London: Hogarth Press.

FREUD, S. (1962). *Civilization and its discontents.* New York: Norton. (Original work published 1930)

*FROMM, E. (1980). *Greatness and limitations of Freud's thought.* New York: New American Library (Mentor).

GOLDMAN, G. D., & MILMAN, D. S. (1978). *Psychoanalytic psychotherapy.* Reading, MA: Addison-Wesley.

HALL, C. (1954). *A primer of Freudian psychology.* New York: New American Library (Mentor).

*HALL, C., & LINDZEY, G. (1978). *Theories of personality* (3rd ed.). New York: Wiley.

HAMACHEK, D. F. (1988). Evaluating self-concept and ego development within Erikson's psychosocial framework: A formulation. *Journal of Counseling and Development, 66,* 354–360.

*HEDGES, L. E. (1983). *Listening perspectives in psychotherapy.* New York: Aronson.

KAPLAN, L. (1978). *Oneness and separateness.* New York: Simon & Schuster.

*KERNBERG, O. F. (1975). *Borderline conditions and pathological narcissism.* New York: Aronson.

KERNBERG, O. F. (1976). *Object-relations theory and clinical psychoanalysis.* New York: Aronson.

KLEIN, M. (1975). *The psycho-analysis of children.* New York: Dell.

KOHUT, H. (1971). *The analysis of the self.* New York: International Universities Press.

KOHUT, H. (1977). *Restoration of the self.* New York: International Universities Press.

KOHUT, H. (1984). *How does psychoanalysis cure?* Chicago: University of Chicago Press.

KOVEL, J. (1976). *A complete guide to therapy.* New York: Pantheon.

KUTASH, I. L., & GREENBERG, J. C. (1986). Psychoanalytic psychotherapy. In I. L. Kutash & A. Wolf (Eds.), *Psychotherapist's casebook* (pp. 22–42). San Francisco: Jossey-Bass.

LANGS, R. L. (1973). *The techniques of psychoanalytic psychotherapy: Vol. 1.* New York: Aronson.

LINDER, R. (1955). *The fifty-minute hour.* New York: Bantam Books.

MAHLER, M. S. (1968). *On human symbiosis or the vicissitudes of individuation.* New York: International Universities Press.

MAHLER, M. S. (1971). A study of the separation and individuation process. In *The psychoanalytic study of the child: Vol. 26* (pp. 403–422). New York: Quadrangle.

*MALCOLM, J. (1981). *Psychoanalysis: The impossible profession.* New York: Random House (Vintage).

MARMOR, J. (1987). The psychotherapeutic process: Common denominators in diverse approaches. In J. K. Zeig (Ed.), *The evolution of psychotherapy* (pp. 226–273). New York: Brunner/Mazel.

*MASTERSON, J. F. (1976). *Psychotherapy of the borderline adult: A developmental approach.* New York: Brunner/Mazel.

*MASTERSON, J. F. (1982). *The narcissistic and borderline disorders: An integrated developmental approach.* New York: Brunner/Mazel.

MASTERSON, J. F. (1983). *Countertransference and psychotherapeutic technique.* New York: Brunner/Mazel.

MASTERSON, J. F. (1985). *The real self: A developmental, self, and object relations approach.* New York: Brunner/Mazel.

*MASTERSON, J. F. (1987). The evolution of the developmental object relations approach to psychotherapy. In J. K. Zeig (Ed.), *The evolution of psychotherapy* (pp. 236–242). New York: Brunner/Mazel.

*NYE, R. (1986). *Three psychologies: Perspectives from Freud, Skinner, and Rogers* (3rd ed.). Pacific Grove, CA: Brooks/Cole.

REIK, T. (1948). *Listening with the third ear.* New York: Pyramid Books.

*ST. CLAIR, M. (1986). *Objects relations and self psychology: An introduction.* Pacific Grove, CA: Brooks/Cole.

SARETSKY, T. (1978). The middle phase of treatment. In G. D. Goldman & D. S. Milman (Eds.), *Psychoanalytic psychotherapy.* Reading, MA: Addison-Wesley.

*SCHULTZ, D. (1990). *Theories of personality* (4th ed.). Pacific Grove, CA: Brooks/Cole.

*SEARLES, H. F. (1979). *Countertransference and related subjects: Selected papers.* New York: International Universities Press.

SPITZ, R. (1965). *The first year of life.* New York: International Universities Press.

SULLIVAN, H. S. (1953a). *Conceptions of modern psychiatry.* New York: Norton.

SULLIVAN, H. S. (1953b). *Interpersonal theory of psychiatry.* New York: Norton.

*SULLIVAN, H. S. (1956). *The psychiatric interview.* New York: Norton.

TARACHOW, S. (1963). *An introduction to psychotherapy.* New York: International Universities Press.

WINNICOTT, D. W. (1965). *The maturational process and the facilitating environment.* New York: International Universities Press.

✓*WOLBERG, L. R. (1987). The evolution of psychotherapy: Future trends. In J. K. Zeig (Ed.), *The evolution of psychotherapy* (pp. 250–259). New York: Brunner/Mazel.

5

ADLERIAN THERAPY

Huxley

ALFRED ADLER

ALFRED ADLER (1870–1937) was the third child in a family of five boys and two girls. One of his brothers died as a young boy. Adler's early childhood was not a happy time, for he was sickly and very much aware of death. At 4 he almost died of pneumonia, and at that time he made a significant decision to become a doctor himself.

Because he was ill so much during the first few years of his life, Adler was pampered by his mother. Later he was "dethroned" by a younger brother. It appears that he developed a trusting relationship with his father and that he did not feel very close to his mother. He was jealous of his oldest brother, which led to strained relationships between the two during childhood and adolescence. His early years were characterized by struggling to overcome childhood weaknesses and feelings of inferiority. It is clear that these family experiences had an impact on the formation of his theory. Nevertheless, he is an example of a person who shaped his own life as opposed to being determined by his fate.

Adler was a poor student, and his teacher advised his father that he would be fit to be a shoemaker but not much else. With determined effort Adler eventually rose to the top of his class. He went on to study medicine at the University of Vienna, entered private practice as an ophthalmologist, and then shifted to general medicine. He eventually specialized in neurology and psychiatry, and he had a keen interest in incurable childhood diseases.

Adler had a passionate concern for the common person. He expressed his social interest by being outspoken on matters of child-rearing practices, school reforms, and prejudices that resulted in conflict. He spoke and wrote in simple and nontechnical language so that the public could understand and apply the principles of his Individual Psychology. After serving in World War I as a medical officer, he created numerous child-guidance clinics in the Vienna public schools and began training teachers, social workers, physicians, and other professionals. He pioneered the practice of teaching professionals through live demonstrations with parents and children before large audiences. The clinics he founded grew in number and in popularity, and he was indefatigable in lecturing and demonstrating his work.

Adler lived by this overcrowded work schedule, yet he still took some time to sing, enjoy music, and be with friends. He ignored the warning of his friends to slow down. In the mid-1920s he began lecturing in the United States, and he later made frequent visits and tours. His packed schedule continued, and on May 28, 1937, while taking a walk before a scheduled lecture in Aberdeen, Scotland, he collapsed and died of heart failure.

INTRODUCTION

Along with Freud and Jung, Adler was a major contributor to the development of the psychodynamic approach to therapy. After eight to ten years of collaboration Freud and Adler parted company, with Freud taking the position that Adler was a heretic and was deserting him. Adler resigned as president of the Vienna Psychoanalytic Society in 1911 and founded the Society for Individual Psychology in 1912. Freud then asserted that it was not possible to support Adlerian concepts and still remain in good standing as a psychoanalyst.

Later, as we saw in Chapter 4, a number of other psychoanalysts deviated from Freud's orthodox position. These Freudian revisionists, who included Karen Horney, Erich Fromm, and Harry Stack Sullivan, agreed that social and cultural factors were of great significance in the shaping of personality. Even though these three therapists are typically called neo-Freudians, it would be more appropriate, as Heinz Ansbacher (1979) has suggested, to refer to them as neo-Adlerians, because they moved away from Freud's biological and deterministic point of view and toward Adler's social-psychological and nondeterministic view of human nature.

Adler stressed the unity of personality, contending that people could be understood as integrated and complete beings. This view emphasizes the purposeful nature of behavior, maintaining that the direction in which we are heading is far more important than where we came from. We are seen as the actors and creators of our lives, and we develop a unique style of life that is an expression of our goals. We create ourselves, rather than merely being shaped by our childhood experiences.

After Adler's death in 1937, Rudolf Dreikurs was the most significant figure in bringing Adlerian psychology to the United States, especially as its principles applied to education and group therapy. Dreikurs is credited with giving impetus to the idea of child-guidance centers and to the training of professionals to work with a wide range of clients. More recently, Oscar Christensen, Don Dinkmeyer, Ray Lowe, Harold Mosak, Bob Powers, Bernard Shulman, and Monford Sonstegard have contributed to translating Adler's and Dreikurs's principles into practical approaches in working with children, parents, teachers, and other human-services workers in the United States.

There are significant similarities between Adlerian psychology and recent developments in the behavioral sciences. Further, the present renaissance of Adler's views is more than a school rising from its own ashes, for his thinking and contributions have continued to influence other therapeutic systems (Allen, 1971, pp. 22–23).

KEY CONCEPTS *Human Nature*

VIEW OF HUMAN NATURE

Adler abandoned Freud's basic theories because he believed that Freud was excessively narrow in his stress on biological and instinctual determination. Like Freud, Adler believed that what the individual became in adult life was largely influenced by the first six years of life. Adler's focus was not simply on exploring past events; rather, he was interested in the person's perception of the past and how this interpretation of early events has a continuing influence. On many theoretical grounds Adler was in opposition to Freud. According to Adler, for example, humans are motivated primarily by social urges rather than by sexual urges. For Adler, behavior is purposeful and goal-directed. Consciousness, not the unconscious, is the center of personality. Unlike Freud, Adler stressed choice and responsibility, meaning in life, and the striving for success or perfection.

Feelings of inferiority can be the wellspring of creativity. These basic inferiority feelings can motivate us to strive for mastery, superiority, and perfection, especially in early life. At around 6 years of age, a life goal is formed. Life goals provide the source of human motivation and are expressed as strivings to achieve security and to overcome inferiority feelings.

From the Adlerian perspective humans are not merely determined by heredity and environment. Instead, they have the capacity to interpret, influence, and create events. Adler believed that *what* we were born with was not the central issue. What is crucial is what we *do* with the abilities we possess. Adlerians recognize that biological and environmental conditions limit our capacity to choose and to create. Although they reject the deterministic stance of Freud, they do not go to the other extreme by maintaining that individuals can become whatever they want.

Because their approach is grounded on a growth model, Adlerians put the focus on reeducating individuals and reshaping society. Adler was the forerunner of a subjective approach to psychology, which emphasizes internal determinants of behavior such as values, beliefs, attitudes, goals, interests, and the individual perception of reality. He was a pioneer of an approach that is holistic, social, goal oriented, and humanistic.

SUBJECTIVE PERCEPTION OF REALITY

Adlerians attempt to view the world from the client's subjective frame of reference, an orientation described as phenomenological. It is phenomenological in that it pays attention to the individual way in which people perceive their world. This "subjective reality" includes the individual's perceptions, beliefs, and conclusions. Behavior is understood from the vantage point of this cognitive perspective. How life is in reality is less important than how the individual believes life to be.

As you will see in the chapters that follow, many contemporary theories have incorporated this notion of the client's subjective world view as a basic factor explaining behavior. Some of the approaches that have a phenomenological perspective are existential therapy, person-centered therapy, Gestalt therapy, the cognitive-behavioral therapies, and reality therapy.

UNITY AND PATTERNS OF HUMAN PERSONALITY

A basic premise of the Adlerian approach, also known as *Individual Psychology,* is that personality can be understood as an indivisible whole. The cornerstone of Adlerian psychology is the assumption that people are social, creative, decision-making beings who have a unified purpose (Sherman & Dinkmeyer, 1987). The human personality becomes unified through the life goal. An individual's thoughts, feelings, beliefs, convictions, attitudes, character, and actions are expressions of his or her uniqueness, and all reflect a plan of life that allows for the movement toward a self-selected life goal. An implication of this holistic view of personality is that the client is an integral part of a social system. There is more focus on interpersonal relationships than on the individual's internal psychodynamics.

Behavior as purposeful and goal oriented.   Individual Psychology assumes that all human behavior has a purpose. Humans set goals for themselves, and behavior becomes unified in the context of these goals. Adler replaced deterministic explanations with teleological (purposeful, goal-oriented) ones. A basic assumption of Individual Psychology is that where we are going and what we are striving for are crucial. Thus, Adlerians are interested in the future, without minimizing the importance of past influences. They assume that decisions are based on the person's past experiences, on the present situation, and on the direction in which the person is moving. They look for continuity by paying attention to themes running through a person's life.

Adlerians use the term *fictional finalism* to refer to an imagined central goal that guides a person's behavior. Adler was influenced by the philosopher Hans Vaihinger's view that people live by fictions (or views of how the world should be). The guiding fiction might be expressed: "Only when I am perfect can I be secure," or "Only when I am important can I be accepted." The fictional goal represents an individual's image of a secure position, which he or she strives for in any given situation. The term *finalism* refers to the ultimate nature of the person's goal and the ever-present tendency to move in a certain direction. Because of this ultimate goal, we have the creative power to choose what we will accept as true, how we will behave, and how we will interpret events. Sometimes, of course, we make mistakes.

The striving for significance and superiority.   Adler stresses that striving for perfection and coping with inferiority by seeking mastery are innate (1979, p. 29). To understand human behavior it is essential to grasp the ideas of basic inferiority and compensation. According to Adler, the second we experience inferiority, we are pulled by the striving for superiority. He maintained that the goal of success pulled people forward toward mastery and enabled them to overcome obstacles. The goal of superiority contributes to the development of human community. However, it is important to note that *superiority*, as used by Adler, does not mean being superior to others but, rather, attaining a greater degree of one's own potential. Superiority is a striving from lower to higher or from minus to plus. We cope with feelings of helplessness by striving for competence, mastery, and perfection. We can seek to change a weakness into a strength, for example, or we can excel in one area of concentration to compensate for defects in other areas. The unique way in which we develop a style of striving for competence is what constitutes individuality.

Contsbract

Lifestyle. The term *lifestyle* refers to an individual's basic orientation to life, or personality, and the themes that characterize the individual's existence. Synonyms are style of life, plan of life, life movement, strategy for living, and road map of life. It is through our lifestyle that we move toward our life goal. Adler saw us as actor, creator, and artist of our life. In striving for goals that have meaning to us, we develop a unique style of life (Ansbacher, 1974). This concept helps explain how all our behavior fits together so that there is some consistency to our actions. Understanding one's lifestyle is somewhat like understanding the style of a composer: "We can begin wherever we choose: every expression will lead us in the same direction — towards the one motive, the one melody, around which the personality is built" (Adler, 1964a, p. 332).

No two people develop exactly the same lifestyle. In striving for the goal of superiority, some develop their intellect; others, their artistic talent; others, athletic talents; and so on. These styles of life consist of people's views about themselves and the world and their distinctive behaviors and habits as they pursue their personal goals. Everything we do is influenced by our unique style of life, which is assumed to be shaped by forces during the first six years of life. Experiences within the family and relationships between siblings contribute to the shaping of the lifestyle (Sherman & Dinkmeyer, 1987). But it is not the childhood experiences in themselves that are crucial; rather, it is our present interpretation of these events.

SOCIAL INTEREST *Construct*

Social interest, or *Gemeinschaftsgefühl,* is probably Adler's most significant and distinctive concept. The term refers to an individual's awareness of being a part of the human community and to the individual's attitudes in dealing with the social world; it includes striving for a better future for humanity. The socialization process, which begins in childhood, involves finding a place in one's society and acquiring a sense of belonging and of contributing (Kefir, 1981). Adler equated social interest with a sense of identification and empathy with others: "to see with the eyes of another, to hear with the ears of another, to feel with the heart of another" (1979, p. 42). The degree to which we successfully share with others and are concerned with the welfare of others is a measure of mental health (Sherman & Dinkmeyer, 1987, p. 12). From the Adlerian perspective, as social interest develops, the individual's feelings of inferiority and alienation diminish. Social interest will develop if it is taught, learned, and used. People express social interest through shared activity and mutual respect, and they develop on the useful side of life. Those without social interest become discouraged and end up on the useless side of life.

Individual Psychology rests on a central belief that our happiness and success are largely related to this social connectedness. Because we are part of a society, we cannot be understood in isolation from the social context. Humans seek a place in the family and in society. There is a basic need to feel secure, accepted, and worthwhile. People need to discover their unique way of contributing and sharing in activities and responsibilities. Many of the problems we experience are related to the fear of not being accepted by the groups we value.

If our sense of belonging is not fulfilled, anxiety is the result. Only when we have a sense of belonging are we able to act with courage in facing and dealing with our problems.

Mosak (1977) contends that we must face and master five life tasks: relating to others (friendship), making a contribution (work), achieving intimacy (love and family relationships), getting along with ourselves (self-acceptance), and developing our spiritual dimension (including values, meaning, life goals, and our relationship with the universe, or cosmos). Furthermore, it is essential that we define our sex roles and learn to relate to others. Because we are not self-sufficient, we need to learn to become interdependent. Work is basic to survival, and therefore it is important that we create meaning in work and that we accept our part in this social enterprise. Our feelings about ourselves and our level of self-acceptance are determinants of how effectively we are able to form interpersonal relationships.

BIRTH ORDER AND SIBLING RELATIONSHIPS

The Adlerian approach is unique in giving special attention to the relationships between siblings and the position in one's family. Adler identified five psychological positions: oldest, second of only two, middle, youngest, and only. It should be noted that actual birth order itself is less important than the individual's interpretation of his or her place in the family. Since Adlerians view most human problems as social in nature, they emphasize intrafamily relationships.

Adler (1958) observes that many people wonder why children in the same family often differ so widely. It is a fallacy to assume that children of the same family are formed in the same environment. Although they share aspects in common in the family constellation, the psychological situation of each child is different from that of the others because of the order of their birth. The following description of the influence of birth order is based on Ansbacher and Ansbacher (1964), Dreikurs (1953), and Adler (1958):

1. The *oldest child* generally receives a good deal of attention, and during the time she is the only child, she is typically somewhat spoiled as the center of attention. She tends to be dependable and hard working and strives to keep ahead. When a new brother or sister arrives on the scene, however, she finds herself ousted from her favored position. She is no longer unique or special. She may readily believe that the newcomer (or intruder) will rob her of the love to which she is accustomed.

2. The *second child* is in a different position. From the time he is born, he shares the attention with another child. The typical second child behaves as if he were in a race and is generally under full steam at all times. It is as though this second child were in training to surpass the older brother or sister. This competitive struggle between the two first children influences the later course of their lives. The younger child develops a knack for finding out the elder child's weak spots and proceeds to win praise from both parents and teachers by achieving successes where the older sibling has failed. If one is talented in a given area, the other strives for recognition by developing other abilities. The second-born is often opposite to the firstborn.

3. The *middle child* often feels squeezed out. She may become convinced of the unfairness of life and feel cheated. This person can assume a "poor me" attitude and can become a problem child.

4. The *youngest child* is always the baby of the family and tends to be the most pampered one. He has a special role to play, for all the other children are ahead of him. The youngest tends to develop characteristics that make it likely that others will shape his life. Youngest children tend to go their own way. They often develop in ways no others in the family thought about.

5. The *only child* has a problem of her own. She has some of the characteristics of the oldest child. She does not learn to share or cooperate with other children but learns to deal with adults well. The only child is often pampered by her mother, and she may become dependently tied to her. She wants to have center stage all of the time, and if her position is challenged, she feels it is unfair. In later life, when she is no longer the center of attention, she tends to have many difficulties.

The birth order and the interpretation of one's position in the family have a great deal to do with how adults interact in the world. They acquired a certain style of relating to others in childhood, and they formed a definite picture of themselves, which they carry into their adult interactions. In Adlerian therapy working with family dynamics, especially relationships among siblings, assumes a key role. Although it is important to avoid stereotyping individuals into a category, it does help to see how certain personality trends that began in childhood as a result of sibling rivalry do have a way of following one throughout the rest of one's life.

The Therapeutic Process — *Change Process*

THERAPEUTIC GOALS

Adlerian counseling rests on a contractual and collaborative arrangement between the client and the counselor. In general, the contract calls for identifying and exploring *mistaken goals* and *faulty assumptions,* followed by a reeducation of the client toward constructive goals. The basic goal of therapy is to develop the client's social interest, which is accomplished by increasing self-awareness and challenging and modifying fundamental premises, life goals, and basic concepts (Dreikurs, 1967).

Adlerians do not see clients as being "sick" and in need of being "cured." Rather, the goal is to reeducate clients so that they can live in society as an equal, both giving to society and receiving from others (Mosak, 1989). Therefore, the counseling process focuses on providing information, teaching, guiding, and offering encouragement to discouraged clients. Encouragement is the most powerful method available for changing a person's beliefs. It helps clients build self-confidence and stimulates courage. Courage is the willingness to act in ways that are consistent with social interest. The loss of courage, or discouragement, results in mistaken and dysfunctional behavior. Discouraged people do not act in line with social interest on the useful side of life; rather, they find their place on the useless side of life. (For a readable and detailed coverage of the encouragement process, consult Dinkmeyer and Losoncy's [1980] *The Encouragement Book: Becoming a Positive Person.*)

Adlerian counselors are engaged in creating a new map, for they are educating clients in new ways of looking at themselves, others, and life:

> The therapist's role aims at enlarging the individual's social interest, helping him or her to overcome feelings of inferiority, helping the individual modify his or her goals, as well as training the client toward greater contribution within interpersonal relationships. The therapeutic process is thus essentially an educative one that results in a tangible movement forward for the individual [Kefir, 1981, p. 403].

Through the process of providing clients with a cognitive map, or a fundamental understanding of the purpose of their behavior, counselors assist them in changing their perceptions. Thus, counselors help clients gain a clearer understanding of their goals and purposes, challenge them to recognize their subjective philosophy of life, and provide a context that allows them to see patterns in their behavior. Mosak (1989, p. 84) lists the following as the goals of the educational process of therapy:

- fostering social interest
- helping clients overcome feelings of discouragement and inferiority
- modifying clients' views and goals — that is, changing their lifestyle
- changing faulty motivation
- assisting clients to feel a sense of equality with others
- helping people become contributing members of society

In addition to the general goal of reeducating clients and helping them acquire values based on social interest, Dreikurs (1967) identifies four aims of the therapeutic process, which correspond to the four phases of therapy. These are discussed in detail later in the chapter. They are:

1. creating and maintaining a good client/therapist relationship
2. identifying the client's dynamics, including his or her lifestyle and goals and how these factors affect the person
3. providing interpretation, which leads to insight
4. achieving a reorientation and reeducation, or translating understanding into action

change process

THERAPIST'S FUNCTION AND ROLE

Inasmuch as Adlerians are not bound to follow any "right" set of techniques, their therapeutic styles often vary. Their techniques are congruent with the basic concepts of Individual Psychology but are adapted to fit the client.

Adlerian counselors focus on the cognitive aspects of therapy. They realize that clients are discouraged emotionally and are functioning ineffectively on a behavioral level because of their faulty cognitions (beliefs and goals). They operate on the assumption that clients will feel and behave better if they discover what is wrong with their thinking. Therapists tend to look for major mistakes in thinking and valuing such as mistrust, selfishness, unrealistic ambitions, and lack of confidence.

A major function of the therapist is to make a comprehensive assessment of the client's functioning. Therapists gather information on the client's *family constellation,* which includes parents, siblings, and others living in the home. They do this by means of a questionnaire, which when summarized and interpreted gives a picture of the individual's early social world. From this information therapists are able to get a perspective on the client's major areas of success and failure and on the critical influences that have had a bearing on the role the client has decided to assume in the world. The counselor also uses *early recollections* as a diagnostic tool. These recollections are of single incidents from childhood that we are able to reexperience. They reflect our current convictions, evaluations, attitudes, and biases (Griffith & Powers, 1984). These memories provide a brief picture of how we see ourselves and others and what we anticipate for our future. After these early recollections are summarized and interpreted, the therapist identifies some of the major successes and mistakes in the client's life. The aim is to provide a point of departure for the therapeutic venture.

By way of summary, in making this diagnostic assessment, therapists do the following: They extract major patterns that appear in the family-constellation questionnaire and thereby get a picture of the client's basic personality. Then, by means of interpreting early recollections, they get a sense of the person's present outlook on life. Mistaken aspects of the client's view of life are identified by comparing his or her current convictions with the framework of social-interest concepts. When this process is completed, the counselor and the client have targets for therapy (Gushurst, 1971).

CLIENT'S EXPERIENCE IN THERAPY

Clients in Adlerian counseling focus their work on their lifestyle, which provides the blueprint for their actions. How do clients maintain their lifestyle, and why do they resist changing it? Generally, people fail to change because they do not recognize the errors in their thinking and behavior, do not know what to do differently, and are fearful of leaving old patterns for new and unpredictable outcomes. Thus, even though their ways of thinking and behaving are not successful, they tend to cling to the familiar patterns (Manaster & Corsini, 1982).

In therapy clients explore what Adlerians call *private logic,* the concepts about self, others, and life that constitute the philosophy on which an individual's lifestyle is based. Clients' problems arise because the conclusions based on their private logic often do not conform to the reality of social living. The core of the therapy experience consists of clients' discovering their basic mistakes and then learning how to correct these faulty assumptions and conclusions.

To provide a concrete example, think of a chronically depressed middle-aged man who begins therapy. After a lifestyle investigation is completed, the following patterns of basic mistakes are identified:

- He has convinced himself that nobody could really care about him.
- He rejects people before they have a chance to reject him.
- He is harshly critical of himself, expecting perfection.
- He has expectations that things will rarely work out well.
- He burdens himself with guilt, since he is convinced that he is letting everyone down.

Even though this man developed these mistaken ideas about life as a small child, he is still clinging to them as rules for living. His expectations, most of which are pessimistic, tend to be fulfilled, because on some level he is seeking to validate his beliefs. In therapy this man will learn how to challenge the structure of his private logic. In his case the syllogism goes as follows:

- "I am basically unlovable."
- "The world is filled with people who are likely to be rejecting."
- "Therefore, I must keep to myself so I won't be hurt."

This person has held onto several basic mistakes. His private logic provides central psychological unity for him. Mosak (1977) would say that there are central themes or convictions in this client's life, some of which may be: "I must get what I want in life." "I must control everything in my life." "I must know everything there is to know, and a mistake would be catastrophic." "I must be perfect in everything I do." It is important for the therapist to listen for the underlying purposes of this client's behavior. Adlerian therapists do not focus directly on *feelings* of depression. Instead, they devote attention to beliefs and convictions, which result in emotional and behavioral disturbances. It is not true that Adlerians discount the role of feelings; rather, they see feelings as being the result of (rather than the cause of) thinking and behaving. So first we think, then feel, and then act. Because emotions are at the service of our cognitive processes, it follows that clients will spend much of their time discussing thoughts, beliefs, and what they are currently doing based on their conceptual framework for living. In short, if clients hope to begin to *feel* better and to *act* better, they must learn better ways of *thinking*. Further, because clients are not perceived by the therapist as "sick," but mainly discouraged, they will receive much *encouragement* that change is possible. Through the therapeutic process, they will discover that they have resources and options to draw on in dealing with significant life issues and life tasks.

RELATIONSHIP BETWEEN THERAPIST AND CLIENT

Adlerians consider a good client/therapist relationship to be one between equals that is based on cooperation, mutual trust, respect, confidence, and alignment of goals. They place special value on the counselor's modeling of communication and acting in good faith. From the beginning of therapy the relationship is a collaborative one, characterized by two persons working equally toward specific, agreed-on goals. Dinkmeyer, Dinkmeyer, and Sperry (1987) maintain that at the outset of counseling, clients should begin to formulate a plan, or contract, detailing what they want, how they plan to get where they are heading, what is preventing them from successfully attaining their goals, how they can change nonproductive behavior into constructive behavior, and how they can make full use of their assets in achieving their purposes. The therapeutic contract sets forth the goals of the counseling process and specifies the responsibilities of both the therapist and the client. However, developing a contract is not a requirement of Adlerian therapy.

The client is not viewed as a passive recipient; rather, the client is an active party in a relationship between equals in which there is no superior and no inferior. Through this *collaborative* partnership clients recognize that they are responsible for their behavior. Although Adlerians view the quality of the therapeutic relationship as relevant to the outcomes of therapy, they do not assume that this relationship, alone, will bring about change. It is the starting point in the process of change. Without initial trust and rapport, the difficult work of changing one's lifestyle is not likely to occur.

APPLICATION: THERAPEUTIC TECHNIQUES AND PROCEDURES—Intervention to 158

Adlerian counseling is structured around four central objectives, which correspond to the four phases of the therapeutic process (Dreikurs, 1967). These phases are not linear and do not progress in rigid steps; rather, they can best be understood as a weaving that leads to a tapestry. As mentioned earlier, these stages are:

1. establishing the proper therapeutic relationship
2. exploring the psychological dynamics operating in the client (analysis and assessment)
3. encouraging the development of self-understanding (insight)
4. helping the client make new choices (reorientation and reeducation)

PHASE 1: ESTABLISHING THE RELATIONSHIP

Methods of therapy

As noted previously, the Adlerian counselor works in a collaborative way with clients, thus increasing their sense of responsibility for their life. This relationship is based on a sense of deep caring, involvement, and friendship. Mozdzierz, Lisiecki, Bitter, and Williams (1984) see the therapist as a human and a friend on whom the client can count in time of need. They see the relationship as a partnership, in which both parties work together for the benefit of the client. Therapeutic progress is possible only when the goals of counseling are clearly defined and when there is an alignment of goals between the therapist and the client. The counseling process, to be effective, must deal with the personal issues that the client recognizes as significant and is willing to discuss and change.

One way to create a working therapeutic relationship is for counselors to help clients become aware of their assets and strengths, rather than dealing continually with their deficits and liabilities. Thus, the Adlerian counselor focuses on positive dimensions and uses encouragement and support. During this initial phase the relationship is created by listening, responding, demonstrating respect in the client's capacity to change, and exhibiting genuine enthusiasm. When clients enter therapy they typically have a diminished sense of self-worth and self-respect, and they lack faith in their ability to cope with the tasks of life. Therapists provide support, which is an antidote to despair and discouragement. For some people this may be one of the few times that they have truly experienced a caring human relationship. Encouragement consists of helping clients use all of their resources. It also includes transforming traits that can be liabilities, such as stubbornness and compulsivity, into assets, such as determination and organization (Dinkmeyer & Losoncy, 1980).

Adlerians pay more attention to the subjective experiences of the client than they do to using techniques. They fit their techniques to the needs of each client. During this initial phase of counseling the main techniques are attending and listening, identifying and clarifying goals, and providing empathy. Attending implies engaging in behaviors such as maintaining eye contact and being psychologically available to the client. Listening entails grasping both the verbal and nonverbal messages of the client. Attending and listening both involve paying attention to the messages conveyed by the client's tone of voice, posture, facial expressions, gestures, and hesitations in speech. The counselor attempts to grasp the core of what the client is experiencing. Empathic understanding involves the therapist's ability to grasp the subjective world of clients and to communicate this understanding to them. If clients are deeply understood and accepted, they are likely to focus on what they want from therapy and thus establish goals.

The initial interview sets a foundation on which the relationship is created and maintained. Powers and Griffith (1987) provide many examples of the typical inquiries during the initial interview such as the following:

- What brought you to see me?
- What have you done about your problem until now?
- How would your life be different if you did not have this problem? (Or what would you do if you were well?)
- What are your expectations of our work together?

PHASE 2: EXPLORING THE INDIVIDUAL'S DYNAMICS

In the second phase the aim of clients is twofold understanding their lifestyle and seeing how it affects their current functioning in all the tasks of life. The counselor begins the initial assessment by exploring how clients are functioning in the various aspects of their lives. As Mozdzierz and his associates (1984) point out, when clients enter therapy, their focus is often narrow and restricted. They often feel overwhelmed by their struggles, their current relationships are strained, they feel stuck, and they feel alienated from their social system. At this stage the counselor's function is to provide a wide-angle perspective that will eventually help them view their world differently. Adlerians help their clients make connections between their past, present, and future behavior. In order to gain a sense of the client's lifestyle, counselors pay close attention to feelings, motives, beliefs, and goals. They explore feelings to understand motives, to develop empathy, and to enhance the quality of the therapeutic relationship. Adlerian therapists go beyond feelings to explore the beliefs underlying them. They then confront faulty beliefs so that clients can become freer.

Adlerians focus on the lifestyle assessment, which systematically deals with a thorough description of the members of the client's family of origin, their relationships, and their circumstances. Mozdzierz and his colleagues (1984) describe the counselor as a "lifestyle investigator" during this phase of therapy. Based on interviewing approaches developed by Adler and Dreikurs, the life-style assessment involves an investigation of the person's family constellation and early childhood history. Counselors also interpret the person's early memories. They seek to understand the whole person as he or she grew up in a social setting. They operate on the assumption that it is the interpretation that people develop about themselves, others, the world, and life that governs what they do. Lifestyle assessment aims at uncovering the private interpretations and private logic of the individual. For example, certain clients hold the mistaken notion that if they are not perfect, they are a failure. Through the assessment process they become aware of their negative thinking and its effects on restricted living.

The counselor explores how the client is functioning with reference to the life tasks of love, work, and friendship and community. Clients are expected to tell the counselor about these areas and also to set out what they want to improve or change. As a part of this assessment clients may be asked to rate their level of success in social relationships, work, sexuality, and feelings about self. They are typically asked questions in each of the above areas. For example: "Do you find satisfaction in your relationships with other people? Do you feel belonging and acceptance? How are things for you in your work? Do you have any special concerns in relating to women [men]? Do you typically feel good about yourself? How much fun do you have? How self-accepting are you?" Besides these questions, broad ones may be raised, such as "What gives your life meaning? What are your goals? How well are you meeting your goals?" Adlerian counselors are especially interested in learning about the ways in which the individual meets the basic demands of life. As Mozdzierz and his colleagues (1984) observe, Adlerians function as "psychological explorers," for they invite their clients on a journey through what has been, what is, and what can be. They help clients explore their options for growth and the paths that lead to a more productive and constructive future.

The family constellation.   As noted earlier, Adlerian assessment relies heavily on the exploration of the client's family constellation, which includes evaluating the conditions that prevailed in the family when the person was a young child in the process of forming lifestyle convictions and basic assumptions. Mosak and Shulman (1988) developed a lifestyle-assessment questionnaire that investigates what Adlerians consider to be influential factors in one's life. These include the child's psychological position in the family, birth order, and interactions between siblings and parents. Questions such as the following are explored: "Who was the favorite child? What was your father's relationship with the children? Your mother's? Which child was most like the father? In what respects? Which was most like the mother? In what ways? What was your relationship with your mother? Your father? Who among the siblings was most different from you? In what ways? Who was most like you? In what respects? What kind of child were you?" The counselor is also likely to ask why the person is seeking counseling and how satisfied he or she is with the way the basic tasks of life are being carried out. The questionnaire is far more comprehensive than these few questions, but this gives an idea of the type of information the counselor is seeking. The aim is to get a picture of clients' self-perception and of the experiences that have affected their development.

Once information on the family constellation has been collected, it is the counselor's task to make a brief summary of the material. The client's overall lifestyle assessment will also include separate summaries of his or her early recollections, dreams, and priorities.

Early recollections.   Another assessment procedure used by Adlerians is asking clients to give their earliest memories, including the feelings and thoughts that accompanied these incidents. Such occurrences must be ones that clients can remember in clear detail. These specific memories reveal beliefs and basic mistakes. To tap such recollections the counselor may proceed as follows: "I would like to hear about your earliest memories. Please start with your earliest concrete and single memory, something that you actually remember that happened to you one time, not something you were told about." Or: "I'd like to hear about a particular incident that you recall in the first seven or eight years of your life. Tell me what happened, what moment most stands out for you, and what you were thinking and feeling at that time." Clients can be asked to close their eyes, let themselves think back to a memory that stands out for them, and share the feelings that are attached to this recollection. The number of early recollections that are elicited varies. Three memories are usually considered a minimum, and some counselors ask for as many as a dozen.

Adlerians value these early recollections as an important clue to the understanding of an individual's lifestyle. They contend that people remember only those events that are consistent with their current views of themselves (Adler, 1958). Once people develop such views, they perceive only those things that fit their views. This limited perception strengthens people's private logic, which in turn helps them maintain their basic convictions. Early recollections thus provide a basic understanding of how we view and feel about ourselves, how we see the world, what our life goals are, what motivates us, what we believe in, and what we value.

The following examples of early recollections are provided for the case of

Stan (who is the central figure in Chapter 13). Stan reported his earliest memory as follows:

> I was about 6. I went to school and I was scared of the other kids and the teacher. When I came home, I cried and told my mother I didn't want to go back to school. She yelled at me and called me a baby. After that I felt horrible and even more scared.

Another of Stan's early recollections was at age 6½:

> My family was visiting my grandparents. I was playing outside, and some neighborhood kid hit me for no reason. We got in a big fight, and my mother came out and scolded me for being such a rough kid. She wouldn't believe me when I told her he had started the fight. I felt angry and hurt that she didn't believe me.

An Adlerian interpreting Stan's early memories is likely to note that he sees life as frightening and unpredictably abusive and that women will be harsh and uncaring. Counselors can learn a great deal about the individual's dynamics from such early recollections. Specifically, they may consider questions such as the following: Is the person an observer or a participant? What are the dominant themes and overall patterns of the memories? What are the typical responses of the person? Is the individual alone or with others? What feelings are expressed in the memories?

Dreams.   Dreams are projections of a client's current concerns and mood. Clients can learn to observe and understand their own internal dynamics by exploring their dreams (Peven & Shulman, 1986). As a part of the lifestyle assessment Adlerians might ask about dreams, which will then be interpreted and discussed. Particular attention is given to childhood dreams as well as to recurrent and recent dreams. From the perspective of Individual Psychology, dreams are seen as rehearsals for possible future courses of action. They serve as a weathervane for treatment, because they bring problems to the surface. In keeping with the Adlerian spirit, dreams are seen as purposeful and unique to the individual. Thus, there is no fixed symbolism in dreams; one cannot understand dreams without understanding the dreamer (Mosak, 1989). As a concrete illustration of a childhood dream, consider Stan's recollection: "I recall nightmares of being chased a lot. I would wake up crying. All I can remember is seeing something ugly chasing me, and sometimes catching me." Two other dreams, which Stan reports that he has often, go as follows:

> I am alone on a desert, dying of thirst. I see people with water, but nobody seems to notice me, and nobody comes over to me to give me any water. I've also dreamed a number of times that I was falling—like falling out of the sky—and I wake up petrified.

One possible interpretation of this dream is that life is basically frightening and that Stan cannot count on others to help him or be there for him. I suggest that you read the rest of Stan's case in Chapter 13 in order to get a better picture of how his dynamics relate to his early recollections and his dreams.

Priorities.   Adlerians believe that assessing clients' priorities is an important road to understanding their lifestyle. The Israeli psychologist Nera Kefir (1981) originally designated four priorities: *superiority, control, comfort,* and *pleasing.* People's main priority, unless challenged, continues to characterize their immediate response to any stress or difficulty. Each priority involves a dominant behavior pattern with supporting convictions that an individual uses to cope. Priorities become a pathway for relating to others and attaining a sense of significance. Kefir describes four behavioral patterns that reflect the four priorities:

- *Superior personalities* strive for significance through leadership or achievement or through any other avenue to make them feel superior. They seek to avoid meaninglessness in life but often complain of being overworked or overburdened.
- *Controlling personalities* look for guarantees against ridicule. They feel a need for complete control of situations so that they will not be ridiculed or humiliated. They do not want to behave in a socially unsuccessful way.
- *Avoiding personalities* strive for comfort. They tend to delay dealing with problems and making decisions, and they do their best to avoid anything that implies stress or pain. Even routine tasks are avoided, because they are seen as stressful.
- *Pleasing personalities* aim to avoid rejection by seeking constant approval and acceptance. Out of their fear of not being liked, they go to great lengths to win approval.

A way for a counselor to pinpoint clients' top priority is to ask them to describe in detail their typical day: what they do, how they feel, and what they think about. Typically, these descriptions reveal a consistent pattern. Clients' main priority can also be determined by discovering what they avoid at all costs and what feelings they consistently evoke in others.

It is *not* the therapist's job to work toward changing clients' main priority. Instead, the goal is to enable them to recognize the feelings they are evoking in others and the price they are paying for clinging to their highest priority. Kefir (1981) asserts that in order to increase our self-awareness we must learn what our priority, or condition for feeling significant, is as well as finding alternative ways to gain significance by using a wider range of behaviors. For example, if one of Stan's priorities is superiority, his behavior may take several forms. He may overstress the value of being competent of accomplishing one feat after another, of winning, of being right at all costs, and of moving ahead in all situations. Rather than attempting to change Stan directly, the therapist helps him make an evaluation of the impact he is having on others and on the price he is paying for making superiority his top priority. With his style of behavior Stan is likely to evoke feelings of inferiority in others. For himself, he may be weighted down with the responsibility of constantly trying to prove himself, and he may experience a tremendous level of stress in working so hard at being competent in all situations. It is likely that Stan's number-one priority is control. He is often overwhelmed by anxiety and feelings of helplessness. Some of the methods he uses to gain control over these feelings are escaping through alcohol, avoiding interpersonal situations that are threatening to him, keeping to himself, and deciding that he can't really count on others for psychological support. Although his style of seeking control apparently curbs some of his anxiety, he pays a steep price for his behavior. The feelings he evokes in others are frustration and lack of interest; for himself, the price he pays is distance from others and diminished spontaneity and creativity. (See Kefir [1981, pp. 403–407] for a further discussion of working with priorities in counseling.)

Integration and summary.   Once material has been gathered from the client's family constellation, early recollections, dreams, and priorities, separate summaries are done for each of these areas. Finally, based on the entire lifestyle-assessment questionnaire, this material is integrated, summarized, and interpreted. This lifestyle investigation reveals a pattern of basic mistakes, such as exaggerations, unfounded conclusions, faulty assumptions, absolutes, and rigid stances that make it difficult for the person to enjoy life. One of the counselor's major tasks is integrating and summarizing the information gathered about the client's family constellation, early recollections, and basic mistakes, as well as his or her assets. This summary is presented to the client and discussed in the session, with the client and counselor together refining specific points. Dinkmeyer, Dinkmeyer, and Sperry (1987) suggest that it is useful for the counselor to read the summary of the lifestyle in the presence of the client. In the following session the client reads the summary aloud. In this way clients have the chance to discuss specific topics and to raise questions. Also, the counselor can learn much about clients from hearing them read and observing their nonverbal reactions.

The summary also contains an analysis of an individual's basic mistakes. Mosak (1989) writes that the lifestyle can be conceived of as a personal mythology. People thus behave as if the myths were true, since for them they *are* true. Mosak lists five basic mistakes:

1. *Overgeneralizations:* "There is no fairness in the world."
2. *False or impossible goals:* "I must please everyone if I am to feel loved."
3. *Misperceptions of life and life's demands:* "Life is so very difficult for me."
4. *Denial of one's basic worth:* "I'm basically stupid, so why would anyone want anything to do with me?"
5. *Faulty values:* "Get to the top, regardless of who gets hurt in the process."

As another example of a summary of basic mistakes, consider the following list of mistaken and self-defeating perceptions that are evident in Stan's autobiography and that show up in his work with various therapists (see Chapter 13):

- Don't get close to people, especially women, because they will suffocate and control you if they can (overgeneralization).
- I was not really wanted by my parents, and therefore it is best for me to become invisible (denial of one's basic worth).

- It is extremely important that people will like me and approve of me. I'll bend over backward doing what people expect (false or impossible goals).

In order to get a clearer idea of the assessment procedures that Adlerians typically use, I suggest that you consult the appendix of *Understanding Life-Style: The Psycho-Clarity Process* (Powers & Griffith, 1987) for a detailed outline of the initial interview, guidelines for the lifestyle assessment, suggestions for making summaries, and notes for the course of therapy. *The Individual Psychology Client Workbook* (Powers & Griffith, 1986) contains a detailed and comprehensive initial-interview protocol and an excellent form for a lifestyle assessment. Also, the *Manual for Life Style Assessment* (Shulman & Mosak, 1988) presents a comprehensive guide for the initial interview and for establishing the lifestyle. The student manual that accompanies this textbook gives a concrete example of the lifestyle assessment as it is applied to the case of Stan. In *Case Approach to Counseling and Psychotherapy* (Corey, 1991) there is a detailed lifestyle assessment done on another hypothetical client, Ruth, which is based on the form by Powers and Griffith (1986). Consulting these references will help you get a concrete grasp of how Adlerian concepts come to life in practice.

The encouragement process.   After the lifestyle investigation is complete, clients can be encouraged to examine their mistaken perceptions, to begin to challenge their conclusions, and to take note of their assets, strengths, and talents. Encouragement is the most distinctive Adlerian procedure, and therefore it is essential that the overall assessment and interpretation include the client's positive qualities, not just a summary of deficits and mistakes. The encouragement process is basic to every phase of counseling. Adlerians seize every opportunity the client provides to introduce and reinforce this process (Powers & Griffith, 1987). Since clients often do not recognize or accept their positive qualities, one of the counselor's tasks is to help them do so. Through the encouragement process clients eventually begin to accept these strengths and assets.

Adlerians believe that discouragement is the basic condition that prevents people from functioning, and they see encouragement as the antidote. Encouragement takes many forms, depending on the phase of the counseling process. In the assessment phase, which is partially designed to illuminate personal strengths, clients are encouraged to recognize that they have the power to choose and to act differently based on their self-knowledge.

PHASE 3: ENCOURAGING INSIGHT

Although Adlerian therapists are supportive, they are also confrontive. They challenge their clients to develop insights into mistaken goals and self-defeating behaviors. Insight into the hidden purposes and goals of behavior tends to emerge not only through encouragement and challenge but also through well-timed interpretations by the therapist that are stated as tentative hypotheses.

Although insight is regarded by the Adlerians as a powerful adjunct to behavioral change, it is not seen as a prerequisite. Insight is viewed as a step toward change, but the emphasis is on translating this self-understanding into constructive action. People are able to make abrupt and significant changes in behavior without much insight.

Interpretation is a technique that facilitates the process of gaining insight. It is focused on here-and-now behavior and on the expectations and anticipations that arise from one's intentions. Adlerian interpretation is done in relationship to the lifestyle. It is concerned with creating awareness of one's direction in life, one's goals and purposes, one's private logic and how it works, and one's current behavior. Typically, interpretation is focused on behavior and its consequences, not on the causes of behavior. Adlerians operate on the assumption that no one knows the truth about another's world, so only guesses can be ventured. When they interpret another's world, therefore, they offer suggestions in the form of questions or qualified statements. Interpretations are presented tentatively in the form of open-ended sharings that can be explored in the sessions. They are hunches and guesses, and they are often stated thusly: "I have a hunch that I'd like to share with you. . . ." "It seems to me that . . ." "Could it be that . . . ?" "This is how it appears to me." Because interpretations are presented in this manner, clients are not led to defend themselves, and they feel free to discuss or argue over the counselor's hunches and impressions. Through this process clients eventually come to understand their own part in creating a problem, the ways in which they are now contributing to the problem, and what they can do to correct the situation.

Powers and Griffith (1987) maintain that learning how to make interpretations is more a matter of virtue than of technique. It is important that practitioners have the courage to extend themselves in empathic and intuitive guessing. These authors believe that as practitioners gain increased confidence in what they have to offer, they also become increasingly capable of empathy and develop more courage to make guesses. They add that it is crucial for counselors to have the humility to acknowledge wrong guesses when they are corrected or rejected by their clients.

PHASE 4: HELPING WITH REORIENTATION

The final stage of the therapeutic process is the action-oriented phase known as reorientation and reeducation, or putting insights into practice. This phase focuses on helping people see new and more functional alternatives. Clients are both encouraged and challenged to develop the courage to take risks and make changes in their life.

During the reorientation phase of counseling, clients make decisions and modify their goals. They are encouraged to act *as if* they were the person they wanted to be, which can serve to challenge self-limiting assumptions. Clients are asked to catch themselves in the process of repeating old patterns that lead to ineffective behavior. Commitment is an essential part of this phase, for if clients hope to change, they must be willing to set tasks for themselves and do something specific about their problems. In this way they translate their new insights into concrete action.

This action-oriented phase is a time for solving problems and making decisions. This is a time when the counselor and the client consider possible alternatives and their consequences, evaluate how these alternatives will meet the client's goals, and decide on a specific course of action. Some of the major techniques that Adlerians often employ during the reorientation phase are described below; the material is adapted from Dinkmeyer, Dinkmeyer, and Sperry (1987). The techniques described are immediacy, paradoxical intention, acting as if, spitting in the client's soup, catching oneself, push button, avoiding the tar baby, task setting and commitment, and terminating and summarizing.

Immediacy. The technique known as immediacy involves dealing with what is going on in the present moment of the counseling session. It may help the client to see how what is occurring in the session is a sample of what goes on in everyday life. For example, assume that your client continually leans on you for advice, based on her conviction that she typically "messes things up" when she makes important decisions. If you make explicit how she is viewing you and treating you in this relationship and tell her how you are being affected by her expecting you to make decisions for her, you are using immediacy. You can show her how she is defeating herself by clinging to her mistaken belief that she is unable to make decisions, which sets her up for failure.

Paradoxical intention. Adler pioneered the paradoxical strategy as a way of changing behavior. This technique has also been called "prescribing the symptom" and "antisuggestion." It involves having clients consciously pay attention to and exaggerate debilitating thoughts and behaviors. As a result the symptoms become markedly out of proportion to the reality of the situation. The paradoxical strategy consists of seemingly self-contradictory and sometimes even absurd therapeutic interventions. The essence of the technique is that it joins the client's resistance rather than opposing it; it contains characteristics of empathy, encouragement, and humor and leads to increased social interest (Mozdzierz, Macchitelli, & Lisiecki, 1976). Adler used a paradoxical strategy to treat insomnia and tension. In the case of depressed individuals, he cautioned it is best to have someone watch them to determine if suicide is a possibility. For suicidal clients hospitalization is recommended.

Paradoxical techniques are sometimes used for individuals who procrastinate. For example, such clients can be told to put off tasks even longer. A client who worries much of the time might be asked to schedule some time each day devoted exclusively to worrying about everything possible. The client who complains about being fearful of talking out in class is encouraged to sit in the back of the classroom and say nothing. In using this procedure, counselors should recommend exaggeration of a behavior pattern for a specific period of time so that clients can see what they might learn from the experiment. The rationale for paradoxical intention is that it assists people in becoming dramatically aware of how they are behaving in certain situations and how they are responsible for the consequences of their behavior. By going *with*, not against, the client's resistance, the therapist makes the behavior less attractive. The symptom is likely to appear foolish in the client's eyes. Further, when the client is confronted with a problem in a magnified way, she can then consider alternative ways of getting what she wants. Ethical issues are involved in the use of paradoxical procedures. Of course, therapists using them must be competent. Such techniques are usually employed after some of the more conventional techniques have failed to work in a given situation.

Acting as if.   The therapist can set up a role-playing situation in which clients imagine and act the way they would like to be. When clients say "If only I could . . . ," they can be encouraged to act out the role of their fantasy for at least a week, just to see what will happen. As an example of this technique, let's return to Stan. Assume that he says that he is troubled over his social inhibitions and that he would very much like to challenge his extreme fears of meeting and talking with women. His counselor may say:

> Stan, for the next week I'd like you to act as if you were very witty, attractive, and charming. Pretend that you have lots to offer and that women are missing out by not getting to know you. I suggest that you approach at least three women that you've been wanting to get to know.

By suggesting this task, the therapist is challenging Stan to take a risk and courageously do what he said he would like to do. By changing his expectations in positive ways, Stan may make his plan work. If he returns next week and says that he was rebuffed by the three women, he and his counselor can discuss what kept these experiences from being good ones.

Spitting in the client's soup.   The counselor determines the purpose and payoff of some behavior and then spoils the game by reducing the usefulness of the behavior in front of the client's eyes. For example, a father may be getting some mileage out of continually telling his children how hard he works so that they can enjoy the finer things in life. The counselor may confront him on his martyr stance and show him how he is seeking appreciation from his children. It is not the counselor's role to persuade him to change his story to his children but, rather, to show him the price he is paying for this style. The client has the choice of continuing with the same behavior, but the payoff is likely to be spoiled because he is no longer as able to deceive himself.

Catching oneself.   In the process of catching oneself, a client becomes aware of some self-destructive behavior or irrational thought but does not engage in self-condemnation. Initially, clients may catch themselves too late, after they have gotten entangled in old patterns; eventually, with practice, they will learn to anticipate events before they happen and thus change their patterns. In the example given above, the father may decide that he wants to avoid using guilt as a way to get gratitude from his children. In spite of his good intentions to change, he may still catch himself reverting to his old patterns from time to time. At these times he can at least pause for a moment and consider other ways of responding to his children.

Push button.   The push-button technique involves having clients picture alternately pleasant and unpleasant experiences and then pay attention to the feelings accompanying these experiences. The aim of the technique is to teach clients that they can create whatever feelings they wish by deciding on their thoughts (Mosak, 1989). In using the push-button technique, an Adlerian counselor will help a client recognize that he has chosen depression and that it is the result of his thinking. The counselor may use a visualization process, asking the client to recall a very pleasant incident, then to recall a very unpleasant incident, and then to imagine an incident that is turning out the way he would like it to. The client is asked to replay the last incident and to add the feeling that is created as an outcome of thinking. The counselor sends the man home with two "buttons" — a depression button and a happy button — and suggests to him that he is in control of which button to push as future incidents are encountered.

Avoiding the tar baby.   Clients bring with them to counseling some of the self-defeating patterns that they employ in daily life. They may cling to certain faulty assumptions because such biased perceptions do have a payoff. For example, some clients are convinced that nobody could really care about them, so they are likely to attempt to set up their counselor to eventually react to them as others have. Counselors need to be careful of falling into such traps and not to reinforce behaviors of clients that keep them stuck in old patterns. Instead counselors are advised to encourage those behaviors that will lead to increased psychological maturity.

Task setting and commitment.   In taking concrete steps to resolve their problems, clients must set tasks and make a commitment to them. Plans should be designed for a limited period. In this way clients can succeed in accomplishing specific tasks, and they can then develop new plans with confidence. Such tasks must be realistic and attainable. If plans do not work out well, they can be discussed and revised at the next session. If clients do meet with success in dealing with their tasks, they can commit to some long-range goals that will help them move in the direction they desire. (You will see this procedure as a basic part of behavior therapy and reality therapy in later chapters.)

Terminating and summarizing the session.   Setting limits for sessions, closing a session without stifling the client's willingness to continue exploring an issue, and summarizing the highlights of a session are all important skills for counselors to master. It is wise not to get into new material as a session is ending. Instead, the counselor can help the client review what was learned. This is a good time to discuss action-oriented "homework assignments" that the client can carry out during the week. In this way he or she is encouraged to apply new learning to everyday situations.

In addition to the techniques mentioned above Adlerians are likely to draw from a wide range of procedures throughout the counseling process. Most of these techniques are also used by therapists of other orientations; Adlerians are pragmatic when it comes to using methods when they are appropriate (Manaster & Corsini, 1982). The following are a few of these techniques:

- *Advice.* Adlerians will sometimes give advice if they think a client is ready to hear it and to accept it.
- *Homework.* Clients are often asked to keep track of their behavior patterns, along with the feelings and thoughts that are associated with specific situations. For instance, a person may feel intimidated about returning defective merchandise. The assignment can consist of monitoring situations in which she feels intimidated and then recording what she does and what she is thinking. She can be encouraged to actually return a defective product to challenge her thinking that she does not have a right to complain.
- *Humor.* Therapeutic use of humor can result in a client's putting problems into perspective. At times, counselors can help clients learn to take themselves less seriously and even laugh at some of the foolishness of their behavior (Mosak, 1987).
- *Silence.* At times in the therapeutic process one of the best techniques a counselor can use is saying nothing. Giving advice too quickly or too often or rescuing clients when they are uncomfortable with silence can be counterproductive.

AREAS OF APPLICATION

Individual Psychology, because it is based on a growth model, not a medical model, is applicable to such varied spheres of life as child-guidance centers, parent/child counseling, marital counseling, family therapy, group counseling, individual counseling with children and adolescents, cultural conflicts, correctional and rehabilitation counseling, and mental-health institutions. Its principles have been widely applied to substance-abuse programs, social problems to combat poverty and crime, problems of the aged, school systems, religion, and business.

Application to education.   Adler had a keen interest in applying his ideas to education, especially in finding ways to remedy faulty lifestyles of schoolchildren. He initiated a process to work with students in groups and to educate parents and teachers. By providing teachers with ways to prevent and correct basic mistakes of children, he sought to promote social interest and mental health in children. Besides Adler, the main proponent of Individual Psychology as a foundation for the teaching/learning process was Rudolf Dreikurs (1968, 1971). Along with Dreikurs, Don Dinkmeyer has made significant contributions to education and has pioneered methods of consultation with teachers (see Dinkmeyer, 1976; Dinkmeyer & Dreikurs, 1963). Raymond Corsini has also been instrumental in translating Adlerian principles into the school (see Pratt, 1986; Pratt & Mastroianni, 1984). In describing Corsini's approach to alternative education, Pratt and Mastroianni write that it rests on four goals for student development: responsibility, respect, resourcefulness, and responsiveness. In the Corsini Four-R schools, children's academic programs are individualized, and students have opportunities to make choices about their studies. The curriculum consists of a traditional academic program, a socialization program, and a creative program. The socialization program helps students learn interpersonal skills, deal effectively with everyday problems, and contribute to group life. The creative program is based on the motto "Let us know what you would like to learn or teach, and we will try to help you learn or teach it." This curriculum, which is aimed at personal and social development, grows out of the interests and curiosities of both the teacher and the learner.

Application to parent education.   The area of parent education has been one of the major Adlerian contributions. The goal is to improve the relationship between parent and child by promoting greater understanding and acceptance. Parents are taught simple Adlerian principles of behavior that can be applied in the home. Initial topics include understanding the purpose of a child's misbehavior, learning to listen, helping children accept the consequences of their behavior, holding family meetings, and using encouragement. The book considered to be the mainstay of many Adlerian parent-study groups is *Children: The Challenge,* by Dreikurs and Soltz (1964). Another book that presents Adlerian parent-education materials is *The Effective Parent* (Dinkmeyer, McKay, Dinkmeyer, & McKay, 1987).

Application to marriage counseling.   Adlerian marital therapy is designed to assess a couple's beliefs and behaviors while educating them in more effective ways to meet their goals. Dinkmeyer and Dinkmeyer (1982) outline four steps in the process of counseling couples, which correspond to the four stages of therapy described earlier:

1. The couple are asked what they expect from counseling, and the therapist discusses with them how their goals can be achieved.
2. The therapist then assesses both partners' lifestyles to determine the assumptions on which they operate, their basic mistaken perceptions, their assets, and their life goals. The lifestyle assessment is applied to marital therapy much as it is in individual counseling.
3. The therapist provides feedback to each partner on the themes and patterns emerging from the lifestyle assessment. The couple gain insight into their own dynamics and their marital system.
4. The couple are confronted by the therapist on their faulty beliefs about their relationship. This begins a reeducation process. The goal of the couple's reorientation is acquiring skills that they can use to carry out their new agreements.

The full range of techniques applicable to other forms of counseling can be used in working with couples. In marriage counseling and marriage education, couples are taught specific techniques that enhance communication and cooperation. Some of these techniques are listening, paraphrasing, giving feedback, having conferences, listing expectations, doing homework, and using paradoxical intention. Additional strategies in marriage counseling include psychodrama, bibliotherapy (recommending books that partners can read together and then discuss points of significance to them), storytelling and humor, and defining roles (Dinkmeyer, McKay, Dinkmeyer, & McKay, 1987).

Adlerians will sometimes see married people as a couple, sometimes individually, and then alternatively as a couple and as individuals. Rather than looking for who is at fault in the relationship, the therapist considers the lifestyles of the partners and the interaction of the two lifestyles. Emphasis is given to helping them decide if they want to maintain their marriage and, if so, what changes they are willing to make. If you want more information on applying Adlerian principles to marriages, you can consult *Training in Marriage Enrichment* (Dinkmeyer & Carlson, 1984).

Application to family counseling.   Adlerian family therapy has its roots in the work of Adler and Dreikurs. With its emphasis on the family constellation, holism, and the freedom of the therapist to improvise, Adler's approach contributed to the foundation of the family-therapy perspective. Adlerians working with families focus on the family atmosphere, the family constellation, and the lifestyle of each member. The family atmosphere is the climate characterizing the relationship between the parents and their attitudes toward life, sex roles, decision making, competition, cooperation, dealing with conflict, responsibility, and so forth. This atmosphere, including the role models that the parents provide, shapes the children as they grow up. The therapeutic process seeks to increase awareness of the interaction of the individual within the family system. Those who practice Adlerian family therapy strive to understand the goals, beliefs, and behaviors of each family member and the family as an entity in its own right. Because behavior has a social purpose, therapists focus on the relationships that characterize each family (Sherman & Dinkmeyer, 1987).

Adlerian family-therapy techniques are tied to the goals of therapy. Although specific goals are unique to each family, there are some general goals that provide direction (Sherman & Dinkmeyer, 1987):

- The interventions are designed to promote active and constructive movement.
- Family members are taught to accept personal responsibility.
- There is a joint effort between the therapist and each member of the family to evaluate goals and the means to achieve them.
- Family therapy has an educational purpose, for the therapist helps members learn ways to solve problems.
- Therapy is aimed at reorganizing family roles and relationships in a more effective and satisfying structure.

A number of techniques are available to family therapists to meet these goals. In addition to using many of the techniques described earlier in this chapter, they use other strategies: teaching communication skills, helping family members observe and interpret their transactions to differentiate between surface issues and real issues, offering encouragement, and confronting family members on their private logic and their purposes. One Adlerian technique is the use of paradox, which has become a major strategy of some family thera-

pists. Many of the other techniques used in family counseling were also pioneered by Adler. One of the standard techniques is the interview.

The *initial interview* begins the process of counseling family groups
(Lowe, 1982). Its purpose is to help the counselor diagnose the children's
goals, evaluate the parents' methods of child rearing, understand the climate in
the home, and make specific recommendations for change in the family situation. This process focuses on encouragement and on the strengths of all members of the family. It is essential that rapport be established so that productive
work can be done. The family constellation is given special attention in this
initial interview. Family members may be asked how they spend a typical day. A
certain view of life begins to emerge, based on the pattern of interaction between siblings and the children's position in the family. The parents are also
asked how they view their family situation. For example, they are asked to talk
about what concerns them about their children. The family counselor then
makes an appraisal of the family atmosphere, methods of training, and the
strengths of the family members. The interview ends with a series of recommendations that involve homework for the parents and significant others.

Application to group work.   Adler and his co-workers used a group approach in their child-guidance centers in Vienna as early as 1921 (Dreikurs,
1969). Dreikurs, a colleague, extended and popularized Adler's work with
groups and used group psychotherapy in his private practice for over 40 years.
Although he introduced group therapy into his psychiatric practice as a way to
save time, he quickly discovered some unique characteristics of groups that
made them an effective way of helping people change. Dreikurs's rationale for
groups is as follows: "Since man's problems and conflicts are recognized in
their social nature, the group is ideally suited not only to highlight and reveal
the nature of a person's conflicts and maladjustments but to offer corrective
influences" (1969, p. 43). Inferiority feelings can be challenged and counteracted effectively in groups, and the mistaken concepts and values that are at the
root of social and emotional problems can be deeply influenced, because the
group is a value-forming agent.

The group provides the social context in which members can develop a
sense of belonging and a sense of community. Dinkmeyer (1975) writes that
group participants come to see that many of their problems are interpersonal in
nature, that their behavior has social meaning, and that their goals can best be
understood in the framework of social purposes. Some of the specific therapeutic factors that he describes operating in Adlerian groups are:

- The group provides a mirror of the person's behavior.
- Members benefit from feedback from other members and the leaders.
- Members both receive help from others and give help.
- The group provides opportunities for testing reality and for trying new
  behavior.
- The group context encourages members to make a commitment to take
  action to change their life.
- Transactions in the group help members understand how they function at

work and at home and also reveal how members seek to find their place in society.

- The group is structured in such a way that members can meet their need for belonging.

SUMMARY AND EVALUATION

SUMMARY

Adler was far ahead of his time, and most of the contemporary therapies have incorporated at least some of his ideas. His Individual Psychology assumes that people are motivated by social factors; are responsible for their own feelings, thoughts, and actions; are the creators of their own lives, as opposed to helpless victims; and are impelled by purposes and goals, looking more toward the future than to the past.

The basic goal of the Adlerian approach is to help clients identify and change their mistaken beliefs about life and thus participate more fully in a social world. Clients are not viewed as mentally sick but as discouraged. The therapeutic process helps them become aware of their patterns and make some basic changes in their beliefs and thinking, which lead to changes in the way they feel and behave. The role of the family in the development of the individual is emphasized. Therapy is a cooperative venture, structured by a contract and geared toward challenging clients to translate their insights into action in the real world.

Adlerian therapists are resourceful in drawing on many methods. The Adlerian viewpoint is applicable to a wide range of human relations, including but not limited to individual and group counseling, marital and family therapy, and the alleviation of social problems.

CONTRIBUTIONS OF THE ADLERIAN APPROACH

The Adlerian approach gives practitioners a great deal of freedom in working with clients. Adlerian counselors are not bound to follow a specific procedure. Instead, they can use their clinical judgment in applying a wide range of techniques that they think will work best for a particular client.

The Adlerian concepts that I most draw on in my work with clients are: (1) the importance of looking to one's life goals, including focusing on the direction they are leading one; (2) the focus on the individual's early experiences in the family, with special emphasis on their current impact; (3) the clinical use of early recollections; (4) the need to understand and confront basic mistakes; (5) the cognitive emphasis, which holds that emotions and behaviors are largely influenced by one's beliefs and thinking processes; (6) the idea of working out an action plan designed to help clients make changes; (7) the collaborative relationship, whereby the client and therapist work toward mutually agreed-on goals; and (8) the emphasis given to encouragement during the entire course of the counseling process.

The Adlerian approach to social factors in personality lends itself exceptionally well to working with individuals in groups. Major Adlerian contributions have been made in the following areas: elementary education, consultation groups with teachers, parent-education groups, marriage counseling, and family counseling. Adler's influence has extended into the community mental-health movement, including the use of paraprofessionals and a team approach (Ansbacher, 1974).

In my opinion one of Adler's most important contributions is his influence on other systems. The following brief overview illustrates this point:

Existential approach.   Viktor Frankl and Rollo May have acknowledged their debt to Adler. Both men see him as a forerunner of the existential movement because of his position that human beings are free to choose and are entirely responsible for what they make of themselves. This view makes Adler the pioneer of the subjective (phenomenological) approach to psychology, which focuses on the internal determinants of behavior: values, beliefs, attitudes, goals, purposes, meaning in life, and the individual's freedom to create his or her own destiny. The importance of the therapeutic relationship as a collaborative partnership and a shared journey is another common focus for both approaches.

Person-centered approach.   The person-centered perspective shares a number of aspects with Adlerian therapy: a holistic view of behavior and of the unity and consistency of personality, a growth orientation, a subjective perspective, the view that humans are always in the process of becoming and striving toward goals, a stress on empathy and acceptance a focus on support and encouragement, a focus on clients' responsibility and capacity to discover ways to more fully encounter reality, the counselor's sharing of power with the client, the counselor's role of active listening and of empathic understanding, the counselor's activity as a role model, and an emphasis on the importance of the client/therapist relationship to the outcomes of therapy.

Gestalt therapy.   Both the Gestalt and Adlerian perspectives are grounded in a phenomenological perspective, stress the client's responsibility for self, see the client as active in the therapy process, focus on the here and now, analyze nonverbal communication, encourage taking risks to live fully, and help clients deal with impasses.

Transactional analysis.   Several TA concepts are borrowed from the Adlerian perspective, including the notion of a life script and the social framework of behavior. Transactional analysis, like Adlerian therapy, focuses on reevaluating old decisions and making new and more appropriate ones, stresses the equality of client and therapist, seeks the alignment of goals, and uses a therapeutic contract. Both approaches are heavily cognitive, and both stress the role of teaching and reeducation in counseling.

Behavior therapy.   Some ways in which behavior therapy shares Adlerian emphases are its use of encouragement and positive reinforcement, its concreteness and specificity in counseling, its focus on behavioral goals, its use of problem-solving techniques, its use of contracts, and its notion that analysis and assessment are crucial at the early phases of counseling. Both approaches emphasize the importance of a good working relationship in therapy yet call for specific skills on the therapist's part and specific techniques to promote behavioral change.

Rational-emotive therapy.   Although the origins of rational-emotive therapy go back to the Stoic philosophers, Albert Ellis gives credit to Adler as the modern therapist who was the main precursor of RET. Both systems hold that people are disturbed not by events but by their interpretation of these events. Both systems view cognition as the key to understanding feelings and behavior. RET's concept of irrational beliefs is much like the Adlerian notion of basic mistakes. Both approaches also focus on learning new orientations, urge clients to confront self-defeating internalized assumptions, use analysis and action methods, rely on bibliotherapy as an adjunct to therapy, and stress the role of teaching and learning in therapy. With the current emphasis on cognitive factors in understanding behavior, contemporary cognitive-behavioral therapy looks much like Adlerian therapy in a number of respects.

Reality therapy.   William Glasser's reality therapy is based in many respects on Adlerian principles. Both therapies stress the role of the client's purposes, and both hold that the client must determine the goals of therapy. Commitment is seen as a prerequisite for change, and there is a focus on developing a specific and realistic therapy plan, as specified by a contract. Reality therapy shares with Adlerian therapy an emphasis on personal responsibility, a phenomenological/existential orientation, an encouragement of the client's assets and personal strengths, a use of reorientation and reality testing, and a focus on values. There is a similarity between reality therapy's concept of a success identity and a failure identity and the Adlerian concept of encouragement and discouragement. Some reality therapists use techniques such as skillful questioning, paradoxical intention, confrontation, and humor, all of which were used by Adler.

As you proceed with your study of the seven remaining therapeutic systems, I encourage you to continue to pay attention to their similarities and differences. Such a comparative perspective will deepen your understanding of the therapeutic process, help you formulate your own approach, and increase the number of practical applications that these systems offer to you as a counselor.

Contributions from a multicultural perspective.   Although the Adlerian approach is called Individual Psychology, its focus is on the person in a social context. Adlerians' interest in helping others, in social interest, in belonging, and in the collective spirit fits well with the value systems of many ethnic groups. Those cultures that stress the welfare of the social group and that emphasize the role of the family will find the Adlerian focus on social interest to be congruent with their values. According to Mozdzierz and his colleagues (1984), Adlerians operate on the assumption that people are basically social, goal-seeking decision makers who live at their best when they cooperate, contribute to the common good, and face the demands of life. Therapists aim at increasing the individual's social interest and helping him or her contribute within an interpersonal framework.

American Indian clients, for example, tend to value cooperation over competition. A client with an Indian cultural background told a story about a group of boys who were in a race. When one boy got ahead of the others, he would slow down and allow them to catch up, and they all made it to the finish line at the same time. Although the coach tried to explain that the point of the race was for an individual to finish first, these boys were socialized to work together cooperatively as a group. A counselor who would push individualistic and competitive values would be showing ignorance of socially oriented values in this case.

Clients who enter therapy are often locked into rigid ways of perceiving, interpreting, and behaving. It is likely that they have not questioned how their culture has influenced them. Thus, they may feel resigned to "the way things are." Mozdzierz and his colleagues (1984) characterize these clients as myopic and contend that one of the therapist's functions is to provide them with another pair of glasses that will allow them to see things more clearly. The Adlerian emphasis on the subjective fashion in which people view and interpret their world leads to a respect for clients' unique values and perceptions. Adlerian counselors use interpretations as an opportunity for clients to view things from a different perspective, yet it is up to the clients to decide whether to open their eyes and to use these glasses. Adlerians do not decide for clients what they should change or what their goals should be rather, they work collaboratively with their clients in ways that enable them to reach their self-defined goals.

Not only is Adlerian theory congruent with the values of many cultural groups, but the approach offers flexibility in applying a range of cognitive and action-oriented techniques to helping clients explore their practical problems. As we have seen, Adlerian practitioners are not wedded to any particular set of procedures. Instead, they are conscious of the value of fitting their techniques to the needs of their clients. Although they utilize a diverse range of methods, most of them do conduct an assessment of each client's lifestyle. This assessment is heavily focused on the structure and dynamics within the client's family. Many ethnic clients have been conditioned to respect their family heritage and to appreciate the impact of their family on their own personal development. It is essential that counselors be sensitive to the conflicting feelings and struggles of their clients. If counselors demonstrate an understanding of these cultural values, it is likely that these clients will be receptive to an exploration of their lifestyle. Such an exploration will involve a detailed discussion of their own place within their family.

It should be noted that different authors give the term *culture* various meanings. Also, if culture is considered as a broad concept (to include age, roles, lifestyle, and gender differences), there can be cultural differences even within a family. The Adlerian approach emphasizes the value of subjectively understanding the unique world of an individual. Culture is one significant dimension for grasping the subjective and experiential perspective of an individual. Pedersen expresses this idea well: "Culture provides a metaphor to better understand the different perspectives within each of us as our different social roles compete, complement, and cooperate with one another in our decisions. It also provides an alternative for better understanding others whose culturally learned assumptions are different from our own" (1990, p. 94).

LIMITATIONS AND CRITICISMS OF THE ADLERIAN APPROACH

Adler was aware of his time limitations, and he had to choose between devoting his efforts to formalizing his theory and teaching others the basic concepts of Individual Psychology. He placed his priority on practicing and teaching, not on organizing and presenting a well-defined and systematic theory. Thus, his writing style is often difficult to follow. Many of his ideas are somewhat loose and oversimplified.

Although Individual Psychology has undergone further development and refinement, many of Adler's original formulations were stated in such a way that it would be difficult to empirically validate the basic hypotheses. Some of his basic concepts were global in nature and poorly defined, such as notions of the struggle for superiority, the creative power of the self, and the inferiority complex. Adler has been criticized for basing most of his approach on a common-sense psychology and for oversimplifying complex concepts.

Limitations from a multicultural perspective.   For those clients with pressing problems who would like quick solutions, Adlerian therapy poses some difficulties. Such clients may have little interest in exploring their early childhood, their early memories, or the dynamics within their family. Instead, they are likely to view the counselor as the "expert" who will give them specific answers to their problems. They may not see any purpose in going into the details of the development of their lifestyle. Adlerians are aware that there are better ways of dealing with life problems than the ones the client is using, but they also know that there is no "one right way." Although therapists have expertise in the problems of living, they are not experts in solving other people's problems. Instead, they view it as their function to teach people alternative methods of dealing with their own problems. Many clients come to counseling, however, with the expectation that the therapist will provide them with the solutions to their problems.

QUESTIONS FOR REFLECTION AND DISCUSSION

1. What are some major areas of contrast between Freud's and Adler's theories? Which perspective appeals to you more, and why? Do you see any basis for reconciling the differences and integrating Freudian and Adlerian concepts in therapeutic practice?
2. When you look at Adler's life experiences and the development of his theory, what do you conclude? To what degree do you think it is possible to separate the theory from the theorist?
3. Adler saw us as the actor, creator, and artist of our life. How does this description fit your own life experience?
4. The Adlerian notion of striving for superiority holds that we seek to change weakness into strength by excelling in a particular area as a compensation for perceived inferiority. What are some ways in which you strive for superiority? Does this process of compensation and striving work well for you?
5. A person's imagined goals guide behavior. People are more affected by the goals they are striving for in the future than by where they have been in the

past. How does the Adlerian concept of *fictional finalism* apply to you? What goals guide your life?

6. Reread the descriptions of the oldest child, the second-born, the middle child, the youngest child, and the only child. What position did you occupy in your family? To what degree do you see your experiences as a child in your family as a factor shaping the person you are now?

7. In addition to focusing on the family constellation, Adlerians ask for a few early recollections. What is your earliest memory? What meaning does this recollection hold for you today?

8. Adlerians pay a lot of attention to "basic mistakes," or "private logic." In thinking about some of the conclusions you formed based on a series of life experiences, can you identify any mistaken assumptions you hold now or have held in the past? How do you think some of your basic mistakes affect the ways in which you think, feel, and act?

9. What Adlerian concepts are likely to be most congruent with the values of ethnic-minority clients? What are the implications of Adler's ideas for multicultural practice?

10. From what you know of Stan's history (Chapter 13), what are some key themes in his life that would be of greatest interest to an Adlerian therapist? If you were to work with Stan, how might you proceed as an Adlerian?

WHERE TO GO FROM HERE

If you would like to learn more about the Adlerian approach, a good place to begin is by selecting any of the books in the "Recommended Supplementary Readings." You might consider seeking training in Individual Psychology or becoming a member of the North American Society of Adlerian Psychology. The society has a professional and nonprofessional membership of over 1200 in North America and abroad. The membership includes individuals, families, local Adlerian organizations, and training institutes. For more information contact:

North American Society of Adlerian Psychology
202 South State Street, Suite 1212
Chicago, IL 60604-1905
Telephone: (312) 939-0834

The society publishes a newsletter and maintains a list of current institutes, training programs, and workshops in Adlerian psychology.

Another source to contact for information is:

Alfred Adler Institute of Chicago
618 South Michigan Avenue
Chicago, IL 60605
Telephone: (312) 294-7100

An institution that offers postgraduate studies and continuing education in Adlerian psychology is the Americas Institute of Adlerian Studies, in San Diego

County. This organization offers a three-course training program for professionals in Individual Psychology. The address is:

Americas Institute of Adlerian Studies
486 Hillway Drive
Vista, CA 92084
Telephone: (619) 758-4658

The quarterly *Individual Psychology: The Journal of Adlerian Theory: Research and Practice* presents current scholarly and professional research dealing with all aspects of the social, psychological, and personality theory founded by Adler. Articles relate to theoretical and research issues as well as concerns of practice and applications of Adlerian psychological methods. Columns on counseling, education, and parent and family education are regular features of the practice and application issues. This journal provides a forum for the finest dialogue pertaining to Adlerian practices, principles, and theoretical development. Information about subscriptions is available by contacting:

Guy J. Manaster and Jon Carlson, Editors
Individual Psychology
Department of Educational Psychology
University of Texas at Austin
Austin, TX 78712

RECOMMENDED SUPPLEMENTARY READINGS

Adlerian Counseling and Psychotherapy (Dinkmeyer, Dinkmeyer, & Sperry, 1987) gives a good presentation of the theoretical foundations of Adlerian counseling and applies its basic concepts to the practice of group counseling. There are excellent chapters dealing with the phases and techniques of the counseling process, Adlerian group counseling, family and marital therapy, consultation with teachers, and parent education.

Understanding Life-Style: The Psycho-Clarity Process (Powers & Griffith, 1987) is one of the best sources of information for doing a lifestyle analysis. This book comes alive with many good clinical examples. Separate chapters deal with interview techniques, lifestyle assessment, early recollections, the family constellation, and methods of summarizing and interpreting information.

Systems of Family Therapy: An Adlerian Integration (Sherman & Dinkmeyer, 1987) explains family organization and dynamics from an Adlerian perspective. The structure of Adlerian family therapy and the basics of change are discussed within the framework of an integrative theory. There is a useful chapter on family-therapy techniques.

REFERENCES AND SUGGESTED READINGS*

ADLER, A. (1958). *What life should mean to you.* New York: Capricorn.
ADLER, A. (1964a). The Individual Psychology of Alfred Adler. In H. L. Ansbacher & R. R. Ansbacher (Eds.), *The Individual Psychology of Alfred Adler.* New York: Harper & Row (Torchbooks).

* Books and articles marked with an asterisk are suggested for further study.

ADLER, A. (1964b). *Social interest: A challenge to mankind.* New York: Capricorn.

*ADLER, A. (1979). *Superiority and social interest: A collection of later writings* (3rd rev. ed.) (H. L. Ansbacher & R. R. Ansbacher, Eds.). New York: Norton.

ALLEN, T. W. (1971). The Individual Psychology of Alfred Adler: An item of history and a promise of revolution. *The Counseling Psychologist, 3,* 2–24.

ANSBACHER, H. L. (1974). Goal-oriented Individual Psychology: Alfred Adler's theory. In A. Burton (Ed.), *Operational theories of personality.* New York: Brunner/Mazel.

*ANSBACHER, H. L. (1979). The increasing recognition of Adler. In A. Adler, *Superiority and social interest: A collection of later writings* (3rd rev. ed.). New York: Norton.

*ANSBACHER, H. L., & ANSBACHER, R. R. (Eds.). (1964). *The Individual Psychology of Alfred Adler.* New York: Harper & Row (Torchbooks).

BITTER, J. (1985). An interview with Harold Mosak. *Individual Psychology, 41,* 386–420.

BITTER, J. (1987). Communication and meaning: Satir in Adlerian context. In R. Sherman & D. Dinkmeyer (Eds.), *Systems of family therapy: An Adlerian integration* (pp. 109–142). New York: Brunner/Mazel.

COREY, G. (1991). *Case approach to counseling and psychotherapy* (3rd ed.). Pacific Grove, CA: Brooks/Cole.

DINKMEYER, D. (1975). Adlerian group psychotherapy. *International Journal of Group Psychotherapy, 25,* 219–226.

DINKMEYER, D. C. (1976). *Developing understanding of self and others (D-2 Kit).* Circle Pines, MN: American Guidance Service.

DINKMEYER, D., & CARLSON, J. (1984). *Training in marriage enrichment.* Circle Pines, MN: American Guidance Service.

*DINKMEYER, D. C., DINKMEYER, D. C., JR., & SPERRY, L. (1987) *Adlerian counseling and psychotherapy* (2nd ed.). Columbus, OH: Charles E. Merrill.

DINKMEYER, D., & DINKMEYER, J. (1982). Adlerian marriage therapy. *Individual Psychology, 38,* 115–122.

DINKMEYER, D., & DREIKURS, R. (1963). *Encouraging children to learn: The encouragement process.* Englewood Cliffs, NJ: Prentice-Hall.

DINKMEYER, D. C., ET AL. (1983). *Systematic training for effective parenting of teens (STEP/Teen).* Circle Pines, MN: American Guidance Service.

DINKMEYER, D., & LOSONCY, L. E. (1980). *The encouragement book: Becoming a positive person.* Englewood Cliffs, NJ: Prentice-Hall.

DINKMEYER, D., & McKAY, G. D. (1982). *The parent's handbook: Systematic training for effective parenting (STEP).* Circle Pines, MN: American Guidance Service.

DINKMEYER, D., McKAY, G., DINKMEYER, D., JR., & McKAY, J. (1987). *The effective parent.* Circle Pines, MN: American Guidance Service.

*DREIKURS, R. (1953). *Fundamentals of Adlerian psychology.* Chicago: Alfred Adler Institute.

DREIKURS, R. (1967). *Psychodynamics, psychotherapy, and counseling: Collected papers.* Chicago: Alfred Adler Institute.

DREIKURS, R. (1968). *Psychology in the classroom* (2nd ed.). New York: Harper & Row.

DREIKURS, R. (1969). Group psychotherapy from the point of view of Adlerian psychology. In H. M. Ruitenbeek (Ed.), *Group therapy today: Styles, methods, and techniques.* New York: Aldine-Atherton.

DREIKURS, R. (1971). *Social equality: The challenge of today.* Chicago: Regnery.

DREIKURS, R., & MOSAK, H. H. (1966). The tasks of life: I. Adler's three tasks. *The Individual Psychologist, 4,* 18–22.

DREIKURS, R., & MOSAK, H. H. (1967). The tasks of life: II. The fourth task. *The Individual Psychologist, 4,* 51–55.

DREIKURS, R., & SOLTZ, V. (1964). *Children: The challenge*. New York: Meridith Press.

*GRIFFITH, J., & POWERS, R. L. (1984). *An Adlerian lexicon*. Chicago: Americas Institute of Adlerian Studies.

GUSHURST, R. S. (1971). The technique, utility, and validity of life style analysis. *The Counseling Psychologist, 3,* 31–40.

KEFIR, N. (1981). Impasse/priority therapy. In R. J. Corsini (Ed.), *Handbook of innovative psychotherapies* (pp. 401–415). New York: Wiley.

LOWE, R. N. (1982). Adlerian/Dreikursian family counseling. In A. M. Horne & M. M. Ohlsen (Eds.), *Family counseling and therapy*. Itasca, IL: F. E. Peacock.

*MANASTER, G. J., & CORSINI, R. J. (1982). *Individual Psychology: Theory and practice*. Itasca, IL: F. E. Peacock.

MOSAK, H. (1977). *On purpose*. Chicago: Alfred Adler Institute.

MOSAK, H. (1987). *Ha, ha, and aha: The role of humor in psychotherapy*. Muncie, IN: Accelerated Development.

*MOSAK, H. (1989). Adlerian psychotherapy. In R. J. Corsini & D. Wedding (Eds.), *Current psychotherapies* (4th ed.) (pp. 65–116). Itasca, IL: F. E. Peacock.

*MOSAK, H., & MANIACCI, M. (1989). The case of Roger. In D. Wedding & R. J. Corsini (Eds.), *Case studies in psychotherapy* (pp. 23–49). Itasca, IL: F. E. Peacock.

MOSAK, H., & MOSAK, B. (1975). *A bibliography of Adlerian psychology*. Washington, DC: Hemisphere.

MOSAK, H., & MOSAK, B. (1985). *A bibliography for Adlerian psychology: Vol. 2*. New York: McGraw-Hill.

*MOSAK, H., & SHULMAN, B. (1988). *Life style inventory*. Muncie, IN: Accelerated Development.

MOZDZIERZ, G. J., LISIECKI, J., BITTER, J. R., & WILLIAMS, A. L. (1984). *Role-functions for Adlerian therapists*. Unpublished paper.

MOZDZIERZ, G. J., MACCHITELLI, F. J., & LISIECKI, J. (1976). The paradox in psychotherapy: An Adlerian perspective. *Journal of Individual Psychology, 32,* 169–184.

PEDERSEN, P. (1990). The multicultural perspective as a fourth force in counseling. *Journal of Mental Health Counseling, 12,* 93–95.

PEVEN, D. E., & SHULMAN, B. H. (1986). Adlerian psychotherapy. In I. L. Kutash and A. Wolf (Eds.), *Psychotherapist's casebook* (pp. 101–123). San Francisco: Jossey-Bass.

*POWERS, R. L., & GRIFFITH, J. (1986). *The Individual Psychology client workbook*. Chicago: The Americas Institute of Adlerian Studies.

*POWERS, R. L., & GRIFFITH, J. (1987). *Understanding life-style: The psycho-clarity process*. Chicago: The Americas Institute of Adlerian Studies.

PRATT, A. B. (1986). *Questions and answers about Corsini Four-R schools*. Columbus, OH: Capital University. (Manual)

PRATT, A. B., & MASTROIANNI, M. (1984). *How Corsini Four-R schools work*. Columbus, OH: Capital University. (Manual)

SCHULTZ, D. (1990). *Theories of personality* (4th ed.). Pacific Grove, CA: Brooks/Cole.

SHERMAN, R., & DINKMEYER, D. (1987). *Systems of family therapy: An Adlerian integration*. New York: Brunner/Mazel.

SHULMAN, B., & MOSAK, H. (1988). *Manual for life style assessment*. Muncie, IN: Accelerated Development.

TERNER, J., & PEW, W. L. (1978). *The courage to be imperfect: The life and work of Rudolf Dreikurs*. New York: Hawthorn Books.

6

EXISTENTIAL THERAPY

VIKTOR FRANKL

VIKTOR FRANKL (b. 1905) was born and educated in Vienna. He founded the Youth Advisement Centers there in 1928 and directed them until 1938. He was also on the staff at several clinics and hospitals. From 1942 to 1945 Frankl was a prisoner in the German concentration camps at Auschwitz and Dachau, where his parents, brother, wife, and children died. Frankl vividly remembers his horrible experiences in these camps; yet he has been able to use them in a constructive way and has not allowed them to dampen his love and enthusiasm for life. In the late 1940s he married his present wife, Elleonara, with whom he now lives in Austria. At the age of 80 he was still hiking in the Alps, and even now he remains active personally and professionally. He has traveled all around the world and still gives lectures in Europe, Latin America, Southeast Asia, and the United States.

Frankl received his M.D. in 1930 and his Ph.D. in 1949, both from the University of Vienna. Additionally, he holds honorary doctorates from more than 120 universities around the world. He became an associate professor at the University of Vienna and later was a distinguished speaker at United States International University in San Diego. He has also been a visiting professor at Harvard, Stanford, and Southern Methodist universities. Frankl's works have been translated into more than 20 languages, and he continues to have a major impact on the development of existential therapy. His compelling book *Man's Search for Meaning* has been a best-seller around the world.

Although Frankl had begun to develop an existential approach to clinical practice before his grim years in the Nazi death camps, his experiences there confirmed his views. He observed and personally experienced the truths expressed by existential philosophers and writers, including the view that love is the highest goal to which humans can aspire and that our salvation is through love (1963, p. 59). That we have choices in every situation was another notion confirmed by his experiences in the concentration camps. Even in terrible situations, he believes, we can preserve a vestige of spiritual freedom and independence of mind. He learned experientially that everything could be taken from a person but one thing: "the last of human freedoms— to choose one's attitude in any given set of circumstances, to choose one's own way" (1963, p. 104). Frankl believes that the essence of being human lies in searching for meaning and purpose. We can discover this meaning through our actions and deeds, by experiencing a value (such as love or achievements through work), and by suffering.

As you will see, there was no single founder of the existential approach, because it had its roots in diverse movements. I have selected Frankl as one of its key figures because of the dramatic way in which his theories were tested by the tragedies of his life. His life is an illustration of his theory, for he lives what his theory espouses. Although others have written about existential concepts, they have not met with the popularity of Frankl.

ROLLO MAY

ROLLO MAY (b. 1909) first lived in Ohio and then moved to Michigan as a young child with his five brothers and sister. He remembers his home life as being unhappy, a situation that had something to do with his interest in psychology and counseling. In his personal life May has struggled with his own existential concerns and the failure of two marriages. These events, though, have not given him a negative outlook on life. At 78, he said he was getting more fun out of life than he had at 58 and certainly more than he had at 38 (Rabinowitz, Good, & Cozad, 1989).

During his youth May spent some time studying ancient Greek civilization, which he thinks gave him a perspective on human nature. He later traveled to Vienna and studied with Alfred Adler. In 1938 he received a master's of divinity from Union Theological Seminary. It was in 1949 that he received the first Ph.D., in clinical psychology, from Columbia University. During the time he was pursuing his doctoral program, he came down with tuberculosis, which resulted in a two-year stay in a sanitarium. During his recovery period he spent much time reading and learning firsthand about the nature of anxiety. This study resulted in his book *The Meaning of Anxiety* (1950), which he considers the watershed of his career (Rabinowitz et al., 1989). In 1953 his next book was published, *Man's Search for Himself*, which dealt with the meaning of existential loneliness and the anxiety that characterizes the contemporary person. This book distinguished him as a key American existentialist and psychoanalytic writer. He also edited *Existential Psychology* (1961),

which helped make him a leader of the human-potential movement during the 1960s. His popular book *Love and Will* (1969) reflected his own personal struggles with love and intimate relationships and mirrored Western society's questioning of its values pertaining to sex and marriage. To date he has authored or co-authored 14 books.

The greatest personal influence on May was the German philosopher Paul Tillich (author of *The Courage to Be*, 1952), who spent much time with him discussing philosophical, religious, and psychological topics. Most of May's writings reflect a concern with the nature of human experience, such as recognizing and dealing with power, accepting freedom and responsibility, and discovering one's identity. He draws from his rich knowledge based on the classics and his existential perspective.

May is considered one of the main proponents of humanistic approaches to psychotherapy, and he is the principal American spokesman of European existential thinking as it is applied to psychotherapy. He believes that psychotherapy should be aimed at helping people discover the meaning of their lives and should be concerned with the problems of *being* rather than with problem solving. Questions of being include learning to deal with issues such as sex and intimacy, growing old, and facing death. According to May, the real challenge is for people to be able to live in a world where they are alone and where they will eventually have to face death. He contends that our individualism should be balanced by what

Adler referred to as social interest. May believes that there is too much concern about the self and not enough concern about society and culture (Rabinowitz et al., 1989). Therapists need to help individuals find ways to contribute to the betterment of the society in which they live. He believes that therapists should address the higher aspirations of the human race, including those values that make life worth living. If individuals in society were grounded in these higher values, therapists might well be out of business.

May now lives in Tiburon, California, where he still keeps an active schedule that includes spending about four hours daily working on an upcoming book, *The Cry for Myth*. He sees private clients in the afternoon, and he makes time for leisure pursuits.

INTRODUCTION

Existential therapy can best be described as an *intellectual* approach to therapeutic practice, or a *philosophy* that a therapist follows. As such it is not a separate school of therapy or a neatly defined model with specific techniques. Thus, this chapter will focus on some of the existential ideas and themes that have significant implications for the existentially oriented practitioner.

The existential approach developed as a reaction to two other major models, psychoanalysis and behaviorism. The psychoanalytic position is that freedom is restricted by unconscious forces, irrational drives, and past events. The behavioristic position is that freedom is restricted by sociocultural conditioning. Although existential therapy accepts the premise that our choices are limited by external circumstances, it rejects the notion that our acts are determined. It is based on the assumption that we are free and therefore responsible for our choices and actions. We are the author, or architect, of our life, and therefore we are always more than the victim of circumstances. Furthermore, the existential view is based on a growth model and conceptualizes health rather than sickness. As Deurzen-Smith (1988) writes, existential counseling is not designed to cure people in the tradition of the medical model. Clients are not viewed as being sick; rather, they are seen as being sick of life or awkward at living. For Deurzen-Smith, such people need help in surveying the terrain and in discovering their own best way. A major aim of therapy is to challenge clients to recognize their range of alternatives and choose among them. Once clients begin realizing how they have passively accepted circumstances and surrendered control, they can start on a path of consciously shaping their own lives.

HISTORICAL BACKGROUND IN PHILOSOPHY

There are many streams in the existential-therapy movement. It was not founded by any particular person or group. Rather, drawing from a major orientation in philosophy, it arose spontaneously in different parts of Europe and among different schools of psychology and psychiatry in the 1940s and 1950s. It grew out of an effort to help people engage the dilemmas of contemporary life, such as isolation, alienation, and meaninglessness. Rather than trying to develop sets of rules for therapy, it focused on understanding these deep human experiences (May & Yalom, 1989).

The thinking of existential psychologists and psychiatrists was influenced by a number of philosophers and writers, extending as far back as the early 19th century. To get some flavor of the philosophical underpinnings of the existential movement, one must have some awareness of such figures as Fyodor Dostoyevski, Soren Kierkegaard, Friedrich Nietzsche, Martin Heidegger, Jean-Paul Sartre, and Martin Buber.

Dostoyevski (1821–1881).   In *Notes from Underground* the great Russian novelist struck out against the new, sophisticated belief that people are determined in their actions by what they believe will yield the most pleasure. Dostoyevski's main character, a nameless man who both identifies himself with a mouse and yet believes he has a far higher degree of consciousness than the successful men of the world around him, argues that our human capacity to act on whim or impulse is far more precious to us than mere pleasure. We can even decide to act *against* our own "best advantage." Consciousness may be painful, and it may not make us decisive, but at least it gives us a great freedom in the conduct of our life.

Kierkegaard (1813–1855).   The Danish philosopher was particularly concerned with *angst*—a Danish and German word whose meaning lies between the English words *dread* and *anxiety*. Without the experience of angst, we may go through life as sleepwalkers. But many of us, especially in adolescence, are awakened into real life by a terrible uneasiness. Life is one contingency after another, with no guarantees beyond the certainty of death. This is by no means a comfortable state, but it is necessary to our becoming human. Becoming human is a *project*.

Nietzsche (1844–1900).   The German philosopher set out to prove that the ancient definition of humans as *rational* was entirely misleading. We are far more creatures of will than we are impersonal intellects, but society has ways of making us impotent by surrounding us with moral, political, and religious injunctions. If, like sheep, we acquiesce in "herd morality," we will be nothing but mediocrities. But if we release ourselves by giving free rein to our will to power, we will thereby tap our potentiality for creativity and originality. This is the way of the leaders, the "supermen."

Heidegger (1889–1976).   The subjective experience of being human that was so dramatically expressed by Dostoyevski, Kierkegaard, and Nietzsche developed into a 20th-century method of studying experience that is called phenomenology. Heidegger's phenomenology reminds us that we exist "in the world" and should not try to think of ourselves as beings apart from the world into which we are thrown. The way we fill our everyday life with superficial conversation and routine shows that we often assume we are going to live forever and can afford to waste day after day. Our moods and feelings (including anxiety about death) are a form of understanding whether we are living authentically or whether we are inauthentically constructing our life around the expectations of others. When we translate this wisdom from vague feeling to explicit awareness, we may develop more resolve about how we want to be.

Sartre (1905–1980).   The philosopher and novelist was convinced, in part by his dangerous years in the French Resistance in World War II, that humans are even more free than earlier existentialists had believed. The existence of a space — nothingness — between the whole of our past and the *now* frees us to choose what we will. But this freedom is hard to face up to, so we like to invent excuses: "I'm this way because I was born on the wrong side of the tracks," or "I can't change now because of my past conditioning." Sartre called these excuses, and all others, "bad faith." No matter what I *have* been, I can choose as I will and thus become something quite different. But to choose is to become committed: this is the responsibility that is the other side of freedom.

Buber (1878–1965).   Leaving Germany to live in the new state of Israel, this thinker took a less individualistic stand than most of the other existentialists. He said that we humans live in a kind of *betweenness;* that is, there is never just an I, but always also an other. The *I,* the person who is the agent, changes depending on whether the other is an it or a thou. But sometimes I make the serious mistake of reducing another person to the status of a mere object. In this case I am manipulating him or her and am not taking into account the response, as autonomous as my own, that is forthcoming from the other. This does not mean, however, that for Buber we do not have different roles or degrees of authority in our relations with others. Buber, in a famous dialogue with Carl Rogers, argued that the therapist and client could never be on the same footing, for it is the latter who comes to the former for help. When the relationship is fully mutual, we have become "dialogic," a fully human condition.

THREE EUROPEAN EXISTENTIAL PSYCHIATRISTS

Ludwig Binswanger, Medard Boss, and Viktor Frankl were early figures of the existential practice of psychiatry. Although they cannot be regarded as making up a cohesive ideological school, they believed, in common, that the therapist must enter the client's subjective world without presuppositions that would get in the way of this experiential understanding. Both Binswanger and Boss were very much influenced by the thinking of Heidegger's seminal work, *Being and Time,* which provided a broad basis they sought for understanding the individual (May, 1958).

Binswanger (1975) contended that crises in therapy were typically major choice points for the client. Although he originally looked to psychoanalytic theory to shed light on psychosis, he moved toward an existential view of his patients. This perspective allowed him to understand the world view and immediate experience of his patients, as well as the meaning of their behavior, as opposed to superimposing his view as a therapist on their experience and behavior.

Boss (1963) traveled a similar path. He was deeply influenced by Freudian psychoanalysis but even more so by Heidegger. His major professional interest was applying Heidegger's philosophical notions to therapeutic practice, and he was especially concerned with integrating Freud's methods with Heidegger's concepts, as seen in his book *Daseinanalysis and Psychoanalysis.*

Frankl (1963, 1965, 1969, 1978) does not systematically credit many of the existential philosophers mentioned earlier with influencing his own formulation of existential therapy (*logotherapy*). It is clear, however, that he did not develop his therapeutic perspective in a vacuum and that he was influenced by their writings. He was a student of Freud's, and thus he began his career in psychiatry with a psychoanalytic orientation. Later he was influenced by the writings of existential philosophers, and he began developing his own existential philosophy and psychotherapy. Sprinkled throughout his works are references to Dostoyevski, Nietzsche, Sartre, and Heidegger. He borrows, for example, from Dostoyevski's statement that "there is only one thing that I dread; not to be worthy of my sufferings" (1963, p. 105). He is also fond of quoting Nietzsche's words: "He who has a *why* to live for can bear with almost any *how*" (1963, pp. 121, 164). Frankl contends that those words could be the guiding motto for all psychotherapeutic practice. Another quotation from Nietzsche seems to capture the essence of Frankl's own experience and his writings: "That which does not kill me, makes me stronger" (1963, p. 130).

Frankl reacted against most of Freud's deterministic notions and built his theory and practice of psychotherapy on basic concepts such as freedom, responsibility, meaning in life, and search for values. He developed logotherapy, which means "therapy through meaning." The central theme running through his works is the *will to meaning*. According to Frankl, the modern person has the means to live but often has no meaning to live for. The malady of our time is meaninglessness, or the "existential vacuum" that is often experienced when people do not busy themselves with routine and with work. The therapeutic process is aimed at challenging individuals to find meaning and purpose through, among other things, suffering, work, and love (Frankl, 1965).

AMERICAN EXISTENTIAL THERAPY

The most significant spokesmen for the existential approach in the United States are Rollo May and Irvin Yalom, whose ideas are cited frequently in this chapter. Of primary importance in introducing existential therapy to the country was the book *Existence: A New Dimension in Psychiatry and Psychology* (May, Angel, & Ellenberger, 1958).

May is the psychologist most responsible for translating European existentialism into the mainstream of American psychotherapeutic theory and practice. He cites a number of the philosophers mentioned earlier as having influenced him in developing his existential perspective. Specifically, May credits Heidegger, as the fountainhead of present-day existential thought, with giving existential psychiatrists a deep and broad basis for understanding human nature (1958, p. 15). May also recognizes the contributions of Binswanger and Boss to existential therapy, especially through their emphasis on viewing the client's own private world rather than seeing clients from an objective stance. May's writings reflect this focus on the subjective dimension of therapy. Readers seeking a more detailed historical overview of this movement can consult May (1958).

Yalom's comprehensive textbook, *Existential Psychotherapy* (1980), is considered a pioneering accomplishment. Yalom acknowledges the influence on his own writings of several novelists and philosophers. More specifically, he draws in his book on the following themes from those philosophers discussed earlier:

- from Dostoyevski: creativity, meaninglessness, and death
- from Kierkegaard: creative anxiety, despair, fear and dread, guilt, and nothingness
- from Nietzsche: death, suicide, and will
- from Heidegger: authentic being, caring, death, guilt, individual responsibility, and isolation
- from Sartre: meaninglessness, responsibility, and choice
- from Buber: interpersonal relationships, I/thou perspective in therapy, and self-transcendence

Yalom has not drawn much from Binswanger and Boss, however, because of what he considers to be the abstruse nature of their writings. He sees them as being out of tune with the American pragmatic tradition in therapy. Yet Yalom does recognize Frankl as an eminently pragmatic thinker who has had an impact on his writing and practice.

KEY CONCEPTS

VIEW OF HUMAN NATURE

The crucial significance of the existential movement for psychotherapy is that it reacts against the tendency to identify therapy with a set of techniques. Instead, it bases therapeutic practice on an understanding of what makes men and women *human* beings. The existential movement stands for respect for the person, for exploring new aspects of human behavior, and for divergent methods of understanding people. It uses numerous approaches to therapy based on its assumptions about human nature.

The existential tradition in Europe emphasized the limitations and tragic dimensions of human existence. Existential philosophies provided the foundation for therapeutic approaches that focused on the alienated and fragmented individual who found no meaning in the family or in the social institutions of the time. It grew out of a desire to help people address themes in contemporary life such as isolation, alienation, and meaninglessness. It addressed itself to people who were experiencing difficulty in finding meaning and purpose in life and in maintaining their identity (Holt, 1986).

The current focus of the existential approach is on being in the world alone and facing the anxiety of this isolation. Rather than trying to develop rules for therapy, existential practitioners strive to understand these deep human experiences (May & Yalom, 1989).

The existential view of human nature is captured, in part, by the notion that the significance of our existence is never fixed once and for all; rather, we continually recreate ourselves through our projects. Humans are in a constant state of transition, emerging, evolving, and becoming. Being a person implies that we are discovering and making sense of our existence. As persons we continually question ourselves, others, and the world. Although the specific questions we raise vary in accordance with our developmental stage in life, the fundamental themes do not vary. We pose questions such as "Who am I? Who have I been? Whom can I become? Where am I going?" There are no preexisting designs and no meanings that are assigned or given to us (Fischer & Fischer, 1983).

The basic dimensions of the human condition, according to the existential approach, include (1) the capacity for self-awareness; (2) freedom and responsibility; (3) creating one's identity and establishing meaningful relationships with others; (4) the search for meaning, purpose, values, and goals; (5) anxiety as a condition of living; and (6) awareness of death and nonbeing. I have developed these propositions by summarizing themes that emerge in the writings of existential therapists.

PROPOSITION 1: THE CAPACITY FOR SELF-AWARENESS

As human beings we can reflect and make choices because we are capable of self-awareness. The greater our awareness, the greater our possibilities for freedom (see Proposition 2).

Thus, to expand our awareness is to increase our capacity to live fully. We become aware that:

- We are finite, and we do not have an unlimited time to do what we want with our life.
- We have the potential to take action or not to act inaction is a decision.
- We choose our actions, and therefore we can partially create our own destiny.
- Meaning is not automatically bestowed on us but is the product of our searching and of our creating a unique purpose.
- Existential anxiety, which is basically a consciousness of our own freedom, is an essential part of living; as we increase our awareness of the choices available to us, we also increase our sense of responsibility for the consequences of these choices.
- We are subject to loneliness, meaninglessness, emptiness, guilt, and isolation.
- We are basically alone, yet we have an opportunity to relate to other beings.

PROPOSITION 2: FREEDOM AND RESPONSIBILITY

A characteristic theme of existential literature is that people are free to choose among alternatives and therefore have a large role in shaping their destinies. Even though we have no choice about being thrust into the world, the manner in which we live and what we become are the result of our choices. Because of the reality of this essential freedom, we must accept the responsibility for directing our lives. However, it is possible to avoid this reality by making excuses for whom we are becoming. In speaking about "bad faith," Sartre (1971) refers to the inauthenticity of not accepting personal responsibility.

Examples of statements of bad faith are "Since that's the way I'm made, I couldn't help what I did." Or "Naturally I'm this way, because I grew up in an alcoholic family." For Sartre we are constantly confronted with the choice of what kind of person we are becoming, and to exist is never to be finished with this kind of choosing.

We are entirely responsible for our lives, for our actions, and for our failures to take action. From Sartre's perspective people are condemned to freedom. He called for a *commitment* to choosing for ourselves. Existential guilt is being aware of having evaded a commitment, or having chosen not to choose. This is the guilt we experience when we do not live authentically. It results from allowing others to define us or to make our choices for us. Sartre said "We are our choices." An inauthentic mode of existence consists of lacking awareness of personal responsibility for our lives and passively assuming that our existence is largely controlled by external forces. By contrast, living authentically implies being true to our own evaluation of what is a valuable existence for ourselves.

For existentialists, then, being free and being human are identical. Freedom and responsibility go hand in hand. We are the authors of our lives in the sense that we create our destiny, our life situation, and our problems (Russell, 1978). Assuming responsibility is a basic condition for change. Clients who refuse to accept responsibility by persistently blaming others for their problems will not profit from therapy.

Frankl (1978) also links freedom with responsibility. He has suggested that the Statue of Liberty on the East Coast be supplemented by a Statue of Responsibility on the West Coast. His basic premise is that freedom is bound by certain limitations, because we are not free from conditions. But our freedom consists of taking a stand against such restrictions. Ultimately, these conditions are subject to our decisions. We are responsible.

PROPOSITION 3: STRIVING FOR IDENTITY AND RELATIONSHIP TO OTHERS

People are concerned about preserving their uniqueness and centeredness, yet at the same time they have an interest in going outside of themselves to relate to other beings and to nature. Each of us would like to discover a self—that is, to find (or create) our personal identity. This is not an automatic process, and it takes courage. Being relational beings, we also strive for a connectedness with others. We must give of ourselves to others and be concerned with them. Many existential writers discuss loneliness, uprootedness, and alienation, which can be seen as the failure to develop ties with others and with nature.

The trouble with so many of us is that we have sought directions, answers, values, and beliefs from the important people in our world. Rather than trusting ourselves to search within and find our own answers to the conflicts in our life, we sell out by becoming what others expect of us. Our being becomes rooted in their being, and we become strangers to ourselves.

The courage to be.   It does take courage to discover our core and to learn how to live from the inside (Tillich, 1952). We struggle to discover, to create, and to maintain the core deep within our being. One of the greatest fears of clients is that they will discover that there is no core, no self, and no substance and that they are merely reflections of everyone's expectations of them. A client may say: "My fear is that I'll discover I'm nobody, that there really is nothing to me. I'll find out that I'm an empty shell, hollow inside, and nothing will exist if I shed my masks."

Existential therapists may begin by asking their clients to allow themselves to intensify the feeling that they are nothing more than the sum of others' expectations and that they are merely the introjects of parents and parent substitutes. How do they feel now? Are they condemned to stay this way forever? Is there a way out? Can they create a self if they find that they are without one? Where can they begin? Once clients have demonstrated the courage to simply recognize this fear, to put it into words and share it, it does not seem so overwhelming. I find that it is best to begin work by inviting clients to accept the ways in which they have lived outside themselves and to explore ways in which they are out of center with themselves.

The experience of aloneness.   The existentialists postulate that part of the human condition is the experience of aloneness. But they add that we can derive strength from the experience of looking to ourselves and sensing our separation. The sense of isolation comes when we recognize that we cannot depend on anyone else for our own confirmation; that is, we alone must give a sense of meaning to our life, and we alone must decide how we will live. If we are unable to tolerate ourselves when we are alone, how can we expect anyone else to be enriched by our company? Before we can have any solid relationship with another, we must have a relationship with ourselves. We must learn to listen to ourselves. We have to be able to stand alone before we can truly stand beside another.

There is a paradox in the proposition that humans are existentially both alone and related, but this very paradox describes the human condition. To think that we can cure the condition, or that it should be cured, is a mistake. Ultimately we are alone.

The experience of relatedness.   We humans depend on relationships with others. We want to be significant in another's world, and we want to feel that another's presence is important in our world. When we are able to stand alone and dip within ourselves for our own strength, our relationships with others are based on our fulfillment, not our deprivation. If we feel personally deprived, however, we can expect little but a clinging, parasitic, symbiotic relationship with someone else.

Perhaps one of the functions of therapy is to help clients distinguish between a neurotically dependent attachment to another and a therapeutic relationship in which both persons are enhanced. The therapist can challenge clients to examine what they get from their relationships, how they avoid intimate contact, how they prevent themselves from having equal relationships, and how they might create therapeutic, healthy, and mature human relationships.

PROPOSITION 4: THE SEARCH FOR MEANING

A distinctly human characteristic is the struggle for a sense of significance and purpose in life. In my experience the underlying conflicts that bring people into counseling and therapy are centered in the existential questions "Why am I here? What do I want from life? What gives my life purpose? Where is the source of meaning for me in life?"

Existential therapy can provide the conceptual framework for helping the client challenge the meaning in his or her life. Questions that the therapist might ask are "Do you like the direction of your life? Are you pleased with what you now are and what you are becoming? Are you actively doing anything to become closer to your self-ideal? Do you even know what you want? If you are confused about who you are and what you want for yourself, what are you doing to get some clarity?"

The problem of discarding old values.   One of the problems in therapy is that clients may discard traditional values (and imposed values) without finding other, suitable ones to replace them. What does the therapist do when clients no longer cling to values that they never really challenged or internalized and now experience a vacuum? They report that they feel like a boat without a rudder. They seek new guidelines and values that are appropriate for newly discovered facets of themselves, and yet for a time they are without them. Perhaps the task of the therapeutic process is to help clients create a value system based on a way of living that is consistent with their way of being.

The therapist's job might well be to trust the capacity of clients to eventually discover an internally derived value system that does provide a meaningful life. They will no doubt flounder for a time and experience anxiety as a result of the absence of clear-cut values. The therapist's trust in them is important in teaching them to trust their own capacity to discover a new source of values.

Meaninglessness.   When the world they live in seems meaningless, clients may wonder whether it is worth it to continue struggling or even living. Faced with the prospect of our mortality, we might ask: "Is there any point to what I do now, since I will eventually die? Will what I do be forgotten once I am gone? Given the fact of mortality, why should I busy myself with anything?" A man in one of my groups captured precisely the idea of personal significance when he said "I feel like another page in a book that has been turned quickly, and nobody bothered to read the page." For Frankl (1978) such a feeling of meaninglessness is the major existential neurosis of modern life.

Creating new meaning.   Logotherapy is designed to help the person find a meaning in life. Challenging the meaning in life is a mark of being human. "The will to meaning" is the individual's primary striving. Life is not meaningful in itself; the individual must create and discover meaning (Frankl, 1978). This project of creating our own meaning cannot be completed as long as we exist.

The therapist's function is not to tell clients what their particular meaning in life should be but to point out that they can discover meaning even in suffering

(Frankl, 1978). This view does not share the pessimistic flavor that some people find in existential philosophy. It holds that human suffering (the tragic and negative aspects of life) can be turned into human achievement by the stand an individual takes in the face of suffering. Frankl also contends that people can face pain, guilt, despair, and death and, in the confrontation, challenge the despair and thus triumph. Yet meaning is not something that we can directly search for and obtain. Paradoxically, the more rationally we seek it, the more we are likely to miss it. Yalom (1980) and Frankl are in basic agreement on the point that, like pleasure, meaning must be pursued obliquely. Finding meaning in life is a by-product of *engagement,* which is a commitment to creating, loving, working, and building.

PROPOSITION 5: ANXIETY AS A CONDITION OF LIVING

Arising from one's personal strivings to survive and to maintain and assert one's being, anxiety must be confronted as an inevitable part of the human condition. Existential therapists differentiate between normal and neurotic anxiety, and they see anxiety as a potential source of growth. Normal anxiety is an appropriate response to an event being faced. Further, this kind of anxiety does not have to be repressed, and it can be used as a motivation to change. Neurotic anxiety, in contrast, is out of proportion to the situation. It is typically out of awareness, and it tends to immobilize the person. Because we could not survive without some anxiety, it is not the therapeutic task to eliminate normal anxiety. Being psychologically healthy entails living with as little neurotic anxiety as possible while accepting and struggling with normal anxiety that is a part of living. Life cannot be lived, nor can death be faced, without anxiety (May & Yalom, 1989).

One constructive form of normal anxiety, existential anxiety, can be a stimulus for growth in that we experience it as we become increasingly aware of our freedom and the consequences of accepting or rejecting that freedom. In fact, when we make a decision that involves reconstruction of our life, the accompanying anxiety can be a signal that we are ready for personal change. The signal is constructive, for it tells us that all is not well. If we learn to listen to the subtle messages of anxiety, we can dare to take steps necessary to change the direction of our life.

Many clients who seek counseling want solutions that will enable them to eliminate anxiety. Although attempts to avoid anxiety by creating the illusion that there is security in life may help us cope with the unknown, we really know on some level that we are deceiving ourselves when we think we have found fixed security. We can blunt anxiety by constricting our life and thus reducing choices. Opening up to new life, however, means opening up to anxiety, and we pay a steep price when we short-circuit anxiety.

People who have the courage to face themselves are, nonetheless, frightened. I am convinced that those who are willing to live with their anxiety for a time are the ones who profit from personal therapy. Those who flee too quickly into comfortable patterns might experience a temporary relief but in the long run seem to experience the frustration of being stuck in their old ways.

According to May (1981) freedom and anxiety are two sides of the same coin; anxiety is associated with the excitement accompanying the birth of a new idea. Thus, we experience anxiety when we use our freedom to move out of the known into the realm of the unknown. Out of fear, many of us try to avoid taking such a leap into the unknown. As May puts it: "We can escape the anxiety only by not venturing — that is, by surrendering our freedom. I am convinced that many people never become aware of their most creative ideas since their inspirations are blocked off by this anxiety before the ideas even reach the level of consciousness" (1981, p. 191).

PROPOSITION 6: AWARENESS OF DEATH AND NONBEING

The existentialist does not view death negatively but holds that awareness of death as a basic human condition gives significance to living. A distinguishing human characteristic is the ability to grasp the reality of the future and the inevitability of death. It is necessary to think about death if we are to think significantly about life. If we defend ourselves against the reality of our eventual death, life becomes insipid and meaningless. But if we realize we are mortal, we know that we do not have an eternity to complete our projects and that the present moment is crucial. Our awareness of death is the source of zest for life and creativity (May, 1981). Death and life are interdependent, and though physical death destroys us, the idea of death saves us (Yalom, 1980).

The recognition of death plays a significant role in psychotherapy, for it can be the factor that helps us transform a stale mode of living into a more authentic one (Yalom, 1980). Thus, one focus in existential therapy is on exploring the degree to which clients are doing the things they value. Without being morbidly preoccupied by the ever-present threat of nonbeing, clients can develop a healthy awareness of death as a way to evaluate how well they are living and what changes they want to make in their life.

The fear of death and the fear of life are related. The fear of death looms over those of us who are afraid to outstretch our arms and fully embrace life. If we affirm life and attempt to live in the present as fully as possible, however, we are not obsessed with the termination of life. Those of us who fear death also fear life, as though we were saying "I fear death because I have never really lived."

Because some of us are afraid of facing the reality of our own death, we might attempt to escape the fact of our eventual nonbeing. When we do try to flee from the confrontation with nothingness, however, we must pay a price. As May puts it, "The price for denying death is undefined anxiety, self-alienation" (1961, p. 65).

THE THERAPEUTIC PROCESS

THERAPEUTIC GOALS

A basic goal of many therapeutic systems is enabling individuals to accept the awesome freedom to act and the responsibility for their action. Existentialism holds that there is no escape from freedom, in the sense that we can always be held responsible. We can relinquish our freedom, however, which is the ultimate inauthenticity. Existential therapy seeks to take clients out of their rigid grooves and to challenge their narrow and compulsive trends, which are blocking their freedom. Although this process gives individuals a sense of release and increased autonomy, the new freedom does bring about anxiety. Freedom is a venture down new pathways, and there is no certainty about where these paths will lead. The "dizziness" and dread of freedom must be confronted if growth is to occur (May, 1981). Many fear the weight of being responsible for who they are now and whom they are becoming. They must choose, for example, whether to cling to the known and the familiar or to risk opening themselves to a less certain and more challenging life. The lack of guarantees in life is precisely what generates anxiety. Thus, existential therapy helps clients face the anxiety of choosing for themselves and accepting the reality that they are more than mere victims of deterministic forces outside themselves. The aim is to enable clients to engage in action that is based on the authentic purpose of creating a worthy existence.

Existential therapy is best considered as an invitation to clients to recognize the ways in which they are not living fully authentic lives and to make choices that will lead to their becoming what they are capable of being. This approach does not focus on curing sickness or merely applying problem-solving techniques to the complex task of authentic living Bugental (1987) writes about life-changing psychotherapy, which is the effort to help clients examine the manner in which they have answered life's existential questions and to challenge them to revise some of their answers in ways that will result in living authentically.

May contends that people come to therapy with the self-serving illusion that they are inwardly enslaved and that someone else (the therapist) can free them. Thus, "The purpose of psychotherapy is not to 'cure' the clients in the conventional sense, but to help them become aware of what they are doing and to get them out of the victim role" (1981, p. 210). The task of existential therapy is to teach clients to listen to what they already know about themselves, even though they may not be attending to what they know. Therapy is a process of bringing out the latent aliveness in the client (Bugental 1986).

The following letter was written by one of my former clients and is presented here with her consent. Her words describe vividly her struggles with awareness, freedom, and responsibility and the anxiety she feels in making daily decisions regarding the way she wants to lead her life.

> Often now I find myself struggling deep within me with who I really am as a person and how I really feel. Emotions don't come easily to me even now. Feelings of love and hate are new to me, and often very scary. Many times I find it hard to reconcile myself to the fact that sometimes I can miss someone I care about one moment and then wish that they would go away the next. This inconsistency in myself, this dependency/independency struggle, is confusing to me at times. Sometimes I think that I would have been better off if I had remained as emotionally dead as I once was. At least then I didn't hurt so much. But I also know that I wasn't fully alive then either.
>
> Today a man embraced me and I felt very warm and safe for a little while. I

like that feeling, and yet I fear it, too. It's so alien to me. I want to trust, and yet I still find it difficult to do so. Perhaps it's because there's always an element of risk involved in any relationship, and I still won't allow myself to accept that risk. I worry about whether I will ever be able to overcome all the old hurts and disappointments and learn to live for today.

Occasionally, when I'm feeling especially alone and lost, I try to imagine what it would be like if I had never entered counseling, if I had never acquired the self-insight that I now have. Or what it would be like if I could magically return in time to an earlier stage of my emotional growth when I felt less threatened, and be able to stay there. I saw no beauty in the world then, and I knew no success, nor did I have much peace of mind, but I felt safer then. The pressures that I live with now didn't exist. It was a simpler, less challenging time for me. And yet if I were magically given the ability to go back, I know that I wouldn't. I'm not always sure where I'm going these days, but I do know where I've been, and I would never knowingly choose to return to what I once was again. I've come too far to go back now. And yet sometimes I still wonder if it's all been worth it.

THERAPIST'S FUNCTION AND ROLE

Existential therapists are primarily concerned with understanding the subjective world of the client in order to help that person come to new understandings and options. The focus is on the client's current life situation, not on helping clients recover a personal past (May & Yalom, 1989). Typically, existential therapists show wide latitude in the methods they employ, varying not only from client to client but also with the same client at different phases of the therapeutic process. On the one hand, they may make use of techniques such as desensitization, free association, or cognitive restructuring, and they may draw insights from therapists of other orientations. No set of techniques is specified or essential (Fischer & Fischer, 1983). On the other hand, some existential therapists abhor techniques, seeing them as suggesting rigidity, routine, and manipulation. Throughout the therapeutic process techniques are secondary to the establishing of a relationship that will enable the counselor to effectively challenge and understand the client. Existential therapists are especially concerned about the client's avoiding responsibility; they invite clients to accept personal responsibility. If clients say "I can't," for example, they will be asked to substitute "I won't." When clients complain about the predicaments they are in and blame others, the therapist is likely to ask them how they created the situation they are in.

Therapists with an existential orientation usually deal with people who have what could be called a *restricted existence*. These clients have a limited awareness of themselves and are often vague about the nature of their problems. They may see few if any options to limited ways of dealing with life situations, and they tend to feel trapped or helpless. A central task of the therapist is to directly confront these clients with the ways they are living a restricted existence and to help them become aware of their own part in creating this condition. Therapists may hold up a mirror, so to speak, so that clients can gradually engage in self-confrontation. In this way clients can see how they got the way they are and how they might enlarge the way they live. By becoming aware of factors in their past and of stifling modes of their present existence, they can begin to accept responsibility for changing their future.

For an example of what an existentially oriented therapist might actually do in a therapeutic session, refer again to the letter of my former client. If this client were to express her feelings to a therapist in a session, the therapist might:

- share his or her own personal reactions to what the client is saying
- engage in some relevant and appropriate personal disclosure of experiences similar to those of the client
- ask the client to express her anguish over the necessity to choose in an uncertain world
- challenge her to look at all the ways in which she is avoiding decisions and to make a judgment concerning this avoidance
- share with her that she is learning that her experience is precisely the unique quality of being human: that she is ultimately alone, that she must decide for herself, that she will experience anxiety over not being sure of her decisions, and that she will have to struggle to define her own meaning in a world that often appears meaningless

CLIENT'S EXPERIENCE IN THERAPY

In existential therapy clients are clearly encouraged to take seriously their own subjective experience of their world. They are challenged to take responsibility for how they *now* choose to be in their world. Effective therapy does not stop with this awareness itself, for the therapist encourages clients to take action on the basis of the insights they develop through the therapeutic process. Clients are expected to go out into the world and decide *how* they will live differently. Further, they must be active in the therapeutic process, for during the sessions they must decide what fears, guilts, and anxieties they will explore. Merely deciding to enter psychotherapy is itself often a scary prospect, as indicated by the notes one of my clients kept for herself during the period of her therapy. Sense the anxiety that she experienced as she chose to leave security and embark on a search for herself:

> I started private therapy today. I was terrified, but I didn't know of what. Now I do. First of all, I was terrified of Jerry himself. He has the power to change me. I'm giving him that power, and I can't go back. That's what's really upsetting me. I can't go back ever. Nothing is the same. . . . I don't know myself yet, only to know that nothing is the same. I'm sad and scared of this. I've sandblasted security right out of my life, and I'm really frightened of who I'll become. I'm sad that I can't go back. I've opened the door into myself, and I'm terrified of what's there, of coping with a new me, of seeing and relating to people differently. I guess I have free-floating anxiety about everything, but most specifically I'm afraid of myself.

In essence, clients in existential therapy are engaged in opening the doors to themselves. The experience is often frightening, exciting, joyful, depressing, or a combination of all of these. As clients wedge open the closed doors, they also begin to loosen the deterministic shackles that have kept them psychologically bound. Gradually, they become aware of what they have been and who they are now, and they are better able to decide what kind of future they want. Through the process of their therapy they can explore alternatives for making their visions become real.

When clients plead helplessness and attempt to convince themselves that they are powerless, May (1981) reminds them that their journey toward freedom begins by putting one foot in front of the other to get to his office. As minute as their range of freedom may be, they can begin building and augmenting that range by taking initial steps.

Another aspect of the experience of being a client in existential therapy is the confronting of ultimate concerns rather than coping with immediate problems. On this issue May writes: "The major experiences such as birth, death, love, anxiety, guilt are not problems to be solved, but paradoxes to be confronted and acknowledged. Thus in therapy we should talk of solving problems only as a way of making the paradoxes of life stand out more clearly" (1981, p. 67). Some major themes of the therapy sessions are anxiety, freedom and responsibility, isolation, alienation, death and its implications for living, and the continual search for meaning.

RELATIONSHIP BETWEEN THERAPIST AND CLIENT

Existential therapists give central prominence to their relationship with the client. The relationship is important in itself, not because it promotes transference. The quality of this person-to-person encounter in the therapeutic situation is the stimulus for positive change. Therapists with this orientation believe that their basic attitudes toward the client and their own personal characteristics of honesty, integrity, and courage are what they have to offer. Therapy is a journey taken by therapist and client, a journey that delves deeply into the world as perceived and experienced by the client. But this type of quest demands that therapists also be in contact with their own phenomenological world. Buber's (1970) conception of the I/thou relationship has significant implications here. It is all too easy for counselors to smile and nod without really listening and attending. Many clients will sense this absence, or lack of presence, and it will negatively affect the relationship.

Therapists share their reactions to clients with genuine concern and empathy, as one way of deepening the therapeutic relationship. Bugental emphasizes the crucial role that the *presence* of the therapist plays in this relationship. In his view many therapists and therapeutic systems overlook its fundamental importance. He contends that therapists are too often so concerned with the content of what is being said that they are not aware of the distance between themselves and their clients. His view differs from the conception of the therapist as a skilled and objective director of the therapeutic venture: "The therapeutic alliance is the powerful joining of forces which energizes and supports the long, difficult, and frequently painful work of life-changing psychotherapy. The conception of the therapist here is not of a disinterested observer-technician but of a fully alive human companion for the client" (1987, p. 49).

May and Yalom (1989) also stress the crucial role of the therapist's capacity to *be there* for clients during the therapy hour, which includes being fully present and intensely involved with the clients. They caution that if therapists feel removed from their clients and look forward to the end of the hour, they are failing to achieve the authentic encounter that their clients so urgently require. The counselor guides the client toward engagement with others by first relating deeply with the client (Yalom, 1980).

The core of the therapeutic relationship is respect, which implies faith in clients' potential to cope authentically with their troubles and in their ability to discover alternative ways of being. The therapist helps clients understand how they, along with circumstances, have restricted their existence. Clients eventually come to view themselves as active and responsible for their existence, whereas before therapy they were likely to see themselves as helpless. They eventually develop an increased ability to accept and confront the freedom they possess.

Sidney Jourard (1971) urges therapists to invite the client to embrace authenticity through their own authentic and self-disclosing behavior. Jourard asks that therapists work toward a relationship of I and thou, in which their spontaneous self-disclosure fosters growth in the client. As he puts it, "Manipulation begets counter-manipulation. Self-disclosure begets self-disclosure" (p. 142). He also points out that the therapeutic relationship can change the therapist as much as it does the client. "This means that those who wish to leave their being and their growth unchanged should not become therapists" (p. 150).

Therapists thus invite clients to grow by modeling authentic behavior. They are able to be transparent when it is appropriate in the relationship, and their own humanity is a stimulus for the client to tap potentials for realness. Jourard contends that if therapists keep themselves hidden during the therapeutic session or if they engage in inauthentic behavior, clients will also remain guarded and persist in their inauthentic ways. Thus, therapists can help clients become less of a stranger to themselves by selectively disclosing their own responses at appropriate times. Of course, this disclosure does not imply an uncensored sharing of every fleeting feeling or thought. Rather, it implies a willingness to share persistent reactions with clients, especially when this sharing is likely to be facilitative.

APPLICATION: THERAPEUTIC TECHNIQUES AND PROCEDURES

As we have seen, the existential approach is unlike most other therapies in that it does not have a well-defined set of techniques. Its eclecticism can include drawing on some psychoanalytic concepts and techniques, as does Bugental (1978, 1981, 1987). It can also incorporate techniques from the cognitive-behavioral therapies. As Baldwin (1987) has written, the use of the therapist's self is the core of therapy. It is in the I/thou encounter, when the deepest self of the therapist meets with the deepest part of the client, that the therapeutic process is at its best. Therapy is a creative, evolving discovery of oneself, which emerges from the trusting bond and meaningful collaboration between the client and therapist.

As one of my colleagues, Don Polkinghorne, points out, existential counselors are not eclectic in the sense of being nontheoretical and guided by the pragmatic criterion of "doing whatever works." Instead, their interventions are based on a philosophical framework. Polkinghorne (personal communication) emphasizes that existential therapy is distinguished by its understanding that the human task is to create an existence characterized by integrity and meaning.

There are three phases in the process of existential counseling. During the initial phase the counselor assists clients in identifying and clarifying their assumptions about the world. Clients are invited to define and question the ways in which they perceive and make sense of their existence. They examine their values, beliefs, and assumptions to determine their validity. For many clients this is a difficult task, because they may initially present their problems as resulting almost entirely from external causes. They may focus on what other people "make them feel" or how others are largely responsible for their action or inaction. The counselor teaches them how to reflect on their own existence and to examine their role in creating their problems in living.

During the middle phase of existential counseling clients are encouraged to more fully examine the source and authority of their value system. This process of self-exploration typically leads to new insights and some restructuring of their values and attitudes. Clients get a better sense of what kind of life they consider worthy. They develop a clearer idea of their internal valuing process.

The final phase of existential counseling focuses on helping clients put what they are learning about themselves into action. The aim of therapy is to enable clients to find ways of applying their examined and internalized values in a concrete way. Clients typically discover their strengths and find ways to put them to the service of living a purposeful existence.

From the existential perspective techniques are viewed as tools to help clients become aware of their choices and accept the responsibility that accompanies the use of their personal freedom. This section deals with the counseling implications of the six major existential propositions developed earlier in the chapter.

1. THE CAPACITY FOR SELF-AWARENESS: COUNSELING IMPLICATIONS

Awareness can be conceptualized in the following way: Picture yourself walking down a long hallway with many doors on each side. Let yourself imagine that you can choose to open some of the doors, either a crack or fully, or to leave them closed. Perhaps if you opened one of the doors, you would not like what you saw — it might be fearsome or ugly. But you might also discover a room filled with beauty. You might debate with yourself whether to leave a door shut or attempt to pry it open.

We can choose to either expand or restrict our consciousness. Because self-awareness is at the root of most other human capacities, the decision to expand it is fundamental to human growth. What follows is a list of some dawning awarenesses that individuals experience in the counseling process:

- They see how they are trading the security of dependence for the anxieties that accompany choosing for themselves.
- They begin to see that their identity is anchored in someone else's definition of them; that is, they are seeking approval and confirmation of their being in others instead of looking to themselves for affirmation.
- They learn that in many ways they are keeping themselves prisoner by some of their past decisions, and they realize that they can make new decisions.
- They learn that although they cannot change certain events in their lives, they can change the way they view and react to these events.
- They learn that they are not condemned to a future similar to the past, for they can learn from their past and thereby reshape their future.
- They realize that they are so preoccupied with death and dying that they are not appreciating living.
- They are able to accept their limitations yet still feel worthwhile, for they understand that they do not need to be perfect to feel worthy.
- They can come to realize that they are failing to live in the present moment because of preoccupation with the past, or planning for the future, or trying to do too many things at once.

Increasing self-awareness, which includes awareness of alternatives, motivations, factors influencing the person, and personal goals, is an aim of all counseling. It is the therapist's task to indicate to the client that a price must be paid for increased awareness. As one becomes more aware, one finds it more difficult to "go home again." Ignorance of one's condition may have brought contentment along with a feeling of partial deadness, but as one opens the doors in one's world, one can expect more struggle as well as the potential for more fulfillment.

2. FREEDOM AND RESPONSIBILITY: COUNSELING IMPLICATIONS

What are the counseling implications of the existential position of linking responsibility to the choices one makes as the designer of one's life? Existential therapists continually focus on clients' responsibility for their situation. They will not allow clients to blame others, to blame external forces, or to blame heredity. If clients do not recognize and accept their responsibility for having created their situation, there is little motivation for them to commit themselves to personal change (May & Yalom 1989; Yalom, 1980).

The therapist assists clients in discovering how they are avoiding freedom and encourages them to learn to risk using it. Not to do so is to cripple clients and make them neurotically dependent on the therapist. Therapists need to teach clients that they can explicitly accept the fact that they have choices, even though they may have devoted most of their life to evading them.

People often come to counselors because they feel that they have lost control of how they are living. They may look to the counselor to direct them, give them advice, or produce magical cures. They may also need to be heard and understood. Two central tasks of the therapist are inviting clients to recognize how they have allowed others to decide for them and encouraging them to take steps toward autonomy. In challenging clients to explore other ways of being that are more fulfilling than their present restricted existence, existential counselors can ask "Although you have lived in a certain pattern, now that you recognize the price of some of your ways, are you willing to consider creating new patterns?" Others may have a vested interest in keeping the client in an old pattern, so the initiative for changing it will have to come from the client.

3. STRIVING FOR IDENTITY AND RELATIONSHIP TO OTHERS: COUNSELING IMPLICATIONS

People who seek therapy are frequently troubled over a sense of loss of self or of being strangers to themselves. They may say that they have lost internal direction, for they are caught up in living a life designed by others. In their attempt to please others and win approval, they often find that they neither win acceptance nor feel self-accepting.

In the process of basing our identity on what others say, we actually become strangers to ourselves. This inauthentic existence consists of "selling out" by becoming what others expect us to become. An inauthentic existence involves playing status-seeking games to gain applause for a life performance. One important lesson for many clients is that they have indeed paid a steep price for striving to play this performance. Not only do they lose contact with themselves, but they also lose any meaningful basis for developing intense or satisfying relationships with others.

The awareness of our ultimate aloneness, like the awareness of our death and our freedom, can be frightening. Just as many shrink from accepting freedom and responsibility out of fear of the risks involved, some may attempt to avoid accepting their aloneness and isolation.

Part of the therapeutic journey consists of therapists' challenging their clients to begin to examine the ways in which they have lost touch with their identity, especially by letting others design their life for them. The therapy process itself is often frightening for clients when they realize that they have surrendered their freedom to others and that in the therapy relationship they will have to assume it back. By refusing to give easy solutions or answers, therapists thus confront clients with the reality that they alone must find their own answers.

4. THE SEARCH FOR MEANING: COUNSELING IMPLICATIONS

The existential therapist tends to think more of restricted existence as a condition that brings people into therapy, rather than of sickness and psychopathology. People who lead a restricted life have only limited self-awareness; many of their potentials are locked up; they find life dull and meaningless; and they often wonder if this is all there is to life. Meaninglessness in life leads to emptiness and hollowness, or a condition that Frankl calls the existential vacuum. At times people who feel trapped by the emptiness of their life withdraw from the struggle of creating a life with purpose. Because there is no preordained design for living, people are faced with the task of creating their own meaning. The issues of experiencing meaninglessness and establishing values that are a part of a meaningful life may well be taken up in counseling.

Related to the concept of meaninglessness is what existential practitioners call existential guilt. This is a condition that grows out of a sense of incompleteness, or a realization that one is not what one might have become. It is the awareness that one's actions and choices express less than one's full range as a person. When one neglects certain potentialities, there is a sense of this existential guilt. This guilt is not viewed as neurotic, nor is it seen as a symptom that needs to be cured. Instead, the existential therapist explores it to see what clients can learn about the ways in which they are living their life. And it can be used to challenge the meaning and direction of life.

5. ANXIETY AS A CONDITION OF LIVING: COUNSELING IMPLICATIONS

Existential anxiety is the sense of uneasiness we experience when we become aware that we are accountable to ourselves for what we make out of our own existence. Because existential anxiety makes us uncomfortable and because the weight of personal responsibility is heavy, we have a tendency to avoid this anxiety and deny the responsibility for what we are becoming. Although we have developed coping strategies to deal with anxiety, these strategies often do not hold up when we face crises of living. Most people seek professional help when their attempts to cope with anxiety no longer work. Often clients enter a counseling office with the expectation that the counselor will remove their suffering or at least provide some formula for the reduction of their anxiety. The existentially oriented counselor is not, however, devoted to mere removal of symptoms or to anxiety reduction per se. In fact, existential counselors do not view anxiety as undesirable. They may work in such a way that the client experiences increased levels of anxiety for a time. Some questions that can be posed are: How is the client coping with anxiety? Is the anxiety a function of growth, or is it a function of clinging to neurotic behaviors? Is the anxiety in proportion to the threat to the client's well-being? Does the client demonstrate the courage to experience the anxiety of the unknown?

Anxiety is the material for productive therapy sessions. If clients experience no anxiety, their motivation for change will be low. Anxiety can be transformed into the needed energy for enduring the risks of experimenting with new behavior. Thus, the existentially oriented therapist can help the client recognize that learning how to tolerate ambiguity and uncertainty and how to live without props can be a necessary phase in the journey from living dependently to becoming a more autonomous person. The therapist and client can explore the possibility that although breaking away from crippling patterns and building new lifestyles will be fraught with anxiety for a while, anxiety will diminish as the client experiences more satisfaction with newer ways of being.

When clients become more self-confident, their anxiety that results from an expectation of catastrophe becomes less.

6. AWARENESS OF DEATH AND NONBEING: COUNSELING IMPLICATIONS

Dying and living are intertwined. In order to grow we must be willing to let go of some of our past. Parts of us must die if new dimensions of our being are to emerge. We cannot cling to the neurotic aspects of our past and at the same time expect a more creative side of us to flourish.

One group technique that I have found useful is to ask people to fantasize themselves in the same room with the same people ten years later. I ask them to imagine that they have not followed through with their decisions and that they have failed to accept opportunities to change themselves in ways they said they most wanted to change. They are to imagine that they have not faced the parts of themselves they fear, that they have not carried out their projects, and that they have chosen to remain as they are rather than to take risks. Then I ask them to talk about their life as if they knew they were going to die. This exercise can mobilize clients to take seriously the time they have, and it can jar them into accepting the possibility that they could accept a zombielike existence in place of a fuller life.

SUMMARY AND EVALUATION

SUMMARY

As humans, according to the existentialist view, we are capable of self-aware-ness, which is the distinctive capacity that allows us to reflect and to decide. With this awareness we become free beings who are responsible for choosing the way we live, and we thus influence our own destiny. This awareness of freedom and responsibility gives rise to existential anxiety, which is another basic human characteristic. Whether we like it or not, we are free, even though we may seek to avoid reflecting on this freedom. The knowledge that we must choose, even though the outcome is not certain, leads to anxiety. This anxiety is heightened when we reflect on the reality that we are mortal beings. Facing the inevitable prospect of eventual death gives the present moment significance, for we become aware that we do not have forever to accomplish our projects. Our task is to create a life that has meaning and purpose. As humans we are unique in that we strive toward fashioning purposes and values that give mean-ing to living. Whatever meaning our life has is developed through freedom and a commitment to make choices in the face of uncertainty.

Existential therapy places central prominence on the person-to-person re-lationship. It assumes that client growth occurs through this genuine en-counter. It is not the techniques a therapist uses that make a therapeutic differ-ence; rather, it is the quality of the client/therapist relationship that heals.

Because this approach is basically concerned with matters such as the goals of therapy, basic conditions of being human, and therapy as a shared journey, practitioners are not bound by specific techniques. Although they can apply techniques from other orientations, their interventions are guided by a philosophical framework about what it means to be human. They do not employ a set of unintegrated techniques and procedures based on different assumptions about the essential nature of human existence.

CONTRIBUTIONS OF THE EXISTENTIAL APPROACH

The existential approach has helped bring the person back into central focus. It has shown that people are constantly in the process of becoming. It has focused sharply on the central facts of human existence: self-consciousness and the consequent freedom. To the existentialists goes the credit for providing a new view of death as a positive force, not a morbid prospect to fear, for death gives life its meaning. The existentialists have contributed a new dimension to the understanding of anxiety, guilt, frustration, loneliness, and alienation.

In my judgment one of the major contributions of the existential approach is its stress on the human quality of the therapeutic relationship. This emphasis lessens the chances of dehumanizing psychotherapy by making it a mechanical process. Also, I find the philosophy underlying existential therapy exciting. I particularly like the emphasis on freedom and responsibility and the person's capacity to redesign his or her life by choosing with awareness. From my viewpoint this perspective provides a sound philosophical base on which to build a personal and unique style of the practice of therapy because it addresses itself to the core struggles of the contemporary person.

The existential tenets have something to offer clinicians regardless of their theoretical orientation. Rejecting the notion that an existential orientation "offers a license for improvisation, for undisciplined woolly therapists to 'do their thing,' " Yalom (1980) concludes that "the existential approach is a valuable, effective psychotherapeutic paradigm, as rational, as coherent, and as systematic as any other" (p. 5). He further contends that the existential approach offers therapists a system to explain an array of clinical data and to formulate a systematic strategy for the therapeutic process. He sees this model as possessing several advantages: it is parsimonious (has few basic assumptions); it is accessible (the assumptions are based on data that people can perceive through looking at their own experience); and it is a humanistically based model consistent with the values of the therapeutic endeavor. Despite these contributions Yalom readily admits that it is best to consider it as *a* paradigm, rather than *the* paradigm; it is useful for many clients but not for all populations, and it can be employed successfully by some therapists but not by all. I agree with his view. Human beings are too complex to be fully understood by way of one avenue.

Areas of application.   What problems are most amenable to an existential approach? For which populations is existential therapy particularly useful? A strength of the perspective is its focus on available choices and pathways toward personal growth. Even for brief counseling, existential therapy can focus clients on significant areas such as assuming personal responsibility, making a commitment to deciding and acting, and expanding their awareness of their current situation. For clients who are struggling with developmental crises, existential therapy is especially appropriate (May & Yalom, 1989). Some examples of these critical turning points that mark passages from one stage of life into another are the struggle for identity in adolescence, coping with possible disappointments in middle age, adjusting to children's leaving home, coping with failures in marriage and work, and dealing with increased physical limitations as one ages. These developmental challenges involve both dangers and opportunities. Uncertainty, anxiety, and struggling with decisions are all part of this process. The existential viewpoint can be appropriately used in either individual or group counseling, and its basic concepts can serve as the foundation for integrating methods from other therapies. According to May and Yalom, the main aim of the founders of existential therapy is that its key concepts and themes become integrated into all therapeutic schools. They think that this integration is clearly occurring.

Contributions to multicultural counseling.   As we have seen, the focus in existential therapy is more on understanding an individual than on mastering techniques. Being existentially oriented gives counselors the freedom to draw on other systems for specific techniques that can be flexibly used in therapeutic work with culturally diverse client populations. Existential counselors have a theory to guide their interventions. Although they assume that using a diversity of unintegrated techniques and procedures based on different assumptions about human development can be more harmful than helpful, they do use a variety of basic counseling skills.

The existential notions of freedom and control can be useful in helping clients deal with their cultural values. At times clients may feel that their lives are out of control, and they may sense that they are being driven rather than doing the driving. There are always consequences of what people do or fail to do. Clients can be challenged to look at the price they are paying for the decisions they have made. Although it is true that some ethnic clients may not feel a sense of freedom, their freedom can be increased through recognition of the social limits they are facing. It is true that their freedom can be hindered by institutions and that their freedom may be limited by their family. In fact, it may be difficult to separate individual freedom from the context of their family structure.

A client who is struggling with feeling limited by her family situation can be invited to look at her part in this process. For example, Marina may be working to attain a professional identity even though her family thinks that she is being selfish and neglecting her primary duties. It is likely that as Marina moves from one culture to another, she will experience culture shock. The family is likely to exert pressure on her to give up her personal interests in favor of what they see as best for the welfare of the entire family. She may be convinced that she can take care of her family and at the same time satisfy her need for involvement in her profession. She may feel trapped in the situation and see no way out, unless she rejects what her family wants. In cases such as this it is useful to explore the client's underlying values and to help her determine whether her values are working for her and for her family. Clients such as Marina who have two cultures have the challenge of weighing values and balancing behaviors based on their biculturality. Ultimately, it will be up to Marina to decide in what ways she will change her situation. But the basic clash is still between her feeling that there is almost nothing that she can do to change her situation and the counselor's invitation to begin to explore what she *can do* to initiate change.

I think that it is essential to respect the purpose that clients have in mind when they initiate therapy. If we pay careful attention to what our clients tell us about what they want, we can operate within an existential framework. Our task then becomes encouraging them to weigh the alternatives and to explore the consequences of what they are doing with their lives. We can help clients see that even though oppressive forces may be severely limiting the quality of their lives, they are not merely the victims of circumstances beyond their control. At the same time that these clients are learning ways to change their external environment, they can also be challenged to look within themselves to recognize their own contribution to their plight. Through the therapy experience they may be able to discover new courses of action that will lead to a change in their situation. To be truly free, however, they must first be aware of culturally learned assumptions.

LIMITATIONS AND CRITICISMS OF THE EXISTENTIAL APPROACH

A major criticism often aimed at this approach is that it lacks a systematic statement of the principles and practices of psychotherapy. It is also frequently criticized as lacking rigorous methods. Some accuse it of mystical language and concepts, and some object to it as a fad based on a reaction against the scientific approach. Those who prefer a counseling practice based on research contend that the concepts should be empirically sound, that definitions should be operational, that the hypotheses should be testable, and that therapeutic practice should be based on the results of research into both the process and outcomes of counseling.

Some therapists who claim adherence to an existential orientation describe their therapeutic style in vague and global terms such as *self-actualization, dialogic encounter, authenticity,* and *being in the world.* This lack of precision causes confusion at times and makes it difficult to conduct research on the process or outcomes of existential therapy.

Another basic limitation that I see in the existential approach is that many of its concepts are quite abstract and difficult to apply in therapeutic practice. Existential theorists such as Kierkegaard, Nietzsche, Heidegger, and Sartre were not writing for practicing counselors and therapists! Both beginning and advanced practitioners who are not of a philosophical turn of mind tend to find many of the existential concepts lofty and elusive. And those counselors who do find themselves close to this philosophy are often at a loss when they attempt to apply it to practice. As we have seen, this approach places primary emphasis on understanding the world of clients. It is assumed that techniques follow understanding. The fact that few techniques are generated by this approach makes it essential for practitioners to develop their own innovative procedures or to borrow from other schools of therapy.

Finally, philosophical insight may not be appropriate for some clients. Thus, the existential approach may be ineffective in working with the seriously disturbed. And yet it should be noted that R. D. Laing (1965, 1967) has used an existential point of view in successfully treating schizophrenic patients. Laing's positive results suggest that existential practitioners may work well with all sorts of populations, treating people in humane ways that are in keeping with this approach while at the same time drawing on some of the more active and directive intervention methods to meet the unique needs of their clients.

Limitations for multicultural counseling.   There are some limitations of the existential approach as it is applied to multicultural populations. A common criticism of the existentialists is that they are excessively individualistic, seeming to suggest that all changes can be internal. Minority clients, however, may operate on the assumption that they have very little choice. They often feel that their environmental circumstances are severely restricting their ability to influence the direction of their lives. Even if they change internally, they see little hope that the external realities of racism, discrimination, and oppression will change. They are likely to experience a deep sense of frustration and feelings of powerlessness when it comes to making changes outside of themselves. This is especially true in an individualistic culture. A good place to begin counseling is to explore these feelings of helplessness and hopelessness and eventually look for ways to overcome certain limitations.

Even accepting the fact of environmental limitations, some degree of freedom can still be exercised. Counselors with an existential orientation can take into account the sociocultural factors that do restrict choices, and at the same time they can challenge these clients to recognize those steps that they can take to change their situation. In working with people of color who come from the barrio or ghetto, for example, it is important to deal with their survival issues. Such clients may be primarily motivated by safety and survival needs. They can use skills for effective parenting, learn how to cope with a crisis over housing, or get help in dealing with unemployment. If counselors consistently tell these clients that they have a choice in making their life better, they may feel patronized and misunderstood. These real-life issues provide a good focus for counseling, assuming the therapist is willing to deal with them.

Another problem with this approach is the lack of direction that clients may get from the counselor. Minority clients are likely to approach counseling expecting answers and concrete solutions to immediate problems, or at least looking for expert advice. Although they may feel better if they have an opportunity to talk and to be understood, they are likely to expect the counselor to do something to bring about a change in their life situation. A major challenge facing the counselor is to provide enough concrete direction for these clients without taking the responsibility away from them. For a counselor to provide the structure that is often desired by some minority clients would be inconsistent with the existential approach. The counselor can still attempt to understand the client's world and at the same time help him or her take action, even if it is only small steps toward change.

QUESTIONS FOR REFLECTION AND DISCUSSION

1. What does personal freedom mean to you? Do you believe that you are what you are now largely as a result of your choices, or do you believe that you are the product of your circumstances?
2. As you reflect on some critical turning points in your life, what decisions appear to have been crucial to your present development?
3. Are you able to accept and exercise your own freedom and make significant decisions alone? Do you attempt to escape from freedom and responsibility? Are you inclined to give up some of your autonomy for the security of being taken care of by others?
4. Do you agree that each person is basically alone? What are the implications for counseling practice? In what ways have you attempted to avoid your experience of aloneness?
5. What is your experience with anxiety? Does your anxiety result from the consideration that you must choose for yourself, the realization that you are alone, the fact that you will die, and the realization that you must create your own meaning and purpose in life? How have you dealt with anxiety in your own life?
6. Do you believe that unless you take death seriously, life has little meaning?
7. What are some specific things that you value most? What would your life be like without them? What gives your life meaning and a sense of purpose?
8. Have you experienced an "existential vacuum"? Is your life at times without substance, depth, and meaning? What is this experience of emptiness like for you, and how do you cope with it?
9. What are your reactions to the existential view of the importance of the client/therapist relationship? To what extent do you see yourself as being able to make the therapeutic journey with a client into unknown territory? To what degree are you open to challenging and changing your own life?
10. Apply the existential approach to Stan's case (Chapter 13). What are some major issues in Stan's life that would be particularly applicable to this approach? How do you imagine that it would be for you to counsel Stan if you were to stay primarily with an existential perspective?

WHERE TO GO FROM HERE

There are no formal organizations for the existential approach, because it is not considered a "school" of therapy. Yet you might consider attending the conferences sponsored by the Association for Humanistic Psychology. At its annual meetings members can participate in various workshops that are based on existential and humanistic concepts. For information about joining this organization or about subscribing to the *Journal of Humanistic Psychology,* contact:

Association for Humanistic Psychology
325 Ninth Street
San Francisco, CA 94103

Membership dues include the quarterly journal, the *AHP Resource Direc-*

tory, a newsletter, priority for attendance at special events, and professional networking services.

RECOMMENDED SUPPLEMENTARY READINGS

Existential Psychotherapy (Yalom, 1980) is a superb treatment of the ultimate human concerns of death, freedom, isolation, and meaninglessness as these issues relate to therapy. This book has depth and clarity, and it is rich with clinical examples that illustrate existential themes. If you were to select just one book on existential therapy, this would be my recommendation as a comprehensive and interesting discussion of the topic.

The Art of the Psychotherapist (Bugental, 1987) is an outstanding book that bridges the art and science of psychotherapy, making places for both. The author is an insightful and sensitive clinician who writes about the psychotherapist's and the client's journey in therapy from an existential perspective.

Psychotherapy and Process: The Fundamentals of an Existential-Humanistic Approach (Bugental, 1978) is a concise yet comprehensive overview. It is highly readable, and the clinical examples provide a sense of reality to the discussion of concepts. An excellent source.

The Discovery of Being: Writings in Existential Psychology (May, 1983) addresses fundamental human concerns that are central to therapy. The author writes about the cultural background of existential psychology and the contributions of existential thinking to therapy.

Existential Psychology (May, 1961) is a reader that examines and evaluates the role of existential psychology. Maslow, May, Rogers, and Allport are among those who have contributed essays.

Man's Search for Himself (May, 1953) is a classic. It deals with key existential themes such as loneliness, anxiety, the experience of becoming a person, the struggle to be, freedom, choice, responsibility, and religion.

The Transparent Self (Jourard, 1971) is a significant work based on the thesis that our lack of openness results in sickness, maladjustment, and alienation. The chapters on psychotherapy, groups, and the "disclosing therapist" are especially relevant to our discussion.

I Never Knew I Had a Choice (Corey & Corey, 1990) is a self-help book written from an existential perspective. It contains many exercises and activities that leaders can use for their group work and that they can suggest as homework assignments between sessions. The topics covered include our struggle to achieve autonomy; the roles that work, love, sexuality, intimacy, and solitude play in our lives; the meaning of loneliness, death, and loss; and the ways in which we choose our values and philosophies of life. Each chapter is followed by numerous annotated suggestions for further reading.

Existential Counselling in Practice (Deurzen-Smith, 1988), a well-written book, develops a practical method of counseling based on concepts of existential philosophy. The author draws on her experience as a psychotherapist in describing numerous case illustrations to highlight the value of applying existential themes.

REFERENCES AND SUGGESTED READINGS*

*BALDWIN, D. C., JR. (1987). Some philosophical and psychological contributions to the use of self in therapy. In M. Baldwin & V. Satir (Eds.), *The use of self in therapy* (pp. 27–44). New York: Haworth Press.

*Books and articles marked with an asterisk are suggested for further study.

*BECKER, E. (1973). *The denial of death*. New York: Free Press.

BINSWANGER, L. (1975). *Being-in-the-world: Selected papers of Ludwig Binswanger*. London: Souvenir Press.

BOSS, M. (1963). *Daseinanalysis and psychoanalysis*. New York: Basic Books.

BUBER, M. (1970). *I and thou* (W. Kaufmann, Trans.). New York: Scribner's.

BUGENTAL, J. F. T. (1976). *The search for existential identity: Patient-therapist dialogues in humanistic psychotherapy*. San Francisco: Jossey-Bass.

BUGENTAL, J. F. T. (1978). *Psychotherapy and process: The fundamentals of an existential-humanistic approach*. Reading, MA: Addison-Wesley.

BUGENTAL, J. F. T. (1981). *The search for authenticity: An existential-analytic approach to psychotherapy* (rev. ed.). New York: Holt, Rinehart & Winston.

BUGENTAL, J. F. T. (1986). Existential-humanistic psychotherapy. In I. L. Kutash & A. Wolf (Eds.), *Psychotherapist's casebook* (pp. 222–236). San Francisco: Jossey-Bass.

*BUGENTAL, J. F. T. (1987). *The art of the psychotherapist*. New York: Norton.

COREY, G. (1990). *Theory and practice of group counseling* (3rd ed.). Pacific Grove, CA: Brooks/Cole.

COREY, G. (1991). *Case approach to counseling and psychotherapy* (3rd ed.). Pacific Grove, CA: Brooks/Cole.

COREY, G., & COREY, M. (1990). *I never knew I had a choice* (4th ed.). Pacific Grove, CA: Brooks/Cole.

*DEURZEN-SMITH, E. (1988). *Existential counselling in practice*. Newbury Park, CA: Sage Publications.

DOSTOYEVSKI, F. (1960). *Notes from underground*. New York: Dutton.

FISCHER, C. T., & FISCHER, W. F. (1983). Phenomenological-existential psychotherapy. In M. Hensey, A. E. Kazdin, & A. S. Bellack (Eds.), *The clinical psychology handbook: Vol. 2*. New York: Pergamon Press.

*FRANKL, V. (1963). *Man's search for meaning*. Boston: Beacon Press.

*FRANKL, V. (1965). *The doctor and the soul*. New York: Bantam Books.

FRANKL, V. (1969). *The will to meaning: Foundations and applications of logotherapy*. New York: New American Library.

FRANKL, V. (1978). *The unheard cry for meaning*. New York: Simon & Schuster (Touchstone).

HEIDEGGER, M. (1962). *Being and time*. New York: Harper & Row.

HOLT, H. (1986). Existential analysis. In I. L. Kutash & A. Wolf (Eds.), *Psychotherapist's casebook* (pp. 177–194). San Francisco: Jossey-Bass.

JOURARD, S. (1971). *The transparent self* (rev. ed.). New York: Van Nostrand Reinhold.

KIERKEGAARD, S. (1944). *The concept of dread*. Princeton, NJ: Princeton University Press.

KIERKEGAARD, S. (1954a). *Fear and trembling*. New York: Doubleday.

KIERKEGAARD, S. (1954b). *The sickness unto death*. New York: Doubleday.

LAING, R. D. (1965). *The divided self*. Baltimore: Pelican.

LAING, R. D. (1967). *The politics of experience*. New York: Ballantine.

LAING, R. D. (1987). The use of existential phenomenology in psychotherapy. In J. K. Zeig (Ed.), *The evolution of psychotherapy* (pp. 203–211). New York: Brunner/Mazel.

*MAHRER, A. R. (1986). *Therapeutic experiencing: The process of change*. New York: Norton.

MASLOW, A. (1968). *Toward a psychology of being* (2nd ed.). New York: Van Nostrand Reinhold.

MASLOW, A. (1970). *Motivation and personality* (2nd ed.). New York: Harper & Row.

MASLOW, A. (1971). *The farther reaches of human nature*. New York: Viking Press.

*MAY, R. (1950). *The meaning of anxiety.* New York: Ronald Press.

MAY, R. (1953). *Man's search for himself.* New York: Dell (Delta).

MAY, R. (1958). The origins and significance of the existential movement in psychology. In R. May, E. Angel, & H. F. Ellenberger (Eds.), *Existence: A new dimension in psychiatry and psychology.* New York: Basic Books.

*MAY, R. (Ed.). (1961). *Existential psychology.* New York: Random House.

MAY, R. (1969). *Love and will.* New York: Norton.

MAY, R. (1972). *Power and innocence: A search for the sources of violence.* New York: Norton.

MAY, R. (1975). *The courage to create.* New York: Norton.

MAY, R. (1981). *Freedom and destiny.* New York: Norton.

*MAY, R. (1983). *The discovery of being: Writings in existential psychology.* New York: Norton.

MAY, R. (1985). *My quest for beauty.* New York: Norton.

*MAY, R. (1989). Black and impotent: The life of Mercedes. In D. Wedding & R. J. Corsini (Eds.), *Case studies in psychotherapy* (pp. 165–176). Itasca, IL: F. E. Peacock.

MAY, R., ANGEL, E., & ELLENBERGER, H. F. (Eds.). (1958). *Existence: A new dimension in psychiatry and psychology.* New York: Basic Books.

*MAY, R., & YALOM, I. (1989). Existential psychotherapy. In R. J. Corsini & D. Wedding (Eds.), *Current psychotherapies* (4th ed.) (pp. 363–402). Itasca, IL: F. E. Peacock.

MOUSTAKAS, C. (1975). *The touch of loneliness.* Englewood Cliffs, NJ: Prentice-Hall.

MOUSTAKAS, C. (1987). Phenomenology, discovery, and meaning. *Michigan Journal of Counseling and Development, 18,* 21–24.

PATTERSON, C. H. (1986). *Theories of counseling and psychotherapy.* New York: Harper & Row. (Chap. 15, Logotherapy)

*RABINOWITZ, F. E., GOOD, G., & COZAD, L. (1989). Rollo May: A man of meaning and myth. *Journal of Counseling and Development, 67,* 436–441.

RUSSELL, J. M. (1978). Sartre, therapy, and expanding the concept of responsibility. *American Journal of Psychoanalysis, 38,* 259–269.

SARTRE, J.-P. (1946). *No exit.* New York: Knopf.

SARTRE, J.-P. (1971). *Being and nothingness.* New York: Bantam Books.

*SIEGEL, B. S. (1988). *Love, medicine, and miracles.* New York: Harper & Row (Perennial Library).

SIEGEL, B. S. (1989). *Peace, Love, and healing: Bodymind communication and the path to self-healing: An exploration.* New York, Harper & Row.

TILLICH, P. (1952). *The courage to be.* New Haven, CT: Yale University Press.

*YALOM, I. D. (1980). *Existential psychotherapy.* New York: Basic Books.

7

PERSON-CENTERED THERAPY

CARL ROGERS

CARL ROGERS (1902–1987), as a major spokesman for humanistic psychology, led a life that reflected the ideas he developed for half a century. He showed a questioning stance, a deep openness to change, and a courage to forge into unknown territory, both as a person and as a professional. In writing about his early years, Rogers (1961) recalls his family atmosphere as characterized by close and warm relationships but also by strict religious standards. Play was discouraged, and the virtues of the Protestant ethic were extolled. His boyhood was a somewhat lonely one in which he pursued scholarly interests instead of social ones.

During his college years Rogers's interests and academic major changed from agriculture to history, then to religion, and finally to clinical psychology. As a sophomore he began studying for the ministry, and in his junior year he was selected to attend a World Student Christian Federation conference in Peking. This was a most significant experience, for it stretched his thinking and led him to recognize the wide divergence in people's religious beliefs. He considered this the time when he achieved his psychological independence: "In major ways I for the first time emancipated myself from the religious thinking of my parents, and realized that I could not go along with them" (1961, p. 7). His years in graduate school were also marked by questioning and deciding. His decision to leave the seminary and to pursue psychology was partly prompted by a student-directed class at the seminary that gave him the opportunity to question the religious dogma he was being taught.

From 1928 to 1939 Rogers directed the Child Guidance Center in Rochester, New York. He held several academic appointments from 1939 to 1963, including positions at the University of Wisconsin, the University of Chicago, and Ohio State University. Because of his disagreement with the educational policies of graduate psychology programs, he decided to leave university life. In 1964 he joined the staff at the Western Behavioral Sciences Institute in La Jolla, California, where he worked with groups of people who were seeking to improve their abilities in human relations. Here he did much to foster the encounter-group movement in the 1960s. In 1968 Rogers and his colleagues established the Center for the Studies of the Person in La Jolla.

In an interview Rogers was asked what he would want his parents to know about his contributions if he could communicate with them. He replied that he could not imagine talking to his mother about anything of significance, because he was sure she would have some negative judgment. Interestingly, a core theme in his theory is the necessity for nonjudgmental listening and acceptance if clients are to change (Heppner, Rogers, & Lee, 1984).

Rogers earned recognition around the world for originating and developing the humanistic movement in psychotherapy, pioneering in research, and influencing all fields related to psychology. During the last 15 years of his life he applied the person-centered approach to politics by training policymakers, leaders, and groups in conflict. Perhaps his greatest passion was directed toward the reduction of interracial tensions and the effort to achieve world peace, for which he was nominated for the Nobel Peace Prize shortly before he died. After a fall in 1987 that resulted in a fractured hip, he successfully underwent an operation. During the night following his surgery, however, his heart failed, and he died a few days later as he had hoped to — "with his boots on and, as always, looking forward" (Cain, 1987a). In writing some reflections, Rogers said that his life at 85 was better than anything he could have dreamed of or expected. He added: "I do not know when I will die, but I do know that I will have lived a full and exciting 85 years!" (1987b, p. 152).

In an assessment of Rogers's impact, Cain (1987b) writes that the therapist, author and person were the same man. Rogers lived his life in accordance with his theory in his dealings with a wide variety of people in diverse settings. His faith in people deeply affected the development of his theories and the way that he related to all those with whom he came in contact. Rogers knew who he was, felt comfortable with his beliefs, and was without pretense. According to Cain, he embodied the characteristics of the fully functioning person. He was not afraid to take a strong position and challenge the status quo throughout his professional career.

INTRODUCTION

HISTORICAL BACKGROUND

The person-centered approach is based on concepts from humanistic psychology, and it can also be classified as a branch of the existential perspective presented in the last chapter. In the early 1940s Rogers developed what was known as *nondirective counseling* as a reaction against the directive and psychoanalytic approaches to individual therapy. His theory emphasized the counselor's creation of a permissive and noninterventionist climate. Rogers caused a furor when he challenged the basic assumption that "the counselor knows best." He also challenged the validity of commonly accepted therapeutic procedures such as advice, suggestion, persuasion, teaching, diagnosis, and interpretation. Based on his conviction that diagnostic concepts and procedures were inadequate, prejudicial, and often misused, he omitted them from his approach. Nondirective counselors avoided sharing a great deal about themselves with clients, and instead they focused mainly on reflecting and clarifying the verbal and nonverbal communications of clients. Rogers's basic assumptions were that people are essentially trustworthy, that they have a vast potential for understanding themselves and resolving their own problems without direct intervention on the therapist's part, and that they are capable of self-directed growth if they are involved in a therapeutic relationship. From the beginning he emphasized the attitudes and personal characteristics of the therapist and the quality of the client/therapist relationship as the prime determinants of the outcome of the therapeutic process. He consistently relegated to a secondary position matters such as the therapist's knowledge of theory and techniques.

Rogers's early interests (1942) were in working with children and in the practice of individual counseling and psychotherapy. He later developed a systematic theory of personality and applied this self theory to the practice of counseling individuals. He renamed his approach *client-centered therapy* to reflect this focus (Rogers, 1951). The approach gradually extended its sphere of influence into a variety of fields far from its point of origin. The client-centered philosophy was applied to education, for example, and was called student-centered teaching. During the 1950s and 1960s Rogers and his associates continued to test the underlying hypotheses of the client-centered approach by conducting extensive research on both the processes and the outcomes of psychotherapy. Rogers was interested in researching the ways in which people best learn in psychotherapy, and he focused his studies on the qualities of the client/therapist relationship as a catalyst leading to personality change. On the basis of this research the approach was further refined (Rogers, 1961).

Because of Rogers's ever-widening scope of influence, including his interest in how people obtain, possess, share, or surrender *power* and *control* over others and themselves, his theory has become known as the *person-centered approach.* In the 1960s and 1970s he did a great deal to spearhead the development of personal-growth groups, and he applied his ideas to the basic encounter group with many populations (Rogers, 1970).

EXISTENTIALISM AND HUMANISM

There is a growing interest among counselors in a "third force" in therapy as an alternative to the psychoanalytical and behavioral approaches. Under this heading fall existential therapy, the person-centered approach, and Gestalt therapy, developed by Fritz Perls (the subject of Chapter 8). Both person-centered therapy and Gestalt therapy are experiential and relationship oriented. They are humanistic approaches that grew out of the philosophical background of the existential tradition.

Partly because of this historical connection and partly because representatives of existentialist thinking and humanistic thinking have not always clearly sorted out their views, the connections between the terms *existentialism* and *humanism* have tended to be confusing for students and theorists alike. The two viewpoints have much in common, and yet there are also significant philosophical differences between them. They share a respect for the client's subjective experience and a trust in the capacity of the client to make positive and constructive conscious choices. They have in common an emphasis on the vocabulary of freedom, choice, values, personal responsibility, autonomy, purpose, and meaning. They differ in that existentialists take the position that we are faced with the anxiety of choosing to create a never secure identity in a world that lacks intrinsic meaning. The humanists, in contrast, take the somewhat less anxiety-evoking position that each of us has within us a nature and potential that we can actualize and through which we can find meaning.

The underlying vision of the humanistic philosophy is captured by the illustration of how an acorn, if provided with the appropriate nurturing conditions, will *automatically* grow in positive ways, pushed naturally toward its actualization as an oak. In contrast, for the existentialist there is nothing that we "are," no internal "nature" we can count on, and we are faced at every moment with a choice about what to make of this condition. The humanistic philosophy on which the person-centered approach rests is expressed in attitudes and behaviors that create a growth-producing climate. According to Rogers (1986b), when this philosophy is lived, it helps people develop their capacities, and it stimulates constructive change in others. Individuals are empowered, and they are able to use this power for personal and social transformation.

As will become evident in this chapter, the existential and person-centered approaches have a number of parallel concepts, especially as they apply to the client/therapist relationship at the core of therapy. Over the years person-centered therapy has moved increasingly toward existentialism (Patterson, 1986). The phenomenology that is basic to the existentialist approach is also fundamental to the person-centered theory. Both approaches focus on the client's perceptions and call for the therapist to enter the client's subjective world.

KEY CONCEPTS

VIEW OF HUMAN NATURE

A consistent theme pervades all of Rogers's writings and activities over the last 50 years of his personal and professional life. This theme is a deep faith in the tendency of humans to develop in a positive and constructive manner *if* a climate of respect and trust is established. Rogers's (1987c) professional experience taught him that if he was able to get to the core of an individual, he found a trustworthy, positive center. He firmly believed that people were resourceful, capable of self-direction, and able to live effective and productive lives (Cain, 1987b).

Rogers showed little sympathy for systems based on the assumption that the individual cannot be trusted and instead needs to be directed, motivated, instructed, punished, rewarded, controlled and managed by others who are in a superior and "expert" position. Throughout his professional life he maintained that there were three therapist attributes that released a growth-promoting climate in which individuals could move forward and become what they were capable of becoming. These attributes are (1) congruence (genuineness, or realness), (2) unconditional positive regard (acceptance and caring), and (3) accurate empathic understanding (an ability to deeply grasp the subjective world of another person). According to Rogers, if these attitudes are communicated by the helper, those being helped will become less defensive and more open to themselves and their world, and they will behave in social and constructive ways. The basic drive to fulfillment implies that people move toward health if the way seems open for them to do so. Thus, the goals of counseling are to set clients free and to create those conditions that will enable them to engage in meaningful self-exploration. When people are free, they will be able to find their own way (Combs, 1989).

In addition to Rogers, Abraham Maslow has been instrumental in developing the humanistic trend in psychology. Maslow (1968, 1970) focused much of his research on the nature of the self-actualizing person. Maslow writes of the "psychopathology of the average." So-called "normals" may never extend themselves to become what they are capable of becoming. Maslow argues that healthy people differ from normals in kind as well as in degree. He criticizes the Freudian preoccupation with the sick and crippled side of human nature. He contends that, if we base our findings on a sick population, we will have a sick psychology. According to Maslow, too much attention has been given to hostility, aggression, neuroses, and immaturities; likewise, too little attention has been given to love, creativity, joy, and "peak experiences." Maslow's (1968, 1970) research with self-actualizing subjects yielded the following characteristics: the capacity to tolerate and even welcome uncertainty in their lives, acceptance of self and others, spontaneity and creativity, a need for privacy and solitude, autonomy, the capacity for deep and intense interpersonal relationships, a genuine caring for others, a sense of humor, an inner-directedness, and an open and fresh attitude toward life.

This positive view of human nature has significant implications for the practice of therapy. Because of the belief that the individual has an inherent capacity to move away from maladjustment toward psychological health, the therapist places the primary responsibility on the client. The person-centered approach rejects the roles of the therapist as the authority who knows best and of the passive client who merely follows the dictates of the therapist. Therapy is thus rooted in the client's capacity for awareness and the ability to make decisions.

Seeing people in this light means that the therapist focuses on the constructive side of human nature, on what is right with the person, and on the assets that people bring with them to therapy. It focuses on how clients act in their world with others, how they can move forward in constructive directions, and how they can successfully encounter obstacles (both from within themselves and outside of themselves) that are blocking their growth. The implication is that therapy is more than "adjustment to norms"; and this approach does not stop with merely solving problems. Instead, practitioners with a humanistic orientation aim at challenging their clients to make changes that will lead to living fully and authentically, with the realization that this kind of existence demands a continuing struggle. People never arrive at a static state of being self-actualiz*ed;* rather, at best they are continually involved in the process of actualiz*ing* themselves.

BASIC CHARACTERISTICS

Rogers did not present the person-centered theory as a fixed and completed approach to therapy. He hoped that others would view his theory as a set of tentative principles relating to how the therapy process develops, not as dogma. Rogers and Wood (1974, pp. 213–214) describe the characteristics that distinguish the person-centered approach from other models. An adaptation of this description follows.

The person-centered approach focuses on clients' responsibility and capacity to discover ways to more fully encounter reality. Clients, who know themselves best, are the ones to discover more appropriate behavior for themselves based on a growing self-awareness.

The approach emphasizes the phenomenal world of the client. With an attempt to apprehend the client's internal frame of reference, therapists concern themselves mainly with the client's perception of self and of the world.

The same principles of psychotherapy apply to all clients — "normals," "neurotics," and "psychotics." Based on the view that the urge to move toward psychological maturity is deeply rooted in human nature, the principles of person-centered therapy apply to those who function at relatively normal levels as well as to those who experience a greater degree of psychological maladjustment.

According to the person-centered approach, psychotherapy is only one example of a constructive personal relationship. Clients experience psychotherapeutic growth in and through the relationship with another person who helps them do what they cannot do alone. It is the relationship with a counselor who is congruent (matching external behavior and expression with internal feelings and thoughts), accepting, and empathic that facilitates therapeutic change for the client. Person-centered theory holds that the therapist's function is to be immediately present and accessible to the client and to focus on the here-and-now experience.

Perhaps more than any other single approach to psychotherapy, person-centered theory has developed through research on the process and outcomes of therapy. The theory is not closed but has grown through years of counseling observations and continues to change as new research yields increased understanding of human nature and the therapeutic process.

Thus, person-centered therapy is not a set of techniques or a dogma. Rooted in a set of attitudes and beliefs that the therapist demonstrates, it is perhaps best characterized as a way of being and as a shared journey in which both therapist and client reveal their humanness and participate in a growth experience.

THE THERAPEUTIC PROCESS

THERAPEUTIC GOALS

The goals of person-centered therapy are different from those of traditional approaches. The person-centered approach aims toward a greater degree of independence and integration of the individual. Its focus is on the person, not on the person's presenting problem. In Rogers's view (1977) the aim of therapy is not merely to solve problems. Rather, it is to assist clients in their growth process, so that they can better cope with problems they are now facing and with future problems.

Rogers (1961) writes that people who enter psychotherapy are often asking: "How can I discover my real self? How can I become what I deeply wish to become? How can I get behind my facades and become myself?" The underlying aim of therapy is to provide a climate conducive to helping the individual become a fully functioning person. Before clients are able to work toward that goal, they must first get behind the masks they wear, which they develop through the process of socialization. Clients come to recognize that they have lost contact with themselves by using these facades. In a climate of safety in the therapeutic session, they also come to realize that there are other possibilities.

When the facades are worn away during the therapeutic process, what kind of person emerges from behind the pretenses? Rogers (1961) describes people who are becoming increasingly actualized as having (1) an openness to experience, (2) a trust in themselves, (3) an internal source of evaluation, and (4) a willingness to continue growing. Encouraging these characteristics is the basic goal of person-centered therapy.

These four characteristics provide a general framework for understanding the direction of therapeutic movement. The therapist does not choose specific goals for the client. The cornerstone of person-centered theory is the view that clients in relationship with a facilitating therapist have the capacity to define and clarify their own goals. Many counselors, however, experience difficulty in allowing clients to decide for themselves their specific goals in therapy. Although it is easy to give lip service to the concept of clients' finding their own way, it takes considerable respect for clients and courage on the therapist's part to encourage clients to listen to themselves and follow their own directions — particularly when they make choices that are not what the therapist hoped for.

THERAPIST'S FUNCTION AND ROLE

The role of person-centered therapists is rooted in their ways of being and attitudes, not in techniques designed to get the client to "do something." Research on person-centered therapy seems to indicate that the attitudes of therapists, rather than their knowledge, theories, or techniques, facilitate personality change in the client. Basically, therapists use themselves as an instrument of change. When they encounter the client on a person-to-person level, their "role" is to be without roles. Their function is to establish a therapeutic climate that helps the client grow.

The person-centered therapist thus creates a helping relationship in which clients experience the necessary freedom to explore areas of their life that are now either denied to awareness or distorted. They become less defensive and more open to possibilities within themselves and in the world. First and foremost, the therapist must be willing to be real in the relationship with a client. Instead of perceiving clients in preconceived diagnostic categories, the therapist meets them on a moment-to-moment experiential basis and helps them by entering their world. Through the therapist's attitudes of genuine caring, respect, acceptance, and understanding, they are able to loosen their defenses and rigid perceptions and move to a higher level of personal functioning.

CLIENT'S EXPERIENCE IN THERAPY

Therapeutic change depends on the clients' perception both of their own experience in therapy and of the counselor's basic attitudes. If the counselor creates a climate conducive to self-exploration, clients have the opportunity to experience and explore the full range of their feelings. What follows is a general sketch of the experience of the client in therapy.

Clients come to the counselor in a state of incongruence; that is, a discrepancy exists between their self-perception and their experience in reality. For example, a college student may see himself as a future physician, and yet his below-average grades might exclude him from medical school. The discrepancy between how he sees himself (self-concept) or how he would *like* to view himself (ideal self-concept) and the reality of his poor academic performance may result in anxiety and personal vulnerability, which can provide the necessary motivation to enter therapy. This client must perceive that a problem exists or, at least, that he is uncomfortable enough with his present psychological adjustment to want to explore possibilities for change.

One of the reasons that clients seek therapy is a feeling of basic helplessness, powerlessness, and inability to make decisions or effectively direct their own life. They may hope to find "the way" through the teachings of the therapist. Within the person-centered framework, however, they soon learn that they can be responsible for themselves in the relationship and that they can learn to be freer by using the relationship to gain greater self-understanding.

As counseling progresses, clients are able to explore a wider range of their feelings (Rogers, 1987e). They can express their fears, anxiety, guilt, shame, hatred, anger, and other emotions that they had deemed too negative to accept and incorporate into their self-structure. With therapy, people constrict less, distort less, and move to a greater acceptance and integration of conflicting and confusing feelings. They increasingly discover aspects within themselves that had been kept hidden. As clients feel understood and accepted, their defensiveness is less necessary, and they become more open to their experience. Because they are not as threatened, feel safer, and are less vulnerable, they become more realistic, perceive others with greater accuracy, and become better able to understand and accept others. They come to appreciate themselves more as they are, and their behavior shows more flexibility and creativity. They become less oriented to meeting others' expectations, and thus they begin to behave in ways that are truer to themselves. These individuals empower themselves to direct their own lives, instead of looking outside of themselves for answers. They move in the direction of being more in contact with what they are experiencing at the present moment, less bound by the past, less determined, freer to make decisions, and increasingly trusting in themselves to effectively manage their own lives. In short, their experience in therapy is like throwing off the self-imposed shackles that had kept them in a psychological prison. With increased freedom they tend to become more mature psychologically and more actualized.

The person-centered approach offers a humanistic base from which to understand the subjective world of clients. It provides clients with the rare opportunity to be truly listened to without evaluation or judgment. They can feel free to experiment with new behavior. They are expected to take responsibility for themselves, and it is *they* who set the pace in counseling. They decide what areas they wish to explore, on the basis of their own goals for change.

Rogers (1987e) points to considerable research that confirms these outcomes of person-centered individual therapy. He maintains that personality and behavioral changes occur when the core therapeutic conditions exist. The six conditions that are deemed necessary and sufficient for such changes to occur are described in the following section.

RELATIONSHIP BETWEEN THERAPIST AND CLIENT

The basic hypothesis of person-centered therapy is summarized in this sentence: "If I can provide a certain type of relationship, the other person will discover within himself the capacity to use that relationship for growth and change, and personal development will occur" (Rogers, 1961, p. 33). Rogers hypothesizes further that "significant positive personality change does not occur except in a relationship" (1967, p. 73).

What are the characteristics of the therapeutic relationship that are conducive to creating a suitable psychological climate in which the client will experience the freedom necessary to initiate personality change? According to Rogers (1987e), the following six conditions are necessary and sufficient for personality changes to occur:

1. Two persons are in psychological contact.
2. The first, whom we shall term the client, is experiencing incongruency.
3. The second person, whom we shall term the therapist, is congruent or integrated in the relationship.
4. The therapist experiences unconditional positive regard or real caring for the client.
5. The therapist experiences an empathic understanding of the client's internal frame of reference and endeavors to communicate this experience to the client.
6. The communication to the client of the therapist's empathic understanding and unconditional positive regard is to a minimal degree achieved [pp. 39–41].

Rogers hypothesizes that no other conditions are necessary. If the six conditions exist over some period of time, constructive personality change will occur. The conditions do not vary according to client type. Further, they are necessary and sufficient for all approaches to therapy and apply to all personal relationships, not just to psychotherapy. The therapist need not have any specialized knowledge. Accurate psychological diagnosis is not necessary and may more often than not interfere with effective therapy. Rogers admitted that his theory was striking and radical. His formulation has generated considerable controversy, for he asserts that many conditions that other therapists commonly regard as necessary for effective psychotherapy are nonessential.

From Rogers's perspective the client/therapist relationship is characterized by equality, for therapists do not keep their knowledge a secret or attempt to mystify the therapeutic process. The process of change in the client depends to a large degree on the quality of this equal relationship. As clients experience the therapist listening in an accepting way to them, they gradually learn how to listen acceptingly to themselves. As they find the therapist caring for and valuing them (even the aspects that have been hidden and regarded as negative), they begin to see worth and value in themselves. As they experience the realness of the therapist, they drop many of their pretenses and are real with both themselves and the therapist.

As we have noted, three personal characteristics, or attitudes, of the therapist form a central part of the therapeutic relationship: (1) congruence, or genuineness, (2) unconditional positive regard, and (3) accurate empathic understanding.

Congruence, or genuineness.   Of the three characteristics, congruence is the most important, according to Rogers's recent writings. Congruence implies that therapists are real; that is, they are genuine, integrated, and authentic during the therapy hour. They are without a false front, their inner experience and outer expression of that experience match, and they can openly express feelings and attitudes that are present in the relationship with the client. Authentic therapists are spontaneously and openly *being* the feelings and attitudes, both negative and positive, that flow in them. By expressing (and accepting) any negative feelings, they can facilitate honest communication with the client.

Through authenticity therapists serve as a model of a human being struggling toward greater realness. Being congruent might necessitate the expression of anger, frustration, liking, attraction, concern, boredom, annoyance, and a range of other feelings in the relationship. This does not mean that therapists should impulsively share all feelings, for self-disclosure must also be appropriate. Nor does it imply that the client is the cause of the therapist's boredom or anger. A pitfall is that counselors can try too hard to be genuine. Sharing because one thinks it will be good for the client, without being genuinely moved to express something regarded as personal, can be incongruent. Therapists must, however, take responsibility for their own feelings and explore with the client persistent feelings that block their ability to be fully present with the client. The goal of counseling is not, of course, for therapists to continually discuss their own feelings with the client. Person-centered therapy also stresses that counseling will be inhibited if the counselor feels one way about the client but acts in a different way. Hence, if the counselor either dislikes or disapproves of the client but feigns acceptance, therapy will not work.

Rogers's concept of congruence does not imply that only a fully self-actualized therapist can be effective in counseling. Because therapists are human, they cannot be expected to be fully authentic. The person-centered model assumes that if therapists are congruent in the relationship with the client, the process of therapy will get under way. Congruence exists on a continuum rather than on an all-or-nothing basis, as is true of all three characteristics.

Unconditional positive regard and acceptance.   The second attitude that therapists need to communicate to the client is a deep and genuine caring for him or her as a person. The caring is unconditional, in that it is not contaminated by evaluation or judgment of the client's feelings, thoughts, and behavior as good or bad. Therapists value and warmly accept the client without placing stipulations on the acceptance. It is not an attitude of "I'll accept you when . . ."; rather, it is one of "I'll accept you as you are." Therapists communicate through their behavior that they value the client as the client is and that he or she is free to have feelings and experiences without risking the loss of the therapist's acceptance. Acceptance is the recognition of the client's right to have feelings; it is not the approval of all behavior. All overt behavior need not be approved of or accepted.

It is important also that therapists' caring be nonpossessive. If the caring stems from their own need to be liked and appreciated, constructive change in the client is inhibited.

According to Rogers (1977), research indicates that the greater the degree of caring, prizing, accepting, and valuing the client in a nonpossessive way, the greater the chance that therapy will be successful. He also makes it clear that it is not possible for therapists to genuinely feel acceptance and unconditional caring at all times.

One implication of this emphasis on acceptance is that therapists who have little respect for their clients or an active dislike or disgust can anticipate that their work will not be fruitful. Clients will sense this lack of regard and become increasingly defensive.

Accurate empathic understanding.   One of the main tasks of the therapist is to understand clients' experience and feelings sensitively and accurately as they are revealed in the moment-to-moment interaction during the therapy session. The therapist strives to sense clients' subjective experience, particularly in the here and now. The aim is to encourage them to get closer to themselves, to feel more deeply and intensely, and to recognize and resolve the incongruity that exists within them.

Empathic understanding implies that the therapist will sense clients' feelings as if they were his or her own without becoming lost in those feelings. By moving freely in the world as experienced by clients, the therapist can not only communicate to them an understanding of what is already known to them but can also voice meanings of experience of which they are only dimly aware. It is important to understand that accurate empathy goes beyond recognition of obvious feelings to a sense of the less clearly experienced feelings of clients.

Empathy entails more than reflecting content to the client, and it is more than an artificial technique that the therapist routinely uses. It is not simply objective knowledge ("I understand what your problem is"), which is an evaluative understanding *about* the client from the outside. Instead, empathy is a deep and subjective understanding *of* the client *with* the client. It is a sense of personal identification with the client. Therapists are able to share the client's subjective world by tuning in to their own feelings that are like the client's feelings. Yet therapists must not lose their own separateness. Rogers believes that when therapists can grasp the client's private world, as the client sees and feels it, without losing the separateness of their own identity, constructive change is likely to occur.

APPLICATION: THERAPEUTIC TECHNIQUES AND PROCEDURES

EVOLUTION OF PERSON-CENTERED METHODS

As Rogers's view of psychotherapy developed, its focus shifted away from therapeutic techniques toward the therapist's personal qualities, beliefs, and attitudes and toward the relationship with the client. The therapeutic relationship, as we have seen, is the critical variable, not what the therapist says or does. In the person-centered framework the 'techniques" are listening, accepting, respecting, understanding, and sharing. A preoccupation with using techniques is seen as depersonalizing the relationship. The techniques must be an honest expression of the therapy; they cannot be used self-consciously, for then the counselor is not genuine.

With its development the approach addressed itself less to prohibitions and allowed counselors greater freedom to participate more actively in the relationship. This change encouraged the use of a wider variety of methods, rather than the traditional listening, reflecting, and communicating understanding. According to Combs (1988), the current person-centered approach is understood primarily as a process of helping clients discover new and more satisfying personal meanings about themselves and the world they inhabit.

Although the person-centered approach has been applied mainly to individual and group counseling, it has broadened considerably beyond therapeutic practice. Important areas of application include education, family life, leadership and administration, organizational development, health care, cross-cultural and interracial activity, international relations, and the search for world peace (Cain, 1986a).

As it has evolved, the approach has encompassed broader social issues, especially conflict resolution among diverse groups of people. The major recent application is an effort to attain world peace. In the last few years of his life Rogers (1984) focused much attention on alternatives to what he called "nuclear planetary suicide." He shared his hope of disengaging the world from a precarious entanglement that threatened human survival (see Rogers, 1987d; Rogers & Malcolm, 1987).

AREAS OF APPLICATION

In addition to its application to both individual and group counseling, the person-centered approach has been used extensively in training professionals and paraprofessionals who work with people in a variety of other settings. This approach is useful in the training of practitioners, because the methods have built-in safety features. It emphasizes staying with clients as opposed to getting ahead of them with interpretations. Hence, this approach is safer than many models of therapy that put the therapist in the directive position of making interpretations, forming diagnoses, probing the unconscious, analyzing dreams, and working toward more radical personality changes. For a person with limited background in counseling psychology, personality dynamics, and psychopathology, the approach offers assurance that prospective clients will not be psychologically harmed.

The person-centered approach has applications for people without advanced psychological education. They are able to benefit by translating the therapeutic conditions of genuineness, empathic understanding, and unconditional positive regard into both their personal and professional lives. The approach's basic concepts are straightforward and easy to comprehend, and they encourage locating power in the person, rather than fostering an authoritarian structure in which control and power are denied to the person. The core skills can be used by many people in the helping professions. These skills are also essential as a foundation for virtually all of the other therapy systems covered in this book. If counselors are lacking in these relationship and communication skills, they will not be effective in carrying out a treatment program for their clients.

An area where I see the person-centered approach as being especially applicable is crisis intervention. Many people in the helping professions (nursing, medicine, education, the ministry) are the first on the scene in a variety of crises. Consider specific life events that can lead to crises, such as an unwanted pregnancy, an illness, or the loss of a loved one. Even if the helping person is not a trained mental-health professional, he or she can do much if the basic attitudes described in this chapter are present. When people are in crisis, one of the first steps is to give them an opportunity to fully express themselves. Sensitive listening, hearing, and understanding are essential at this point. Although a person's crisis is not likely to be resolved by one or two contacts with a helper, such contacts can pave the way for an openness to receiving help later. If the person in crisis does not feel understood and accepted, the situation will probably become more aggravated, so that the person may lose hope of "returning to normal" and may not seek help in the future. Genuine support, caring, and nonpossessive warmth can go a long way in building bridges that can motivate people to *do* something to work through and resolve a crisis. People in trouble do not need false reassurances that "everything will be all right." Yet the presence of and psychological contact with a caring person can do much to bring about healing.

Summary and Evaluation

SUMMARY

Person-centered therapy is based on a philosophy of human nature that postulates an innate striving for self-actualization. Further, Rogers's view of human nature is phenomenological; that is, we structure ourselves according to our perceptions of reality. We are motivated to actualize ourselves in the reality that we perceive.

Rogers's theory rests on the assumption that clients can understand the factors in their life that are causing them to be unhappy. They also have the capacity for self-direction and constructive personal change. Change will occur if a congruent therapist is able to establish with the client a relationship characterized by genuineness, acceptance, and accurate empathic understanding. Therapeutic counseling is based on an I/thou, or person-to-person, relationship in the safety and acceptance of which clients drop their rigid defenses and come to accept and integrate aspects that they have denied or distorted. The person-centered approach emphasizes this personal relationship between client and therapist; the therapist's attitudes are more critical than are knowledge, theory, or techniques. Clients are encouraged to use this relationship to unleash their growth potential and become more of the person they choose to become.

This approach places primary responsibility for the direction of therapy on the client. Clients are confronted with the opportunity to decide for themselves and come to terms with their own personal power. The general goals of therapy are becoming more open to experience, achieving self-trust, developing an internal source of evaluation, and being willing to continue growing. Specific goals are not imposed on clients; rather, clients choose their own values and goals. Current applications of the theory emphasize more active participation by the therapist or facilitator than was the case earlier. More latitude is given for them to express values, reactions, and feelings as they are appropriate to what is occurring in therapy. Counselors can be fully involved as persons in the relationship.

CONTRIBUTIONS OF THE PERSON-CENTERED APPROACH

Rogers had a major impact on the field of counseling and psychotherapy when he introduced his revolutionary ideas about therapeutic practice in 1940. As has been mentioned, his influence went beyond the practice of individual counseling and extended into the field of human relations in many settings. Interestingly, today there are few person-centered graduate programs in the United States, although this approach is taught in most counseling programs. If one wants to study person-centered philosophy and practice, it appears that there are more opportunities to do so in several European countries, South America, and Japan.

Smith (1982) conducted a survey of clinical and counseling psychologists to determine their primary theoretical orientation. Out of 422 respondents, fewer than 9% identified themselves as holding a person-centered orientation. In the same study Rogers was ranked at the top of the list as the psychologist who had made the greatest impact on the field of counseling and psychotherapy. One might wonder about this discrepancy. Perhaps it can be resolved by understanding that Rogers consistently opposed the formation of a client-centered "school." Likewise, he reacted negatively to the idea of the founding of institutes, the granting of certificates, and the setting of standards for membership. He viewed this institutionalization as leading to an increasingly narrow, rigid, and dogmatic perspective.

During the 1980s, however, person-centered therapists took the initiative to move toward increased organization. The Association for the Development of the Person-Centered Approach, founded by David Cain in 1981, has the purpose of fostering innovation in person-centered therapy, education, and supervision. The organization is also aimed at creating a system of networks to increase awareness of and access to those interested in the person-centered approach.

Cain (1988) organized and edited a "roundtable" article to pursue the question "Why do you think there are so few person-centered practitioners or scholars, considering that literally thousands of persons throughout the world attest to the enormous impact Carl Rogers has had on their personal and professional lives?" Some of the responses given were:

- Person-centered therapy is viewed as too simple.
- It is seen as limited to techniques of attending and reflecting.

- Some see it as ineffective and as leading to undirected rambling by the client.
- Some do not like the emphasis given to the counselor as a person and would rather focus on developing a variety of techniques that can be applied to solving specific problems.
- Some prefer more emphasis on systematic training in counseling skills and less focus on the attitudes of the counselor.
- Many practitioners do not accept the assumption that individuals have within them a growth potential or actualizing tendency.
- Some counselors resist putting faith in their clients' capacity to trust their own inner direction and find their own answers.
- Some do not want to give up their role of authority, and they find it essential to advise and direct clients.

Rogers warned that too much loyalty to a method, a school of thought, or a technique could have a counterproductive effect on the counseling process. The advice Rogers often gave to students in training and followed in his own life was: "There is one *best* school of therapy. It is the school of therapy you develop for yourself based on a continuing critical examination of the effects of your way of being in the relationship" (1987c, p. 185).

One of the strengths of the person-centered approach is that it is not dogmatic and that practitioners have the latitude to develop their own counseling style. Specific techniques are not the focus; rather, the attitudes of the counselor are considered crucial. Thus, therapists can learn to express themselves through their work. In his personal evaluation of Rogers's necessary and sufficient conditions of therapeutic change, Braaten (1986) discusses his own struggles with finding a therapeutic style. Although Braaten agrees on the basics of the person-centered approach, he contends that it is acceptable to differ on minor matters and refinements. He thinks that the major problem with adopting someone else's therapy model is that it is, by definition, external to one's own personality. He encourages all clinicians to seriously undertake the task of personalizing a counseling theory.

To its credit, this approach allows for diversity and does not foster practitioners who become mere followers of a guru. Counselors can be person-centered and practice in a diversity of ways, so long as they demonstrate a belief in the core therapeutic conditions and so long as their practices do not undercut the capacity of clients to discover the best path for themselves.

Emphasis on research.   One of Rogers's contributions to the field of psychotherapy was his willingness to state his concepts as testable hypotheses and to submit them to research. He literally opened the field of psychotherapy to research. He was truly a pioneer in his insistence on subjecting the transcripts of therapy sessions to critical examination and applying research technology to counselor/client dialogue (Combs, 1988). Even his critics give him credit for having conducted and inspired others to conduct the most extensive research on counseling process and outcome of any school of psychotherapy. He presented a challenge to psychology to design new models of scientific investigation capable of dealing with the inner, subjective experiences of the person His theories of therapy and personality change have had a tremendous heuristic effect, and though much controversy surrounds this approach, his work has challenged practitioners and theoreticians to examine their own therapeutic styles and beliefs.

Person-centered research has been conducted predominantly on the hypothesized necessary and sufficient conditions of therapeutic personality change (Cain, 1986a, 1987b). Most of the other counseling approaches covered in this book have incorporated the importance of the therapist's attitude and behavior in creating a therapeutic relationship that is conducive to the use of their techniques. For instance, the cognitive behavioral approaches have developed a wide range of strategies designed to help clients deal with specific problems. These approaches are based on the assumption that a trusting and accepting client/therapist relationship is necessary for successful application of these procedures. Yet these practitioners contend that the working relationship is not sufficient to produce change. Active procedures are needed to bring it about.

From my own perspective, the therapeutic core conditions are necessary for therapy to occur, yet I do not see them as being sufficient conditions for change. I see them as the necessary foundation on which counselors must then build the *skills* of therapeutic intervention. Even though the appropriate use of techniques and application of skills in counseling are important, I do think that there is a tendency to place too much emphasis on the skills of counseling, to the neglect of the development of the personal characteristics and attitudes of the counselor. On this issue Combs (1988) suggests that training should focus less on the counselor's techniques and more on the counselor's belief systems. Counselors need to reexamine the basic assumptions of therapy and the beliefs that guide their practice. Bozarth and Brodley have observed that one of the major misunderstandings of the person-centered approach is to view it as a "way of doing" rather than a "way of being" (1986, p. 268).

Contributions to multicultural counseling.   Person-centered therapy has made significant contributions to the field of human relations and to practice in multicultural settings. In fact, this approach has been applied to bringing people of diverse cultures together to develop mutual understanding. Rogers (1987d) has elaborated on a theory of reducing tension among antagonistic groups that he began developing in 1948.

Rogers has had a global impact, for his work has reached over 30 countries, and his writings have been translated into 12 languages. Following are some examples of ways in which this approach has influenced various cultures:

- In several European countries, there has been a significant impact on the practice of counseling as well as on education cross-cultural communication, and reduction of racial and political tensions. For instance, international encounter groups have provided participants with multicultural experiences.
- Japan, Australia, South America, and Mexico have all been receptive to person-centered concepts and have adapted practices to fit their culture.

- In the 1970s Rogers and his associates began conducting workshops promoting cross-cultural communication. Well into his 80s he led large workshops in many parts of the world. He and his colleagues facilitated intensive groups in South Africa with equal numbers of Black and White participants. He also facilitated a group from Belfast, Northern Ireland, composed of militant Protestants, militant Catholics, and English. He conducted similar workshops with different types of factional differences in Italy, Poland, France, Brazil, Japan, Mexico, the Philippines, and the United States.

- Shortly before his death Rogers conducted workshops in both Moscow and Tbilisi in the Soviet Union. He reported that these intensive workshops with Soviet professionals had demonstrated that their concerns differed very little from the concerns felt by a similar professional group in the United States and that it was important to learn that the psychological climate that produced certain predictable results in other countries produced the same results in the Soviet Union (Rogers, 1987a).

- The nature of the impact on counseling research and practice from 1940 to the 1970s in the United States was described earlier in this chapter.

Cain sums up the far-reaching extent of the person-centered approach to cultural diversity: "Our international family consists of millions of persons worldwide whose lives have been affected by Carl Rogers's writings and personal efforts as well as his many colleagues who have brought his and their own innovative thinking and programs to many corners of the earth" (1987c, p. 149).

Person-centered groups have become popular in Japan, and a good deal of research has been done on these groups. In the past 15 years 165 articles have been published in Japan on the behavior of facilitators and on cross-cultural studies (Murayama, Nojima, & Abe, 1988). Murayama and his colleagues came to the conclusion that "person-centered groups have been a great factor in the orientation of persons living in Japanese society. The application of person-centered theory has contributed to the development of a more mature and knowledgeable human being" (1988, p. 490).

LIMITATIONS AND CRITICISMS OF THE PERSON-CENTERED APPROACH

A vulnerability of the person-centered approach is the tendency of some practitioners to be very supportive without being challenging. Out of their misunderstanding of the basic concepts of the approach, some have limited the range of their responses to reflections and empathic listening. Although there is value in really hearing a client and in reflecting and communicating understanding, psychotherapy is more than that. Perhaps listening and reflecting are prerequisites for a therapeutic relationship, but they should not be confused with therapy itself.

One limitation of the approach is the way in which some practitioners become "client centered" and lose a sense of their own personhood and uniqueness. Paradoxically, counselors may focus on the client to such an extent that they diminish the value of their own power as a person and thus lose the impact of their personality on the client.

It should be remembered that this approach is something more than merely a listening and reflecting technique. It is based on a set of attitudes that the therapist brings to the relationship, and more than any other quality, the therapist's genuineness determines the power of the therapeutic relationship. If therapists submerge their unique identity and style in a passive and nondirective way, they may not be harming many clients; but they may also not be really affecting clients in a positive way. Therapist authenticity and congruence are so vital to this approach that practitioners must feel natural and must find a way to express their own reactions to clients. If not, there is a real possibility that person-centered therapy will be reduced to a bland, safe, and ineffectual pablum.

According to Combs (1988), one issue that needs increased attention is the teaching role of the counselor. Over the years the person-centered approach has largely opposed the counselor's functioning as a teacher, since the counselor does not necessarily know what is best for the client. This approach therefore focuses on self-initiated learning by clients. Combs, in contrast, describes counseling as a process to help clients learn better and more satisfying ways of being in the world. He adds that counselors cannot help teaching and influencing their clients by their verbal and nonverbal behavior. He contends that they should recognize and accept their teaching role and use it to help clients attain their goals. I think that counselors can carry out both therapeutic and educational functions. They can teach clients, yet they can also encourage them to move toward independence.

Criticisms of research.   Although I have applauded person-centered therapists for their willingness to subject their hypotheses and procedures to empirical scrutiny, some researchers have been critical of methodological errors they see as being part of some of these studies. Some examples of these scientific shortcomings include using control subjects who are not candidates for therapy; failing to use an untreated control group; failing to account for placebo effects; reliance on self-reports as a major way to assess the outcomes of therapy; and using inappropriate statistical procedures. Therefore, before concluding that person-centered therapy has been demonstrated to be effective, it would be well to examine the rigor and sophistication of its research procedures (Prochaska, 1984). In an evaluation of the empirical studies of Rogers's hypotheses of the necessary and sufficient conditions for effective psychotherapy, Watson (1984) found that none of the studies had met all of the conceptual and methodological criteria for rigorous research: "After 25 years of research on Rogers's hypotheses, there is not yet research of the rigor required for drawing conclusions about the validity of this important theory" (p. 40).

Rogers (1986a) saw that solid research would be essential to the future development of the person-centered approach. He acknowledged that there was relatively little new knowledge being developed in the field, and he expressed concern that the person-centered approach could become dogmatic and restrictive. For Rogers the way to avoid this regression of the approach was through "studies — simultaneously hardheaded and tender minded — which open new vistas, bring new insights, challenge our hypotheses, enrich our theory, expand our knowledge, and involve us more deeply in an understanding of the phenomena of human change" (1986a, p. 259).

Combs (1988) contends that the early momentum of person-centered research has declined significantly to a point at which few person-centered therapists are engaging in any form of research. One reason for this decline of interest in research is that most practitioners interested in therapy are involved in private practice or in providing therapeutic services in community agencies. Combs asserts that without this firm research base, the practice of counseling is difficult to defend, and the profession is deprived of a critical source of growth.

A good theory is necessary for continued development in the areas of research and practice in counseling. According to Cain (1986a), very little new theory has been proposed by person-centered theorists since an article by Rogers in 1959. Cain contends that it is essential to refine existing theoretical constructs as well as to develop new concepts. "Person-centered theory of personality, psychopathology, social relations, and group and organizational behavior remains rudimentary and relatively unchanged in the last 25 years" (Cain, 1986a, pp. 120–121). Combs (1988, 1989) also sees the need for a more adequate theory on which to base the thinking and practice of person-centered therapy. An adequate theory "ought to be comprehensive, accurate, internally consistent, systematic, appropriate to its problems, and adaptable to changing demands and conditions" (1988, p. 264). Combs maintains that most person-centered practitioners do not have a theory that can meet these criteria. It seems clear that without continued development of person-centered theory, further research and advancement in practice will be limited.

Limitations for multicultural counseling.   Although the person-centered approach has made significant contributions to the counseling of people with diverse social, political, and cultural backgrounds, there are some limitations to practicing exclusively within this framework. Many of the clients who come to a community mental-health clinic or who are involved in some type of outpatient treatment tend to want more structure than is provided by this approach. Some ethnic-minority clients seek professional help to deal with a crisis, to alleviate psychosomatic symptoms, or to learn certain coping skills in dealing with everyday problems. When these clients do seek professional help, it may be as a last resort after their other resources have not worked. Some ethnic clients are looking for expert guidance, and they often wait for active probing by the counselor or for an expressed invitation to speak. They expect a directive counselor and can be put off by one who does not provide some structuring (Chu & Sue, 1984).

A second limitation of the person-centered approach is that it is difficult to translate the core conditions into actual practice in certain cultures. The way in which counselors communicate these core conditions needs to be consistent with the client's cultural framework. Consider, for example, the expression of therapist congruence. Some clients may be accustomed to indirect communication and may therefore be uncomfortable with the openness and directness of the counselor. Chu and Sue (1984) provide a useful guideline: practitioners must be sensitive to the cultural values of ethnic clients while at the same time avoiding stereotyping of individuals. Respect can be shown by recognizing and appreciating the rich diversity that exists within any group of people.

A third limitation in applying the person-centered approach to ethnic clients pertains to the fact that this approach extols the value of an internal locus of evaluation. Yet some ethnic groups value an external locus of evalua- tion. For example, they may look to traditional expectations for their direction. They are likely to be highly influenced by societal expectations and not simply motivated by their own personal preference. Also, the focus on the develop- ment of the individual is often at odds with the cultural value that stresses the common good. It may be viewed as selfish to think about one's personal growth rather than being primarily concerned with what is best for the group. Lupe, a Hispanic client, may well consider her role as a mother and a wife and the interests of her family before she focuses on what she wants for herself. Al- though it is possible that she might "lose her own identity" by being overly concerned with her role in taking care of others in the family to the exclusion of her personal interests, a counselor could make a mistake by pushing her to think about what she wants for herself apart from being a wife and a mother. The context of her cultural values and her level of commitment to these values must be considered in working with her. The counselor may well encourage Lupe to explore how well her values are working for her, but it would be inappropriate for the counselor to impose a vision of the kind of woman she should be.

Although there are distinct limitations to working exclusively within a person-centered perspective with ethnic-minority clients, it should not be con- cluded that this approach is unsuitable for these clients. There is great diversity among any group of people, so there is room for a variety of therapeutic styles. Although some clients prefer an active style on the counselor's part, other clients respond well to a less directive counselor. The literature suggests that the appropriateness and effectiveness of counseling styles depend largely on the cultural values and world view embraced by an individual (Mokuau, 1987). It is a mistake to assume that one counseling style will be effective for all ethnic clients. Mokuau has observed that the prescription of a directive counseling style with Asian-American clients is limiting, because it is based on a monocul- tural perspective of an Asian world view and values. She challenges the notion that an active counseling style fits for all Asian-American clients.

I am becoming more convinced that the person-centered approach sup- plies an ideal foundation for establishing a solid relationship with ethnically diverse clients (see Patterson, 1985, chap. 10). Counselors are likely to find it necessary to utilize some structure while maintaining a climate that fosters self-direction in their clients. If a counselor simply waits for clients to bring up their personal issues, they may become dissatisfied with counseling and quit. It seems to me that more activity and structuring may be called for than is usually the case in a person-centered framework. However, the potential positive im- pact of a counselor who responds empathically to a minority client cannot be underestimated. Empathy is a powerful tool to communicate that the client is being understood. Many clients have never met someone who is able to truly listen and understand.

Questions for Reflection and Discussion

1. The relationship that the therapist creates with the client is the cornerstone of the person-centered approach. Rogers considered the core therapeutic conditions to be both necessary and sufficient for change to occur. Do you agree with this position? If not, what other therapeutic conditions or procedures do you see as essential?

2. Rogers eliminated diagnosis, because he found such procedures to be unnecessary and frequently misused. What are your thoughts on the purpose and usefulness of diagnosis?

3. The person-centered approach stresses listening to the deeper meanings of the client's behavior and allowing the client to provide the direction for the session. Are there any circumstances under which you might want to interpret the meaning of your client's behavior? Do you think you would have any difficulty in fully listening to the meanings conveyed by your clients? Can you think of any situations in which you might want to actively intervene by making suggestions or leading your client?

4. In counseling clients who have a different cultural background from yours, what potential advantages or disadvantages can you see in adopting a person-centered perspective?

5. Regardless of which approach guides your practice, the core therapeutic conditions and the type of relationship emphasized in the person-centered approach seem to serve as the foundation for counseling. What are the basic concepts of this theory that you might consider incorporating into your personal style of counseling?

6. Would you be able to accept your client? What would you do if you did not feel accepting of a certain person? Do you see any conflict between genuineness and acceptance?

7. How congruent, or real, could you be if you withheld your own values, feelings, and attitudes from your client? If you feel like making suggestions but refrain from doing so, are you being inauthentic?

8. What factors might interfere with your being genuine with a client? What about your need for the client's approval? Is there a danger that you might avoid a confrontation because you wanted to be liked?

9. What within yourself might make accurate empathic understanding difficult for you? Do you have broad life experiences that will help you identify with your client's struggles?

10. By this time you should be getting to know Stan, as depicted in Chapter 13. How might you feel if you were his counselor and you stayed within a person-centered framework? To what degree do you think you can understand Stan? Do you have any basis for identifying with him from your own experience?

Where to Go from Here

As I hope you will do with all the approaches, consider going beyond the introduction that you have been given here. An excellent place to begin is by selecting at least one source from the annotated reading suggestions (especially one of Rogers's works). Then consider attending a workshop offered by a center or an institute. If you are interested in participating in learning activities and workshops, you can write:

Center for Studies of the Person
1125 Torrey Pines Road
La Jolla, CA 92037

An organization that you might consider joining is the Association for the Development of the Person-Centered Approach. The association is an interdisciplinary and international organization with over 250 members. Membership includes a subscription to the *Person-Centered Review*, the association's quarterly newsletter, a membership directory, and a discount for attending the annual meeting. It also provides information about continuing education and supervision and training in the person-centered approach. General membership is $45 a year. Contact David Cain at:

Person-Centered Association
2831 Cedarwood Way
Carlsbad, CA 92008
Telephone: (619) 434-6080

If you are interested in obtaining training and supervised experience in the person-centered approach, you might be interested in the Carl Rogers Institute of Psychotherapy Training and Supervision. The institute conducts four training programs each year, including a one-month intensive program. For more information, contact:

Norman E. Chambers
Center for Studies of the Person
1125 Torrey Pines Road
La Jolla, CA 92037
Telephone: (619) 459-3861

An In-Depth Training Program in the Person-Centered Approach is designed to bring together person-centered theory and practice in an interactive group process. The format consists of ten weekends per year. For more information, contact:

Center for Interpersonal Growth
Box 271
Port Jefferson, NY 11777
Telephone: (516) 331-2061

RECOMMENDED SUPPLEMENTARY READINGS

One of the best ways to stay current in the area of theory, research, and application of the person-centered approach is by reading the *Person-Centered Review*. This journal is published quarterly— in February, May, August, and November—by Sage Publications,

2111 West Hillcrest Drive, Newbury Park, CA 91320. Its aim is to carry forward the work of Rogers and his pioneering spirit as well. This is an excellent journal, featuring personal reactions from person-centered practitioners, articles on the current state of theory applied to practice, and reviews of research.

One of the best primary sources for further reading is Rogers's *On Becoming a Person* (1961), a collection of his articles on the process of psychotherapy, its outcomes, the therapeutic relationship, education, family life, communication, and the nature of the healthy person.

A Way of Being (Rogers, 1980) contains a series of writings on Rogers's personal experiences and perspectives, as well as chapters on the foundations and applications of the person-centered approach. Especially useful are his chapters on new challenges to the helping professions and on the world of tomorrow and the person of tomorrow.

A Theory of Therapy: Guidelines for Counseling Practice (Combs, 1989) is a very important work based on a person-centered and humanistic philosophy. The author discusses topics such as the self in therapy, the nature of health and the goal of therapy, therapy as a learning process, the therapist as an instrument of change, and becoming a counselor.

REFERENCES AND SUGGESTED READINGS*

*AXLINE, V. (1964). *Dibs: In search of self.* New York: Ballantine.

BARRETT-LENNARD, G. T. (1988). Listening. *Person-Centered Review, 3,* 410–425.

BOZARTH, J. D., & BRODLEY, B. T. (1986). Client-centered psychotherapy: A statement. *Person-Centered Review, 1,* 262–271.

*BRAATEN, L. J. (1986). Thirty years with Rogers' necessary and sufficient conditions of therapeutic personality change: A personal evaluation. *Person-Centered Review, 1,* 37–50.

CAIN, D. J. (1986a). Editorial: A call for the "write stuff." *Person-Centered Review, 1,* 117–124.

CAIN, D. J. (1986b). Editor's introduction to the *Person-Centered Review. Person-Centered Review, 1,* 3–14.

CAIN, D. J. (1986c). What does it mean to be "person-centered"? *Person-Centered Review, 1,* 251–256.

CAIN, D. J. (1987a). Carl Rogers' life in review. *Person-Centered Review, 2,* 476–506.

*CAIN, D. J. (1987b). Carl R. Rogers: The man, his vision, his impact. *Person-Centered Review, 2,* 283–288.

CAIN, D. J. (1987c). Our international family. *Person-Centered Review, 2,* 139–149.

CAIN, D. J. (Ed.). (1988). Roundtable discussion: Why do you think there are so few person-centered practitioners or scholars considering that literally thousands of persons throughout the world attest to the enormous impact Carl Rogers has had on their personal and professional lives? *Person-Centered Review, 3,* 353–390.

CAIN, D. J., LIETAER, G., SACHSE, R., & THORNE, B. (1989). Proposals for the future of client-centered and experiential psychotherapy. *Person-Centered Review, 4,* 11–26.

CHU, J., & SUE, S. (1984). Asian/Pacific-Americans and group practice. In L. E. Davis (Ed.), *Ethnicity in social group work practice.* New York: Haworth.

COMBS, A. W. (1988). Some current issues for person-centered therapy. *Person-Centered Review, 3,* 263–276.

*COMBS, A. W. (1989). *A theory of therapy: Guidelines for counseling practice.* Newbury Park, CA: Sage Publications.

*Books and articles marked with an asterisk are suggested for further study.

COREY, G. (1990). *Theory and practice of group counseling* (3rd ed.). Pacific Grove, CA: Brooks/Cole.

COREY, G. (1991). *Case approach to counseling and psychotherapy* (3rd ed.). Pacific Grove, CA: Brooks/Cole.

FISCHER, C. T. (1987). Beyond transference. *Person-Centered Review, 2,* 157–164.

GENDLIN, E. T. (1988). Carl Rogers (1902–1987). *American Psychologist, 43,* 127–128.

GIESEKUS, U., & MENTE, A. (1986). Client empathic understanding in client-centered therapy. *Person-Centered Review, 1,* 163–171.

HEPPNER, P. P., ROGERS, M. E., & LEE, L. A. (1984). Carl Rogers: Reflections on his life. *Journal of Counseling and Development, 63,* 14–20.

HOWARD, G. S. (1987). The person in research. *Person-Centered Review, 2,* 50–65.

JENNINGS, J. L. (1986). The dream is the dream is the dream: A person-centered approach to dream analysis. *Person-Centered Review, 1,* 310–333.

LAMBERT, M. J. (1986). Future directions for research in client-centered psychotherapy. *Person-Centered Review, 1,* 185–200.

*LEVANT, R. F., & SHLIEN, J. M. (Eds.). (1984). *Client-centered therapy and the person-centered approach: New directions in theory, research, and practice.* New York: Praeger.

LIETAER, G. (1984). Unconditional positive regard: A controversial basic attitude in client-centered therapy. In R. F. Levant & J. M. Shlien (Eds.), *Client-centered therapy and the person-centered approach: New directions in theory, research, and practice* (pp. 41–58). New York: Praeger.

LIETAER, G., & NEIRINCK, M. (1986). Client and therapist perceptions of helping processes in client-centered/experiential psychotherapy. *Person-Centered Review, 1,* 436–455.

MADDI, S. R. (1986). On the importance of the present. *Person-Centered Review, 2,* 171–180.

MASLOW, A. (1968). *Toward a psychology of being* (rev. ed.). New York: Van Nostrand Reinhold.

MASLOW, A. (1970). *Motivation and personality* (rev. ed.). New York: Harper & Row.

MASLOW, A. (1971). *The farther reaches of human nature.* New York: Viking Press.

McILDUFF, E., & COGHLAN, D. (1989). Process and facilitation in a cross-cultural communication workshop: Questions and issues. *Person-Centered Review, 4,* 77–98.

MEARNS, D., & McLEOD, J. (1984). A person-centered approach to research. In R. F. Levant & J. M. Shlien (Eds.), *Client-centered therapy and the person-centered approach: New directions in theory, research, and practice* (pp. 370–398). New York: Praeger.

MOKUAU, N. (1987). Social workers' perceptions of counseling effectiveness for Asian-American clients. *Journal of the National Association of Social Workers, 32,* 331–335.

MURAYAMA, S., NOJIMA, K., & ABE, T. (1988). Person-centered groups in Japan: A selected review of the literature. *Person-Centered Review, 3,* 479–492.

*NATIELLO, P. (1987). The person-centered approach: From theory to practice. *Person-Centered Review, 2,* 203–216.

NYE, R. D. (1986). *Three psychologies: Perspectives from Freud, Skinner, and Rogers* (3rd ed.). Pacific Grove, CA: Brooks/Cole.

O'HARA, M. (1986). Heuristic inquiry as psychotherapy: The client-centered approach. *Person-Centered Review, 1,* 172–184.

O'LEARY, C. J. (1987). The lover's quarrel with the non-directive method. *Renaissance, 4,* 1–3.

PATTERSON, C. H. (1985). *The therapeutic relationship: Foundations for an eclectic psychotherapy.* Pacific Grove, CA: Brooks/Cole.

PATTERSON, C. H. (1986). *Theories of counseling and psychotherapy* (4th ed.). New York: Harper & Row.

PROCHASKA, J. O. (1984). *Systems of psychotherapy: A transtheoretical analysis* (2nd ed.). Pacific Grove, CA: Brooks/Cole.

*RASKIN, N. J., & ROGERS, C. R. (1989). Person-centered therapy. In R. J. Corsini & D. Wedding (Eds.), *Current psychotherapies* (4th ed.) (pp. 155–194). Itasca, IL: F. E. Peacock.

ROGERS, C. (1942). *Counseling and psychotherapy.* Boston: Houghton Mifflin.

ROGERS, C. (1951). *Client-centered therapy.* Boston: Houghton Mifflin.

*ROGERS, C. (1957). The necessary and sufficient conditions of therapeutic personality change. *Journal of Consulting Psychology, 21,* 95–103.

ROGERS, C. (1959). A theory of therapy, personality, and interpersonal relationships, as developed in the client-centered framework. In S. Koch (Ed.), *Psychology: A study of a science: Vol. 3.* New York: Basic Books.

*ROGERS, C. (1961). *On becoming a person.* Boston: Houghton Mifflin.

ROGERS, C. (1967). The conditions of change from a client-centered viewpoint. In B. Berenson & R. Carkhuff (Eds.), *Sources of gain in counseling and psychotherapy.* New York: Holt, Rinehart & Winston.

*ROGERS, C. (1970). *Carl Rogers on encounter groups.* New York: Harper & Row.

*ROGERS, C. (1977). *Carl Rogers on personal power: Inner strength and its revolutionary impact.* New York: Delacorte Press.

ROGERS, C. (1980). *A way of being.* Boston: Houghton Mifflin.

ROGERS, C. (1983). *Freedom to learn in the 80's.* Columbus, OH: Charles E. Merrill.

ROGERS, C. (1984). One alternative to nuclear planetary suicide. In R. Levant & J. M. Shlien (Eds.), *Client-centered therapy and the person-centered approach: New directions in theory, research, and practice* (pp. 400–422). New York: Praeger.

ROGERS, C. (1986a). Carl Rogers on the development of the person-centered approach. *Person-Centered Review, 1,* 257–259.

*ROGERS, C. (1986b). Client-centered therapy. In I. L. Kutash & A. Wolf (Eds.), *Psychotherapist's casebook* (pp. 197–208). San Francisco: Jossey-Bass.

ROGERS, C. (1986c). Reflections of feelings. *Person-Centered Review, 1,* 375–377.

*ROGERS, C. R. (1987a). Inside the world of the Soviet professional. *Counseling and Values, 32,* 46–66.

ROGERS, C. R. (1987b). Our international family. *Person-Centered Review, 2,* 139–149.

ROGERS, C. R. (1987c). Rogers, Kohut, and Erickson: A personal perspective on some similarities and differences. In J. K. Zeig (Ed.), *The evolution of psychotherapy* (pp. 179–187). New York: Brunner/Mazel.

ROGERS, C. R. (1987d). Steps toward world peace, 1948–1986: Tension reduction in theory and practice. *Counseling and Values, 32,* 38–45.

ROGERS, C. R. (1987e). The underlying theory: Drawn from experiences with individuals and groups. *Counseling and Values, 32,* 38–45.

*ROGERS, C. R. (1989). The case of Mrs. Oak. In D. Wedding & R. J. Corsini (Eds.), *Case studies in psychotherapy* (pp. 63–85). Itasca, IL: F. E. Peacock.

ROGERS, C. R., & MALCOLM, D. (1987). The potential contribution of the behavioral scientist to world peace. *Counseling and Values, 32,* 10–11.

ROGERS, C., & WOOD, J. (1974). Client-centered theory: Carl Rogers. In A. Burton (Ed.), *Operational theories of personality.* New York: Brunner/Mazel.

RYBACK, D. (1989). An interview with Carl Rogers. *Person-Centered Review, 4,* 99–112.

SANFORD, R. C. (1987). An inquiry into the evolution of the client-centered approach to psychotherapy. In J. K. Zeig (Ed.), *The evolution of psychotherapy* (pp. 188–197). New York: Brunner/Mazel.

SEEMAN, J. (1984). The fully functioning person: Theory and research. In R. F. Levant & J. M. Shlien (Eds.), *Client-centered therapy and the person-centered approach: New directions in theory, research, and practice* (pp. 131–152). New York: Praeger.

SEEMAN, J. (1988). Self-actualization: A reformulation. *Person-Centered Review, 3,* 304–315.

SIMS, J. M. (1989). Client-centered therapy: The art of knowing. *Person-Centered Review, 4,* 27–41.

SMITH, D. (1982). Trends in counseling and psychotherapy. *American Psychologist, 37,* 802–809.

TAUSCH, R. (1988). The relationship between emotions and cognitions. *Person-Centered Review, 3,* 277–291.

WATSON, N. (1984). The empirical status of Rogers' hypotheses of the necessary and sufficient conditions for effective psychotherapy In R. F. Levant & J. M. Shlien (Eds.), *Client-centered therapy and the person-centered approach: New directions in theory, research, and practice* (pp. 17–40). New York: Praeger.

WHITELEY, J. M. (1987). The person-centered approach to peace. *Counseling and Values, 32,* 5–8.

8

GESTALT THERAPY

FRITZ PERLS

FREDERICK S. (FRITZ) PERLS (1893–1970) was the originator and developer of Gestalt therapy. Born in Berlin in a lower-middle-class Jewish family, he identified himself as a source of much trouble for his parents. Although he failed the seventh grade twice and was expelled from school because of difficulties with the authorities, he still managed to complete his schooling and receive an M.D. with a specialization in psychiatry. In 1916 he joined the German Army and served as a medic in World War I.

* After the war Perls worked with Kurt Goldstein at the Goldstein Institute for Brain-Damaged Soldiers in Frankfurt. It was through this association that he came to see the importance of viewing humans as a whole rather than as a sum of discretely functioning parts. Later he moved to Vienna and began his psychoanalytic training. Perls was analyzed by Wilhelm Reich, a psychoanalyst who pioneered methods of self-understanding and personality change by working with the body. He was also supervised by several other key figures in the psychoanalytic movement, including Karen Horney.

Perls broke away from the psychoanalytic tradition around the time that he emigrated to the United States in 1946.

He later established the New York Institute for Gestalt Therapy in 1952. Eventually, he settled in Big Sur, California, and gave workshops and seminars at the Esalen Institute, carving out his reputation as an innovator in psychotherapy. Here Perls had a great impact on people, partly through his professional writings but mainly through personal contact in his workshops.

Personally Perls was both vital and perplexing. People typically either responded to him in awe or found him harshly confrontive and saw him as meeting his own needs through showmanship. He was viewed variously as insightful, witty, bright, provocative, manipulative, hostile, demanding, and inspirational. Unfortunately, some of the people who attended his workshops became followers of the "guru" and then went out to spread the gospel of Gestalt therapy. Even though Perls mentioned in one of his books his concern over those who mechanically functioned as Gestalt therapists and promoted phoniness, it appeared to many that he did little to discourage this kind of cult.

Readers who want a firsthand account of the life of Perls should read his autobiography, *In and Out of the Garbage Pail* (1969b).

INTRODUCTION

As developed by Perls, Gestalt therapy is an existential approach based on the premise that people must find their own way in life and accept personal responsibility if they hope to achieve maturity. The basic, initial goal is for clients to gain *awareness* of what they are experiencing and doing. Through this awareness they gain self-understanding and the knowledge that they can change.

Hence, they learn that they are *responsible* for what they are thinking, feeling, and doing. The approach is *phenomenological* in its focus on the client's perceptions of reality. The approach is *existential* in that it is grounded in the here and now. Being in the present moment involves a transition between one's past and one's future. Thus, clients are asked to bring any concerns about what was or will be into the present and directly experience these concerns. In this way Gestalt therapy is lively and promotes direct experiencing, rather than the abstractness of talking about situations. The approach is *experiential* in that clients come to grips with what they are thinking, feeling, and doing as they interact with another person, the therapist. Gestalt therapy places a premium on the willingness of the therapist to be fully present during the therapeutic encounter. Growth occurs from genuine contact between these two persons, not from the therapist's interpretations or techniques.

Perls originally focused on the awareness and responsibility that clients develop by looking inward at their own direct experiencing. One of the therapist's roles is to devise *experiments* designed to increase clients' self-awareness of what they are doing and how they are doing it. This awareness makes it possible for them to see alternatives for changing themselves. Clients are expected to do their own seeing, feeling, sensing, and interpreting, as opposed to waiting passively for the therapist to give them insight and answers.

Perls was influenced by a number of intellectual trends of his time, including psychoanalysis, Gestalt psychology, psychodrama, and existentialism and phenomenology. Reich's influence on Gestalt therapy is found in its focus on experiencing one's body, such as working with breathing, energy level, and blockages in a certain area of the body. Although Perls was influenced by psychoanalytic concepts, he took issue with Freud's theory on a number of grounds. Whereas Freud's view of human beings was basically mechanistic, Perls stressed a holistic approach to personality. Freud focused on repressed intrapsychic conflicts from one's early childhood; Perls valued examining one's present situation. This approach focuses much more on process than on content. Emphasis is given to what is being presently experienced, rather than to the content of what clients reveal. Perls believed that *how* individuals behave in the present moment is far more crucial to self-understanding than *why* they behave as they do.

KEY CONCEPTS

VIEW OF HUMAN NATURE

The Gestalt view of human nature, as we have seen, is rooted in existential philosophy and phenomenology. Genuine knowledge is the product of what is immediately evident in the experience of the perceiver. Therapy aims not at analysis but at integration of sometimes conflicting dimensions within the person. The process of "reowning" parts of oneself that have been disowned and the unification process proceed step by step until clients become strong enough to carry on their own personal growth. By becoming aware, one becomes able to make choices and thus live a meaningful existence.

A basic assumption of Gestalt therapy is that individuals can themselves deal effectively with their life problems, especially if they make full use of awareness of what is happening in and around them. Because of certain problems in development, people form various ways of avoiding problems and, therefore, reach impasses in their personal growth. Therapy provides the necessary intervention and challenge to help them proceed toward integration and a more authentic and vital existence.

THE NOW

For Perls nothing exists except the "now." Because the past is gone and the future has not yet arrived, only the present is significant. One of the main contributions of the Gestalt approach is its emphasis on learning to appreciate and fully experience the present moment. Focusing on the past can be a way to avoid coming to terms with the present.

In speaking of the "now ethos," Polster and Polster (1973) develop the thesis that "power is in the present." For many people the power of the present is lost; instead of being in the present moment, they invest their energies in bemoaning their past mistakes and ruminating about how life could and should have been different, or they engage in endless resolutions and plans for the future. As they direct their energy toward what was or what might have been, the power of the present diminishes. However, Erving Polster (1987a) points out that there is a danger in limiting the focus of therapy to the here and now. In his current thinking he stresses the importance of having clients flesh out their stories, which may include working with the past, present, and future.

To help the client make contact with the present moment, the Gestalt therapist asks "what" and "how" questions but rarely asks "why" questions. In order to promote "now" awareness, the therapist encourages a dialogue in the present tense by asking such questions as "What is happening now? What is going on now? What are you experiencing as you sit there and attempt to talk? What is your awareness at this moment? How are you experiencing your fear? How are you attempting to withdraw at this moment?" Perls (1969a) contends that without an intensification of feelings the person would speculate *why* he or she felt this way. According to Perls, "why" questions lead only toward rationalizations and "self-deceptions" and away from the immediacy of experiencing. "Why" questions lead to an endless and heady rumination about the past that only serves to encourage resistance to present experience.

The questions and exercises used by the Gestalt therapist point up the specific methods the client is using to escape. Most people can stay in the present for only a short while. They are inclined to find ways of interrupting the flow of the present. Instead of experiencing their feelings in the here and now, they often *talk about* their feelings, almost as if their feelings were detached from their present experiencing. Perls's aim was to help people make contact with their experience with vividness and immediacy rather than merely talking about the experience. Thus, if a client begins to talk about sadness, pain, or confusion, the therapist makes every attempt to have the client experience that sadness, pain, or confusion *now*. Talking about problems can become an endless word game that leads to unproductive discussion and exploration of hidden meanings. It is one way of resisting growth and also a way of engaging in self-deception; clients attempt to trick themselves into believing that because they are facing their problems and talking about them, they are resolving their problems and growing as persons. To lessen the danger of this, attempts are made to intensify and exaggerate certain feelings. In a group setting, for example, the therapist may ask a client who reports how conscious he or she is of pleasing others and meeting others' expectations to choose several persons in the group and to strive at that very moment to please each one.

Is the past ignored in the Gestalt approach? It is not accurate to say that Gestalt therapists have no interest in a person's past; the past is important when it is related in some way to significant themes in the individual's present functioning. When the past seems to have a significant bearing on one's present attitudes or behavior, it is dealt with by bringing it into the present as much as possible. Thus, when clients speak about their past, the therapist may ask them to bring it into the now by reenacting it as though they were living it now. The therapist directs clients to "bring the fantasy here" and strive to relive the feelings they experienced earlier. For example, rather than *talking about* a past childhood trauma with their father, clients *become* the hurt child and talk directly to the father in fantasy. Through this process there is a reliving of the hurt and a potential to change it to understanding and resolution.

UNFINISHED BUSINESS

Another key concept is unfinished business, or unexpressed feelings such as resentment, rage, hatred, pain, anxiety, grief, guilt, abandonment, and so on. Even though the feelings are unexpressed, they are associated with distinct memories and fantasies. Because the feelings are not fully experienced in awareness, they linger in the background and are carried into present life in ways that interfere with effective contact with oneself and others. Unfinished business persists until the individual faces and deals with the unexpressed feelings. In speaking of the effects of unfinished business, Polster and Polster (1973) maintain that "these incomplete directions *do seek* completion and when they get powerful enough, the individual is beset with preoccupation, compulsive behavior, wariness, oppressive energy and much self-defeating behavior" (p. 36).

An example of how unfinished business nags at one and manifests itself in current behavior can be seen in a man who never really felt loved and accepted by his mother. He developed resentment of his mother, for, no matter how he sought her approval, he was always left feeling that he was not adequate. In an attempt to deflect the direction of this need for maternal approval, he may look to women for his confirmation of worth as a man. In developing a variety of games to get women to approve of him, he reports that he is still not satisfied. The unfinished business has prevented him from authentic intimacy with women, because the need was that of a child rather than an adult. He needs to experience closure of the unfinished business before he can experience real

satisfaction; that is, he needs to return to the old business, express his unacknowledged feelings of disappointment and rage, and resolve the old impasse.

Unacknowledged feelings create unnecessary emotional debris that clut-
ters present-centered awareness. According to Perls (1969a), resentment is the
most frequent and worst kind of unfinished business. In his view when people
are resentful, they become stuck, for they can neither let go nor engage in
authentic communication until they express the resentment. Thus, Perls contends that it is imperative to express resentments. Unexpressed resentment
frequently converts to guilt. "Whenever you feel guilty, find out what you are
resenting and express it and make your demands explicit" (Perls, 1969a, p. 49).

AVOIDANCE

A concept related to unfinished business is avoidance, which refers to the
means people use to keep themselves from facing unfinished business and
from experiencing the uncomfortable emotions associated with unfinished
situations. Perls (1969a) writes that most people would rather avoid experiencing painful emotions than do what is necessary to change. Therefore, they
become stuck and are unable to get through the impasse, blocking their possibilities of growth.

Because we have a tendency to avoid confronting and fully experiencing
our anxiety, grief, guilt, and other uncomfortable emotions, the emotions become a nagging undercurrent that prevents us from being fully alive. Perls
spoke of the catastrophic expectations that we conjure up and that keep us
psychologically stuck: "If I express my pain fully, people will be embarrassed,
and they won't have anything to do with me"; "If I were to express my anger to
the significant people in my life, they would abandon me"; "If I ever allowed
myself to mourn over my losses, I might sink so deep into depression that I'd
never get out of that hole."

Perls maintained that these fantasies keep us from living, because we use
them to avoid taking the necessary risks that growth demands. Thus, the Gestalt
therapist encourages expressing in the now of the therapeutic session intense
feelings never directly expressed before. If a client says that she is afraid of
getting in touch with her feelings of hatred and spite, she may be encouraged by
the therapist to become her hateful and spiteful side and express these negative
feelings. By experiencing the side of herself that she works so hard at disown-
ing, she begins a process of integration and allows herself to get beyond the
impasse that keeps her from growing. By going beyond our avoidances, we
make it possible to dispose of unfinished business that interferes with our
present life, and we move toward health and integration.

LAYERS OF NEUROSIS —*way to change*

Perls (1970) likens the unfolding of adult personality to the peeling of an
onion. In order for individuals to achieve psychological maturity, they must
strip off five layers of neurosis. These superimposed growth disorders are

(1) the phony, (2) the phobic, (3) the impasse, (4) the implosive, and (5) the explosive. The first layer we encounter, the *phony layer,* consists of reacting to others in stereotypical and inauthentic ways. This is the level where we play games and get lost in roles. By behaving *as if* we are a person that we are not, we are trying to live up to a fantasy that we or others have created. Once we become aware of the phoniness of game playing and become more honest, then we experience unpleasantness and pain.

The next layer we encounter is the *phobic layer.* At this level we attempt to avoid the emotional pain that is associated with seeing aspects of ourselves that we would prefer to deny. At this point our resistances to accepting ourselves the way we actually are pop up. We have catastrophic fears that if we recognize who we really are and present that side of ourselves to others, they will surely reject us.

Beneath the phobic layer is the *impasse,* or the point where we are stuck in our own maturation. This is the point at which we are sure that we will not be able to survive, for we convince ourselves that we do not have the resources within ourselves to move beyond the stuck point without environmental support. Typically, this is the time when we attempt to manipulate the environment to do our seeing, hearing, feeling, thinking, and deciding for us. At the impasse we often feel a sense of deadness and feel that we are nothing. If we hope to feel alive, it is essential that we get through the impasse.

If we allow ourselves to fully experience our deadness, rather than denying it or running away, then the *implosive level* comes into being. Perls (1970) writes that it is necessary to go through this implosive layer in order to get to the authentic self. By getting into contact with this layer, or our deadness and inauthentic ways, we expose our defenses and begin to make contact with our genuine self.

Perls contends that peeling back the implosive layer creates an explosive state. When we contact the *explosive layer,* we let go of phony roles and pretenses, and we release a tremendous amount of energy that we have been holding in by pretending to be who we are not. To become alive and authentic, it is necessary to achieve this explosion, which can be an explosion into pain and into joy.

CONTACT AND RESISTANCES TO CONTACT

In Gestalt therapy contact is necessary if change and growth are to occur. When we make contact with the environment, change is inevitable. Contact is made by seeing, hearing, smelling, touching, and moving. Effective contact means interacting with nature and with other people without losing one's sense of individuality. It is the continually renewed creative adjustment of individuals to their environment (M. Polster, 1987). Prerequisites for good contact are clear awareness, full energy, and the ability to express oneself (Zinker, 1978). Miriam Polster claims that contact is the lifeblood of growth. It entails zest, imagination, and creativity. There are only moments of this type of contact, so it is most accurate to think of levels of contact, rather than a final state to achieve.

After a contact experience there is typically a withdrawal to integrate what has been learned.

The Gestalt therapist also focuses on resistances to contact. From a Gestalt perspective resistance refers to defenses that we develop to prevent us from experiencing the present in a full and real way. The five layers of neurosis represent a person's style of keeping energy pent up in the service of maintaining pretenses. There are also ego-defense mechanisms that prevent people from being authentic. Polster and Polster (1973) describe five major channels of resistance that are challenged in Gestalt therapy: introjection, projection, retroflection, deflection, and confluence.

Introjection is the tendency to uncritically accept others' beliefs and standards without assimilating them to make them congruent with who we are. These introjects become alien to us, because we have not analyzed and restructured them. When we introject, we passively incorporate what the environment provides, spending little time on getting clear what we want or need. If we remain in this stage, our energy is bound up in taking things as we find them.

Projection is the reverse of introjection. In projection we disown certain aspects of ourselves by assigning them to the environment. When we are projecting, we have trouble distinguishing between the inside world and the outside world. Those attributes of our personality that are inconsistent with our self-image are disowned and put onto other people. By seeing in others the very qualities that we refuse to acknowledge in ourselves, we avoid taking responsibility for our own feelings and the person who we are, and this keeps us powerless to initiate change.

Retroflection consists of turning back to ourselves what we would like to do to someone else or doing to ourselves what we would like someone else to do to us. If we lash out and injure ourselves, for example, we are often directing aggression inward that we are fearful of directing toward others. This process seriously restricts engagement between the person and his or her environment. Typically, these maladaptive styles of functioning are adopted out of our awareness; part of the process of Gestalt therapy is to help us discover a self-regulatory system so that we can deal realistically with the world.

Deflection is the process of distraction so that it is difficult to maintain a sustained sense of contact. People who deflect attempt to diffuse contact through the overuse of humor, abstract generalizations, and questions rather than statements (Frew, 1986). They engage their environment on an inconsistent basis, which results in their feeling a sense of emotional depletion. Deflection involves a diminished emotional experience. People who deflect speak through and for others.

Confluence involves a blurring of awareness of the differentiation between the self and the environment. For people who are oriented toward blending in, there is no clear demarcation between internal experience and outer reality. Confluence in relationships involves an absence of conflicts, or a belief that all parties experience the same feelings and thoughts. Confluence is a style of contact that is characteristic of clients who have a high need to be accepted and liked. It is a way of staying safe by going along with others and not expressing one's true feelings and opinions. Conflicts can be very anxiety-producing for individuals who rely on confluence as a style of contact (Frew, 1986). Confluence makes it difficult for people to have their own thoughts and to speak for themselves. Such people tend to avoid conflicts. This condition makes genuine contact extremely difficult. A therapist might assist clients who use this channel of resistance by asking questions such as "What are you doing now? What are you experiencing at this moment? What would you want right now?"

Introjection, projection, retroflection, deflection, and confluence represent styles of resisting contact. The concern of Gestalt therapists is the interruption of contact with the environment when the individual is unaware of this process. Terms such as *resistance to contact* or *boundary disturbance* refer to the characteristic styles that people employ in their attempt to control their environment. The premise in Gestalt therapy is that contact is both normal and healthy. Therefore, a discussion of these styles of resistance to contact focuses on the degree to which these processes are in the individual's awareness. Clients in Gestalt therapy are encouraged to become increasingly aware of their dominant style of blocking contact.

ENERGY AND BLOCKS TO ENERGY

In Gestalt therapy special attention is given to where energy is located, how it is used, and how it can be blocked. Blocked energy is another form of resistance. It can be manifested by tension in some part of the body, by posture, by keeping one's body tight and closed, by a quivering of some body part, by looking away from people when speaking as a way to avoid contact, and by speaking with a restricted voice, to mention only a few.

In commenting on the value of focusing on the client's energy in therapeutic work, Zinker (1978) writes that clients may not be aware of their energy or where it is located, and they may experience it in a negative way. From his perspective therapy at its best involves a dynamic relationship that awakens and nourishes the client without sapping the therapist of his or her own energy. Zinker maintains that it is the therapist's job to help clients locate the ways in which they are blocking energy and to help them transform this blocked energy into more adaptive behaviors. This process is best accomplished when resistance is not viewed as a client's refusal to cooperate and as something simply to be gotten around. Instead, therapists can learn to welcome resistance and use it as a way of deepening therapeutic work. Clients can be encouraged to recognize how their resistance is being expressed in their body, and rather than trying to rid themselves of certain bodily symptoms, they can actually delve fully into tension states. By allowing themselves to exaggerate their tight mouth and shaking legs, they can discover for themselves how they are diverting energy and keeping themselves powerless.

THE THERAPEUTIC PROCESS

THERAPEUTIC GOALS

Gestalt therapy is basically an existential encounter between people, out of which clients tend to move in certain directions. These directions, or the general goals of the Gestalt process, are outlined by Zinker (1978). As an outgrowth of a genuine therapeutic encounter, it is expected that clients will:

- move toward increased awareness of themselves
- gradually assume ownership of their experience (as opposed to making others responsible for what they are thinking, feeling, and doing)
- develop skills and acquire values that will allow them to satisfy their needs without violating the rights of others
- become more aware of all of their senses
- learn to accept responsibility for what they do, including accepting the consequences of their actions
- move from outside support toward increasing internal support
- nevertheless be able to ask and get help from others and to give to others

In keeping with the humanistic spirit, Perls contends that most of us use only a fraction of our potential. This view is like Maslow's concept of the "psychopathology of the average": our lives are patterned and stereotyped; we play the same roles again and again and find very few ways to reinvent our existence and make full use of the possibilities of the present moment. Perls contends that if we find out how we are preventing ourselves from realizing the full measure of our human potential, we can learn many ways to make life richer. This potential is based on the attitude of living each moment freshly. A major goal of therapy, therefore, is to help the client live a fuller life.

An immediate aim of the Gestalt process is the attaining of awareness. Increased and enriched awareness, by and of itself, is seen as curative. Without awareness clients do not possess the tools for personality change. With awareness they have the capacity to face and accept denied parts of their being and to get in touch with subjective experiences and with reality. They can become unified and whole. When clients stay with their awareness, important unfinished business will always emerge so that it can be dealt with in therapy

THERAPIST'S FUNCTION AND ROLE

The Gestalt therapist focuses on the client's feelings, awareness at the moment, body messages, energy, avoidance, and blocks to awareness. Perls demonstrated an anti-intellectual bias, asserting that much of our thinking is a way of avoiding feeling. His often-quoted dictum is "Lose your mind and come to your senses." In the current practice of Gestalt therapy there is less of an anti-intellectual spirit. It is possible to keep your mind and awareness and still "come to your senses."

Gestalt therapy involves getting in touch with the obvious, according to Perls (1969a), who contends that neurotics do not see the obvious. They are unaware of their tightly clenched fist, of their controlled voice, or of not having responded to the therapist's suggestion. Thus, the therapist's job is to challenge clients so that they learn to use their senses fully and get in touch with body messages. Perls asserts that the total being of a person is before the therapist. Gestalt therapy uses the eyes and ears of the therapist to stay in the now. The therapist avoids abstract intellectualization, diagnosis, interpretation, and excessive verbiage.

Although the Gestalt approach is concerned with the obvious, its simplicity should not be taken to mean that the therapist's job is easy. If therapists do not use their personhood as an instrument of therapeutic change, they become little more than responders, catalysts, and technicians who play therapeutic games with clients. Developing a variety of Gestalt gimmicks is easy, but employing the techniques in a mechanical fashion allows the clients to continue inauthentic living. If clients are to become authentic, they need contact with an authentic therapist. In *Creative Process in Gestalt Therapy* Zinker (1978) emphasizes the role of the therapist as a creative agent of change, an inventor, and a compassionate and caring human being. Zinker, although borrowing from Perls, has carried Gestalt therapy beyond the Perlsian style.

Polster and Polster, like Zinker, have developed their own style of Gestalt practice. The Polsters discuss the concept of the "therapist as his own instrument" (1973, pp. 18–22). Like artists who need to be in touch with what they are painting, therapists are "artistic participant[s] in the creation of new life." Polster and Polster implore therapists to use their own experiences as essential ingredients in the therapy process. According to them, therapists are more than mere responders or catalysts. If they are to function effectively, they must be in tune with the persons before them, and they must also be in tune with themselves. Thus, therapy is a two-way engagement on a genuine I/thou basis. Not only does the client change, but so does the therapist. If the therapist is not sensitively tuned in to his or her own qualities of tenderness, toughness, and compassion and to reactions to the client, then "he becomes a technician, ministering to another person and not living the therapy with the full flavor that is available." In other words, therapists must also be aware and functioning sensitively in the present if they are to foster these qualities in the client.

How does Gestalt therapy proceed, and what are the functions of the therapist in the process? What follows are Perls's (1969a) key ideas about the role of the therapist. To begin with, the therapist's aim is the client's maturation and the removal of "blocks that prevent a person from standing on his own feet." The therapist's job is to help the client make the transition from external to internal support, and this is done by locating the impasse. The impasse is the point at which individuals avoid experiencing threatening feelings because they feel uncomfortable. It is a resistance to facing one's self and to changing. People often express resistance by saying: "I feel frustrated — like I'm spinning my wheels and getting nowhere. I don't know where to go from here. I can't do thus and so. I feel stuck." According to Perls, people experience "being stuck" because of their "catastrophic expectations." They imagine that something terrible will happen. Their catastrophic fantasies prevent them from fully living, and because of their unreasonable fears they refuse to take the necessary risks to become more mature. Typically, "catastrophic expectations" take the form of statements such as "If I am a certain way or have certain feelings, then I won't be loved, or accepted, or approved of. I'll be stupid. I'll perish. I'll feel like a fool. I'll be abandoned."

At the moment of impasse clients attempt to maneuver their environment by playing roles of weakness, helplessness, stupidity, and foolishness. The therapist's task is to help them get through the impasse so that growth is possible. This is a difficult task, for at the point of impasse clients believe that they have no chance of survival and that they will not find the means for survival within. The therapist assists them in recognizing and working through the impasse by providing situations that encourage them to experience fully their conditions of being stuck. By fully experiencing the blockage, they are able to get into contact with their frustrations. Perls contends that frustration is essential for growth, for without frustration people have no need to muster their own resources and to discover that they can well do on their own what they are manipulating others to do for them. If therapists are not careful, they too will be sucked into clients' manipulations.

An important function of the Gestalt therapist is paying attention to the client's body language. The client's nonverbal cues provide the therapist with rich information, because they often betray feelings of which the client is unaware. Perls (1969a) writes that a client's posture, movements, gestures, voice, hesitations, and so on tell the real story. He warns that verbal communication is usually a lie and that if therapists are content-oriented they miss the essence of the person. Real communication is beyond words.

Thus, the therapist needs to be alert for splits in attention and awareness and for incongruities between verbalizations and what clients are doing with their body. Clients demonstrate from moment to moment their lack of full contact with their present-centered actuality. Thus, the therapist might direct clients to speak for and become their gestures or body parts. Gestalt therapists often ask: "What do your eyes say? If your hands could speak at this moment, what would they say? Can you carry on a conversation between your right and left hands?" Clients may verbally express anger and at the same time smile. Or they may say that they are in pain and at the same time laugh. The therapist can ask them to recognize that their laughter is covering up their pain. Clients may be asked to become aware of how they are using their laughter to mask feelings of anger or pain. Attention to the messages that clients send nonverbally are grist for the mill, and the therapist needs to focus on the nonverbal cues.

In addition to calling attention to a client's nonverbal language, the Gestalt counselor places emphasis on the relationship between language patterns and personality. This approach suggests that clients' speech patterns are often an expression of their feelings, thoughts, and attitudes. The Gestalt approach focuses on overt speaking habits as a way to increase clients' awareness of themselves, especially by asking them to notice whether their words are congruent with what they are experiencing or instead are distancing them from their emotions.

A function of the Gestalt counselor is to gently confront clients by interventions that help them become aware of the effects of their language patterns. By focusing on language, clients are able to increase their awareness of what they are experiencing in the present moment and of how they are avoiding coming into contact with this here-and-now experience. What are some of the aspects of language that the Gestalt counselor might focus on? The following are some examples:

- *"It" talk.* When clients say "it" instead of "I," they are using depersonalizing language. The counselor may ask them to substitute personal pronouns for impersonal ones so that they will assume an increased sense of responsibility. For example, a client says "It is difficult to make friends." The client could be asked to restate this by making an "I" statement — "I have trouble making friends."
- *"You" talk.* The counselor will point out generalized use of "you" and ask the client to substitute "I" when this is what is meant. When clients say "You feel sort of hurt when people don't accept you," they may be asked to look at how they are distancing themselves from intense feelings by using a generalized "you." Again, they can be encouraged to change this impersonal "you" into an "I" statement such as "I feel hurt when I am not accepted." They can be asked to notice the difference in their feelings when they say each.
- *Questions.* Questions have a tendency to keep the questioner hidden, safe, and unknown. Gestalt counselors often ask clients to change their questions into statements. In making personal statements, clients begin to assume responsibility for what they say. They may become aware of how they are keeping themselves mysterious through a barrage of questions and how this serves to prevent them from making declarations that express themselves. For example, without stating their investment behind their question, group members often question one another by probing for information. If a member were to ask another member: "Why do you try so hard to get your father's approval when it seems so futile?" I would be likely to ask the questioning member: "Could you tell her what prompts you to ask her this question? Would you be willing to make a statement about yourself, rather than expecting her to answer your question?" Of course, not all questions are seen as resistances to change. Some questions are genuine requests for information.
- *Language that denies power.* Some clients have a tendency to deny their personal power by adding qualifiers or disclaimers to their statements. When a client says "I want to stop feeling like a victim, but I feel powerless to change," he or she is adding to the powerlessness with the appendage of "but." Often what follows a "but" serves to discount the first part of the statement. The counselor may also point out to clients how certain qualifiers subtract from their effectiveness. In this way clients become aware of how qualifiers keep them ambivalent. Experimenting with omitting qualifiers such as "maybe," "perhaps," "sort of," "I guess," "possibly," and "I suppose" can help clients change ambivalent messages into clear and direct statements. Likewise, when clients say "I can't," they are really implying "I won't." Asking them to substitute "won't" for "can't" assists them in owning and accepting their power by taking responsibility for their decisions. Other words that deny power are the "shoulds" and "oughts" that some people habitually use. Clients can at least become aware of the frequency with which they tell themselves and others that they "should" or "ought" to do this or that. By changing these "I shoulds" to "I choose to" or "I want to" they can begin taking active steps that reduce the

feeling of being driven and not in control of their life. The counselor must be careful in intervening so that clients do not feel that everything they say is subject to scrutiny. Rather than fostering a morbid kind of introspection, the counselor hopes to foster awareness of what is really being expressed through words.

• *Listening to a client's metaphors.* In his workshops Erving Polster emphasizes the importance of a therapist's learning how to listen to the metaphors of clients. By paying attention to metaphors, the therapist gets rich clues to a client's internal struggles. Examples of metaphors that can be amplified include client statements such as these: "It's hard for me to spill my guts in here." "At times I feel that I don't have a leg to stand on." "I need to be prepared in case someone blasts me." "I felt ripped to shreds after you confronted me last week." Beneath a metaphor may lie a suppressed internal dialogue that represents critical unfinished business. The art of therapy consists of translating the meaning of these metaphors into manifest content so that they can be dealt with in therapy.

• *Listening for language that uncovers a story.* Polster also teaches the value of what he calls "fleshing out a flash." He contends that clients often use language that is elusive but contains significant clues to their life struggles. He suggests that therapists learn to pick out a small part of what someone says and then to focus and develop this element. Clients are likely to slide over pregnant phrases, but the alert therapist can ask questions that will help them flesh out their story line. It is essential for therapists to pay attention to what is fascinating about the person who is sitting before them and get that person to tell a story.

CLIENT'S EXPERIENCE IN THERAPY

The general orientation of Gestalt therapy is toward clients' assumption of more and more responsibility for themselves — for their thoughts, feelings, and behavior. The therapist confronts them with the ways in which they are avoiding their personal responsibilities and asks them to make decisions about continuing therapy, about what they wish to learn from it, and about how they want to use their therapy time. Other issues that can become the focal point of therapy include the client/therapist relationship and the similarities in the ways clients relate to the therapist and to others in their environment. Clients in Gestalt therapy, then, are active participants who make their own interpretations and meanings. It is they who increase awareness and decide what they will or will not do with their personal meaning.

Miriam Polster (1987) describes a three-stage integration sequence that characterizes client growth in therapy. The first part of this sequence consists of *discovery.* Clients are likely to reach a new realization about themselves or to acquire a novel view of an old situation, or they may take a new look at some significant person in their life. Such discoveries often come as a surprise to them.

The second stage of the integration sequence is *accommodation,* which involves clients' recognizing that they have a choice. They are not bound tightly to one course, but there are alternative ways of behaving. Clients begin by trying out new behaviors in the supportive environment of the therapy office, and then they expand their awareness of the world. Making new choices is often done awkwardly, but with support clients can gain skills in coping with difficult situations. The therapeutic task is to mobilize the support system of the client and to encourage practice and experimentation with alternate ways of behaving. Clients are likely to carry out homework assignments that are aimed at achieving success.

The third stage of the integration sequence is *assimilation,* which involves clients' learning how to influence their environment. At this phase clients feel capable of dealing with the surprises they encounter in everyday living. They are now beginning to do more than passively accept the environment. Behavior at this stage may include a client's taking a stand on a critical issue. Eventually, clients develop confidence in their ability to improve and improvise. They are able to make choices that will result in getting what they want. The therapist points out that something has been accomplished and acknowledges the changes that have taken place within the client. At this phase clients have learned what they can do to maximize their chances of getting what is needed from their environment.

RELATIONSHIP BETWEEN THERAPIST AND CLIENT

As an existential brand of therapy, Gestalt practice involves a person-to-person relationship between the therapist and the client. The therapist's experiences, awareness, and perceptions provide the background of the therapy process, and the client's awareness and reactions constitute the forefront. It is important that therapists actively share their own present perceptions and experiences as they encounter clients in the here and now. Further, the therapist gives feedback, particularly of what clients are doing with their body. Feedback allows clients to develop an awareness of what they are actually doing. The therapist must encounter clients with honest and immediate reactions and challenge their manipulations without rejecting them as persons. The therapist needs to explore with clients their fears, catastrophic expectations, blockages, and resistances.

Therapists are responsible for the quality of their presence, for knowing themselves and the client, and for remaining open to the client. They are also responsible for establishing and maintaining a therapeutic atmosphere that will foster a spirit of work on the client's part. The I/thou relationship is given primary importance, which means that there is a dialogue and contact between therapist and client. It is from this interaction that clients learn about themselves and are able to change. It is not so much a matter of techniques used by therapists, but rather who they *are* as persons and what they are *doing* (Yontef & Simkin, 1989).

A number of writers have given central importance to the I/thou relationship and the quality of the therapist's presence, as opposed to technical skills. They warn of the dangers of becoming technique-bound and losing sight of their own being as they engage the client. Techniques are not the issue; rather, the therapist's attitudes and behavior and the relationship that is established are what really count (Polster & Polster, 1973; Yontef & Simkin, 1989).

APPLICATION: THERAPEUTIC TECHNIQUES AND PROCEDURES

Before examining the variety of Gestalt methods that you could include in your repertoire of counseling procedures, it is helpful to differentiate between exercises and experiments. *Exercises* are ready-made techniques that are sometimes used to evoke certain emotions (such as the expression of anger) in clients. *Experiments,* in contrast, grow out of the interaction between client and therapist. They can be considered the very cornerstone of experiential learning.

Miriam Polster (1987) says that an experiment is a way to bring out some kind of internal conflict by making this struggle an actual process. It is aimed at facilitating a client's ability to work through the stuck points of his or her life. Experiments encourage spontaneity and inventiveness by bringing the possibilities for action directly into the counseling session. By dramatizing or playing out problem situations or relationships in the relative safety of therapy, clients increase their range of flexibility of behavior. According to Polster, Gestalt experiments can take many forms: imagining a threatening future encounter; setting up a dialogue between a client and some significant person in his or her life; dramatizing the memory of a painful event; reliving a particularly profound early experience in the present; assuming the identity of one's mother or father through role playing; focusing on gestures, posture, and other nonverbal signs of inner expression; or carrying on a dialogue between two conflicting aspects within the person. The main point is that experiments bring struggles to life by inviting clients to enact them in the safety of the therapy session. Through these experiments clients actually experience the feelings associated with their conflicts, as opposed to merely talking about their problems in a detached fashion. Zinker (1978) sees therapy sessions as a series of experiments, which are the avenues for clients to learn experientially. What is learned from an experiment is a surprise to both the client and the counselor. Gestalt experiments are a creative adventure, a way of thinking out loud, and a way for clients to express themselves behaviorally.

PREPARING FOR GESTALT EXPERIMENTS

Sometimes I hear students maintain that Gestalt therapy relies too much on techniques and that they would be afraid to introduce many of these methods into a counseling session for fear that their clients would perceive them as being slightly odd. Unless these techniques are experienced, they may seem strange. After all, who would talk to an empty chair? Moreover, who would expect the chair to answer back? Asking clients to "become" an object in one of their dreams, for instance, can seem silly and pointless to some. It is a good practice for counselors to be familiar with the experiments they introduce (or the kinds of experiment they create and suggest). It is important for counselors to *personally* experience the power of Gestalt experiments and to feel comfortable suggesting them to clients. For those who are interested in Gestalt self-experiments I highly recommend James and Jongeward (1971); Passons (1975);

Perls, Hefferline, and Goodman (1951); Rainwater (1979); Stevens (1971); and Zinker (1978).

It is also essential that counselors establish a relationship with their clients, so that the clients will feel trusting enough to participate in the learning that can result from Gestalt experiments. Clients will get more from Gestalt experiments if they are oriented and prepared for them. Through a trusting relationship with the therapist, clients are likely to challenge their resistance and allow themselves to participate in these experiments.

If clients are to cooperate, counselors must avoid directing them in a commanding fashion to carry out an experiment. Typically, I ask people if they are willing to try out an experiment to see what they might learn from it, and I take care to emphasize that no specific result is expected. I also tell clients that they can stop when they choose to, so the power is with them. Clients at times say that they feel silly or self-conscious or that the task feels artificial or unreal. At such times I am likely to respond with something like: "Oh, why not go ahead and be silly? Will the roof cave in if you act foolish? Are you willing to give it a try and see what happens?" I cannot overemphasize the power of the therapeutic relationship and the necessity for trust as the foundation for implementing any technique. If I meet with resistance, I tend to be interested in exploring the client's reluctance. It is helpful to know the reason that the client is stopping. The reluctance to become emotionally involved often is a function of the client's cultural background. Some clients have been conditioned to work hard to maintain emotional control. They may have reservations about expressing intense feelings openly, even if they are in an emotional state. This can well be due to their socialization and to cultural norms that they abide by. In some cultures it is considered rude to express emotions openly. And there are certain cultural injunctions against showing one's vulnerability or psychological pain. If clients have had a long history of containing their feelings, it is understandable that they will be reluctant to participate in exercises that are designed to bring their emotions to the surface. Of course, White males have been socialized not to express intense feelings. Their reluctance to allow themselves to be emotional needs to be dealt with in a respectful manner.

Other clients may resist becoming emotionally involved because of their fear, lack of trust, concern over being foolish, or some other concern. The *way* in which the client resists doing an experiment reveals a great deal about the client's personality and his or her way of being in the world. Therefore, resistance does not have to be met with therapist defensiveness. I find that when I respect resistance and go with it, some of these defenses melt away. I attempt to show clients that I am willing to go as far as they are and that I will not push them to do what they say they do not want to do. Further, I hope that they can discover for themselves the meaning of their patterns of behavior through the experiment or through their resistance to it.

What about clients who refuse to participate in a given Gestalt experiment? I do not see that much is gained by pushing clients who are unwilling to try an experiment. In fact, by not respecting the limits and resistances of clients, the counselor may induce increased defensiveness. In those cases when clients decline to go along with an experiment, I generally like to explore their reasons. In a group situation, for example, a client may not want to role-play. There are many possible reasons for her reluctance, some of which are not wanting to look foolish, fearing that she will be judged by others in the group, not quite understanding the purpose of role playing, not trusting the group leader, being afraid that she will tap into intense emotions that she won't be able to control, or feeling pressured to "perform" by the group leader or the other members. Rather than persuading her to go along with a Gestalt experiment, I see much more value in pursuing her reluctance, but in a respectful way.

It is well to remember that the techniques of Gestalt therapy are designed to expand the client's awareness and to help him or her experiment with new modes of behavior. These techniques are only means to the end of helping people change, not ends in themselves. The following guidelines, largely taken from Passons (1975) and Zinker (1978), are suggestions I find useful both in preparing clients for Gestalt experiments and in carrying them out in the course of therapy:

- It is important for counselors to be sensitive enough to know when to leave the client alone.
- To derive maximum benefit from Gestalt experiments, the counselor must be sensitive to introducing them at the right time.
- The nature of the experiment depends on the individual's problems, what the person is experiencing, and the life experiences that both the client and the therapist bring to the session
- Experiments require the client's active role in self-exploration.
- Gestalt experiments work best when the therapist is respectful of the client's cultural background and is in good contact with the person.
- If counselors meet with hesitation on the client's part, it is a good idea to nondefensively explore its meaning for the client.
- It is important that counselors be flexible in using techniques, paying particular attention to how the client is responding.
- Counselors should be ready to scale down tasks so that clients have a good chance to succeed in their efforts. It is not helpful to suggest experiments that are too advanced for a client.
- It is helpful for counselors to learn which experiments can best be practiced in the session itself and which can best be performed outside.

ROLE OF CONFRONTATION

I have found that students are sometimes put off by Gestalt therapy because of their perception that a Gestalt counselor's style is direct and confrontational. They base this perception on the few quotations I have given from Perls or whatever of his they have read. I tell them that it is a mistake to equate the practice of Gestalt therapy with the personality of Perls. Although he could be highly confrontational and sharp with clients, it is still possible to incorporate Gestalt approaches into one's counseling style in a way that is both challenging and gentle.

It is true that most of the Gestalt techniques that I describe *are* confrontational. Counselors who use these methods must be willing to be active and at times challenging. Clients must also be willing to take risks and challenge themselves, and in that sense self-confrontation becomes crucial. I agree with Passons (1975) that some people tend to ascribe too much power to Gestalt techniques. He views these experiments as designed to enhance awareness, with no power of their own; the power lies in the person who uses the techniques. If they are used in a caring and appropriate manner, they can heighten the experiencing of clients. The skill comes in challenging clients to push beyond their usual level of resistance and avoidance without fostering increased defensiveness.

I think it is fair to state that confrontation is a part of most Gestalt techniques, yet it does not have to be viewed as a harsh attack. Confrontation can be done in such a way that clients cooperate, especially when they are *invited* to examine their behaviors, attitudes, and thoughts. Counselors can encourage clients to look at certain incongruities, especially gaps between their verbal expression and nonverbal expression. If a client is speaking of a painful event yet smiling at the same time, calling attention to the lack of congruence between her smile and her stated feelings can be confrontational to the extent that she may become aware of her attempt to avoid feeling the intensity of her pain. Further, confrontation does not have to be aimed at weaknesses or negative traits; clients can be challenged to recognize the ways in which they block their strengths and ways in which they are not living as fully as they might. In this sense confrontation can and should be a genuine expression of caring that results in positive changes in a client.

Perhaps one of the most essential ingredients in effective confrontation is respect for the client. Counselors who care enough to make demands on their clients are telling them, in effect, that they could be in fuller contact with themselves and others. Ultimately, however, clients must decide for themselves if they want to accept this invitation to learn more about themselves. This caveat needs to be kept in mind with all of the techniques that are to be described.

There have been some changes in Gestalt practice from the style of Perls. These recent trends include more softness, more direct self-expression by the therapist, less reliance on techniques, more emphasis on self-acceptance, and a greater trust in the client's experiencing. While the typical Gestalt therapist is still challenging, support and a soft demeanor are also likely to be present (Yontef & Simkin, 1989).

TECHNIQUES OF GESTALT THERAPY

Techniques can be useful tools to help the client gain fuller awareness, experience internal conflicts, resolve inconsistencies and dichotomies, and work through an impasse that is preventing completion of unfinished business.

Levitsky and Perls provide a brief description of a number of techniques, including (1) the dialogue exercise, (2) making the rounds, (3) unfinished business, (4) "I take responsibility," (5) "I have a secret," (6) playing the projection, (7) reversals, (8) the rhythm of contact and withdrawal, (9) "rehearsal," (10) "exaggeration," (11) "May I feed you a sentence?" (12) marriage-counseling games, and (13) "Can you stay with this feeling?" (1970, pp. 144–149). The following discussion is based on some of the exercises described by Levitsky and Perls, although I have modified the material and added suggestions for implementing these techniques.

The dialogue exercise. As we saw earlier, a goal of Gestalt therapy is to bring about integrated functioning and the acceptance of aspects of one's personality that have been disowned and denied. Gestalt therapists pay close attention to splits in personality function. A main division is between the "top dog" and the "underdog." Often therapy focuses on the war between the two.

The top dog is righteous, authoritarian, moralistic, demanding, bossy, and manipulative. This is the "critical parent" that badgers with "shoulds" and "oughts" and manipulates with threats of catastrophe. The underdog manipulates by playing the role of victim; by being defensive, apologetic, helpless, and weak; and by feigning powerlessness. This is the passive side, the one without responsibility, and the one that finds excuses. The top dog and the underdog are engaged in a constant struggle for control. The struggle helps to explain why one's resolutions and promises often go unfulfilled and why one's procrastination persists. The tyrannical top dog demands that one be thus-and-so, whereas the underdog defiantly plays the role of disobedient child. As a result of this struggle for control, the individual becomes fragmented into controller and controlled. The civil war between the two sides continues, with both sides fighting for their existence.

The conflict between the two opposing poles in the personality is rooted in the mechanism of introjection, which involves incorporating aspects of others, usually parents, into one's ego system. Perls implies that the taking in of values and traits is both inevitable and desirable; the danger is in the uncritical and wholesale acceptance of another's values as one's own, which makes becoming an autonomous person difficult. It is essential that one become aware of one's introjects, especially the toxic introjects that poison the system and prevent personality integration.

The empty-chair technique is one way of getting the client to externalize the introject. In this technique two chairs are used. The therapist asks the client to sit in one chair and be fully the top dog and then shift to the other chair and become the underdog. The dialogue can continue between both sides of the client. Essentially, this is a role-playing technique in which all the parts are played by the client. In this way the introjects can surface, and the client can experience the conflict more fully. The conflict can be resolved by the client's acceptance and integration of both sides. This technique helps clients get in touch with a feeling or a side of themselves that they may be denying; rather than merely talking about a conflicted feeling, they intensify the feeling and experience it fully. Further, by helping clients realize that the feeling is a very real part of themselves, the technique discourages them from disassociating the feeling. The technique can help clients identify distasteful parental introjects. For example, a client might say "That sounds exactly like my father in me!"

Parental introjections can keep a "self-torture" game alive as clients swallow parental injunctions and use them to punish and control themselves.

The dialogues between opposing tendencies have as their aim the promotion of a higher level of integration between the polarities and conflicts that exist in everyone. The aim is not to rid oneself of certain traits but to learn to accept and live with the polarities. Perls argues that other therapeutic approaches place too much emphasis on change. He contends that change cannot be forced but that through the acceptance of polarities an integration can occur, and the client can stop the badgering self-torture game. Many common conflicts lend themselves to the game of dialogue. Some that I find applicable include (1) the parent inside versus the child inside, (2) the responsible one versus the impulsive one, (3) the puritanical side versus the sexual side, (4) the "good boy" versus the "bad boy," (5) the aggressive self versus the passive self, (6) the autonomous side versus the resentful side, and (7) the hard worker versus the goof-off.

The dialogue technique can be used in both individual and group counseling. Let me describe one example of a common conflict between the top dog and underdog that I have found to be a powerful agent in helping a client become more intensely aware of the internal split and of which side would become dominant. The client, in this case a woman, plays the weak, helpless, dependent game of "poor me." She complains that she is miserable and that she hates and resents her husband, yet she fears that if he leaves her, she will disintegrate. She uses him as the excuse for her impotence. She continually puts herself down, always saying: "I can't," "I don't know how," "I am not capable." If she decided that she was miserable enough to want to change her dependent style, I would probably ask her to sit on one chair in the center of the room and become fully the underdog martyr and to exaggerate this side of herself. Eventually, if she got disgusted with this side, I would ask her to be the other side — that is, the top-dog side that puts her down — and talk to the "poor me." Then I might ask her to pretend that she were powerful, strong, and independent and to act as if she were not helpless. I might ask "What would happen if you were strong and independent and if you gave up your clinging dependency?" That technique can often energize clients into really experiencing the roles they continue to play, the result frequently being the reinvention of the autonomous aspects of self.

Making the rounds.   Making the rounds is a Gestalt exercise that involves asking a person in a group to go up to others in the group and either speak to or do something with each. The purpose is to confront, to risk, to disclose the self, to experiment with new behavior, and to grow and change. I have employed the technique when I sensed that a participant needed to face each person in the group with some theme. For example, a group member might say: "I've been sitting here for a long time wanting to participate but holding back because I'm afraid of trusting people in here. And besides, I don't think I'm worth the time of the group anyway." I might counter with "Are you willing to do something right now to get yourself more invested and to begin to work on gaining trust and self-confidence?" If the person answers affirmatively, my suggestion could well be "Go around to each person and finish this sentence: I don't trust you be-cause . . ." Any number of exercises could be invented to help individuals involve themselves and choose to work on the things that keep them frozen in fear.

Some other related illustrations and examples that I find appropriate for the making-the-rounds technique are reflected in clients' comments such as these: "I would like to reach out to people more often." "I'm bored by what's going on in this group." "Nobody in here seems to care very much." "I'd like to make contact with you, but I'm afraid of being rejected [or accepted]." "It's hard for me to accept good stuff; I always discount good things people say to me." "It's hard for me to say negative things to people; I want to be nice always." "I'd like to feel more comfortable in touching and getting close." If it is appropriate, group members can be asked to respond.

"I take responsibility for . . ."   The therapist may ask the client to make a statement and then add "and I take responsibility for it." Some examples: "I'm feeling bored, and I take responsibility for my boredom." "I'm feeling ex-cluded and lonely, and I take responsibility for my feelings of exclusion." "I don't know what to say now, and I take responsibility for my not knowing." This technique is an extension of the continuum of awareness, and it is designed to help clients recognize and accept their feelings instead of projecting their feelings onto others. Although this technique may sound mechanical, it can be very meaningful.

Playing the projection.   The dynamics of projection consist of one's seeing clearly in others the very things one does not want to see and accept within oneself. One can invest much energy in denying feelings and imputing motives to others. Often, especially in a group setting, the statements an individual makes toward and about others are in fact projections of attributes he or she possesses.

In the playing-the-projection game the therapist asks the person who says "I can't trust you" to play the role of the untrustworthy person — that is, to become the other — in order to discover the degree to which the distrust is an inner conflict. In other words, the therapist asks the person to "try on for size" certain statements he or she makes to others in the group.

The reversal technique.   Certain symptoms and behavior often represent reversals of underlying or latent impulses. Thus, the therapist could ask a person who claims to suffer from severe inhibitions and excessive timidity to play the role of an exhibitionist in the group. I remember the woman in one of our groups who had difficulty in being anything but sugary sweet. I asked her to reverse her typical style and be as negative as she could be. The reversal worked well; soon she was playing her part with real gusto and later was able to recog-nize and accept her "negative side" as well as her "positive side."

The theory underlying the reversal technique is that clients take the plunge into the very thing that is fraught with anxiety and make contact with those parts of themselves that have been submerged and denied. This technique can thus help clients begin to accept certain personal attributes that they have tried to deny.

Another time I asked one of the women in a group to become an evil witch. I asked her to go around to all the others in the group to place her curse on them, to wish evil on them, and to tell them the very thing they feared most. As part of her act she delivered a chilling, evil lecture. This was a woman who, because she had never really been allowed to recognize her demonic side, had repressed her devils. She stored up hostility and resentment as by-products of repression. When she was encouraged to release her personal demons, to become fully the witch she had never allowed herself to express, the results were dramatic. She intensely felt her denied side and gradually was able to integrate that side into her personality, becoming more assertive and outspoken.

The rehearsal exercise.   According to Perls, much of our thinking is rehearsing. We rehearse in fantasy for the role we think we are expected to play in society. When it comes to the performance, we experience stage fright, or anxiety, because we fear that we will not play our role well. Internal rehearsal consumes much energy and frequently inhibits our spontaneity and willingness to experiment with new behavior.

The members of a therapy group can share their rehearsals with one another in order to become more aware of the many preparatory means they use in bolstering their social roles. They become increasingly aware of how they try to meet the expectations of others, of the degree to which they want to be approved, accepted, and liked, and of the extent to which they go to attain acceptance.

The exaggeration exercise.   One aim of Gestalt therapy is that clients become more aware of the subtle signals and cues they are sending through body language. Movements, postures, and gestures may communicate significant meanings, yet the cues may be incomplete. The person is asked to exaggerate the movement or gesture repeatedly, which usually intensifies the feeling attached to the behavior and makes the inner meaning clearer.

Some examples of behavior that lends itself to the exaggeration technique are habitually smiling when expressing painful or negative material, trembling (shaking hands, legs), slouched posture and bent shoulders, clenched fists, tight frowning, facial grimacing, crossed arms, and so forth. If a client reports that his or her legs are shaking, for instance, the therapist may ask the client to stand up and exaggerate the shaking. Then the therapist may ask the client to put words to the shaking limbs.

As a variation verbal behavior also lends itself to the exaggeration exercise. The therapist can ask a client to repeat a statement that he or she had glossed over and to repeat it each time louder and louder. Frequently, the effect is that clients begin to really listen to and hear themselves.

Staying with the feeling.   At key moments when a client refers to a feeling or a mood that is unpleasant and from which he or she has a great urge to flee, the therapist urges the client to stay with, or retain, the feeling.

Most clients desire to escape from fearful stimuli and to avoid unpleasant feelings. The therapist may ask clients to remain with whatever fear or pain they are experiencing at present and encourage them to go deeper into the feeling and behavior they wish to avoid. Facing, confronting, and experiencing feelings not only take courage but are also a mark of a willingness to endure the pain necessary for unblocking and making way for newer levels of growth.

The Gestalt approach to dream work.   In psychoanalysis dreams are interpreted, intellectual insight is stressed, and free association is used as one method of exploring the unconscious meanings of dreams. The Gestalt approach does not interpret and analyze a dream. Instead, the intent is to bring the dream back to life and relive it as though it were happening now. The dream is not told as a past event but is acted out in the present, and the dreamer becomes a part of his or her dream. The suggested format for working with dreams includes making a list of all the details of the dream, remembering each person, event, and mood in it, and then becoming each of these parts by transforming oneself, acting as fully as possible and inventing dialogue. Because each part of the dream is assumed to be a projection of oneself, one creates scripts for encounters between various characters or parts. All of the different parts of a dream are expressions of one's own contradictory and inconsistent sides. Thus, by engaging in a dialogue between these opposing sides, one gradually becomes more aware of the range of one's own feelings.

Perls's concept of projection is central in his theory of dream formation. According to him, every person and every object in the dream represent a projected aspect of the dreamer. Perls (1969a) suggests that "we start with the impossible assumption that whatever we believe we see in another person or in the world is nothing but a projection ' (p. 67). He writes that the recognition of the senses and the understanding of projections go hand in hand. Thus, Perls did not interpret dreams, play intellectual guessing games, or tell clients the meaning of their dreams. Clients do not think about or analyze the dream but use it as a script and experiment with the dialogue among the various parts of the dream. Because clients can act out a fight between opposing sides, eventually they can appreciate and accept their inner differences and integrate the opposing forces. Whereas Freud calls the dream the royal road to the unconscious, to Perls (1969a) it is the "royal road to integration" (p. 66).

According to Perls (1969a), the dream is the most spontaneous expression of the existence of the human being. It represents an unfinished situation, but it is more than an uncompleted situation or an unfulfilled wish. Every dream contains an existential message of oneself and one's current struggle. Everything is to be found in dreams if all the parts are understood and assimilated. Each piece of work done on a dream leads to some assimilation. Perls asserts that if dreams are properly worked with, the existential message becomes clearer. According to him, dreams serve as an excellent way to discover personality voids by revealing missing parts and the client's methods of avoidance. If people do not remember dreams, they are refusing to face what is wrong with their life. At the very least, the Gestalt counselor asks clients to talk to their missing dreams. For example, as directed by her therapist, a client reported the following dream in the present tense, as though she were still dreaming:

> I have three monkeys in a cage. One big monkey and two little ones! I feel very attached to these monkeys, although they are creating a lot of chaos in a cage that is divided into three separate spaces. They are fighting with one another — the big monkey is fighting with the little monkey. They are getting out of the cage, and they are clinging onto me. I feel like pushing them away from me. I feel totally overwhelmed by the chaos that they are creating around me. I turn to my mother and tell her that I need help, that I can no longer handle these monkeys because they are driving me crazy. I feel very sad and very tired, and I feel discouraged. I am walking away from the cage, thinking that I really love these monkeys, yet I have to get rid of them. I am telling myself that I am like everybody else. I get pets, and then when things get rough, I want to get rid of them. I am trying very hard to find a solution to keeping these monkeys and not allowing them to have such a terrible effect on me. Before I wake up from my dream, I am making the decision to put each monkey in a separate cage, and maybe that is the way to keep them.

The therapist then asked his client, Brenda, to "become" different parts of her dream. Thus, she "became" the cage, and she "became" and had a dialogue with each monkey, and then she "became" her mother, and so forth. One of the most powerful aspects of this technique was Brenda's reporting her dream as though it were still happening. She quickly perceived that her dream expressed a struggle that she was having with her husband and her two children. From her dialogue work, Brenda discovered that she both appreciated and resented her family. She learned that she needed to let them know about her feelings and that together they might work on improving an intensely difficult lifestyle. She did not need an interpretation from her therapist to understand the clear message of her dream.

In a paper on dream work as theater, Zinker (1971) describes a very creative way of working with a client's dream in the context of a group. The dream is reported by a group member and then first worked through on an individual basis. Then a group experiment is created in such a way that other members can reap the benefits from the original imagery of the dreamer. The other members take parts in the drama and actively participate in acting out various themes of the dream. The dreamer, the original creator of the drama, does not get lost in this process, for he or she can experience the unfolding of the dream in the group. The dreamer can step in and change the action, can take over different roles, can coach others, or can experiment with different outcomes. Through this approach to exploring a dream in a group context, everyone has an opportunity to become involved and to learn experientially.

SUMMARY AND EVALUATION

SUMMARY

Gestalt therapy is an experiential therapy stressing here-and-now awareness. The major focus is on the *what* and *how* of behavior and the role of unfinished business from the past that prevents effective functioning in the present. Some of the key goals of the approach are accepting personal responsibility, living in the immediate moment, and direct experiencing as opposed to abstract talking about experiences. The approach helps clients deal with avoidance, unfinished business, and impasses.

A central therapeutic aim is to challenge the client to move more fully into self-support. Expansion of awareness, which is viewed as curative of itself, is a basic goal. With awareness clients are able to reconcile polarities and dichotomies within themselves and thus proceed toward the reintegration of all aspects of themselves.

In this approach the therapist assists clients to experience all feelings more fully, and this enables them to make their own interpretations. The therapist avoids making interpretations and instead focuses on how clients are behaving. Clients identify their own unfinished business and they work through the blockages impeding their growth. They do this largely by reexperiencing past situations as though they were happening in the present. Therapists have many techniques at their disposal, all of which have two things in common: they are designed to intensify direct experiencing and to integrate conflicting feelings.

CONTRIBUTIONS OF GESTALT THERAPY

I make frequent use of Gestalt methods. I am impressed with the action approach, which brings conflicts and human struggles to life. Through such techniques, I have found, people actually experience their struggles, as opposed to merely talking about problems endlessly in a detached manner. In doing so, they are able to increase their awareness of what they are experiencing in the present moment. I especially like the range of experiments and exercises that a therapist can suggest to help clients discover new facets of themselves.

Another of Gestalt therapy's contributions is the exciting way in which the past is dealt with in a lively manner by bringing relevant aspects into the present. Practitioners challenge clients in creative ways to become aware of and work with issues that are obstructing current functioning. Further, paying attention to the obvious verbal and nonverbal leads provided by the client is a useful way to approach a counseling session. Through the skillful and sensitive use of Gestalt approaches, practitioners can assist people in heightening their present-centered awareness of what they are thinking and feeling as well as what they are doing. Through this awareness they are enabled to assume an increased share of personal responsibility for what they are experiencing.

I especially value the compassionate confrontational aspect of this approach in refusing to accept helplessness as an excuse for not changing. The client is provided with a wide range of tools, in the form of Gestalt experiments, for making decisions about changing the course of living.

The Gestalt approach to working with dreams is a unique pathway for people to increase their awareness of key themes in their life. By seeing each aspect of a dream as a projection of themselves, clients are able to bring the dream to life, to interpret its personal meaning, and to assume responsibility for it.

The Gestalt approach is a perspective on growth and enhancement, not merely a system of techniques to treat disorders. With the emphasis given to the existential relationship between client and therapist, there is a creative spirit in suggesting, inventing, and carrying out experiments aimed at increasing awareness. Of all the approaches, Gestalt therapy has the greatest potential for creativity.

Contributions to multicultural counseling.   There are opportunities to sensitively and creatively use Gestalt methods, if they are timed appropriately, with culturally diverse populations. One of the advantages of drawing on Gestalt experiments is that they can be tailored to fit the unique way in which an individual perceives and interprets his or her culture. Furthermore, Gestalt methods can allow the client and the therapist to break down certain cross-cultural barriers between them. One of my colleagues goes to Japan almost every year for three months and teaches a combination of body work, Rolfing (or structural integration, as developed by Ida Rolf), and Gestalt therapy. He finds the Japanese he teaches to be very receptive to Gestalt methods, for many of the principles are grounded on Eastern notions.

Gestalt therapy is particularly effective in helping people integrate the polarities within themselves. Many bicultural clients experience an ongoing struggle in reconciling what appear to be diverse aspects of the two cultures in which they live. In one of our weeklong groups a dynamic piece of work was done by a woman with European roots. Her struggle consisted of integrating her American side with her experiences in Germany as a child. I asked her to "bring her family into this group" by talking to selected members in the group as though they were members of her family. She was asked to imagine that she was 8 years old and that she could now say to her parents and siblings things that she never expressed. I asked her to speak in German (since this was her primary language as a child). The combined factors of her trust in the group, her willingness to recreate an early scene by reliving it in the present moment, and her symbolic work with fantasy helped her achieve a significant breakthrough. She was able to put a new ending to an old and unfinished situation through her participation in this Gestalt experiment.

LIMITATIONS AND CRITICISMS OF GESTALT THERAPY

A chief criticism of the Perlsian style of Gestalt therapy involves its deemphasis of the cognitive factors of personality. Perls did discourage thinking about one's experience, and many Gestaltists have stressed becoming aware of and expressing feelings to the neglect of examining thoughts. Some practitioners view an intellectual process, or even attempting to bring cognitive structuring to something they experience in therapy, as a defense against feeling and fully experiencing in the here and now. To some degree, however, this one-sidedness is changing, with many therapists integrating cognitive work. It appears that more attention is being given to theoretical instruction, theoretical exposition, and cognitive factors in general (Yontef & Simkin, 1989).

Although Gestalt therapy discourages interrupting the process of immediate experiencing and integration by focusing on cognitive explanations, clients do clarify their thinking, explore beliefs, and put meaning to experiences they are reliving in therapy. Gestalt therapy also discourages the therapist from *teaching* clients, as opposed to *facilitating* the clients' own process of self-discovery and learning. It seems to me, however, that clients can engage in self-discovery *and* at the same time benefit from appropriate teaching by the therapist. Why should therapy exclude information giving, suggestions, cognitive processing, explanations, interpretations, and coaching on the therapist's part? As you will see, I favor blending the emotional and experiential work of Gestalt therapy with theoretical concepts and techniques of the cognitive and behavioral approaches (especially transactional analysis, behavior therapy, and, to some extent, reality therapy). This type of integration of approaches would answer my major criticism of Gestalt therapy as it is often practiced.

Current Gestalt practice places a high value on the contact and dialogue between the therapist and client. This implies an existential encounter in the therapy process that can be used for the client's benefit. For Gestalt therapy to be effective, I think, the therapist must have a high level of personal development. Being aware of one's own needs and seeing that they do not interfere with the client's process, being present in the moment, and being willing to be nondefensive and self-revealing all demand a lot of the therapist. There is a danger that power-hungry therapists who are inadequately trained will be primarily concerned with impressing and manipulating clients.

Cautions about techniques.   For Gestalt experiments to be effective, clients must be prepared for them. Thus, care must be taken to avoid springing techniques on clients who are left wondering about their purpose. It behooves the counselor to lay the necessary groundwork and to build trust with the client so that the techniques do not appear to be mere gimmicks. Gestalt therapy worked well for Perls, because he invented it, and it also fit his personality.

As exciting and dynamic as Gestalt methods are, however, they are not for all clients. According to Shepherd (1970), the appropriate application of Gestalt techniques hinges on questions of "When?" "With whom?" and "In what situation?" She indicates that, in general, Gestalt therapy is most effective with overly socialized, constricted individuals, often described as neurotic, phobic, perfectionistic, ineffective, and depressed. On the other hand, Gestalt work with less organized, more severely disturbed, or psychotic individuals is more problematic and requires caution, sensitivity, and patience.

A major concern I have about Gestalt therapy is the potential danger for abusing techniques. Typically, Gestalt therapists are highly active and directive, and if they do not have the characteristics mentioned by Zinker (1978) — sensitivity, timing, inventiveness, empathy, and respect for the client — their experiments can easily boomerang.

With an approach that can have powerful effects on clients, either constructive or destructive, ethical practice depends on the level of training and supervision of its therapists. The most immediate limitation of Gestalt, or any other therapy is the skill, training, experience, and judgment of the therapist. Probably the most effective application of Gestalt techniques comes from personal therapeutic experiences gained in professional training workshops and work with competent therapists and supervisors (Shepherd, 1970).

The Gestalt approach can be dangerous, because of the therapist's power to manipulate the client with techniques. An ethical issue is raised by inept therapists who use powerful techniques to stir up feelings and open up problems that clients have kept from full awareness, only to abandon the clients once they have managed to have a dramatic catharsis. The failure to stay with clients, by helping them work through what they experience and bring some closure to the experience, can be detrimental.

It is easy to see that many Gestalt techniques offer a tempting place for therapists to hide their personal responses instead of authentically contacting their clients. Through the use of confrontive techniques they can direct the pressure primarily toward the client. The therapist's willingness to encounter clients with his or her honest and immediate responses and to challenge them without rejecting them is crucial (Shepherd, 1970). Gestalt practitioners need to learn how to confront in a manner that does not entrench the client's resistance. A blend of support and challenge goes a long way in creating the kind of I/thou relationship that enables clients to explore their defensiveness.

Limitations for multicultural counseling.   To a greater extent than is true of most other approaches, there are definite hazards in too quickly utilizing some Gestalt techniques with ethnic clients. As is evident from this chapter, Gestalt techniques tend to produce a high level of intense feelings. This focus on affect has some clear limitations with those clients who have been culturally conditioned to be emotionally reserved. As mentioned earlier, some ethnic clients believe that expressing feelings openly is a sign of weakness and a display of one's vulnerability. Counselors who operate on the assumption that catharsis is necessary for any change to occur are likely to find certain clients becoming increasingly resistant, and such clients may prematurely terminate counseling. Other clients have strong cultural injunctions prohibiting them from directly expressing their emotions to their parents (such as "Never show your parents that you are angry at them" or "Strive for peace and harmony, and avoid conflicts"). For instance, I recall a client from another culture who was asked by his counselor to "bring your father into the room." The client was very reluctant to even symbolically tell his father of his disappointment with their relationship. In his culture the accepted way to deal with his father was to use his uncle as a go-between, and it was considered highly inappropriate to express any negative feelings toward one's father. The client later said that he would have felt terrible guilt if he had symbolically told his father what he sometimes thought and felt.

Some practitioners make the mistake of too rigidly pushing such injunctions as "Always be in the present" or "Take responsibility for yourself." There are some situations, as in the case just mentioned, in which stopping what clients are doing and asking them to bring something into the here and now would be quite counterproductive. Gestalt therapists who have truly integrated their approach are sensitive enough to practice in a flexible way. They consider the client's cultural framework and are thus able to adapt techniques that are likely to be well received. They strive to help clients experience themselves as fully as possible in the present, yet they are not rigidly bound by dictates, nor do they routinely intervene whenever clients stray from the present. Sensitively staying in contact with a client's flow of experiencing entails the ability to focus on the person and not on the mechanical use of techniques for a certain effect.

QUESTIONS FOR REFLECTION AND DISCUSSION

1. What are the values and limitations of the Gestalt focus on the here and now? Do you think that this approach adequately deals with one's past and one's future? Explain.
2. Gestalt therapy discourages "why" questions and focuses instead on the "what" and "how" of experiencing. What are your reactions to this emphasis? Do you agree or disagree that "why" questions generally lead to heady ruminations?
3. Gestalt therapy tends to focus on what people are *feeling* moment to moment. Do you think that this emphasis precludes thinking about one's experiencing? Explain.
4. Gestaltists tend to be confrontational in their work. Although this confrontation can be done with care, respect, and sensitivity for clients, there are also some dangers. In your view what risks are inherent in this approach?
5. A wide variety of techniques and experiments was described in this chapter. How comfortable do you think you would feel in using some of the techniques? Do you think that it is important that *you* experience these techniques first *as a client* before you attempt to use them with others? How might you prepare your clients so that they would be more likely to benefit from Gestalt exercises?
6. What specific aspects (either techniques or concepts) of Gestalt therapy would you be most likely to incorporate in your own style of counseling? Explain.
7. Compare Gestalt therapy with the psychoanalytic approach. Do you see any basis for integrating Gestalt techniques within a psychoanalytic framework? Discuss.
8. Gestalt therapy and person-centered therapy share some philosophical views regarding human nature. At the same time, the former model relies on techniques, whereas the latter deemphasizes techniques and therapist direction. Do you see any basis for integrating Gestalt approaches with some person-centered concepts? Why or why not?
9. What are the implications of Gestalt therapy for your own personal growth? How can you use some of the techniques, experiments, and concepts as a way of furthering self-understanding and promoting personality change in yourself?
10. Assume that Stan has come to you for Gestalt therapy. How might you prepare him for the Gestalt techniques that you will employ? Select a few of his current struggles, and show what specific Gestalt experiments you would suggest. How comfortable would you feel in working with him in this modality?

WHERE TO GO FROM HERE

If you have become excited about including Gestalt techniques in your counseling style, I encourage you to attend a Gestalt workshop led by a competent professional. I have real concerns about practitioners who employ Gestalt techniques if they have not experienced them personally. Although reading is surely of value, it is not sufficient to produce skillful clinicians. In addition to personally experiencing Gestalt experiments, it is crucial to have careful supervision, to learn the theoretical framework underlying these techniques, and to be well aware of the boundaries of one's competence.

Some resources for training in Gestalt therapy are:

Gestalt Institute of Cleveland
1588 Hazel Drive
Cleveland, OH 44106

Gestalt Training Center
P.O. Box 2189
La Jolla, CA 92038

Gestalt Therapy Institute of
Los Angeles
620 Venice Boulevard
Venice, CA 90291

Gestalt Institute of San Francisco
1790 Union Street
San Francisco, CA 94123

New York Institute for Gestalt
Therapy
7 West 96th Street
New York, NY 10025

Gestalt Institute of the Southwest
7700 Alabama Street
El Paso, TX 79904

Since no national Gestalt therapy organization exists, each of the institutes establishes its own standards and criteria for membership and training.

RECOMMENDED SUPPLEMENTARY READINGS

Gestalt Therapy Verbatim (Perls, 1969a) is one of the best places to get a firsthand account of the style in which Perls worked. If you like that book and want to know more about Perls as a person, I recommend *In and Out of the Garbage Pail* (Perls, 1969b).

Gestalt Approaches in Counseling (Passons, 1975) is one of the books about Gestalt therapy that I most highly recommend, as it deals with the practical applications of Gestalt concepts in a wide variety of counseling situations. It is an excellent resource for techniques, and it stresses the importance of preparing clients for these techniques.

Gestalt Therapy Integrated: Contours of Theory and Practice (Polster & Polster, 1973) is a superb source for those who want a more advanced and theoretical treatment of this model.

Creative Process in Gestalt Therapy (Zinker, 1978) is a beautifully written book that is a delight to read. Zinker captures the essence of Gestalt therapy as a combination of phenomenology and behavior modification by showing how the therapist functions much like an artist in creating experiments that encourage clients to expand their boundaries. His concepts are fleshed out with rich clinical examples. The book shows how Gestalt can be practiced in a creative, eclectic, and integrative style.

The Gestalt Journal, published twice yearly, offers articles, reviews, and commentaries of interest to the practitioner, theoretician, academician, and student. For subscription information write: P.O. Box 990, Highland, NY 12528.

References and Suggested Readings*

COREY, G. (1990). *Theory and practice of group counseling* (3rd ed.). Pacific Grove, CA: Brooks/Cole.

COREY, G. (1991). *Case approach to counseling and psychotherapy* (3rd ed.). Pacific Grove, CA: Brooks/Cole.

DOWNING, J., & MARMORSTEIN, R. (Eds.). (1973). *Dreams and nightmares: A book of Gestalt therapy sessions.* New York: Harper & Row.

*FAGAN, J. (1970). The tasks of the therapist. In J. Fagan & I. Shepherd (Eds.), *Gestalt therapy sessions.* New York: Harper & Row.

*FAGAN, J., & SHEPHERD, I. (Eds.). (1970a). *Life techniques in Gestalt therapy.* New York: Harper & Row.

FAGAN, J., & SHEPHERD, I. (Eds.). (1970b). *What is Gestalt therapy?* New York: Harper & Row.

FEDER, B., & RONALL, R. (Eds.). (1980). *Beyond the hot seat: Gestalt approaches to group work.* New York: Brunner/Mazel.

FREW, J. E. (1986). The functions and patterns of occurrence of individual contact styles during the development phase of the Gestalt group. *Gestalt Journal, 9,* 55–70.

*JAMES, M., & JONGEWARD, D. (1971). *Born to win: Transactional analysis with Gestalt experiments.* Reading, MA: Addison-Wesley

LEVITSKY, A., & PERLS, F. (1970). The rules and games of Gestalt therapy. In J. Fagan & I. Shepherd (Eds.), *Gestalt therapy now* (pp 140–149). New York: Harper & Row (Colophon).

*PASSONS, W. R. (1975). *Gestalt approaches in counseling.* New York Holt, Rinehart & Winston.

PATTERSON, C. H. (1986). *Theories of counseling and psychotherapy: Chap. 13.* New York: Harper & Row.

*PERLS, F. (1969a). *Gestalt therapy verbatim.* Moab, UT: Real People Press.

*PERLS, F. (1969b). *In and out of the garbage pail.* Moab, UT: Real People Press.

PERLS, F. (1970). Four lectures. In J. Fagan & I. Shepherd (Eds.), *Gestalt therapy now* (pp. 14–38). New York: Harper & Row (Colophon).

*PERLS, F. (1973). *The Gestalt approach and eye witness to therapy.* New York: Bantam Books.

*PERLS, F. (1989). The case of Jane. In D. Wedding & R. J. Corsini (Eds.), *Case studies in psychotherapy* (pp. 145–162). Itasca, IL: F. E. Peacock.

PERLS, F., HEFFERLINE, R., & GOODMAN, P. (1951). *Gestalt therapy integrated: Excitement and growth in the human personality.* New York: Dell.

POLSTER, E. (1987a). Escape from the present: Transition and storyline. In J. K. Zeig (Ed.), *The evolution of psychotherapy* (pp. 326–340). New York: Brunner-Mazel.

POLSTER, E. (1987b). *Every person's life is worth a novel.* New York: Norton.

*POLSTER, E., & POLSTER, M. (1973). *Gestalt therapy integrated: Contours of theory and practice.* New York: Brunner/Mazel.

POLSTER, M. (1987). Gestalt therapy: Evolution and application. In J. K. Zeig (Ed.), *The evolution of psychotherapy* (pp. 312–325). New York: Brunnel/Mazel.

*RAINWATER, J. (1979). *You're in charge! A guide to becoming your own therapist.* Los Angeles: Guild of Tutors Press.

SHEPHERD, I. (1970). Limitations and cautions in the Gestalt approach. In J. Fagan & I. Shepherd (Eds.), *Gestalt therapy now* (pp 234–238). New York: Harper & Row (Colophon).

* Books and articles marked with an asterisk are suggested for further study.

*SIMKIN, J. S., SIMKIN, A. N., BRIEN, L., & SHELDON, C. (1986). Gestalt therapy. In I. L. Kutash & A. Wolf (Eds.), *Psychotherapist's casebook* (pp. 209–221). San Francisco: Jossey-Bass.

SMITH, E. W. L. (Ed.). (1976). *The growing edge of Gestalt therapy.* New York: Brunner/Mazel.

SMITH, E. (1985). *The body in psychotherapy.* Jefferson, NC: MacFarland & Co.

STEVENS, J. O. (1971). *Awareness: Exploring, experimenting, experiencing.* Moab, UT: Real People Press.

VAN DE RIET, V., & KORB, M. (1980). *Gestalt therapy: An introduction.* New York: Pergamon Press.

*YONTEF, G. M., & SIMKIN, J. S. (1989). Gestalt therapy. In R. J. Corsini & D. Wedding (Eds.), *Current psychotherapies* (4th ed.) (pp. 323–361). Itasca, IL: F. E. Peacock.

ZINKER, J. (1971). Dream work as theater: An innovation in Gestalt therapy. *Voices, 7,* 2.

ZINKER, J. (1978). *Creative process in Gestalt therapy.* New York: Random House (Vintage).

9

TRANSACTIONAL ANALYSIS

ERIC BERNE

ERIC BERNE (1910–1970), the originator of transactional analysis, received an M.D. from McGill University in Montreal in 1935, and he completed his psychiatric residency at Yale University shortly thereafter. It was during the time he served in the U.S. Army (1943–1946) that he began experimenting with group therapy. Excited by the possibilities of group work, Berne gradually lost interest in individual psychoanalytic therapy.

After the war Berne made his home in Carmel, California, and resumed his psychoanalytic studies with Erik Erikson. He practiced psychiatry in San Francisco and Carmel, where he continued to observe his clients and to draw conclusions about the structure and functioning of the personality. His investigations resulted in ideas that were diametrically opposed to those of most psychiatrists in the mid-1950s. At 46 years of age he was turned down for membership in the Psychoanalytic Institute. He challenged the basic assumptions of traditional psychoanalytic therapy, abandoned his traditional training, and began practicing what he called transactional analysis.

In 1964 his book *Games People Play* became an international best-seller. At the same time, his new therapeutic approach, which represented a radical departure from psychoanalysis, achieved wide popularity. By the late 1960s his theory was almost complete.

Steiner (1974), who refers to Berne as a "far-reaching pioneer and a radical scientist in the field of psychiatry," also writes about Berne as a person. Berne behaved independently and acted as if he were self-sufficient. Like his father he chose the medical profession and made curing others his mission in life. Dedicated to his practice of psychiatry and to writing books, Berne sacrificed his personal life for his professional achievements. Although Berne loved and admired children and appreciated the ability of adults who could allow themselves to play as children do, he did not give himself permission to overcome his shyness and to express his fun-loving side unless it was safe to do so. Steiner concluded that Berne, who had developed the concept of "life scripts," was himself under the influence of a script that called for an early death of a broken heart. Berne accepted messages against expressing love for others and against accepting love from others. He followed in the path of his mother; they both died at the age of 60 from coronary failure.

INTRODUCTION

Transactional analysis (TA) is set apart from most other approaches in that it is contractual and decisional. The contract, which is developed by the client, clearly states the goals and direction of the therapeutic process. It also focuses on early decisions that each person has made, and it stresses the capacity to make new decisions. TA emphasizes the thinking, feeling, and behavioral aspects of personality and is oriented toward increasing awareness so that clients will be able to make such new decisions and alter the course of their lives. The contractual nature of the psychotherapeutic process tends to equalize the power of the therapist and the client. It is the responsibility of clients to decide what they will change. To make their desires into reality, clients actively change their behavior. Because of the operational nature of TA, including its use of a contract, a client's degree of change can be objectively evaluated.

This approach, as developed by Berne, supplies a framework for the analysis of transactions between people and within a single person, based on the concept of three ego states: *Parent, Adult,* and *Child.* Other key words in the TA vocabulary are *decision, redecision, game, life script, racket, stroke,* and *discounting.* Berne began to develop TA in the mid-1950s. Four phases in its development have been identified by Dusay and Dusay (1989).

The *first phase* of TA (1955–1962) began with Berne's identification of the ego states (Parent, Adult, and Child), which provided a perspective from which to explain thinking, feeling, and behaving. He decided that the way to study personality was to observe here-and-now phenomena such as the client's voice, gestures, and vocabulary. These observable criteria provide a basis for inferring a person's past history and for predicting future problems. The *second phase* (1962–1966) focused on transactions and "games." It was during this period that TA became popular because of its straightforward vocabulary and because people could recognize their own games. At this time TA was primarily a cognitive approach, with little attention given to emotions. The *third phase* (1966–1970) gave attention to life scripts and script analysis. A life script is an internal plan that determines the direction of one's life. The *fourth phase* (1970 to the present) is characterized by the incorporation of new techniques into TA practice (such as those from the human-potential movement, Gestalt therapy, encounter groups, and psychodrama). TA is moving toward the direction of active and emotive models as a way of balancing its early emphasis on cognitive factors and insight (Dusay & Dusay, 1989, p. 448).

Classical transactional analysis had been largely developed by the late 1960s. Since then, however, TA practitioners have moved in various directions and have modified many of the basic concepts that Berne formulated. Because there are several models of TA, it is difficult to discuss practices that apply to all of them. This chapter will be primarily concerned with the basic concepts and therapeutic procedures developed by Berne, which were later built on and expanded by Mary and Robert Goulding (1979), leaders of the *redecisional school* of TA. The Gouldings are the co-directors of the Western Institute for Group and Family Therapy in Watsonville, California. Developed by the Gouldings, redecision therapy began with psychoanalysis, included key concepts of Berne's system, incorporated techniques of Perls's Gestalt therapy, and became an integration of all three systems in novel ways (Madison, 1985; McCormick & Pulleyblank, 1985). The Gouldings emphasize that people are able to restructure their ways of thinking, feeling, and behaving through making updated decisions about themselves and the world. The redecisional approach aims at helping people challenge themselves to discover ways in which they are playing victimlike roles and to take charge of their lives by deciding for themselves how they will change.

KEY CONCEPTS

VIEW OF HUMAN NATURE

Transactional analysis is rooted in an antideterministic philosophy. It places faith in the person's capacity to rise above habit patterns and to select new goals and behavior. This does not imply that people are free from the influences of social forces, nor does it mean that they arrive at critical life decisions totally by themselves. It acknowledges that they were influenced by the expectations and demands of significant others, especially because their early decisions were made at a time in life when they were highly dependent on others. But decisions can be reviewed and challenged, and if early decisions are no longer appropriate, new ones can be made.

This view of human nature has definite implications for the practice of TA therapy. The therapist recognizes that one reason a person is in therapy is because he or she has entered into conspiracies and game playing with others. The therapist will not accept "I tried," "I couldn't help it," and "Don't blame me, because I'm stupid." Because of the basic premise that the person can make choices, can make new decisions, and can act, excuses, or "cop-outs," are not accepted in the therapeutic practice of TA. Therefore, if clients are able to see how these decisions helped them survive as a child in their family but are no longer working for their welfare today, they can choose to redesign their life in new and effective ways. People make certain decisions in order to survive at some point in life. Yet these need not be permanent decisions, for people can make new ones later and thus change the course of their life.

EGO STATES

As mentioned earlier, transactional analysis delineates three distinct patterns of behavior, or ego states: Parent, Adult, and Child (P-A-C).

The Parent part of the personality is an introject of the parents and parental substitutes. In the Parent ego state we reexperience what we imagined were our own parents' feelings in a situation, or we feel and act toward others as our parents felt and acted toward us. The Parent ego state contains "shoulds" and "oughts." We each have a "Nurturing Parent" and a "Critical Parent."

The Adult ego state is the processor of data. It is the objective part of the person, which gathers information about what is going on. It is not emotional or judgmental but works with the facts and with external reality. The Adult is without passionate convictions, but many problems also require empathy and intuition to be resolved.

The Child ego state consists of feelings, impulses, and spontaneous acts. The Child in each of us can be the "Natural Child," the "Little Professor," or the "Adapted Child." The Natural Child is the impulsive, untrained, spontaneous, expressive infant in each of us. The Little Professor is the unschooled wisdom of a child. It is manipulative, egocentric, and creative. It is that part of the Child ego state that is intuitive and plays on hunches. The Adapted Child exhibits modifications of the Natural Child's inclinations. The modifications are the result of traumatic experiences, demands, training, and decisions about how to get attention. The Adapted Child whines, complies, and rebels.

TA clients are taught how to recognize the ego state in which they are functioning when there is a problem. In this way they can make conscious decisions about the particular ego state in which they want to function. For example, if Susan becomes aware that she typically responds to her children in the same critical way in which her own mother responded to her, she is then in a position to change this stance.

As clients become more aware of the ego state they are in, they also become more aware of their adaptive behavior (both to their internal Parent and to the outside world). With this awareness they are better able to choose other options knowingly.

AN INTEGRATED THEORY

The following sections, which present further key concepts of TA, are to a large extent an adaptation of the writings of the Gouldings. The theory of TA integrates the following concepts: Children grow up with *injunctions,* and on the basis of these parental messages they make *early decisions* These early decisions are aimed at receiving parental *strokes* (recognition and attention), as well as at ensuring basic survival. *Games* develop as a way of supporting one's early decisions. *Rackets* are familiar bad feelings that people save up. In many families certain feelings are not allowed. For example, perhaps no one, or only one person, is allowed to be angry; the other family members must substitute another feeling. Thus, someone strongly forbidden to be angry may feel sad instead and may make a racket of calling up this sadness to mask anger or resentment. All of these elements fit into the *life script,* which includes our expectations of how our life drama will be played out. A major contribution of the Gouldings to therapeutic practice is the focus on the client's capacity to make *redecisions* about this script.

Injunctions and early decisions. The Gouldings' redecision work is grounded in the TA concepts of injunctions and early decisions (M. Goulding, 1987, p. 288). An injunction is a message given to the child by the parents' internal Child out of the circumstances of the parents' own pains—anxiety, anger, frustration, and unhappiness. These messages tell children what they have to do and be in order to get recognition. Although some of these injunctions may be given in a verbal and direct manner, more often than not they are inferred from parental behavior and translated as "Don't be separate from me," "Don't be the sex you are," "Don't want," "Don't need," "Don't think," "Don't feel," and "Don't be a child" (M. Goulding, 1987; M. Goulding & Goulding, 1979).

According to Mary Goulding (1987), as children we decide either to accept these parental messages or to fight against them. If we accept certain injunctions, we decide precisely how we will accept them. We then make early decisions that become a basic part of our permanent character structure.

The Gouldings maintain that injunctions are not inserted in our heads as an electrode would be. Rather, as children we may have invented them or misinterpreted messages from our parents, and thus in some cases we gave ourselves our own injunctions to avoid danger and to survive. Although many of these injunctions may have been appropriate in certain situations in childhood, they are now inappropriate as they are carried into adulthood. A major part of the therapeutic process of TA consists of increasing awareness of the specific nature of injunctions that are leading to present difficulties. The following list, based on an adaptation of the works of the Gouldings, includes common injunctions and some possible decisions that could be made in response to them (M. Goulding, 1987; M. Goulding & Goulding, 1979; R. Goulding, 1987; R. Goulding & Goulding, 1976, 1978):

1. *"Don't."* Given by scared parents, this injunction tells children not to do normal things for fear that they could lead to disaster. Children who accept this injunction will believe that nothing they do is right or safe, and they will look to others to protect them and decide for them.
   Possible decisions: "I can't decide for myself, so I look to others to tell me what to do." "I'll never decide for myself again." "I'm scared of making wrong decisions for fear I'll make mistakes, so I won't decide."
2. *"Don't be."* As one of the most lethal of all messages, this one is often delivered nonverbally through the way the parent holds (or does not hold) the child. The message might be "I wish you hadn't been born, and then I wouldn't have had to put up with all I have!" This "Don't exist" message may be implied by brutality or indifference.
   Possible decisions: "I'll get you to love me, even if it kills me." "I'll do what you want and pretend I don't exist in this family." "If things get too bad, I'll kill myself."
3. *"Don't be close."* This parental message can be given by parents who are not physically close or who push the child aside. Related to this injunction are the messages "Don't trust" and "Don't love."
   Possible decisions: "I won't allow myself to get close, for when I do people leave me." "I won't get close, and that way I won't be hurt." "I'll never trust a woman [man] again."
4. *"Don't be important."* In some way children may feel personally discounted when they speak, and thus they may decide not to be important and not to ask for what they want and need.
   Possible decisions: "I'll never be or feel important." "If I ever do become important, I can never let anyone know about it."
5. *"Don't be a child."* A message that oldest children often get is to be responsible and take care of the rest of the children. As they grow up, they may find it extremely difficult to allow themselves to have fun or to be a child.
   Possible decisions: "I'll always be mature and won't do anything childish." "I'll take care of others, and I won't ask for anything for myself."
6. *"Don't grow."* A series of parental messages may include these: "Don't grow beyond infancy." "Don't grow up and leave me." "Stay a

child and don't become sexual." This injunction may be given by parents who are frightened that they cannot handle the fact that their children are able to grow.

Possible decisions: "I won't be sexual, and in that way my father won't reject me." "I'll stay little and helpless, for then I'll get goodies from my parents."

7. *"Don't succeed."* If parents typically criticize children, this message comes across: "You can't make it." "You never do anything right." These children actually get stroked for failing, and thus they may buy the "Don't succeed" message.

Possible decisions: "I'm basically stupid and meant to be a loser." "I'll show you that I can make it, even if it kills me.' 'No matter how good I am, I'll never be good enough."

8. *"Don't be you."* This message is given by parents with the implication that "you are the *wrong sex.* You should have been a girl [boy], and then I would have loved you." In the attempt to win parental acceptance, children may decide to try to become whatever their parents want them to be.

Possible decisions: "No matter what I ever do or am, I'll never please them." "I'll pretend I'm a boy [girl]."

9. *"Don't be sane"* and *"Don't be well."* Some children receive most of their strokes when they are physically ill or when in some way they act crazy. Crazy behavior may be rewarded and modeled.

Possible decisions: "I'll be crazy [ill], and then I ll get noticed." "I am crazy."

10. *"Don't belong."* This message may indicate that a family feels that it does not belong in the community or with any group.

Possible decisions: "Nobody will ever like me because I don't belong anywhere." "I'll never feel at home anywhere."

Strokes. In this description of basic injunctions and early decisions, I have referred to the strokes that children strive for in their interactions with parents. In TA terminology strokes are a form of recognition. We use them to communicate with each other. *Positive strokes* say "I like you," and they may be expressed by warm physical touches, accepting words, and friendly gestures. *Negative strokes* say "I don't like you," and they too can be expressed both verbally and nonverbally. *Conditional strokes* say "I will like you *if* and *when* you are a certain way"; they are received for *doing* something. *Unconditional strokes* say "I am willing to accept you for who you are and for being who you are, and we can negotiate our differences."

TA theory pays attention to how people structure their time to get strokes. It also looks at the life plan of individuals to determine which kind of strokes they both get and give. According to TA. it behooves us to become aware of the strokes we survive on, the strokes that we both ask for and receive, and the strokes that we give others.

Positive stroking is essential for healthy psychological development. It takes the form of expressions of affection or appreciation. If strokes are authentic, we are nourished. Negative stroking by parents leads to thwarting a child's growth. Negative strokes rob people of dignity by diminishing, humiliating, or ridiculing them. As bad as they may be, negative strokes appear to be preferable to no strokes at all.

Games.   A game is an ongoing series of transactions that ends with a bad feeling for at least one player. By their very nature games are designed to prevent intimacy. They develop for the purpose of supporting original decisions, and they are a part of a person's life script (a plan for life, or a conclusion that was reached about how to behave in order to survive in this world). For example, assume that a person was given the message "Don't make it." Also assume that she made the early decision not to succeed, for if she encountered any success, it would bring anxiety. As a child she may have engaged in games that were designed to help her fail. As time passes, she may arrange her life in such a way that she continues to sabotage any chances of enjoying success. Thus, games are a vital part of a person's interactions with others, and they need to be understood if the person wants to decrease game-playing behavior and live authentically. In short, one of the aims of TA is to help people understand the nature of their transactions with others so that they can respond to others with directness, wholeness, and intimacy. Game playing is then reduced.

TA views games as exchanges of strokes that lead to payoffs of bad feelings and advance the script. Games might give the appearance of intimacy, but people who engage in game-playing transactions create distance between them. Common games include Poor Me; Martyr; Yes, But; If It Weren't for You; Look What You Made Me Do! Harried; Uproar; and Wooden Leg. Parents often resort to a battery of games to control their children, and children counter by becoming competent game-players themselves. For example, children are masterful at inventing games to avoid doing chores. The problem with a game is that the ulterior motive for it is buried, and the players end up feeling not OK.

The Karpman Drama Triangle (see Figure 9-1) is a useful device to help people understand games. The triangle has a Persecutor, a Rescuer, and a Victim. For example, a family drama may include the interplay of family members, each operating from a different point on the Drama Triangle. The Victim plays the Kick Me game by inviting another person to "kick" him or her. Often the Victim persecutes another person until he or she kicks the Victim. To complete the triangle, another family member may rush in to save the poor, helpless, kicked Victim from the ruthless Persecutor. It is not uncommon for the Victim to then persecute the Rescuer. The Rescuer, in the guise of being helpful, works to keep others in dependent positions. The feature that distinguishes a game from a straight transaction is the very fast "switch" from one position in the triangle to another, such as the switch from Rescuer to Persecutor or from Victim to Persecutor, as illustrated in Figure 9-1.

Rackets.   The unpleasant feelings that we experience after a game are called rackets. These chronic feelings that we hold on to are the ones we often experienced with our parents. They are the feelings that we got (from the strokes we received) when we acted in certain ways as children. Like games, rackets sup-

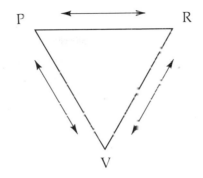

Figure 9-1   The Karpman Drama Triangle *(From "Fairy Tales and Script Drama Analysis," by S. Karpman. In* Transactional Analysis Bulletin, *1968, 7, 39–43. Reprinted by permission.)*

port early decisions, and they are a basic part of one's life script. People can develop an anger racket, a guilt racket, or a depression racket, to mention a few. These rackets are maintained by actually choosing situations that will support unpleasant and chronic feelings. For example, if a woman in order to survive has bought the "Don't be close" injunction and made the decision not to trust people and not to get close, she may save up bad feelings of anger to justify her need for distance. If for some reason it appears that she might be getting close to someone, she will probably find certain characteristics or behaviors of the other person that result in her angry feelings, and in this way she does not get close. If she collects enough bad feelings, she can eventually prove that she was right all along—that it is dangerous to get close.

Life scripts.   As mentioned earlier, a life script in many ways resembles a drama with a plot. Our script may have been formed very early in life, when we learned that for psychological or physiological survival we had to be a certain way. Our life script includes parental messages we have incorporated the decisions we have made in response to these injunctions, the games we play to maintain our early decisions, the rackets we experience to justify our decisions, and our expectations of the way we think our life drama will be played out and how the story will end. Some TA writers, such as Berne (1964, 1972), Harris (1967), and Steiner (1974), have stressed the script theory. Berne writes that children are "scripted" and that they need direction from a strong Parent figure in the therapist if they hope to change their life scripts. Other TA theorists and practitioners reject this scripting theory. Goulding and Goulding (1978, 1979) assert that we make decisions in response to real or imagined injunctions and thereby "script" ourselves: "We believe that the individual writes his own script and can rewrite it with the help of a strong Parent he builds himself, rather than incorporates from a therapist" (1979, p. 42).

   People's life plan is based on their early existential decisions about themselves and others. As children they assume a basic life position that they are either OK as a person or not OK. This early decision is reinforced by others in both verbal and nonverbal ways. In childhood people also decide whether other people are OK or not and whether they are to be trusted or not. This decision-making process about self and others becomes our basic belief system (Dusay & Dusay, 1989).

Mary Goulding (1987) contends that people are capable of transcending their early programming and choices by coming to understand their past decisions and by making new choices in the present that will affect their future. She believes that clients discard and grow beyond their Child decisions. In doing so, they learn to free themselves from the self-restricting straitjackets of their past.

Life scripts seem to operate in physical diseases, such as cancer. In his excellent book *Love, Medicine, and Miracles* Siegel (1988) writes about personality programming as a significant factor in disease. He reports that many of his patients with cancer are convinced that the only way they can receive love is by dying. They have made a "Don't exist" or "Don't be well" decision. Siegel says that some of his patients tend to get the same diseases as their parents and to die at the same age. They appear doomed to reenact their parents' scripts. He contends that one's psychological conditioning is at least as critical as genetic predisposition in leading to disease. He arrived at this conclusion after observing people change their negative conditioning once they became aware of it. A good illustration of this fatalistic life script was given by a nurse who said to Siegel after one of his lectures: "I think you may have saved my life. I've been waiting to die of cancer, since my mother has it and my father had it. It never occurred to me that I didn't have to have it" (Siegel, 1988, p. 88).

Apparently, Siegel believes that the life script is a significant factor in why some people seem to *need* an illness such as cancer. He believes that sickness gives those people "permission" to do things they would otherwise be inhibited from doing. For example, their illness may allow them to take the time to reflect, meditate, and chart a new course of life.

Redecisions.   Throughout their writings, the Gouldings stress that once early decisions have been made, they are not irreversible. In their view we cooperated in making the early decisions that direct our lives, so we can now make new decisions that are appropriate and that will allow us to experience life anew. In working with clients in the redecision process, they have them go back to the early childhood scenes in which they made these decisions. Then, from the Child ego state, they work with them to facilitate a new decision. Simply making an intellectual decision to be different is rarely enough to counteract years of past conditioning. It thus becomes necessary for clients to reexperience the original situation emotionally and to make the new decision emotionally as well as intellectually. For example, if a man were struggling to change an early decision of not wanting to live (in response to the "Don't be" messages that he accepted as a child), he would be encouraged to go back to an early scene with his parents, work through feelings he had with them at that time, and eventually tell himself (and his parents symbolically) that he will live, that he deserves to live even if they wished he had never been born, and that he will make a new decision to stop his self-destructive ways and live to the fullest, *for himself!*

With each of the ten basic injunctions (and some possible decisions that flow from them), there are countless possibilities for new decisions. In each case the therapist chooses an early scene that fits the client's injunction/decision pattern, so that the scene will help this client make a specific redecision. For example, a client may return to a scene in which she was stroked for not succeeding or was negatively stroked for succeeding and thus decided "I won't make it." After some work on the feelings this early scene stirs up, she can make a new decision: "Whether you like it or not, I *am* succeeding and I like it."

The process of redecision is a beginning rather than an ending. Once clients experience a redecision through fantasy work, they and their therapists design experiments so that they can practice new behavior to reinforce their decision. Such people tend to think, feel, and behave in different ways. They discover an ability to be autonomous, and they can experience a sense of freedom, excitement, and energy (M. Goulding, 1987; M. Goulding & Goulding, 1979).

THE THERAPEUTIC PROCESS

THERAPEUTIC GOALS

The basic goal of transactional analysis, as we have seen, is to help clients make new decisions about their present behavior and the direction of their lives. Individuals learn alternatives to sterile and deterministic ways of living. The essence of therapy is to substitute an autonomous lifestyle characterized by awareness, spontaneity, and intimacy for a lifestyle characterized by manipulative game playing and a self-defeating life script. Individuals learn to "write their own script" instead of being passively "scripted." According to Mary Goulding (1987), the essence of redecision therapy consists of contractual change. Working together, the counselor and client establish the specific goals of therapy. Clients are then assisted in taking control of their thoughts, feelings, and actions.

Various other views of TA goals have been expressed, a few of which are:

- being a catalyst to enable clients to mobilize their efforts (Dusay & Dusay, 1989)
- helping clients obtain a friendly "divorce" from their parents (Berne, 1964)
- helping clients break through a series of impasses that stem from injunctions and early decisions (M. Goulding & Goulding, 1979)
- teaching clients to move freely among the Child Adult, and Parent ego states (Harris, 1967)

THERAPIST'S FUNCTION AND ROLE

Transactional analysis is designed to gain both emotional and intellectual insight, but with the focus clearly on rational aspects, the role of the therapist is largely to pay attention to didactic and cognitive issues. The therapist assists clients in discovering the disadvantageous conditions of the past under which they made certain early decisions, adopted life plans, and developed strategies in dealing with people that they might now wish to reconsider. The therapist does not function in the role of a detached, aloof, superior expert who is there to cure the "sick patient." Most TA theorists stress the importance of an equal relationship and point to the contract for therapy as evidence that the therapist and the client are partners in the therapeutic process. Hence, therapists bring their knowledge to bear in the context of a clear, specific contract that the client initiates.

The therapist's job is to help clients acquire the tools necessary for change. The therapist encourages and teaches clients to rely on their own Adult rather than on the therapist's Adult. Contemporary TA practice emphasizes that the key job of the counselor is to help clients discover their inner power to change by making more appropriate decisions *now,* as opposed to continuing to live by archaic decisions they made in childhood. The therapist's real job is to *allow* clients to find their own power.

CLIENT'S EXPERIENCE IN THERAPY

One basic prerequisite for being a TA client is the capacity and willingness to understand and accept a therapeutic contract. The contract contains a specific statement of objectives that the client will attain and the criteria to determine whether these goals have been effectively met. The therapist and client focus only on material in the contract, so that the client knows what he or she is coming to the therapist for. When the terms of the contract are completed, the relationship is terminated unless a new contract is established.

The contract reflects the fact that clients are active agents in the therapeutic process. From the outset they state and clarify their own therapeutic goals. To carry out these goals, the client and therapist may design "assignments" for therapy sessions and for everyday life. Clients experiment with new ways of behaving, and thus they can determine whether they prefer the old or the new behavior. In this way the therapeutic process does not become an interminable one in which clients are dependent on the wisdom of the therapist. Clients demonstrate their willingness to change by actually doing, not by merely "trying" and not by endlessly exploring the past and talking about insights. For therapy to succeed, clients *act* to bring about desired changes.

RELATIONSHIP BETWEEN THERAPIST AND CLIENT

Dusay and Dusay (1989) write that TA therapy is based on an Adult-to-Adult agreement between the therapist and the client on both goals and process. The therapist raises the question that is a basic part of contractual therapy: "How will both you and I know when you get what you came for?" The basic attitude is that they are allies and will work together to accomplish a mutually agreed-on goal. During the course of therapy, Dusay and Dusay write, the therapist and client define their responsibilities in achieving the goal. The therapist does not assume a passive, spectator role, nor does the client sit back passively and wait for the therapist to perform a magical cure.

Mary Goulding and Robert Goulding (1979) agree that the contract sets the focus for treatment and determines the basis of the therapeutic relationship. They write that clients decide the specific beliefs, emotions, and behaviors they plan to change about themselves in order to reach self-designated goals. Clients then work with the therapist to determine the nature of the contract, with the therapist serving as both the witness and facilitator. A therapist will support and work with a contract that is therapeutic for the client.

The emphasis on specific contracts is one of TA's major contributions to counseling and therapy. Without contracts it is easy to wander aimlessly in therapy without looking at goals or without taking personal responsibility for change. Many clients seek a therapist as the source of a cure-all or to play a familiar role in their script, and they begin therapy in a passive and dependent stance. They may attempt to continue their life script by shifting responsibility to their therapist. The contractual approach of TA is based on the expectation that clients focus on their goals and make a commitment. It emphasizes the division of responsibility and provides a point of departure for working.

The contract approach clearly implies a joint responsibility. Through sharing responsibility with the therapist, the client becomes a colleague in his or her treatment. There are several implications of this relationship. First, there is no unbridgeable gap of understanding between the client and the therapist. They share the same vocabulary and concepts and have a similar comprehension of the situation. Second, the client has full and equal rights while in therapy. This means that the client is not forced to make any disclosures he or she chooses not to make. Third, the contract reduces the status differential and emphasizes equality between the client and the therapist.

APPLICATION: THERAPEUTIC TECHNIQUES AND PROCEDURES

In their redecision therapy Mary Goulding and Robert Goulding (1979) work within the framework of TA theory, yet their methods are a combination of TA, Gestalt therapy, interactive group therapy, behavior modification, family therapy, psychodrama, and desensitization methods. Realizing the importance of combining the affective and the cognitive levels the Gouldings draw heavily from TA theory for cognitive structure; they use Gestalt techniques to provide the highly emotional work that breaks through resistance and impasses. In their intensive residential-group format participants stay together anywhere from a weekend to a month.

Following is a brief description of some of the more commonly used processes, procedures, and techniques in TA practice. Most of them can be applied to both individual psychotherapy and group counseling.

THERAPEUTIC PROCEDURES

Structural analysis.   Structural analysis is a tool by which a person becomes aware of the content and functioning of his or her Parent, Adult, and Child. TA clients learn how to identify their own ego states. Structural analysis helps them resolve patterns that they feel stuck with. It allows them to find out which ego state their behavior is based on. With that knowledge they can determine their options.

Two problems related to the structure of personality can be considered by structural analysis: contamination and exclusion. Contamination exists when the contents of one ego state are mixed with those of another. The Parent, the Child, or both intrude within the boundaries of the Adult ego state and interfere with the clear thinking and functioning of the Adult (see Figure 9-2). Contamination from the Parent is typically manifested through prejudiced ideas and attitudes; contamination from the Child involves distorted perceptions of reality. When contamination of the Adult by the Parent, the Child, or both exists, "boundary work" is called for so that the demarcation of each ego state is clearly drawn. When the ego-state boundaries are realigned, the person understands his or her Child and Parent rather than being contaminated by them. Examples of statements reflecting contamination from the Parent are "Don't mix with people who are not of our kind"; "Never trust Italians"; "Watch out for mechanics; they'll cheat you every time"; "You can't depend on teenagers." Examples of statements reflecting contamination from the Child are "Everyone's always picking on me. Nobody treats me right"; "Anything I want I should get right now"; "Who could possibly ever want me for a friend?"

Exclusion exists when, for example, an Excluding-Child ego state can "block out" the Parent or when an Excluding-Parent ego state can "block out" the Child — that is, when rigid ego-state boundaries do not allow for free movement. The person may be restricted to relating primarily as Parent, as Child, or as Adult. The Constant Parent (see Figure 9-3) excludes the Adult and Child and can typically be found in people who are so duty-bound and work-oriented that they cannot play. Such people may be judgmental, moralistic, and demanding of others. They often behave in a domineering and authoritarian manner. The Constant Child excludes the Adult and Parent and, at the extreme, is a sociopath

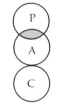

The Parent
contaminating
the Adult

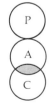

The Child
contaminating
the Adult

Both the Parent
and the Child
contaminating
the Adult

Figure 9-2   Contamination

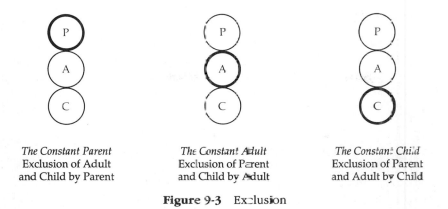

The Constant Parent
Exclusion of Adult
and Child by Parent

The Constant Adult
Exclusion of Parent
and Child by Adult

The Constant Child
Exclusion of Parent
and Adult by Child

Figure 9-3 Exclusion

without a conscience. People operating mainly from the Constant Child are perpetually childlike — they refuse to grow up. They do not think or decide for themselves but attempt to remain dependent in order to escape the responsibility for their own behavior. They seek someone who will take care of them. The Constant Adult, who excludes the Parent and the Child, is objective — that is, involved and concerned with facts. The Constant Adult is an individual who appears robotlike, with little feeling and little spontaneity.

Transactional analysis.   Transactional analysis is basically a description of what people do and say themselves and to each other. Whatever happens between people involves a transaction between their ego states; when messages are sent, a response is expected. There are three types of transaction: complementary, crossed, and ulterior. Complementary transactions occur when a message sent from a specific ego state gets the predicted response from a specific ego state of the other person. An example is the playful Child/Child transaction illustrated in Figure 9-4. Crossed transactions occur when an unexpected response is made to a message that a person sends out, as shown in Figure 9-5. Ulterior transactions are complex. They involve more than two ego states, and a disguised message is sent, as is illustrated in Figure 9-6.

Family modeling.   Family modeling, another approach to working with structural analysis, is particularly useful in working with a Constant Parent, a Constant Adult, or a Constant Child. The client is asked to imagine a scene including as many significant persons in the past as possible, including himself or herself. The client becomes the director, producer, and actor. He or she

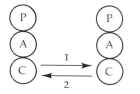

1. "I'd love to go sledding in the snow with you."

2. "Hey, that sounds like fun! Let's go!"

Figure 9-4   Complementary transactions

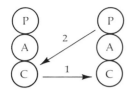

1. "I'd love to go sledding with you in the snow."

2. "Oh, grow up and act your age! I don't have time to waste on foolishness like that!"

Figure 9-5   Crossed transactions

defines the situation and uses other members of the group as substitutes for family members. The client places them in the way he or she remembers the situation. The subsequent discussion, action, and evaluation can then heighten the awareness of a specific situation and the personal meanings it still holds for the client.

Analysis of rituals and pastimes.   Analysis of transactions includes identification of rituals and pastimes that are used in the structuring of time. Time structuring is important material for discussion and examination, because it reflects the decisions of the script about how to transact with others and how to get strokes. People who fill their time chiefly with rituals and pastimes are probably experiencing stroke deprivation, and thus they lack intimacy in their transactions with others. Because ritual and pastime transactions have low stroke value, such people's social transacting may lead to complaints such as emptiness, boredom, lack of excitement, feeling unloved, and a sense of meaninglessness.

Analysis of games and rackets.   The analysis of games and rackets is an important aspect of understanding transactions with others. Berne (1964) describes a game as "an ongoing series of complementary ulterior transactions progressing to a well-defined, predictable outcome" (p. 48). A payoff for most games is a "bad" feeling that the player experiences. It is important to observe and understand why the games are played, what payoffs result, what strokes are received, and how these games maintain distance and interfere with intimacy. Learning to understand a person's racket and how the racket relates to the person's games, decisions, and life script is an important process in TA therapy.

As I mentioned earlier, a racket consists of the calling up and collection of feelings that one uses to justify one's life script and, ultimately, one's decisions. For example, if Jane saves up feelings of depression, the games she plays with

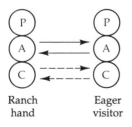

Overt messages (Adult to Adult)
Ranch hand: Can I show you the barn?
Eager visitor: Yes. I'm interested in architecture.

Covert messages (Child to Child)
Ranch hand: How about a roll in the hay?
Eager visitor: Let's go now!

Figure 9-6   Ulterior transactions

others most often have depression as the payoff. When she has finally gathered enough feelings of depression, she feels justified in suicide, which is the action called for to conclude the life script. This is true of the person who has incorporated the "Don't be" message. A person may learn to convert anger to sadness and eventually depression after years of feeling impinged on and never, in anger, telling the aggressors to stop. Or so much anger may be stored and converted that eventually the person can no longer stomach any more, and the rage breaks out in violence to self or others.

Rackets involve the "collection of stamps" that are later traded for a psychological prize. The individual collects archaic feelings by persecuting or rescuing others in order to feel rejected, angry, depressed, abandoned, guilty, and so on. The person invites others to play certain roles. For example, Jane, a group member, may invite other members to react to her with anger. She could program this reaction by being extremely closed and hostile and by persuading herself that nobody could ever understand her, much less care for her. Any genuine approach from others would be rebuffed by her refusal to accept anything from anyone. Eventually, Jane would collect enough stamps to prove to the entire group that she was right all along, and then she could say "See, I told you nobody cares about me."

Rackets are as important as games in manipulating others, for they are the primary method of masking a person from the real world. It takes a competent therapist to distinguish between anger, sadness, and fear that are used as a racket and the honest expression of emotions. The competent and skillful therapist squarely challenges a client's racket in such a manner that the client becomes aware of the behavior without being driven off.

Script analysis.   People's lack of autonomy stems from their commitment to their scripting — that is, to a life plan decided on at an early age. An important aspect of the life script is the compelling quality that drives people to play it out.

Scripting initially occurs nonverbally in infancy, from parents' messages. During the early years of development, one learns about one's worth as a person and one's place in life. Later, scripting occurs in direct as well as indirect ways. In a family, for example, such messages as the following may be picked up: "In this family, the man is the boss of the house." "Children are to be seen but not heard." "We always expect the best from you." "The way you are, you'll never amount to a hill of beans." "Never question our authority, and strive to be respectful and obedient." Because the life script forms the core of a person's identity and destiny, life experiences may lead the person to conclude, on the one hand: "I'm really dumb, because nothing I do ever turns out right. I suppose I'll always be stupid." On the other hand, the person may conclude: "I can do almost anything that I really decide I want to do. I know I can attain my goals if I channel my efforts in a direction I want to go in.'

Script analysis is a part of the therapeutic process by which the life pattern that clients follow is identified. It can demonstrate to clients the process by which they acquired the script and the ways in which they justify their script actions. When clients become aware of their life script, they are in a position to do something about changing their programming. People are not condemned to be a victim of early scripting, for, through awareness, redecision is possible. Script analysis opens up new alternatives from which to choose as people go through life; they need no longer feel compelled to play games to collect payoffs to justify a certain action that is called for in their life script.

Script analysis can be carried out by means of a script checklist, which contains items related to life positions, rackets, and games — all of which are key functional components of a person's life script. I encourage you to take time to fill out the life-script questionnaire in the student manual that accompanies this book.

APPLICATION TO GROUPS

The practice of TA is ideally suited to groups. Berne believed that group therapy yielded information about one's personal plan for life that would take much more time to obtain through individual therapy. In a group people are able to observe others changing, giving them models and increasing their own options. They come to understand the structure and functioning of their individual personality and learn how they transact with others. By seeing how others play games and act out their script, group members are better able to identify their own games and script. This whole process of watching others proceed at various speeds and levels of change validates clients' pacing of their own changes. Clients are able to focus on their early decisions, which may never have been subject to scrutiny. Interaction with other group members gives them ample opportunity to practice assignments and fulfill their contracts. The transactions in the group enable the members to increase their awareness of both self and others and thus to focus on the changes and redecisions they will make in their lives.

Redecisional therapy, as practiced by the Gouldings, is done in a group context in which members can experience their script coming to life by reliving early memories and by interacting with others in the group. From a redecisional perspective group therapy is the treatment of choice. People change more rapidly than they do in individual therapy (R. Goulding, 1987). There are many avenues of self-understanding through analyzing transactions within the group. In much the same way that Gestalt groups function in the here and now, TA groups ask clients to relive past scenes as though they were happening in the present. The presence of group members facilitates action, because they can represent family members from the past as well as people in the present. Because of the interaction within the group, members are given many opportunities to review and challenge their past decisions and experiment with new ones. One rationale for group counseling is that it provides a living experience that participants can implement in their interactions in everyday life. In their redecision groups the Gouldings integrate TA's theoretical base with techniques drawn from a variety of other approaches, including Gestalt therapy, psychodrama, fantasy and imagery, behavior therapy, desensitization, and family therapy.

Through the group process members experience the point at which they feel stuck. They relive the context in which they made earlier decisions, some of which are no longer functional, and they learn to make appropriate new decisions. The group process helps members discover ways in which they are viewing themselves in victimlike roles and enables them to increasingly control their lives by beginning to act differently both in the group and in everyday life.

Summary and Evaluation

SUMMARY

Transactional analysis is grounded on the assumption that we make current decisions based on past premises — premises that were at one time appropriate to our survival needs but that may no longer be valid. TA emphasizes the cognitive, rational, and behavioral aspects of the therapeutic process. More specifically, it stresses the capacity of the person to change decisions and is oriented toward increasing awareness with the goal of enabling people to make new decisions (redecide) and thereby alter the course of their life. To achieve this goal, TA clients learn how to recognize the three ego states (Parent, Adult, and Child) in which they function. They also learn how their current behavior is affected by the rules and regulations they received and incorporated as children and how they can identify the life script that determines their actions. Underlying TA therapy is this theory of a life script, which is similar to Adler's concept of the lifestyle. Early in life each of us fashions a script that we carry out, usually without awareness.

TA emphasizes that as children we reacted to environmental stresses, received injunctions, and then made early decisions about self and others based on such messages. Such basic decisions show up in our current ways of thinking, feeling, and behaving. TA therapists encourage clients to recall and reexperience situations in childhood where faulty learning originated. Ultimately, clients come to realize that they have the power to redecide and initiate a new direction in life and that they can change what is *not* working while retaining what serves them well.

TA therapists are guided in their work by the contracts their clients develop with them. In carrying out this therapeutic work, counselors can employ a variety of procedures. Some of these are structural analysis, transactional analysis, role playing, family modeling, analysis of games and rackets, teaching, and script analysis. TA's concepts and techniques can be adapted to individual, group, marital, and family therapy. They can also be applied to a wide range of clients,

CONTRIBUTIONS OF TRANSACTIONAL ANALYSIS

I find TA's contract method very useful, and I believe that any orientation to counseling can incorporate it. In my judgment it helps the client assume more personal responsibility for the outcomes of the counseling experience. The analysis of the games that we all play, another contribution of TA, teaches clients to become more aware of game structures and to free themselves from game-playing behavior. They can move from ulterior behavior to straightforward behavior.

Another contribution of TA that I have incorporated into my counseling is challenging clients to become more aware of their early decisions. A lot of people drag behind them these decisions about their self-worth and personal power, and they fail to come to terms with their power because they cling to parental messages that they rehearse over and over in their heads. I favor asking people to talk out loud about these inner rehearsals of the messages, many of which keep them in an emotional straitjacket. Examining here-and-now transactions with others to determine what people get from some of their behavior styles is another useful procedure.

Further, the integration of TA concepts and practices with certain concepts from Gestalt therapy is extremely helpful. I frequently use some of the concepts from TA, such as early parental messages or the subtle ways people behave as their parents behaved, as catalysts for role playing or psychodrama. For example, instead of allowing group participants to carry on a lengthy monologue about why they have difficulty expressing affection to those they care about, I will request that they reenact some early scene with their parents that depicts how they learned that "you aren't supposed to get too close." Role playing, which can tap the deeper feelings of a current difficulty, tends to be far more meaningful than having people talk about an early decision. Another strength is the open stance that many TA practitioners have in integrating techniques from other theoretical approaches. These practitioners use TA as a theory of personality that offers a perspective for therapeutic work. Within this theoretical framework they are free to borrow procedures from any other approach.

Contributions to multicultural counseling.   To my way of thinking two of the major assets of TA as applied to multicultural counseling are its focus on cultural and familial injunctions and its emphasis on early decisions. Consider some of the following injunctions, any of which you are likely to hear if you work with ethnic clients: "Live up to the expectations of your parents and your family." "Don't shame the family." "Don't be too concerned about yourself." "Do not show your weaknesses." "Don't talk about your family or about family problems with strangers." "Don't put your own good above the social good." These cultural injunctions provide a good starting point for counseling. It is important that the counselor respect clients' cultural injunctions yet at the same time challenge clients to evaluate the basis for their beliefs. Naturally, some injunctions, and the decisions based on them, may remain unchanged if the client determines that change is not necessary.

TA provides a structured approach that teaches clients how their early decisions have continued to influence their behavior. The structure allows clients to see connections between what they learned in their family and their attitudes toward others. Its cognitive approach enables individuals to examine many of their basic assumptions. The analysis of the life script can be especially useful in structuring the counseling sessions.

Another strength of TA as applied to multicultural counseling lies in the manner in which this approach deals with power. People of color often experience a lack of the power to make a difference in society, especially in the dominant mainstream culture. TA has specific techniques to enhance personal responsibility that often result in empowerment. TA's contractual approach also provides a means for clients to assume increased personal power, because they decide what they are willing to change and what steps they can take to bring these changes about. Their contract can also act as a safeguard against therapists' imposing their cultural values. Thus, this approach can help clients who have been robbed of their power by society and who have also contributed to their own feelings of powerlessness by their attitudes and behavior (Dusay & Dusay, 1989).

LIMITATIONS AND CRITICISMS OF TRANSACTIONAL ANALYSIS

I personally have some trouble with much of the terminology used in transactional analysis. I'm concerned that clients might get lost in the specialized terminology and structure of this theory, in spite of the claim by many proponents that TA is simple and can easily be understood by children.

TA's emphasis on structure is another disquieting aspect for me. I believe that it is very possible for therapists who are well schooled in TA to become expert in diagnosing game patterns—indicating to the client what type of transaction he or she is now in, labeling every bit of behavior with some cliché phrase, detecting to what degree a person is "OK," and sorting out all kinds of scripting—and yet still practice therapy in such a manner that they leave themselves (their values, feelings, reactions to the client, and so on) out of the transaction with a client. In other words, I do not see in TA a great emphasis on the authenticity of the therapist or on the quality of the person-to-person relationship with the client. The TA therapist can hide under the blanket of categories, structures, labeling, transaction analysis, and the figurative job of directing traffic.

The danger is that TA can be primarily an intellectual experience. TA clients can understand intellectually all sorts of things but perhaps not feel and experience those aspects of themselves. Is the client in TA encouraged to work toward a synthesis of head and gut? Reliance on TA as an exclusive way of growth seems to be limiting in that it stresses understanding on a cognitive level. In my opinion one of the shortcomings of the Gestalt approach is that is deemphasizes intellectual factors. In Gestalt therapy clients are frequently called to task if they think, and they are told that they are "bullshitting" or, even worse, "elephant-shitting"! In TA, however, one of the shortcomings is its deemphasis of the affective domain. Thus, it is the marriage of many of the concepts and techniques of Gestalt with those of TA that is most useful.

A major criticism of TA from a behavioral perspective is that concepts and procedures have not been subjected to testing for scientific validation. TA needs to specify how constructs such as Parent, Child, and Adult can be experimentally tested. Attention also needs to be given to specifying with which problems and under what conditions TA works best (Prochaska, 1984). The literature is sorely lacking when it comes to objective empirical research studies of TA. For the most part, case studies are used for support. TA theory could profit from well-designed studies using behavioral outcome measures.

Limitations for multicultural counseling.   A limitation of applying TA to multicultural counseling is that the terminology may not be meaningful to some ethnic-minority clients. Even though TA therapists assert that their approach is simple and easy to understand, many clients may have difficulty with the complexity of concepts such as crossed transactions, the structure and dynamics of games, and the subcomponents of the various ego states. Before therapists challenge the life scripts of ethnic-minority clients, it is well for them to establish a trusting relationship and make sure that these clients demonstrate a readiness to question the specifics of what it was like growing up in their family. One caution is that therapists should avoid challenging clients too quickly, thus lessening the chances of premature termination. A safeguard is to work with clients in developing a contract, for in this way they are deciding which values they may want to challenge.

QUESTIONS FOR REFLECTION AND DISCUSSION

1. How are you like your mother? like your father? How are you different from them?
2. What are some games and strategies you used as a child with your family and that you are aware of still using in your present relationships with people? What do these games do for you?
3. Can you trace some of the basic early decisions that you made about yourself during your childhood? Are those decisions still operating in your present behavior? Are you aware of changing any of your basic decisions? If so, which ones?
4. What are some parental injunctions that you can identify in your life? Can you identify with any of the following? "Don't enjoy." "Don't think." "Don't touch." "Don't talk." "Don't look." "Don't be close." "Don't succeed." "Don't fail." "Don't let us down." "Don't enjoy." "Don't trust." "Don't be you." "Don't be sexy." "Don't be angry." "Don't fight." "Don't be selfish." "Don't be."
5. What are some "dos," "oughts," and "shoulds" in your life? Which of the following fit for you? "Be perfect." "You should be productive." "You ought to work to your potential." "You should do what is expected of you." "You ought to be responsible." "Succeed at everything." "Be tough." "Do what is right."
6. Can you see how some injunctions that you have internalized might have some effect on you as you counsel others? For example, if you have trouble being spontaneous or being childlike, how might you be affected in working with clients who are impulsive and tend to live for the moment?
7. How do you get your strokes? Are they mainly negative or mainly positive? Do you get strokes from your family? from work? from friends? Are you able to ask for the strokes you want, or are you limited in the amount of positive stroking you can tolerate?

8. Do you really believe that most people are able to change the early decisions that they made about themselves, others, and life? What forces operate against a person in his or her attempt to change and make new decisions? How can a person make and retain new decisions?

9. How essential is a contract as the basis for a therapeutic relationship? What are some possible advantages of a contract? Are there any disadvantages? What do you think of this statement by Dusay and Dusay (1989): "Throughout the therapy contract, each will be defining their mutual responsibilities in achieving the goal; the therapist will not enter in a passive spectator position and the client will not sit back waiting for the therapist to perform a miracle" (pp. 427–428)?

10. In thinking about Stan's case, what are the major injunctions that he was apparently given? What early decisions do you think he made? How might a TA therapist proceed with Stan? What aspects of TA might you draw from if he were your client?

WHERE TO GO FROM HERE

According to Dusay (1986), TA is recognized as a complete theory of personality and an entire system of psychotherapy. The regulatory body, the International Transactional Analysis Association, certifies the therapists who enroll in its rigorous training program. TA is practiced internationally, by both professionals and paraprofessionals. Prison inmates, schizophrenic patients, people in drug-rehabilitation programs, and outpatient clients from all socioeconomic levels have participated in TA treatment programs.

If you want to learn more about TA, I encourage you to consider attending a teaching workshop where you can apply TA principles to counseling in various settings. For further information contact:

International Transactional Analysis Association
1772 Vallejo Street
San Francisco, CA 94123
Telephone: (415) 885-5992

This association provides guidelines for becoming a Certified Clinical Member. Before certification is granted, candidates must pass both a written and an oral examination, in which samples of their work are reviewed by a board of examiners to determine their level of clinical competence.

RECOMMENDED SUPPLEMENTARY READINGS

The *Transactional Analysis Journal* is a good source for keeping current with the developments of TA theory, clinical applications, and research. The subscription rate is $25 annually, and the journal is published quarterly. For information concerning dues for various membership classifications and journal subscriptions, contact the ITAA office, 1772 Vallejo Street, San Francisco, CA 94123.

Redecision Therapy: Expanded Perspectives (Kadis, 1985) is a collection of articles on the theory and technique of redecision therapy, as well as the applications of this approach to specific settings.

For a popular account of transactional analysis, an excellent place to begin is *Born to Win: Transactional Analysis with Gestalt Experiments* (James & Jongeward, 1971), which gives a good overview of TA principles and also includes many Gestalt experiments dealing with stroking, sexual identity, game playing, adulthood, and autonomy.

TA: The Total Handbook of Transactional Analysis (Woollams & Brown, 1979) contains a variety of excellent exercises aimed at understanding TA concepts.

What Do You Say After You Say Hello? (Berne, 1972) presents an overall theory of personality, with emphasis on scripts.

Scripts People Live: Transactional Analysis of Life Scripts (Steiner, 1974) is one of the best accounts of life scripts. Attention is given to political and social institutions, to oppression, and to social action.

If you are interested in a more advanced treatment of transactional analysis as a theory with specific applications to therapeutic practice in groups, I highly recommend *Changing Lives through Redecision Therapy* (M. Goulding & Goulding, 1979). This is a very readable work that gives a clear and concise overview of TA. It deals in depth with such topics as injunctions and early decisions, contracts, stroking, dealing with emotions, redecisions, and the blending of TA theory with Gestalt techniques. It is an excellent example of integrating the cognitive and the affective dimensions in helping clients work through early decisions and toward new decisions.

References and Suggested Readings*

BERNE, E. (1961). *Transactional analysis in psychotherapy.* New York: Grove Press.
*BERNE, E. (1964). *Games people play.* New York: Grove Press.
BERNE, E. (1966). *Principles of group treatment.* New York: Oxford University Press.
BERNE, E. (1970). *Sex in human loving.* New York: Simon & Schuster.
*BERNE, E. (1972). *What do you say after you say hello?* New York: Grove Press.
*BERNE, E. (1989). A terminated case with follow-up. In D. Wedding & R. J. Corsini (Eds.), *Case studies in psychotherapy* (pp. 179–192). Itasca, IL: F. E. Peacock.
COREY, G. (1990). *Theory and practice of group counseling* (3rd ed.). Pacific Grove, CA: Brooks/Cole.
COREY, G. (1991). *Case approach to counseling and psychotherapy* (3rd ed.). Pacific Grove, CA: Brooks/Cole.
*DUSAY, J. M. (1986). Transactional analysis. In I. L. Kutash & A. Wolf (Eds.), *Psychotherapist's casebook* (pp. 413–423). San Francisco: Jossey-Bass.
*DUSAY, J. M., & DUSAY, K. M. (1989). In R. J. Corsini & D. Wedding (Eds.), *Current psychotherapies* (4th ed.) (pp. 405–453). Itasca, IL: F. E. Peacock.
GLADFELTER, J. (1985). Dreamwork from a redecision approach. In L. B. Kadis (Ed.), *Redecision therapy: Expanded perspectives* (pp. 104–105). Watsonville, CA: Western Institute for Group and Family Therapy.
GOULDING, M. M. (1985a). The joy of psychotherapy. In L. B. Kadis (Ed.), *Redecision therapy: Expanded perspectives* (pp. 4–8). Watsonville, CA: Western Institute for Group and Family Therapy.
GOULDING, M. M. (1985b). A redecision exercise. In L. B. Kadis (Ed.), *Redecision therapy: Expanded perspectives* (pp. 65–67). Watsonville, CA: Western Institute for Group and Family Therapy.
GOULDING, M. M. (1987). Transactional analysis and redecision therapy. In J. K. Zeig (Ed.), *The evolution of psychotherapy* (pp. 285–299). New York: Brunner/Mazel.

* Books and articles marked with an asterisk are suggested for further study.

*GOULDING, M., & GOULDING, R. (1979). *Changing lives through redecision therapy.* New York: Brunner/Mazel.

GOULDING, R. (1985). History of redecision therapy. In L. B. Kadis (Ed.), *Redecision therapy: Expanded perspectives* (pp. 9–11). Watsonville, CA: Western Institute for Group and Family Therapy.

GOULDING, R. (1986). Discussion of therapist transparency. *International Journal of Group Psychotherapy, 36,* 25–27.

*GOULDING, R. L. (1987). Group therapy: Mainline or sideline? In J. K. Zeig (Ed.), *The evolution of psychotherapy* (pp. 300–311). New York: Brunner/Mazel.

GOULDING, R., & GOULDING, M. (1976). Injunctions, decision, and redecision. *Transactional Analysis Journal, 6,* 41–48.

*GOULDING, R., & GOULDING, M. (1978). *The power is in the patient: A TA/Gestalt approach to psychotherapy.* San Francisco: TA Press.

*HARRIS, T. (1967). *I'm OK—You're OK.* New York: Avon.

HEYER, N. R. (1987). Empirical research on ego state theory. *Transactional Analysis Journal, 17,* 286–293.

JAMES, M., & JONGEWARD, D. (1971). *Born to win: Transactional analysis with Gestalt experiments.* Reading, MA: Addison-Wesley.

*KADIS, L. B. (Ed.). (1985). *Redecision therapy: Expanded perspectives.* Watsonville, CA: Western Institute for Group and Family Therapy.

KARPMAN, S. (1968). Fairy tales and script drama analysis. *Transactional Analysis Bulletin, 7,* 39–43.

MADISON, P. (1985). Redecision therapy: What it is, how and why it works. In L. B. Kadis (Ed.), *Redecision therapy: Expanded perspectives* (pp. 20–25). Watsonville, CA: Western Institute for Group and Family Therapy.

McCORMICK, P. (1971). *Guide for use of a life script questionnaire in transactional analysis.* San Francisco: Transactional Publications.

McCORMICK, P., & PULLEYBLANK, E. (1985). The stages of redecision therapy. In L. B. Kadis (Ed.), *Redecision therapy: Expanded perspectives* (pp. 51–59). Watsonville, CA: Western Institute for Group and Family Therapy.

NOVELLINO, M. (1987). Redecision analysis of transference: The unconscious dimension. *Transactional Analysis Journal, 1,* 271–276.

PATTERSON, C. H. (1986). *Theories of counseling and psychotherapy* (4th ed.). New York: Harper & Row.

PRICE, R. (1985). Paradoxical possibilities in redecision therapy. In L. B. Kadis (Ed.), *Redecision therapy: Expanded perspectives* (pp. 26–35). Watsonville, CA: Western Institute for Group and Family Therapy.

PROCHASKA, J. O. (1984). *Systems of psychotherapy: A transtheoretical analysis* (2nd ed.). Pacific Grove, CA: Brooks/Cole.

SIEGEL, B. (1988). *Love, medicine, and miracles.* New York: Harper & Row (Perennial Library).

SIMKIN, J. S., & YONTEF, G. M. (1984). Gestalt therapy. In R. Corsini (Ed.), *Current psychotherapies* (3rd ed.). Itasca, IL: F. E. Peacock.

STEINER, C. (1967). A script checklist. *Transactional Analysis Bulletin, 6*(22), 38–39; 56.

STEINER, C. (1971). *Games alcoholics play: The analysis of life scripts.* New York: Grove Press.

STEINER, C. (1974). *Scripts people live: Transactional analysis of life scripts.* New York: Grove Press.

*WOOLLAMS, S., & BROWN, M. (1979). *TA: The total handbook of transactional analysis.* Englewood Cliffs, NJ: Prentice-Hall.

10

BEHAVIOR THERAPY

ARNOLD LAZARUS

ARNOLD A. LAZARUS (b. 1932) was born and educated in Johannesburg, South Africa. The youngest of four children (his sisters were 17 and 14 when he was born, and his brother was 9), he grew up in a neighborhood where there were very few children, and he remembers being lonely and frightened. He learned to play the piano at an early age and performed on Saturday mornings at a movie theater during intermission, for which he received the equivalent of $1 ("a small fortune for a 7-year-old when 8 cents got you into a movie, and an ice cream cone cost 1 cent"). "When I was 7,' he says, "I used to play like a talented 12-year-old, but when I turned 14 and still played like a 12-year-old, I decided to quit!" At that time his interests changed to bodybuilding, weight lifting, boxing, and wrestling. "I was a pathetically skinny kid, often beaten up and bullied, so I started training rather frantically." Through sheer determination he ended up winning boxing and weight-lifting competitions and planned to own and operate a gym or health center.

Although Lazarus grew up in South Africa, he strongly identified with the United States. "I loved to read Superman and Batman Comics, and these heroes espoused liberty, justice, and the American (not South African) way." At an early age he felt that racism and discrimination were totally unacceptable. These views got him into lots of fights, which was another reason he took up boxing and weight lifting.

He entered college intending to major in English with a view to journalism as a career, "but the English professors were stodgy and boring, so I switched my majors to psychology and sociology, where the subject matter soon intrigued me and where there were three or four inspiring teachers." He obtained a master's degree in experimental psychology in 1957 and a Ph.D. in clinical psychology in 1960, and then he went into full-time private practice in Johannesburg. In 1963 he was invited by Albert Bandura to teach at Stanford University. "So my wife, Daphne, my 4-year-old daughter, Linda, my 2-year-old son, Cliff, and I set out for California." Although Lazarus found his year at Stanford "amazingly stimulating," he was extremely homesick, so he returned to Johannesburg and went back into full-time private practice. But he had tasted America and Academia and found life in South Africa "politically untenable," so in 1966 he returned to California with his wife and children to head the Behavior Therapy Institute.

In 1967 he was appointed a full professor at Temple University Medical School in Philadelphia, where he worked with Dr. Joseph Wolpe, who had been his mentor. When Lazarus criticized Wolpe for being too rigid and narrow in his outlook, they parted company. In 1970 Lazarus went to Yale University as Director of Clinical Training, and in 1972 he received the rank of Distinguished Professor at Rutgers University, where he teaches in the Graduate School of Applied and Professional Psychology. He has a private practice in Princeton, New Jersey.

Lazarus's *Behavior Therapy and Beyond* (1971) is one of the first books on cognitive-behavioral therapy, and it subsequently evolved into his systematic and comprehensive approach called *multimodal therapy*. Out of his 11 books and 150 articles, 3 books and 36 papers are on the multimodal orientation, which is gaining recognition both in the United States and abroad. In addition, Lazarus has been affiliated with several professional and scientific societies, and has served on editorial boards. But he insists: "What sets me apart from most of my colleagues is that they seem to live for their work, whereas I work in order to live. My wife and kids have always come first, followed by the cultivation of really meaningful friendships, and the pursuit of fun."

INTRODUCTION

Behavior therapy offers various action-oriented methods to help people take steps to change what they are doing and thinking. Many techniques, particularly those developed within the last decade, emphasize cognitive processes. In this chapter the terms *behavior modification* and *behavior therapy* are used synonymously. Although some writers differentiate between the terms, most use them interchangeably. Two definitions will provide a sense of the focus of behavior therapy and show how it differs from most of the other approaches in this book. Behavior modification, or behavior therapy, has been defined as "(1) the use of a broadly defined set of clinical procedures whose description and rationale often rely on the experimental findings of psychological research, and (2) an experimental and functionally analytic approach to clinical data, relying on objective and measurable outcomes" (Craighead, Kazdin, & Mahoney, 1976, p. 19). A second definition of behavior modification is "the application of basic research and theory from experimental psychology to influence behavior for purposes of resolving personal and social problems and enhancing human functioning" (Kazdin, 1978).

HISTORICAL BACKGROUND

The behavioral approach had its origin in the 1950s and early 1960s as a radical departure from the dominant psychoanalytic perspective. During this time the behavior-therapy movement differed from other therapeutic approaches in its application of principles of classical and operant conditioning to the treatment of a variety of problem behaviors. Today, behavior therapy can no longer be defined so simply (Wilson, 1989). Spiegler (1983) compares the historical development of behavior therapy to the stages of human development. During the late 1950s behavior therapy was able to survive its "birth trauma," in spite of the harsh criticism leveled against it by adherents of other schools of therapy. In the 1960s the approach was challenged to establish its own identity. As Franks (1987) has observed, this was a pioneering era of ideology in which behavior therapists mobilized their energy against the opponents. It was during the 1970s that behavior therapy emerged as a major force in psychotherapy and education and also experienced a significant growth spurt. During this adolescence the approach was credited with developing new techniques and expanding its areas of competence. In this period there was an increased emphasis on self-control procedures that enabled clients to make significant changes on their own. This decade also gave rise to the development of cognitive-behavioral therapies, which legitimized the place of subjective events (thoughts and attitudes) in therapy. During the 1980s behavior therapy was in its early adulthood. It was giving up some of its adolescent idealism yet replacing it with a more realistic and mature evaluation of both its strengths and limitations. This was a period characterized by a search for new horizons in concepts and methods. Behavior therapists continued to subject their methods to empirical scrutiny and to consider the impact of the practice of therapy on both their clients and the larger society. The 1980s were characterized by a search for new horizons, which included the development of new concepts and methods that went beyond traditional learning theory (Franks, 1987). More attention was given to the role of affect in therapeutic change. Also, there was more focus on the role that biological factors play in many of the disorders that are treated with behavioral methods.

Behavior therapy today is marked by a diversity of views. There is now a wide variety of procedures with different theoretical rationales (Wilson, 1989). Behavior therapy is much more diverse than it was in the 1950s, either theoretically or methodologically (Karoly & Harris, 1986). In some sense it is experiencing a midlife crisis, in that there is uncertainty about the movement's future directions.

THREE AREAS OF DEVELOPMENT

Contemporary behavior therapy can be understood by considering three major areas of development: classical conditioning, operant conditioning, and cognitive therapy. First is the approach of *classical conditioning,* in which certain respondent behaviors, such as knee jerks and salivation, are elicited from a passive organism. In the 1950s Joseph Wolpe and Arnold Lazarus of South Africa and Hans Eysenck of England began using the findings of experimental research with animals to help treat phobias in clinical settings. They based their work on Hullian learning theory and Pavlovian (or classical) conditioning. An underlying characteristic of the work of these pioneers was the focus on experimental analysis and evaluation of therapeutic procedures. Wolpe's contribution to the development of the technique of systematic desensitization, which is described later in this chapter, is based on the classical-conditioning model, and it illustrates how principles of learning derived from the experimental laboratory can be applied clinically.

Second is the approach of *operant conditioning.* Operant behavior consists of actions that operate on the environment to produce consequences. Examples of operant behaviors include reading, writing, driving a car, and eating with utensils. Such behaviors include most of the significant responses we make in everyday life. If the environmental changes brought about by the behavior are reinforcing (if they provide some reward to the organism or eliminate aversive stimuli), the chances are strengthened that the behavior will occur again. If the environmental changes produce no reinforcement, the chances are lessened that the behavior will recur.

At the same time that Wolpe, Lazarus, and Eysenck were carrying out their experiments in the 1950s, B. F. Skinner was studying the use of the principles of operant conditioning with psychotic patients in the United States. Skinner's view of controlling behavior is based on the principles of operant conditioning, which rest on the assumption that changes in behavior are brought about when that behavior is followed by a particular kind of consequence. Skinner contends that learning cannot occur in the absence of some kind of reinforcement, either positive or negative. For him actions that are reinforced tend to be repeated, and those that are discouraged tend to be extinguished. His general writings apply concepts of operant conditioning to society. His model is based on reinforcement principles and has the goal of identifying and controlling environmental factors that lead to behavioral change.

Positive reinforcement is a procedure in which a response is followed by the presentation of a stimulus. It involves the addition of something (such as praise or money) as a consequence of certain behavior. The stimulus is a positive reinforcer, which is something the organism seeks, such as food. For example, a child may whine when she wants candy. If her father gives her the candy each time she whines, to quiet her, her whining has become positively reinforced. Negative reinforcement involves the removal of unpleasant stimuli from a situation once a certain behavior has occurred. Negative reinforcers are generally unpleasant, so that the individual is motivated to exhibit a desired behavior in order to avoid the unpleasant condition. For example, I will eventually go to the woodpile and bring in logs for the stove, because I have learned that if I don't, my wife will tell me how lazy I am or the house will get cold. I have learned to interrupt my work long enough to fetch wood, because if I don't, there are some unpleasant consequences.

Third is the *cognitive trend* in behavior therapy. The behaviorists of both the classical-conditioning and operant-conditioning models excluded any reference to mediational concepts (such as the role of thinking processes, attitudes, and values), perhaps as a reaction against the insight-oriented psychodynamic approaches. Since the 1970s the behavioral movement has conceded a legitimate place to thinking, even to the extent of giving cognitive factors a central role in the understanding of and treating of behavioral problems (see Bandura, 1969, 1986; Beck, 1976; Beck & Weishaar, 1989; Goldfried & Davison, 1976; Lazarus, 1971, 1981, 1989; London, 1985; Mahoney, 1977, 1979; Meichenbaum, 1977, 1985). According to Franks (1987), cognitive-behavioral therapy is now established as a part of mainstream behavior therapy. Some writers believe that "to ignore the role of cognitive factors in the conceptualization and modification of human behavior would seriously interfere with the behavior therapist's ability to deal with many of the problems he is confronted with clinically" (Goldfried & Davison, 1976, p. 12).

Behavior therapy has undergone important changes and has expanded considerably. It is no longer grounded exclusively in learning theory, nor is it a narrowly defined set of techniques. Contemporary behavior therapy encompasses a variety of conceptualizations, research methods, and treatment procedures to explain and change behavior, as well as considerable debate about evidence of efficacy (Kazdin & Wilson, 1978). Lazarus (1971) is considered one of the pioneers of clinical behavior therapy, for he has contributed to broadening its conceptual bases and introducing innovative clinical techniques (Wilson, 1989, p. 244).

This chapter will describe some of the basic behavior-therapy principles as well as clarify important characteristics of the therapeutic process. The bulk of the chapter describes the application of therapeutic techniques to many different populations. The next chapter will be devoted to Albert Ellis's rational-emotive therapy and other cognitive-behavioral approaches.

KEY CONCEPTS

VIEW OF HUMAN NATURE

Modern behavior therapy is grounded on a scientific view of human behavior that implies a systematic and structured approach to counseling. This view does not rest on a deterministic assumption that humans are a mere product of their sociocultural conditioning. Rather, the current view is that the person is the producer *and* the product of his or her environment (Bandura, 1974, 1977, 1986).

Whereas the "radical behaviorists" such as Skinner (1948, 1971) rule out the possibility of self-determination and freedom, the current trend is toward developing procedures that actually give control to clients and thus increase their range of freedom. Behavior modification aims to increase people's skills so that the number of their response options is increased. By overcoming debilitating behaviors that restrict choices, people are freer to select from possibilities that were not available earlier. Thus, as behavior modification is typically applied, it will increase rather than stifle individual freedom (Kazdin, 1978).

Philosophically, the behavioristic and the humanistic approaches have often been viewed as polar opposites. The writings of contemporary behavior therapists suggest that bridges are being built, allowing the possibility of a fruitful synthesis. The strict environmental view of human nature that is based on a stimulus/response model of behavior has been criticized by the pioneer of social-learning theory, Albert Bandura (1974, 1977, 1986). He rejects the mechanistic and deterministic model of human behavior because of its exclusive reliance on environmental determinants. He contends that this view, which holds that we are passive agents subjected to the influences of our surroundings, does indeed fail to take into account our capacity to actually affect our environment.

Other writers have made a case for using behavioristic methods to attain humanistic ends (Mahoney & Thoresen, 1974; Meichenbaum, 1977; Thoresen & Coates, 1980; Watson & Tharp, 1989). According to Thoresen and Coates, greater attention is being given to the emerging similarities among theories. They identify three interrelated themes that characterize this convergence. First is the focus on therapy as an action-oriented approach. Clients are being asked to act rather than to reflect passively and introspect at length on their problems. They are being helped to take specific actions to change their life. Second is the increasing concern of behavior therapists with how stimulus events are mediated by cognitive processes and private or subjective meanings. Third is the increasing emphasis on the role of responsibility for one's behavior. Given the techniques and skills of self-change, people have the capacity to improve their life by altering one or more of the various factors influencing their behavior. The above three converging themes provide a conceptual framework for a bridge between the behavioral and humanistic approaches.

THE SCIENTIFIC METHOD

Behavior therapy is separated from other approaches by its strict reliance on the principles of the scientific method. Concepts and procedures are stated explicitly, tested empirically, and revised continually. Further, treatment and assessment are interrelated, for they occur simultaneously. Research is considered essential to providing effective treatments and advancing beyond current therapeutic practices.

Regardless of the concepts or procedures employed, the common denominator in all behavior-therapy research is the commitment to applying experimental methods to the analysis of therapeutic practices (Goldfried & Davison, 1976). A defining characteristic is the insistence on rigorous standards of evidence for the efficacy of any technique employed. An important question that serves as a guide for this evaluation is "What treatment, by *whom*, is the most effective for *this* individual with that specific problem and under *which* set of circumstances?" (Paul, 1967, p. 111).

BASIC CHARACTERISTICS AND ASSUMPTIONS

Because the behavioral approach is so diverse, it is difficult to enumerate a set of common premises and features that apply to the entire field. The following characteristics apply widely, if not universally, to the behavioral approaches:

- Behavior therapies are based on experimentally derived principles of learning that are systematically applied to help people change maladaptive behaviors.
- These therapies focus on the client's current problems and the factors influencing them, as opposed to their historical determinants.
- They emphasize overt behavior changes as the main criteria by which treatment should be evaluated, yet cognitive processes are not excluded.
- They specify treatment goals in concrete and objective terms in order to make replication of treatment interventions possible.
- The distinguishing characteristic of behavioral practitioners is their systematic adherence to specification and measurement. In fact, without specifying and recording problems and goals, there is no true behavior therapy (Kuehnel & Liberman, 1986). Throughout the course of therapy there is assessment of problem behaviors and the conditions that are maintaining them. Behavioral concepts and procedures are stated explicitly, tested empirically, and revised continually.

- Research is considered essential to providing effective treatments and to advancing beyond current therapeutic practices.
- Behavior therapy is largely educational in nature. There is an emphasis on teaching clients skills of self-management, with the expectation that they will be responsible for transferring what they learn in the office to their everyday lives.
- Behavioral procedures are tailored to fit the unique needs of each client.

These common characteristics represent a basis for unity within the heterogeneity of the behavioral approaches. The basic assumption is that disorders commonly treated in therapy are best understood from the perspective of experimental psychology (Wilson, 1978). The principles that are derived from a variety of psychological experiments can be applied in clinical practice to the goal of changing behavior.

THE THERAPEUTIC PROCESS

THERAPEUTIC GOALS

Goals occupy a place of central importance in behavior therapy. The general goal is to create new conditions for learning. The assumption is that learning can ameliorate problem behaviors. The client usually formulates the goals, which are specifically defined at the outset of the therapeutic process. Continual assessment throughout therapy determines the degree to which these goals are being met. Assessment and treatment occur together.

Kuehnel and Liberman (1986) describe the core of behavior therapy as a six-step process of pinpointing and specifying a client's behavioral problems. The first step in this behavioral assessment is to identify behaviors that are considered maladaptive or problematic. The next step consists of determining the client's assets and strengths. The third step is to put the information gathered into the context in which the problem behaviors occur. This phase includes specifying the probable antecedents and consequences of behavioral problems. The fourth step involves setting up a strategy to measure each of the identified problem behaviors. Assessing the frequency of the target behaviors produces a baseline evaluation, which can be used as a reference point to determine the effectiveness of the interventions. In the fifth step the client's potential reinforcers are surveyed to identify those people, activities, and things that can provide motivation for treatment and for maintaining changes after therapy ends. The sixth and final step of the assessment process involves the formulation of treatment goals. Cooperatively, the client and clinician explore alternative behaviors that could resolve the problem. Included in this assessment are the client's functioning in the affective, cognitive, behavioral, and interpersonal domains. The therapist's task is to apply principles of human learning to facilitate the replacement of maladaptive behaviors with more adaptive ones.

There are several misconceptions about the goals of behavior therapy. One common myth is that the overall goal is simply to remove the symptoms of a disturbance and that once this is done, new symptoms will appear because the underlying causes were not treated. Most behavior therapists would not accept the notion that their approach is merely treatment of symptoms, for they see the therapist's task as eliminating maladaptive behavior and assisting the client to replace it with more adjustive behavior. The focus of therapy is on factors influencing current behavior and what can be done to change that behavior. Furthermore, research into the outcomes of therapy demonstrates that symptom substitution does not occur (Kazdin & Wilson, 1978; Sloane, Staples, Cristol, Yorkston, & Whipple, 1975).

Another common misconception is that client goals are determined and imposed by the behavior therapist. A clear trend in the modern behavioral therapies is toward involving the client in the selection of goals. G. T. Wilson (1989) asserts that "because it is fundamental to behavior therapy that the client should have the major say in setting treatment goals, it is important that the client is fully informed, and consents to and participates in setting goals" (p. 257). In addition, a good working relationship between the therapist and the client is seen as necessary (though not sufficient) in order to clarify therapeutic goals and cooperatively work toward the means to accomplish them. Whereas the early proponents of this approach seem to have emphasized the expert role of the therapist in deciding goals and behavior, recent practitioners make it clear that therapy cannot be imposed on an unwilling client.

Goals serve three important functions in counseling. Goals that are clearly defined reflect specific areas of client concern, and thus they provide a meaningful direction for counseling. Goals also provide a basis for selecting and using particular counseling strategies and interventions. Most important of all, goals provide a framework for evaluating the outcome of counseling.

The goals of therapy must be refined so that they are clear, concrete, understood, and agreed on by the client and the counselor. This process of determining therapeutic goals entails a negotiation between the client and the counselor, which results in a contract that guides the course of therapy. Behavior therapists and clients alter goals throughout the therapeutic process as needed.

The sequence of selecting and defining goals is described by Cormier and Cormier (1985, pp. 220–221). This process demonstrates the essential nature of a collaborative relationship between the therapist and the client:

- The counselor explains the purpose of goals.
- The client specifies the positive changes desired as a result of counseling.
- The client and counselor determine whether the stated goals are changes "owned" by the client.
- Together they explore whether the goals are realistic.
- They discuss the possible advantages of the goals.
- They discuss the possible disadvantages of the goals.
- On the basis of the information obtained about client-stated goals, the counselor and the client make one of the following decisions: to continue counseling, to reconsider the client's goals, or to seek a referral.

Once the above process of selecting and agreeing to goals is accomplished, a process of defining the goals begins. This process includes a joint effort in which the counselor and client discuss the behaviors associated with the goals, the circumstances of change, the level of behavioral change, the nature of subgoals, and a plan of action to work toward these goals.

A case can be made for the use of behavioral technology as a means for accomplishing both societal goals and the individual's goals. As previously noted, behavioral techniques do not threaten to eliminate or reduce freedom of choice. For example, behavior-modification programs in hospitals and other institutions have established goals endorsed by society. These aims include returning an individual to the community, fostering self-help, increasing social skills, and alleviating bizarre behaviors. In outpatient therapy clients come to treatment with a goal: to acquire a skill or to alleviate a problem. The primary function of the behavior therapist is providing a means to attain the goal of the individual. Relieving people of behaviors that interfere with effective living is consistent with the democratic value that individuals should be free to pursue their own goals as long as these goals are consistent with the general social good (Kazdin, 1978).

THERAPIST'S FUNCTION AND ROLE

Behaviorally oriented practitioners function in some ways as other clinicians do. They pay attention to the clues given by clients, and they are willing to follow their clinical hunches. They use techniques such as summarizing, reflection, clarification, and open-ended questioning. But there are two functions that distinguish behavioral clinicians: they focus on specifics, and they systematically attempt to get information about situational antecedents, the dimensions of the problem behavior, and the consequences of the problem (Goldfried & Davison, 1976).

As an example of how a behavior therapist might perform these functions, assume that a client comes to therapy to reduce her anxiety, which is preventing her from leaving the house. The therapist is likely to begin with a specific analysis of the nature of her anxiety. The therapist will ask how she experiences the anxiety of leaving her house, including what she actually *does* in these situations. Systematically, the therapist gathers information about this anxiety. When did it begin? In what situation(s) does it arise? What does she do at these times? What are her feelings and thoughts in these situations? How do her present fears interfere with living effectively? What are the consequences of her behaviors in threatening situations? After this assessment specific behavioral goals will be developed, and strategies will be designed to help the client reduce her anxiety to a manageable level. The therapist will get a commitment from her to work toward the specified goals, and the two of them will evaluate her progress toward meeting these goals throughout the duration of therapy.

Another important function of the therapist is role modeling for the client. Bandura (1969, 1971a, 1971b, 1977, 1986) maintains that most of the learning that occurs through direct experiences can also be acquired through observation of others' behavior. One of the fundamental processes by which clients learn new behavior is through imitation. The therapist, as a person, becomes a significant model. Because clients often view the therapist as worthy of emulation, they pattern attitudes, values, beliefs, and behavior after him or her. Thus, therapists should be aware of the crucial role that they play. To be unaware of the power they have in influencing the client's way of thinking and behaving is to deny the central importance of their own personhood in the therapeutic process.

Some critics have voiced the concern that behavior therapists impose values on clients and thus are overly directive. Other writers, however, contend that it is the client's responsibility to decide on the direction in which their behavior will be modified. In behavior therapy the client typically determines *what* behavior is to be changed, and the therapist determines *how* it will be changed. Bandura (1969) emphasizes the therapist's role as primarily one of exploring alternative courses of action that are available (along with the probable consequences). With this knowledge clients can make informed choices about therapy. Of course, this process involves the therapist's values, so it is a good practice for the therapist to identify the ways in which these values might affect his or her evaluation of the therapeutic goals. Because behavior therapists recognize that counseling involves a process of social influence, they emphasize specific, client-oriented behavioral objectives (Wilson, 1989).

CLIENT'S EXPERIENCE IN THERAPY

One of the unique contributions of behavior therapy is that it provides the therapist with a well-defined system of procedures to employ within the context of a well-defined role. It also provides the client with a clear role, and it stresses the importance of client awareness and participation in the therapeutic process. Clients are actively involved in the selection and determination of goals. They must be motivated to change and must be willing to cooperate in carrying out therapeutic activities, both during therapy sessions and in their life. If the client is not involved in this way, the chances that therapy will be successful are slim.

Clients are encouraged to experiment in enlarging their repertoire of adaptive behaviors. They are helped to generalize and to transfer the learning acquired within the therapeutic situation to situations outside therapy. Counseling is not complete unless actions follow verbalizations. Clients are expected to do more than merely gather insights; they need to be willing to make changes. Success and setbacks in the attempts to adopt new behavior are a vital part of the therapeutic adventure.

RELATIONSHIP BETWEEN THERAPIST AND CLIENT

Some critics characterize the relationship between the behavior therapist and the client as mechanically manipulative and highly impersonal. Most behavioral writers, however, assert that establishing a good interpersonal relationship is an essential aspect of the therapeutic process. Behavior therapists do not have to be cast in an impersonal role that reduces them to programmed machines that impose a set of techniques on robotlike clients. Contemporary behavior therapy does rest on a scientific view of human behavior that calls for a structured and systematic approach to counseling. However, this focus does not play down the importance of the therapeutic relationship or the value of clients' choosing for themselves.

Some clinical and research evidence suggests that a therapeutic relationship, even in the context of a behavioral orientation, can contribute significantly to the process of behavior change. Spiegler (1983) agrees that behavior therapy cannot be carried out in a rigid fashion. He emphasizes that it requires a good therapeutic relationship, which increases the chances that the client will be receptive to therapy. Not only is it important that the client cooperate with the therapeutic procedures, but the client's positive expectations about the effectiveness of therapy often contribute to successful outcomes. The skilled behavior therapist is one who can conceptualize problems behaviorally and make use of the client/therapist relationship in facilitating change.

As you will recall, the experiential therapies (existential therapy, person-centered therapy, and Gestalt therapy) place primary emphasis on the nature of the engagement between the counselor and client. In psychoanalysis the transference relationship serves as the stage on which therapy is played. In contrast, most behavioral practitioners do not assign an all-important role to relationship variables. Instead, they contend that factors such as warmth, empathy, authenticity, permissiveness, and acceptance are considered necessary, but not sufficient, for behavior change to occur. It is not a matter of the importance of the relationship per se but, rather, the role of the relationship as a foundation on which therapeutic strategies are built to help clients change in the direction they wish. Lazarus (1989b) maintains that unless clients respect their therapist, it will be difficult to develop the trust necessary for them to engage in significant self-disclosure. Yet he adds that counselors need an array of clinical skills and techniques to employ once an effective client/therapist relationship has been established. Likewise, Goldstein and Myers argue that "with such a relationship, client change is possible, or even probable, but not inevitable. Other, more specific, change measures must typically be utilized in addition" (1986, p. 63).

It is clear that behavior therapy demands a high level of skills and sensitivity and an ability to form a working relationship with clients. Behavior therapists tend to be active and directive and to function as consultants and problem solvers. Because they use a coping model in instigating behavioral change in the client's natural environment, it is important that they be personally supportive.

APPLICATION: THERAPEUTIC TECHNIQUES AND PROCEDURES

One of the major strengths of the behavioral approaches to counseling and psychotherapy is the development of specific therapeutic procedures that lend themselves to refinement through the scientific method. As we have seen, behavioral techniques must be shown to be effective through objective means, and there is a constant effort to improve them. Although behavior therapists may make mistakes in analysis or in applying therapeutic procedures, the results of their mistakes are obvious to them, for they receive continual direct response from their clients. The main finding produced by research into the behavioral therapies is that treatment outcomes are multifaceted. Changes are not all or nothing. Improvements are likely to occur in some areas but not in others, all improvements do not emerge at one time, and gains in some areas may be associated with problems emerging in other areas (see Kazdin, 1982; Voltz & Evans, 1982).

In the contemporary behavior therapies any technique that can be demonstrated to change behavior may be incorporated into a treatment plan. Lazarus (1989c) advocates the use of diverse techniques, regardless of their theoretical origin. He outlines a wide range of techniques that he has used in his clinical practice to supplement behavioral methods. In his view the more extensive the range of therapy techniques, the more potentially effective is the therapist. It is clear that behavior therapists do not have to restrict themselves strictly to methods derived from learning theory. Likewise, behavioral techniques can be incorporated into other approaches.

The therapeutic techniques and procedures used by behavior therapists are specifically appropriate for a particular client, rather than randomly selected from a "bag of techniques." Therapists are often quite creative in their design of interventions. In the following sections I will describe a range of behavioral techniques available to the practitioner: relaxation training, systematic desensitization, modeling methods, assertion-training programs, self-management programs, and multimodal therapy. I want to emphasize that these techniques do not encompass the full spectrum of behavioral procedures. In a brief overview it is difficult to capture the diversity and scope of the field, which is continually developing.

RELAXATION TRAINING AND RELATED METHODS

Relaxation training has become increasingly popular as a method of teaching people to cope with the stresses produced by daily living. It is aimed at achieving muscle and mental relaxation and is easily learned. After clients learn the basics of relaxation procedures, it is essential that they practice these exercises daily in order to obtain maximum results.

Jacobson (1938) is credited with initially developing the progressive-relaxation procedure. It has since been refined and modified, and relaxation procedures are frequently used in combination with a number of other behavioral techniques. These include imaginal-desensitization procedures, systematic desensitization, assertion training, self-management programs, tape-recorded instruction, biofeedback-induced relaxation, hypnosis, meditation, and autogenic training—teaching control of bodily and imaginal functions through autosuggestion.

Relaxation training involves several components that typically require from four to eight hours of instruction. Clients are given a set of instructions that asks them to relax. They assume a passive and relaxed position in a quiet environment while alternately contracting and relaxing muscles. Deep and regular breathing is also associated with producing relaxation. At the same time, clients learn to mentally "let go," perhaps by focusing on pleasant thoughts or images. Relaxation becomes a well-learned response, which can become a habitual pattern if practiced daily for 20 or 25 minutes. During these exercises it helps clients to actually feel and experience the tension building up, to notice their muscles getting tighter and study this tension, and to hold and fully experience the tension. Also, it is useful to experience the difference between a tense and a relaxed state.

Until the last few years relaxation training was primarily used as a part of systematic-desensitization procedures (which will be described later). Recently, relaxation procedures have been applied to a variety of clinical problems, either as a separate technique or in conjunction with related methods. The most common use has been with problems related to stress and anxiety, which often are manifested in psychosomatic symptoms. Other ailments for which relaxation training is helpful include high blood pressure and other cardiovascular problems, migraine headaches, asthma, and insomnia.

SYSTEMATIC DESENSITIZATION

Systematic desensitization, which is based on the principle of classical conditioning, is one of the most widely employed and empirically researched behavior-therapy procedures. The basic assumption underlying this technique is that an anxiety response is learned, or conditioned, and can be inhibited by substituting an activity that is antagonistic to it. The procedure is used primarily for anxiety and avoidance reactions. It involves, first, a behavioral analysis of stimuli that evoke anxiety and the constructing of a hierarchy of anxiety-producing situations; then relaxation procedures are taught and are paired with imagined scenes. Situations are presented in a series that moves from the least to the most threatening. Anxiety-producing stimuli are repeatedly paired with relaxation training until the connection between those stimuli and the response of anxiety is eliminated (Wolpe, 1958, 1969).

Before desensitization begins, the therapist conducts an initial interview to identify specific information about the anxiety and to gather relevant background information about the client. This interview, which may last several sessions, gives the therapist a good understanding of who the client is. The therapist questions the client about the particular circumstances that elicit the conditioned fears. For instance, under what circumstances does the client feel anxious? If the client is anxious in social situations, does the anxiety vary with the number of people present? Is the client more anxious with people of the same sex or the other sex? The client is asked to begin a self-monitoring process consisting of observing and recording situations during the week that elicit anxiety responses. Some therapists also administer a questionnaire to gather additional data about situations leading to anxiety.

If the decision is made to use the desensitization procedure, the therapist gives the client a rationale for the procedure and briefly describes what is involved. Morris (1986) outlines three steps in the use of systematic desensitization: (1) relaxation training, (2) development of the anxiety hierarchy and (3) systematic desensitization proper.

1. During the first few sessions the client is taught how to relax. The steps in this relaxation training are based on a modified version of the technique developed by Jacobson (1938) and described in detail by Wolpe (1969). The therapist uses a very quiet, soft, and pleasant voice to teach progressive muscular relaxation. The client is induced to create imagery of previously relaxing situations, such as sitting by a lake or wandering through a beautiful field. It is important that the client reach a state of calm and peacefulness. The client is then taught how to relax all the muscles while visualizing the various parts of the body, with emphasis on the facial muscles. The arm muscles are relaxed first, followed by the head, the neck and shoulders, the back, abdomen, and thorax, and then the lower limbs. The client is instructed to practice relaxation outside the session for about 30 minutes each day.

2. After completing the initial interview and during the relaxation-training phase, the therapist works with the client to develop an anxiety hierarchy for each of the identified areas. Stimuli that elicit anxiety in a particular area, such as rejection, jealousy, criticism, disapproval, or any phobia, are analyzed. The therapist constructs a ranked list of situations that elicit increasing degrees of anxiety or avoidance. The hierarchy is arranged in order from the worst situation that the client can imagine down to the situation that evokes the least anxiety. If it has been determined that the client has anxiety related to fear of rejection, for example, the highest-anxiety-producing situation might be rejection by the spouse, next rejection by a close friend, and then rejection by a co-worker. The least disturbing situation might be a stranger's indifference toward the client at a party.

3. Desensitization does not begin until several sessions after the initial interview has been completed. Enough time is allowed for clients to learn relaxation in the office, to practice it at home, and to construct the anxiety hierarchy. The desensitization process begins with the client's reaching complete relaxation with eyes closed. A neutral scene is presented, and the client is asked to imagine it. If the client remains relaxed, he or she is asked to imagine the least anxiety-arousing scene on the hierarchy of situations that has been developed. The therapist moves progressively up the hierarchy until the client signals that he or she is experiencing anxiety, at which time the scene is terminated. Relaxation is then induced again, and the client continues up the hierarchy. Treatment ends when the client is able to remain in a relaxed state while imagining the scene that was formerly the most disturbing and anxiety producing.

Homework and follow-up are essential components of successful desensitization (Cormier & Cormier, 1985). Clients can practice selected relaxation procedures daily, at which time they visualize scenes completed in the previous session. Gradually, they also expose themselves to real-life situations as a further way to manage their anxieties.

Systematic desensitization is an appropriate technique for treating phobias, but it is a misconception that it can be applied only to the treatment of anxiety. It has also been used effectively in dealing with nightmares, anorexia nervosa, obsessions, compulsions, stuttering, and depression. Cormier and Cormier (1985) indicate that historically, desensitization probably has the longest track record of any behavioral technique in dealing with fears, and its results have been frequently documented.

MODELING METHODS

The terms *modeling, observational learning, imitation, social learning,* and *vicarious learning* have been used interchangeably. All refer to the process by which the behavior of an individual or a group (the model) acts as a stimulus for similar thoughts, attitudes, and behaviors on the part of observers. Through the process of observational learning, clients can learn to perform desired acts themselves without trial-and-error learning. Bandura (1969, 1971a, 1971b, 1977, 1986) has emphasized the role of modeling in the development and the modification of much of human behavior. For example, he has suggested that most fears are developed through social transmission rather than through direct experience with aversive stimuli.

Effects of modeling.   Bandura outlines three major effects of modeling, each of which has significant implications for clinical practice. First is the acquisition of new responses or skills and the performance of them. This observational-learning effect refers to integrating new patterns of behavior based on watching a model or models. Examples include learning skills in sports, learning language patterns, training autistic children to speak through the use of models, learning social skills, and teaching hospital patients coping skills necessary for their return to the community.

The second effect of modeling is an inhibition of fear responses, which occurs when the observers' behaviors are inhibited in some way. In this case the model who performs an inhibited fear response either does not suffer negative consequences or, in fact, meets with positive consequences. Examples include models who handle snakes and are not bitten, models who perform daring feats and do not get hurt, and models who perform prohibited acts. An example of the latter is the worker who walks off the job and strikes. If the person does not lose his or her job, fellow workers may follow suit.

The third effect of modeling is a facilitation of responses, in which a model provides cues for others to emulate. The effect is to increase behaviors that the individual has already learned and for which there are no inhibitions. Examples include models such as attractive teenagers who talk on a television commercial about a brand of jeans. Other youths who see the ad may follow the fad. Another model who channels or influences behavior is the person who is the first one to leave a social gathering. Typically, others soon follow this action.

Types of model.   Several types of model can be used in therapeutic situations. A *live model* can teach clients appropriate behavior, influence attitudes and values, and teach social skills. For example, therapists can model the very characteristic that they hope the clients will acquire. Through their actual behavior during sessions, therapists can best teach self-disclosure, risk taking, openness, honesty, compassion, and the like. Therapists are constantly serving as a live model for their clients — for better or for worse! In addition to modeling desired behaviors and attitudes, therapists can also adversely influence their clients by modeling rigidity, lack of regard and respect, fear, rudeness, coldness, and aloofness.

Behavior therapists also use *symbolic models.* A model's behaviors are shown on films, videotapes, and other recording devices. In reviewing the research evidence, Bandura (1969) writes that symbolic models have been used successfully in a variety of situations. One example is clients who experience fears. By observing a model or models who successfully encounter certain fearful situations without negative consequences, such clients can decrease or eliminate certain fears.

Multiple models are especially relevant in group therapy. The observer can change attitudes and learn new skills through observation of successful peers in the group (or through observing coleaders). An advantage of multiple models is that observers learn some alternative ways of behaving, for they see a variety of appropriate and successful styles of behavior.

What are the characteristics of effective models? Reviews of research (Bandura, 1969) indicate that a model who is similar to the observer with respect to age, sex, race, and attitudes is more likely to be imitated than a model who is unlike the observer. Models who have a degree of prestige and status are more likely to be imitated than those who have a low level of prestige. However, the status level of the model should not be so high that the observer sees the model's behavior as unrealistic. Further, models who are competent in their performances and who exhibit warmth tend to facilitate modeling effects.

Clinical uses of modeling methods.   Perry and Furukawa (1986) present a comprehensive survey of the uses of modeling with a variety of special populations and problem areas. Clinical applications include treating snake phobias and helping to alleviate fears of children facing surgery. Modeling is used to teach new behaviors to socially disturbed children in the classroom, basic survival skills to retarded individuals, and verbal and motor skills to autistic children. Psychotic adults are taught the social skills they will need on returning to their community, and drug addicts and alcoholics learn interpersonal skills.

Modeling is also used in teaching counseling skills to staff members in clinical settings. It appears that counselor trainees can learn to increase their empathic level of responding to clients through a combination of modeling with other behavioral methods such as role playing, feedback, and reinforcement.

Modeling is part of other treatments, particularly those involving role playing, in which the therapist may rehearse and enact alternative behaviors. However, modeling by itself in the manner that Bandura has described is not typically used in clinical situations. Perry and Furukawa (1986) write that a review of recent studies, in comparison with earlier ones, reveals a trend toward treatment packages, in which modeling is one component. These programs include modeling as an established behavioral procedure.

ASSERTION TRAINING

A behavioral approach that has gained popularity is assertion training, which is one form of social-skills training. At each developmental stage in life important social skills must be mastered. Children need to learn how to make friends, adolescents need to learn how to interact with the opposite sex, and adults must learn how to effectively relate to mates, peers, and supervisors. People who lack social skills frequently experience interpersonal difficulties at home, at work, at school, and during leisure time. Behavioral methods have been designed to teach such individuals ways of interacting successfully. Many people have difficulty in feeling that it is appropriate or right to assert themselves. Assertion training can be useful for the following people: (1) those who cannot express anger or irritation, (2) those who have difficulty in saying no, (3) those who are overly polite and who allow others to take advantage of them, (4) those who find it difficult to express affection and other positive responses, and (5) those who feel that they do not have a right to express their thoughts, beliefs, and feelings.

The basic assumption underlying assertion training is that people have the right (but not the obligation) to express their feelings, thoughts, beliefs, and attitudes. One goal of assertion training is to increase people's behavioral repertoire so that they can make the *choice* of whether to behave assertively in certain situations. Another goal is teaching people to express themselves in a way that reflects sensitivity to the feelings and rights of others. Assertion does not mean aggression; thus, truly assertive people do not stand up for their rights at all costs, ignoring the feelings of others.

Many assertion-training methods are based on principles of the cognitive-behavioral therapies, which will be covered in the next chapter. For now, it is sufficient to say that most assertion-training programs focus on a client's negative self-statements, self-defeating beliefs, and faulty thinking. People often behave in unassertive ways because they think that they do not have a right to state a viewpoint or ask for what they want or deserve. Thus, their thinking leads to passive behavior. Effective assertion-training programs do more than merely giving people skills and techniques for dealing with difficult situations. Such programs challenge people's beliefs that accompany their lack of assertiveness and teach them to make constructive self-statements and to adopt a new set of beliefs that will result in assertive behavior.

Assertion training is not a panacea, but it is a treatment of choice for most clients with interpersonal difficulties. Although counselors can adapt assertion-training procedures to suit their own style, it is important to include behavioral rehearsal and continual assessment as basic aspects of the program. According to Alberti and Emmons (1986a), there are many advantages to conducting assertiveness training in a group setting. The group provides a laboratory for members to work on common problems and goals. It offers the support and guidance that is necessary to experiment with new behaviors. There are also diverse perspectives for feedback on interpersonal issues. Because the assertion-training group focuses on social situations that involve anxiety, it offers a realistic opportunity for people to face and challenge their difficulties in a structured and safe environment. As members are learning new skills, they have the advantage of social reinforcement. Alberti and Emmons indicate that assertiveness-training groups are not appropriate for all people. They therefore recommend an assessment of individual clients before assigning them to a group. Furthermore, they recommend that members be prepared for the group experience. They stress the importance of a trusting atmosphere in order for productive work to occur. If you are interested in learning more about the issues involved in assertion training and how to set up such a program, I suggest you consult *Your Perfect Right: A Guide to Assertive Behavior* (Alberti & Emmons, 1986a).

SELF-MANAGEMENT PROGRAMS AND SELF-DIRECTED BEHAVIOR

There is a growing trend toward integrating cognitive and behavioral methods to help clients manage their own problems (Kanfer & Goldstein, 1986). A related trend, toward "giving psychology away," involves psychologists' sharing their knowledge so that "consumers" can increasingly lead self-directed lives and not be dependent on experts to deal with their problems. Psychologists who share this perspective are primarily concerned with teaching people the skills they will need to manage their own lives effectively.

Self-management is a relatively recent phenomenon in counseling and therapy, and reports of clinical applications have burgeoned since 1970. Self-management strategies include, but are not limited to, self-monitoring, self-reward, self-contracting, and stimulus control. Self-management strategies have been applied to many populations and many problems, such as anxiety, depression, and pain.

The basic idea of self-management assessments and interventions is that change can be brought about by teaching people to use coping skills in problematic situations. Generalization and maintenance of the outcomes are enhanced by encouraging clients to accept the responsibility for carrying out these strategies in daily life (Rehm & Rokke, 1988).

In self-management programs people make decisions concerning specific behaviors they want to control or change. Some common examples include control of smoking, drinking, and drugs; learning study and time-management skills; and dealing with obesity and overeating. People frequently discover that a major reason that they do not attain their goals is the lack of certain skills. It is in such areas that a self-directed approach can provide the guidelines for change and a plan that will lead to change.

Five characteristics of an effective self-management program are identified by Cormier and Cormier (1985, p. 520):

1. A combination of self-management strategies is usually more useful than a single strategy.
2. Consistent use of strategies is essential. If self-management efforts are not employed regularly over a sustained period, their effectiveness may be too limited to produce any significant change.
3. It is necessary to set realistic goals and then evaluate the degree to which they are being met.
4. The use of self-reinforcement is an important component of self-management programs.
5. Environmental support is necessary to maintain changes that result from a self-management program.

Watson and Tharp offer a model designed for self-directed change. The following four stages of the model are based on material drawn from several sources, including Watson and Tharp (1989), Cormier and Cormier (1985), Kanfer and Gaelick (1986), and Williams and Long (1983):

1. *Selection of goals.* The initial stage begins with specifying what changes are desired. Goals should be established one at a time, and they should be measurable, attainable, positive, and significant for the person. This last requirement is extremely important, for if the individual develops a self-change program based on goals determined by someone else, the program has a real possibility of failing.

2. *Translating goals into target behaviors.* Next, the goals selected in the initial stage are translated into target behaviors. To that effect, questions such as the following are relevant: "What specific behaviors do I want to increase or decrease? What chain of actions will produce my goal?"

3. *Self-monitoring.* A major first step in self-directed change is the process of self-monitoring, which consists of deliberately and carefully attending to one's own behavior (Kanfer & Gaelick, 1986). This monitoring presumably leads to awareness, focused on concrete and observable behaviors rather than on historical events or feeling experiences. A *behavioral diary* is one of the simplest methods for observing one's behavior. The occurrence of a particular behavior is recorded, along with comments about the relevant antecedent cues and consequences. If you want to change your eating habits, for example, the behavioral diary will contain entries of what you eat, events and situations before eating or snacking, meal frequency, types of food eaten, and so forth. Total counts can also be transferred at the end of each day or week to a chart, providing a visual illustration of progress (or the lack of it) toward self-selected goals. Cormier and Cormier (1985) maintain that self-monitoring is indispensable as a measuring device to define problems and to collect evaluative data. They add that although it is necessary and useful for many clients, it is often not sufficient unless it is used in conjunction with other self-management procedures, such as stimulus control, self-reward and self-punishment, and self-contracting (see below).

4. *Working out a plan for change.* This stage begins with a comparison between the information obtained from self-monitoring and the individual's standards for a specific behavior. After clients make the evaluation of behavioral changes they want to acquire, they need to devise an action program to bring about actual change. Plans help to gradually replace an unwanted action with a desirable one or to increase a desirable action. Such a plan of action entails some type of self-reinforcement system and the negotiating of a working contract.

Self-reinforcement, such as participating in pleasant activities, is a basic part of the plan for change. Self-praise can be a useful reinforcer, because it can be easily applied after a target behavior occurs. The use of reinforcement to change behavior is the cornerstone of modern behavior therapy. It is important to choose appropriate self-rewards, ones that are personally motivating. Watson and Tharp suggest that the purpose of self-reinforcement is to make desired behavior so successful that the natural consequences of daily life will sustain it. In other words, self-reinforcement is a temporary strategy to be used until people can implement new behaviors in everyday life.

Self-contracting is the other facet of a plan for change. It is a strategy that involves determining in advance the external and internal consequences that will follow the execution of the desired or undesired action. Such contracts can help clients keep their commitment to carry out their action plan with some degree of consistency.

Evaluating the plan for change is essential to determine the degree to which clients are achieving their goals. After the plan of action is set forth, it must be readjusted and revised as clients learn other ways to meet their goals. Evaluation is an ongoing process rather than a one-time occurrence. Watson and Tharp (1989) point out that a perfect plan for a problem does not exist. But they list these characteristics of successful plans:

- rules that state which behaviors and techniques for change will be used in various situations
- explicit goals and subgoals
- a system of getting feedback on one's progress, derived largely from self-observation
- a comparison of feedback with one's goals and subgoals to measure progress
- adjustments in the plan as conditions change

Counselors who encourage their clients to utilize self-management programs need to ensure that the plan developed and selected meets the above characteristics to a large degree. The value of such programs lies in learning responsibility for one's own actions.

MULTIMODAL THERAPY

Multimodal therapy is a comprehensive, systematic, holistic approach to behavior modification developed by Lazarus (1971, 1986, 1987b, 1989b, 1989c). It is an open system and encourages a *technical eclecticism.* New techniques are constantly being introduced, and existing techniques are refined, but these techniques are never used in a shotgun manner (Lazarus, 1989b). Multimodal therapists ask the question "Who or what is best for this particular person?" Thus, they take great care not to fit the unique client to a predetermined treatment. Instead, a careful attempt is made to determine precisely what relationship and what treatment strategies would work best with each client and under which particular circumstances. The underlying assumption of this approach is that because individuals are troubled by a variety of specific problems, it is appropriate that a multitude of treatment strategies be used in bringing about change. Multimodal therapists are constantly adjusting their procedures to effectively achieve the client's goals in therapy (Lazarus, 1989b).

Most of the techniques listed by Lazarus (1989c) are standard behavioral procedures. His multimodal schema serves as an example of how behavior therapists can draw on methods from the three major thrusts of the behavioral approach, the classical, operant, and cognitive.

The BASIC ID. The essence of the multimodal approach is the premise that human beings' complex personality can be divided into seven major areas of functioning: (1) B = behavior, (2) A = affective responses, (3) S = sensations, (4) I = images, (5) C = cognitions, (6) I = interpersonal relationships, and (7) D = drugs, biological functions, nutrition, and exercise (Lazarus, 1989b, 1989c). Although these modalities are interactive, they can be considered discrete functions (Roberts, Jackson, & Phelps, 1980).

The multimodal therapist takes the view that a complete assessment and treatment program must account for each modality of this BASIC ID. Thus, the BASIC ID is the cognitive map that ensures that each aspect of personality receives explicit and systematic attention (Lazarus, 1989c). Further, comprehensive therapy entails the correction of irrational beliefs, deviant behaviors, unpleasant feelings, bothersome images, stressful relationships, negative sensations, and possible biochemical imbalances. Enduring change is seen as a function of combined strategies and tactics.

Multimodal therapy begins with a comprehensive assessment of the seven modalities of human functioning. Clients are asked questions pertaining to the BASIC ID. What follows is a modification of this assessment process based on Lazarus's questions (1982, 1989b, 1989c):

- *Behavior.* This modality refers primarily to overt behaviors, including acts, habits, and reactions that are observable and measurable. Some questions asked are "What would you like to change?" "How active are you?" "How much of a doer are you?" "What would you like to start doing?" "What would you like to stop doing?" "What are some of your main strengths?" "What specific behaviors keep you from getting what you want?"
- *Affect.* This modality refers to emotions, moods, and strong feelings. Questions sometimes asked include ' How emotional are you?" "What emotions do you experience most often?" "What makes you laugh?" "What makes you cry?" "What makes you sad, mad, glad, scared?" "What emotions are problematic for you?"
- *Sensation.* This area refers to the five basic senses of touch, taste, smell, sight, and hearing. Examples of questions asked are "Do you suffer from unpleasant sensations, such as pains, aches, dizziness, and so forth?" "How much do you focus on sensations?" "What do you particularly like or dislike in the way of seeing, smelling, hearing, touching, and tasting?"
- *Imagery.* This modality pertains to ways in which we picture ourselves, and it includes memories and dreams. Some questions asked are "What are some bothersome recurring dreams and vivid memories?" "Do you engage in fantasy and daydreaming?" "Do you have a vivid imagination?" "How do you view your body?" "How do you see yourself now?" "How would you like to be able to see yourself in the future?"
- *Cognition.* This modality refers to insights, philosophies, ideas, and judg-

ments that constitute one's fundamental values, attitudes, and beliefs. Questions include "How much of a thinker are you?" "What are some ways in which you meet your intellectual needs?" "How do your thoughts affect your emotions?" "What are the values and beliefs you most cherish?" "What are some negative things that you say to yourself?" "What are some of your central irrational beliefs?" "What are the main 'shoulds,' 'oughts,' and 'musts' in your life? How do they get in the way of effective living?"

- *Interpersonal relationships.* This modality refers to interactions with other people. Examples of questions include "How much of a social being are you?" "To what degree do you desire intimacy with others?" "What do you expect from the significant people in your life?" "What do they expect from you?" "Are there any relationships with others that you would hope to change?" "If so, what kinds of changes do you want?"
- *Drugs/biology.* This modality includes more than drugs; it takes into consideration one's nutritional habits and exercise patterns. Some questions asked are "Are you healthy and health conscious?" "Do you have any concerns about your health?" "Do you take any prescribed drugs?" "What are your habits pertaining to diet, exercise, and physical fitness?"

It should not be thought that the above list is a complete representation of the BASIC ID, but a preliminary investigation brings out some central and significant themes that can be productively explored. The preliminary questioning is followed by a detailed life-history questionnaire. Once the main profile of a person's BASIC ID has been established, the next step consists of an examination of the interactions among the different modalities. This second phase of work intensifies specific facets of the person's problem areas and allows the therapist to understand the person more fully as well as devise effective coping and treatment strategies.

Technical eclecticism. As mentioned earlier, multimodal therapists are aware that people have unique and diverse needs and expectations, and therefore they require a wide range of therapeutic styles. Based on the assumption that many clients come to therapy needing to learn skills, therapists are willing to teach, coach, train, model, and direct their clients. They typically function directively by providing information, instruction, and feedback. They challenge self-defeating beliefs, offer constructive feedback, provide positive reinforcement, and are appropriately self-disclosing. It is most essential that therapists start where the client is and then move into other productive areas for exploration. Failure to apprehend the client's situation can easily lead the client to feel alienated and misunderstood (Lazarus, 1989b).

Multimodal therapists "borrow" techniques from many other therapy systems. Some of these principal techniques that they employ in individual psychotherapy are anxiety-management training, behavior rehearsal, bibliotherapy, biofeedback, communication training, contingency contracting, hypnosis, meditation, modeling, paradoxical strategies, positive imagery, positive reinforcement, relaxation training, self-instruction training, sensate-focus training, social-skills and assertiveness training, time projection, and thought stopping. (See Lazarus, 1987a, for a detailed description of these methods.)

Several basic assumptions about the therapist have implications for the practice of multimodal therapy. First, therapists must be effective as persons. Second, they need a broad range of skills and techniques to deal with the range of problems posed by their clients. Third, they must have "technical eclecticism"; that is, they should be able to employ any techniques that have been demonstrated to be effective in dealing with specific problems (Roberts et al., 1980).

The kind of technical eclecticism that Lazarus (1987b) contends is needed is scientific and has three other qualities: breadth, depth, and specificity. In espousing technical (or systematic) eclecticism Lazarus is not arguing in favor of a *theoretical* eclecticism. According to him, there are some basic problems in being theoretically eclectic, because different therapeutic systems sometimes have contradictory notions. In calling for technical eclecticism, he endorses using a variety of techniques within a theoretical structure that is open to verification and disproof. He adds that useful techniques can be derived from many sources, which can be divorced from their origins. Lazarus (1989b) points out that all multimodal therapists are eclectic, yet not all eclectics are multimodal therapists.

SUMMARY AND EVALUATION

SUMMARY

Contemporary behavior therapy (unlike traditional behaviorism and radical behaviorism) places emphasis on the interplay between the individual and the environment. Cognitive factors and the subjective reactions of people to the environment now have a place in the practice of behavior therapy. Thus, behavioral technology can be used to attain humanistic ends. It is clear that bridges can connect the humanistic and the behavioristic therapies, especially with the current focus of attention on self-directed approaches and multimodal therapy.

Behavior therapy is diverse with respect not only to basic concepts but also to techniques that can be applied in coping with specific problems. The behavioral movement includes three major areas of development: classical conditioning, operant conditioning, and increasing attention to the cognitive factors influencing behavior (the subject of the next chapter). A unique characteristic of behavior therapy is its strict reliance on the principles of the scientific method. Concepts and procedures are stated explicitly, tested empirically, and revised continually. Treatment and assessment are interrelated, for they occur simultaneously. Research is considered to be a basic aspect of the approach, so that therapeutic techniques can be continually refined.

A hallmark of behavior therapy is the identification of specific goals at the outset of the therapeutic process. In helping clients achieve their goals, behavior therapists typically assume an active and directive role. Although the client generally determines *what* behavior will be changed, the therapist typically determines *how* this behavior can best be modified. In designing a treatment plan, behavior therapists employ techniques and procedures that are specifically appropriate for a particular client. In selecting these strategies, therapists have a wide range of options, a few of which include relaxation training, systematic desensitization, modeling methods, assertion-training programs, and self-management programs. The approach of multimodal therapy provides a context in which therapists can borrow techniques from a variety of therapeutic systems and apply them to the unique needs of each client. Such an approach provides for the therapeutic flexibility and versatility required to effectively achieve a diverse range of goals.

CONTRIBUTIONS OF BEHAVIOR THERAPY

Behavioral practitioners have contributed to the counseling field with their focus on specifics and their systematic way of applying counseling techniques. They challenge us to reconsider our global approach to counseling. Although we may assume that we know what a client means by the statement "I feel unloved; life has no meaning," the behavior therapist will work with the client in defining what is meant so that therapy can proceed. Whereas a humanist may nod in acceptance to such a statement, the behaviorist may retort with: "Who specifically is not loving you? What is going on in your life to bring about this meaninglessness? What are some specific things that you may be doing that contribute to the state you're in? What would you most like to change?"

Another contribution is the wide variety of specific behavioral techniques at the disposal of the therapist. Because behavior therapy stresses *doing,* as opposed to merely talking about problems and gathering insights, practitioners have many strategies to assist clients in actively changing their behavior.

Over the past decade there has been a considerable broadening of the research and conceptual base of behavioral methods. These methods have been applied to a wide array of problems. Behavior therapy has gone well beyond the usual areas of clinical practice. It is deeply enmeshed in medicine, geriatrics, pediatrics, rehabilitation programs, and stress management. The behavioral approaches have also expanded the range of populations for whom intervention is possible. New techniques can be used to address problems of the mentally retarded, autistic children, and aggressive children and adolescents. Few other techniques with *demonstrated* efficacy are available for these populations. Behavioral techniques have been used effectively in treating problems related to anxiety, phobic behaviors, relationship problems, substance abuse, adult psychotic behaviors, and childhood and adolescent problem behaviors. Compared with alternative approaches, behavioral techniques have generally been shown to be at least as effective and frequently more effective in changing target behaviors (Spiegler, 1983).

What follows is a summary of other selected problem areas for which behavior therapy appears to be an effective treatment, as discussed by Wilson (1989):

- *Anxiety disorders.* Studies have demonstrated the success of behavior therapy in treating phobias, such as fear of open places.

- *Depression.* The combination of cognitive and behavioral procedures has yielded promising results in the treatment of depression.
- *Sexual disorders.* Behavior therapy is the preferred treatment for sexual problems such as impotence, premature ejaculation, orgasmic dysfunction, and vaginismus.
- *Prevention and treatment of cardiovascular disease.* Certain behavior patterns and lifestyles have been associated with an increased risk of premature cardiovascular disease, and modification of these behaviors is likely to produce a reduction of the disease. Behavioral methods have been effectively used in curbing cigarette smoking, overeating, and overdrinking. They are of value in helping people stick to an exercise plan and in managing stress and hypertension. In fact, behavioral medicine, the wellness movement, and approaches to holistic health incorporate behavioral strategies as a part of their practice.

Another major contribution of behavior therapy is its emphasis on research and assessment of treatment outcomes. It is up to practitioners to demonstrate that therapy is working. If progress is not being made, they take a careful look at the original analysis and the treatment plan that was formulated. Of all the therapies presented in this book, no other approach and its techniques have been subjected to the degree of empirical research that behavior therapy has. This scrutiny may account for the fact that this model has changed so dramatically since its origin. Behavior therapists now raise more specific research questions. In the early years of research, investigators framed questions in terms of global outcomes. Now they ask "Which type of client, meeting with which type of counselor, using which type of treatment, will yield what outcome?" It is recognized that some techniques and therapists are appropriate for certain clients but not for others. Furthermore, almost no procedure can be expected to lead to behavior change in all clients or to correct all the problems of any client (Kanfer & Goldstein, 1986). This kind of focused research is more characteristic of behavior therapy than of any other approach, and it provides a framework for studies that could be used to evaluate techniques that flow from other schools.

Contributions to ethical practice.   A related strength is ethical accountability. Perhaps more than any other approach, behavior therapy provides a basis for responsible practice. Although some critics think that behavior therapy poses ethical problems that do not exist with other therapeutic approaches, Spiegler (1983) writes that it is ethically neutral in that it does not dictate whose behavior or what behavior should be changed. At least in cases of voluntary counseling, the behavioral practitioner only specifies how to change those behaviors that the client targets as goals for change. Thus, in deciding what the goals of therapy will be, clients actually have a good deal of control and freedom in behavior therapy.

Behavior therapists, in general, are particularly concerned with the ethical aspects of practice. Although they have powerful means of modifying behavior at their disposal, their willingness to involve clients in the various stages of therapy seems to serve as a good safeguard. The therapist helps clients in considering alternative courses of action and in evaluating the goals they are pursuing.

Contributions to multicultural counseling. Behavior therapy has some clear advantages over many other theories in working with multicultural populations. Because of their cultural and ethnic backgrounds, some clients hold values that are contrary to the free expression of feelings and the sharing of personal concerns. Behavioral counseling does not place emphasis on experiencing catharsis but, rather, on changing specific behaviors and developing problem-solving skills. Clients who are looking for action plans and behavioral change are likely to cooperate with this approach, for this approach offers them concrete methods for dealing with their problems of living.

Behavioral procedures ideally take into consideration the social and cultural dimensions of the client's life. Kanfer and Goldstein (1986) maintain that simply having a catalog of available techniques is not sufficient preparation for competent therapeutic practice. They mention that behavioral research and publications emphasize the need to give careful consideration to the client's life setting, personal values, and biological and sociopsychological characteristics. They also point out that various sociocultural developments contribute to psychological problems and to violence and abuse in personal relationships. It seems clear that the behavioral approach has moved beyond treating clients for a specific symptom or behavioral problem. Instead, it stresses a thorough evaluation of the person's life circumstances, to ascertain not only whether the target behavior is amenable to change but also whether such a change is likely to lead to a significant improvement in the client's total life situation. In designing a change program for clients, effective behavioral practitioners conduct a functional analysis of the problem. This assessment includes the cultural context in which the problem behavior occurs, the consequences both to the client and to the client's sociocultural environment, the resources within the environment that can promote change, and the impact that change is likely to have on others in the client's surroundings (Kanfer & Goldstein, 1986).

Behavior therapy tends to be short-term, to be effective, and to rely on the client to specify the particular focus of therapy. Because the behavioral practitioner educates clients about the therapeutic process and the specific procedures to be used, they have a good chance of knowing what to expect and how best to participate. Other factors that contribute to the usefulness of the behavioral approach include its specificity, task-orientation, focus on objectivity, focus on cognition and behavior, and problem-solving orientation. Social and political influences play a significant role in the lives of people of color. Some of these are discriminatory practices, economic problems, and demands made by the environment that are inconsistent with the person's cultural values or background. Clients learn coping strategies and acquire survival techniques that help them deal with the realities present in their environment. A problem-solving approach is more likely to appeal to some ethnic clients than a lengthy introspective therapy. As we have seen, multimodal therapists are constantly adapting their techniques to the unique backgrounds and needs of their clients. The aim of this approach is to come up with the best methods for each client, rather than attempting to squeeze all clients into a common mold.

LIMITATIONS AND CRITICISMS OF BEHAVIOR THERAPY

In my view one of the central limitations of this approach is that it deemphasizes the role of feelings in the therapeutic process. I do not think that behavior therapy deals with emotional processes as fully or as adequately as do the experiential therapies. A general criticism of both the behavioral and the cognitive approaches is that clients are not encouraged to experience their emotions. In concentrating on how clients are behaving or thinking, counselors play down the working through of emotional issues. Generally, I favor initially focusing on what clients are feeling and then working with the behavioral and cognitive dimensions. This criticism leads to a related concern that I have — namely, the tendency of some behaviorally oriented practitioners to overly stress problem solving and treating of a condition. Behavior therapists need to listen very carefully to their clients and to allow them to express and explore their feelings *before* implementing a treatment plan. The basic therapeutic conditions that are stressed by the person-centered therapist — such as active listening, accurate empathy, positive regard, genuineness, respect, and immediacy — can be integrated into a behavioral framework. However, too often counselors are so anxious to work toward resolution of client problems that they are not fully present with their clients. A mistake some counselors make is only getting at a minor problem as they focus on the presenting issue, which they then work with instead of listening to the client's deeper message.

Five criticisms.   Below are some common criticisms and misconceptions that people often have about behavior therapy, together with my reactions.

Criticism 1: Behavior therapy may change behaviors, but it does not change feelings. Some critics argue that feelings must change before behavior can change. Behavioral practitioners generally contend that if clients can change their behavior, they are likely to change their feelings also. They hold that empirical evidence has not borne out the criticism that feelings must be changed first. Although they do not focus primarily on feelings, behavioral clinicians do in actual practice deal with feelings as an overall part of the treatment process. Kanfer and Goldstein (1986) indicate that increasing attention is being given to the affective dimensions in behavior and the role of emotional variables in modifying cognitive and behavioral events.

Criticism 2: Behavior therapy ignores the important relational factors in therapy. The charge is often made that the importance of the relationship between the client and the therapist is discounted in behavior therapy. Although it appears to be true that behavior therapists do not place primary weight on the relationship variable, this does not mean that the approach is condemned to a mechanical and nonhumanistic level of functioning. As we have seen, behavior therapists contend that a good working relationship with their clients is a basic foundation necessary for the effective use of techniques. As Lazarus and Fay (1984) write, "The relationship is the soil that enables the techniques to take root" (p. 493).

Research has not shown that the behavioral therapies are any different from other therapeutic orientations in the relationship variables that emerge (Sloane et al., 1975). It may be true that some therapists are attracted to behavior therapy because they can be directive, can play the role of expert, or can avoid the anxieties and ambiguities of establishing a more personal relationship. This is not an intrinsic characteristic of the approach, however, and I think that many behavior therapists are more humanistic in practice than some of the therapists are who profess to practice humanistic therapy.

Criticism 3: Behavior therapy does not provide insight. If this assertion is indeed true, behavior-modification theorists would probably respond that insight isn't necessary. They would maintain that they do not focus on insight because of the absence of clear evidence that insight is critical to outcome. Behavior is changed directly. If the goal of achieving insight is an eventual change of behavior, then behavior therapy, which has proven results, has the same effect. Moreover, a change in behavior often leads to a change in understanding; it is a two-way street. Nevertheless, many people want not just to change their behavior but also to gain an understanding of why they behave the way they do. The answers are often buried deep in past learning and in historical events. Although it is possible for behavior therapists to give explanations in this realm, in fact they usually do not.

Criticism 4: Behavior therapy ignores the historical causes of present behavior. The psychoanalytic assumption is that early traumatic events are at the root of present dysfunction. The progression is from discovering original causes to reliving past situations in the therapeutic relationship and to facilitating insight. This process is thought to lead to changing present behavior. Behavior therapists may acknowledge that deviant responses have historical origins, but they contend that history is seldom important in the maintenance of current problems. Thus, behavior therapy focuses on providing the client with opportunities to acquire the new learning needed for effectively coping with problem situations.

Related to this criticism is the notion that unless historical causes of present behavior are therapeutically explored, new symptoms will soon take the place of those that were "cured." Behaviorists rebut this assertion on both theoretical and empirical grounds. They do not accept the assumption that symptoms are manifestations of underlying intrapsychic conflicts. Furthermore, they assert that there is no empirical evidence that symptom substitution occurs after behavior therapy has successfully eliminated unwanted behavior (Kazdin & Wilson, 1978; Sloane et al., 1975; Spiegler, 1983).

Criticism 5: Behavior therapy involves control and manipulation by the therapist. As already noted, concerns are often voiced about the clinical practitioner's power to exert control over a client's behavior. Some people are alarmed by the behavior therapist's power to shape and direct the values and behaviors of clients. Many ethical criticisms of behavior therapy relate to the contention that its practices control clients to the degree that they are robbed of their freedom and autonomy. In replying to this criticism, Spiegler (1983) retorts that after successful behavior therapy clients have increased alternatives and more ways of behaving than before therapy. His point is that behavior therapy provides the procedures for achieving various therapeutic goals but does not specify goals for clients. Ultimately, clients decide for themselves what behavior is desirable or undesirable, and thus they choose their own goals.

Other writers have clearly acknowledged that therapists do have control and that this capacity to manipulate relevant variables is not necessarily undesirable or unethical. Goldfried and Davison (1976) and London (1985) take the position that we cannot argue that what therapeutic practitioners do is valuable and justified and at the same time maintain that such professionals are not in the business of changing people's behavior. Surely, in all therapeutic approaches there is control by the therapist, and the therapist hopes to change behavior in some way. This does not mean, however, that clients are helpless victims who are at the mercy of the whims and values of therapists. Clients do become involved in formulating goals as well as selecting treatment interventions in cases where to do so would be appropriate. As was mentioned earlier, the success of behavior therapy is determined in a large degree by the active involvement and cooperation of the client. Contemporary behavior therapists employ techniques aimed at increased self-direction and self-control, which are skills that clients actually learn in the therapeutic process.

Limitations in multicultural counseling. Perhaps a major limitation of behavioral counseling rests more with certain practitioners than with the approach itself. There is a tendency for some behavioral counselors to focus on using a variety of techniques in narrowly treating a specific behavioral problem. Instead of viewing clients in the context of their sociocultural environment, these practitioners concentrate too much on symptoms, and in doing so they may overlook significant issues in the lives of clients. Such practitioners are not likely to bring about beneficial changes for ethnic clients.

The fact that behavioral interventions often work well raises an interesting issue in multicultural counseling. When clients make significant personal changes, it is very likely that others in their environment will react to them differently. Before deciding too quickly on goals for therapy, the counselor and client need to discuss the advantages and disadvantages of change. It is essential for therapists to conduct a thorough assessment of the interpersonal and cultural dimensions of the problem. Clients should be helped in assessing the possible consequences of some of their newly acquired social skills. Once goals are determined and therapy is under way, they should have opportunities to talk about the problems they encounter as they become different people in their home and work settings. For example, a client may want to become more assertive with her husband and children and may strive for increased independence. It is conceivable that as she becomes more assertive and independent, divorce may result. Her culture may place a premium on compliance with tradition, and being assertive can lead to problems if she decides to stay within that culture. As a divorced woman she could find herself without any support from relatives and friends, and she might eventually regret making the changes she did.

Questions for Reflection and Discussion

1. Compare behavior therapy with the other therapeutic approaches you have studied thus far. In what ways do you think behavior therapy is unique? What are some distinct advantages? What are some disadvantages or limitations?
2. In what ways might the behavioral therapies be amalgamated with the humanistic, relationship-oriented approaches? What are the bases on which bridges can be built between the two approaches?
3. Assume that you had a client very much like yourself. Knowing what you do about yourself, what specific steps would you take in working with this client from a behavioral perspective? What would be your focus in therapy? What techniques would you tend to use? How would you attempt to enlist the cooperation of your client? What problems might you expect as the therapeutic process unfolds? How would you deal with these problems as they arise?
4. Assume that Stan is your client and that he requests a behavioral self-management program to deal with his concerns. How would you teach him to set up such a program? Which of his problems might be helped most by this program? Can you think of other specific problems of Stan's that would be amenable to behavioral techniques? Which problems? Which techniques?
5. Which behavioral techniques would you be most inclined to use in your practice? Why? Explain what types of problem and client would be best suited for the techniques you have selected.
6. What ethical issues are involved in the use of behavior-therapy techniques? List the techniques, as well as the issues, that you see as being central.
7. Some criticize behavior therapy for working too well; that is, they are concerned that conditioning techniques will be too effective and will be used to manipulate the client. What are your reactions to using behavioral strategies for social control?
8. What is your view of this approach's stress on empirical research to validate therapy results? As a practitioner, how might you attempt to assess the process and the outcomes of therapy?
9. How can the concepts and techniques of the other therapy systems that you have studied be integrated into a behavioral framework? Can you think of ways to develop an eclectic style as a counselor, while still staying within the behavioral spirit?
10. What aspects of behavior therapy could you apply to yourself in order to increase your own level of effective functioning in everyday life? Mention some specific problem areas you have or behaviors you want to change, and then discuss the behavioral strategies you could draw on in making the changes you desire.

WHERE TO GO FROM HERE

Because the literature in this field is so extensive and diverse, it is not possible in one brief survey chapter to present a comprehensive discussion of behavioral techniques. I hope that you will be challenged to examine any misconceptions you may hold about behavior therapy and be stimulated to do some further reading of selected sources.

If you have an interest in further training in behavior therapy, the Association for Advancement of Behavior Therapy is an excellent source. It is a professional organization with a membership of over 3000. Members are from many disciplines, such as psychology, psychiatry, social work, nursing, and education. There is also a student-member category. The association publishes a *Directory of Graduate Study in Behavior Therapy,* which gives information on nearly 300 programs in clinical/counseling psychology, internship programs in psychology and psychiatry, and social work. It also publishes the *Journal of Psychopathology and Behavioral Assessment,* as well as a monthly newsletter called *The Behavior Therapist.* There is an annual convention that features workshops and special sessions as a way of keeping current in behavioral research and practice. The address of the AABT is 15 West 36th Street, New York, NY 10018.

Interested readers can keep up with this ever-expanding field by consulting other journals devoted exclusively to behavior therapy: *Advances in Behavior Research and Therapy, Behaviour Research and Therapy, Behavioral Assessment, Behavior Modification, Journal of Behavior Therapy and Experimental Psychiatry, Journal of Behavioral Assessment, Journal of Applied Behavior Analysis,* and *Cognitive Therapy and Research.*

RECOMMENDED SUPPLEMENTARY READINGS

The literature in the field of behavior therapy is vast. One excellent starting place is a comprehensive textbook for counselors that emphasizes techniques and procedures: *Interviewing Strategies for Helpers: Fundamental Skills and Cognitive Behavioral Interventions* (Cormier & Cormier, 1985).

For readings on self-management and on using behavioral principles to initiate and direct self-change programs, I most recommend *Self-Directed Behavior: Self-Modification for Personal Adjustment* (Watson & Tharp, 1989) and *Toward a Self-Managed Life-Style* (Williams & Long, 1983).

In *Clinical Behavior Therapy,* Goldfried and Davison (1976) do an excellent job of describing their clinical practice. The book is highly readable.

Helping People Change: A Textbook of Methods (Kanfer & Goldstein, 1986) is an excellently edited overview of the main behavioral methods in use today.

The Practice of Multimodal Therapy (Lazarus, 1981) is interesting, easy to read, and highly informative. It is a fine perspective or integrating diverse techniques in an eclectic framework.

Review of Behavior Therapy: Theory and Practice: Vol. 11 (Wilson, Franks, Kendall, & Foreyt, 1987) provides up-to-date and comprehensive coverage of most aspects of research, theory, and application.

Behavior Modification in Applied Settings (Kazdin, 1980) focuses on the application of operant-conditioning principles and procedures in classrooms and institutions for the retarded.

REFERENCES AND SUGGESTED READINGS*

AGRAS, W. S. (Ed.). (1978a). *Behavior modification: Principles and clinical applications* (2nd ed.). Boston: Little, Brown.

AGRAS, W. S. (1978b). The token economy. In W. S. Agras (Ed.), *Behavior modification: Principles and clinical applications* (2nd ed.). Boston: Little, Brown.

*ALBERTI, R. E., & EMMONS, M. L. (1986a). *Your perfect right: A guide to assertive behavior* (5th ed.). San Luis Obispo, CA: Impact.

*ALBERTI, R. E., & EMMONS, M. L. (1986b). *Your perfect right: A manual for assertiveness trainers.* San Luis Obispo, CA: Impact.

AYLLON, T., & AZRIN, N. (1968). *The token economy: A motivation system for therapy and rehabilitation.* New York: Appleton-Century-Crofts.

AZRIN, N. H., STUART, R. B., RISELY, T. R., & STOLZ, S. (1977). Ethical issues for human services. *AABT Newsletter, 4,* 11.

BANDURA, A. (1969). *Principles of behavior modification.* New York: Holt, Rinehart & Winston.

BANDURA, A. (Ed.). (1971a). *Psychological modeling: Conflicting theories.* Chicago: Aldine-Atherton.

BANDURA, A. (1971b). Psychotherapy based upon modeling principles. In A. E. Bergin & S. L. Garfield (Eds.), *Handbook of psychotherapy and behavior change.* New York: Wiley.

BANDURA, A. (1974). Behavior therapy and the models of man. *American Psychologist, 29,* 859–869.

BANDURA, A. (1977). *Social learning theory.* Englewood Cliffs, NJ: Prentice-Hall.

BANDURA, A. (1986). *Social foundations of thought and action: A social cognitive theory.* Englewood Cliffs, NJ: Prentice-Hall.

BARLOW, D. H. (1978). Aversive procedures. In W. S. Agras (Ed.), *Behavior modification: Principles and clinical applications* (2nd ed.). Boston: Little, Brown.

*BECK, A. T. (1976). *Cognitive therapy and emotional disorders.* New York: New American Library.

*BECK, A. T. (1989). An interview with a depressed and suicidal patient. In D. Wedding & R. J. Corsini (Eds.), *Case studies in psychotherapy* (pp. 125–142). Itasca, IL: F. E. Peacock.

BECK, A. T., & WEISHAAR, M. E. (1989). Cognitive therapy. In R. J. Corsini & D. Wedding (Eds.), *Current psychotherapies* (4th ed.) (pp. 285–320). Itasca, IL: F. E. Peacock.

BELLACK, A. S., & HERSEN, M. (1977). *Behavior modification: An introductory textbook.* Baltimore: Williams & Wilkins.

COREY, G. (1990). *Theory and practice of group counseling* (3rd ed.). Pacific Grove, CA: Brooks/Cole.

*COREY, G. (1991). *Case approach to counseling and psychotherapy* (3rd ed.). Pacific Grove, CA: Brooks/Cole.

CORMIER, W. H., & CORMIER, L. S. (1985). *Interviewing strategies for helpers: Fundamental skills and cognitive behavioral interventions* (2nd ed.). Pacific Grove, CA: Brooks/Cole.

* Books and articles marked with an asterisk are suggested for further study.

CRAIGHEAD, W. E., KAZDIN, A. E., & MAHONEY, M. J. (1976). *Behavior modification: Principles, issues, and applications.* Boston Houghton Mifflin.

*DOBSON, D. S. (Ed.). (1988). *Handbook of cognitive-behavioral therapies.* New York: Guilford Press.

*FLANAGAN, S. G., & LIBERMAN, R. P. (1982). Ethical issues n the practice of behavior therapy. In M. Rosenbaum (Ed.), *Ethics and values in psychotherapy: A guidebook.* New York: Free Press.

FRANKS, C. M. (1987). Behavior therapy: An overview. In G. T. Wilson, C. M. Franks, P. C. Kendall, & J. P. Foreyt (Eds.), *Review of behavior therapy: Theory and practice: Vol. 11* (pp. 1–39). New York: Guilford Press.

*GOLDFRIED, M. R., & DAVISON, G. C. (1976). *Clinical behavior therapy.* New York: Holt, Rinehart & Winston.

GOLDSTEIN, A. P., & MYERS, C. R. (1986). Relationship-enhancement methods. In F. H. Kanfer & A. P. Goldstein (Eds.), *Helping people change* (3rd ed.) (pp. 19–65). New York: Pergamon Press.

GOTTMAN, J. M., & LEIBUM, S. (1974). *How to do psychotherapy and how to evaluate it.* New York: Holt, Rinehart & Winston.

HAAGA, D. A., & DAVISON, G. C. (1986). Cognitive change methods. In F. H. Kanfer & A. P. Goldstein (Eds.), *Helping people change: A textbook of methods* (3rd ed.) (pp. 236–282). New York: Pergamon Press.

JACOBSON, E. (1938). *Progressive relaxation.* Chicago: University of Chicago Press.

KANFER, F. H., & GAELICK, L. (1986). Self-management methods. In F. H. Kanfer & A. P. Goldstein (Eds.), *Helping people change: A textbook of methods* (3rd ed.) (pp. 283–345). New York: Pergamon Press.

KANFER, F. H., & GOLDSTEIN, A. P. (1986). Introduction. In F. H. Kanfer & A. P. Goldstein (Eds.), *Helping people change: A textbook of methods* (3rd ed.) (pp. 1–18). New York: Pergamon Press.

KAROLY, P., & HARRIS, A. (1986). Operant methods. In F. H. Kanfer & A. P. Goldstein (Eds.), *Helping people change: A textbook of methods* (3rd ed.) (pp. 111–144). New York: Pergamon Press.

KAZDIN, A. E. (1978). *History of behavior modification: Experimental foundations of contemporary research.* Baltimore: University Park Press.

*KAZDIN, A. E. (1980). *Behavior modification in applied settings* (rev. ed.). Homewood, IL: Dorsey Press.

KAZDIN, A. E. (1982). Symptom substitution, generalization, and response covariation: Implications for psychotherapy outcome. *Psychological Bulletin, 91,* 349–365.

KAZDIN, A. E., & WILSON, G. T. (1978). *Evaluation of behavior therapy: Issues, evidence, and research strategies.* Cambridge, MA: Ballinger.

KINKADE, K. (1972). *A Walden Two experiment: The first five years of Twin Oaks community.* New York: Morrow.

KRASNER, L. (1982). Behavior therapy: On roots, contexts, and growth. In G. T. Wilson & C. M. Franks (Eds.), *Contemporary behavior therapy: Conceptual and empirical foundations* (pp. 11–62). New York: Guilford Press.

KUEHNEL, J. M., & LIBERMAN, R. P. (1986). Behavior modification. In I. L. Kutash & A. Wolf (Eds.), *Psychotherapist's casebook* (pp. 240–262). San Francisco: Jossey-Bass.

LAZARUS, A. A. (1971). *Behavior therapy and beyond.* New York: McGraw-Hill.

*LAZARUS, A. A. (1981). *The practice of multimodal therapy.* New York: McGraw-Hill.

LAZARUS, A. A. (1982). Multimodal group therapy. In G. M. Gazda (Ed.), *Basic approaches to group psychotherapy and group counseling* (3rd ed.). Springfield, IL: Charles C Thomas.

*LAZARUS, A. A. (1986). Multimodal therapy. In J. C. Norcross (Ed.), *Handbook of eclectic psychotherapy* (pp. 65–93). New York: Brunner/Mazel.

LAZARUS, A. A. (1987a). The multimodal approach with adult outpatients. In N. S. Jacobson (Ed.), *Psychotherapists in clinical practice.* New York: Guilford Press.

*LAZARUS, A. A. (1987b). The need for technical eclecticism: Science, breadth, depth, and specificity. In J. K. Zeig (Ed.), *The evolution of psychotherapy* (pp. 164–178). New York: Brunner/Mazel.

LAZARUS, A. A. (Ed.). (1988). *Casebook of multimodal therapy.* New York: Guilford Press.

*LAZARUS, A. A. (1989a). The case of George. In D. Wedding & R. J. Corsini (Eds.), *Case studies in psychotherapy* (pp. 227–238). Itasca, IL: F. E. Peacock.

*LAZARUS, A. A. (1989b). Multimodal therapy. In R. Corsini & D. Wedding (Eds.), *Current psychotherapies* (4th ed.) (pp. 503–544). Itasca, IL: F. E. Peacock.

*LAZARUS, A. A. (1989c). *The practice of multimodal therapy.* Baltimore: John Hopkins University Press.

LAZARUS, A. A., & FAY, A. (1984). Behavior therapy. In T. B. Karasu (Ed.), *The psychiatric therapies* (pp. 483–538). Washington, DC: American Psychiatric Association.

LONDON, P. (1985). *The modes and morals of psychotherapy* (2nd ed.). Washington, DC: Hemisphere.

MAHONEY, M. J. (1977). Reflections on the cognitive-learning trend in psychotherapy. *American Psychologist, 32,* 5–13.

*MAHONEY, M. J. (1979). *Self-change: Strategies for solving personal problems.* New York: Norton.

MAHONEY, M. J., & THORESEN, C. E. (1974). *Self-control: Power to the person.* Pacific Grove, CA: Brooks/Cole.

MASTERS, J. C., BURISH, T. G., HOLLON, S. D., & RIMM, D. C. (1987). *Behavior therapy: Techniques and empirical findings* (3rd ed.). New York: Harcourt Brace Jovanovich.

McMULLIN, R. E. (1986). *Handbook of cognitive therapy techniques.* New York: Norton.

*MEICHENBAUM, D. (1977). *Cognitive behavior modification: An integrative approach.* New York: Plenum.

MEICHENBAUM, D. (1985). *Stress inoculation training.* New York: Pergamon Press.

MEICHENBAUM, D. (1986). Cognitive behavior modification. In F. H. Kanfer & A. P. Goldstein (Eds.), *Helping people change: A textbook of methods* (3rd ed.) (pp. 346–380). New York: Pergamon Press.

*MEICHENBAUM, D., & CAMERON, R. (1982). Cognitive-behavior therapy. In G. T. Wilson & C. M. Franks (Eds.), *Contemporary behavior therapy: Conceptual and empirical foundations* (pp. 310–338). New York: Guilford Press.

MORRIS, R. J. (1986). Fear reduction methods. In F. H. Kanfer & A. P. Goldstein (Eds.), *Helping people change: A textbook of methods* (3rd ed.) (pp. 145–190). New York: Pergamon Press.

*O'LEARY, K. D., & WILSON, G. T. (1987). *Behavior therapy: Application and outcome* (2nd ed.). Englewood Cliffs, NJ: Prentice-Hall.

PATTERSON, C. H. (1986). *Theories of counseling and psychotherapy* (4th ed.). New York: Harper & Row.

PAUL, G. L. (1966). *Insight vs. desensitization in psychotherapy.* Stanford, CA: Stanford University Press.

PAUL, G. L. (1967). Outcome research in psychotherapy. *Journal of Consulting Psychology, 31,* 109–188.

PERRY, M. A., & FURUKAWA, M. J. (1986). Modeling methods. In F. H. Kanfer & A. P.

Goldstein (Eds.), *Helping people change: A textbook of methods* (3rd ed.) (pp. 66–110). New York: Pergamon Press

REHM, L. P., & ROKKE, P. (1988). Self-management therapies. In K. S. Dobson (Ed.) *Handbook of cognitive-behavioral therapies* (pp. 136–166). New York: Guilford Press.

ROBERTS, T. K., JACKSON, L. J., & PHELPS, R. (1980). Lazarus's multimodal therapy model applied in an institutional setting. *Professional Psychology, 11,* 150–156.

SKINNER, B. F. (1948). *Walden II.* New York: Macmillan.

SKINNER, B. F. (1953). *Science and human behavior.* New York: Macmillan.

SKINNER, B. F. (1971). *Beyond freedom and dignity.* New York: Knopf.

SKINNER, B. F. (1976). *Particulars of my life.* New York: Knopf.

SKINNER, B. F. (1979). *The shaping of a behaviorist.* New York: Knopf.

SLOANE, R. B., STAPLES, F. R., CRISTOL, A. H., YORKSTON, N. J., & WHIPPLE, K. (1975). *Psychotherapy versus behavior therapy.* Cambridge, MA: Harvard University Press.

SPIEGLER, M. D. (1983). *Contemporary behavioral therapy.* Palo Alto, CA: Mayfield.

STOLZ, S. B., & ASSOCIATES. (1978). *Ethical issues in behavior modification.* San Francisco: Jossey-Bass.

THORESEN, C. E., & COATES, T. J. (1980). What does it mean to be a behavior therapist? In C. E. Thoresen (Ed.), *The behavior therapist.* Pacific Grove, CA: Brooks/Cole.

VOLTZ, L. M., & EVANS, I. M. (1982). The assessment of behavioral interrelationships in child behavior therapy. *Behavioral Assessment, 4,* 131–165.

*WATSON, D. L., & THARP, R. G. (1989). *Self-directed behavior: Self-modification for personal adjustment* (5th ed.). Pacific Grove, CA: Brooks/Cole.

*WILLIAMS, R., & LONG, J. (1983). *Toward a self-managed life-style* (3rd ed.). Boston: Houghton Mifflin.

WILSON, G. T. (1978). Cognitive behavior therapy: Paradigm shift or passing phase? In J. P. Foreyt & D. P. Rathjen (Eds.), *Cognitive behavior therapy: Research and applications.* New York: Plenum.

WILSON, G. T. (1984). Behavior therapy. In R. Corsini (Ed.), *Current psychotherapies* (3rd ed.) (pp. 239–276). Itasca, IL: F. E. Peacock.

WILSON, G. T. (1987). Clinical issues and strategies in the practice of behavior therapy. In G. T. Wilson, C. M. Franks, P. C. Kendall, & J. P. Foreyt (Eds.), *Review of behavior therapy: Theory and practice: Vol. 11* (pp. 288–317). New York: Guilford Press.

WILSON, G. T. (1989). Behavior therapy. In R. J. Corsini & D. Wedding (Eds.), *Current psychotherapies* (4th ed.) (pp. 241–282). Itasca, IL: F. E. Peacock.

WILSON, G. T., & FRANKS, C. M. (Eds.). (1982). *Contemporary behavior therapy: Conceptual and empirical foundations.* New York: Guilford Press.

WILSON, G. T., FRANKS, C. M., KENDALL, P. C., & FOREYT, J. P. (Eds.). (1987). *Review of behavior therapy: Theory and practice: Vol. 11.* New York: Guilford Press.

WOLPE, J. (1958). *Psychotherapy by reciprocal inhibition.* Stanford, CA: Stanford University Press.

WOLPE, J. (1969). *The practice of behavior therapy.* New York: Pergamon Press

11

RATIONAL-EMOTIVE THERAPY AND OTHER COGNITIVE-BEHAVIORAL APPROACHES

ALBERT ELLIS

ALBERT ELLIS (b. 1913) was born in Pittsburgh but escaped to the wilds of New York at the age of 4 and has lived there (except for a year in New Jersey) ever since. He was hospitalized nine times as a child, mainly with nephritis, and developed renal glycosuria at the age of 19 and diabetes at the age of 40. But by rigorously taking care of his health and stubbornly refusing to make himself miserable about it, he has lived an unusually robust and energetic life.

He grew up on the streets of the Bronx, where he often played handball, stickball, and touch football. In many ways he reared himself (and helped rear his younger brother and sister), since his father and mother were nice enough people but were both neglectful parents. He mapped out his own educational career after deciding, at the age of 12, to be a writer. He went to the High School of Commerce and to the City College of New York as a business administration major in the hopes of making enough money in business to be able to write anything he wanted.

The Great Depression of the 1930s influenced Ellis to give up the idea of being a rich businessman, but he continued to write and write, finishing 20 book-length manuscripts, including fiction, poetry, plays, and nonfiction, by the time he was 28. Several of his manuscripts came within a hair of being published but never quite made it. Undaunted, he continued his research and writing in the areas of sex, love, and marriage and became such an authority in these areas that many of his friends and relatives sought his advice about their personal problems.

Realizing that he could counsel people skillfully and that he greatly enjoyed doing so, Ellis decided to become a psychologist. Eight years after he had graduated from college, he matriculated in the clinical psychology program at Teachers College, Columbia. He began practicing in the areas of marriage, family, and sex therapy. Ellis, believing psychoanalysis to be the deepest form of psychotherapy, was analyzed and supervised by a training analyst of the Karen Horney school. From 1947 to 1953 he practiced classical analysis and analytically oriented psychotherapy.

After coming to the conclusion that psychoanalysis was a relatively superficial and unscientific form of treatment, he experimented with several other systems. Early in 1955 he combined humanistic, philosophical, and behavioral therapy to form rational-emotive therapy (RET). Ellis is rightly known as the father of RET and the grandfather of cognitive-behavioral therapy. In an interview he was asked how he would like to be remembered after his death. He replied:

> In the field of psychotherapy, I would like them to say that I was the main pioneering cognitive and cognitive behavioral theorist and therapist, that I fought very hard to get cognition accepted in psychotherapy, and that, largely as a result of my efforts, it has finally been accepted, albeit a little belatedly [Dryden, 1989, p. 545].

To some extent Ellis developed his approach as a method of dealing with his own problems during his youth. At one point in his life, for example, he had exaggerated fears of speaking in public. During his adolescence he was extremely shy around girls. At age 19 he forced himself to talk to 100 girls in the Bronx Botanical Gardens over a period of one month. Although he never managed to get a date from these brief encounters, he does report that he desensitized himself to his fear of rejection by women. By applying cognitive-behavioral methods, he has managed to conquer some of his worst blocks (Ellis, 1962, 1979c). Moreover, he has learned to actually *enjoy* public speaking and other activities about which he was once highly anxious.

People who hear Ellis lecture often comment about his abrasive, humorous, and flamboyant style (Dryden, 1989). He does see himself as more abrasive than most in his workshops, and he also considers himself humorous and startling in some ways. In his workshops it seems that he takes delight in giving vent to his eccentric side. He enjoys his work, which is his primary commitment in life.

Ellis is a highly energetic and productive person and is surely one of the most prolific writers in the field of counseling and psychotherapy. In his busy professional life he sees as many as 80 clients a week for individual sessions, conducts 5 group-therapy sessions weekly, and gives about 200 talks and workshops to professionals and the public each year. He has published over 50 books and more than 600 articles, mostly on the theory and applications of RET.

INTRODUCTION

Rational-emotive therapy (RET) departs radically from several of the other systems presented in this book — namely, the psychoanalytic, person-centered, and Gestalt approaches. I have selected it for inclusion because it is a challenging perspective on many of the basic issues of counseling and psychotherapy. RET has much in common with the therapies that are oriented toward cognition, behavior, and action, in that it stresses thinking, judging, deciding, analyzing, and doing. RET is highly didactic, very directive, and concerned as much with thinking as with feeling. It is based on the assumption that cognitions, emotions, and behaviors interact significantly and have a reciprocal cause-and-effect relationship. Throughout its development RET has continued to emphasize all three of these modalities and their interactions, thus characterizing it as a multimodal and eclectic approach (Ellis, 1979a, 1979c, 1979e, 1987a, 1989).

DEVELOPMENT OF RET

Ellis developed rational-emotive therapy after finding that his training as a psychoanalyst was inadequate for dealing with his clients. Ellis (1988) argues that the psychoanalytic approach is more than inefficient, because people often seem to get worse instead of better. Out of this conviction he began to persuade and impel his clients to *do* the very things they were most afraid of doing, such as risking rejection by significant others. Gradually, he became much more eclectic and more active and directive as a therapist.

RET became a general school of psychotherapy aimed at providing clients with the tools to restructure their philosophical and behavioral styles (Ellis & Yeager, 1989). Although RET is generally conceded to be the parent of today's cognitive-behavioral therapies, it had precursors. The interrelationship among cognitions, emotions, and behaviors was noted by several ancient Eastern and Western philosophers (Ellis, 1984b). Ellis acknowledges his debt to the ancient Greeks, especially the Stoic philosopher Epictetus, who is quoted as having said in the first century A.D. "People are disturbed not by things, but by their view of things" (Dryden & Ellis, 1988, p. 214). He also gives credit to Adler as an influential modern forerunner of RET. As you will recall, Adler contends that our emotional reactions and lifestyle are associated with our basic beliefs and are therefore cognitively created. Like the Adlerian approach, RET emphasizes the role of social interest in determining psychological health. There are other Adlerian influences on RET, such as the importance of goals, purposes, values, and meanings in human existence; the focus on active and directive teaching; the use of cognitive persuasive methods; and teaching about therapy by giving live demonstrations before an audience (Dryden & Ellis, 1988).

RET's basic hypothesis, then, is that our emotions stem mainly from our beliefs, evaluations, interpretations, and reactions to life situations. Through the rational-emotive therapeutic process, clients learn skills that give them the tools to identify and dispute irrational beliefs that have been acquired and are now maintained by self-indoctrination. They learn how to replace such ineffective ways of thinking with effective and rational cognitions, and as a result they change their emotional reactions to situations. The therapeutic process allows clients to apply RET principles not only to a particular presenting problem but also to many other problems in life or to future ones they might encounter. Several therapeutic implications flow from these assumptions: The focus is on working with *thinking* and *acting* rather than primarily with expressing feelings. Therapy is seen as an *educational* process. The therapist functions in many ways like a *teacher,* especially in giving homework assignments and in teaching strategies for straight thinking; and the client is a *learner,* who practices the skills in everyday life that are being acquired in therapy.

The concepts of rational-emotive therapy raise several key questions that it would be well to keep in mind as you read this chapter: Is psychotherapy essentially a process of reeducation? Is it appropriate for therapists to use persuasion and highly directive methods? How effective is it to attempt to rid clients of their "irrational beliefs" by using logic, advice, information, and interpretations? Will changing one's thoughts necessarily lead to changing how one feels and acts?

RELATIONSHIP BETWEEN RET AND
OTHER COGNITIVE-BEHAVIORAL THERAPIES

In the 1950s RET and behavior therapy had little in common, except that Ellis employed behavioral techniques as a part of his integrative repertoire. He was interested in changing clients' ideas that mediated their emotions, not merely in changing their behavior. RET practitioners have consistently theorized that because humans are innately predisposed to think, emote, and behave interactionally, they rarely make and sustain basic cognitive changes unless they also forcefully work on their feelings and unless they consistently practice new behaviors. RET stresses cognitive, affective, and behavioral techniques and encourages therapists to present these techniques in an active and directive manner (Dryden & Ellis, 1988; Ellis, 1984b, 1987a, 1989a).

As was mentioned in the previous chapter, behavior therapy began to broaden in the 1960s to include cognitions as legitimate behavior that could be learned and modified. As RET became more widely accepted and practiced, behavior therapists developed their own views of the cognitive dimensions of an individual's problems and devised techniques to modify cognitions. The basic assumption of this cognitive approach is that people contribute to their own psychological problems, as well as specific symptoms, by the way in which they interpret events and situations in their life. To a large degree cognitive-behavioral therapy is based on the assumption that a reorganization of one's self-statements will result in a corresponding reorganization of one's behavior. Donald Meichenbaum (1977) writes that within a learning-theory framework the client's cognitions are explicit behaviors that can be modified in their own right, just as are overt behaviors that can be directly observed. Thus, the behavioral techniques that have been used to modify overt behaviors, such as operant conditioning, modeling, and behavioral rehearsal (practicing a skill in a therapy session in preparation for an anticipated situation), can also be applied to the more covert and subjective processes of thinking and internal dialogue. Both RET and other cognitive-behavioral therapies include a variety of behavioral strategies. Later in this chapter I will give an overview of two selected cognitive-behavioral approaches, Aaron T. Beck's *cognitive therapy* and Meichenbaum's *cognitive behavior modification*.

A difference between RET and other cognitive-behavioral therapies pertains to relationship procedures. The other cognitive-behavioral approaches give more value to the role of empathy and personal warmth than is true of RET. However, RET does emphasize the therapist's unconditional acceptance of the client.

Another feature that distinguishes RET is its systematic exposing of irrational beliefs that result in emotional and behavioral disturbance (Ellis, 1986b; Wessler & Wessler, 1980). In comparing RET with most of the cognitive-behavioral therapies, Ellis asserts that it is unique in that it teaches clients to look for their *unconditional "shoulds"* and their *absolutistic "musts."* RET reveals to clients their underlying *must*urbatory philosophies, tries to help them surrender these faulty beliefs, and provides them with alternative rational statements. The main goal of RET is to help clients make a profound philosophical change that will result in deep-seated emotional and behavioral change. It does this by teaching clients the basics of the scientific method and helping them internalize this method so that they can use it to solve their own emotional and behavioral problems for the rest of their life (Ellis, 1984a, 1987a, 1987b, 1988; Ellis & Dryden, 1987).

KEY CONCEPTS

VIEW OF HUMAN NATURE

Rational-emotive therapy is based on the assumption that human beings are born with a potential for both rational, or straight, thinking and irrational, or crooked, thinking. People have predispositions for self-preservation, happiness, thinking and verbalizing, loving, communion with others, and growth and self-actualization. They also have propensities for self-destruction, avoidance of thought, procrastination, endless repetition of mistakes, superstition, intolerance, perfectionism and self-blame, and avoidance of actualizing growth potentials.

Taking for granted that humans are fallible, RET attempts to help them accept themselves as creatures who will continue to make mistakes yet at the same time learn to live more at peace with themselves. Ellis (1979b) lists some of the key RET assumptions:

- People condition themselves to feel disturbed, rather than being conditioned by external sources.
- People have the biological and cultural tendency to think crookedly and to needlessly disturb themselves.
- Humans are unique in that they invent disturbing beliefs and keep themselves disturbed about their disturbances.
- People have the capacity to change their cognitive, emotive, and behavioral processes; they can choose to react differently from their usual patterns, refuse to allow themselves to become upset, and train themselves so that they can eventually remain minimally disturbed for the rest of their life.

Ellis (1989c) has concluded that humans are *self-talking, self-evaluating,* and *self-sustaining.* They develop emotional and behavioral difficulties when they take *simple preferences* (desires for love, approval, success) and make the mistake of thinking of them as dire needs. Ellis also affirms that humans have inborn tendencies toward growth and actualization, yet they often sabotage their movement toward growth as a result of their inborn tendency toward crooked thinking and also the self-defeating patterns they have learned (Ellis & Dryden, 1987).

VIEW OF EMOTIONAL DISTURBANCE

We originally learn irrational beliefs from significant others during our childhood. Additionally, we create irrational dogmas and superstitions by ourselves. Then we actively reinstill false beliefs by the processes of autosuggestion and self-repetition. Hence, it is largely our own repetition of early-indoctrinated irrational thoughts, rather than a parent's repetition, that keeps dysfunctional attitudes alive and operative within us.

RET insists that blame is the core of most emotional disturbances. Therefore, if we are to cure a neurosis or a personality disorder, we had better stop blaming ourselves and others. Instead, it is important that we learn to accept ourselves despite our imperfections. Ellis (1987b) hypothesizes that virtually all people are born with the ability to think rationally; however, we also have strong tendencies to escalate our desires and preferences into dogmatic, absolutistic "shoulds," "musts," "oughts," demands, and commands. If we stay with preferences and rational beliefs, we will not become inappropriately depressed, hostile, and self-pitying. It is when we live by demands that we disturb ourselves. Our unrealistic and illogical ideas create disruptive feelings. Crazy ideas create dysfunctional behaviors (Ellis, 1987b).

Ellis (1988) contends that because we largely create our own disturbed thoughts and feelings, we have the power to control our emotional destiny. He suggests that when we are upset, it is a good idea to look to our hidden dogmatic "musts" and absolutistic "shoulds." Absolutistic cognitions are at the core of human misery, because most of the time these beliefs impede and obstruct people in their pursuit of their goals and purposes. Practically all human misery and serious emotional turmoil are quite unnecessary. We create, both consciously and unconsciously, the ways we think and, hence, the ways we feel in a variety of situations. Because we have the capacity for self-awareness, we can observe and evaluate our goals and purposes and, thus, can change them. We can usually change our feelings, no matter what happens to us. We are able to creatively decide to feel differently about a situation and therefore stubbornly refuse to make ourselves severely anxious or depressed about anything (Ellis, 1988).

RET contends that people do not *need* to be accepted and loved, even though it may be highly desirable. The therapist teaches clients how to feel undepressed even when they are unaccepted and unloved by significant others. Although RET encourages people to experience sadness over being unaccepted, it attempts to help them find ways of overcoming depression, anxiety, hurt, loss of self-worth, and hatred.

Here are some irrational ideas that we internalize and that inevitably lead to self-defeat (Dryden & Ellis, 1988; Ellis, 1987b, 1988):

- "I *must* have love or approval from all the significant people in my life."
- "I *must* perform important tasks competently and perfectly well."
- "Because I strongly desire that people treat me considerately and fairly, they *absolutely must* do so!"
- "If I don't get what I want, it's terrible, and I can't stand it."
- "It's easier to avoid facing life's difficulties and responsibilities than to undertake more rewarding forms of self-discipline."

Most humans have a strong tendency to make and keep themselves emotionally disturbed by internalizing self-defeating beliefs such as the ones listed above. Therefore, they find it virtually impossible to consistently achieve and maintain good mental health (Ellis, 1987b).

A-B-C THEORY OF PERSONALITY

As we have seen, the basic tenet of RET is that emotional disturbances (as distinguished from feelings of sorrow, regret, and frustration) are largely the product of irrational thinking. The irrational quality comes from *demanding* that the universe *should, ought to,* and *must* be different. From the RET perspective, many therapists err by focusing on past history and activating events, as if anything could be done to change the client's early childhood. Other therapists make the mistake of overemphasizing the effort to have clients recognize, express, and ventilate feelings. Some urge clients to relive early events and feelings in the present. Ellis would say that this tactic is not too productive, because emotional consequences will not vanish merely because feelings have been intensified and expressed. Instead, the client and the therapist work together to dispute the irrational beliefs that are causing negative emotional consequences. They work toward transforming an unrealistic, immature, demanding, and absolute style of thinking into a realistic, mature, logical, and empirical approach to thinking and behaving. This results in more appropriate feeling reactions to life's situations.

The following diagram will clarify the interaction of the various components being discussed:

A (activating event) ◄——— B (belief) ———► C (emotional and behavioral consequence)

D (disputing intervention) ———► E (effect) ———► F (new feeling)

The A-B-C theory of personality is central to RET theory and practice. A is the existence of a fact, an event, or the behavior or attitude of an individual. C is the emotional and behavioral consequence or reaction of the individual; the reaction can be either appropriate or inappropriate. A (the activating event) does not cause C (the emotional consequence). Instead, B, which is the person's belief about A, largely causes C, the emotional reaction. For example, if a person experiences depression after a divorce, it may not be the divorce itself that causes the depressive reaction but the person's *beliefs* about being a failure, being rejected, or losing a mate. Ellis would maintain that the beliefs about the rejection and failure (at point B) are what mainly cause the depression (at point C), not the actual event of the divorce (at point A). Thus, human beings are largely responsible for creating their own emotional reactions and disturbances. Showing people how they can change the irrational beliefs that directly cause their disturbed emotional consequences is the heart of RET (Ellis, 1979b).

How is an emotional disturbance fostered? It is fed by the illogical sentences that the person continually repeats to himself or herself, such as "I am totally to blame for the divorce," "I am a miserable failure, and everything I did was wrong," "I am a worthless person." Ellis repeatedly makes the point that "you mainly feel the way you think." Disturbed emotional reactions such as depression and anxiety are initiated and perpetuated by the self-defeating belief system, which is based on irrational ideas that one has incorporated and invented.

After A, B, and C comes D, disputing. Essentially, D is the application of the scientific method to help clients challenge their irrational beliefs. Because the principles of logic can be taught, they can be used to destroy any unrealistic, unverifiable hypothesis. Ellis and Bernard (1986) describe three components of this disputing process: detecting, debating, and discriminating. First, clients learn how to *detect* their irrational beliefs, particularly their absolutistic "shoulds" and "musts," their "awfulizing," and their "self-downing." Then clients *debate* their dysfunctional beliefs by learning how to logically and empirically question them and to vigorously argue themselves out of and act against believing them. Finally, clients learn to *discriminate* irrational beliefs from rational beliefs.

Although RET uses many other cognitive, emotive, and behavioral methods to help clients surrender their irrational beliefs, it stresses this process of disputing both during the therapy sessions and in outside life. Eventually they arrive at E, an effective philosophy, which has a practical side. A new and effective rational philosophy consists of replacing inappropriate thoughts with appropriate ones. If we are successful in doing this, we also create F, or a new set of feelings. Instead of feeling seriously anxious or depressed, we feel appropriately in accord with a situation. The best way to begin to feel better is to develop an effective and rational philosophy. Thus, instead of berating oneself and punishing oneself with depression over the divorce, one would reach a rational and empirically based conclusion: "Well, I'm genuinely sorry that our marriage didn't work out and that we divorced. Although I wish we could have worked things out, we didn't, and that isn't the end of the world. Because our marriage failed doesn't mean that I'm a failure in life, and it's foolish for me to continue blaming myself and making myself fully responsible for the breakup." According to RET theory, the ultimate effect is the minimizing of feelings of depression and self-condemnation.

In sum, philosophical restructuring to change our dysfunctional personality involves the following steps: (1) fully acknowledging that we are largely responsible for creating our own problems; (2) accepting the notion that we have the ability to change these disturbances significantly; (3) recognizing that our emotional problems largely stem from irrational beliefs; (4) clearly perceiving these beliefs; (5) seeing the value of disputing such foolish beliefs, using rigorous methods; (6) accepting the fact that if we expect to change, we had better work hard in emotive and behavioral ways to counteract our beliefs and the dysfunctional feelings and actions that follow; and (7) practicing RET methods of uprooting or changing disturbed consequences for the rest of our life (Ellis, 1979d, 1988).

THE THERAPEUTIC PROCESS

THERAPEUTIC GOALS

The many roads taken in rational-emotive therapy lead toward the one destination of clients' minimizing their emotional disturbances and self-defeating behaviors by acquiring a more realistic philosophy of life. Other important therapeutic goals include reducing a tendency for blaming oneself or others for what goes wrong in life and learning ways to effectively deal with future difficulties.

RET strives for a thorough philosophical reevaluation based on the assumption that human problems are philosophically rooted. Thus, it is not aimed primarily at removing symptoms. It is mainly designed to induce people to examine and change some of their most basic values, especially those values that keep them disturbed. If a client's fear is of failing in her marriage, the aim is not merely to reduce that specific fear; instead, the therapist attempts to work with her exaggerated fears of failing in general.

Following are specific goals toward which RET therapists work with their clients: self-interest, social interest, self-direction, tolerance, flexibility, acceptance of uncertainty, commitment, scientific thinking, self-acceptance, risk taking, nonutopianism, high tolerance of frustration, and self-responsibility for disturbance (Ellis, 1979c; Ellis & Bernard, 1986; Ellis & Dryden, 1987).

THERAPIST'S FUNCTION AND ROLE

To achieve the aims just detailed, the therapist has specific tasks. The first step is to show clients that they have incorporated many irrational "shoulds," "oughts," and "musts." Clients learn to separate their rational beliefs from their irrational ones. To foster this client awareness, the therapist serves the function of a scientist who challenges the self-defeating idea that the client originally accepted or invented without question as truth. The therapist encourages, persuades, and at times even directs the client to engage in activities that will counter this propaganda.

A second step in the therapeutic process takes clients beyond the stage of awareness. It demonstrates that they keep their emotional disturbances active by continuing to think illogically and by repeating self-defeating meanings and philosophies. In other words, because clients keep reindoctrinating themselves, they are largely responsible for their own problems. That the therapist merely shows clients that they have illogical processes is not enough, for a client is likely to say: "Now I understand that I have fears of failing and that these fears are exaggerated and unrealistic. But I'm still afraid of failing!"

To get beyond clients' mere recognition of irrational thoughts and feelings, the therapist takes a third step: helping them modify their thinking and abandon their irrational ideas. Rational-emotive psychology assumes that their illogical beliefs are so deeply ingrained that clients will not normally change them by themselves. The therapist therefore assists clients in understanding the vicious circle of the self-blaming process.

The fourth and final step in the therapeutic process is to challenge clients to develop a rational philosophy of life so that in the future they can avoid becoming the victim of other irrational beliefs. Tackling only specific problems or symptoms can give no assurance that new illogical fears will not emerge. What is desirable, then, is for the therapist to attack the core of the irrational thinking and to teach clients how to substitute rational beliefs and attitudes for the irrational ones; the more scientific and tolerant clients become, Ellis contends, the less disturbed they will be.

A therapist who works within the RET framework functions differently from most other practitioners. Because RET is essentially a cognitive and directive behavioral process, it often minimizes the intense relationship between the therapist and the client. The therapist mainly employs a persuasive methodology that emphasizes education. Ellis outlines what the rational-emotive practitioner does (1989, pp. 215–216):

- encourages clients to discover a few basic irrational ideas that motivate much disturbed behavior
- challenges clients to validate their ideas
- demonstrates to clients the illogical nature of their thinking
- uses absurdity and humor to confront the irrationality of clients' thinking
- uses a logical analysis to minimize clients' irrational beliefs
- shows how these beliefs are inoperative and how they will lead to future emotional and behavioral disturbances
- explains how these ideas can be replaced with more rational ideas that are empirically grounded
- teaches clients how to apply the scientific approach to thinking so that they can observe and minimize present or future irrational ideas and illogical deductions that foster self-destructive ways of feeling and behaving
- uses several emotive and behavioral methods to help clients work directly on their feelings and to act against their disturbances

Wessler and Wessler (1980) describe the evolution of a typical RET case. During the critical first session the focus is on building rapport and creating the kind of client/therapist relationship that will encourage the client to talk freely. Once a collaborative and therapeutic alliance is formed, the relationship aspect is given less emphasis. Therapy proceeds by identifying those problems that will be targeted for exploration. Therapists ask open-ended questions such as "What problems do you most want help with? What would you most want from therapy?" Goal setting is a major task during the early phase of therapy. Clients identify feelings, beliefs, and actions that they would like to acquire or increase as well as merely listing ones they want to reduce or eliminate. A therapist might ask "In what ways would you like to feel, think, and act differently than you do now?"

Clients are then oriented to the basic principles and practices of RET. Rational-emotive therapists take the mystery out of the therapeutic process. They teach clients about the cognitive hypothesis of disturbance, showing how irrational beliefs lead to negative consequences. When clients understand that certain irrational beliefs they hold lead to dysfunctional emotions and behaviors, the therapist challenges them to examine why they are clinging to old misconceptions instead of letting go of them.

Homework is carefully designed, aimed at getting clients to carry out positive actions and induce emotional and attitudinal change. These assignments are checked in later sessions, and clients learn effective ways to dispute self-defeating thinking. Toward the end of therapy, clients review their progress, make plans, and identify strategies for dealing with continuing or potential problems.

In summary, RET therapists actively *teach* clients that self-condemnation is one of the main causes of emotional disturbance; that it is possible to stop *rating* themselves on their performances; and that by hard work and by carrying out behavioral homework assignments, they can rid themselves of irrational thinking that leads to disturbances in feeling and behaving.

RET differs from many other therapeutic approaches in that it does not place much value on free association, working with dreams, focusing on the client's past history, endlessly expressing and exploring feelings, and obsessive dealing with transference phenomena. Ellis (1989) believes that devoting any length of time to these factors is "indulgence therapy," which might result in clients' *feeling* better but will rarely aid them in *getting* better.

CLIENT'S EXPERIENCE IN THERAPY

Clients typically think that their emotional and behavioral problems are externally caused. Through RET they learn that these problems are mainly the result of erroneous beliefs. Once clients begin to accept that their beliefs are the primary cause of their emotions and behaviors, they are able to participate effectively in the cognitive-restructuring process (Ellis & Yeager, 1989). Thus, to a large measure, the client's role in RET is that of a student, or learner. Psychotherapy is viewed as a reeducative process whereby the client learns how to apply logical thought to problem solving and emotional change.

According to Dryden and Ellis (1988), in order to bring about a philosophical change, clients need to do the following:

- Accept the reality that although they largely create their own disturbances, they do have the ability to significantly change them.
- Understand that their personality problems stem mainly from irrational and absolutistic beliefs, rather than from actual events.
- Learn to detect their irrational beliefs and to dispute them to the point that they incorporate rational alternatives.
- Commit themselves to working and practicing toward the internalization of a new, rational philosophy by using cognitive, emotive, and behavioral methods of change.

The therapeutic process focuses on the client's experience in the present. Like the person-centered and existentially oriented approaches to therapy, RET mainly emphasizes here-and-now experiences and clients' present ability to change the patterns of thinking and emoting that they acquired earlier. The therapist does not devote much time to exploring clients' early history and making connections between their past and present behavior. Nor does the therapist usually explore in depth their early relationships with their parents or siblings. Instead, the therapeutic process stresses that regardless of clients' basic, irrational philosophies of life, they are presently disturbed because they still believe in their self-defeating view of themselves and their world. Questions of where, why, or how they acquired their irrational philosophy are of secondary importance. The central issue is how clients can become aware of their self-defeating tacit philosophies and challenge and act against them.

According to RET theory, superficial insight alone does not typically lead to personality change, for at best it teaches people that they have problems and that there are factors antecedent to these disturbances. Even when insight is correct, it does not automatically make a situation better. Insight can help us see exactly how we are continuing to sabotage ourselves and what we can do to change. Insight alone can be misleading, however, because activating events (A) do not *cause* dysfunctional behavior. Instead people mainly cause their own upsets (C) by the way they interpret what happens to them (B) (Ellis, 1984a, 1988, 1989). What is necessary to bring about change is the awareness of one's irrational beliefs, the willingness to consistently confront dysfunctional thinking and replace it with rational thinking, and the willingness to begin behaving in different ways.

Ellis (1979e, 1988) describes three main levels of insight in RET. The first level refers to the fact that we choose to disturb ourselves about events in our lives. We largely upset ourselves at point C (consequences) and do not merely get upset by the events at point A (activating events). We upset ourselves by accepting and inventing irrational beliefs. The second level of insight pertains to the ways in which we acquired our irrational beliefs originally and how we are choosing to maintain them. How, when, or why we originally became emotionally disturbed is not important; rather, we remain this way today because we keep reindoctrinating ourselves with our absolutistic beliefs. Our self-conditioning is more important than our early conditioning by others. The third level of insight involves the recognition that there are no magical ways for us to change our personality and our tendencies to upset ourselves. We can usually change only if we are willing to work and practice. Mere acceptance that a belief is irrational is generally not enough to bring about change. No matter how clearly we see that we are upsetting ourselves and making ourselves miserable, we will rarely improve unless we actively change our disturbance-creating beliefs and act against them. It is essential to persistently and strongly challenge our beliefs cognitively, emotively, and behaviorally if we hope to break the perpetuation of the disturbance cycle.

For an illustration of these three levels of insight, let us assume that Stan, who is featured in Chapter 13, is working on his fear of women. He feels threatened by attractive women, and he is afraid of how he might react to a powerful woman and what she might do to him. On the first level of insight Stan becomes aware that there is some antecedent cause of his fear of women. This cause is not that his mother tried, for example, to dominate him. Rather, it is his irrational beliefs that she should not have tried to dominate him and that it was, and still is, awful that she did try and that other women may dominate him, too.

On the second level of insight Stan recognizes that he is still threatened by women and feels uncomfortable in their presence because he still believes in, and keeps repeating endlessly to himself, the irrational beliefs that he once accepted. He sees that he keeps himself in a state of panic with women because he continues to tell himself "Women can castrate me!" or "They'll expect me to be a superman!" or some other irrational notions.

The third level of insight consists of Stan's acceptance that he will rarely improve unless he works diligently and practices changing his irrational beliefs by actively disputing them and actually doing things of a counter-propaganda nature. Thus, his homework assignment might be to approach an attractive woman and ask her for a date. While on this date, he can challenge his irrational notions and his catastrophic expectations of what might happen. Merely talking about his fears will not do much to change his behavior. What is important is that he engage in activity and in cognitive reconstruction that will torpedo the underpinnings of his irrational fears. Since Stan is also afraid of rejection, his therapist will teach him ways to cope with possible rejection as well as teaching him how to keep from being immobilized by fear of rejection.

RET stresses the second and third levels of insight — namely, Stan's acknowledgment that it is he who is keeping the originally disturbing ideas and feelings alive and that he had better rationally/emotively face them, think about them, and work to eliminate them.

RELATIONSHIP BETWEEN THERAPIST AND CLIENT

The issue of the personal relationship between the therapist and the client takes on a different meaning in RET than it has in most other forms of therapy. In close agreement with the person-centered concept of unconditional positive regard is RET's concept of *full acceptance,* or *tolerance.* The basic idea here is to help clients avoid self-condemnation. Although clients may evaluate their behavior, the goal is for them to refuse to rate themselves as persons, no matter how ineffectual some of their behavior is. Therapists show their full acceptance by refusing to evaluate their clients as persons while at the same time being willing to relentlessly confront clients' nonsensical thinking and self-destructive behaviors. Unlike the relationship-oriented therapies, RET does not place a premium on personal warmth and empathic understanding, on the assumption that too much warmth and understanding can be counterproductive by fostering a sense of dependence for approval from the therapist. In fact, RET therapists can accept their clients as imperfect beings without giving personal warmth, instead using a variety of impersonal techniques such as teaching, bibliotherapy, and behavior modification (Ellis, 1989) but always modeling as well as teaching unconditional full acceptance.

Some RET practitioners, however, give more emphasis to the importance of building rapport and a collaborative relationship than does Ellis. Wessler and Wessler (1980) agree that Rogers's therapeutic conditions (unconditional positive regard, empathy, and therapist genuineness) do facilitate change, yet they add: "We also believe that these conditions for change are important, but they can be conveyed in a directive as well as a nondirective situation. If they are not conveyed, however, all the techniques in the world will be unlikely to lead to a successful outcome" (p. 21).

The development of good rapport between client and therapist is seen by Walen, DiGiuseppe, and Wessler (1980) as a key ingredient in maximizing therapeutic gains. Like Wessler and Wessler, they stress that being active and directive is not incompatible with developing a professional relationship based on competence, credibility, respect, and a commitment to help the client change.

Rational-emotive therapists are often open and direct in disclosing their own beliefs and values. Some are willing to share their own imperfections as a way of disputing the client's unrealistic notion that therapists are "completely put together" persons. Along this line, transference is not encouraged, and when it does occur, the therapist is likely to attack it. The therapist wants to show that a transference relationship is based on the irrational belief that the client must be liked and loved by the therapist (or parent figure) (Ellis, 1989).

APPLICATION: THERAPEUTIC TECHNIQUES AND PROCEDURES

THE PRACTICE OF RATIONAL-EMOTIVE THERAPY

Rational-emotive therapists are multimodal and integrative and use a variety of cognitive, affective, and behavioral techniques, tailoring them to individual clients. These techniques are applied to the treatment of a range of common clinical problems such as anxiety, depression, anger, marital difficulties, poor interpersonal skills, parenting failures, personality disorders, obsessive/compulsive disorders, eating disorders, psychosomatic disorders, addictions, and psychotic disorders (Warren & McLellarn, 1987). What follows is a brief summary of the major cognitive, emotive, and behavioral techniques Ellis describes (Dryden & Ellis, 1988; Ellis, 1979a, 1986a; Ellis & Dryden, 1987; Ellis & Yeager, 1989).

Cognitive methods.   RET practitioners usually incorporate into the therapeutic process a forceful cognitive methodology. RET demonstrates to clients in a quick and direct manner what it is that they are continuing to tell themselves. Then it teaches them how to deal with these self-statements so that they no longer believe them; it encourages them to acquire a philosophy based on reality. RET relies heavily on thinking, disputing, debating, challenging, interpreting, explaining, and teaching. A few of these cognitive techniques that are available to the RET therapist are:

1. *Disputing irrational beliefs.* The most common cognitive method of RET consists of the therapist's actively disputing clients' irrational beliefs and teaching them how to do this challenging on their own. The therapist shows clients that they are disturbed not because of certain events or situations but because of their perceptions of these events and because of the nature of their self-statements. The therapist quickly challenges irrational beliefs by asking questions such as "Where is the evidence for your beliefs? Why is it *terrible* and *horrible* if life is not the way you want it to be? Where is it written that you *cannot stand* a situation? Why do you assume that you are a *rotten person* because of the way you behave? Would it really be catastrophic if your worst fantasies were to come true?" Through a series of refutations, therapists are instrumental in raising the consciousness of their clients to a more rational

(self-helping) level. Clients work on a major irrationality (especially an absolutistic "must") in a systematic way on a daily basis. Clients go over a particular "must," "should," or "ought" until they no longer hold the irrational belief, or at least until it is diminished in strength. Some examples of questions or statements that clients learn to tell themselves are "Why *must* people treat me fairly?" "Where did I learn that I will be a total flop if I don't succeed in everything I try?" "If I don't get the job I want, it may be disappointing, but I can certainly stand it." "If life doesn't always go the way I would like it to, it isn't *awful,* just inconvenient."

2. *Cognitive homework.* RET clients are expected to make lists of their problems, look for their absolutistic beliefs and dispute these beliefs. They are given homework assignments, which is a way of tracking down the absolutistic "shoulds" and "musts" that are a part of their internalized self-messages. Part of homework consists of applying the A-B-C theory of RET to many of the problems they encounter in daily life. They often fill out the RET Self-Help Form (which is reproduced in the student manual of this text). Clients are encouraged to put themselves in risk-taking situations that will allow them to challenge their self-limiting beliefs. For example, a person with a talent for acting who is afraid to act in front of an audience because of fear of failure may be asked to take a small part in a stage play. The person is instructed to replace negative self-statements such as "I will fail," "I will look foolish," or "No one will like me" with more positive messages such as "Even if I do behave foolishly at times, this does not make me a foolish *person.* I can act. I will do the best I can. It's nice to be liked, but not everybody will like me, and that isn't the end of the world." The theory behind this and similar assignments is that people often create a negative, self-fulfilling prophecy and actually fail because they told themselves in advance that they would. Clients are encouraged to carry out specific assignments during the sessions and, especially, in everyday situations between sessions. In this way they gradually learn to deal with anxiety and challenge basic irrational thinking.

Because therapy is seen as an educational process, clients are also encouraged to read rational-emotive self-help books, such as Ellis's *How to Stubbornly Refuse to Make Yourself Miserable about Anything — Yes, Anything!* (1988). They also listen to and criticize tapes of their own therapy sessions. Making changes is hard work, and doing work outside of the sessions is of real value in revising one's thinking, feeling, and behaving.

3. *Changing one's language.* RET contends that imprecise language is one of the causes of distorted thinking processes. Practitioners pay particular attention to the language patterns of their clients on the grounds that language shapes thinking and that thinking shapes language. Clients learn that "musts," "oughts," and "shoulds" can be replaced by *preferences.* Instead of saying "It would be absolutely awful if . . ." they can learn to say "It would be inconvenient if. . . ." Clients who use language patterns that reflect helplessness and self-condemnation can learn to employ new self-statements. They can assume personal power by replacing their "shoulds" and "musts" with nonabsolutistic preferences. Through the process of changing their language patterns and

making new self-statements, clients come to think and behave differently. As a consequence they also begin to feel differently.

4. *Use of humor.* A survey has revealed that humor is one of the most popular techniques of rational-emotive therapists (Warren & McLellarn, 1987). Ellis himself tends to use a good deal of humor as a way to combat exaggerated thinking that leads clients into trouble (1986a). RET contends that emotional disturbances often result from taking oneself too seriously and losing one's sense of perspective and humor over the events of life. Consequently, counselors employ humor to counterattack the overserious side of individuals and to assist them in disputing their musturbatory philosophy of life. In his workshops and therapy sessions Ellis typically uses rational, humorous songs, and he encourages people to sing to themselves or in groups when they feel depressed or anxious (Ellis & Yeager, 1989). He believes that humor shows the absurdity of certain ideas that clients steadfastly maintain. It is one approach that can be of value in helping clients take themselves much less seriously.

Emotive techniques.   Emotively, RET practitioners use a variety of procedures, including unconditional acceptance, rational-emotive role playing, modeling, rational-emotive imagery, and shame-attacking exercises. Clients are taught the value of unconditional acceptance. Even though their behavior may be difficult to accept, they can decide to see themselves as worthwhile persons. They are taught how destructive it is to engage in "putting oneself down" for perceived deficiencies. One of the main techniques that therapists employ to teach clients how to accept themselves is modeling. Therapists are able to be themselves in the sessions; they avoid seeking the approval of their clients, do not live by "shoulds" and "musts," and are willing to risk themselves as they continue to challenge their clients. They also model or display full acceptance of difficult clients.

It should be noted that regardless of the client's presenting problem, rational-emotive therapists do not necessarily focus on all its details, nor do they attempt to get the client to extensively express feelings surrounding the problem. They do not encourage "long tales of woes, sympathetically getting in tune with emotionalizing or carefully and incisively reflecting feelings" (Ellis, 1989, pp. 214–215). Although RET employs a variety of emotive and forceful therapeutic strategies, it does so in a selective and discriminating manner. These strategies are used both during the therapy sessions and as homework assignments in daily life. The purpose of such techniques is not simply to provide a cathartic experience but to help clients *change* some of their thoughts, emotions, and behavior (Ellis & Yeager, 1989). Some of these evocative and emotive therapeutic techniques include the following:

1. *Rational-emotive imagery.* This technique is a form of intense mental practice designed to establish new emotional patterns. Clients imagine themselves thinking, feeling, and behaving exactly the way they would like to think, feel, and behave in real life (Maultsby, 1984). They can also be shown how to imagine one of the worst things that could happen to them, how to feel inappropriately upset about this situation, how to intensely experience their feelings,

and then how to change the experience to an appropriate feeling (Ellis & Yeager, 1989). Once they are able to change their feelings to appropriate ones, they stand a better chance of changing their behavior in the situation. Such a technique can be usefully applied to interpersonal and other situations that are problematic for the individual. Ellis (1988) maintains that if we keep practicing rational-emotive imagery several times a week for a few weeks, we will reach the point that we no longer feel upset over such events. (If you are interested in an illustration of rational-emotive imagery, see Ellis, 1979a.)

2. *Role playing.* There are both emotional and behavioral components in role playing. The therapist often interrupts to show clients what they are telling themselves to create their disturbances and what they can do to change their inappropriate feelings to appropriate ones. Clients can rehearse certain behaviors to bring out what they feel in a situation. The focus is on working through the underlying irrational beliefs that are related to unpleasant feelings. For example, a woman may put off applying to a graduate school because of her fears of not being accepted. Just the thought of not being accepted to the school of her choice brings out her feelings of "being stupid." She role-plays an interview with the dean of graduate students, notes her anxiety and the irrational beliefs leading to it, and challenges the irrational thoughts that she absolutely *must* be accepted and that not gaining such acceptance means that she is a stupid and incompetent person.

3. *Shame-attacking exercises.* Ellis (1988) has developed exercises to help people get rid of irrational shame over behaving in certain ways. He thinks that we can stubbornly refuse to feel ashamed by telling ourselves that it is not catastrophic if someone thinks we are foolish. The main point of these exercises is that clients work to feel unashamed even when others clearly disapprove of them. This procedure typically involves both emotive and behavioral components. Clients may be given a homework assignment to take the risk of doing something that they are ordinarily afraid to do because of what others might think. Clients are not encouraged to engage in exercises that will bring harm to themselves or others. Minor infractions of social conventions often serve as useful catalysts. For example, clients may shout out the stops on a bus or a train, wear "loud" clothes designed to attract attention, sing at the top of their lungs, ask a silly question at a lecture, ask for a left-handed monkey wrench in a grocery store, or refuse to tip a waitress or waiter who gives them poor service. By carrying out such assignments, clients are likely to find out that other people are not really that interested in their behavior. They work on themselves so that they do not feel ashamed or humiliated. They continue practicing these exercises until they realize that their feelings of shame are self-created and until they are able to behave in less inhibited ways. Clients eventually learn that they often have no reason for continuing to let others' reactions or possible disapproval stop them from doing the things they would like to do.

4. *Use of force and vigor.* Ellis has suggested the use of force and energy as a way to help clients go from intellectual to emotional insight. Clients are also shown how to conduct forceful dialogues with themselves in which they express their irrational beliefs and then powerfully dispute them. Sometimes the therapist will engage in reverse role playing by strongly clinging to the client's

self-defeating philosophy; the client is asked to vigorously debate with the therapist in an attempt to persuade him or her to give up these dysfunctional ideas. Force and energy are a basic part of the shame-attacking exercises described above.

Behavioral techniques.   RET practitioners use most of the regular behavior-therapy procedures, especially operant conditioning, self-management principles, systematic desensitization, relaxation techniques, and modeling. Behavioral homework assignments to be carried out in real-life situations are particularly important. These assignments are done systematically and are recorded and analyzed on a form. Many involve desensitization, skill training, and assertiveness training. RET clients are encouraged to desensitize themselves gradually and also, at times, to perform the very things they dread doing. For example, a person with a fear of elevators may stare down his or her fears by going up and down in one 20 or 30 times in a day. Clients actually *do* new and difficult things, and in this way they put their insights to use in the form of concrete action. By acting differently, they also tend to change their irrational beliefs, such as "I'll always fail because I have failed so many times up to now."

APPLICATIONS OF RET TO CLIENT POPULATIONS

RET has been widely applied to the treatment of anxiety, hostility, character disorders, psychotic disorders, and depression; to problems of sex, love, and marriage; to child rearing and adolescence; and to social-skills training and self-management (Ellis, 1979b). Ellis does not assert that all clients can be helped through logical analysis and philosophical reconstruction. Some are not bright enough to follow a rigorous rational analysis. Some are too detached from reality. Some are too old and inflexible. Some are too philosophically prejudiced against logic to accept rational analysis. Some are chronic avoiders or shirkers who insist on looking for magical solutions. Some are simply unwilling to do the hard work that RET demands. And some seem to enjoy clinging to their misery and refuse to make any basic changes.

Some of the main areas of application are (1) individual therapy, (2) group therapy, (3) brief therapy, (4) marital therapy, and (5) family therapy (Ellis, 1989).

1. Application to individual therapy.   In one-to-one work RET tends to be focused on a specific problem and relatively short term. Ellis (1989) writes that most clients who are seen individually have one session weekly for anywhere from 5 to 50 sessions. The clients begin by discussing their most pressing problems and describing their most upsetting feelings. Then the therapist discovers the precipitating events that lead to the upsetting feelings. He or she also gets the clients to see the irrational beliefs that they associated with the events and gets them to dispute their irrational beliefs by assigning them homework activities that will help them directly work on undoing their irrational ideas and assist them in practicing more rational ways of being. Each week the therapist checks their progress, and the clients continually learn how to dispute their irrational system until they do more than merely lose their symptoms — that is, until they learn a more tolerant and rational way of living.

Ellis recommends that clients with severe emotional disturbances continue either individual or group therapy for up to a year so that they can practice what they are learning

2. Application to group therapy.   RET is very suitable for group therapy, for all the members are taught to apply RET principles to one another in the group setting. They get an opportunity to practice new behaviors that involve taking risks, and they get abundant opportunities to do homework assignments. Members also have an opportunity to experience assertiveness training, role playing, and a variety of risk-taking activities. They can learn social skills and practice interacting with others in after-group sessions. Both other group members and the leader can observe their behavior and give feedback. In individual therapy a client usually gives after-the-fact reports, but in a group setting clients are able to engage in contacts designed to foster a radical philosophical change. Ellis recommends that most RET clients experience group as well as individual therapy at some point.

3. Brief therapy.   By design, RET is appropriate as a brief therapy. For clients who will be in therapy for a relatively short time, the A-B-C approach to both understanding and starting to work on changing basic disturbance-creating attitudes can be done in from one to ten sessions. For people with specific problems — such as coping with the loss of a job or dealing with retirement — RET can be of help in a brief period. In such cases clients are taught how to apply RET principles to treat themselves, often with supplementary didactic materials (books, tapes, self-help forms, and the like). A useful device is for clients to tape their therapy sessions and then frequently listen to the entire tape on their own time. By engaging in this process, they get a better grasp on the nature of their problems and begin to see ways for coping with them.

For both professional mental-health workers and paraprofessionals, RET offers a useful perspective and tools for helping people who are experiencing a crisis. In most crises our cognitive perspective has a lot to do with how a particular event affects us. It is not simply the crisis itself that leads to disturbance, but how we interpret and react to the event. For example, consider a middle-aged man (Sam) who is suddenly told by his wife that she is leaving him, that she has been having a long-standing affair, and that she has never really felt love for him. Sam could approach a therapist feeling absolutely devastated, saying over and over that this proves that he is basically an "unlovable creep who will never be able to have a relationship with any woman!" In working with Sam it would be useful to think of an analogy to a computer program. How can Sam process this new information? If for years he has viewed his wife as a person who loved and appreciated him and as a person who would be eternally faithful to him, then accepting what is happening to him will be most difficult. The therapist could work with Sam's expectations, as well as with the self-damning things he is saying to himself. Although Sam might feel appropriately hurt, sad, and shocked, he could learn not to feel totally immobilized and devastated by his wife's actions. By using the tools of RET, Sam could challenge his limiting view that no woman would want anything to do with him. If he wanted a relationship with a woman eventually, he could challenge himself by doing what is necessary to go out and meet women. He might take a critical look at the ways he elevated his wife and the power he gave to her. In a relatively brief time Sam could begin to successfully cope with his emotional upsets by working on his thinking and self-verbalizations and by actually doing something differently.

4. Marital therapy.   RET practitioners typically see couples together. The therapist listens to each person's complaints but soon attempts to minimize guilt, depression, and hostility. The partners are taught the principles of RET so that they can work out their differences or at least become less disturbed about such differences. The couple are expected to decide whether they want to work on the relationship. If they are committed to dealing with some of their basic conflicts, they make contracts, discuss compromises, and learn how to speak directly and rationally with each other. The concern is with each person as an individual, not in keeping the relationship together at all costs. But communication, sexual, and other skills are also taught. As each person applies RET principles individually, the relationship often improves (Ellis & Dryden, 1987).

5. Application to family therapy.   The goals of RET family therapy are basically the same as those of individual therapy. Essentially, members of a family are helped to see that they are responsible for disturbing themselves by taking the actions of other members too seriously. They are encouraged to consider letting go of the demand that others in the family behave in ways they would like them to. Instead, RET teaches family members that they are primarily responsible for their own actions and for changing their own reactions to the family situation. The rational-emotive perspective is that one family member actually has little power to directly change another person in the family. As a family they are shown that each member has the power to control his or her individual thinking and feeling patterns. Thus, each person is in control of modifying his or her behavior, which may have an indirect effect on the family as a unit.

BECK'S COGNITIVE THERAPY

The approach known as *cognitive therapy,* developed by Beck, has a number of basic similarities to RET. Cognitive therapy shares with RET an active, directive, time-limited, structured approach (Beck, Rush, Shaw, & Emery, 1979). It is an insight therapy that emphasizes recognizing and changing negative thoughts and maladaptive beliefs. Beck's approach is based on the theoretical rationale that the way people feel and behave is determined by how they structure their experience. He did his work independently of Ellis, but their approaches have the same goal of helping clients recognize and discard self-defeating cognitions.

The basic theory of Beck's cognitive model of emotional disorders holds that in order to understand the nature of an emotional episode or disturbance, it is essential to focus on the cognitive content of an individual's reaction to the upsetting event or stream of thoughts (DeRubeis & Beck, 1988). The goal is to change the way the client thinks. Cognitive therapy has been successfully applied in treating depression, general anxiety, social anxiety, test anxiety, phobias, psychosomatic disorders, eating disorders, anger and chronic-pain problems (Beck, 1987, pp. 149, 158).

Principles of cognitive therapy.   Beck, a practicing psychoanalytic therapist for many years, grew interested in his clients' "automatic thoughts" (personalized notions that are triggered by particular stimuli that lead to emotional responses). He asked them to observe these thoughts, which seem to "just happen" as if by reflex and are difficult to "turn off.' Further, it appears that these negative thoughts persist even though they are contrary to objective evidence. People with emotional difficulties tend to commit "characteristic logical errors," which tilt objective reality in the direction of self-deprecation. Beck has concluded that the internal dialogue of clients plays a major role in behavior. The ways in which they monitor and instruct themselves, give themselves praise or criticism, interpret events, and make predictions shed considerable light on the dynamics of emotional disorders, such as depression.

Cognitive therapy is based on the assumption that cognitions are the major determinants of how we feel and act. Beck (1976) writes that, in the broadest sense, "cognitive therapy consists of all the approaches that alleviate psychological distress through the medium of correcting faulty conceptions and self-signals" (p. 214). For Beck the most direct route to changing dysfunctional emotions and behaviors is by modifying inaccurate and dysfunctional thinking. The following common distortions in processing information have been identified as leading to faulty assumptions and misconceptions (Beck et al., 1979; Beck & Weishaar, 1989):

• *Arbitrary inference* refers to reaching conclusions without sufficient and relevant evidence. This distortion includes "catastrophizing," or thinking of the absolute worst scenario for a situation. You may begin your first job as a counselor with the conviction that you will not be liked or valued by either your colleagues or your clients. You are convinced that you fooled your professors and somehow just managed to get your degree, but now people will certainly see through you.

• *Selective abstraction* consists of forming conclusions based on an isolated detail of an event and, thus, missing the significance of the overall context. The assumption is that the events that matter are those dealing with failure and deprivation. As a counselor you may measure your worth by your errors and weaknesses, not by your successes.

• *Overgeneralization* is a process of holding extreme beliefs on the basis of a single incident and applying them inappropriately to dissimilar events or settings. If you have difficulty in working with one adolescent, for example, you may conclude that you will not be effective in counseling any adolescents. You may also conclude that this proves that you will not be effective in working with *any* clients!

• *Magnification and exaggeration* consists of overestimating the significance of negative events. You could make this cognitive error by assuming that even minor mistakes in counseling a client could easily create a crisis and maybe even result in psychological damage.

• *Personalization* is a tendency for people to relate external events to themselves, even when there is no basis for making this connection. If a client does not return for a second counseling session, you may be absolutely convinced that this absence is due to your terrible performance during the initial session.

• *Polarized thinking* involves thinking and interpreting in all-or-nothing terms, or categorizing experiences in either/or extremes. With such dichotomous thinking, events are labeled in "good or bad" terms. For example, you may give yourself no latitude for being an imperfect person and an imperfect counselor. You may view yourself as being either the perfectly competent counselor (which means you always succeed with all clients) or a total flop if you are not fully competent (which means there is no room for any mistakes).

The cognitive therapist teaches clients how to identify distorted and dysfunctional cognitions through a process of evaluation. Through the collaborative therapist/client effort, clients learn to discriminate between their own thoughts and reality. They learn the influence that cognition has on their feelings, behaviors, and even environmental events. Clients are taught to recognize, observe, and monitor their own thoughts and assumptions, especially their negative "automatic thoughts."

After they have gained insight into how their unrealistically negative thoughts are affecting them, clients are trained to subject these automatic thoughts to reality testing, by examining the evidence for and against their cognitions. This process involves homework assignments, gathering data on the assumptions they make, keeping a record of activities, and forming alternative interpretations. Clients form hypotheses about their behavior and eventually learn to use specific problem-solving and coping skills. Like RET, cognitive therapy borrows heavily from the behavioral approaches. Eventually, clients learn to substitute realistic and accurate interpretations for their biased cognitions. They also learn to modify the dysfunctional beliefs and assumptions that predispose them to distort their experience (Beck et al., 1979).

The client/therapist relationship in cognitive therapy.   One of the main ways in which cognitive therapy differs from rational-emotive therapy is its emphasis on the therapeutic relationship. As you will recall, Ellis views the therapist largely as a teacher and does not think that a warm personal relationship with a client is essential, though it may have advantages. In contrast, Beck (1987) stresses the quality of the therapeutic relationship as basic to the application of cognitive therapy. Successful counseling rests on a number of desirable characteristics of the therapist, such as genuine warmth, accurate empathy, nonjudgmental acceptance, and the ability to establish trust and rapport with clients. The core therapeutic conditions described by Rogers in his person-centered approach are viewed by cognitive therapists as being necessary, but not sufficient, to produce the optimum therapeutic effect.

Techniques are most effectively applied in the context of a *therapeutic collaboration* between the therapist and client. Cognitive therapists are continuously active and deliberately interactive with clients; they also strive to engage the client's active participation throughout all phases of the therapy. The therapist and client work together to frame the client's conclusions in the form of a testable hypothesis. This process of co-investigation as a way to uncover and examine faulty interpretations is called *collaborative empiricism*. The assumption is that lasting changes in the client's thinking and behavior will be most likely to occur with the client's understanding, awareness, and effort (Beck, 1987; Beck et al., 1979).

Other differences from RET.   In both Beck's cognitive therapy and RET the reality testing is highly organized. Clients come to realize on an experiential level that they have misconstrued situations. Yet there are some important differences between RET and cognitive therapy, especially with respect to therapeutic methods and style. As is clear by now, RET is often highly directive, persuasive, and confrontive. In contrast, Beck emphasizes more of a Socratic dialogue, he places more stress on helping clients discover their misconceptions for themselves, and he generally applies more structure than RET. Further, cognitive therapy relates different disorders to clients' different cognitive styles, and therefore it uses different therapeutic interventions depending on the disorder. RET uses different methods depending on the individual personality and resistance of the client. In cognitive therapy the therapist does have preconceptions about the forms that maladaptive thinking frequently takes (as described earlier), but the therapist works with the client in collaborative ways more than is the case with RET, which is more educational.

Beck takes exception to RET's concept of irrational beliefs, asserting that telling clients that they are "thinking irrationally" can be detrimental, for many clients believe that they are "seeing things as they really are" (1976, p. 246). Instead, the therapist helps clients look for the evidence that supports or contradicts their views and hypotheses. Beck stresses *inaccurate conclusions.* He maintains that certain ideas are not irrational but, rather, too absolute, broad, and extreme. For Beck people live by *rules* (premises or formulas): they get into trouble when they label, interpret, and evaluate by a set of rules that is unrealistic or when they use the rules inappropriately or excessively. If clients make the determination that they are living by rules that are likely to lead to misery, the therapist may *suggest* alternative rules for them to consider, without indoctrinating them. Although cognitive therapy often begins by recognizing the client's frame of reference, the therapist continues to ask for evidence for a belief system. "Where is the evidence for . . . ?" is a question often posed to the client.

There are several other differences between Beck's therapy and RET, but many of them are trivial and depend on which style the therapist uses; many RET practitioners can be mild and slow-moving, and many cognitive therapists can be highly confrontative and fast-moving. Ellis himself uses a variety of styles with different clients and sometimes would appear to be much like Beck and Meichenbaum.

Rational-emotive therapists use virtually all the techniques used by Beckians but mainly differ as follows:

- RET holds that distorted cognitions often consist of distorted and over-generalized inferences and misperceptions of reality but that they usually stem from absolutistic, musturbatory thinking. Other cognitive therapists, including Beck, often ignore these tacit demands and commands.
- RET aims at deliberately getting clients to seek out their dogmatism and absolutistic thinking and to vigorously and repetitively minimize it.
- RET strives in most cases to enable clients to make a profound philosophical change, so that they become, preferably for the rest of their lives, more scientific, flexible thinkers.
- RET stresses unconditional self-acceptance instead of self-rating and actively teaches clients how to fully accept themselves *whether or not* they perform well and *whether or not* they are approved of and loved by significant others. Ideally, it strives to help clients *only* to rate their acts and traits and *not* to rate themselves.
- RET contends that people often forcefully hold on to their dogmatic thinking and that therapists therefore will succeed by using highly emotive, evocative techniques to help them vigorously and forcefully change this irrational thinking and behaving.
- RET stresses supplementary techniques, such as bibliotherapy, recordings, talks, workshops, group therapy, marathons, and intensive sessions, whereas cognitive therapy puts less emphasis on these educational methods.
- RET distinguishes between clients' strong, emotionally held rules, standards, and values, which it usually does not challenge, and their "musts" and demands *about* these values, which it usually does challenge. Unlike Beck, Meichenbaum, and other cognitive therapists, RET counselors hypothesize that people *learn* rules of living but often innately *transmute* these into absolutistic commands. Thus, RET shows them how to become more scientific and flexible and to abjure all dogmas and rigidities.

An example of applying cognitive therapy.   The following example represents an approach that a client might take in developing alternative interpretations of events and thus changing the feelings surrounding these events (Beck, 1976):

The *situation* is that your professor does not call on you during a particular class session. Your *feelings* may include depression. *Cognitively* you are thinking to yourself and telling yourself: "My professor thinks that I'm stupid and don't have much of value to offer the class. What's more, he's right, because everyone else is brighter and more articulate than I am." Some possible *alternative interpretations* are that the professor wants to include others in the discussion, that he is short on time and wants to move ahead, or that he already knows your views.

As can be readily seen from this example, Beck attempts to have clients become aware of the distortions in their thinking patterns. He has them look at their inferences, which may be faulty. They see how they sometimes come to a conclusion (your decision that you are stupid, with little of value to offer) when evidence for such a conclusion is lacking. Clients also learn about the process of magnification of thinking, which involves exaggeration of the meaning of an event (obviously the professor thinks you are stupid because he did not acknowledge you on this one occasion). Beck also stresses such distortions as disregarding important aspects of a situation, overly simplified and rigid thinking, and generalizing from a single incident of failure.

Treatment of depression.   Cognitive therapy was originally devised as a treatment for depression. Beck rejects the notion that depression results from anger turned inward. Instead, he focuses on the content of the depressive's negative thinking. Among depressed clients he found negative biases and cognitive errors (DeRubeis & Beck, 1988). Because he is considered one of the leading authorities on the subject of depression, I will illustrate how his therapeutic techniques can be applied in treating it.

Beck (1987) writes about the cognitive triad as a pattern that triggers depression. According to this model, three components contribute to the depression syndrome. In the first component of the triad clients hold a negative view of themselves. They blame their setbacks on personal inadequacies without considering circumstantial explanations. They are convinced that they lack the qualities that are essential to bring them happiness. The second component of the triad consists of the tendency to interpret experiences in a negative manner. It almost seems as if depressed people select certain facts that conform to their negative conclusions. The third component of the triad pertains to depressed clients' gloomy vision and projections about the future. They expect their present difficulties to continue, and they can anticipate only failure.

Depression-prone people often set rigid, perfectionistic goals for themselves, which are impossible to attain. The negative expectations of such people are so strong that even if they experience success in specific tasks, they anticipate failure the next time. They screen out successful experiences that are not consistent with their negative self-concept. The thought content of depressed individuals centers on significant loss. This sense of irreversible loss and negative expectation results in emotional states of sadness, disappointment, and apathy.

The Beck Depression Inventory (BDI) was designed as a standardized device to assess the depth of depression. The items are based on observations of the symptoms and basic beliefs of depressed people. The inventory contains the following 21 areas of symptoms and attitudes: (1) sadness, (2) pessimism, (3) sense of failure, (4) dissatisfaction, (5) guilt, (6) sense of punishment, (7) self-dislike, (8) self-accusations, (9) suicidal ideation, (10) crying spells, (11) irritability, (12) social withdrawal, (13) indecision, (14) distorted body image,

(15) work inhibition, (16) sleep disturbance, (17) tendency to become fatigued, (18) loss of appetite, (19) weight loss, (20) somatic preoccupations, and (21) loss of libido (Beck, 1975).

Applied to treating depressed clients, Beck's therapeutic approach focuses on specific problem areas (symptoms) and the reasons that clients give for such symptoms. Some of the behavioral symptoms of depression are inactivity, withdrawal, and avoidance. Clients report that they are too tired to do anything, that they will feel even worse if they become active, and that they will fail at anything they try. The therapist is likely to probe with Socratic questioning such as "What would be lost by trying? Will you feel worse if you are passive? How do you know that it is pointless to try?" Therapeutic procedures include setting up an activity schedule, with graded tasks to be completed. Clients are asked to complete easy tasks first, so that they will begin to be active, meet with some success, and become slightly more optimistic. The point is to enlist the client's cooperation with the therapist, on the assumption that *doing something* will lead to feeling better than *doing nothing.*

At times some depressed clients may harbor suicidal wishes. Behind these symptoms the following attitudes are often expressed: "I'm a burden to others. I can't cope with my problems. There is no point in going on. Since I'm so miserable, I need to escape." Cognitive-therapy strategies may include exposing the client's ambivalence, devising alternatives, and reducing problems to manageable proportions. For example, the therapist may ask the client to list the reasons for living and for dying. Further, if the client can develop alternative views of a problem, alternative courses of action can be thought of. This process can result in a client's not only feeling better but also behaving in more effective ways.

A central characteristic of most depressive people is self-criticism. Underneath the person's self-hate are attitudes of weakness, inadequacy, and lack of responsibility. A number of therapeutic strategies can be used. Clients can be asked to identify and provide reasons for their excessively self-critical behavior. The therapist may ask the client "If I were to make a mistake the way you do, would you despise me as much as you do yourself?" A skillful therapist may play the role of the depressed client, portraying himself or herself as inadequate, inept, and weak. This technique can be effective in demonstrating the client's cognitive distortions and arbitrary inferences. The therapist can then discuss with the client how the "tyranny of shoulds" can lead to self-hate and depression.

Depressed clients typically experience painful emotions. They may say that they cannot stand the pain or that nothing can make them feel better. One therapeutic procedure to counteract painful affect is humor. A therapist can demonstrate the ironical aspects of a situation. If clients can even briefly experience some light-heartedness in their life situation, it can serve as an antidote to their sadness. Such a shift in their cognitive set is simply not compatible with their self-critical attitude.

Another specific characteristic of depressed people is an exaggeration of external demands, problems, and pressures. Such people often exclaim that they feel overwhelmed and that there is so much to accomplish that they can never do it. A cognitive therapist may focus on problem resolution by asking the client to list things that need to be done, set priorities, check off tasks that have been accomplished, and break down an external problem into manageable units. When problems are discussed, clients often become aware of the ways in which they are magnifying the importance of these difficulties. Through rational exploration clients are able to regain a perspective on defining and accomplishing tasks.

The therapist typically has to take the lead in helping clients make a list of their responsibilities, set priorities, and develop a realistic plan of action. Because carrying out such a plan is often inhibited by self-defeating thoughts, it is well for therapists to use cognitive-rehearsal techniques in both identifying and changing negative thoughts. If clients can learn to combat their self-doubts in the therapy session, they may be able to apply their newly acquired cognitive and behavioral skills in real-life situations.

MEICHENBAUM'S COGNITIVE BEHAVIOR MODIFICATION

Another major alternative to rational-emotive therapy is Meichenbaum's cognitive behavior modification (CBM). His self-instructional therapy, which is basically a form of cognitive restructuring, focuses on changing the client's self-verbalizations. According to Meichenbaum (1977), self-statements affect a person's behavior in much the same way as statements made by another person. A basic premise of CBM is that, as a prerequisite to behavior change, clients must notice how they think, feel, and behave and the impact they have on others. For change to occur, clients need to interrupt the scripted nature of their behavior so that they can evaluate their behavior in various situations (Meichenbaum, 1986).

This approach shares with RET and Beck's cognitive therapy the assumption that distressing emotions are typically the result of maladaptive thoughts. There are differences, however, between RET and Meichenbaum's approach. Whereas RET is more direct and confrontational in uncovering and attacking irrational thoughts, Meichenbaum's self-instructional therapy focuses more on helping clients become aware of their self-talk. The therapeutic process consists of training clients to modify the instructions they give to themselves so that they can cope more effectively with the problems they encounter. The emphasis is on acquiring practical coping skills for problematic situations such as impulsive and aggressive behavior, fear of taking tests, and fear of public speaking.

Cognitive restructuring plays a central role in Meichenbaum's approach. He describes *cognitive structure* as the organizing aspect of thinking, which seems to monitor and direct the choice of thoughts (1977). Cognitive structure implies an "executive processor," which "holds the blueprints of thinking" that determine when to continue, interrupt, or change thinking.

How behavior changes.   Meichenbaum proposes that "behavior change occurs through a sequence of mediating processes involving the interaction of inner speech, cognitive structures, and behaviors and their resultant outcomes"

(1977, p. 218). He describes a three-phase process of change in which those three aspects are interwoven. According to him, focusing on only one aspect will probably prove insufficient.

Phase 1: Self-observation. The beginning step in the change process consists of clients' learning how to observe their own behavior. When they begin therapy, their internal dialogue is characterized by negative self-statements and imagery. A critical factor is their willingness and ability to *listen* to themselves. This process involves an increased sensitivity to their thoughts, feelings, actions, physiological reactions, and ways of reacting to others. If depressed clients hope to make constructive changes, for example, they must first realize that they are not a "victim" of negative thoughts and feelings. Rather, they are actually contributing to their depression through the things they tell themselves. Although self-observation is seen as a necessary process if change is to occur, it is not sufficient, per se, for change. As therapy progresses, clients acquire new cognitive structures that enable them to view their problems in a new light. This reconceptualization process comes about through a collaborative effort between the client and therapist.

Phase 2: Starting a new internal dialogue. As a result of the early client/ therapist contacts, clients learn to notice their maladaptive behaviors, and they begin to see opportunities for adaptive behavioral alternatives that will lead to behavioral, cognitive, and affective changes. If clients hope to change, what they say to themselves must initiate a new behavioral chain, one that is incompatible with their maladaptive behaviors. Clients learn to change their internal dialogue through therapy. Their new internal dialogue serves as a guide to new behavior. In turn, this process has an impact on the client's cognitive structures.

Phase 3: Learning new skills. The third phase of the modification process consists of teaching clients more effective coping skills, which are practiced in real-life situations. (For example, clients who can't cope with failure may avoid appealing activities for fear of not succeeding at them. Cognitive restructuring can help them change their negative view of failure, thus making them more willing to engage in desired activities.) At the same time, clients continue to focus on telling themselves new sentences and observing and assessing the outcomes. As they behave differently in situations, they typically get different reactions from others. The stability of what they learn is greatly influenced by what they say to themselves about their newly acquired behavior and its consequences.

Coping-skills programs.   The rationale for coping-skills programs is that we can acquire more effective strategies in dealing with stressful situations by learning how to modify our cognitive "set." In brief, there is a five-step treatment procedure designed to teach these coping skills by:

1. exposing clients to anxiety-provoking situations by means of role playing and imagery
2. requiring clients to evaluate their anxiety level
3. teaching clients to become aware of the anxiety-provoking cognitions they experience in stressful situations

4. helping clients examine these thoughts by reevaluating their self-statements
5. having clients note the level of anxiety following this reevaluation

Research studies have demonstrated the success of coping-skills programs when applied to problems such as speech anxiety, test anxiety, phobias, anger, social incompetence, addictions, alcoholism, sexual dysfunctions, and social withdrawal in children (Meichenbaum, 1977, 1986).

A particular application of a coping-skills program is teaching clients stress-management techniques by way of a strategy known as "stress inoculation." Using cognitive techniques, Meichenbaum (1985) has developed stress-inoculation procedures that are a psychological and behavioral analog to immunization on a biological level. Individuals are given opportunities to deal with relatively mild stress stimuli in successful ways, so that they gradually develop a tolerance for stronger stimuli. This training is based on the assumption that we can affect our ability to cope with stress by modifying our beliefs and self-statements about our performance in stressful situations. Meichenbaum's stress-inoculation training is concerned with more than merely teaching people specific coping skills. His program is designed to prepare clients for intervention and motivate them to change, and it deals with issues such as resistance and relapse. Stress-inoculation training (SIT) consists of a combination of information giving, Socratic discussion, cognitive restructuring, problem solving, relaxation training, behavioral rehearsals, self-monitoring, self-instruction, self-reinforcement, and modifying environmental situations. This approach is designed to teach coping skills that can be applied to both present problems and future difficulties.

Meichenbaum (1985) has designed a three-stage model for stress-inoculation training: (1) the conceptual phase, (2) the skills-acquisition and rehearsal phase, and (3) the application and follow-through phase.

During the initial stage of SIT — the *conceptual phase* — the primary focus is on creating a working relationship with clients. This is mainly done by helping them gain a better understanding of the nature of stress and reconceptualizing it in social-interactive terms. The therapist enlists the client's collaboration during this early phase. Together the two rethink the nature of the problem(s). Initially, clients are provided with a conceptual framework in simple terms designed to help them understand the ways in which they are responding to a variety of stressful situations. They learn about the role that cognitions and emotions play in creating and maintaining stress. They are taught this by didactic presentations, through Socratic questioning, and by a process of guided self-discovery.

Clients often begin treatment feeling that they are the victims of external circumstances, thoughts, feelings, and behaviors over which they have no control. Training includes teaching them to become aware of their own role in creating their stress. They acquire this awareness by systematically observing the statements they make internally as well as monitoring the maladaptive behaviors that flow from this inner dialogue. Such self-monitoring continues throughout all the phases. As is true in cognitive therapy, clients typically keep an open-ended diary in which they systematically record their specific thoughts, feelings, and behaviors. In teaching these coping skills, therapists strive to be flexible in their use of techniques and to be sensitive to the individual, cultural, and situational circumstances of their clients.

The second stage of SIT—the *skills-acquisition and rehearsal phase*—focuses on giving clients a variety of behavioral and cognitive coping techniques to apply to stressful situations. This phase involves *direct actions,* such as gathering information about their fears, learning specifically what situations bring about stress, arranging for ways to lessen the stress by doing something different, and learning methods of physical and psychological relaxation. The training involves *cognitive coping;* clients are taught that adaptive and maladaptive behaviors are linked to their inner dialogue. They acquire and rehearse a new set of self-statements. Meichenbaum (1986) provides some examples of coping statements that are rehearsed in this phase of SIT:

- "How can I prepare for a stressor?" ("What do I have to do? Can I develop a plan to deal with the stress?")
- "How can I confront and deal with what is stressing me?" ("What are some ways I can handle a stressor? How can I meet this challenge?")
- "How can I cope with feeling overwhelmed?" ("What can I do right now? How can I keep my fears in check?")
- "How can I make reinforcing self-statements?" ("How can I give myself credit?")

As a part of the stress-management program, clients are also exposed to various behavioral interventions, some of which include relaxation training, social-skills training, time-management instruction, and self-instructional training. They are helped to make lifestyle changes such as reevaluating priorities, developing support systems, and taking direct action to alter stressful situations. Clients are introduced to a variety of methods of relaxation and are taught to use these skills to decrease arousal due to stress. Through teaching, demonstration, and guided practice, clients learn the skills of progressive relaxation, which are to be practiced regularly. Other approaches that are recommended for learning to relax include meditation, yoga, tensing and relaxing muscle groups, and breath-control techniques. Relaxation also includes activities such as walking, jogging, gardening, knitting, or other physical activities. Meichenbaum stresses that relaxation is as much a state of mind as it is a physical state.

In the third phase of SIT—the *application and follow-through phase*—the focus is on carefully arranging for transfer and maintenance of change from the therapeutic situation to the real world. It is clear that teaching coping skills is a complex procedure that relies on varied treatment programs. For clients to merely say new things to themselves is generally not sufficient to produce change. They need to practice these self-statements and apply their new skills in real-life situations. Once they have become proficient in cognitive and behavioral coping skills, they practice behavioral assignments, which become increasingly demanding. Clients are asked to write down the homework assignments that they are willing to complete. The outcomes of these assignments are carefully checked at subsequent meetings, and if clients do not follow through with them, the trainer and the client collaboratively consider the reasons for the failure. Follow-up and booster sessions typically take place at 3-, 6-, and 12-month periods as an incentive for clients to continue practicing and refining their coping skills. SIT can be considered part of an ongoing stress-management program that extends the benefits of training into the future.

Stress-management training has potentially useful applications for a wide variety of problems and clients, both for remediation and prevention. Some of these applications include anger control, anxiety management, assertion training, improving creative thinking, treating depression, and dealing with health problems. The approach has also been used in treating obese people, hyperactive children, social isolates, and schizophrenics (Meichenbaum, 1977, 1935).

SUMMARY AND EVALUATION

SUMMARY

RET is a form of cognitively oriented behavioral therapy. It has evolved into a comprehensive and eclectic approach that emphasizes thinking, judging, deciding, and doing. The approach retains Ellis's highly didactic and directive quality, and RET is as much concerned with the cognitive dimensions as with feelings. It starts with clients' disturbed emotions and behaviors and reveals and disputes the thoughts that directly create them.

Although RET assumes that we have the capacity for straight thinking, the tendencies toward crooked thinking and environmental factors make it difficult to avoid subscribing to irrational beliefs that are at the root of our problems in thinking, feeling, and behaving. In order to block the self-defeating beliefs that are reinforced by a process of self-indoctrination, RET therapists employ active and directive techniques such as teaching, suggestion, persuasion, and homework assignments, and they challenge clients to substitute a rational belief system for an irrational one. They do this by continually urging clients to validate their observations and ideas and showing them how to do this type of refutation themselves. They demonstrate how and why irrational beliefs lead to negative emotional and behavioral results. They teach clients how to think scientifically and how to annihilate new self-defeating ideas and behaviors that might occur in the future.

It is crucial that therapists demonstrate full acceptance and tolerance. They do so by refusing to judge the person while at the same time confronting self-destructive behaviors. Also given primary importance is the therapist's skill and willingness to challenge, confront, probe, and convince the client to practice activities (both inside and outside of therapy) that will lead to constructive changes in the client's thinking and behaving. RET stresses action — doing something about the insights one gains in therapy. Change comes about mainly by a commitment to consistently practice new behaviors that replace old and ineffective ones.

Rational-emotive therapists are typically eclectic in selecting therapeutic strategies. They draw heavily on cognitive and behavioral techniques that are geared to uprooting the irrational beliefs that lead to self-defeating feelings and behaviors and to teaching clients how to replace this negative process with a rational philosophy of life. Therapists have the latitude to develop their own personal style and to exercise creativity; they are not bound by fixed techniques for particular problems. As long as they stay within the spirit of rational-emotive theory, therapists have the freedom to bring themselves into their therapeutic work in inventive ways.

As we have seen, RET is the forerunner of other cognitive-behavioral therapies. Two therapies that are considered modifications and, in some ways, extensions of RET are Beck's *cognitive therapy* and Meichenbaum's *cognitive behavior modification*. These therapies stress the importance of cognitive processes as determinants of behavior. They maintain that how people *feel* and what they actually *do* is largely influenced by their subjective assessment of situations. Because this appraisal of life situations is influenced by beliefs, attitudes, assumptions, and internal dialogue, such cognitions become the major focus of therapy.

CONTRIBUTIONS OF THE RATIONAL-EMOTIVE APPROACH

There are aspects of RET that I find to be very valuable as I work with clients, either individually or in groups. I believe that significant others in our past have contributed to the shaping of our current lifestyle and philosophy of life. Yet, in strong agreement with Ellis, I contend that we are the ones who are responsible for maintaining certain self-destructive ideas and attitudes that influence our daily transactions. We may have learned that we should be perfect and that it is essential to be loved and approved of by everyone; the problem, however, is that we still apply these notions relentlessly to ourselves. I see value in confronting clients with questions such as "What are your assumptions and basic beliefs? Have you really scrutinized some of the core ideas that you live by to determine if they are your own values or merely introjects?"

In addition, I value thinking as well as feeling and experiencing in psychotherapy. I am critical of many group approaches, particularly encounter and sensitivity groups, where thinking, judging, and evaluating are looked on with scorn and where experiencing here-and-now feelings and "gut reactions" is seen as equivalent to psychological health. After a person has experienced a cathartic or highly intensive emotional experience related to earlier traumas, some attempt at conceptualization and giving meaning to the experience is essential if it is to have any lasting effect. RET does offer the cognitive dimension and does challenge clients to examine the rationality of many of their decisions and values.

Another contribution of RET is its emphasis on putting newly acquired insights into action. The homework-assignment method is well suited to enabling clients to practice new behaviors and assisting them in the process of their reconditioning. Reality therapy, Adlerian therapy, behavior therapy, and transactional analysis share with RET this action orientation. Clients can gain a multitude of insights and can become very aware of the nature of their problems, but I question the value of self-understanding unless specific plans that lead to behavioral changes desired by the client are implemented. RET insists on this action phase as a crucial part of the therapy process.

A major contribution of RET is its emphasis on a comprehensive and eclectic therapeutic practice. Numerous cognitive, emotive, and behavioral techniques can be employed in changing one's emotions and behaviors by changing the structure of one's cognitions. Further, RET is open to using therapeutic procedures derived from other schools, especially from behavior therapy

Another contribution is the nondeterministic stance that we are not helpless victims of past unfortunate events. RET has built on the Adlerian notion that events themselves do not have the power to shape us; rather, it is our interpretation of these events that is crucial. The A-B-C model simply and clearly illustrates how human disturbances occur and the ways that problematic behavior can be changed. This approach has shed light on how the therapist can focus on the subjective process whereby clients interpret and react to what happens to them, rather than making situations and events the prime focus in therapy.

Although there are other advantages of RET one more that I would like to mention is the benefit of teaching clients ways that they can carry on their own therapy without the direct intervention of a therapist. I applaud RET's emphasis on supplementary approaches such as listening to tapes, doing action-oriented homework, keeping a record of what they do (as well as what they think and feel) during the week, reading self-help books, and attending lectures and workshops. In this way they can further the process of change in themselves without becoming excessively dependent on a therapist.

Research efforts in RET.   RET is characterized by a growing collection of therapeutic strategies for helping people change their maladaptive cognitions. Therapists typically use a combination of cognitive, behavioral, and emotive methods within a single session with any given client. If a particular technique does not seem to be producing results, the therapist is likely to switch to another one. This type of technical eclecticism and therapeutic flexibility makes controlled research difficult (Wessler, 1986).

In spite of these difficulties both RET and other cognitive-behavioral therapies have been subjected to extensive research. There are methodological shortcomings in many of these studies, such as inadequate control groups (DiGiuseppe, Miller, & Trexler, 1979). Most of this research focuses either on the cognitive dimension as a key factor in emotional disturbance or on therapeutic outcomes.

In one of his articles Ellis (1979c) deals with a review of research literature that supports cognitive-behavioral therapy in general as well as RET in particular. He concludes that RET has "immense — indeed, almost awesome — research backing" (p. 103). In a review of outcome studies of RET from 1977 to 1982, McGovern and Silverman (1986) report general findings that support the efficacy of RET. Of the 47 studies reviewed, 31 had significant findings in favor of the RET position. In the remaining studies the RET-treatment groups showed improvement, and in no study was another treatment technique significantly superior. Recent reviews have also shown that RET has clinical effectiveness (Engels & Dienstra, 1987; Haaga & Davison, 1989; Jcrm, 1987). One of the strengths of RET and other cognitive-behavioral approaches is their willingness to conduct research to assess the effectiveness of techniques.

Other cognitive approaches.   Most of the therapies considered in this book can be considered "cognitive," in a general sense, because they have the aim of changing clients' subjective views of themselves and the world. But the cognitive-behavioral therapies explored in this chapter are different in their focus both on undermining faulty assumptions and beliefs and on teaching clients effective coping skills needed to deal with their problems.

Beck's key concepts are very similar to Ellis's, though there are some differences with reference to therapeutic techniques. Beck made pioneering efforts in the treatment of anxiety, phobias, and depression. He developed specific cognitive procedures that are useful in challenging a depressive client's assumptions and beliefs and in providing a new cognitive perspective that can lead to optimism and changed behavior. In a review of the empirical status of Beck's cognitive therapy, Haaga and Davison (1986) conclude that its effects on depression and hopelessness seem to be maintained for at least one year after treatment. A number of experiments support the efficacy of his approach for depressed clients.

As we have seen, Meichenbaum is one of the leading figures in cognitive-behavioral therapy. His work in self-instruction therapy and stress-inoculation training has been applied successfully to a variety of client populations and specific problems. Of special note is his contribution to understanding how stress is largely self-induced through inner dialogue. His specific therapy techniques are particularly applicable to teaching stress management. But he has gone beyond simply adding a few cognitive techniques to behavior therapy and has actually broadened its theoretical base through his demonstration of the importance of self-talk (Patterson, 1986). Meichenbaum (1986) cautions cognitive-behavioral practitioners against the tendency to become overly preoccupied with techniques. Instead, he suggests that if progress is to be made, cognitive behavior modification must develop a testable theory of behavior change. He reports that some attempts have been made to formulate a cognitive social-learning theory that will explain behavior change and that will specify the best methods of intervention.

Contributions of rational-emotive and cognitive-behavioral therapy from a multicultural perspective.   RET and the other cognitive-behavioral therapies have certain advantages in cross-cultural situations. If ethnic clients are not challenged too quickly, they can be effectively invited to examine the premises on which they base their behavior. Consider an Asian-American client (let's call her Sung) from a particular culture that stresses values such as doing one's best, cooperating, and working hard. Sung is struggling with feelings of guilt because she perceives that she is not living up to the expectations and standards set for her by her family and her community. She feels that she is bringing shame to her family by going through a divorce.

If a counselor confronts Sung too quickly on living by the expectations of others, the results are likely to be counterproductive. In fact, she may leave counseling because she feels misunderstood. A sensitive RET or other cognitive-behavioral practitioner may, however, encourage her to begin to question how she might have uncritically accepted all of the messages from her cultural background. Without encouraging her to abandon respect for her heritage, the therapist can still challenge her to examine the consequences of basing her behavior totally on her belief system. If Sung maintains that she is worried about letting her parents down and that she feels as though she is a failure because she did not make her marriage work, it is not wise to judge her basic values and beliefs as "irrational." If her therapist understands the cultural context in which divorce is interpreted as being shameful, she can be helped to sort out the rational components from those beliefs that are leading to her difficulties. Also, she can gradually begin to understand some of the consequences of trying as hard as she does to live up to both her own standards and those of her family As is the case for many other ethnic-minority clients, Sung is likely to be torn between two cultures. So it is crucial for a counselor to help her explore her values and gain a full awareness of her conflicting feelings. It is important to point out that she may retain many facets of her culture even though she chooses to make certain modifications in her beliefs and practices.

Because counselors with a cognitive-behavioral orientation function as teachers, their focus is on imparting skills to deal with the problems of living. In speaking with colleagues who work with culturally diverse populations, I have learned that their clients tend to appreciate an emphasis on cognition and action as well as on relationship issues. Beck's cognitive therapy certainly stresses modes of thinking and acting as well as the quality of the interpersonal relationship between the client and the counselor. His collaborative approach offers ethnic clients the structure they often feel they need, yet the therapist still makes every effort to enlist their active cooperation and participation. Clients are challenged to think about their thinking to determine the impact their beliefs have on what they do.

Another advantage of the cognitive-behavioral approaches is that they play down the notion of mental illness and cures. Although the sense of shame surrounding mental illness may be characteristic of nonethnic clients, as well, it is even more pronounced with many minority clients. Life can be more fulfilling if clients learn better ways to think about the issues that are confronting them. The counselor teaches the client how she became disturbed by using the A-B-C model of personality or by helping her assess her cognitive errors. One of the counselor's functions is to teach her how to dispute her faulty thinking and how to change her self-defeating style of life. With the help of the therapist the client learns new ways of thinking and behaving, which result in new feelings.

LIMITATIONS AND CRITICISMS OF RATIONAL-EMOTIVE THERAPY

My major criticisms directed against RET involve the aspects of the client's life that are denied and ignored by the approach As you will recall, rational-emotive therapists do not listen to a client's history, and they surely do not encourage clients to recount "long tales of woes." They make little use of unconscious dynamics, free association, dream work, and the transference relationship. Although some RET practitioners emphasize the building of rapport and a collaborative relationship between the therapist and the client, Ellis maintains that dimensions such as personal warmth, liking for the client, and personal interest or caring are not essential ingredients for effective therapy.

In my view of therapeutic practice there is value in paying attention to a client's past, without getting lost in this past and without assuming a fatalistic stance about earlier traumatic experiences. I find it hard to believe that clients can make lasting and significant changes until they first recognize and accept their history and then come to terms with past unfinished conflicts so that these feelings do not interfere with their present functioning. I also value the therapeutic power of tools such as free association, dream work, and working with transference as it appears in the therapy relationship. When transference appears, Ellis would attack it on the ground that the client is inventing a false connection between the therapist and some significant other in the client's past. I think that such feelings can teach clients about areas in their life that they still need to explore and resolve. Attacking such feelings hardly helps the client to work therapeutically with them.

Many clients can easily be intimidated by such quick confrontation, especially *before* the therapist has *earned* their respect and trust by building a solid relationship. If clients feel that they are not being listened to or that they are not really being cared about, there is a good chance that they may prematurely leave therapy. Here is where person-centered therapy can be coupled nicely with some of the active and directive procedures of RET. It seems important to me that the core therapeutic conditions in creating a relationship expounded by Rogers and the other person-centered practitioners are an excellent way to begin the therapy venture. Once the client and the therapist have worked on trust issues and after the client *feels* heard, accepted, and cared for by the therapist, challenge and confrontation are in order.

Finally, a concern I have about RET as it is sometimes practiced is that clients can easily acquiesce in a therapist's power and authority by readily accepting the therapist's views without really challenging them or without internalizing new ideas. As a precaution it seems essential for therapists to know themselves well and to take care not to merely impose their own philosophy of life on their clients. The issue of what constitutes rational behavior is central here. The fact that the rational-emotive therapist assumes such a confrontive and directive position creates certain dangers. The therapist's level of training, knowledge, skill, perceptiveness, and accuracy of judgment are particularly important in RET. Because the therapist has a large degree of power by virtue of persuasion and directiveness, psychological harm is more possible in RET than in the less directive person-centered approach. The therapist must be aware of when to "push" clients and when not to. There is the danger that an untrained therapist who uses RET might view therapy as "beating down" clients with persuasion, indoctrination, logic, and advice. Thus, a practitioner can misuse RET by reducing it to dispensing quick-cure methods—that is, by telling clients what is wrong with them and how they should change.

Ways to limit hazards.   If RET is done in the manner prescribed by Ellis, however, these dangers are considerably lessened. Ellis rarely questions his clients' desires, preferences, values, or morality. What he does question is their "musts," "shoulds," and irrational demands. Thus, if someone says "I want romantic love" or "I prefer to be sexually abstinent," Ellis would rarely disagree. However, if the person said instead "I *must* be loved romantically" or "I *have* to be abstinent under all conditions," he would challenge such *must*urbatory views and encourage the client to change them to strong preferences. It is Ellis's belief that his brand of RET, by showing clients that even rationality is *desirable* but not *necessary,* minimizes bigotry, absolutism, and emotional disturbance.

It is well to underscore that RET can be done by many people in a manner different from Ellis's style. Because he has so much visibility, it is worth distinguishing between the principles and techniques of RET and his very confrontational way of doing RET. A therapist can be soft-spoken and gentle and still use RET concepts and methods. At times new RET practitioners may assume that they *must* follow the fast pace of Ellis. Walen et al. (1980) maintain that this assumption is not correct, because the novice therapist may not be able to replicate Ellis's performance. RET practitioners use many effective styles. Wessler and Wessler (1980), agreeing that there is no one way to practice RET, write that a therapist may use different styles, depending on the client and what is happening during a particular session. They add: "Thus, RET is not synonymous with a particular style. Nor is it synonymous with particular techniques. RET therapists differ in techniques used, amount of activity, and degree of directiveness, although we are all to some degree active and directive" (p. 20).

In his critique of Meichenbaum's cognitive behavior modification, Patterson (1986) raises some excellent questions that can apply to most cognitive-behavioral therapies. The basic issue is discovering the best way to change a client's internal dialogue. Is directly teaching the client the most effective approach? Is the client's failure to think rationally or logically always due to a lack of understanding of reasoning or problem solving? Is the most effective way to modify client self-statements through didactic instruction? Is learning by self-discovery more effective and longer lasting than being taught by a therapist?

A criticism that I have of all the cognitive-behavioral approaches, including RET, is that they are less concerned with unconscious factors and ego defenses than I would like. I question the assumption of these approaches that most problems can be resolved without exploring unconscious material. I also question the view of most cognitive therapists that exploring the client's past is ineffective in helping clients change faulty thinking and behavior. In some cases not enough emphasis is given to encouraging clients to express and explore their feelings. I think that cognitive therapy can work best once clients have experienced their feelings, which often occurs when they relive and work through emotional issues from their past.

Limitations of RET from a multicultural perspective.   Since exploring values plays such an important role in RET, it is crucial for the therapist to have some understanding of clients' cultural background and to be sensitive to their struggles. Luis might say: "All my life I've been taught to respect my father. Although I do have respect and love for him, I'm thinking that there are some choices that I want to make about my life that are not in line with his choice for me. I've always told myself that I simply can't disappoint my father, so I've subjugated my wishes and followed his will." A therapist who would insensitively confront Luis's beliefs as irrational would not be respecting his values and would be ignoring his strengths. Even though it might be therapeutic for him to question some of his beliefs, it is critical that the counselor not err by imposing mainstream standards on him. Therapists would do well to use caution in challenging ethnic clients until they clearly understand the cultural context of their beliefs and behavior patterns.

One limitation of RET in multicultural settings stems from its negative interpretation of dependency. Many cultures view dependency as necessary to good mental health. According to Ellis (1989), "To keep clients from becoming and remaining unduly dependent, RET therapists often deliberately use hardheaded methods of convincing clients that they had damned well better resort to more self-discipline" (p. 198). Clients with certain long-cherished cultural values pertaining to dependency are not likely to respond favorably to such "hardheaded methods" of persuasion.

Haaga and Davison (1986) express a concern over the RET emphasis on the individual's being self-sufficient and tough enough to cope with life's difficulties without needing love and support from others. As mentioned before, the Asian culture (and certain other non-Western cultures as well) promotes interdependence as opposed to individualism, stressing the importance of the individual's tailoring his or her behavior to the needs of the family and the larger community. For clients who place considerable value on cooperation and harmony in their family context, the emphasis on not needing others' support could lead to increased difficulties for both them and others in their family. If they are told that they do not need (but merely prefer) such approval and support, they are likely to experience even greater conflict. An effective RET therapist, however, does not challenge their strong desires and values but, rather, their absolutist demands that family members support them.

A potential limitation of RET and other cognitive-behavioral therapies is that ethnic-minority clients could become dependent on the counselor to make decisions about what constitutes rationality and about the appropriate ways to solve problems. If the therapist is not well qualified, it would be easy to assume a highly directive stance that would keep the client in a dependent position. In some cultures, however, this dependency may be viewed positively. The RET clinician walks a fine line between being directive and promoting dependence. Although RET practitioners may be active and directive, it is important that they teach their clients to question and to assume an active role in the therapeutic process. This is especially important with clients from some ethnic groups, who may have been conditioned to accept the counselor's word because they see the counselor as an authority figure.

QUESTIONS FOR REFLECTION AND DISCUSSION

1. Do you believe that it is desirable for one to "think" one's way through "irrational" aspects of life such as joy, ecstasy, craziness, sadness, despair, abandonment and loneliness, rage, fear, and hatred? Should one be "cured" of those feelings? What would life be like if one were almost exclusively rational?

2. RET views anxiety as frequently the result of self-blame. Ellis maintains that blaming ourselves or others is pernicious. Do you agree? Is it desirable to remove all guilt? If one gets to a point where one never experiences guilt, does this mean that one is an accomplished psychopath? What kind of guilt is healthy? What kind is unhealthy?

3. Do you agree with the contention that one does not need love and acceptance from other significant people? Is it realistic to teach a client ways of enjoying life while feeling unloved? Is this a persuasive form of denial?

4. Can you apply to yourself the view that one tends to keep irrational ideas alive by repeating those ideas to oneself? What are some examples in your own life?

5. Review Ellis's list of common irrational ideas that many of us have learned in society. What is your evaluation of these ideas? What other irrational ideas could you add to the list? What ideas can you relate to personally? In what ways do you still cling to some irrational premises? Have you tried to eradicate them?

6. What do you consider to be some of the major contributions of the cognitive-behavioral therapies? How do you think that cognitive factors influence one's emotions and behaviors?

7. Assume that a client came to you with a specific goal of learning how to effectively manage stress. Using Meichenbaum's stress-inoculation techniques, how might you design a program to help this client?

8. In working with a culturally diverse population, what are some guidelines you would follow to determine when and how to use some of the more active and forceful RET techniques? What are your thoughts about showing respect for clients' cultural values and beliefs and at the same time challenging them on what you consider dysfunctional beliefs?

9. What are some of the basic characteristics of Beck's cognitive therapy? How is it similar to Ellis's RET? What are the differences between the two?

10. Assume that Stan is still your client and that he has yet to be "cured." What are his central irrational beliefs? As a cognitive therapist how would you challenge his faulty thinking? What might you say? And what might you do?

WHERE TO GO FROM HERE

The Institute for Rational-Emotive Therapy in New York City offers a variety of professional training programs involving a primary certificate, an intermediate certificate, an associate fellowship, and a fellowship program. Each of these programs has different requirements, including clinical experience, supervision, and experience in personal therapy. Several affiliated branches of RET around the world offer official programs of study. You can get a catalog describing RET workshops, books, cassette tapes, films, self-help forms, software items, and an order form for publications by contacting:

Institute for Rational-Emotive Therapy
45 East 65th Street
New York, NY 10021-6593
Telephone: (212) 535-0822

The *Journal of Rational Emotive and Cognitive-Behavior Therapy* is published by Human Sciences Press, Inc., 72 Fifth Avenue, New York, NY 10011-8004. This journal is an excellent way to keep informed of the developments in RET. It is published quarterly.

RECOMMENDED SUPPLEMENTARY READINGS

Handbook of Rational-Emotive Therapy: Vol. 2 (Ellis & Grieger, 1986) is a comprehensive and updated work that deals with the theoretical and conceptual foundations of RET, the dynamics of emotional disturbance, specific techniques to promote change, and applications of RET.

Handbook of Cognitive-Behavioral Therapies (Dobson, 1988a) is a well-balanced collection of chapters on problem-solving therapies, self-management therapies, cognitive-behavioral methods with children, RET, Beck's cognitive therapy, and an overview of the current status and future of the cognitive-behavioral therapies.

The Practice of Rational-Emotive Therapy (Ellis & Dryden, 1987) specifically shows how RET is used individually, with couples and families, in groups, and in other ways.

Cognitive Therapy of Depression (Beck, Rush, Shaw, & Emery, 1979) describes techniques used with depressed clients. The wide range of cognitive techniques included make this a useful handbook for practitioners.

New Directions in Cognitive Therapy: A Casebook (Emery, Holland, & Bedrosian, 1981) emphasizes the clinical application of the cognitive approach in working with a variety of special populations. The casebook also describes treatment of a range of specific clinical problems and the use of special techniques in cognitive therapy.

Cognitive Behavior Modification: An Integrative Approach (Meichenbaum, 1977) merges techniques of behavior therapy with the clinical concerns of cognitive approaches. The author summarizes both empirical studies and clinical techniques, and he offers a number of innovative procedures such as self-instructional training and stress-inoculation training.

Stress Inoculation Training (Meichenbaum, 1985) provides a framework for understanding ways to reduce and prevent maladaptive stress reactions. The author clearly describes specific stages and techniques of his model for helping clients cope with stress.

REFERENCES AND SUGGESTED READINGS*

BECK, A. T. (1967). *Depression: Clinical, experimental, and theoretical aspects.* New York: Harper & Row.

* Books and articles marked with an asterisk are suggested for further study.

BECK, A. T. (1975). *Depression: Causes and treatment.* Philadelphia: University of Pennsylvania Press.

*BECK, A. T. (1976). *Cognitive therapy and emotional disorders.* New York: International Universities Press.

BECK, A. T. (1987). Cognitive therapy. In J. K. Zeig (Ed.), *The evolution of psychotherapy* (pp. 149–178). New York: Brunner/Mazel.

BECK, A. T., & EMERY, G. (1985). *Anxiety disorders and phobias: A cognitive perspective.* New York: Basic Books.

*BECK, A., RUSH, A., SHAW, B., & EMERY, G. (1979). *Cognitive therapy of depression.* New York: Guilford Press.

BECK, A. T., & WEISHAAR, M. E. (1989). In R. J. Corsini & D. Wedding (Eds.), *Current psychotherapies* (4th ed.) (pp. 285–320). Itasca, IL: F. E. Peacock.

COREY, G. (1990). *Theory and practice of group counseling* (3rd ed.). Pacific Grove, CA: Brooks/Cole.

COREY, G. (1991). *Case approach to counseling and psychotherapy* (3rd ed.). Pacific Grove, CA: Brooks/Cole.

DeRUBEIS, R. J., & BECK, A. T. (1988). Cognitive therapy. In K. S. Dobson (Ed.), *Handbook of cognitive-behavioral therapies* (pp. 273–306). New York: Guilford Press.

DiGIUSEPPE, R. A., MILLER, N. J., & TREXLER, L. D. (1979). A review of rational-emotive psychotherapy outcome studies. In A. Ellis & J. M. Whiteley (Eds.), *Theoretical and empirical foundations of rational-emotive therapy* (pp. 218–235). Pacific Grove, CA: Brooks/Cole.

DOBSON, K. S. (Ed.). (1988a). *Handbook of cognitive-behavioral therapies.* New York: Guilford Press.

DOBSON, K. S. (1988b). The present and future of the cognitive-behavioral therapies. In K. S. Dobson (Ed.), *Handbook of cognitive-behavioral therapies* (pp. 387–414). New York: Guilford Press.

DOBSON, K. S., & BLOCK, L. (1988). Historical and philosophical bases of the cognitive-behavioral therapies. In K. S. Dobson (Ed.), *Handbook of cognitive-behavioral therapies* (pp. 3–38). New York: Guilford Press.

DRYDEN, W. (1986). Vivid methods in rational-emotive therapy. In A. Ellis & R. Grieger (Eds.), *Handbook of rational-emotive therapy: Vol. 2* (pp. 221–245). New York: Springer.

DRYDEN, W. (1989). Albert Ellis: An efficient and passionate life. *Journal of Counseling and Development, 67,* 539–546.

DRYDEN, W., & ELLIS, A. (1988). Rational-emotive therapy. In K. S. Dobson (Ed.), *Handbook of cognitive-behavioral therapies* (pp. 214–272). New York: Guilford Press.

*ELLIS, A. (1962). *Reason and emotion in psychotherapy.* New York: Lyle Stuart.

ELLIS, A. (1967). Rational-emotive psychotherapy. In D. Arbuckle (Ed.), *Counseling and psychotherapy.* New York: McGraw-Hill.

ELLIS, A. (1969). A weekend of rational encounter. In A. Burton (Ed.), *Encounter: The theory and practice of encounter groups.* San Francisco: Jossey-Bass.

*ELLIS, A. (1971). *Growth through reason.* Hollywood, CA: Wilshire Books.

*ELLIS, A. (1973). *Humanistic psychotherapy: The rational-emotive approach.* New York: Julian Press.

ELLIS, A. (1977a). The basic clinical theory of rational-emotive therapy. In A. Ellis & R. Grieger (Eds.), *Handbook of rational-emotive therapy: Vol. 1* (pp. 3–34). New York: Springer.

ELLIS, A. (1977b). *A garland of rational songs.* New York: Institute for Rational-Emotive Therapy.

ELLIS, A. (1979a). The practice of rational-emotive therapy. In A. Ellis & J. Whiteley (Eds.), *Theoretical and empirical foundations of rational-emotive therapy* (pp. 61–100). Pacific Grove, CA: Brooks/Cole.

ELLIS, A. (1979b). Rational-emotive therapy. In A. Ellis & J. M. Whiteley (Eds.), *Theoretical and empirical foundations of rational-emotive therapy* (pp. 1–6). Pacific Grove, CA: Brooks/Cole.

ELLIS, A. (1979c). Rational-emotive therapy: Research data that support the clinical and personality hypotheses of RET and other modes of cognitive-behavior therapy. In A. Ellis & J. M. Whiteley (Eds.), *Theoretical and empirical foundations of rational-emotive therapy* (pp. 101–173). Pacific Grove, CA: Brooks/Cole.

ELLIS, A. (1979d). The theory of rational-emotive therapy. In A. Ellis & J. Whiteley (Eds.), *Theoretical and empirical foundations of rational-emotive therapy* (pp. 33–60). Pacific Grove, CA: Brooks/Cole.

ELLIS, A. (1979e). Toward a new theory of personality. In A. Ellis & J. Whiteley (Eds.), *Theoretical and empirical foundations of rational-emotive therapy* (pp. 7–32). Pacific Grove, CA: Brooks/Cole.

ELLIS, A. (1982). Rational-emotive family therapy. In A. M. Horne & M. M. Ohlsen (Eds.), *Family counseling and therapy.* Itasca, IL: F. E. Peacock.

ELLIS, A. (1984a). Is the unified-interaction approach to a cognitive-behavior modification a reinvention of the wheel? *Clinical Psychology Review, 4,* 215–217.

ELLIS, A. (1984b). Maintenance and generalization in rational-emotive therapy. *The Cognitive Behaviorist, 6,* 2–4.

*ELLIS, A. (1985). *Overcoming resistance: Rational-emotive therapy with difficult clients.* New York: Springer.

ELLIS, A. (1986a). Rational-emotive therapy. In I. L. Kutash & A. Wolf (Eds.), *Psychotherapist's casebook* (pp. 277–287). San Francisco: Jossey-Bass.

*ELLIS, A. (1986b). Rational-emotive therapy and cognitive behavior therapy: Similarities and differences. In A. Ellis & R. Grieger (Eds.), *Handbook of rational-emotive therapy: Vol. 2* (pp. 31–45). New York: Springer.

*ELLIS, A. (1987a). The evolution of rational-emotive therapy (RET) and cognitive behavior therapy (CBT). In J. K. Zeig (Ed.), *The evolution of psychotherapy* (pp. 107–132). New York: Brunner/Mazel.

*ELLIS, A. (1987b). The impossibility of achieving consistently good mental health. *American Psychologist, 42,* 364–375.

*ELLIS, A. (1988). *How to stubbornly refuse to make yourself miserable about anything — yes, anything!* Secaucus, NJ: Lyle Stuart.

*ELLIS, A. (1989). Rational-emotive therapy. In R. J. Corsini & D. Wedding (Eds.), *Current psychotherapies* (4th ed.) (pp. 197–238). Itasca, IL: F. E. Peacock.

*ELLIS, A., & BERNARD, M. E. (1986). What is rational-emotive therapy (RET)? In A. Ellis & R. Grieger (Eds.), *Handbook of rational-emotive therapy: Vol. 2* (pp. 3–30). New York: Springer.

*ELLIS, A., & DRYDEN, W. (1987). *The practice of rational-emotive therapy.* Secaucus, NJ: Lyle Stuart.

*ELLIS, A., & GRIEGER, R. (1977). *Handbook of rational-emotive therapy: Vol. 1.* New York: Springer.

*ELLIS, A., & GRIEGER, R. (1986). *Handbook of rational-emotive therapy: Vol. 2.* New York: Springer.

*ELLIS, A., & HARPER, R. (1975). *A new guide to rational living* (rev. ed.). Hollywood, CA: Wilshire Books.

ELLIS, A., SICHEL, J., YEAGER, R., DiMATTIO, D., & DiGIUSEPPE, R. (1969). *Rational emotive couples therapy.* New York: Pergamon Press.

*ELLIS, A., & WHITELEY, J. M. (Eds.). (1979). *Theoretical and empirical foundations of rational-emotive therapy.* Pacific Grove, CA: Brooks/Cole.

ELLIS, A., & YEAGER, R. J. (1989). *Why some therapies don't work.* Buffalo, NY: Prometheus Books.

EMERY, G. (1981). *A new beginning: How you can change your life through cognitive therapy.* New York: Simon & Schuster (Touchstone Books)

*EMERY, G., HOLLAND, S. D., & BEDROSIAN, R. C. (1981). *New directions in cognitive therapy: A casebook.* New York: Guilford Press.

ENGELS, G., & DIENSTRA, R. (1987). *Efficacy of rational-emotive therapy: A quantitative review.* Unpublished manuscript, University of Reiden.

GRIEGER, R. M. (1986a). From a linear to a contextual model of the ABC's of RET. In A. Ellis & R. Grieger (Eds.), *Handbook of rational-emotive therapy: Vol. 2* (pp 59–80). New York: Springer.

*GRIEGER, R. M. (1986b). The process of rational-emotive therapy. In A. Ellis & R. Grieger (Eds.), *Handbook of rational-emotive therapy: Vol. 2* (pp. 203–212). New York: Springer.

HAAGA, D. A., & DAVISON, G. C. (1986). Cognitive change methods. In F. H. Kanfer & A. P. Goldstein (Eds.), *Helping people change: A textbook of methods* (3rd ed.) (pp. 236–282). New York: Pergamon Press.

HAAGA, D. A., & DAVISON, G. C. (1989). Outcome studies of rational-emotive therapy. In M. E. Bernard & R. DiGiuseppe (Eds.), *Inside rational-emotive therapy.* San Diego: Academic Press.

HARRELL, T. H., BEIMAN, I., & LAPOINTE, K. (1986). Didactic persuasion techniques in cognitive restructuring. In A. Ellis & R. Grieger (Eds.), *Handbook of rational-emotive therapy: Vol. 2* (pp. 213–220). New York: Springer.

JORM, A. P. (1987). Modifiability of a personality trait which is a risk factor for neurosis. Paper presented at the World Psychiatric Association, Reykjavik, Iceland.

MAHONEY, M. J. (1977). Reflections on the cognitive-learning trend in psychotherapy. *American Psychologist, 32,* 5–13.

MAHONEY, M. J. (1988). The cognitive sciences and psychotherapy: Patterns in a developing relationship. In K. S. Dobson (Ed.), *Handbook of cognitive-behavioral therapies* (pp. 357–386). New York: Guilford Press.

MAULTSBY, M. C. (1984). *Rational behavior therapy.* Englewood Cliffs, NJ: Prentice-Hall.

McGOVERN, T. E., & SILVERMAN, M. (1986). A review of outcome studies of rational-emotive therapy from 1977 to 1982. In A. Ellis & R. Grieger (Eds.), *Handbook of rational-emotive therapy: Vol. 2* (pp. 81–102). New York: Springer.

McMULLIN, R. E. (1986). *Handbook of cognitive therapy techniques.* New York: Norton.

MEICHENBAUM, D. (1977). *Cognitive behavior modification: An integrative approach.* New York: Plenum.

MEICHENBAUM, D. (1985). *Stress inoculation training.* New York: Pergamon Press.

MEICHENBAUM, D. (1986). Cognitive behavior modification. In F. H. Kanfer & A. P. Goldstein (Eds.), *Helping people change: A textbook of methods* (pp. 346–380). New York: Pergamon Press.

MEICHENBAUM, D., & CAMERON, R. (1982). Cognitive-behavior therapy. In G. T. Wilson & C. M. Franks (Eds.), *Contemporary behavior therapy: Conceptual and empirical foundations* (pp. 310–338). New York: Guilford Press.

PATTERSON, C. H. (1986). *Theories of counseling and psychotherapy* (4th ed.). New York: Harper & Row.

REHM, L. P., & ROKKE, P. (1988). Self-management therapies. In K. S. Dobson (Ed.), *Handbook of cognitive-behavioral therapies* (pp. 136–166). New York: Guilford Press.

*WALEN, S., DiGIUSEPPE, R., & WESSLER, R. L. (1980). *A practitioner's guide to rational-emotive therapy*. New York: Oxford University Press.

WARREN, R., & McLELLARN, R. W. (1987). What do RET therapists think they are doing? An international survey. *Journal of Rational-Emotive Therapy, 5,* 92–107.

WARREN, R., McLELLARN, R. W., & ELLIS, A. (1987). Albert Ellis' personal responses to the survey of rational-emotive therapists. *Journal of Rational-Emotive Therapy, 5,* 71–91.

WEINRACH, S. G. (1980). Unconventional therapist: Albert Ellis. *Personnel and Guidance Journal, 59,* 152–160.

WESSLER, R. L. (1986). Varieties of cognitions in the cognitively oriented psychotherapies. In A. Ellis & R. Grieger (Eds.), *Handbook of rational-emotive therapy: Vol. 2* (pp. 46–58). New York: Springer.

*WESSLER, R. A., & WESSLER, R. L. (1980). *The principles and practice of rational-emotive therapy*. San Francisco: Jossey-Bass.

12

REALITY THERAPY

WILLIAM GLASSER

WILLIAM GLASSER (b. 1925) was educated in Cleveland and finished medical school at Case Western Reserve University in 1953. He became a chemical engineer at 19 and a physician at 28. He then took his psychiatric training at the Veterans Administration Center in West Los Angeles, did his final year at the University of California at Los Angeles in 1957, and was board-certified in 1961. During his training he began to be more and more aware that there was a vast difference between what he was being taught to do (follow the Freudian model) and what seemed to him to work. The difference centered on two main points: (1) rather than aloofness and detachment, he found, close and warm involvement backed by personal interest and some self-revelation seemed necessary for a good outcome, and (2) rather than being victims of their own impulses or victims of those around them, he found, clients actually seemed to choose what they did with their lives; they were never lifelong victims unless they chose to be so. Glasser was reluctant to express his dissatisfaction with psychoanalytic therapy until he met a sympathetic faculty supervisor, G. L. Harrington, to whom he gives full credit for many contributions to these ideas as they formed.

In 1956 Glasser became a consulting psychiatrist at the Ventura School for Girls, a California state facility for the treatment of delinquent adolescents. This experience convinced him even further of the futility of classical psychoanalytic concepts and techniques, so he began to develop and experiment with a different therapeutic approach that in many ways was antithetical to Freudian psychoanalysis. In 1961 Glasser published his first book, *Mental Health or Mental Illness?* which laid the foundation for reality therapy.

By 1965, when he published *Reality Therapy,* he was able to state his fundamental beliefs, which are that we are all responsible for what we choose to do with our lives and that in a warm, accepting, nonpunitive therapeutic environment we are willing to learn more effective choices, or more responsible ways to live our lives.

During the 1960s Glasser worked as a consultant in public education, where he put into practice his basic concepts of reality therapy. This work was the beginning of his efforts to apply these powerful ideas to systems rather than to individuals, and the result was his first major book on education, *Schools without Failure* (1969). At this time he turned his professional interests to how teachers and students interacted with each other, how learning in schools could be connected to the lives of the learners, how schools often contributed to a "failure identity," and how they could be changed to make learning come alive. He continued to flesh out his ideas, and by 1972, when he published *The Identity Society,* he had already begun to lay the groundwork for what would be his acceptance and support of *control theory,* which explained not only how we functioned as individuals, both psychologically and physiologically, but also how we functioned as groups and even as societies.

Although the ideas of control theory are not original with Glasser, most of the recent work on this new theory and how it can be applied to systems is based on his observations, which are summarized in his 1985 book, *Control Theory*. How this theory can be applied to education has been well summarized in *Control Theory in the Classroom* (1986b). His most recent book, *The Quality School* (1990), applies these ideas to school management.

Glasser has been married to his wife, Naomi, for over 40 years. They have three children, who, in entering the professions of counseling, teaching, and medicine, have to a great extent followed in his foot-steps. His wife has been highly supportive of his career and helps unstintingly with the work of the nonprofit Institute for Reality Therapy, through which the ideas are taught throughout the world. Over 2500 people have been certified by the institute as proficient in these ideas. She has also edited two important books of cases that explain in great detail how this therapy is actually done. These are *What Are You Doing?* (1980) and *Control Theory in the Practice of Reality Therapy* (1989). William Glasser lectures widely on these ideas all over the world.

INTRODUCTION

Reality therapy rests on the central idea that we choose our behavior and are therefore responsible not only for what we are doing but also for how we think and feel. The basic philosophy of reality therapy is shared by the existential approach and rational-emotive therapy. The general aim of this therapeutic system is to provide conditions that will help clients develop the psychological strength to evaluate their present behavior and, if it does not meet their needs, to acquire more effective behavior. This process of learning effective behavior is facilitated by the application of the basic principles of reality therapy, which include a warm, accepting counseling environment and various counseling procedures.

In *Stations of the Mind* Glasser (1981) began to explain control theory, which is now the neurological and psychological basis for his clinical approach. Control theory is grounded in the assumption that we create an inner world that satisfies our needs. Also important is the idea that this inner world does not reflect the way the real world exists but, rather, the way we perceive it to exist, a major concept of phenomenology. Behavior is the attempt to control our perceptions of the external world to fit this internal and need-satisfying world. Glasser has used this theory to explain the basic premise of reality therapy, which is that all behavior is generated from within ourselves and that people have choices in what they do. It is assumed that people who learn control theory will be able to take more effective control of their lives. Thus, by putting the principles of control theory into practice, people can prevent many potential problems that could lead them into therapy (Glasser, 1985).

Practitioners of reality therapy concentrate on what clients can do in their present situation to change the behavior that is designed to fulfill their needs. A central task of the therapist is to establish a therapeutic involvement with clients, which encourages them to make an assessment of their current style of living. This assessment enables them to determine how well their chosen behaviors are working for them. Reality therapy focuses on current actions and thoughts rather than on insight, feelings, past experiences, or unconscious motivations. Individuals can improve the quality of their lives through a process of honest self-examination. Clients are taught the basic needs and are asked to identify their wants (which is how they are going to satisfy these needs). They are challenged to evaluate if what they are doing will satisfy their needs. If it will not, they are encouraged to formulate a plan for change, to commit themselves to such a plan, and to follow through with their commitment.

Reality therapy was selected for inclusion in this book for several reasons. First, this approach (as does Ellis's rational-emotive therapy) provides a good contrast to most of the other counseling approaches explored. It raises questions and issues that you will want to explore. Second, reality therapy continues to be popular among school counselors, teachers, principals, rehabilitation workers, and those who counsel in community agencies. The principles of control theory need not be restricted to psychotherapists; rather, they can be used by parents, ministers, doctors, and spouses in working on interpersonal relationships. Third, it presents many of the basic issues in counseling underlying such questions as: What motivates people to behave? Should therapists teach their clients? How can clients be challenged to evaluate what they are doing and whether their current behavior is working for them? What model should the counselor provide? What is the role of values in counseling? As you read this chapter, keep these questions in mind, and compare reality therapy with the other therapeutic approaches you have studied.

Key Concepts

VIEW OF HUMAN NATURE

Control theory, as we have seen, rests on the notion that human behavior is purposeful and originates from within the individual rather than from external forces. Although external forces have an influence on our decisions, our behavior is not *caused* by these environmental factors. Rather, we are motivated completely by internal forces, and all of our behavior is our best attempt to get what we want and in doing so to gain effective control of our lives.

Our behavior is geared to fulfilling our basic human needs. Glasser (1985, 1989) identifies them as the four psychological needs for *belonging, power, freedom,* and *fun* and the physiological need for *survival.* Control theory explains how we attempt to satisfy our needs, which are the powerful forces that drive us. According to control theory, our brain functions as a control system to aid us in getting what we want. When our psychological needs are thwarted, the behaviors we choose feel painful, and we are not satisfied with life. When we meet these needs in a responsible way, however, we develop an identity characterized by success and self-esteem, and the behaviors we use to meet them feel good.

Although we all possess these needs, each of us fulfills them in various ways. We develop an inner "picture album" of specific wants, which contains precise pictures of how we would best like to fulfill our needs. A major goal of reality therapy is to teach people better and more effective ways of getting what they want from life. It is important that therapists understand that clients live in the external world but always try to control it so that it is as close as possible to their own internal world (W. Glasser, 1989).

Clearly, then, control theory challenges the deterministic philosophy of human nature. In a democratic society if people wish to make the effort, they can change and live more effectively. They can behave for a purpose: to mold their environment, as a sculptor molds clay, so it matches their own inner pictures of what they want. These goals are achievable only through hard work (Wubbolding, 1988b). When people make choices that infringe on others' freedom, their behavior is irresponsible. Through the practice of reality therapy people learn how to achieve freedom so that others do not suffer in the process.

A CONTROL-THEORY EXPLANATION OF BEHAVIOR

In his workshops Glasser frequently explains the concept of *total behavior* by comparing how we function to how a car functions. Just as the four wheels guide a car, so do the four components of our total behavior determine our direction in life. These components of total behavior are *doing* (or active behaviors, such as getting up and going to work); *thinking* (thoughts and self-statements); *feeling* (such as anger, joy, pain, depression, anxiety); and *physiology* (such as sweating or developing psychosomatic symptoms). Although these behavioral components always blend to make a whole, or total, behavior, one is usually more prominent than the others (W. Glasser, 1989).

Control theory is grounded on the assumption that it is impossible to choose a total behavior and not choose all its components. Glasser (1989) gives emphasis to the "two front wheels" (doing and thinking), which steer us, just as the front wheels steer the direction of a car. It is difficult to directly change how we are feeling separately from what we are doing or thinking. However, we have almost complete ability to change what we are doing and thinking in spite of how we might be feeling. Therefore, the key to changing a total behavior lies in choosing to change what we do and think, thus changing our emotional and physiological reactions in the process.

All we will ever do from birth to death is behave, and every total behavior is always our best attempt to get what we want. In this context behavior is purposeful because it is designed to close the gap between what we want and what we perceive that we are getting. Specific behaviors are always generated from this discrepancy. Wubbolding (1988b) writes that we are all sculptors of our behavior as we strive to change the world outside of us to match our internal pictures of what we want. Our behaviors come from the inside, and thus we are choosing our destiny.

Glasser says that to speak of being depressed, having a headache, being angry, or being anxious implies passivity and lack of personal responsibility, and it is inaccurate. It is more accurate to think of these as parts of total behaviors and as such use the verb forms *depressing, headaching, angering,* and *anxiety-ing* to describe them. Glasser speaks of people depressing or angering themselves, rather than being depressed or being angry. When people choose misery by developing a range of "paining" behaviors, it is because these are the best behaviors that they are able to devise at the time, and these behaviors often get them what they want. But why does it make sense to choose misery? Glasser (1985) answers this question by discussing these three reasons: (1) to keep anger under control, (2) to get others to help us, and (3) to excuse our unwillingness to do something more effective. From this perspective depression can be explained as an active choice that we make. This process of "depressing" keeps anger in check, and it also allows us to ask for help. Glasser contends that as long as we cling to the notion that we are victims of depression and that misery is something that happens to us, we will not change for the better. When people begin to say "I am choosing to depress," there will be fewer people making this choice.

CHARACTERISTICS OF REALITY THERAPY

Control theory provides the conceptual framework for reality therapy. This theory underlies the principles and practices that a counselor applies to helping people change. A few of the distinguishing characteristics of reality therapy are described below. Later, in the section on the practice of reality therapy, I will give a more detailed discussion of the counseling environment and procedures (known as the "cycle of counseling").

Rejection of the medical model.   Discarding the orthodox concept of mental illness, including neurotic and psychotic disorders, has been a driving force of reality therapy since its origin. Formulations such as "schizophrenic" and "depressive psychosis" are based on the notion that these illnesses are reactions to external events. Reality therapists contend that "neurotic" or "psychotic" behavior is not something that merely happens to us; rather, it is behavior that we choose as a way of attempting to control our world. Even though certain behaviors (such as psychosomatic disorders and addictions to drugs and alcohol) may be both painful and ineffective, they work to some extent, or we would not use them. It is Glasser's contention (1984a, 1985) that we choose most of these unsatisfactory behaviors as a way of closing the gap between what we want and what we have. Thus, external factors that we call "stressful" are identified as such because we are not able to control them satisfactorily with the behaviors we choose. Glasser maintains that stress is a subjective phenomenon. What is stressful to some is joyful to others — for example, parachute jumping. Our reactions to the environment are unique, and we can control almost all stressful situations.

Success identity and positive addiction.   The concept of *success identity* is essential to understanding reality therapy. People who possess a success identity see themselves as being able to give and receive love, feel that they are significant to others, feel powerful, possess a sense of self-worth, and meet their needs in ways that are not at the expense of others. Those people with a success identity possess *strength,* which helps them create a satisfying life. Glasser (1976a) also develops the idea of *positive addiction* as a major source of psychological strength in our life. Two ways of developing positive addiction are running and meditation.

Emphasis on responsibility. Reality therapy has consistently emphasized responsibility, which Glasser (1984a, 1984b, 1985) defines as behavior that satisfies one's needs in ways that do not interfere with others' fulfilling their needs. Responsible people are autonomous in the sense that they know what they want from life and make plans for meeting their needs and goals. In short, responsibility means that people have learned to take effective control of their lives. Glasser emphasizes avoiding criticism, either from the therapist or from ourselves. We can learn to live and behave responsibly without becoming harshly self-critical. Searching for our faults and criticizing ourselves certainly does not help us.

Deemphasis on transference. Rejecting the idea of transference as a misleading concept, Glasser (1984a) contends that conventional therapists are putting ideas into the client's head by imposing that notion. Reality therapy sees transference as a way for the therapist to remain hidden as a person. It calls for therapists to be themselves and not to think or teach that they are playing the role of the client's mother or father. The reality therapist deals with whatever perceptions clients have, and there is no attempt to teach clients that their reactions and views are other than what they state. Since the inception of reality therapy Glasser has taught that clients do not look for a repeat of unsuccessful involvements in their past but, rather, seek a satisfying human involvement with a person in their present existence. Instead of dwelling on a client's past failures, reality therapists look to the past for evidences of the client's ability to successfully control the world, and they help clients deal with situations that are directly related to their present lives.

THE THERAPEUTIC PROCESS

THERAPEUTIC GOALS

The overall goal of reality therapy is for individuals to find more effective ways of meeting their needs for belonging, power, freedom and fun. At his workshops Glasser stresses that counseling consists of helping clients learn ways to regain control of their lives and to live more effectively. This includes confronting clients to examine what they are doing, thinking, and feeling, to figure out if there is a better way for them to function.

Reality therapy focuses on what clients are conscious of and then helps them increase their level of awareness. As clients become aware of the ineffective behaviors they are using to control the world, they are more open to learning alternative ways of behaving. Unlike many other approaches, reality therapy is concerned with teaching people these more effective ways to deal with the world. The core of reality therapy is to help clients evaluate whether their wants are realistic and whether their behavior is helping them. It is the clients who decide if what they are doing is getting them what they want, and they determine what changes, if any, they are willing to make. After they make this assessment, they are assisted by the counselor in designing a plan for change as a way of translating talk into action. Glasser (1989) emphasizes that the only person's behavior that we can control is our own, which means that the best way to control events around us is through what we do.

THERAPIST'S FUNCTION AND ROLE

The reality therapist's job is to get involved with clients and to develop a relationship with them that will lay the groundwork for the rest of the counseling process. The counselor functions as a teacher by being active in the sessions, helping clients formulate specific plans of action, offering them behavioral choices, and teaching them control theory (see N. Glasser, 1989).

Therapists challenge clients with the basic question of reality therapy: "Is what you are choosing to do getting you what you want?" If clients make the judgment that what they are doing is not working, therapists may suggest an alternative course of action (W. Glasser, 1989). The counselor also teaches clients how they can create a success identity by recognizing and accepting accountability for their own chosen behaviors (Glasser, 1986c). This role requires counselors to perform several functions:

- providing a model for responsible behavior and for a life based on a success identity
- establishing rapport based on care and respect
- focusing on the individual's strengths and potentials that can lead to success
- actively promoting discussion of clients' current behavior and discouraging excuses for irresponsible or ineffective behavior
- introducing and fostering the process of evaluating realistically attainable wants
- teaching clients to formulate and carry out plans to change their behaviors
- establishing a structure and limits for the sessions
- helping clients find ways to meet their needs and refusing to give up easily, even if clients become discouraged

CLIENT'S EXPERIENCE IN THERAPY

People who come for counseling are typically behaving in ineffective ways. Their behavior is an attempt to meet their needs, yet what they are doing is not working well. Therefore, clients who initiate counseling with the presenting complaint of depression are doing what they can to close the gap between what they want and what they have.

In his workshops Glasser often relates the case of a man ("Melvyn") who is "depressing" after his wife left him. Melvyn wants his wife back, and he wants to feel loved and accepted. He complains that he is depressed, that he is not going to work, that he is unable to sleep, and that he wants to know how to get his wife to return to him. He is focused on his wife, and he can see few options for changing his misery. The balance has been tipped, and he is striving to regain control of his life.

From the perspective of reality therapy Melvyn is choosing to depress. By depressing, he is hoping to control his wife to get her to do what he would like her to do. His choice to depress is his best attempt to deal with a difficult life situation. He is focusing on one component of total behavior, feeling miserable. In reality therapy he is expected to deal with his total behavior, yet the focus is on what he is doing. With the help of his therapist he can be in a position to choose more effective ways of acting and thinking. In his situation he has more control over his actions and thoughts (the front wheels) than he does his feelings and physiology (the rear wheels). If Melvyn learns to steer the front wheels in a different direction, he will discover that his emotional upsets and his physical symptoms will decrease.

RELATIONSHIP BETWEEN THERAPIST AND CLIENT

Before effective therapy can occur, an involvement between the client and the counselor must be established. Clients need to know that the helping person cares enough about them both to accept them and to help them fulfill their needs in the real world. Reality therapy emphasizes an understanding and supportive relationship. An important factor is the willingness of counselors to develop their own individual therapeutic style. Sincerity and being comfortable with one's style are crucial traits in being able to carry out therapeutic functions, according to Glasser:

> If the counselor is not perceived as being sincere, the client will not experience the immediate sense of belonging that is an essential part of the need-fulfilling approach which is basic to reality therapy. If the counselor is not perceived as being comfortable, the client will see this as a lack of skill and have little confidence in the counseling process [1986c, p. 19].

For this involvement between the therapist and the client to occur, the counselor must have certain personal qualities, including warmth, understanding, acceptance, concern, respect for the client, openness and the willingness to be challenged by others. One of the best ways to develop this goodwill and therapeutic friendship is simply by listening to clients. Involvement is also promoted by talking about a wide range of topics that have relevance for the client. Once involvement has been established, the counselor confronts clients with the reality and consequences of their *current* behavior.

APPLICATION: THERAPEUTIC TECHNIQUES AND PROCEDURES

THE PRACTICE OF REALITY THERAPY

The practice of reality therapy can best be conceptualized as the *cycle of counseling,* which consists of two major components: (1) the counseling environment and (2) specific procedures that lead to changes in behavior. The art of counseling is to weave these components together in ways that lead clients to evaluate their lives and decide to move in more effective directions.

How do these components blend in the counseling process? The cycle of counseling begins, as we have seen, with establishing a working relationship with clients. The process proceeds through an exploration of their wants, needs, and perceptions. Clients then explore their total behavior and make their own evaluation of how effective they are in getting what they want. If clients decide to try new behavior, they make plans that will lead to change, and they commit themselves to their plan. During this process counselors do not accept excuses for failing to follow through with plans, do not criticize clients, and do not easily give up on them. The cycle of counseling includes following up on how well clients are doing and offering further consultation as needed.

It is important to keep in mind that although the concepts discussed below may seem simple as they are presented, being able to translate them into actual therapeutic practice takes considerable skill and creativity. Although the principles will be the same when used by any counselor who is certified in reality therapy, the manner in which they are applied does vary depending on the counselor's style and personal characteristics. Just because the principles are applied in a progressive manner, they should not be thought of as discrete and rigid categories. Glasser (1986c) stresses that the art of practicing reality therapy involves far more than following procedures in a step-by-step, or "cookbook," fashion. He has also said that it takes approximately two years to see the world through the window of reality therapy and its underlying control theory.

The discussion that follows is best considered as an aid for teaching reality therapy, but it should not be thought of as a replacement for the extensive training that is needed to counsel effectively. It is an integrated summary and adaptation of material from various sources (Glasser, 1965, 1969, 1976b, 1980, 1981, 1984a, 1984b, 1985, 1986a, 1986b, 1986c; Wubbolding, 1988b).

THE COUNSELING ENVIRONMENT

Personal involvement with the client.   The practice of reality therapy begins with the counselor's efforts to create a supportive environment within which clients can begin to make changes in their lives. To create this therapeutic climate, counselors must become involved in their clients' lives and establish rapport. This involvement occurs through a combined process of listening to the client's story and skillfully questioning. One of the most effective ways of building this relationship is for the counselor to explore the pictures in the client's mind as well as his or her wants, needs, and perceptions.

Counselor attitudes and behaviors that promote change.   Counselors consistently attempt to focus clients on what they are *doing now*. They also avoid discussing clients' feelings or physiology as though these were separate from their total behavior. Counselors help their clients see connections between what they are feeling and their concurrent actions and thoughts. Although reality therapists focus on the actions and thoughts of clients (the front wheels that drive the car), they consider it quite legitimate to talk about feelings and physiology. When people begin to act differently, they will also begin to feel differently.

Counselors hope to teach their clients to value the attitude of accepting responsibility for their total behavior. Thus, they accept no excuses for irresponsible behavior, even though they recognize that ineffective behavior is still the client's best attempt to get what is wanted. If clients do not follow through with their agreed-on plans for change, counselors are likely to help them reassess the situation, yet they are firm in their refusal to accept excuses. Reality therapists show clients that excuses are a form of self-deception that may offer temporary relief but ultimately leads to failure and to the cementing of a failure identity. By refusing to accept excuses, counselors convey their belief in the client's ability to regain control.

Reality therapy holds that punishment is not a useful means of changing behavior. This principle is especially useful in applying reality therapy to parenting or management. Specific punishments that are avoided include chastising individuals for what they have failed to do and making deprecating remarks to them. Instead of being punished, individuals can learn to accept the *reasonable consequences* that flow from their actions. By not making critical comments, by refusing to accept excuses, and by remaining nonjudgmental, counselors are in a position to ask clients if they are really interested in changing.

It is important that counselors not easily give up their belief in the client's ability to find a more responsible life, even if the client makes little effort to follow through. If the counselor gives up, it tends to confirm the client's belief that no one cares enough to help (Glasser, 1986a, 1986c). Those with a failure identity *expect* others to give up on them. Such people are rarely helped if the counselor acts on the assumption that they will never change or that they are hopeless.

In addition to the counselor's attitudes mentioned above that create an environment conducive to client change, Wubbolding (1988b) emphasizes the importance of practitioners' being willing to seek consultation with someone else who is trained in reality therapy. Regardless of how well a person practices reality therapy, Wubbolding contends, there is room for improvement. It can be achieved both by consultation and by developing an ongoing plan for professional development.

PROCEDURES THAT LEAD TO CHANGE

Exploring wants, needs, and perceptions.   Reality therapists ask "What do you want?" Through the therapist's skillful questioning, clients are encouraged to recognize, define, and refine how they wish to meet their needs. Part of counseling consists of the exploration of their "picture album" and the ways in which their behavior is aimed at moving their perception of the external world closer to their inner world of wants.

The skill of reality therapy involves counseling in a noncriticizing and accepting way so that clients will reveal what is in this special world. Clients are given the opportunity to explore every facet of their lives, including what they want from their family, friends, and work. Furthermore, it is useful for them to define what they expect and want from the counselor and from themselves (Wubbolding, 1988b). This exploration of wants, needs, and perceptions should continue throughout the counseling process, because the client's pictures change. Some useful questions to help clients pinpoint what they want include "If you were the person you want to be, what kind of person would you be?" "If you had what you want, what would you have?" "What would your family be like if your wants and their wants matched?" "What would you be doing if you were living the way you wish?" This line of questioning sets the stage for the application of other procedures in reality therapy. After clients explore their picture album, they are later asked to look at their behavior to determine if what they are doing is getting them what they want.

Focus on current behavior.   Reality therapy stresses current behavior and is concerned with past events only insofar as they influence how the client is behaving now. The focus on the present is characterized by the question so often asked by the reality therapist: "What are you doing?" Even though problems may be rooted in the past, clients need to learn how to deal with them in the present by learning better ways of getting what they want. Glasser (1989) contends that no matter how frustrating the past was, there is no way that either the client or the therapist can undo these frustrations. What can be done now is to help clients make more need-satisfying choices.

The past may be discussed if doing so will help clients plan for a better tomorrow. For example, if an adult client was sexually abused as a child, Glasser stresses the value of working on the problem that this client has now. If it becomes necessary to working through her present problems, she can explore her childhood abuse. Glasser is distrustful of going back too far in childhood. For him the task of the counselor consists of steering this client into dealing with her present situation. She needs to learn how to live her life despite what happened to her earlier.

Early in counseling it is essential to discuss with clients the overall direction of their lives, including where they are going and where their behavior is taking them. This exploration is preliminary to the subsequent evaluation of whether it is a desirable direction. The therapist functions by holding a mirror before the client and asking "What do you see for yourself now and in the future?" For this reflection to become clear to clients, some time is necessary for them to be able to verbally express their perceptions (Wubbolding, 1988b).

Reality therapy concentrates on changing current total behavior, not merely attitudes and feelings. That doesn't imply that attitudes are dismissed as unimportant; rather, total behavioral change is easier to effect than attitudinal change and of greater value in the therapeutic process. For that reason a client who expressed feelings of helplessness would not be questioned about the reasons for the feelings but would be encouraged to describe a time when he was not helpless. What was he doing then that is different from what he is doing now? Although the reality therapist might encourage the client to discuss feelings, the focus would clearly be on the acting and thinking parts of the total behavioral system. The therapist would urge the person to identify those thoughts and actions that accompanied the feelings. The aim is to help clients understand *their* responsibilities for their own feelings. Questions such as the following are likely to be asked: "What are you doing now?" "What did you actually do this past week?" "What did you want to do differently this past week?" "What stopped you from doing what you say you want to do?" "What will you do tomorrow?"

Listening to clients talk about feelings can be productive, but only if it is linked to what they are doing. When an emergency light on the car dashboard lights up, the driver is alerted that something is wrong and that immediate action is necessary to remedy a problem. In a similar way when clients talk about problematic feelings, the counselor, rather than focusing on these feelings, needs to encourage them to take action by changing what they are doing and thinking. According to Glasser (1980, 1981, 1985, 1989), what we are doing is easy to see and impossible to deny, and thus it serves as the proper focus in therapy. Discussions centering on feelings, without strongly relating them to what people are doing, are counterproductive (Glasser, 1980). Briefly, then, the focus of reality therapy is on gaining awareness of current total behavior, because this process contributes to helping a person get what he or she wants and to develop a positive self-image.

Getting clients to evaluate their behavior.   The core of reality therapy, as we have seen, is to ask clients to make the following evaluation: "Does your present behavior have a reasonable chance of getting you what you want now, and will it take you in the direction you want to go?" (Glasser, 1986a, 1986c). Through skillful questioning the counselor helps clients evaluate their behavior. These questions include "Is what you are doing helping or hurting you?" "Is what you are doing now what you want to be doing?" "Is your behavior working for you?" "Is what you are doing against the rules?" "Is what you want realistic or attainable?" "Does it help you to look at it that way?" "How committed are you to the therapeutic process and to changing your life?" (Wubbolding, 1988b). Counselors can encourage clients to make value judgments by asking them questions about their wants, perceptions and total behavior. It is the counselor's task to confront clients with the consequences of their behavior and to get *them* to judge the quality of their actions. Without this self-assessment clients will not change.

Asking clients to evaluate each component of their total behavior is a major task in reality therapy. When therapists ask a depressing client if this behavior is helping in the long run, they introduce the idea of choice to the client. The process of evaluation of the doing, thinking, feeling, and physiological components of total behavior is within the scope of the client's responsibility. The therapist is careful not to take on the responsibility for the answers (Thatcher, 1987).

From the reality therapist's perspective it is acceptable to be directive with certain clients at the beginning of treatment. This is done to help them recognize that some behaviors are not effective. In working with clients who are in crisis, for example, it is sometimes necessary to suggest straightforwardly what will work and what will not. Other clients need direction early in the course of treatment, such as alcoholics and children of alcoholics, for they often do not have the thinking behaviors in their control system to be able to make consistent evaluations of when their lives are seriously out of effective control. These clients are likely to have blurred pictures and, at times, not to be aware of what they want or whether their wants are realistic. As they grow and continually interact with the counselor, they learn to make the evaluations with less help from the counselor (Wubbolding, 1988b).

Some clients insist that they do not have a problem and that their behavior is not getting them into trouble. It is essential to recognize that clients behave according to their perceptions. Counseling cannot be successful unless the counselor can accept that what the client perceives may be far different from what the counselor and others who are close to the client may see (Glasser, 1986c). In such cases, Glasser (1986a, 1986c) suggests that counselors should then continue to focus on the clients' present behaviors through the process of skillful questioning. He says that patience is important, for difficult clients may take considerable time to realize that certain behavior patterns are not getting them what they want and that their behavior is not taking them in a direction they want to go.

Planning and commitment.   Once clients determine what they want to change, they are generally ready to explore other possible behaviors and formulate an action plan. After plans have been formulated by a joint effort between the counselor and the client, a commitment must be made to carry them out.

Much of the significant work of counseling consists of helping clients identify specific ways to fulfill their wants. The process of creating and carrying out plans is how people gain control over their lives. This is clearly the teaching phase of counseling, which is best directed toward providing clients with new information and helping them find more effective ways of getting what they want. The purpose of the plan is to arrange for successful experiences. Throughout this planning phase the counselor continually urges clients to assume responsibility for their own choices and actions. This is done by reminding them that no one in the world will do things for them or live their life for them.

Wubbolding (1988b) devotes a chapter to planning and commitment, explaining that clients gain more effective control over their lives with plans that have the following characteristics:

- The plan should be within the limits of the motivation and capacities of each client. Skillful counselors help members identify plans that involve greater need-fulfilling payoffs. A client might be asked "Do you really want to stop depressing?"
- Good plans are simple and easy to understand. Although they need to be specific, concrete, and measurable, they should be flexible and open to modification as clients gain a deeper understanding of the specific behaviors that they want to change.

- Plans should be realistic and attainable. Counselors can help clients recognize that even small plans will help them take significant steps toward their desired changes.
- The plan should involve a positive action, and it should be stated in terms of what the client is willing to do.
- Counselors should encourage clients to develop plans that they can carry out independently of what others do. Plans that are contingent on others lead clients to sense that they are not steering their own ship but are at the mercy of the ocean.
- Effective plans are repetitive and, ideally, are performed daily. For example, clients can choose to take the initiative by approaching others first, to achieve something, to have fun, and to act independently.
- Plans should be carried out as soon as possible. Counselors can ask questions such as "What are you willing to do today to begin to change your life?" "You say you would like to stop depressing. What are you going to do now to attain this goal?"
- Effective planning involves process-centered activities. For example, clients may plan to do any of the following: apply for a job, write a letter to a friend, take a yoga class, substitute nutritious food for junk food, devote two hours a week to volunteer work, and take a vacation that they have been wanting.
- Before clients carry out their plan, it is a good idea for them to evaluate it with their therapist to determine if it is realistic and attainable and if it relates to what they need and want. After the plan has been carried out in real life, it is useful to evaluate it again. The counselor needs to ask "Is your plan helpful?" If a plan does not work, it can be reevaluated, and alternatives can be considered.
- In order for clients to commit themselves to their plan, it is useful for them to firm it up in writing.

Resolutions and plans are empty unless there is a commitment to carry them out. It is up to each client to determine ways of taking these plans outside the restricted world of therapy and into the everyday world. Effective therapy can be the catalyst that leads to self-directed, responsible living.

SPECIAL PROCEDURES IN REALITY THERAPY

This section describes four special procedures that can be appropriately used to augment the practice of reality therapy. These procedures are (1) the skillful use of questioning, (2) self-help techniques for a personal growth plan, (3) the use of humor, and (4) paradoxical techniques (Wubbolding, 1988b). Of course, reality therapists do not have a patent on these procedures, and they can be used in many of the other therapeutic approaches that have been discussed.

The art of skillful questioning. Because reality therapy uses questioning to a greater degree than many other approaches, counselors need to develop extensive questioning skills. Four main purposes for questioning procedures are (1) to enter the inner world of the client, (2) to gather information, (3) to give information, and (4) to help clients take more effective control of their lives (Wubbolding, 1988b).

Questioning is often misused by counselors, especially those who are inexperienced. Closed questions, or ones that simply tap information, can be overdone and tend to result in defensiveness and resistance. Open questions that are well-timed, however, can lead clients to think about what they want and to evaluate whether their behavior is leading them in the direction they want to go. In the next section examples of skillful questions are given.

Self-help procedures for a personal-growth program.   Wubbolding describes his version of an approach to personal growth in his "replacement program." This program helps clients identify specific need-fulfilling wants as well as specific behaviors as targets for change. "Replacements" include "do-it behaviors" in place of "give-up behaviors" and "positive-symptom behaviors" instead of "negative-symptom behaviors."

Regardless of their theoretical orientation, counselors can ask questions such as the following to help clients evaluate their wants: "Do you really want to change your life?" "If right now you had what you want, how do you imagine that your life would be different?" "What do you want that you don't seem to be getting from life?" "What do you think stops you from making the changes you would like?" Some of the following questions can help clients think about what they are doing: "Describe a time when you felt a sense of accomplishment. Specifically, what were you doing?" "Describe a time in your life when you felt that you were in charge. What were you doing?" "What are some of the things you do that bring you the greatest satisfaction?" "What are some of the things you are doing that you would like to stop doing?" "If you had only a year to live, what would you be doing differently?"

Key questions help clients focus on what they are doing and thinking and how they are feeling. Strategic questions can have the effect of getting clients to identify specific ways in which they can replace a failure identity with a positive identity. Instead of being cemented to negative addictions, clients can develop positive addictions. (For a more detailed discussion of positive addictions see Glasser [1976a], and for a discussion of the "replacement program" see Wubbolding [1988b].)

The use of humor.   Several practitioners have written about the role that fun and humor have in psychotherapy (see Ellis, 1977; Greenwald, 1975). To be effective, humor must be timed appropriately. It is usually unwise to employ humor until the therapeutic relationship has been well established. Once this involvement with a client exists, it is far more likely that humor will result in positive outcomes. Therapeutic humor has an educative, corrective message, and it helps clients put situations in perspective. Such humor does not involve hostility, ridicule, or a lack of respect.

On the other hand, harmful humor exacerbates a client's problems, undermines a sense of personal worth, and leaves the person feeling resentful (Saper,

1987). It goes without saying that humor that undermines the self-esteem of clients by deprecating and humiliating them is never appropriate, for it works against therapeutic aims

Using paradoxical techniques.   Clients in reality therapy are generally encouraged to change by direct and straightforward procedures. Yet there are times when clients seem especially resistant to making plans, or if they do make plans, they may be resistant to carrying them out. At such times reality therapists have the option of doing the unexpected. By looking at the principles and procedures of reality therapy in a different light, it is possible to identify paradox. This attention to the subtle dimension often facilitates change (Wubbolding, 1988b).

Paradoxical techniques place clients in a double bind, so that therapeutic change occurs regardless of the paradoxical directives. Clients may be asked to exaggerate and even perfect a problematic behavior. Clients who complain that they cannot sleep are directed to attempt to stay awake. Clients who are deathly afraid of making mistakes are directed to try to make mistakes. A client who is depressing is told: "Maybe you should not give up this symptom too quickly. It does get you the attention that you say you want. If you stop depressing, then your family may not notice you." By accepting the therapist's directives and thus maintaining the symptom, clients demonstrate control over it and are no longer helpless. And if clients choose to resist the directives and let go of a particular symptom, the behavior is not merely controlled but eliminated.

Paradoxical procedures are powerful interventions, and thus they should be used only by practitioners who have been adequately trained in this technique or are under close supervision. Research findings reveal that paradoxical techniques have been successfully applied in dealing with depression, insomnia, phobias, and anxiety disorders. They also appear to be especially well suited for resistant clients with specific behaviorally defined problems (Huddleston & Engels, 1986).

Paradoxical procedures are usually not used until the more conventional procedures of reality therapy have been tried. Also, sarcasm would not be an acceptable paradoxical technique in reality therapy. Furthermore, there are ethical and clinical issues involved in using paradoxical interventions. Ethical practice demands that therapists know when paradoxical procedures should be avoided. These procedures are not advisable in crisis situations, suicide, homicide, violence, abuse, or excessive drinking. Paradox in these situations is not likely to have a therapeutic effect and will probably be counterproductive and irresponsible (Weeks & L'Abate, 1982).

In summary, the value of paradoxical procedures depends largely on the therapist's training and experience. They can be misused when counselors employ them for shock value or as a way to enjoy power (Weeks & L'Abate, 1982). When these procedures are used in a timely and appropriate way, however, they can be powerful therapeutic tools. They can have a similar impact as humor in helping clients cast their problems in a new light. Clients may actually learn how to laugh at their foibles, which could make change a much easier matter.

Dowd and Milne (1986, p. 278) suggest that the appropriate use of paradoxical interventions requires that this question be raised: "What technique used by what counselor causes what change with what type of client in what situation?" In addition to this standard question other questions a counselor can raise to determine when the use of paradox is appropriate include "Have I established a strong bond of trust between myself and the client?" "Might the use of paradox have a boomerang effect, so that the client feels tricked and thus becomes even more resistant?" "How has the client responded to the use of other techniques?" "Am I clear on what I expect to accomplish, and do I have an educated sense of how my client might react to this procedure?"

If you would like to pursue the topic of the use of paradox, see Wubbolding (1988b), Weeks and L'Abate (1982), Dowd and Milne (1986), Huddleston and Engels (1986), and Frankl (1960).

APPLICATIONS OF REALITY THERAPY

Reality therapy is a relatively short-term intervention that is applicable to individual counseling, marriage and family therapy, group counseling, social work, education, crisis intervention, corrections and rehabilitation, institutional management, and community development. It is a popular approach in schools, correctional institutions, general hospitals, state mental hospitals, halfway houses, and substance-abuse centers. Most of the military clinics that treat drug and alcohol abusers use reality therapy as their preferred therapeutic approach.

Glasser (1984a) maintains that reality therapy is applicable to people "with any sort of psychological problem, from mild emotional upset to complete psychotic withdrawal." It is used with children, adolescents, adults, and the aged. According to Glasser, the only factor limiting its applicability is the technical skill of the therapist.

Marriage counseling is often practiced by the reality therapist. Although the sessions are generally kept to about ten, therapy can be of a longer duration. After the ten sessions an evaluation is made to determine what progress has been made and whether continued sessions are in order. It is important to establish at the outset whether the couple are (1) deciding to terminate the relationship, (2) exploring the pros and cons of continuing the relationship, (3) sharing a commonality of perceptions, wants, and behaviors, or (4) quite sure they wish to remain married but seeking help in improving their relationship. Therapists are encouraged to be active. Some questions that they are likely to pose are "What are you doing that makes you feel good [bad] about yourself? What is your spouse doing that makes you feel good [bad] about yourself? What specific changes would each of you be willing to make to help your marriage?"

What Are You Doing? (N. Glasser, 1980) demonstrates how more than two dozen reality therapists worked with a variety of clients. Examples of cases include dealing with the problems of a divorced parent, therapy with depressed clients, helping an alcoholic find a new life, helping suicidal adolescents develop a sense of purpose, working with people with severe handicaps, helping a mentally retarded boy learn to assume increasing responsibility, assisting a principal in helping teachers, and providing teachers and school counselors with ways of helping children. The therapists who worked with these cases took the basic tools provided in reality therapy and found an individualistic way of using them effectively to help the clients look at their life and design constructive behavioral alternatives.

In her more recent book, *Control Theory in the Practice of Reality Therapy: Case Studies,* Naomi Glasser (1989) provides illustrations of how reality therapy can be applied to diverse populations, including children and adolescents, survivors of incest, abused children, prisoners, and people with eating disorders.

Summary and Evaluation

SUMMARY

The reality therapist functions as a teacher and a model, who confronts clients in ways that help them evaluate what they are doing and whether their behavior is fulfilling their basic needs without harming themselves or others. The heart of reality therapy is accepting personal responsibility and gaining more effective control. People take charge of their life rather than being the victim of circumstances beyond their control. Thus, practitioners of reality therapy focus on what clients are *able and willing to do* in the *present* to change their behavior.

The practice of reality therapy weaves together two components, the counseling environment and specific procedures that lead to changes in behavior. This process enables clients to move in the direction of getting what they want.

CONTRIBUTIONS OF REALITY THERAPY

Among the advantages of reality therapy are its relatively short-term focus and the fact that it deals with conscious behavioral problems. One of its more recent ideas is the importance of clarifying what clients want, or exploring with them their "picture album." Clients are confronted with the necessity of making value judgments about their behavior. Insight and awareness are not enough; a plan of action and a commitment to following through are the core of the therapeutic process. I like the focus on strongly encouraging clients to evaluate their life situations, to decide if what they are doing is working, and to commit themselves to make changes.

Reality therapy provides a structure in which both clients and therapists can measure the degree and nature of changes. The contract approach is one such method that can lead to specificity and accountability. Although I like the idea of not accepting excuses for violating contracts, I also like the avoidance of punishment and blaming that is basic to reality therapy. If clients do not carry out their plans, it is important to frankly explore with them the implications of this situation and to make a new plan.

Although Glasser's control theory teaches the necessity for assuming more responsibility for one's own perceived world, it is important to avoid criticizing oneself, for this only makes matters worse. It seems to me that Glasser and Ellis are very close on this point of insisting that self-blaming and harsh self-criticism lead to an increase in one's problems. Both also stress the value of accepting people while encouraging them to change certain aspects of their behavior.

View of psychosis.   In contemporary reality therapy mental health is equated with the responsible fulfilling of one's needs or drives, and mental illness is what occurs when people are unable to control the world to satisfy their needs. However, their behavior is still their best attempt to deal with reality at that particular time. On this point Glasser (1985) has written that reality therapists believe that psychosis can be directly related to unfulfilled needs. Psychotic persons may have been unable to figure out satisfying behavior and therefore have turned to living with distortions. In their perceived world they have created unrealistic (psychotic) ways of reducing the pain they experience in attempting to cope with reality.

In many respects I am in agreement with reality therapy's view of mental health and mental illness. I certainly think that we choose the way we behave to a large extent, and thus we also choose how we feel and how we think. In my view the disease concept can easily be an excuse for not accepting the consequences of our behavior. It seems almost fashionable to have a disease label attached to most forms of human misery. Although it may be easier for people to convince themselves that they are the victims of a disease (such as depression or some type of addiction), this conviction renders them passive and powerless to change their situation. By accepting their own role in creating situations, individuals empower themselves to discover more effective ways of living. However, the reality of psychiatric disease does exist, and not all mental and emotional disturbance can be reduced to a "cop-out" for responsible behavior. As therapists we need to distinguish between psychiatric disorders and irresponsible actions.

Contributions to multicultural counseling.   The core principles of reality therapy have much to offer in the area of multicultural counseling. In cross-cultural therapy it is essential that counselors respect the differences in world view between themselves and their clients. Counselors demonstrate their respect for the cultural values of their clients by helping them explore how satisfying their current behavior is both to themselves and to others. Once clients make this assessment, they can formulate realistic plans that are consistent with their cultural values. It is a further sign of respect that the counselor refrains from deciding what behavior should be changed. Through skillful questioning on the counselor's part, ethnic-minority clients can be helped to determine the degree to which they have acculturated into the dominant society. It is possible for them to find a balance, retaining their ethnic identity and values while integrating some of the values and practices of the dominant group. Again, the counselor does not determine this balance for clients but challenges them to arrive at their own answer. With this focus on acting and thinking rather than on identifying and exploring feelings, many clients are less likely to display resistance to counseling.

Clients identify particular problems that are causing them difficulty, and these problems become the targets for change. Thus, counseling becomes a teaching/learning process, which appeals to many ethnic-minority clients. This process teaches clients that they have the power to control their destiny by changing their behavior.

To its credit this approach provides clients with tools to make the desired changes. This is especially true during the planning phase that is so central to the process of reality therapy. The focus is on positive steps that can be taken, not on what cannot be done. Within this context clients can be assisted in taking specific measures to move the external world closer to their perceived world of wants. This type of specificity, and the direction that is provided by an effective plan, are certainly assets in counseling ethnic-minority clients.

A professional colleague who trains counselors and social workers in Hong Kong tells me that school counselors there have found this approach highly effective. In fact, an increasing number of mental-health professionals in Hong Kong with educational and religious backgrounds are choosing reality therapy as their primary orientation.

LIMITATIONS AND CRITICISMS OF REALITY THERAPY

In my estimation one of the main limitations of reality therapy is that it does not give adequate emphasis to the role of these aspects of the counseling process: the unconscious, the power of the past and the effect of traumatic experiences in early childhood, the therapeutic value of dreams, and the place of transference. It seems to me that reality therapy focuses almost exclusively on consciousness and, by doing so, does not take into account factors such as repressed conflicts and the power of the unconscious in influencing how we think, feel, behave, and choose. The psychoanalytic analogy of consciousness as only the tip of the iceberg makes sense to me, for I do not see how clients can truly choose or make changes without awareness of influential factors in their development. Likewise, past unfinished business and childhood experiences have a great deal of therapeutic power if they are connected to our present functioning. Some painful early experiences need to be recognized, *felt fully*, reexperienced, and worked through in therapy before people can free themselves of restrictive influences. Notice that I do place value on giving attention to the expression and exploration of *feelings* as well as on challenging clients to eventually make new decisions and to translate what they learn in the therapeutic situation into constructive changes in their current ways of thinking, feeling, behaving, and choosing.

From my vantage point dreams are powerful tools in helping people recognize their internal conflicts. Yet the analysis of dreams is not part of the reality therapist's repertoire. From Glasser's (1984a) standpoint there is virtually no evidence to indicate that working with dreams is of any therapeutic value, and such work can be used as a defense to avoid talking about one's behavior. Again, my colleagues and I continue to be impressed by the richness of an individual's dream, which can be a shorthand message of his or her central struggles, hopes, and visions of the future. Asking clients to recall, report, share, and relive their dreams in the here and now of the therapeutic session has helped unblock them and has paved the way for taking a different course of action.

Similarly, I have a difficult time accepting Glasser's view of transference as a misleading concept, for I find that clients are able to learn that significant people in their life have a present influence on how they perceive and react to others. True, a focus on transference can be an avoidance on both the therapist's and the client's part, yet to rule out an exploration of this special type of projection that distorts accurate perception of others seems narrow.

A lack of depth.   Most of the strategies of reality therapists are simple, direct, and straightforward. It seems to me, however, that many of these interventions are directed mainly at solving immediate problems rather than exploring unfinished business from the past that is blocking a client's effective functioning. Many of the behavioral methods used in reality therapy do not seem to address some of the deeper and long-lasting personal struggles. There is a danger that therapists can use reality therapy as a way of dealing exclusively with the client's surface concerns, ignoring more profound issues. This criticism does depend largely on the skill level of the therapist, and current reality therapy does allow for a broader range of interventions than merely teaching clients problem-solving skills.

Reality therapy is vulnerable to the practitioner who assumes the role of an expert in deciding for others such questions as how life should be lived, what is realistic or unrealistic, what is right or wrong behavior, and what constitutes responsible behavior. Thus, counselors who are unaware of their own needs to "straighten people out" can stunt a client's growth and autonomy by becoming overly moralistic and by strongly influencing the client to accept their view of reality. If counselors do this, however, they are perverting the basic concepts inherent in reality therapy, for the approach calls on clients to make their own value judgments.

Limitations for multicultural counseling.   One of the shortcomings in working with ethnic-minority clients is that they may not feel that this approach takes into account some very real environmental forces that operate against them in their everyday lives. Discrimination and racism are unfortunate realities, and these forces do limit many minority clients in getting what they want from life. If counselors do not accept these environmental restrictions, such clients are likely to feel misunderstood. There is a danger that some reality therapists will too quickly or too forcefully stress the ability of these clients to take charge of their lives.

Another problem that needs to be taken into account is that some ethnic-minority clients are very reluctant to say what they need. Their culture has not reinforced them in assertively asking for what they want, and in fact, they may be socialized to think more of what is good for the social group than of their individual wants. In working with people with these values, counselors must "soften" reality therapy somewhat. Such clients should not be pushed to assertively declare their wants. If this method is not applied sensitively, these clients are likely to leave therapy, because they will perceive what is being asked of them as foreign to them. Reality therapy needs to be used artfully and not blindly. Many of its principles and concepts can be incorporated in a dynamic and personal way into the style of counselors, and there is a basis for integrating them with most of the other therapeutic approaches covered in this book.

QUESTIONS FOR REFLECTION AND DISCUSSION

1. Control theory is based on the premise that although outside events influence us, we are not determined by them. To what degree do you agree with the assumption that our actions, thoughts, and emotions are the product of our choices? What are the implications for counseling practice of the way you answer this question?
2. Control theory rests on the assumption that everything we do, think, and feel is generated by what happens inside us. What are the implications of this perspective for counseling practice? How would this view influence the interventions that you make?
3. What is the importance of defining and clarifying wants, or "pictures"? What are the implications of counselors' helping clients express realistic wants?
4. If you were working with a man who was depressing and he insisted that he couldn't help the way he felt, how would you deal with him by teaching him control theory? Assume that he told you that he was coming to you because he was not capable of getting out of his pit of depression. How would you proceed?
5. In what specific areas or situations might you have trouble in allowing your clients to make value judgments for themselves? Might you be inclined to impose your values on your clients?
6. What might you do in a situation with clients who consistently refused to make any plans to change? How would you intervene with clients who made plans but then did not carry them out?
7. What are your reactions to reality therapy's focus on current behavior and its lack of interest in exploring the past? Compare and contrast this view of the role of the past with the psychoanalytic approach's view.
8. Although reality therapists do not ignore dealing with feelings, they certainly do not encourage clients to focus on feelings as if they were separate from actions and thoughts. What is your reaction to this tactic?
9. If you were working with culturally diverse populations, how well do you think the concepts of control theory and the practices of reality therapy might work? Assume that your clients wanted to focus on factors such as institutional racism, environmental barriers, and economic injustices that they were dealing with daily. How would it be for you (and for your clients) if you worked exclusively with reality therapy?
10. Stan is still with you, and he is about ready to give up on counseling (and on you as a counselor)! As a last-ditch effort, how can you work with Stan's giving up? Assume that he makes plans with you, says that he *really* wants to change, but does not stick by his commitments. What will you say or do?

WHERE TO GO FROM HERE

The programs offered by the Institute for Reality Therapy are designed to teach the concepts of control theory and the practice of reality therapy. The institute offers a certification process involving a one-week intensive basic seminar, in which participants take part in discussions, demonstrations, and role playing, followed by a supervised practicum designed specifically to best meet the needs of each individual trainee. A second intensive week and second practicum follow. The basic and advanced practicums each entail a minimum of 30 hours over at least a six-month period. For further information about these training programs contact either of these two organizations:

Institute for Reality Therapy
7301 Medical Center Drive, Suite 407
Canoga Park, CA 91307
Telephone: (818) 888-0688

Center for Reality Therapy
7777 Montgomery Road
Cincinnati, OH 45236
Telephone: (513) 561-1911

The *Journal of Reality Therapy* publishes manuscripts concerning research, theory development, and specific descriptions of the successful application of reality therapy in field settings. If you are interested in subscribing, contact:

Dr. Lawrence Litwack, Editor
Journal of Reality Therapy
203 Lake Hall, Boston-Bouve College
Northeastern University
360 Huntington Avenue
Boston, MA 02115

RECOMMENDED SUPPLEMENTARY READINGS

Control Theory: A New Explanation of How We Control Our Lives (Glasser, 1985) gets my top recommendation. In this popular and easy-to-read book, Glasser discusses how we can choose to change our actions and thus gain better control of our thoughts and feelings and live healthier and more productive lives. His central thesis is that everything that we do, think, and feel is generated by what happens inside of us, not what occurs in our external environment. He shows how our behavior makes sense in light of our attempt to meet our basic needs, which are the powerful forces that drive us. Other interesting topics that are explored include choosing misery, craziness and responsibility, psychosomatic illness as a creative process, addictive drugs, taking control of our health, and how to start using control theory.

Reality Therapy: A New Approach to Psychiatry (Glasser, 1965) outlines the basic concepts and gives examples of how this approach works for clients in various settings. It will give you a good understanding of the ideas that Glasser initially stressed.

Control Theory in the Practice of Reality Therapy: Case Studies (N. Glasser, 1989) is a book of cases showing how control theory is applied to the practice of reality therapy with a diverse range of clients. It brings the concepts of reality therapy up to date by showing how therapists integrate the concepts of control theory into their practice. These cases demonstrate how the key ideas of control theory actually work in helping clients to ask themselves the question "Is what I am choosing to do now getting me what I want?"

Using Reality Therapy (Wubbolding, 1988b) extends the principles of reality therapy by presenting case studies that can be applied to marital and family counseling as well as individual counseling. He has summarized control theory into five clear principles. This book is clearly written, with practical guidelines for implementing the principles of reality therapy in practice. There are excellent questions and brief examples that clarify ways of using reality-therapy concepts. There are chapters on guidelines for creating an effective counseling relationship as well as on specific procedures used by the reality therapist to facilitate change. The author has extended the scope of practicing reality therapy by describing other procedures such as paradoxical techniques, humor, skillful questioning, supervision, and self-help. He presents reality therapy as a philosophy of life rather than a doctrinaire theory or set of prescriptions.

REFERENCES AND SUGGESTED READINGS*

COREY, G. (1990). *Theory and practice of group counseling* (3rd ed.). Pacific Grove CA: Brooks/Cole.

COREY, G. (1991). *Case approach to counseling and psychotherapy* (3rd ed.). Pacific Grove, CA: Brooks/Cole.

DOWD, E. T., & MILNE, C. R. (1986). Paradoxical interventions in counseling psychology. *The Counseling Psychologist, 14,* 237–282.

ELLIS, A. (1977). Fun as psychotherapy. *Rational Living, 12,* 2–6

EVANS, D. B. (1982). What are you doing? An interview with William Glasser. *Personnel and Guidance Journal, 60,* 460–465.

FRANKL, V. E. (1960). Paradoxical intention: A logotherapeutic technique. *American Journal of Psychotherapy, 14,* 520–535.

GLASSER, N. (Ed.). (1980). *What are you doing? How people are helped through reality therapy.* New York: Harper & Row.

*GLASSER, N. (Ed.). (1989). *Control theory in the practice of reality therapy: Case studies.* New York: Harper & Row.

GLASSER, W. (1961). *Mental health or mental illness?* New York: Harper & Row.

GLASSER, W. (1965). *Reality therapy: A new approach to psychiatry.* New York: Harper & Row.

GLASSER, W. (1969). *Schools without failure.* New York: Harper & Row.

GLASSER, W. (1972). *The identity society.* New York: Harper & Row.

GLASSER, W. (1976a). *Positive addiction.* New York: Harper & Row.

GLASSER, W. (1976b). Reality therapy. In V. Binder & B. Rimland (Eds.), *Modern therapies.* Englewood Cliffs, NJ: Prentice-Hall.

*GLASSER, W. (1980). Reality therapy. An explanation of the steps of reality therapy. In N. Glasser (Ed.), *What are you doing? How people are helped through reality therapy.* New York: Harper & Row.

*GLASSER, W. (1981). *Stations of the mind.* New York: Harper & Row.

* Books and articles marked with an asterisk are suggested for further study.

*GLASSER, W. (1984a). Reality therapy. In R. Corsini (Ed.), *Current psychotherapies* (3rd ed.) (pp. 320–353). Itasca, IL: F. E. Peacock.

*GLASSER, W. (1984b). *Take effective control of your life.* New York: Harper & Row.

*GLASSER, W. (1985). *Control theory: A new explanation of how we control our lives.* New York: Harper & Row (Perennial Paperback).

*GLASSER, W. (1986a). *The basic concepts of reality therapy* (chart). Canoga Park, CA: Institute for Reality Therapy.

GLASSER, W. (1986b). *Control theory in the classroom.* New York: Harper & Row (Perennial Paperback).

*GLASSER, W. (1986c). *The control theory–reality therapy workbook.* Canoga Park, CA: Institute for Reality Therapy.

*GLASSER, W. (1989). Control theory in the practice of reality therapy. In N. Glasser (Ed.), *Control theory in the practice of reality therapy: Case studies* (pp. 1–15). New York: Harper & Row.

*GLASSER, W. (1990). *The quality school.* New York: Harper & Row.

GREENWALD, H. (1975). Humor in psychotherapy. *Journal of Contemporary Psychotherapy, 7,* 113–116.

HUDDLESTON, J. E., & ENGELS, D. W. (1986). Issues related to the use of paradoxical techniques in counseling. *Journal of Counseling and Human Service Professions, 1,* 127–133.

PARISH, T. S. (1988). Why reality therapy works. *Journal of Reality Therapy, 7,* 31–32.

SAPER, B. (1987). Humor in psychotherapy: Is it good or bad for the client? *Professional Psychology: Research and Practice, 18,* 360–367.

THATCHER, J. A. (1987). Value judgments: A significant aspect of reality therapy. *Journal of Reality Therapy, 7,* 23–25.

WEEKS, G. R., & L'ABATE, L. (1982). *Paradoxical psychotherapy: Theory and practice with individuals, couples, and families.* New York: Brunner/Mazel.

WUBBOLDING, R. E. (1988a). Professional ethics: Intervention in suiciding behaviors. *Journal of Reality Therapy, 7,* 13–17.

*WUBBOLDING, R. E. (1988b). *Using reality therapy.* New York: Harper & Row (Perennial Library).

WUBBOLDING, R. E. (1989). Professional issues: Four stages of decision making in suicidal client recovery. *Journal of Reality Therapy, 8,* 57–61.

WUBBOLDING, R. E. (1990). *Reality therapy training: Intensive workshop.* Cincinnati, OH: Center for Reality Therapy.

13

CASE ILLUSTRATION: COMPARISON OF APPROACHES

INTRODUCTION

This chapter illustrates how the various therapies could deal with the same client, Stan. We will examine their answers to questions such as these: What themes in Stan's life merit special attention in therapy? What concepts explain the nature of his problems? What are the general goals of his therapy? What possible techniques and methods would best meet these goals? What are some characteristics of the relationship between Stan and his therapist? How might the therapist proceed?

A single case can illustrate both contrasts and parallels among the approaches. It will also help you understand the practical applications of the nine models and will provide some basis for integrating them. Try to sharpen your focus on certain attributes of each approach that can be incorporated into a personalized style of counseling.

To make this chapter more meaningful, you might imagine yourself to be, like Stan, in psychological counseling. Provide your own background information, and develop goals for what you hope to accomplish. Then, *as a client,* work through each of these therapies.

THE CASE OF STAN

The setting is a community mental-health agency, where both individual and group counseling by a qualified staff are available. Stan is coming to counseling because of a court order as a stipulation of his probation. He was charged for driving under the influence of alcohol. Although he does not think he has a serious drinking problem, the judge determined that he needed professional help.

Stan arrives for an intake interview and provides the counselor with this information:

> At 25 years old I'm working as a construction worker. I like building houses, but I'm pretty sure I don't want to stay in construction for the rest of my life. When it comes to my personal life, I've always had a rough time getting along with people. I suppose you could call me a "loner." I like having people in my life, but I just don't seem to know how to go about making friends or getting close to people. Probably the reason I sometimes drink a bit too much is because I'm so scared when it comes to mixing with people. Even though I hate to admit it, when I've been drinking, things don't seem quite so overwhelming. When I look at others, they seem to know the right things to say. Next to them I feel so dumb. I'm afraid that people will be bored with me and that if they really knew me, they wouldn't want anything to do with me. Sure, I'd like to turn my life around, and I'm trying, but sometimes I just don't know where to begin. That's why I went back to school. Besides my work in construction I'm also a part-time college student majoring in psychology. I want to better myself. In one of my classes, Psychology of Personal Adjustment, we talked about ourselves and how we wanted to change, and we also had to write an autobiographical paper. Should I bring it in?

That is the essence of Stan's introduction. The counselor says that she very much wants to read his autobiography. He hopes it will give her a better understanding of where he has been, where he is now, where he would like to go, and what he wants for himself. It reads as follows:

Where am I *currently* in my life? At 25, I feel that I have wasted most of my life. By now I should be finished with college and into a good job, but instead I'm only a junior. I cannot afford to really commit myself to pursuing college full time, because I need to work to support myself. Even though construction work is hard, I like the satisfaction I get by looking at what I helped build.

Although I would like to build things as a hobby, I want to get into some profession where I could work with people, if I could ever get over my fears of what people thought of me. Someday, I am hoping to get a master's degree in counseling or in social work and eventually work as a counselor with kids who are in trouble. I feel I was helped by someone who cared about me, and I would like to have a similar influence on young people.

At this time I live alone, have very few friends, and feel scared with people my own age or older. I feel good when I am with kids, because they are so honest. But I worry a lot whether I am smart enough to get through all the studies I will need to do before I can become a counselor.

One of my problems is that I drink heavily and frequently get drunk. This happens mostly when I feel alone and scared that I'll always feel as lonely and isolated as I do now. At first drinking makes me feel better, but later on I really feel rotten. I used to do drugs heavily, and once in a while I still get loaded. People really scare me, and I feel overwhelmed when I am around strong and attractive women. I feel all cold, sweaty, and terribly uptight when I am with a woman. Maybe I think they're judging me, and I know they will find out that I am not much of a man. I am afraid I will not measure up to being a man — *always* having to be strong, tough, and perfect. I am not any of those, so I often wonder if I am adequate as a man. I really have trouble in seeing myself as sexually adequate. When I do have sex, I get uptight and worry that I will not be able to perform, and then I really feel terrible.

I feel a terrible anxiety much of the time particularly at night. Sometimes I get so scared that I feel like running, but I just cannot move. It is awful, because I often feel as if I am dying at times like this. And then I fantasize about committing suicide and wonder who would care. Sometimes I see my family coming to my funeral feeling very sorry that they did not treat me better. I even made a weak attempt to do myself in a couple of years ago. Much of the time I feel guilty that I have not worked up to my potential, that I have been a failure, that I have wasted much of my time, and that I let people down a lot. I can really get down on myself and wallow in my guilt, and I feel very *depressed*. At times like this I think about how rotten I am, how I will never be able to change, and how I would be better off dead. Then I would not have to hurt anymore, and I would not want anything either. It is very difficult for me to get close to anyone. I cannot say that I have ever loved a person, and I know that I have never felt fully loved or wanted.

Everything is not bleak, because I did have enough guts to leave a lot of my shady past behind me, and I did get into college. I like my determination — I *want* to change. I am tired of feeling like a loser, and I know that nobody is going to change my life for me. It is up to me to get what I want. Even though I feel scared a lot, I like it that I can *feel* my feelings and that I am willing to take risks. I hate being a quitter.

What was my past like? What are some significant events and turning points in my life? A major turning point was the confidence my supervisor had in me at the youth camp where I worked the past few summers. He helped me get my job, and he also encouraged me to go to college. He said he saw a lot of potential in me for being able to work well with young people. That was hard for me to *really* believe, but his faith inspired me to begin to believe in myself. Another turning point was my marriage and divorce. This "relationship" did not last long before my wife left me. Wow, that really made me wonder about what kind of man I was! She was a strong and dominant woman who was always telling me how worthless I was and how she could not stand to get near me. We met in a gambling casino in Las Vegas, and we tied the knot shortly after that. We had sex only a few times, and most of the time I was impotent. That was hard to take—a real downer! I am so afraid to get close to a woman. I am afraid she will swallow me up. My parents never got a divorce, but I wish they had. They fought most of the time. I should say, my mother did most of the fighting. She was dominant and continually bitching at my father, whom I always saw as weak, passive, and mousy next to her. He would *never* stand up to her. There were four of us kids at home. My folks always compared me unfavorably to my older sister (Judy) and older brother (Frank). They were "perfect" children, successful honor students. My younger brother (Karl) and I fought a lot, and he was the one who was spoiled rotten by them. I really do not know what happened to me and how I turned out to be the failure of the bunch.

In high school I got involved with the wrong crowd and took a lot of drugs. I was thrown into a youth rehabilitation facility for stealing. Later I was expelled from regular school for fighting, and I landed in a continuation high school, where I would go to school in the mornings and have afternoons for on-the-job training. I got into auto mechanics and was fairly successful and even managed to keep myself employed for three years as a mechanic.

Back to my parents. I remember my father telling me: "You're really dumb. Why can't you be like your sister and brother? You'll never amount to a hill of beans! Why can't you ever do anything right?" And my mother treated me much the way she treated my father. She would say: "Why do you do so many things to hurt me? Why can't you grow up and be a man? You were a mistake—I wish I didn't have you! Things are so much better around here when you're gone." I recall crying myself to sleep many nights, feeling so terribly alone and filled with anger and hate. And feeling so disgusted with myself. There was no talk of religion in my house, nor was there any talk about sex. In fact, I always find it hard to imagine my folks ever having sex.

Where would I like to be five years from now? What kind of person do I want to become, and what changes do I most want in my life? Most of all, I would just like to start feeling better about myself. I would really like to be able to stop drinking altogether and still feel good. I have an inferiority complex, and I know how to put myself down. I want to like myself much more than I do now. I hope I can learn to love at least a few other people, most of all, women. I want to lose my fear that women can destroy me. I would like to feel equal with others and not always have to feel apologetic for my existence. I do not want to suffer from this anxiety and guilt. And I hope that I can begin to think of myself as an OK person. I really want to become a good counselor with kids, and to do this I know I am going to have to change. I am not certain how I will change or even what all the changes are I hope for. I do know that I want to get free of my self-destructive tendencies and learn to trust people more. Maybe when I begin to like myself more, I will be able to trust that others might find something about me that is worth liking.

After the intake session, using the DSM III-R, the counselor gave the following primary diagnosis: Histrionic Personality Disorder. As a secondary diagnosis Stan fit the criteria for Psychoactive Substance Abuse, with alcohol dependence. (In the next chapter the DSM-III-R is discussed, and the issue of diagnosis is explored in greater detail.)

THE VARIOUS APPROACHES

Effective therapists, regardless of their theoretical orientation, pay attention to suicidal ideation. In Stan's autobiography he says that he fantasizes about committing suicide and wonders who would care. At times, he also doubts that he will ever change and wonders if he'd be better off dead. Certainly, before embarking on treatment the therapist would make an assessment of Stan's current ego strength, which would include a discussion of his suicidal thoughts and feelings. (Refer to the discussion of specific guidelines for the assessment of suicidal risk in Chapter 3.)

PSYCHOANALYTIC THERAPY

The psychoanalytic approach would focus on the unconscious psychodynamics of Stan's behavior. Considerable attention might be given to material that he has repressed, such as his anxiety related to the threatened breakthrough of his sexual and aggressive impulses. In his past he had to rigidly control both these impulses, and when he did not, he got into trouble. He also developed a strong superego by introjecting parental values and standards and making them his own. These aspirations were unrealistic, for they were perfectionistic goals. He could be loved only if he became perfect; yet no matter what he attempted, it never seemed adequate. He internalized his anger and guilt, which became depression. At the extreme he demonstrated a self-destructive tendency, which is a way of inflicting punishment on himself. Instead of directing his hostility toward his parents and siblings, he turned it inward toward himself. Stan's preoccupation with drinking could be hypothesized as evidence of an oral fixation. Because he never received love and acceptance during his early childhood, he is still suffering from this deprivation and still desperately searching for approval and acceptance from others. Stan's sex-role identification was fraught with difficulties. He learned the basis of female/male relationships through his early experiences with his parents. What he saw was fighting, bickering, and discounting. His father was the weak one who always lost, and his mother was the strong, domineering force who could and did hurt men. He identified with his weak and impotent father; he generalized his fear of his mother to all women. It could be further hypothesized that he married a woman who was similar to his mother and who reinforced his feelings of impotence in her presence.

The opportunity to develop a transference relationship and work through it would be the core of the therapy process. An assumption is that Stan will eventually relate to his therapist as he did to his mother and that the process will be a valuable means of gaining insight into the origin of his difficulties with women. The analytic process would stress an intensive exploration of his past. The goal would be to make the unconscious conscious, so that he would no longer be determined by unconscious forces. He would devote much therapy time to reliving and exploring his early past. As he talked, he would gain increased understanding of the dynamics of his behavior. He would begin to see connections between his present problems and early experiences in his childhood. Thus, he would explore memories of relationships with his siblings and with his mother and father and also explore how he has generalized his view of women and men from his view of these family members. It could be expected that he would reexperience old feelings and would uncover buried feelings related to traumatic events. Some questions for Stan could include "What did you do when you felt unloved? What did you have to do as a child with your negative feelings? Could you express your rage, hostility, hurt, and fears? What effects did your relationship with your mother have on you? What did this teach you about all women?"

The analytic process would focus on key influences in Stan's developmental years. As he came to understand how he had been shaped by these past experiences, he would become increasingly able to exert control over his present functioning. Many of his fears would become conscious, and then his energy would not have to remain fixed on defending himself from unconscious feelings. Instead, he could make new decisions about his current life. He could do this only if he worked through the transference relationship, however, for the depth of his endeavors in therapy would largely determine the depth and extent of his personality changes.

From the framework of psychoanalytic therapy (as opposed to traditional psychoanalysis), there would be more frequent use of supportive interventions, such as reassurance, expressions of empathy, suggestions, and more self-disclosure by the therapist. There would also be more focus on dealing with Stan's pressing practical issues than on working with his fantasy material. The couch would be less likely to be used, there would be fewer sessions, and the therapy would be structured by more limited objectives.

If the therapist operated from a contemporary psychoanalytic orientation, her focus would be on Stan's developmental sequences. Particular attention would be paid to understanding his current behavior in the world as largely a repetition of one of his earlier developmental phases. Because of his dependency it would be useful in understanding his behavior to see that he is now repeating patterns that he formed with his mother during his infancy. Viewed from this perspective, he has not accomplished the task of separation and individuation. He is still "stuck" in the symbiotic phase on some levels, he is unable to obtain his confirmation of worth from himself, and he has not resolved the dependence/independence struggle. Looking at his behavior from the viewpoint of self psychology can help the therapist deal with his difficulties in forming intimate relationships.

ADLERIAN THERAPY

The basic aims of an Adlerian therapist would be fourfold, corresponding to the four stages of counseling: (1) establishing and maintaining a good working relationship with Stan, (2) exploring his dynamics, (3) encouraging him to develop insight and understanding, and (4) helping him see new alternatives and make new choices.

The first goal would be to develop mutual trust and respect. The therapist would pay close attention to Stan's subjective experience and attempt to get a sense of how he has reacted to the turning points in his life. During the initial session he reacts to his counselor as an expert who has the answers. In fact, he is convinced that he has made a mess of his life and that when he attempts to make decisions, he always ends up regretting what happens. Thus, he approaches his counselor out of desperation and almost pleads for a prescription for coping with his problems. Because she views counseling as a relationship between equals, she would initially focus on his feeling of being unequal to most other people. A good place to begin might be exploring his feelings of inferiority. The goals of counseling would be developed mutually, and the counselor would avoid deciding for him what his goals should be. She would also resist giving him the simple formula he is requesting.

The second stage of the counseling process would deal with an analysis and assessment of Stan's style of life. This assessment would be based on a questionnaire to tap information about his early years, especially his experiences in his family. (See the student manual for a complete description of this lifestyle assessment form as it is applied to Stan.) As mentioned earlier, this assessment would certainly include a determination of whether he poses a danger to himself, since he did mention suicidal inclinations. During this assessment phase, which might take a few sessions, the counselor would explore his social relationships, his relationships with members of his family, his work responsibilities, his role as a male, and his feelings about himself. She would place considerable emphasis on his goals in life and his priorities. She would not pay a great deal of attention to his past, except to show him the consistency between his past and present as he is moving toward the future. Having gathered the data about his family constellation, his early recollections, and his dreams, she would summarize and interpret this information for him. She would pay particular attention to identifying what Adlerians call "basic mistakes," which are faulty conclusions about life and self-defeating perceptions. In Stan's case some of the mistaken conclusions that form the core of his style of life are:

- "I must not get close to people, because they will surely hurt me."
- "Because my own parents did not want me and did not love me, I will never be desired or loved by anybody.'
- "If only I could become perfect, maybe people would acknowledge and accept me."
- "Being a man means not showing emotions."

The information that the counselor summarized and interpreted would lead to insight and increased self-understanding on Stan's part. He would become more aware of how he is functioning and how his *thinking* is contributing to his behavior and feelings. He would learn that he is not "sick" and in need of being "cured"; rather, he is discouraged and needs to be encouraged to reorient his life goals. Through continued emphasis on his beliefs, goals, and intentions, Stan would come to see how his private logic is inaccurate. In his case the core of his style of life can be explained in this way: (1) "I am unloved, insignificant, and do not count"; (2) "the world is a threatening place to be, and life is unfair"; (3) "therefore, I must find ways to protect myself and keep safe." During this third phase of the process his counselor would make interpretations centering on his lifestyle, his current direction, his goals and purposes, and how his private logic works. Of course, he would be expected to carry out homework assignments that would assist him in translating his insights into new behavior. In this way he would be an active participant in his therapy.

In the final, or reorientation, phase of therapy Stan and his counselor would work together to consider alternative attitudes, beliefs, and actions. By now he would see that he does not have to be locked into past patterns, would feel encouraged, and would realize that he does have the power to change his life. He would accept that he will not change merely by gaining insights and would know that he will have to make use of these insights by carrying out an action-oriented plan. He would begin to feel that he can create a new life for himself and not remain the victim of circumstances.

EXISTENTIAL THERAPY

The counselor with an existential orientation would approach Stan with the view that he has the capacity to increase his self-awareness and decide for himself the future direction of his life. She would want him to realize more than anything else that he does not have to be the victim of his past conditioning but can be the architect in redesigning his future. He can free himself of his deterministic shackles and accept the responsibility that comes with directing his own life. This approach would not stress techniques but would emphasize the importance of the therapist's understanding of Stan's world, primarily by establishing an authentic relationship as a means to a fuller degree of self-understanding.

What possible dimensions might be explored with Stan? He could be confronted with the ways in which he is attempting to escape from his freedom through alcohol and drugs. He is demonstrating what Sartre would call "bad faith," which refers to his inauthenticity of not accepting personal responsibility. Examples of his implicit statements of bad faith include "Since my family never really cared for me, this is why I feel unworthy most of the time." "Since that's the way I am, I can't help what I do." "Naturally I'm a loser, because I've been rejected so many times." Eventually, his counselor would confront him with the passivity that is keeping him unfree. She would reaffirm that he is now entirely responsible for his life, for his actions, and for his failure to take action. She could do this in a kind manner, but she would still be firm in challenging him.

The counselor would not see Stan's anxiety as something that needs to be "cured"; rather, he needs to learn that realistic anxiety is a vital part of living with uncertainty and freedom. Because there are no guarantees and because the individual is ultimately alone, he can expect to experience some degree of healthy anxiety, aloneness, guilt, and even despair. These conditions are not neurotic in themselves, but the way in which he orients himself to these conditions and how he copes with his anxiety would be seen as critical.

Stan talks about feeling so low at times that he fantasizes about suicide. Certainly, the therapist would investigate further to determine if he posed an immediate threat to himself. In addition to this assessment to determine lethality, the existential therapist might view his thoughts of "being better off dead" as symbolic. Could it be that he feels that he is dying as a person? Is he using his human potential? Is he choosing a dead way of merely existing instead of affirming life? Is he mainly trying to elicit sympathy from his family? The existentially oriented therapist would confront him with the issue of the meaning and purpose in his life. Is there any reason for him to want to continue living? What are some of the projects that enrich his life? What can he do to find a sense of purpose that will make him feel more significant and more alive?

Stan needs to accept the reality that he may at times feel alone, because choosing for oneself and living from one's own center accentuates the experience of aloneness. He is not, however, condemned to a life of isolation, alienation from others, and loneliness. The existential therapist would help him discover his own centeredness and live by the values he chooses and creates for himself. By doing so, he can become a more substantial person and learn to appreciate himself more. When he does, the chances are lessened that he will have a clinging need to secure approval from others, particularly his parents and parental substitutes. Instead of forming a dependent relationship, he could relate to others out of his strength. Only then would there be the possibility of overcoming his feelings of separateness and isolation.

PERSON-CENTERED THERAPY

Stan's autobiography indicates that he has a fairly clear idea of what he wants for his life. The person-centered approach would rely on his self-report of the way he views himself rather than on a formal assessment and a diagnosis. The person-centered therapist is concerned with understanding him from his internal frame of reference. He has stated goals that are meaningful for him. He is motivated to change and seems to have sufficient anxiety to work toward these desired changes. The person-centered counselor would thus have faith in his ability to find his own way and would trust that he has within himself the necessary resources for personal growth. She would encourage him to speak freely about the discrepancy between the person he sees himself as being and the person he would like to become; about his feelings of being a failure, being inadequate, or being unmanly; about his fears and uncertainties; and about his hopelessness at times. She would strive to create an atmosphere of freedom and security that would facilitate his exploring of threatening aspects of himself. To do this, the counselor would not merely reflect the content of his verbalizations. As he revealed his feelings to her, she would listen intently not only to his words, but to the manner in which he delivered his message. She would attempt to accurately understand what it must be like to live in his world. As more than a mechanical technique, her authentic relationship with him would be based on a concern, a deep understanding and appreciation of his feelings, a nonpossessive warmth and acceptance, and a willingness to allow him to explore any and all of his feelings during the therapeutic hour. She would convey to him the basic attitudes of understanding and accepting, and through this positive regard he might well be able to drop his pretenses and more fully and freely explore his personal concerns.

Stan has a low evaluation of his self-worth. Although he finds it difficult to believe that others really like him, he wants to feel loved ("I hope I can learn to love at least a few people, most of all, women"). He wants to feel equal to others and not have to apologize for his existence, yet most of the time he is keenly aware that he feels inferior. If his therapist can create a supportive, trusting, and encouraging atmosphere, he is likely to feel that she is genuinely interested in him. Basically, Stan would grow personally in the relationship with his therapist. He could use the relationship to learn to be more accepting of himself, with both his strengths and limitations. He would have the opportunity to openly express his fears of women, of not being able to effectively work with people, and of feeling inadequate and stupid. He could explore how he feels judged by his parents and by authorities. He would have an opportunity to express his guilt—that is, his feelings that he has not lived up to his parents' expectations and that he has let them and himself down. He could also relate his feelings of hurt over not having ever felt loved and wanted. He could express the loneliness and isolation that he so often feels, as well as the need to dull these feelings with alcohol or drugs.

In relating his feelings, Stan would no longer be totally alone, for he would take the risk of letting his therapist into his private world. In doing so, how would he be helped? Through the relationship with her he would gradually get a sharper focus on his experiencing and would be able to clarify his own feelings and attitudes. He would be seen as having the capacity to muster his own strengths and make his own decisions. In short, the therapeutic relationship would tend to free him from his self-defeating ways. Because of the caring and faith he would experience from his therapist, he would be able to increase his own faith and confidence in his ability to resolve his difficulties and discover a new way of being.

Therapy would be successful if Stan came to view himself in a more positive light. He would be more sensitive to listening to messages within himself and less dependent on confirmation from others around him. He would gradually discover that there is someone in his life that he can depend on—himself.

GESTALT THERAPY

The Gestalt-oriented therapist would surely want to focus on the unfinished business that Stan has with his parents, siblings, and ex-wife. It would appear that this unfinished business consists mainly of feelings of resentment, yet he turns this resentment inward toward himself. His present life situation would be spotlighted, but he might also need to reexperience past feelings that could be interfering with his present attempts to develop intimacy with others. From his cultural conditioning he has learned to hide rather than reveal his emotions.

Understanding this about him, his counselor would explore his hesitations and concerns about "getting into feelings." She would recognize that he is hesitant in expressing his emotions and thus would help him assess whether it is important to him to become more emotional.

On the assumption that Stan decides that he does want to experience his emotions, rather than to deny them, the therapist would not merely ask him to talk about past experiences. Instead, she would ask him to imagine himself in earlier scenes with his wife, as though the painful situation were occurring in the here and now. He would symbolically relive and reexperience the situation, perhaps by talking "directly" to his wife. He could tell her of his resentments and hurts and eventually complete his unfinished business with her. It would also be important that he speak with his older brother and sister, toward whom he feels resentment because they were always seen as the "perfect" children in the family. However, more important than speaking to them in reality is his willingness to talk to them symbolically as a part of a therapy session. He would also need to talk symbolically with his mother and father, as though he were a child again. The therapist might use the empty-chair technique to "bring" a sibling or parent into therapy. It is not necessarily a part of the Gestalt approach that he actually speak with these significant people in real life, but it is essential that he deal with them in his therapy sessions. He would be encouraged to "say" to them what he had never told them before. The therapist might ask "What are your resentments toward each of these people? What did you want from them that you never received? How would you have liked to be treated by them? What do you need to tell them now so that you can keep from being destroyed by your resentments?"

Through awareness of what he is now doing and how he keeps himself locked into his past, Stan can increasingly assume personal responsibility for his own life. In working toward this end, he might engage in a "game of dialogue" in which his "top-dog" side talks with his "underdog" side. These dimensions within himself are struggling for control. He would play both parts for himself, and again, the empty-chair technique could be used. Through this procedure, it is hoped, he could become aware of the self-torture game he is continuing to play with himself. Stan also maintains that he has difficulty in feeling like a man, especially in relationships with strong women. He might become the little boy in exaggerated fashion and talk to a powerful woman (in the empty chair), and then he could become the threatening woman and talk back to his little-boy side. The main point is that he would face his fears and engage in a dialogue with the polarities that exist within him. The aim would not be to extract his feelings but to learn to live with his polarities. Why must he be either a "little boy" or a "powerful superman"? Can he not learn to be a man who at times feels threatened and weak?

Most of the Gestalt exercises would serve one main function for Stan helping him gain a fuller sense of what he is doing in the present to keep significant figures alive and powerful within himself. As he gained more complete awareness of his dependency, he would also find an internal capacity to strive for his own wishes, rather than remaining controlled by the expectations of others.

TRANSACTIONAL ANALYSIS

Stan would begin TA therapy by developing with his therapist a contract that specified areas of his life he desires to change. A general area that he would like to modify is learning how to feel "OK," for now he feels "not OK" much of the time. How might his therapy proceed with a TA orientation? Although the focus would be on present behavior, transactions with others, and his attitudes toward himself, exploration of the past would also be important, to the extent that early decisions could be identified. Essentially, he would need to learn that his decision about the way he had to be in order to survive when he was a child might no longer be appropriate. The decision was "I am stupid, and it would be better if I were not here. I am a loser." Now he can modify this early decision by redeciding what may be currently appropriate.

In addition to making this early decision, Stan accepted a list of injunctions and messages that he still lives by, including "Don't be"; "Be a man" (which means "Always be strong"); "Don't trust women"; "You'll never become anything"; and "You can't do anything right." Perhaps the basic injunction, and the most dangerous one, is the message "Don't be." In many ways Stan was programmed with the message "You were an accident, and the best way for you to be is to become invisible." Perhaps his suicidal thoughts are related to following the script that he is best off being invisible. TA therapists are very likely to insist on what they refer to as a "no-suicide" contract. Such a contract with Stan would involve a statement by his Adult that he will monitor himself in order to guard against his self-destructive impulses. He would guarantee his therapist that he would not take his life for a specified period of time. The therapist would then explore with him what is going on in his life, with a focus on his perception of the unsolved problems that he is using as a justification for ending his life. Therapy would be directed toward solving these problems once he decides that he does want to live in spite of his problems. If he is not confronted on this issue, he could easily sabotage any therapeutic progress by telling himself "If things don't get better, I could always end my life."

In addition to the injunctions mentioned above, Stan has been influenced by cultural injunctions. The TA therapist would be interested in exploring his cultural background, including his values and the values characteristic of his culture. With this focus it is likely that he may identify some of the following cultural injunctions: "Don't talk about your family with strangers, and don't hang out your dirty linen in public." "Don't confront your parents, for they deserve respect." "Don't be too concerned about yourself." "Don't show your vulnerabilities; hide your feelings and weaknesses." Although Stan's counselor would respect the cultural context in which he grew up, she would still strive to create a therapeutic climate that would allow him to question the degree to which he has accepted certain messages that are no longer functional. Although he can decide to retain those aspects of his cultural background that he prizes, he is also in a position to modify certain cultural expectations.

Certainly, the strokes that Stan asks for and receives would be a focus of therapy. In his childhood, he received many negative strokes, and he was discounted as a person of worth. Now he finds it difficult to maintain intimate relationships and to accept positive strokes. He has invested considerable energy in collecting "bad feelings," including his feelings of anxiety, guilt, self-deprecation, and suicidal thoughts, which would be explored as part of the therapeutic process.

The TA therapist would probably confront Stan with the games that he is playing, such as "Poor Me," "Victim," "Martyr," and "Helpless One." His "racket," the collection of feelings that he uses to justify his life script and his early decision, is at once both a guilt racket and a depression racket. He appears to be saving up his feelings of guilt and depression, and the games he plays with others often have depression and guilt as a payoff. In his case, when he finally gathered up enough self-condemnation and depression, he could feel justified in taking his life, which is the concluding action that his life script calls for. His accepting of the message "don't be" is a particular problem that would be essential to explore in therapy.

Throughout the course of his therapy Stan would be taught how to analyze his life script. He would be shown that he has based his lifetime plan on a series of decisions and adaptations. Through script analysis he would identify the life patterns he appears to be following, and as he became more aware of his life script, he would be able to actively change his programming. It is through increased awareness that he can break free of his early scripting.

Stan's autobiography indicates that he has introjected a Critical Parent who punishes him and drives him to feel that whatever he does is not quite enough. If he hopes to learn how to love others more fully, it would be important for him to learn how to be kinder to and less demanding of himself. He must be able to nourish himself, accept his successes, and open himself to others.

BEHAVIOR THERAPY

Working with Stan from a behavioral perspective, the therapist might begin with a comprehensive assessment utilizing the categories that are a part of the multimodal approach. In Stan's case many specific and interrelated problems can be identified by using the following BASIC ID diagnosis:

Behavior

- is defensive, avoids eye contact, speaks hesitantly
- uses alcohol excessively
- has gotten into trouble with the law because of his drinking
- has a poor sleep pattern
- pounds his leg with his fist, turning his anger inward
- displays various avoidance behaviors

Affect

- feels anxiety
- panics (especially at night when trying to sleep)
- experiences depression
- fears criticism and rejection
- feels worthless

- feels stupid
- feels isolated and alienated
- has resentment toward his siblings

Sensation

- feels dizziness
- suffers from impotence
- has palpitations
- gets headaches

Imagery

- receives ongoing negative parental messages
- has an unfavorable body image and poor self-image
- sees himself as a failure in life
- has suicidal fantasies at times
- views himself in an inferior light in the presence of women
- sees himself as homely
- fantasizes himself as being shunned by others

Cognition

- asks self-identity questions ("Who and what am I?")
- has worrying thoughts (death and dying)
- questions his right to succeed in his projects
- has many self-defeating thoughts and beliefs
- is governed by categorical imperatives ("shoulds," "oughts," "musts")
- seeks new values
- compares himself with others
- engages in fatalistic thinking

Interpersonal characteristics

- is unassertive
- has an unsatisfactory relationship with his parents
- has very few friends
- is afraid of contact with women and fears intimacy
- feels like an outcast
- feels socially inferior

Drugs and biological factors

- abuses alcohol
- has used illegal drugs
- lacks an exercise program
- has various physical complaints
- shows no organic pathology

After completing this assessment of Stan, his therapist would focus on helping him define the specific areas where he would like to make changes. She and Stan would then talk about how the therapy sessions (and his work outside of them) could help him reach his goals. Early during treatment she would help him translate some of his general goals into concrete and measurable ones. Thus, if he said "I want to feel better about myself," she would help him define more specific goals. If he said "I want to get rid of my inferiority complex," she might counter with "What are some situations in which you feel inferior?" "What do you actually do that leads to feelings of inferiority?" In his case some concrete aims include his desire to function without drugs or alcohol. He might be asked to keep a record of when he drinks and what events lead up to his drinking.

Stan indicated that he does not want to feel apologetic for his existence. He might then be asked to engage in some assertiveness-training exercises with his therapist. If he has trouble talking with his boss or co-workers, for example, the therapist could demonstrate how to approach them more directly and confi- dently. This procedure would include modeling, role playing, and behavior rehearsal. He could then try more effective behaviors with his therapist, who would play the role of the boss and then give feedback on how strong or apologetic he seemed.

Stan's anxiety about women could also be explored by behavior-rehearsal methods. The therapist could play the role of a woman whom Stan wants to date. He could practice being the way he would like to be with his date and could say the things to his therapist that he might be afraid to say to his date. He could thus explore his fears, get feedback on the effects of his behavior, and experiment with more assertive behavior.

Systematic desensitization might be appropriate in working with Stan's fear of failing. First, he would learn relaxation procedures during the sessions, and he would then practice them daily at home. Next he would list his specific fears relating to failure. Stan identifies his greatest fear as sexual impotence with a woman. The least fearful situation he identifies is being with a female student for whom he does not feel an attraction. He would then imagine a pleasant scene and begin a desensitization process beginning with his lesser fears and working up to the anxiety associated with his greatest fear.

Therapy would focus on modifying the behavior that results in Stan's feel- ings of guilt and anxiety. This approach would not place importance on his past except to the extent necessary to modify his faulty learning. The therapist would not explore his childhood experiences but would work directly with the present behaviors that are causing his difficulties. Insight would not be seen as important, nor would having him experience or reexperience his feelings. The assumption would be that if he can learn more appropriate coping behaviors, eliminate unrealistic anxiety and guilt, and acquire more adaptive responses, his presenting symptoms will decrease and he will report a greater degree of satisfaction.

RATIONAL-EMOTIVE AND COGNITIVE-BEHAVIORAL THERAPY

The rational-emotive or cognitive-behavioral therapist would have as a broad objective minimizing Stan's self-defeating attitudes and helping him acquire a more realistic outlook on life. In essence the goal would be to teach him how to

identify those thoughts that result in his feeling upset and how to make functional self-statements. To begin with, he would be taught that he is keeping
alive some of his irrational ideas by reindoctrinating himself in an unthinking
manner and that he can learn to challenge the source of his difficulties. If he
learned how to think more rationally, he might begin to feel better. What are
some of the steps that the therapist might employ to assist him in ridding
himself of irrational beliefs and in internalizing a rational philosophy of life?

First, the therapist would challenge Stan to examine the many "shoulds,"
"oughts," and "musts" that he had blindly accepted. She would confront him
on the issue of his continued repetition of specific illogical sentences and
irrational beliefs, which in his case are "I always have to be strong, tough, and
perfect. I'm not a man if I show any signs of weakness. If everyone didn't love
me and approve of me, things would be catastrophic. If a woman rejected me, I
really would be diminished to a 'nothing.' If I fail, I'm a rotten person. I'm
apologetic for my existence, because I don't feel equal to others."

Second, the therapist would ask Stan to evaluate the ways in which he keeps
reindoctrinating himself with those self-defeating sentences. She would not
only attack specific problems but also confront the core of his irrational thinking with ideas such as the following:

> You're not your father, and you don't need to continue telling yourself that
> you're just like him. You no longer need to accept without question your
> parents' value judgments about your worth. You say that you're such a failure
> and that you feel inferior. Do your present activities support this? Why do you
> continue to be so hard on yourself? Does having been the scapegoat in your
> family mean that you need to continue making yourself the scapegoat?

Third, once Stan has understood the nature of his irrational beliefs and has
become aware of how he is maintaining faulty notions about himself, the therapist would urge him to work diligently at attacking them by engaging in coun-
terpropaganda. He would continue to work and practice on looking for evidence to support some of his conclusions. The counselor would give him
specific homework assignments to help him deal with his fears. At some point,
for instance, she would probably ask him to explore his fears of attractive and
powerful women and his reasons for continuing to tell himself "They can
castrate me. They expect me to be strong and perfect. If I'm not careful, they
will dominate me." His homework could include approaching a woman for a
date. If he succeeded in getting the date, he could challenge his catastrophic
expectations of what might happen. What would be so terrible if she did not like
him or if she refused the date? Why does he have to get all his confirmation from
one woman? Stan tells himself over and over that he must be *approved of*
by women and that if any woman rebuffs him, the consequences are more than
he can bear. With awareness of the unrealistic demands he is accepting, he
eventually begins to tell himself that although he prefers acceptance to rejection, it is not the end of the world if he does not get what he wants. He learns to
substitute preferences and desires for "musts" and "shoulds."

In addition to using homework assignments, the therapist might employ
many other behavioral techniques, such as role playing, humor, modeling,

behavior rehearsal, and desensitizaticn. Stan might be asked to read Ellis's book *How to Stubbornly Refuse to Make Yourself Miserable about Anything — Yes, Anything!* He could use these ideas as he works and practices on changing. Basically, she would work in an active, directive manner and would focus on cognitive and behavioral dimensions. She would pay little attention to Stan's past. Instead, she would highlight his present functioning and his illogical thinking and would teach him to rethink and reverbalize in a more logical and constructive way. Thus, he could learn how to be different by telling himself a new set of statements, which might include "I can be lovable. I'm able to succeed as well as fail at times. I need not make all women into my mother. I don't have to punish myself by making myself feel guilty over past failures, because it is not essential to always be perfect."

In addition to rational-emotive techniques Stan could benefit from the range of cognitive-behavioral procedures aimed at helping him learn to make constructive self-statements. He could profit from cognitive restructuring, which would proceed as follows: First, the therapist would assist him in learning ways to observe his own behavior in various situations. This could best be accomplished by his completing a written rational self-analysis. He could do this by completing the RET Self-Help Form, and it would be a good idea for him to bring what he writes on the form to his therapy session. (See the student manual for a sample copy of the form.) During the week he could take a particular situation that is problematic for him, paying particular attention to his automatic thoughts and internal dialogue. What is he telling himself as he approaches a difficult situation? How is he setting himself up for failure with his self-talk? Second, as he learned to attend to his maladaptive behaviors, he would begin to see that what he tells himself has as much impact as others' statements about him. He would also see the connections between his thinking and his behavioral problems. With this awareness he would be in an ideal place to begin to learn a new, more rational internal dialogue. Third, he could also learn new coping skills, which he could practice first in the sessions and then in real-life situations. It would not be enough for him to merely say new things to himself, for to become proficient in new cognitive and behavioral coping skills he would need to apply them in various daily situations. As he experienced success with his assignments, these tasks could become increasingly demanding.

REALITY THERAPY

The reality therapist would be guided by the key concepts of control theory to identify Stan's behavioral dynamics, to provide a direction for him to work toward, and to teach him about better alternatives for getting what he wants. Although he is aware that he is suffering when he initially comes to therapy, he is convinced that he is the victim of past events over which he has no control. The reality therapist would show him that he does not have to be a victim of his past unless he chooses to be. Although she would have compassion for his suffering and the difficulties he continues to face, she would want him to realize that if he decides to change, he has many options. She might have a hunch that he wants to focus on talking about his past because that is easier than facing the present, which would involve considerable work. His counselor would grant that all of his behavior was the best attempt to get what he wanted, yet she would also help him see that what he is doing is not working very well. As counseling progressed, he would learn that even though most of his problems did indeed begin in childhood, there is little he can now do to undo what happened. He would eventually realize that he has little control over changing others but has a great deal of control over what he can do now.

Initially, Stan would want to tell his counselor how miserable he feels. He would do this by attempting to focus on his major symptoms: depression, anxiety, inability to sleep, and other psychosomatic symptoms. He would very much need someone who is willing to listen to him and not criticize him for what he says. Most of his life he has had people criticize him, so now as he presents his story, he expects criticism and invites it from his counselor. During the early phase of counseling the therapist would listen to him and continue to reinforce the idea that she will not criticize him. She would work at establishing involvement with him to provide a good foundation on which to support future therapy. Although she would listen, she would also challenge him, especially as he focused on his misery and his symptoms. She would explain to him that he has an ideal picture of what he wants his life to be, yet he does not possess effective behaviors for meeting his needs. The counselor would talk to him about his needs and how this type of therapy would teach him how to satisfy them in effective ways. She would also explain that his total behavior is made up of acting, thinking, feeling, and physiology. Even though he says he hates feeling anxious most of the time, he would learn that much of what he is doing and thinking is directly leading to his unwanted feelings and physiological reactions. When Stan complained of feeling depressed much of the time, anxious at night, and overcome by panic attacks, the counselor would let him know that she is more interested in what he is doing and thinking, since these components can be directly changed more easily than what he is feeling. She would teach him that instead of being depressed he is, on some level, actually choosing to be depressed; that is, he is *depressing*.

The counselor might well suggest to Stan that he read Glasser's book *Control Theory*, which they would then discuss in each session until he was clearly aware of ways to apply the concepts of this approach to his life. As the sessions progressed, she would ask him in a number of ways the basic question of reality therapy: "Is what you are doing now getting you where you want to be?" It would be up to him to answer this pivotal question. He has admitted that he is seeking counseling because he knows that there is a large gap between what he has and what he wants.

In his therapy Stan tells his counselor about the pictures in his head, a few of which include becoming a counselor, acting confident in meeting people, thinking of himself as a worthwhile person, and enjoying life. Through therapy he makes the evaluation that much of what he is doing is not getting him closer to the pictures in his head or getting him what he wants. After he decided that he was willing to work on himself to be different, the majority of time in the sessions would be devoted to making plans and discussing their implementation. Together he and the therapist would focus on many steps that he can take right now to bring about the changes he would like. Instead of waiting for others to initiate contacts, he could practice seeking out those people he would like to get to know better. He might get involved in volunteer work with young people at a community agency, especially since this is the kind of activity that he finds meaningful. The point is that he would be encouraged to actually do more of the things he wants to do, rather than focusing on what he perceives to be his deficits. As he continued to carry out plans in the real world, he would gradually begin to experience success. When he did backslide, his counselor would not put him down but would help him to do better. Together they would develop a new plan that they felt more confident about. She would not be willing to give up on him, which would be a source of real inspiration for him to keep working on himself.

WORKING WITH STAN: INTEGRATION OF THERAPIES

In this section I work toward integrating therapeutic concepts and techniques from the nine theoretical perspectives. As I describe how I would counsel Stan on the levels of *thinking, feeling,* and *doing,* based on information presented in his autobiography, I will indicate from what orientations I am borrowing ideas at the various stages of his therapy. As you read, think about interventions you might make with Stan that would be either similar to or different from mine. At the end of the chapter are questions that can guide you as you reflect about being his counselor.

A PLACE TO BEGIN

I would start by giving Stan a chance to say how he feels about coming to the initial session. Questions that I might explore with him are:

- "What brings you here? What has been going on in your life recently that gave you the impetus to seek professional help?"
- "What expectations do you have of therapy? of me? What are your hopes, fears, and any reservations? What goals do you have for yourself through therapy?"
- "Could you give me a picture of some significant turning points in your life? Who have been the important people in your life? What are some significant decisions you've made? What are some of the struggles and conflicts you've dealt with, and what are some of these issues that are current for you?"
- "What was it like for you to be in your family? How did you view your parents? How did they react to you? What about your early development?" (It would be useful to administer the Adlerian lifestyle questionnaire, the TA life-script questionnaire, or both.)

CLARIFYING THE THERAPEUTIC RELATIONSHIP

I do not want to give the impression that I would bombard Stan with all of the preceding questions at once. Early in our sessions, however, those would be some of the questions I would have in the back of my mind. At the outset I would work with Stan to develop a working contract, which would involve a discussion of our mutual responsibilities and a clear statement of what he wants from these sessions and what he is willing to do to obtain it. I believe that it is important to openly discuss any factors that might perpetuate a client's dependency on the therapist, so I would invite his questions about this therapeutic relationship. One goal would be to demystify the therapy process; another would be to get some focus for the direction of our sessions.

In establishing the therapeutic relationship, I am influenced by the person-centered, existential, Gestalt, and Adlerian approaches. They do not view therapy as something that the therapist *does* to a *passive* client. Counseling is far more than administering techniques. It is a deeply personal relationship that Stan can use in his learning. Although I think it is essential for me to be familiar with the various theories of counseling and to possess specific skills in implementing techniques in a timely manner, I must apply this knowledge in the context of a working relationship characterized by mutual trust and respect. A few questions that I see as helpful to ask myself are: To what degree am I able to listen to and hear Stan in a nonjudgmental way? Am I able to respect and care for him? Do I have the capacity to enter his subjective world without losing my own identity? Am I able to share with him my own thoughts and feelings as they pertain to our relationship? This relationship is critical at the initial stages of therapy, but it must be maintained during all stages if therapy is to be effective.

My contract with Stan would specify his rights and responsibilities as a client and my role as his therapist. Expectations would be explored, goals would be defined, and there would be a basis for therapy as a collaborative effort. This emphasis is consistent with several of the therapeutic approaches: Adlerian therapy, TA, the behavior therapies, and reality therapy. An excellent foundation for building a working partnership is openness by the counselor about the process of therapy. I think it is a mistake to hide behind "professionalism" as a way of keeping distance from the client. Therefore, I would begin by being as honest as I could be with Stan as the basis for creating this relationship.

CLARIFYING THE GOALS OF THERAPY

It is not enough simply to ask clients what they hope they will leave with at the conclusion of therapy. Typically, I find that clients are vague, global, and unfocused about what they want. Especially from behavior therapy, Adlerian therapy, TA, and reality therapy I borrow the necessity of getting clients to be specific in defining their goals. Thus, Stan may say: "I want to stop playing all these games with myself and others. I'd hope to stop putting myself down. I want to get rid of the terrible feelings I have. I want to feel OK with myself and begin living." My reply is: "Let's see if we can narrow down some of these broad goals into specific enough terms that both you and I will know what you're talking about. What exactly are these games you talk about? In what ways do you put yourself down? What are some of these terrible feelings that bother you? In what specific ways do you feel that you're not living now? What would it take for you to begin to feel alive?"

Again, I would not barrage Stan with all these questions at once. They are merely illustrations of ways in which I would work with him toward greater precision and clarity. If we merely talked about lofty goals of self-actualization I fear, we would have directionless sessions. Thus, I value focusing on concrete language and specific goals that both of us can observe and understand. Once this is ascertained, Stan can begin to observe his own behavior, both in the sessions and in his daily life. This self-monitoring itself is a vital step in any effort to bring about change.

IDENTIFYING FEELINGS

The person-centered approach stresses that one of the first stages in the therapy process involves identifying, clarifying, and learning how to express feelings. Because of my relationship with Stan I would expect him to feel increasingly free to mention feelings that he has kept to himself. In some cases these feelings are out of his awareness. Thus, I would encourage him to talk about any feelings that are a source of difficulty. Again drawing on the person-centered model, I would expect these feelings to be vague and difficult to identify at first.

Therefore, during the early stages of our sessions I would rely on empathic listening. If I can really hear Stan's verbal and nonverbal messages, some of which may not be fully clear to him, I can respond to him in a way that lets him know that I have some appreciation for what it is like in his world. I need to do more than merely reflect what I hear him saying; I need to share with him my reactions as I listen to him. As I come to communicate to him that he is being deeply understood and accepted for the feelings he has, he has less need to deny or distort his feelings. His capacity for clearly identifying what he is feeling at any moment gradually increases.

There is a great deal of value in letting Stan tell his story in a way he chooses. The way he walks into the office, his gestures, his style of speech, the details he chooses to go into, and what he decides to relate and not to relate — to mention a few elements — provide me with clues to his world. If I do too much structuring too soon and if I am too directive, I will interfere with his typical style of presenting himself. So at this stage I agree with the Adlerians, who stress attending and listening on the counselor's part and who focus on the productive use of silence. Although I am not inclined to promote long silences early in counseling, there is value in not jumping in too soon when silences occur. Instead of coming to the rescue, it is better to explore the meanings of the silence.

EXPRESSING AND EXPLORING FEELINGS

My belief is that it is my authenticity as a person that encourages Stan to begin to identify and share with me a range of feelings. But I do not believe that an open and trusting relationship between us is sufficient to change his personality and behavior. I am convinced that I must also use my knowledge, skills, and experiences.

As a way of helping Stan express and explore his feelings, I would tend to draw heavily on Gestalt techniques. Eventually, I would ask him to avoid merely talking about situations and about feelings. Rather, I would encourage him to bring whatever reactions he is having into the present. For instance, if he reported feeling tense, I would ask him *how* he experiences this tension and *where* it is located in his body. One of the best ways that I have found to encourage clients to make contact with their feelings is to ask them to "be that feeling." Thus, if Stan has a knot in his stomach, he can intensify his feeling of tension by "becoming the knot, giving it voice and personality." If I notice that he has moist eyes, I may direct him to "be his tears now." By putting words to his tears, he avoids merely abstractly intellectualizing about all the reasons *why* he is sad or tense. Before he can change his feelings, he must allow himself to *fully experience* these feelings. And the experiential therapies give me valuable tools for guiding him to the expression of feelings.

WORKING WITH STAN'S ALCOHOLISM

Although none of the nine therapeutic approaches addresses drug and alcohol use, it would be imperative at some point in Stan's therapy to confront him on the probability that he is a chemically dependent person. In this section I describe my approach to working with his dependence as well as giving some brief background information on the alcoholic personality and on treatment approaches.

Some basic assumptions.   I would establish a good relationship with Stan before launching into the treatment phase of his possible alcoholism. He has given a number of significant clues suggesting that I should determine whether he is a chemically dependent person and, if so, what course of treatment would be indicated. From the information that he has provided, it is clear that he has many of the personality traits that are typically found in alcoholics, including low self-concept, anxiety, sexual dysfunctions, underachievement, feelings of social isolation, inability to love himself or to receive love from others, hypersensitivity, impulsivity, dependence, fear of failure, feelings of guilt, self-pity, and suicidal impulses. In addition, he has used drugs and alcohol as a way of blunting anxiety and attempting to control what he perceives as a painful reality. He has switched from drugs to alcohol, which is a common attempt to control the disastrous effects of addiction.

Once our therapeutic relationship is firmly established, I would confront Stan (in a caring and concerned manner) on his self-deception that he is doing something positive by not getting loaded with drugs but is merely getting drunk. He needs to see that alcohol *is* a drug, and I would surely want him to make an honest evaluation of his behavior so that he can recognize the degree to which his drinking is interfering in his living. Although he might well resort to excuses, rationalizations, denials, distortions, and minimizations about his drinking patterns, I would provide some information that he could use to examine his confused system of beliefs. Johns Hopkins University Hospital in Baltimore has designed a questionnaire that is useful in assessing the preliminary signs of addiction. A few questions are "Have you lost time from work due to drinking? Do you drink to escape from worries? Do you drink to build up your self-confidence? Have you ever felt remorse after drinking? Do you drink because you're shy with other people? Does drinking cause you to have difficulty in sleeping?" From what we already know of Stan, it is likely that he would answer yes to several of these questions, if he responded honestly. "Yes" answers to even one or two of these questions would indicate enough of a problem to warrant further assessment for chemical dependency.

A supplementary treatment program.   Let's assume that Stan eventually recognizes that he does indeed have a problem with alcoholism and that he is willing to do something about this problem. I would tell him that alcoholism is considered by most substance-abuse experts to be a disease in itself, rather than a symptom of another underlying disorder, that it is a chronic condition that can be treated, and that it is a progressive disorder that eventually results in death if it is not arrested. It will be helpful for him to know that long-term recovery is based on the principle of total abstinence from all drugs and alcohol and that such abstinence is a prerequisite to effective counseling. In addition to his weekly individual therapy sessions with me, I would provide him with a referral to deal with his chemical dependence.

I would encourage Stan to join Alcoholics Anonymous and attend their meetings. The 12-step program of AA has worked very well for many alcoholics. It does not have to be a substitute for therapy, but it can be an ideal supplement. Once Stan understands the nature of his chemical dependence and no longer uses drugs, the chances are greatly increased that we can focus on the other aspects of his life that he sees as problematic and would like to change. In short, it is possible to treat his alcoholism and at the same time carry out a program of individual therapy geared to changing his ways of thinking, feeling, and behaving.

WORKING WITH STAN'S PAST, PRESENT, AND FUTURE

Dealing with the past.   Some therapies (for example, reality therapy and rational-emotive therapy) do not place much emphasis on the client's history. Their rationale is that early childhood experiences do not necessarily have much to do with the maintenance of present ineffective behavior. My inclination, in contrast, is to give weight to understanding, exploring, and working with Stan's early history and to connect up his past with what he is doing today. My view is that themes running through our life can become evident if we come to terms with significant turning points in our childhood. The use of an Adlerian lifestyle questionnaire would indicate some of these themes that originate from Stan's childhood. The psychoanalytic approach, of course, emphasizes uncovering and reexperiencing traumas in early childhood, working through the places where we have become "stuck," and resolving unconscious conflicts. Although I agree that Stan's childhood experiences were influential in contributing to his present personality (including his ways of thinking, behaving, and feeling), it does not make sense to me to assume that these factors have

determined him. I favor the Gestalt approach of having him bring to the surface his "toxic introjects" by dealing in the here and now with people in his life
with whom he feels unfinished. This can be accomplished by fantasy exercises
and a variety of role-playing techniques. In this way his past comes intensely to
life in the present moment of our sessions.

Dealing with the present.   Being interested in Stan's past does not mean that
we get lost in history or that we dwell on reliving traumatic situations. In fact, by
paying attention to what is going on in the here and now of the counseling
session, we get excellent clues to what is unfinished for him in his past. There is
no need to go on digging expeditions, because the present is rich with material.
He and I can direct attention to his immediate feelings as well as his thoughts
and actions. It seems essential to me that we work with all three dimensions —
what he is thinking, what he is actually doing, and how his thoughts and behaviors affect his feeling states. Again, by directing his attention to what is going on
with him during our sessions, I can show him how he interacts in his world apart
from therapy.

Dealing with the future.   Adlerians are especially interested in where the
client is heading. Humans are pulled by goals, strivings, and aspirations. It
would help to know what Stan's goals in life are. What are his intentions? What
does he want for himself? If he decides that his present behavior is not getting
him what he wants, he is in a good position to think ahead about the changes he
would like and what he can do *now* to actualize his aspirations. The present-
oriented behavioral focus of reality therapy is a good reference point for getting
him to dream about what he would like to say about his life five years hence.
Connecting present behavior with future plans is an excellent device for helping him formulate a concrete plan of action. He will have to actually *create* his
future.

THE THINKING DIMENSION IN THERAPY

Once Stan has gotten in touch with some intense feelings and perhaps experienced catharsis (release of pent-up feelings), some kind of cognitive work is
essential. He needs to be able to experience his feelings fully, and he may need
to express them in symbolic ways. This may include getting his anger toward
women out by hitting a pillow and by saying angry things that he has never
allowed himself to say. Yet eventually he needs to begin to make sense of the
emotional range of material that is surfacing.

   To bring in this cognitive dimension, I would draw heavily on transactional
analysis to focus Stan's attention on parental messages that he has incorporated
and on the decisions that he made as a child. I would get him to think about the
reason that he made certain early decisions — namely, to ensure basic psychological survival. Then I would challenge him to think about the degree to which
he still needs to cling to some archaic and nonfunctional decisions. I would
challenge him to look at his decisions about life, about himself, and about
others and to make necessary revisions that can lead him to getting on with his
living.

The Adlerian perspective is highly cognitive. After getting basic information about Stan's life history (by means of the lifestyle assessment form), I
would summarize and interpret it. For example, I might interpret some connections between his present fears of developing intimate relationships and his
history of rejection by his siblings and his parents. Thus, I would be interested
in his family constellation and his early recollections. Rather than working
exclusively with his feelings, I would want him to begin to understand (cognitively) how these early experiences affected him then and how they still influence him today. I concur with the Adlerians in their therapeutic interest in
identifying and exploring basic mistakes. Here my emphasis would be on
having Stan begin to question the conclusions he came to about himself, others,
and life. What is his private logic? What are some of his mistaken, self-defeating
perceptions that grew out of his family experiences? In ways similar to those of
TA, an Adlerian perspective provides tools for doing some productive cognitive
work both in and out of the therapy sessions.

From rational-emotive therapy I especially value the emphasis on learning
to think rationally. I would look for the ways in which Stan contributes to his
negative feelings by the process of self-indoctrination with irrational beliefs. I
would get him to really test the validity of the dire consequences that he
predicts. I value the stress put on doing hard work in demolishing beliefs that
have no validity and replacing them with sound and rational beliefs. Surely, I do
not think that he can merely think his way through life or that merely examining
his faulty logic is enough by itself for personality change. But I do see this
process as an essential component of therapy.

The cognitive-behavioral therapies have a range of cognitive techniques
that could help Stan recognize connections between his cognitions and his
behaviors. He should also learn about his inner dialogue and the impact it has
on his day-to-day behavior. Eventually, our goal would be some cognitive-restructuring work by which he could learn new ways to think, new things to tell
himself, and new assumptions about life. This would provide a basis for change
in his behavior.

WORKING TOWARD REDECISIONS

When Stan has identified and explored both his feelings and his faulty beliefs
and thinking processes, it does not mean that therapy is over. Becoming aware
of early decisions, including some of his basic mistakes and his irrational ideas,
is the starting point for change. It is essential that he find ways to translate his
emotional and cognitive insights into new ways of thinking, feeling, and behaving. Therefore, as much as possible I structure situations in the therapy sessions
that will facilitate new decisions on his part on both the emotional and cognitive
levels. In encouraging him to make these new decisions, I draw on cognitive,
emotive, and behavioral techniques. A few techniques that I might employ are
role playing, fantasy and imagery, assertion-training procedures, and behavioral
rehearsals. Both reality therapy and Adlerian therapy have a lot to offer on
getting clients to decide on a plan of action and then make a commitment to
carry out their program for change.

DOING: ANOTHER ESSENTIAL COMPONENT OF THERAPY

Stan can spend countless hours in gathering interesting insights about why he is the way he is. He can learn to express feelings that he kept inside for so many years. And he can think about the things he tells himself that lead to defeat. Yet in my view feeling and thinking are not enough to a complete therapy process. *Doing* is a way of bringing these feelings and thoughts together by applying them to real-life situations in various action programs. I am indebted to Adlerian therapy, behavior therapy, reality therapy, rational-emotive therapy, and transactional analysis, all of which give central emphasis to the role of action as a prerequisite for change.

Behavior therapy offers a multitude of techniques for behavioral change. In Stan's case I would be especially inclined to work with him in developing self-management programs. For example, he complains of often feeling tense and anxious. Daily relaxation procedures are one way that he can gain more control of his physical and psychological tension. Perhaps by a combination of meditation and relaxation procedures he can get himself centered before he goes to his classes, meets women, or talks to friends. He can also begin to monitor his behavior in everyday situations to gain increased awareness of what he tells himself, what he does, and then how he feels. When he gets depressed, he tends to drink to alleviate his symptoms. He can carry a small notebook with him and actually record events that lead up to his feeling depressed (or anxious or hurt). He might also record what he actually did in these situations and what he might have done differently. By paying attention to what he is doing in daily life, he is already beginning to gain more control of his behavior.

This behavioral monitoring can ideally be coupled with both Adlerian and rational-emotive approaches. My guess is that Stan gets depressed, engages in self-destructive behavior (drinking, for one), and then feels even worse. I would work very much on both his behaviors and cognitions and would show him how many of his actions are influenced by what he is telling himself. For example, he might want to go out and apply for a job but be afraid that he might "mess up" in the interview and not get the job. This would be an ideal time to use behavioral rehearsal. Together we would work on how he is setting himself up for failure by his self-defeating expectations. True to the spirit of rational-emotive therapy, we would explore his irrational assumptions that he *must* be perfect and that if he does not get the job, life will be unbearable. There would be many opportunities to help him see connections between his cognitive processes and his daily behavior. I would encourage him to begin to behave differently and then look for changes in his feeling states and his thinking.

With this in mind I would ask Stan to think of as many ways as possible of actually bringing into his daily living the new learning that he is acquiring in our sessions. Practice is essential. Homework assignments (preferably ones that he could give himself) are an excellent way for him to become an active agent in his therapy. He must do something himself for change to occur. I would hope that he sees that the degree to which he will change is directly proportional to his willingness to get out in life and experiment. I would want him to learn from his new behavior in life. Thus, each week we would discuss his progress toward meeting his goals and review how well he is completing his assignments. If he failed in some of them we could use this as an opportunity to learn how he might adjust his behavior. I would insist on a commitment from him that he have an action plan for change and that he continually look at how well his plan was working.

INCLUDING THE SPIRITUAL DIMENSION IN THERAPY

In my work with Stan I would want to make room for an exploration of spiritual values if that is a part of his world view. From my perspective spirituality entails the belief in a higher power than ourselves, and it involves an attempt to align our life toward this higher power. Stan's struggles deal with finding meaning in his life, resolving feelings of guilt, discovering his identity, and finding a framework for personal direction. Although I do not see it as my role to impose on Stan any specific religious values, especially my own, I do think that a comprehensive view of therapy involves a willingness of the therapist to help Stan explore and clarify struggles of a spiritual and religious nature. Thus, I consider it appropriate to invite him to tell me about his experiences with religion. I am likely to ask him questions such as "Do you consider religion to be an important aspect of your life?" "What were some of your experiences with religion during your childhood and adulthood?" "In what ways might a religious or spiritual orientation help you in finding meaning and purpose in your life?" "What were some of your positive and negative experiences with religion?" "To what degree have you challenged your religious beliefs and integrated them into the practice of your daily life?"

MOVING TOWARD TERMINATION OF THERAPY

The process that I have been describing might take weeks or months, and it could even take a couple of years. My basic point has been to show that it is possible to draw simultaneously on a variety of therapeutic systems in working with Stan's thoughts, feelings, and behaviors. Although in this illustration I have described these dimensions separately, do keep in mind that I tend to work in an integrated fashion.

Eventually, this process would lead to a time when Stan could continue what he has learned in therapy but without my assistance. Termination of therapy is as important as the initial phase, for now the challenge is to put into practice what he has learned in the sessions by applying new skills and attitudes to daily social situations. I hope that he will bring up a desire to "go it alone." If he does, we will talk about his readiness to end therapy and his reasons for thinking about termination. I will also share with him my perceptions of the directions I have seen him take. This is a good time to talk about where he can go from here. Together we can spend a few sessions developing an action plan and talking about how he can best maintain his new learning. He might want to join a therapeutic group. He could find support in a variety of social networks. In essence, he can continue to challenge himself by doing things that are difficult for him yet at the same time broaden his range of choices. If he wants, he might take some dancing classes that he previously has avoided out of a fear of failing. Now he can take the risk and be his own therapist, dealing with feelings as they arise in new situations.

In a behavioral spirit, evaluating the process and outcomes of therapy seems essential. This evaluation can take the form of devoting a session or two to discussing Stan's specific changes in therapy. A few questions for focus might be: "What stands out the most for you, Stan? What did you learn that you consider the most valuable? How did you learn these lessons? What can you do now to keep practicing new behaviors that work better for you than the old patterns? What will you do if you experience setbacks? How will you handle any regression to old ways or temporary defeats?" With this last question it is helpful for him to know that his termination of formal therapy does not mean that he cannot return for a visit or session when he considers it appropriate. Rather than coming for weekly sessions, he might well decide to come in at irregular intervals for a "checkup." Of course, he would be the person to decide what new areas to explore in these follow-up sessions.

QUESTIONS FOR REFLECTION AND DISCUSSION

1. As you work through each of the theory chapters, it is a good idea to refer to Stan's case and attempt to apply the basic concepts and techniques of each therapeutic approach to him. In doing so, consider these questions: What unique perspectives does this approach offer from which you can understand Stan's dynamics and work with him in counseling? What specific techniques would you be most likely to use from this approach? Why?

2. As you think about meeting Stan for the first session, what might you be thinking and feeling? From what you know about him from his autobiography and from reading this chapter on his work with nine different therapists, how might you approach him?

3. Briefly state how you see Stan in terms of his current psychodynamics, his most pressing conflicts, and the major themes of his life. What are your thoughts about his capacity to understand himself and to translate this insight into action plans leading to behavioral change?

4. On the matter of identifying and clarifying therapeutic goals, what would guide your interventions? Who would be responsible for setting the goals? How would you help Stan make his goals concrete? What goals do you think you might have for him based on what you already know of him?

5. If you were interested in gathering life-history data in order to make an initial assessment of Stan's problems, from which therapeutic approaches would you probably draw? What specific information would you be most interested in obtaining? Once you gathered this information, how might you use it in the initial stages of counseling?

6. What value do you place on the quality of the relationship that you would establish with Stan? Specifically, how might you go about creating a relationship that would allow the two of you to work together productively? Can you think of anything that might get in the way of creating this relationship, either in you or in him?

7. As therapy proceeds, demonstrate how you might select concepts and techniques from all of the nine therapeutic models so that you could work with Stan on a basis of *thinking, feeling,* and *behaving.* What might be your focus? Which theories might you draw on at the various stages of your therapy with him?

8. What do you see your role as being? For example, are you Stan's teacher? model? coach? friend? How would your theory guide your interventions? How would your theory determine your role with him?

9. In what areas might you be most confrontive with Stan? most supportive? What kind of balance might you establish between providing support and confrontation?

10. How might you prepare Stan for termination? What experiences would you want for him, both in the therapy sessions and in daily life, before he ended the counseling relationship? What specific topics would you explore with him in the final phases of counseling? Again, how would your theoretical leaning influence your focus in the later stages of counseling?

RECOMMENDED SUPPLEMENTARY READINGS

Case Studies in Psychotherapy, edited by Danny Wedding and Raymond J. Corsini (Itasca, IL: F. E. Peacock, 1989), consists of 12 cases by practitioners such as Rogers, Ellis, Beck, Perls, May, Berne, and Lazarus. Each of the cases has some therapist/client dialogue as well as a commentary of the case.

Case Approach to Counseling and Psychotherapy (3rd ed.), by Gerald Corey (Pacific Grove, CA: Brooks/Cole, 1991) uses the same sequencing of theory chapters as this textbook. One case (Ruth) is given central focus, and the nine therapeutic approaches are applied to it. Practitioners with an expertise in the given theories (such as Ellis, Glasser, and Lazarus) discuss their methods of assessment and treatment of Ruth. Then I follow up and show how I would work with Ruth using each of the nine theories. There are other cases for the reader to attempt, and guidelines are provided for applying theory to practice in each of them.

14

AN INTEGRATIVE
PERSPECTIVE

INTRODUCTION

This chapter will help you think about areas of convergence and divergence among the nine therapeutic systems. Although the approaches all have at least some of the same goals, there are many differences when it comes to the best route to achieve these aims. Some therapies call for an active and directive stance on the therapist's part, and others place value on the client's being the active agent. Some therapies focus on bringing out feelings, others stress identifying cognitive patterns, and still others concentrate on actual behavior. The key challenge is for you to find ways to integrate certain features of each of these therapies so that you can work with clients on all three levels of human experience.

Although this book has examined only 9 theoretical orientations, the field of psychotherapy is characterized by a diverse range of specialized models. Corsini (1981) lists over 240 different forms of psychotherapy, and Herink (1980) describes more than 250 therapies. With all the diversity in systems of counseling, is there any hope that a practitioner can develop skills in all of the existing techniques? Although it certainly does not appear that we need to develop any additional theories of counseling, models that integrate existing approaches would be useful. According to Norcross (1986a), the proliferation of therapy systems has been accompanied by a deafening cacophony of rival claims. He pleads for networks of practitioners who are willing to work toward rapprochement and eclecticism.

There are clear indications that since the early 1980s psychotherapy has been characterized by a rapidly developing movement toward integration and eclecticism. The Society for the Exploration of Psychotherapy Integration is an international organization that was formed in 1983. Its members are professionals who are working toward the development of a therapeutic approach that is not necessarily associated with a single theoretical orientation. There are both promises and pitfalls in this trend toward integrating perspectives. Goldfried and Safran (1986) caution that if this trend toward eclecticism is carried to its extreme, there is a danger of constructing too many eclectic models in the future. They are concerned that the growing interest in integration could result in competition to determine who can formulate the best eclectic system.

This chapter considers the advantages of developing an integrated perspective on the theory and practice of counseling. It also presents a framework for helping you begin to integrate concepts and techniques from various approaches. As you read, attempt to formulate your personal perspective of counseling and how it best proceeds. Rather than merely reviewing the basic issues, look for a basis to begin synthesizing what sometimes appear to be diverse elements of different theories. As much as possible, be alert for ways in which these systems can function in harmony.

A DESCRIPTION OF ECLECTIC COUNSELING

Eclectic counseling is the process of selecting concepts and methods from a variety of systems. Surveys of clinical and counseling psychologists conducted in the 1970s and 1980s consistently revealed that from 30% to 50% of the respondents considered themselves to be eclectic in their therapeutic practice (Messer, 1986). In one study a group of clinical and counseling psychologists endorsed an approach clearly identified as *systematic eclecticism* (Zook & Walton, 1989). Practitioners of all persuasions are increasingly seeking a rapprochement among various systems and an integration of therapeutic techniques (Norcross, 1986a). Psychologists generally believe that the best hope for a truly comprehensive therapeutic approach lies with eclecticism (Norcross & Prochaska, 1988; Smith, 1982).

Although a large and increasing number of therapists identify themselves as "eclectics," this category covers a broad range of practice. Perhaps at its worst, eclectic practice consists of a haphazard picking of techniques without any overall theoretical rationale. In this brand of "sloppy" eclecticism the practitioner grabs for anything that seems to work, often making no attempt to determine whether the therapeutic procedures are indeed effective. Haphazard eclecticism is primarily an outgrowth of relying on a few techniques. This unsystematic approach is eclecticism "by default," in which its practitioners lack the knowledge and skill to meaningfully select interventions (Norcross, 1986a). The aim of eclecticism is not to produce such tremendous openness to every new development that a practitioner merely goes from one fad to another. Such a hodgepodge is no better than a narrow and dogmatic orthodoxy (Lazarus, 1986). According to Norcross (1986a), eclecticism should instead be thought of as a way to harmoniously blend theoretical concepts and methods into a congruent framework: "The promise of eclecticism is the development of a comprehensive psychotherapy based on a unified and empirical body of work. It is the opportunity to construct a new integrative paradigm and, at the same time, to transcend more narrow 'schools' of therapy" (p. 11).

As one of the reviewers of this book pointed out, ultimate reality has more than one explanation, and thus *theoretical pluralism* is called for to make sense of it. At its best, however, eclectic practice entails a *systematic integration* of underlying principles and methods common to a range of therapeutic approaches. Systematic eclecticism implies that its practitioners are thoroughly grounded in a number of theories, that they are open to the idea that these theories can be unified in some ways, and that they are willing to continually test their hypotheses to determine how well they are working. Such counselors are able to wisely select a range of techniques to meet the special needs of clients. Systematic eclecticism is the product of a great deal of clinical practice, and it involves considerable research and theorizing.

There is some evidence that practitioners prefer the term *integrative* to *eclectic* in describing their practices. Norcross and Prochaska (1988) found that 40% of their respondents favored the term *integrative* and 25% favored *eclectic.* The primary distinction is that eclecticism tends to be technical and pragmatic, whereas integrationism tends to refer to a conceptual or theoretical creation beyond a blending of techniques. It was also found that three central themes for defining eclecticism were (1) pragmatically selecting whichever method best fits for a particular client or problem (34% of the sample), (2) combining a couple of theories in therapy practice (18%), and (3) integrating a number of therapies (21%). Norcross and Prochaska write that relying on a single theory and a few techniques may be a product of inexperience. Experience seems to result in diversity and resourcefulness. From the perspective of theoretical pluralism practitioners may find that several theories play a crucial role in their personal counseling approach. Each theory has its unique contributions. By accepting that each theory has strengths and weaknesses and is, by definition, "different" from the others, practitioners have some basis to begin developing a theory that fits for them. Developing an integrative perspective is a lifelong endeavor that is refined with experience.

THE TREND TOWARD AN ECLECTIC PERSPECTIVE

An increasing number of writers point to the advantages of developing an eclectic approach (see Beutler, 1983, 1986; Brabeck & Welfel, 1985; Brammer, Shostrom, & Abrego, 1989; Garfield, 1980, 1986; Garfield & Kurtz, 1977; Goldfried & Safran, 1986; Hart, 1983, 1986; Lazarus, 1986, 1989; Messer, 1986; Murray, 1986; Norcross, 1986a, 1986b; Norcross & Prochaska, 1988; Rychlak, 1985; Smith, 1982; Young, Feller, & Witmer, 1989). One reason for the trend toward eclectic and integrative perspectives is the recognition that no single theory is comprehensive enough to account for the complexities of human behavior, especially when the range of client types and their specific problems are taken into consideration. Clinicians are challenged with selecting the techniques that best fit a given client. According to Garfield (1980), given the current state of knowledge in the field, it seems justified to place confidence in empirical results and tenable hypotheses instead of adhering to a single theory. In the absence of research data, Garfield contends, therapists must rely on their clinical experiences and evaluate their interventions as therapy proceeds. His view of the eclectic approach places responsibility on the therapist to make an adequate appraisal of the client and then to work out a plan for therapy that seems appropriate.

Smith (1982) asked clinical and counseling psychologists what theoretical orientation guided their practice and found that *eclectic* was the most popular perspective. He cites literature indicating a trend in the direction of "creative synthesis, masterful integration, and systematic eclecticism." His findings show the following orientations:

Eclectic	41.20%
Psychoanalytic	10.84%
Cognitive-behavioral	10.36%
Person-centered	8.67%
Behavioral	6.75%
Adlerian	2.89%
Family	2.65%
Existential	2.17%
Gestalt	1.69%
Rational-emotive	1.69%
Reality	0.96%
Transactional analysis	0.96%
Other	9.16%

The "other" category includes developmental orientation, social-learning theory, career theory, and personal-effectiveness training. The findings indicate a continued decline in the popularity of psychoanalytic therapy and a trend toward the cognitive-behavioral therapies.

In a study done by Young, Feller, and Witmer (1989) counselor educators and mental-health counselors were surveyed to determine their primary theoretical orientation. The results, in alphabetical order, are as follows:

Theoretical orientation	Percent	Counselor educators	Mental-health counselors
Adlerian	2%	1.5%	1%
Behavior modification	3%	3%	3%
Cognitive-behavioral	6%	8%	4%
Eclectic	32%	30%	30%
Ericksonian hypnosis	2%	—	3%
Existential	0.8%	—	1%
Family systems	10%	5%	14%
Gestalt	2%	1.5%	1%
Multimodal	3%	3%	3%
Person-centered	22%	32%	10%
Psychoanalytic	5%	—	10%
Psychoeducational	3%	5%	1%
Rational-emotive	2%	—	3%
Reality	4%	8%	4%
Other	9%	5%	9%
$N=$		66	69

A similar survey of the theoretical orientations of clinical and counseling psychologists by Zook and Walton (1989) revealed that more than three-fourths of the sample drew from at least two theoretical orientations. *Younger clinical* psychologists preferred behavioral approaches, whereas *older clinical* psychologists preferred psychodynamic approaches. *Younger counseling* psychologists favored behavioral approaches, and *older counseling* psychologists favored humanistic approaches.

Theoretical orientation	Percent	Clinical psychologists	Counseling psychologists
Psychodynamic	24.2%	34.5%	15.4%
Psychoanalytic	6.2%	9.9%	3.0%
Psychodynamic	18.0%	24.6%	12.4%
Humanistic	29.0%	18.7%	37.8%
Existential	2.7%	2.9%	2.5%
Gestalt	4.0%	2.9%	5.0%
Humanistic	4.0%	1.8%	3.5%
Person-centered	18.5%	9.9%	25.9%
Transactional analysis	1.1%	1.2%	1.0%

Theoretical orientation	Percent	Clinical psychologists	Counseling psychologists
Behavioral	36.8%	34.5%	38.8%
Behavioral	6.5%	8.2%	5.0%
Cognitive-behavioral	20.2%	17.5%	22.4%
Rational-emotive	5.4%	4.1%	6.5%
Reality	2.2%	1.2%	3.0%
Social-learning	2.7%	3.5%	2.0%
Systems	4.6%	5.3%	3.5%
Other	5.4%	6.4%	4.5%

In this study the respondents were not given the option to list eclecticism as their preferred orientation. Thus, it is more difficult to compare it with the previous study (Young et al., 1989). In this study, however, a high number of respondents chose two or three of the approaches, often changing major categories (psychodynamic, humanistic, and behavioral) in the process. Among both the younger clinical and counseling psychologists there seems to be a move toward cognitive-behavioral approaches. Of those respondents listing three orientations, more than 60% selected cognitive-behavioral approaches as one of the three. The humanistic orientations, particularly the person-centered approach, continue to be popular, especially among counseling psychologists.

The nine systems discussed in this book have evolved in the direction of broadening their theoretical and practical bases, becoming less restrictive in their focus. Thus, many practitioners who claim allegiance to a particular system of therapy are expanding their theoretical outlook and developing a wider range of therapeutic techniques to fit a more diverse population of clients. Norcross (1986a) contends that the profession has developed to a point at which it is more receptive to integrative efforts than it has ever been before: "The psychotherapy *Zeitgeist* of the 1980s is rapprochement, convergence, and integration" (p. ix).

I predict that the *Zeitgeist* of the 1990s will continue with this trend toward convergence and integration and that there will also be an increased emphasis on a spiritual perspective. According to Bergin (1988) it is timely to add a spiritual keystone to the building blocks provided by other therapeutic approaches, because such an orientation contributes to an understanding of techniques and provides a moral frame of reference to values that influence a client's behavior. Miller (1988) writes about the value of including clients' spiritual perspectives in cognitive-behavioral therapy. He endorses a collaborative approach that respects the integrity of the individual's belief system. Miller suggests that once clients clarify their basic assumptions, it is the therapist's task to help them examine the consequences of their beliefs. Counseling can help clients gain insight into the ways in which their core beliefs and values are reflected in their behavior. Clients may discover that what they are doing is based on beliefs that are no longer functional. If this is the case, they can consider alternative assumptions. It seems clear that an integrative perspective allows for the inclusion of the client's spiritual values in the exploration of key life issues. If you are interested in the issue of the possibilities of integrating a spiritual orientation into counseling I recommend consulting the following sources: Bergin (1988), Miller (1988), Miller and Martin (1988), and Peck (1978).

THE CHALLENGE OF DEVELOPING AN INTEGRATIVE PERSPECTIVE

In addressing the issue of the proper degree of eclecticism to introduce into counseling practice, Messer (1986) concludes that the debate will continue between adherents of a single theoretical system and those who favor moving toward a unified theory of therapy.

A survey of approaches to counseling and psychotherapy reveals that no common philosophy unifies them. Many of the theories have different views of human nature and different concepts of therapy that are rooted in those views (see Tables 14-1 and 14-2*). Your philosophical assumptions are important, because they specify how much reality you are able to perceive, and they direct your attention to the variables that you are "set" to see. A word of caution, then: beware of subscribing exclusively to any one central or universal view of human nature; remain open and selectively incorporate a framework for counseling that is consistent with your own personality and your belief system.

In developing a personal eclecticism, however, it is important to be alert to the problem of attempting to mix theories with incompatible underlying assumptions. As Lazarus (1986) has noted, for eclectic therapists to choose their theories and techniques primarily on the basis of subjective appeal can lead to confusion. In working toward the goal of integration one needs to be aware of irreconcilable differences among the systems that make rapprochement impossible. The basic philosophies of classical psychoanalysis and radical behaviorism, for example, do not lend themselves to a merger. Furthermore, many of the concepts of the psychoanalytic approach are fundamentally different from those of control theory.

Despite such divergences in theories, there are possibilities for a creative synthesis among some models. Thus, an existential orientation does not necessarily preclude using techniques drawn from behavior therapy or from some of the more objective, rationally oriented cognitive theories. That all these theories represent different vantage points from which to look at human behavior does not mean that one theorist has "the truth" and the others are in error. Each point of view can offer the counselor a perspective for helping clients in their search for self. I encourage you to study all the major theories, to resist being converted to any single point of view, and to remain open to what you might take from the various orientations as a basis for an integrative perspective that will guide your practice.

You will not be in a position to conceptualize a completely developed integrative perspective after your first course in counseling theory. But the combination of this course and this book can provide you with the tools to begin

---

* All tables referred to in the text can be found near the end of this chapter.

the process of integration. With additional study and practical experience you will be able to expand and refine your emerging personal philosophy of counseling.

ISSUES RELATED TO THE THERAPEUTIC PROCESS

THERAPEUTIC GOALS

The goals of counseling are almost as diverse as are the theoretical approaches. Goals include restructuring personality, uncovering the unconscious, creating social interest, finding meaning in life, curing an emotional disturbance, examining old decisions and making new ones, developing trust in oneself, attaining self-actualization, reducing anxiety, shedding maladaptive behavior and learning adaptive patterns, and gaining more effective control of one's life (see Table 14-3). Is there a common denominator in this range of goals? Can there be any integration of the various theoretical viewpoints on the issue of goals?

This diversity can be simplified by considering the degree of generality or specificity of goals. Goals can be seen as existing on a continuum from specific, concrete, and short-term to general, global, and long-term. The cognitive-behavioral therapies stress the former; the relationship-oriented therapies tend to stress the latter. The goals at opposite ends of the continuum are not necessarily contradictory; it is just a matter of how specifically they are defined.

Who should establish the goals of counseling? Almost all theories are in accord that it is the client's responsibility to decide the objectives of counseling. Goal definition is a joint and evolutionary process—that is, something that is done by the client and the therapist as therapy proceeds. The counselor has general goals, and each client has personal goals. In my view therapy ought to begin with an exploration of the client's expectations and goals. Clients initially tend to have vague ideas of what they expect from therapy. They may be seeking solutions to problems, they may want to stop hurting, they may want to change others so they can live with less anxiety, or they may seek to be different so that some significant persons in their lives will be more accepting of them. In some cases clients may have no goals; they are in the therapist's office simply because they were sent there by their parents, probation officer, or teacher, and all they want is to be left alone. So where can a counselor begin? The intake session can be used most productively by focusing on the client's goals or lack of them. The therapist may begin by asking such questions as "What do you expect from counseling? Why are you here? What do you want? What do you hope to leave with? How is what you are presently doing working for you? What about yourself or your life situation would you most like to change?"

It is frustrating for therapists to hear clients make statements such as "I'd just like to understand myself more, and I'd like to be happy." Counselors, however, can bring such global and diffuse wishes into sharper focus by asking "What is keeping you from feeling happy? What *do* you understand about yourself *now*? What would you like to understand about yourself that you don't now understand?" The main point is that setting goals seems unavoidable, and if there is to be any productive direction, the client and counselor need to explore what they hope to obtain from the counseling relationship. The two need to decide from the outset whether they can work with each other and whether their goals are compatible.

THERAPIST'S FUNCTION AND ROLE

Just as the various theories are guided by different goals, so, too, do the therapist's functions vary among the models. In working toward an integrative perspective, we need to address a number of questions about the counselor's behaviors, such as: How do the counselor's functions change depending on the stage of the counseling process? Does the counselor maintain a basic role, or does this role vary in accordance with the characteristics of the client? How does the counselor determine how active and directive to be? How is structuring handled as the course of therapy progresses? When and how much does the counselor self-disclose?

Defining the role.   A basic issue that all therapists must face concerns the definitions of their role. Is the therapist a friend? an expert? a teacher? an advice giver? an information giver? a provider of alternatives? a confronter? Do counselors have each of these functions at various times, and if so, what is their *basic* role in the counseling process? What influence does the setting in which therapists practice have on their roles? What do counselors do when they are in conflict with the agency's view of what they should be doing?

The fact that a range of appropriate roles exists often confuses beginning counselors. There is no simple and universal answer to the question of the therapist's proper role. Factors such as the type of counseling, the counselor's level of training, the clientele to be served, and the therapeutic setting all need to be considered.

Mental-health workers often find themselves in jobs that demand that they function in multiple roles and perform tasks that do not mix well. In a state hospital where my colleagues and I provided training workshops for the treatment staff, for example, we learned that employees had to switch between several diverse roles. Psychiatric technicians, psychologists, and social workers were expected to function as therapists to a group of involuntarily committed clients, many of whom had been diagnosed as mentally disordered sex offenders, psychotics, and sociopaths. In addition to providing one-to-one contacts, they were expected to regularly hold group-therapy sessions. Yet at the same time they were responsible for making a determination of when the patients were ready to be released and returned to the community. These mental-health workers were expected to carry out multiple functions: therapist, sponsor, nurse, friend, teacher, parent, administrator, guard, and judge.

This mixture of responsibilities proved to be a major burden for many of these workers, because they knew that some of their clients might commit future offenses (including rape, child molestation, or murder). Clients were aware that these workers would make judgments concerning their detention or release. In many cases these clients learned the "right" language aimed at impressing the treatment team, even though many of them had not made any substantial changes in their attitudes or behavior.

Although having to perform the dual roles of therapist and evaluator may be far less than ideal, it is often impractical and unrealistic to think that such workers can involve themselves strictly in therapeutic functions. Like it or not, the reality of most institutions demands that they participate in treatment-team staffings and meetings in which they make evaluative judgments about their clients and decisions that may affect their ability to create a climate of trust in which they can function ideally. Therefore, it is probably best that these workers frankly tell their clients at the outset about this situation and then not apologize for it. This type of directness with clients can go a long way in establishing trust.

Counselors would do well to make a critical evaluation of appropriate counseling functions. They could benefit from deciding in advance those functions that they feel are inconsistent with real counseling. From my perspective the central function of counseling is to help clients recognize their own strengths, discover what is preventing them from using their strengths, and clarify what kind of person they want to be. Counseling is a process by which clients are invited to look honestly at their behavior and lifestyle and make certain decisions about the ways in which they want to modify the quality of their life. In this framework counselors need to provide support and warmth yet care enough to challenge and confront. Counselors need to do more than administer techniques. Lazarus (1986) writes that the therapist's personality and style are integral to the therapy process and outcomes; the mechanisms of change cannot be separated from the person who administers the therapeutic procedures. Counselors need to appropriately reveal themselves in the relationship with clients; they can then sift through the responses they receive and make appropriate decisions.

Control of client behavior.   A related issue is the degree to which the therapist exercises control over the client's behavior both during and outside the session. What is the counselor's job in structuring the therapeutic process? All the approaches are in basic agreement on the need for some type of structure in the counseling experience, although they disagree over its nature and degree. Rational-emotive and cognitive-behavioral therapists, for example, operate within a directive and didactic structure. They frequently prescribe homework assignments that are designed to get clients to practice new behavior outside therapy sessions. By contrast, person-centered therapists operate in a much looser and less defined structure.

Garfield (1986) writes that structuring depends on the particular client and the specific circumstances. He is the most highly structured during the initial session. He asks clients to talk about the problems that led them to seek therapy, and then he makes an assessment. After this initial interview, however, the client typically determines the content of the sessions. From early in the therapy process Garfield attempts to create the expectancy that the client will be an active participant in the process.

Structuring is but one way to control clients' behavior, and it is essential that counselors become aware of the subtle ways in which their behavior influences clients. They would do well to monitor what they say and do in terms of its impact on their clients. It is a good practice for counselors to frequently ask themselves "What am I doing? Whose needs are being met — my client's or my own? What is the effect of my behavior on my client?"

Division of responsibility.   Another basic issue regarding structuring involves division of responsibility. This issue needs to be clarified at the intake session. Early during the course of counseling it is the counselor's responsibility to discuss specific matters such as length and overall duration of the sessions, confidentiality, general goals, and methods used to achieve goals. (Review the discussion of informed consent in Chapter 3.) Both the therapist and the client need to assume responsibility for the direction of therapy. If therapists primarily decide what clients should talk about and are overdirective, they perpetuate clients' dependency. Clients should be encouraged to assume as much responsibility as possible in the early stages of therapy.

It is important to be alert to clients' efforts to get the counselor to assume responsibility for directing their lives. Many clients seek a "magic answer" as a way of escaping the anxiety of making their own decisions. Client-initiated contracts and specific assignments are helpful in keeping the focus of responsibility on the client. Contracts can be changed, and new ones can be developed. Formulating contracts can continue during the entire counseling relationship. As counselors we must ask ourselves "Are my clients doing now what will move them toward greater independence and toward a place where they can increasingly find their answers within?" Perhaps the best measure of our general effectiveness as counselors is the degree to which clients are able to say to us "I appreciate what you've been to me, and because of your faith in me, I feel I can now go it alone." Eventually, if we are good enough, we will be out of business!

CLIENT'S EXPERIENCE IN THERAPY

What expectations do clients have as they approach therapy? What are their responsibilities in the process? Is therapy only for the "disturbed"? Can the relatively healthy person benefit from it? Are there any commonalities among the diverse types of clients?

Most clients share some degree of suffering, pain, or at least discontent. There is a discrepancy between how they would like to be and how they are. Some initiate therapy because of their awareness of wanting to cure a specific symptom or set of symptoms: they want to get rid of migraine headaches, free themselves of chronic anxiety attacks, lose weight, or get relief from depression. They may have conflicting feelings and reactions, may struggle with low self-esteem, or may have limited information and skills. Many seek some resolution to conflicts with a marital partner in the hope that they can enjoy their marriage. Increasingly, people are entering therapy with existential problems; their complaints are less defined but relate to the experiences of emptiness, meaninglessness in life, boredom, dead personal relationships, a lack of intense feelings, and a loss of the sense of self.

The initial expectations of many clients are expert help and a fast result. They often have great hope for major changes in their lives with little effort on their part. As therapy progresses, they discover that they must be active in the process; they need to select their own goals and work for them, both in the therapy sessions and in daily living.

What about the involuntary clients who sit before you because the judge ordered them to do so? It is possible for clients to benefit from therapy even if they do not initiate the process.

Practitioners who work with involuntary clients must begin by openly and directly discussing the nature of the relationship. They must promise nothing that they cannot or will not deliver and must make clear the limits of confidentiality as well as any other factors that might affect the course of therapy. In working with involuntary clients, it is especially important to *prepare* them for the process. Questions to consider are: What is the therapy about? What are the joint responsibilities of both parties? How might therapy help them get what they want? What can the client do to increase the chances that the therapy experience will be positive? What are the potential risks and dangers? What can the client expect in the general course of treatment? This kind of preparation can go a long way toward dealing with resistance. Often, in fact, resistance is brought about by a counselor who omits preparation and merely assumes that all clients are open and ready to benefit from therapy.

In thinking about your integrative perspective on counseling practice, you should consider the characteristics of each client who seeks your help. Some clients can benefit from recognizing and expressing pent-up feeling, others will need to examine their beliefs and thoughts, others will most need to begin behaving in different ways, and others will benefit from talking about their relationships with the significant people in their lives. In deciding what interventions are most likely to be helpful, it is essential to take into account the client's cultural, ethnic, and socioeconomic background. Also, at different phases in the counseling process the focus of counseling may change with each of these clients. Although some clients initially feel a need to be listened to and allowed to express deep feelings, they can profit later from examining the thought patterns that are contributing to their psychological pain. And certainly, at some point in therapy it is essential that clients translate what they are learning about themselves into concrete action. The client's given situation in the environment provides a framework for selecting interventions that are most appropriate.

RELATIONSHIP BETWEEN THERAPIST AND CLIENT

Most approaches share common ground in accepting the importance of the therapeutic relationship. The existential, Gestalt and person-centered views are based on the personal relationship as the crucial determinant of treatment outcomes. It is clear that some other approaches, such as rational-emotive and cognitive-behavioral therapy, do not ignore the relationship factor, even though they do not give it a place of central importance (see Table 14-4).

Counseling is a personal matter that involves a personal relationship, and evidence indicates that honesty, sincerity, acceptance, understanding, and spontaneity are basic ingredients of successful outcomes. Therapists' degree of caring, their interest and ability in helping the client, and their genuineness are factors that influence the relationship. Lazarus (1986) describes what he considers to be the common characteristics of "highly successful therapists": a genuine respect for people, flexibility, a nonjudgmental attitude, a good sense of humor, warmth, authenticity, and the willingness to recognize and reveal their shortcomings. Clients also contribute to the relationship with variables such as their motivation, cooperation, interest, concern, attitudes, perceptions, expectations, behavior, and reactions to the counselor.

As you think about developing your personal counseling perspective, give consideration to the issue of the match between client and counselor. I certainly do not advocate changing your personality to fit your perception of what each client is expecting. It is important that you *be yourself* as you meet clients. You also need to consider the reality that you are not likely to work effectively with every client whom you initially meet, a result that is not determined solely by your knowledge and your technical competence. Some clients will work better with counselors who have another type of personal and therapeutic style than yours. Thus, I recommend sensitivity in assessing what your clients need, along with good judgment about the appropriateness of the match between you and a potential client. Although you do not have to be like your clients or have experienced their same problems to be effective with them, it is critical that you be able to understand their world and respect them. The matter of matching client and counselor has interesting implications for multicultural counseling. You might ask yourself how well prepared you feel to counsel clients from a different cultural background. To what degree do you think you can successfully establish a therapeutic relationship with a client of a different race? ethnic group? gender? age? socioeconomic group? Do you see any potential barriers in yourself that would make it difficult to form a working relationship with certain clients? (This would be a good time to review the discussion of the culturally skilled counselor in Chapter 2 and to consult Tables 14-9 and 14-10.)

THE PLACE OF TECHNIQUES, ASSESSMENT, AND EVALUATION IN COUNSELING

LEARNING TO USE TECHNIQUES APPROPRIATELY

As I've mentioned, I see it as a mistake for you to restrict yourself to a few techniques that you apply to most clients in dealing with most problems. Instead, you would do well to incorporate a wide range of procedures into your therapeutic style. At times, reflection of feeling and simply listening to a client's verbal and nonverbal messages are what is called for, but to restrict yourself to these procedures exclusively is to hamper your effectiveness.

There will be times when it is appropriate to confront clients with their evasions of reality or their illogical thinking. Again, for you to focus primarily on this behavior is to restrict yourself unnecessarily. At times you may need to be interpretive, and at other times you will invite clients to interpret for themselves the meaning of their behavior. Sometimes it may be appropriate to be very directive and structured, and at other times it may be appropriate to flow without a clear structure. So much depends on the purpose of therapy, the setting, the personality and style of the therapist, the qualities of the particular client, and the problems selected for intervention.

Beutler (1983) addresses the question "What therapy activities are most appropriate for what type of problem, by which therapist, for what kind of client?" Regardless of what model you may be working with, you must decide *what* techniques, procedures, or intervention methods to use, *when* to use them, and with *which clients* (see Tables 14-5 and 14-6). It is critical to be aware of how clients' cultural backgrounds contribute to their perceptions of their problems. As we have seen, each of the nine therapeutic approaches has both strengths and limitations when applying its techniques to culturally diverse client populations (see Tables 14-9 and 14-10). Although it is unwise to stereotype clients because of their cultural heritage, it is useful to assess how the cultural context has a bearing on the client's concerns. Some techniques are contraindicated because of a client's socialization. Thus the client's responsiveness (or lack of it) to certain techniques is a critical barometer in judging the effectiveness of these methods.

The multimodal therapy of Lazarus (1986, 1989) is an excellent example of *technical eclecticism*. According to him, therapists who hope to be effective with a wide range of problems and with different client populations must be flexible, versatile, and technically eclectic. The basic questions they ask are What works for whom under which particular circumstances? Why are some procedures helpful and others unhelpful? What can be done to ensure long-term success and positive follow-ups? Lazarus (1986) emphasizes that technical eclecticism draws on many effective techniques without necessarily subscribing to the theories that give rise to them. He notes that some clients respond to warm, informal counselors but that others want more formal counselors. Whereas some clients work well with counselors who are quiet and nonforceful, other clients work best with directive and outgoing counselors. Further, the same client may respond favorably to various therapeutic techniques and styles at different times. (For a review of multimodal procedures and their rationale, refer to Chapter 10, "Behavior Therapy.")

You are your best technique.   Although counselors can learn attitudes and skills and acquire certain knowledge about personality dynamics and the therapeutic process, much of effective therapy is the product of artistry. I think it is misleading to imbue students with the idea that counseling is a science that is distinct from the behavior and personality of the counselor. In many ways I believe that *you,* as a counselor or therapist, are your very best technique. There is no substitute for developing techniques that are an expression of your personality and that fit for you. It is really impossible to effectively separate the techniques you use from your personality and the relationship you have with your clients. There is the ever-present danger of becoming a mechanical technician and simply administering techniques to clients without regard for the relationship variables. Techniques should not be used as a substitute for the hard work that it takes to develop a constructive client/therapist relationship.

This would be a good time to review the charts on the therapeutic relationship and therapeutic techniques (Tables 14-4 and 14-5).

I encourage students and those with whom I consult to experience a wide variety of techniques themselves *as clients.* Reading about a technique in a book is one thing; actually experiencing it from the vantage point of a client is quite another. If you have actually practiced relaxation exercises, for example, you will have a much better feel for how to administer them and will know more about what to look for as you work with clients. If you have carried out real-life homework assignments as a part of your own self-change program, you will have a lot more empathy for your clients and their potential problems. If you have experienced guided imagery, you are likely to suggest fantasy exercises to your clients in a more sensitive and effective manner. Realize that particular techniques may be better suited to one therapist's personality than to another's.

Reasons for applying techniques.   Another question that counselors need to ask themselves frequently is *why* they use a certain technique. There should be a rationale for the techniques used, and they should be tied into the goals of therapy. This does not mean that counselors should attempt to draw on accepted techniques and procedures within a single model; quite the contrary. However, effective counselors avoid using techniques in a hit-or-miss fashion, to fill time, or to get things moving.

Counselors would do well to honestly examine their motivations for using or avoiding certain techniques. This process is a continuing one. It could be useful to reflect on the following questions to determine which techniques you see yourself as favoring:

- Do you use a lot of questions in your counseling? If so, are they *open* questions, which encourage further client talk and exploration, or *closed* questions, which have a simpler answer or do not lead to deeper self-exploration? Do you ask "what," "how," or "why" questions most frequently?
- Are your techniques mainly cognitive? or affective? or behavioral?
- Do the techniques you use fall within a particular school or therapeutic approach? Or are they representative of various approaches?
- Do your techniques intensify what a client is feeling, or do they have the effect of closing up certain feelings? How comfortable are you with pain? anger? jealousy? conflict?
- Who does most of the talking during the session, you or the client?
- Do you use techniques to get clients moving, or do you wait until they express some conflict or feeling and then develop a technique geared to help them experience this feeling more fully?
- What techniques have you personally experienced from the vantage point of a client? What were some of your positive experiences? Did you have any negative experiences?
- How do you imagine it would be if you avoided using any techniques or counseling procedures other than simply being with your clients and relating to them in dialogues?

I see it as a mistake to equate counselor effectiveness simply with proficiency in a single technique or even a set of techniques. For example, some counselors might become specialists in confrontational techniques. They might develop a style of relating to clients geared to provoking them, goading them to "get their anger expressed," or merely focusing on techniques to deal with anger. These therapists might derive a sense of power from becoming "confrontation specialists." For a different set of motives, other counselors might limit themselves to techniques of reflection and clarification. Perhaps they are fearful of getting involved with clients on more than the empathic and supportive level; thus, they continue to reflect because there are few risks involved, and in this way they never have a real interaction with a client. By reviewing the models presented in this book and the techniques that flow from them, it is possible to learn that effective counseling involves proficiency in a combination of *cognitive, affective,* and *behavioral* techniques. Such a combination is necessary to help clients *think* about their beliefs and assumptions, *experience* on a *feeling* level their conflicts and struggles, and actually translate their insights into *action* programs by behaving in new ways in day-to-day living.

At this point I suggest that you review the charts on the applications, contributions, and limitations of the various therapeutic approaches (Tables 14-6, 14-7, and 14-8). These charts should help you identify elements from the various approaches that you may want to incorporate into your own counseling perspective.

THE ROLE OF DIAGNOSIS IN COUNSELING

Psychodiagnosis is the analysis and explanation of a client's problems. It may include an explanation of the causes of the client's difficulties, an account of how these problems developed over time, a classification of any disorders, a specification of preferred treatment procedure, and an estimate of the chances for a successful resolution.

The purpose of diagnosis in counseling and psychotherapy is to identify disruptions in a client's present behavior and lifestyle. Once problem areas are clearly identified, the counselor and client are able to establish the goals of the therapy process, and then a treatment plan can be tailored to the unique needs of the client. A diagnosis is not a final category; rather, it provides a working hypothesis that guides the practitioner in understanding the client. The therapy sessions provide useful clues about the nature of the client's problems. Thus, diagnosis begins with the intake interview and continues throughout the duration of therapy.

The "bible" for guiding practitioners in making diagnostic assessments is the American Psychiatric Association's (1987) *Diagnostic and Statistical Manual of Mental Disorders,* which is also known as the DSM III-R. Clinicians who work in community mental-health agencies, private practice, and other human-service settings are expected to assess client problems within the framework of the DSM-III-R. This manual cautions practitioners that it represents only an initial step in a comprehensive evaluation. There is also a caution about the necessity of gaining additional information about the person being evaluated, rather than merely relying on the information presented in the diagnostic manual.

Although some clinicians view diagnosis as central to the counseling process, others view it as unnecessary and even a detriment to counseling. They contend that diagnosis is an inappropriate application of the medical model of mental health to therapeutic practice. There are those who maintain that practitioners can become too focused on the client's history and thus fail to pay sufficient attention to present attitudes and behavior. They maintain that the diagnostic process needs to be rooted in the individual's current lifestyle if it is to be effective (Brammer et al., 1989). As you review the arguments for and against this practice, think about your own position on this issue.

Arguments for psychodiagnosis.   Those who favor the use of diagnosis in therapy generally argue that it enables the practitioner to acquire enough knowledge about the client's past and current behavior to develop an appropriate plan of treatment. They typically contend that (1) diagnostic labels allow professionals to communicate effectively, because each category specifies behavioral characteristics; (2) diagnosis points the way to appropriate treatment strategies for different disorders; (3) diagnosis is helpful in predicting the course of particular disorders; and (4) it provides a framework for research into various treatment approaches.

Psychoanalytically oriented therapists favor psychodiagnosis, because this form of therapy was patterned after the medical model of mental health and stresses the understanding of past situations that have contributed to a dysfunction. Practitioners with a behavioral orientation also favor a diagnostic stance, for different reasons, inasmuch as they emphasize specific treatment programs. These practitioners value observation and other objective means of appraising both a client's specific symptoms and the factors that have led up to the client's malfunctioning. Such an appraisal, they would argue, enables them to use the techniques that are appropriate for a particular disorder and to evaluate the effectiveness of the treatment program.

Brammer and his colleagues (1989) see diagnosis as being broader than simply labeling clients with some category, and they warn against accepting a narrow and rigid diagnostic approach. They argue in favor of diagnosis as a general descriptive statement identifying a client's style of functioning. Such information can motivate clients to change their behavior. They contend that practitioners must make some decisions, do some therapeutic planning, be alert for signs of pathology in order to avoid serious mistakes in therapy, and be in a position to make some prognoses. They propose that a therapist "simultaneously understand diagnostically and understand therapeutically" (1989, p. 148). Some of the questions they suggest reveal how counselors can incorporate diagnosis and assessment in their work with clients: "How serious is the client's behavior?" "What is the most appropriate therapeutic strategy at this time?" "What are the basic dynamics that help to explain the client's current behavior?"

Arguments against psychodiagnosis.   Critics see diagnosis as unnecessary or harmful. Generally, existential or relationship-oriented therapists fall into this group. Their arguments against diagnosis include the following:

- Diagnosis typically involves observing a person's behavior from an external viewpoint, without reference to the subjective perception of the person.
- The best vantage point for understanding another person is through his or her subjective world, not through a general system of classification.
- Diagnosis can lead people to accept self-fulfilling prophecies or to despair over their condition.
- Diagnosis can narrow therapists' vision by encouraging them to look for behavior that fits a certain disease category.
- There are many potential dangers in reducing human beings to diagnostic categories, one of which is failing to consider the uniqueness of the individual.

Laing (1967) expresses concern about the effects of traditional diagnosis, both on those who are being classified and on those who are doing the categorizing. For clients being classified diagnosis can result in a self-fulfilling prophecy, so that they act as they are expected to act. Thus, a person who knows that he or she has been diagnosed as a schizophrenic may take great delight in telling ward attendants: "After all, I'm crazy! What can you expect from me?" In turn, hospital personnel may see people only through the stereotypes associated with various diagnoses. If they expect certain behaviors from the patients, there is a good chance that the patients will adopt these behaviors and live up to the staff's expectations.

A danger of the diagnostic approach is the possible failure of counselors to consider ethnic and cultural factors in certain patterns of behavior. Unless cultural variables are considered, some clients may be subjected to an erroneous diagnosis. Certain behaviors and personality styles may be labeled neurotic or deviant simply because they are not characteristics of the dominant culture. Sue (1981) gives the example of some mental-health professionals' assertions that Asian Americans are the most repressed of all clients. Such statements indicate that these therapists expect all clients to be self-disclosing, emotionally expressive, and assertive These counselors do not recognize that the cultural upbringing of many Asian Americans places a value on restraint of strong feelings and on a reluctance to discuss personal matters with anyone outside the family. Thus, counselors who work with Blacks, Asian Americans, Hispanics, and American Indians may erroneously conclude that a client is repressed, inhibited, passive, and unmotivated, all of which are seen as undesirable by Western standards.

In assessments of clients with different ethnic and cultural backgrounds the DSM-III-R emphasizes the importance of being aware of unintentional bias and keeping an open mind to the presence of distinctive cultural patterns that could influence the diagnostic process:

> When the DSM-III-R classification and diagnostic criteria are used to evaluate a
> person from an ethnic or cultural group different from that of the clinician's,

and especially when diagnoses are made in a non-Western culture, caution should be exercised in the application of DSM-III-R diagnostic criteria to assure that their use is culturally valid. It is important that the clinician not employ DSM-III-R in a mechanical fashion, insensitive to differences in language, values, behavioral norms, and idiomatic expressions of distress [American Psychiatric Association, 1987, p. xxvi].

A personal commentary on diagnosis.   Is there a way to bridge the gap between the extreme view that diagnosis is the essential core of therapy and the extreme view that it is a detrimental factor? I conceive of diagnosis as a continuing process that focuses on understanding the client. Both the therapist and the client are engaged in the search-and-discovery process from the first session to the last. Even though practitioners may avoid formal diagnostic procedures and terminology, it seems that they raise certain questions, such as: What is going on in the client's life now, and what does the client want from therapy? What are the client's strengths and limitations? What is the client like in the counseling setting, and what does this behavior reveal about the client's actions outside of therapy? How far should therapy go? What is the client learning from therapy, and to what degree is he or she applying this learning to daily living? In dealing with these questions, the therapist is formulating some conception about what clients want and how they might best attain their goals. Thus, diagnosis becomes a form of making tentative hypotheses, and these hunches can be formed with clients and shared with them throughout the process.

I do have serious reservations about pinning on clients shorthand labels such as *paranoid, schizophrenic,* or *psychopathic.* These labels frequently categorize and stereotype a client, and an entire staff might react to the label and treat the "schizophrenic patient" the way they expect that type of "case" to behave.

From my perspective diagnosis should be associated with treatment, and it should help the practitioner conceptualize a case. Ethical dilemmas are often created when diagnosis is done strictly for insurance purposes, which often entails arbitrarily assigning a client a diagnostic classification. However, it is an ethical (and sometimes legal) obligation of therapists to screen clients for life-threatening problems such as organic disorders, schizophrenia, manic-depression, and suicidal types of depression. Students need to learn the clinical skills necessary to do this type of screening, which is a form of diagnostic thinking. In order to function in most mental-health agencies, practitioners need to become skilled in understanding and utilizing diagnostic procedures.

GUIDELINES FOR THE USE OF TESTING IN COUNSELING

The place of testing in counseling and therapy is another controversial issue. Models that emphasize the objective view of counseling are inclined to use testing procedures to get information about clients or to provide them with information so that they can make more realistic decisions. The person-centered and existential orientations view testing much as they do diagnosis, as an external form of understanding that has little to do with effective counseling.

A wide variety of tests can be used for counseling purposes, including measures of interest, aptitude, achievement, attitudes and values, and personal characteristics and traits. In my view tests can be used as an adjunct to counseling; valuable information, which can add to a client's capacity to make decisions, can be gleaned from them. From my experiences in working in a university counseling center, I have formulated some cautions and guidelines regarding the use of tests:

- Clients should be involved in the test-selection process. They should decide which categories of tests, if any, they wish to take.
- Clients' reasons for wanting tests, as well as their past experience with tests, should be explored.
- A client needs to be aware that tests are only tools, and imperfect ones at that. As means to an end tests do not provide "the answer," but at best they provide additional information that can be explored in counseling and used in coming to certain decisions.
- The counselor needs to clarify the purposes of the tests and point out their limitations. This role implies that the counselor has a good grasp of what the test is about and that he or she has taken it.
- The test results, not simply scores, should be given to the client, and their meanings should be explored. In interpreting the results, the counselor should be tentative and neutral. Testing is only one avenue for gaining information, and the information derived needs to be validated by other measures. In presenting the results, the counselor needs to refrain from judgments as much as possible and allow clients to formulate their own meanings and conclusions.
- In using tests as a part of the counseling process, ethical considerations need to be taken into account. In the AACD's *Ethical Standards* (1988) counselors are required to provide information for those taking tests so that the results can be considered along with other relevant factors. It is especially important to consider the ways in which socioeconomic, ethnic, and cultural factors can affect test scores.

In sum, many clients seek tests in the hope of finding "answers." It is important to explore why a person wants to take a battery of tests and to teach the person the values and limitations of tests. If that is done, there is less chance that tests will be undertaken in a mechanical fashion or that unwarranted importance will be attributed to the results. A discussion with clients about tests and testing can open the possibilities of counseling to them. Instead of seeking shortcut methods, they may be willing to invest in counseling as a way to clarify their thinking and to aid their decision making. Thus, tests are best thought of as tools that can be used as an adjunct to the counseling process.

EVALUATING THE EFFECTIVENESS OF COUNSELING AND THERAPY

Research in psychotherapy gained little momentum until the 1950s. Since the late 1950s and the early 1960s research has mainly addressed the process and outcomes of psychotherapy. Its central purpose is to gain a clearer understanding of what constitutes therapeutic change and how it comes about, so that more effective therapeutic methods can be developed (Strupp, 1986; VandenBos, 1986).

The acceleration of public funding for all types of human-service programs during the 1960s also stirred a keen interest in evaluation research. In essence, if government funds were to continue to be allocated to human-service agencies, the burden of proof rested on researchers and practitioners to demonstrate the effectiveness of psychotherapy by using scientific methods. The central question raised was "Of what value is psychotherapy to the individual and society?" (Strupp, 1986).

This brief section examines issues pertaining to the effectiveness of counseling and psychotherapy in achieving the goals of personality and behavior change. Questions that can be asked are: Does therapy make a significant difference? Are people substantially better after therapy than they were without it? Can therapy actually be more harmful than helpful? Because a thorough discussion of these questions is beyond the scope of this book, I will not review the vast literature related to therapy outcomes. Instead, I will address a few basic issues related to evaluating the effectiveness of psychotherapy.*

There are problems in lumping together many research efforts to answer the general question "Does psychotherapy work?" A basic part of the problem is that each of the multitude of therapeutic systems is applied by a practitioner with individual characteristics that are difficult to measure. Further, clients themselves have much to do with therapeutic outcomes. If they choose to engage in activities that are self-destructive, this behavior will cancel out the positive effects of therapy. To add to the problem, effects resulting from unexpected and uncontrollable events in the environment can destroy gains that are made in psychotherapy. It should be clear that evaluating how well counseling and psychotherapy work is far from simple.

One of the first issues relates to the extent of research that has been done on the therapeutic approaches presented in this book. Most of the studies have been done by two divergent groups: the behavior therapists, who have based their therapeutic practice on empirical studies, and the person-centered researchers, who have made significant contributions to the understanding of both process and outcome variables. To a lesser extent rational-emotive therapy has also been subjected to research to support its main hypotheses, although the empirical rigor of these studies has been called into question by several other researchers with a behavioral orientation. Finally, an analytically oriented group of practitioners has also been concerned with the evaluation of psychotherapy. Aside from these four approaches, most of the other models that were covered in this book have not produced significant empirical research dealing with how well therapy works.

---

* For those who are interested in such a review and other articles on psychotherapy research I suggest the following sources: Bergin (1971), Bergin and Lambert (1978), Bergin and Strupp (1972), Cohen, Sargent, and Sechrest (1986), Eysenck (1966), Garfield (1987), Garfield, Prager, and Bergin (1971), Gendlin (1986), Imber and his colleagues (1986), Luborsky, Singer, and Luborsky (1975), Meltzoff and Kornreich (1970), Morrow-Bradley and Elliott (1986), Stiles, Shapiro, and Elliott (1986), Strupp (1986), Strupp, Hadley, and Gomes-Schwartz (1977), and VandenBos (1986).

By about 1980 there was a consensus that psychotherapy was demonstrably more effective than no treatment (VandenBos, 1986). Yet if we are looking for hard data to support the concepts and procedures of most of the therapeutic approaches discussed in this book, we will be disappointed. One reason is that one approach's "cure" is another approach's "resistance." In other words, because each approach works toward different outcomes, it is almost impossible to compare them. Despite the wide range of purportedly distinct psychotherapeutic treatments, most reviews of outcome research show little or no differential effectiveness of the various psychotherapies (Stiles, Shapiro, & Elliott, 1986). Factors other than scientific data must be considered if we are to determine the validity and usefulness of most of the therapeutic approaches.

Lambert (1986) contends that eclecticism provides the broad base needed for the integration of research findings. He concludes that systematic eclecticism has a natural compatibility with and affinity for research. He further identifies four conclusions about outcome research: (1) A substantial number of outpatients improve spontaneously without the benefit of formal psychotherapy. (2) Most of the major therapy approaches have been put to the test of empirical research, which has led to the basic conclusion that psychotherapy is generally effective. (3) Various factors that are common across therapy systems account for a substantial degree of the improvement found in clients. These common factors that are associated with positive outcomes include *support factors* (therapist warmth, respect, acceptance, and other factors associated with a positive relationship); *learning factors* (insight, cognitive learning, and self-acceptance); and *action factors* (facing one's fears, reality testing, modeling, practice, and working through). (4) Specific techniques can be selected for dealing with specific problems on the basis of their effectiveness.

Garfield (1980) argues that the question "Is psychotherapy effective?" is a poor one destined to receive poor answers. He makes the point that psychotherapy is not a clearly defined and uniform process and that there is thus no basis for any objective answer to the question. As VandenBos (1986) concludes, it now appears that outcome research aimed at proving the efficacy of therapy should be a "thing of the past." He contends that future research should be focused on exploring the relative advantages and disadvantages of alternative treatment strategies for clients with different specific psychological and behavioral problems. Included in this research should be factors such as relative cost, length of time necessary to effect change, and nature and extent of change. Whatever form it takes, it does appear that research will play an increasingly important role in determining the future of psychotherapy (Strupp, 1986).

A guideline for improving on this global question is provided by Paul (1967) with the following question: 'What treatment, by whom, is the most effective for this individual with that specific problem, and under what set of circumstances?" It is clear that there is a need for greater precision and specificity of theory and method in research (Stiles et al., 1986). Thus, the question of the effectiveness of psychotherapy needs to be narrowed down to a specific type of therapy and usually narrowed further to a certain technique. It is not sufficient, however, merely to conduct studies of certain therapeutic approaches. Practitioners who adhere to the same approach may function differently. For instance, they are likely to use techniques in various ways and relate to clients in diverse fashions. They may function differently depending on the type of client and the clinical setting.

I am in full agreement with Garfield (1980), who contends that if we expect to improve research designs to meaningfully measure the effectiveness of therapeutic procedures, we must state questions more precisely: What therapeutic procedures will work best with what clients? What kind of therapist will work best with what procedures and with what clients? He contends that we need to individualize our therapeutic procedures and systematically investigate their effectiveness for specific problems.

SUMMARY AND REVIEW CHARTS

I believe that an integration of therapeutic perspectives provides the best vantage point from which to help clients. Creating an eclectic stance is truly a challenge, however, for it does not simply mean picking bits and pieces from theories in a random and fragmented manner. In forming an integrated perspective, it is important to ask: Which theories provide a basis for understanding the *cognitive* dimension? How about the *feeling* aspects? And how about the *behavioral* dimension? Most of the nine therapeutic orientations focus on one of these dimensions of human experience. Although the other dimensions are not necessarily ignored, they are often given short shrift.

Developing an integrated theoretical perspective requires much reading, thinking, and actual counseling experience. Unless you have an accurate and in-depth knowledge of these theories, you cannot formulate a true synthesis. A central message of this book has been to encourage you to remain open to each theory, to do further reading, and to reflect on how the key concepts of each theory fit your personality. Building your personalized theory of counseling, which is based on what you consider to be the best features of several theories, is a long-term venture. In addition to considering your own personality, think about what concepts and techniques work best with a range of clients. It requires knowledge, skill, art, and experience to be able to determine what techniques are suitable for particular problems. It is also an art to know when and how to use a particular therapeutic intervention.

At this point it would be useful for you to reflect on the major insights you have gained through taking this course and reading this book. Most of all, think about what theories seemed to have the most practical application in helping you understand your present life situation. You might consider what changes you are interested in making and which approaches could provide you with strategies to modify specific thoughts, feelings, and behaviors. This is a good time to review what you may have learned about your ability to establish effective relationships with other people. Especially important is a review of any personal characteristics that could either help or hinder you in developing solid working relationships with clients. Some questions you might ask yourself are "What have I learned about my personal needs and how they are likely to operate in a counseling relationship?" "What did I learn about my values and how my attitudes and beliefs could work either for or against establishing effective relationships with clients?" "What steps can I take now to increase the chances of becoming an effective person and counselor?"

After you make this review of significant personal learning, I suggest that you ponder what you have learned about the counseling process. It could help to identify a particular theory that you might adopt as a foundation for establishing your own perspective on counseling theory and practice. As you review the following charts summarizing the nine theories, consider what particular therapies you would be most inclined to draw from with respect to the following aspects: (1) underlying assumptions, (2) major concepts, (3) therapeutic goals, (4) therapeutic relationship, and (5) techniques and procedures. Also consider the major applications of each of the therapies, as well as their basic limitations and major contributions (see Tables 14-7 through 14-10).

TABLE 14-1
The Basic Philosophies

Psychoanalytic therapy	Human beings are basically determined by psychic energy and by early experiences. Unconscious motives and conflicts are central in present behavior. Irrational forces are strong; the person is driven by sexual and aggressive impulses. Early development is of critical importance, because later personality problems have their roots in repressed childhood conflicts.
Adlerian therapy	A positive view of human nature is stressed. Humans are motivated by social interest, by striving toward goals, and by dealing with the tasks of life. People are in control of their fate, not victims of it. Each person at an early age creates a unique style of life, which tends to remain relatively constant throughout life.
Existential therapy	The central focus is on the nature of the human condition, which includes capacity for self-awareness, freedom of choice to decide one's fate, responsibility, anxiety as a basic element, the search for a unique meaning in a meaningless world, being alone and being in relation with others, and finiteness and death.
Person-centered therapy	The view of humans is positive; humans have an inclination toward becoming fully functioning. In the context of the therapeutic relationship the client experiences feelings that were previously denied to awareness. The client actualizes potential and moves toward increased awareness, spontaneity, trust in self, and inner directedness.
Gestalt therapy	The person strives for wholeness and integration of thinking, feeling, and behaving. The view is antideterministic, in that the person is viewed to have the capacity to recognize how earlier influences are related to present difficulties. Growth involves moving from environmental support to self-support.
Transactional analysis	The person has potential for choice. What was once decided can be redecided. Although the person may be a victim of early decisions and past scripting, self-defeating aspects can be changed with awareness

(continued)

TABLE 14-1
The Basic Philosophies *(continued)*

Behavior therapy	Behavior is the product of learning. We are both the product and the producer of environment. No set of unifying assumptions about behavior can incorporate all the existing procedures in the behavioral field.
Rational-emotive and cognitive-behavioral therapy	Humans are born with potentials for rational thinking but also with tendencies toward crooked thinking. They tend to fall victim to irrational beliefs and to reindoctrinate themselves with these beliefs. Therapy is oriented toward cognition, behavior, and action and stresses thinking, judging, analyzing, doing, and redeciding. This model is didactic and directive. Therapy is a process of reeducation.
Reality therapy	Based on the assumption that people are ultimately self-determining and in charge of their life, the approach is both antideterministic and positive. The model describes how people attempt to control the world around them. It teaches them ways to more effectively satisfy their needs.

TABLE 14-2
Key Concepts

Psychoanalytic therapy	Normal personality development is based on successful resolution and integration of psychosexual stages of development. Faulty personality development is the result of inadequate resolution of some specific stage. Id, ego, and superego constitute the basis of personality structure. Anxiety is a result of repression of basic conflicts. Ego defenses are developed to control anxiety. Unconscious processes are centrally related to current behavior.
Adlerian therapy	Based on a growth model, this approach emphasizes the individual's positive capacities to live in society cooperatively. It also stresses the unity of personality, the need to view people from their subjective perspective, and the importance of life goals that give direction to behavior. People are motivated by social interest and by finding goals to strive for. Therapy is a matter of providing encouragement and assisting clients in changing their cognitive perspective.
Existential therapy	Essentially an approach to counseling and therapy rather than a firm theoretical model, it stresses core human conditions. Normally personality development is based on the uniqueness of each individual. Sense of self develops from infancy. Self-determination and tendency toward growth are central ideas. Focus is on the present and on what one is becoming; that is, the approach has a future orientation. It stresses self-awareness before action. It is an experiential therapy.

TABLE 14-2
(continued)

Person-centered therapy	The client has the potential for becoming aware of problems and the means to resolve them. Faith is placed in the client's capacity for self-direction. Mental health is a congruence of ideal self and real self. Maladjustment is the result of a discrepancy between what one wants to be and what one is. Focus is on the present moment and on the experiencing and expressing of feelings.
Gestalt therapy	Emphasis is on the "what" and "how" of experiencing in the here and now to help clients accept their polarities. Key concepts include personal responsibility, unfinished business, avoiding, experiencing, and awareness of the now. Gestalt is an experiential therapy that stresses feelings and the influence of unfinished business on contemporary personality development.
Transactional analysis	Focus is on games played to avoid intimacy in transactions. The personality is made up of Parent, Adult, and Child. Clients are taught how to recognize which ego state they are functioning in with given transactions. Games, rackets, early decisions, scripting, injunctions, and redecisions are key concepts.
Behavior therapy	Focus is on overt behavior, precision in specifying goals of treatment, development of specific treatment plans, and objective evaluation of therapy outcomes. Therapy is based on the principles of learning theory. Normal behavior is learned through reinforcement and imitation. Abnormal behavior is the result of faulty learning. This approach stresses present behavior.
Rational-emotive and cognitive-behavioral therapy	Neurosis is irrational thinking and behaving. Emotional disturbances are rooted in childhood but are perpetuated through reindoctrination in the now. A person's belief system is the cause of emotional problems. Thus clients are challenged to examine the validity of certain beliefs.
Reality therapy	The basic focus is on what clients are doing and how to get them to evaluate whether their present ways are working for them. People create their feelings by the choices they make and by what they do. The approach rejects many notions of conventional therapy (such as focusing on the client's past, feelings, or insight; transference; the unconscious; and dreams).

TABLE 14-3
Goals of Therapy

Psychoanalytic therapy	To make the unconscious conscious. To reconstruct the basic personality. To assist clients in reliving earlier experiences and working through repressed conflicts. Intellectual awareness.

(continued)

TABLE 14-3
Goals of Therapy *(continued)*

Adlerian therapy	To challenge clients' basic premises and goals. To offer encouragement so they can develop socially useful goals. To change faulty motivation and help them feel equal to others.
Existential therapy	To help people see that they are free and become aware of their possibilities. To challenge them to recognize that they are responsible for events that they formerly thought were happening to them. To identify factors that block freedom.
Person-centered therapy	To provide a safe climate conducive to clients' self-exploration, so that they can recognize blocks to growth and can experience aspects of self that were formerly denied or distorted. To enable them to move toward openness, greater trust in self, willingness to be a process, and increased spontaneity and aliveness.
Gestalt therapy	To assist clients in gaining awareness of moment-to-moment experiencing. To challenge them to accept responsibility for internal support as opposed to depending on external support.
Transactional analysis	To help clients become script-free, game-free, autonomous people capable of choosing how they want to be. To assist them in examining early decisions and making new decisions based on awareness.
Behavior therapy	Generally to eliminate maladaptive behaviors and learn more effective behaviors. To focus on factors influencing behavior and find what can be done about problematic behavior. Clients have an active role in setting treatment goals and evaluating how well these goals are being met.
Rational-emotive and cognitive-behavioral therapy	To eliminate clients' self-defeating outlook on life and assist them in acquiring a more tolerant and rational view of life. To help them apply the scientific method in solving their emotional and behavioral problems for the rest of their life.
Reality therapy	To help people become more effective in meeting their needs. To challenge them to evaluate what they are doing and to assess how well this behavior is working for them.

TABLE 14-4
The Therapeutic Relationship

Psychoanalytic therapy	The analyst remains anonymous, and clients develop projections toward him or her. Focus is on reducing the resistances that develop in working with transference and on establishing more rational control. Clients undergo long-term analysis, engage in free association to uncover conflicts, and gain insight by talking. The analyst makes interpretations to teach them the meaning of current behavior as related to the past.

TABLE 14–4
(continued)

Adlerian therapy	The emphasis is on joint responsibility, on mutually determining goals, on mutual trust and respect, and on equality. A cooperative relationship is manifested by a therapeutic contract. Focus is on examining lifestyle, which is expressed by the client's every action.
Existential therapy	The therapist's main tasks are to accurately grasp clients' being in the world and to establish a personal and authentic encounter with them. The relationship is seen as critically important. Clients discover their own uniqueness in the relationship with the therapist. The human-to-human encounter, the presence of the client/therapist relationship, and the authenticity of the here-and-now encounter are stressed. Both the client and the therapist can be changed by the encounter.
Person-centered therapy	The relationship is of primary importance. The qualities of the therapist, including genuineness, warmth, accurate empathy, respect, and permissiveness, and the communication of these attitudes to clients are stressed. They use this real relationship with the therapist to help them transfer their learning to other relationships.
Gestalt therapy	The therapist does not interpret for clients but assists them in developing the means to make their own interpretations. Clients are expected to identify and work on unfinished business from the past that interferes with current functioning. They do so by reexperiencing past traumatic situations as though they were occurring in the present.
Transactional analysis	An equal relationship exists, with deemphasis on the status of the therapist. The client contracts with the therapist for the specific changes desired; when the contract is completed, therapy is terminated. Transference and dependence on the therapist are deemphasized.
Behavior therapy	The therapist is active and directive and functions as a teacher or trainer in helping clients learn more effective behavior. Clients must be active in the process and experiment with new behaviors. Although a personal relationship between them and the therapist is not highlighted, a good working relationship is the groundwork for implementing behavioral procedures.
Rational-emotive and cognitive-behavioral therapy	The therapist functions as a teacher and the client as a student. A personal relationship is not essential. Clients gain insight into their problems and then must practice actively in changing self-defeating behavior.
Reality therapy	Therapists show their concern for clients by a process of involvement throughout the course of therapy. They find out what clients want; ask what they are choosing to do; invite them to evaluate present behavior; help them make plans for change; and get them to make a commitment.

TABLE 14–5
Techniques of Therapy

Psychoanalytic therapy	The key techniques are interpretation, dream analysis, free association, analysis of resistance, and analysis of transference. All are designed to help clients gain access to their unconscious conflicts, which leads to insight and eventual assimilation of new material by the ego. Diagnosis and testing are often used. Questions are used to develop a case history.
Adlerian therapy	Adlerians draw from many techniques, a few of which are paraphrasing, providing encouragement, confrontation, interpretation, gathering life-history data (family constellation, early recollections), therapeutic contracts, homework assignments, paradoxical intention, and suggestions.
Existential therapy	Few techniques flow from this approach, because it stresses understanding first and technique second. The therapist can borrow techniques from other approaches and incorporate them into an existential framework. Diagnosis, testing, and external measurements are not deemed important. The approach can be very confrontive.
Person-centered therapy	This approach uses few techniques but stresses the attitudes of the therapist. Basic techniques include active listening and hearing, reflection of feelings, clarification, and "being there" for the client. This model does not include diagnostic testing, interpretation, taking a case history, and questioning or probing for information.
Gestalt therapy	A wide range of techniques is designed to intensify experiencing and to integrate conflicting feelings. Techniques include confrontation, dialogue with polarities, role playing, staying with feelings, reaching an impasse, and reliving and reexperiencing unfinished business in the forms of resentment and guilt. Gestalt dream work is very useful. Formal diagnosis and testing are not done. Interpretation is done by the client instead of by the therapist. Confrontation is often used to call attention to discrepancies. "How" and "what" questions are used.
Transactional analysis	A script-analysis checklist, or questionnaire, is useful in recognizing early injunctions. Many techniques of TA and Gestalt can be fruitfully combined. Some type of diagnosis may be useful to assess the nature of a problem. Clients participate actively in diagnosis and are taught to make their own interpretations and value judgments. Confrontation is often used, and contracts are essential. Questioning is a basic part of the TA approach.
Behavior therapy	The main techniques are systematic desensitization, relaxation methods, reinforcement techniques, modeling, cognitive restructuring, assertion and social-skills training, self-management programs, behavioral rehearsal, coaching, and various multimodal-therapy techniques. Diagnosis or assessment is done at the outset to determine a treatment plan. Questions are used, such as "what," "how," and "when" (but not "why"). Contracts and homework assignments are also typically used.

TABLE 14 – 5
(continued)

Rational-emotive and cognitive-behavioral therapy	RET therapists use a variety of cognitive, affective, and behavioral techniques; diverse techniques are tailored to suit individual clients. *Cognitive* methods include disputing irrational beliefs, carrying out cognitive homework, and changing one's language and thinking patterns. *Emotive* techniques include role-playing, imagery, and shame-attacking exercises. A wide range of active and practical *behavioral* techniques is used to engage clients in doing the hard work required by therapy.
Reality therapy	An active, directive, and didactic therapy. Various techniques may be used to get clients to evaluate what they are presently doing to see if they are willing to change. If they decide that their present behavior is not effective, they develop a specific plan for change and make a commitment to follow through with their plan.

TABLE 14 – 6
Applications of the Approaches

Psychoanalytic therapy	Candidates for analytic therapy include professionals who want to become therapists, people who have had intensive therapy and want to go further, and those who are in pain and are genuinely suffering. Analytic therapy is not recommended for self-centered and impulsive clients or for severely impaired psychotics. Techniques can be applied to individual and group therapy.
Adlerian therapy	Can be applied to all spheres of life, such as parent/child counseling, marital and family therapy, individual counseling with children and adolescents, correctional and rehabilitation counseling, group counseling, substance-abuse programs, and dealing with problems of the aged. Being a growth model, it is ideally suited to preventive mental health and alleviating a broad range of conditions that interfere with growth.
Existential therapy	Can be especially suited to people facing a developmental crisis or a transition in life. Useful for clients with existential concerns (making choices, dealing with freedom and responsibility, coping with guilt and anxiety, making sense of life, and finding values). A useful approach for those seeking personal enhancement. Can be applied to both individual and group counseling, marital and family therapy, crisis intervention, and community mental-health work.
Person-centered therapy	Has wide applicability to individual and group counseling. It is especially well suited for the initial phases of crisis-intervention work. Its principles have been applied to marital and family therapy, community programs, administration and management, and human-relations training. It is a useful approach to teaching, parent/child relations, and working with groups composed of people from diverse cultural backgrounds.

(continued)

TABLE 14-6
Applications of the Approaches *(continued)*

Gestalt therapy	Addresses a wide range of problems and populations: crisis intervention, treatment of a range of psychosomatic disorders, marital and family therapy, awareness training of mental-health professionals, behavior problems in children, teaching and learning, and organizational development. It is well suited to both individual and group counseling. The methods are powerful catalysts for opening up feelings and getting clients into contact with their present-centered experience.
Transactional analysis	Particularly suited for group situations but also applicable to individual counseling, marital and family therapy, and parent/child relations. It can be used with all ages and for many types of problem: criminal behavior, alcoholism and drug addiction, "reparenting" of schizophrenics, and interpersonal problems.
Behavior therapy	A pragmatic approach based on empirical validation of results. Enjoys wide applicability to individual, group, marital, and family counseling. Some problems to which the approach is well suited are phobic disorders, depression, sexual disorders, children's behavioral disorders, stuttering, and prevention of cardiovascular disease. Beyond clinical practice, its principles are applied in fields such as pediatrics, stress management, behavioral medicine, education, and geriatrics.
Rational-emotive and cognitive-behavioral therapy	Has been widely applied to sex therapy, education, group work, assertion training, depression, child therapy, and a wide range of problems suited for individual therapy. RET uses all the main therapeutic modalities, including group therapy, marathon encounter groups, brief therapy, crisis intervention, and marital and family therapy. The approach is especially useful for assisting people in modifying their cognitions. Many self-help approaches utilize the principles of RET.
Reality therapy	Geared to teaching people ways to control their life effectively. It has been applied to individual counseling with a wide range of clients, group counseling, working with youthful law offenders, and marital and family therapy. In some instances it is well suited to brief therapy and crisis intervention.

TABLE 14-7
Contributions of the Approaches

Psychoanalytic therapy	More than any other system, this approach has generated controversy as well as exploration and has stimulated further thinking and development of therapy. It has provided a detailed and comprehensive description of personality structure and functioning. It has brought into prominence factors such as the unconscious as a determinant of behavior and the role of trauma during the first six years of life. It has developed several techniques for tapping the unconscious. It has shed light on the dynamics of transference and countertransference, resistance, anxiety, and the mechanisms of ego defense.

TABLE 14-7
(continued)

Alderian therapy	One of the first approaches to therapy that was humanistic, unified, and goal oriented and that put an emphasis on social and psychological factors. One of the major contributions is the influence that Adlerian ideas have had on other systems and their integration into the mainstream of other contemporary therapies. Many basic concepts of other systems bear a strong resemblance to those of this approach.
Existential therapy	Its major contribution is a recognition of the need for a subjective approach based on a complete view of the human condition. It calls attention to the need for a philosophical statement on what it means to be a person. Stress on the I/thou relationship lessens the chances of dehumanizing therapy. It provides a perspective for understanding anxiety, guilt, freedom, death, isolation, and commitment.
Person-centered therapy	Unique contribution is having the client take an active stance and assume responsibility for the direction of therapy. The approach has been subjected to empirical testing, and as a result both theory and methods have been modified. It is an open system. People without advanced training can benefit by translating the therapeutic conditions to both their personal and professional lives. Basic concepts are straightforward and easy to grasp and apply. It is a foundation for building a trusting relationship applicable to all therapies.
Gestalt therapy	Main contribution is an emphasis on direct experiencing and doing, rather than on merely talking about feelings. It provides a perspective on growth and enhancement, not merely a treatment of disorders. It uses clients' behavior as the basis for making them aware of inner creative potential. The approach to dreams is a unique, creative tool to help clients discover basic conflicts. Therapy is viewed as an existential encounter; it is process oriented, not technique oriented. It recognizes nonverbal behavior as a key to understanding.
Transactional analysis	Major contributions are the contract as a guide to the therapeutic process, an emphasis on the client's doing, the equal relationship between client and therapist, and the ease with which its basic concepts can be understood. TA recognizes the influence of early decisions and stresses the fact that clients have the power to make new, more appropriate decisions to replace archaic, disfunctional ones.
Behavior therapy	Emphasis is on assessment and evaluation techniques, thus providing a basis for accountable practice. Specific problems are identified, and clients are kept informed about progress toward their goals. The approach has demonstrated effectiveness in many areas of human functioning. The roles of the therapist as reinforcer, model, teacher, and consultant are explicit. The approach has undergone extensive expansion, and research literature abounds. No longer is it a mechanistic approach, for it now makes room for cognitive factors and encourages self-directed programs for behavioral change.

(continued)

TABLE 14–7
Contributions of the Approaches *(continued)*

Rational-emotive and cognitive-behavioral therapy	Major contributions include emphasis on a comprehensive and eclectic therapeutic practice; numerous cognitive, emotive, and behavioral techniques; an openness to incorporating techniques from other approaches; and a methodology for attacking irrational thinking. It emphasizes that past events alone are not important in contributing to emotional disorders; rather, it is one's beliefs about such situations that are critical. It makes full use of supplementary approaches to therapy, such as action-oriented homework, listening to tapes, keeping records on behavior, and reading. The principles and procedures of RET can be applied to other systems.
Reality therapy	Consists of simple and clear concepts that are easily grasped in many helping professions; thus, it can be used by teachers, nurses, ministers, educators, social workers, and counselors. It is a positive approach, with an action orientation. Due to the direct methods, it appeals to many clients who are often seen as resistant to therapy. It is a short-term approach that can be applied to a diverse population. It has been a significant force in challenging the medical model of therapy.

TABLE 14–8
Limitations of the Approaches

Psychoanalytic therapy	Requires lengthy training for therapists and much time and expense for clients. The model stresses biological and instinctual factors to the neglect of social, cultural, and interpersonal ones. Its methods are not applicable to clients in lower socioeconomic classes and are not appropriate for many ethnic and cultural groups. Many clients lack the degree of ego strength needed for "transference neurosis" therapy. It is inappropriate for the typical counseling setting.
Adlerian therapy	Weak in terms of precision, testability, and empirical validity. Few attempts have been made to validate the basic concepts by scientific methods. Tends to oversimplify some complex human problems and is based heavily on common sense.
Existential therapy	Many basic concepts are fuzzy and ill-defined, making its general framework abstract at times. Lacks a systematic statement of principles and practices of therapy. Has limited applicability to lower-functioning and nonverbal clients and to clients in extreme crisis who need direction.
Person-centered therapy	Possible danger from the therapist who remains passive and inactive, limiting responses to reflection. Many clients feel a need for greater direction, more structure, and more techniques. Clients in crisis may need more directive measures. Applied to individual counseling, some cultural groups will expect more counselor activity. The theory needs to be reassessed in light of current knowledge and thought if rigidity is to be avoided.

TABLE 14-8
(continued)

Gestalt therapy	Techniques lead to intense emotional expression; if these feelings are not explored and if cognitive work is not done, clients are likely to be left unfinished and will not have a sense of integration of their learning. Clients who have difficulty in imagining and fantasizing may not profit from Gestalt techniques.
Transactional analysis	Not much empirical research has been conducted to support the basic concepts of TA theory. Practitioners and clients alike tend to focus too much on intellectual understanding and explaining, thus relegating feelings to an unimportant role. The focus on terminology can be a distraction. However, when TA is combined with role playing, Gestalt, and body work, the danger of its being overly cognitive is lessened.
Behavior therapy	Major criticisms are that it may change behavior but not feelings; that it ignores the relational factors in therapy; that it does not provide insight; that it ignores historical causes of present behavior; that it involves control and manipulation by the therapist; and that it is limited in its capacity to address certain aspects of the human condition. Many of these assertions are based on misconceptions, and behavior therapists have addressed these charges. A basic limitation is that behavior change cannot always be objectively assessed because of the difficulty in controlling environmental variables.
Rational-emotive and cognitive-behavioral therapy	A danger is prematurely identifying irrational beliefs and forcefully attacking them; such confrontation may scare clients away. The approach is highly cognitive, almost to the degree that feelings are not really addressed in therapy (except by way of changing one's thinking, which is supposedly a route to changing feelings). The therapist may browbeat clients, substituting his or her own belief system for their irrational system.
Reality therapy	Discounts the therapeutic value of exploration of the client's past, dreams, the unconscious, early childhood experiences, and transference. The approach is limited to less complex problems. It is a problem-solving therapy that tends to discourage exploration of deeper emotional issues. It is vulnerable to practitioners who want to "fix" clients quickly.

TABLE 14-9
Contributions to Multicultural Counseling

Psychoanalytic therapy	Its focus on family dynamics is appropriate for working with many minority groups. The therapist's formality appeals to clients who expect professional distance. Notion of defense is helpful in understanding inner dynamics and dealing with environmental stresses.

(continued)

TABLE 14–9
Contributions to Multicultural Counseling (*continued*)

Adlerian therapy	Its focus on social interest, doing good for society, importance of family, goal orientation, and striving for belongingness is congruent with Eastern cultures. Focus on person-in-environment allows for cultural factors to be explored.
Existential therapy	Focus is on understanding client's phenomenological world, including cultural background. This approach leads to empowerment in an oppressive society. It can help clients examine their options for change, within the context of their cultural realities.
Person-centered therapy	Focus is on breaking cultural barriers and facilitating open dialogue among diverse cultural populations. Main strengths are respect for client's values, active listening, welcoming of differences, nonjudgmental attitude, understanding, willingness to allow clients to determine what will be explored in sessions, and prizing of cultural pluralism.
Gestalt therapy	Its focus on expressing oneself nonverbally is congruent with those cultures that look beyond words for messages. Provides many techniques in working with clients who have cultural injunctions against freely expressing feelings. Can overcome language barrier with bilingual clients. Focus on bodily expressions is a subtle way to help clients recognize their conflicts.
Transactional analysis	Its focus on the contractual method acts as a safeguard against the therapist's imposing values that may not be congruent with a client's culture. This approach offers a basis for understanding the impact of cultural and familial injunctions. Its structure will help clients understand what is expected of them in counseling.
Behavior therapy	Its focus on behavior, rather than on feelings, is compatible with many cultures. Strengths include a collaborative relationship between counselor and client in working toward mutually agreed-on goals, continual assessment to determine if the techniques are suited to the client's unique situation, assisting clients in learning practical skills, an educational focus, and stress on self-management strategies.
Rational-emotive and cognitive-behavioral therapy	The focus is on questioning one's beliefs and identifying values that may no longer be helpful to clients. The emphasis on thinking and rationality (as opposed to expressing feelings) is likely to be acceptable to many clients. The focus on teaching/learning process tends to avoid the stigma of mental illness. Clients may value leader directiveness and stress on homework.
Reality therapy	Focus is on members' making own evaluation of behavior (including how they respond to their culture). Through personal assessment they can determine the degree to which their needs and wants are being satisfied. They can find a balance between retaining their own ethnic identity and integrating some of the values and practices of the dominant society.

TABLE 14–10
Limitations in Multicultural Counseling

Psychoanalytic therapy	Its focus on insight, intrapsychic dynamics, and long-term treatment is often not valued by clients who prefer to learn coping skills for dealing with pressing daily concerns. Internal focus is often in conflict with cultural values that stress an interpersonal and environmental focus.
Adlerian therapy	This approach's detailed interview about one's family background can conflict with cultures that have injunctions against disclosing family matters. Counselor needs to make certain that the client's goals are respected.
Existential therapy	Values of individuality, freedom, autonomy, and self-realization often conflict with cultural values of collectivism, respect for tradition, deference to authority, and interdependence. Some may be deterred by the absence of specific techniques. Others will expect more focus on surviving in their world.
Person-centered therapy	Some of the core values of this approach may not be congruent with the client's culture. Lack of counselor direction and structure are unacceptable for clients who are seeking help and immediate answers from a knowledgeable professional.
Gestalt therapy	Clients who have been culturally conditioned to be emotionally reserved may not embrace Gestalt techniques. The quick push for expressing feelings could cause premature termination of therapy by the client. Some may not see how "being aware of present experiencing" will lead to solving their problems.
Transactional analysis	Terminology may distract clients of some cultures with a different perspective. Counselor must establish clear contract of what client wants before challenging client's life scripts, cultural and familial injunctions, and decisions. Caution required in probing into family patterns.
Behavior therapy	Counselors need to help clients assess the possible consequences of making behavioral changes. Family members may not value clients' newly acquired assertive style, so clients must be taught how to cope with resistance by others.
Rational-emotive and cognitive-behavioral therapy	If counselor has a forceful and directive leadership style, clients may retreat. It is necessary to understand client's world before confronting beliefs perceived as irrational by counselor.
Reality therapy	This approach stresses taking charge of one's own life, yet some clients hope to change their external environment. Counselor needs to appreciate the role of discrimination and racism and help clients deal with social and political realities.

QUESTIONS FOR REFLECTION AND DISCUSSION

1. There appears to be a growing trend toward eclecticism. What do you think this movement signifies? What are the advantages and disadvantages of this trend?
2. If you were asked in a job interview to state your theoretical orientation, what would you say? Be sure to describe what you mean by your preference. (For example, if you would say "I am eclectic," clearly spell out what theoretical concepts will guide the techniques you employ.)
3. Taking the key concepts of all nine approaches that you have studied, how could you classify these concepts under the three separate headings of thinking, feeling, and behaving?
4. Again, assume that you were asked in a job interview to state your view of the goals of psychotherapy. In what ways could you categorize the nine therapy systems in terms of goals under one of the three areas of focus: thinking, feeling, and doing?
5. What is your view of your role and function as a therapist? How would you answer this question in an interview by bringing several theoretical perspectives together?
6. How essential is the client/therapist relationship to therapeutic outcomes? Specifically, what do you think you would do to create the relationship with your clients that you deem ideal?
7. Assume that you are still in the interview situation. You are told that in this agency the clients come from diverse socioeconomic and cultural backgrounds. Explain which approaches might be most helpful to you in effectively working with a multicultural population.
8. After reading about the issues involved in diagnosis and testing, what is your thinking about the proper role of diagnosis in the counseling process? What are some of your guidelines in using tests?
9. In working with clients who have a different ethnic and cultural background from yours, what guidelines would you employ in making diagnostic assessments or in using tests?
10. Which of the nine theories of counseling provide(s) you with the best frame of reference for understanding yourself? Which basic ideas from these theories stand out as especially useful for you?

WHERE TO GO FROM HERE

At the beginning of the introductory course in theories and techniques of counseling, my students' typical reaction is "How will I ever be able to learn all these theories, and how can I make sense out of what appears to be a mass of knowledge?" By the end of the course these students are often surprised by how much work they have done *and* by how much they have learned. Although an introductory survey course will not make students into accomplished counselors, it generally gives them the basis for selecting from the many models to which they are exposed.

At this point you may be able to begin putting the theories together in some meaningful way for yourself. This book will have served its central purpose if it has encouraged you to read further and to expand your knowledge of the theories that most caught your interest. I hope that you have made friends with some theories that were unknown to you before and that you have seen something of value that you can use from each of the approaches described. Further, I hope that this book has introduced you to some of the major professional and ethical issues that you will eventually encounter, that it has stimulated you to think about your position on them, and that you have been convinced that there is no single theory that contains the total truth. Finally, the book will have been put to good use if it has challenged you to think about the ways in which your philosophy of life, your values, your life experiences, and the person you are becoming are vitally related to the quality of counselor you can become and to the impact you can have on those who establish a relationship with you personally and professionally. If you have read the chapters in the order presented in the book, I suggest that you make the time to reread Chapters 2 and 3, as they can help you put some of the personal issues in perspective.

Now that you have finished this book, I would be very interested in hearing about your experience with it and with your course. The comments of readers over the years have been helpful to me in revising each edition, and I welcome your feedback along with remarks about your experience in your course. You can write to me in care of Brooks/Cole Publishing Company, Pacific Grove, CA 93950-5098, and you can complete the reaction sheet at the end of the book.

RECOMMENDED SUPPLEMENTARY READINGS

At this stage you may be interested in books that deal with an eclectic approach to psychotherapy, as resources to help you develop a basis for integrating the various theories and applying them to practice.

Handbook of Eclectic Psychotherapy (Norcross, 1986b) is the state-of-the-art description of the major systems and principles of eclectic psychotherapy. This edited volume gives a comprehensive overview of the major eclectic approaches. If you have time to read only one source on integrative therapy, this is my recommendation.

Casebook of Eclectic Psychotherapy (Norcross, 1987) is designed as an extension and elaboration of the *Handbook of Eclectic Psychotherapy*. This volume presents 13 cases that illustrate the practice of eclectic therapy in its varied manifestations.

The Practice of Multimodal Therapy (Lazarus, 1989) describes a pragmatic and empirical approach. The author presents a highly readable account of his systematic and comprehensive therapy; he also describes in detail the concept of technical eclecticism.

Therapeutic Psychology: Fundamentals of Counseling and Psychotherapy (Brammer, Shostrom, & Abrego, 1989) provides a fine comprehensive review of the counseling process and counseling procedures from an eclectic framework. It has clear descriptions of commonly used counseling techniques.

Eclectic Psychotherapy: A Systematic Approach (Beutler, 1983) is an excellent source. The book describes an eclectic psychotherapy that can be applied in a relatively consistent and reliable fashion. It attempts to define the ingredients of good therapy and to maximize their effective use by matching clients with both therapists and techniques.

Modern Eclectic Therapy: A Functional Orientation to Counseling and Psychotherapy (Hart, 1983) integrates many techniques and theories into an integrative framework. The author draws on behavioral, insight, and humanistic perspectives.

For those who are interested in an advanced treatment of the various therapy approaches, I recommend *Theories of Counseling and Psychotherapy* (Patterson, 1986), which also contains an excellent chapter on the convergences and divergences among the major systems.

REFERENCES AND SUGGESTED READINGS*

AMERICAN ASSOCIATION FOR COUNSELING AND DEVELOPMENT. (1988). *Ethical standards* (rev. ed.). Alexandria, VA: Author.

AMERICAN PSYCHIATRIC ASSOCIATION. (1987). *Diagnostic and statistical manual of mental disorders* (3rd ed., rev.). Washington, DC: Author.

ATKINSON, D. R., MORTEN, G., & SUE, D. W. (Eds.). (1989). *Counseling American minorities: A cross cultural perspective* (3rd ed.). Dubuque, IA: William C. Brown.

BERGIN, A. E. (1971). The evaluation of therapeutic outcomes. In A. E. Bergin & S. L. Garfield (Eds.), *Handbook of psychotherapy and behavior change: An empirical analysis.* New York: Wiley.

BERGIN, A. E. (1988). Three contributions of a spiritual perspective to counseling, psychotherapy, and behavioral change. *Counseling and Values, 33,* 21–31.

BERGIN, A. E., & LAMBERT, M. J. (1978). The evaluation of therapeutic outcomes. In S. L. Garfield & A. E. Bergin (Eds.), *Handbook of psychotherapy and behavior change* (2nd ed.). New York: Wiley.

BERGIN, A. E., & STRUPP, H. H. (1972). *Changing frontiers in the science of psychotherapy.* Chicago: Aldine-Atherton.

*BEUTLER, L. E. (1983). *Eclectic psychotherapy: A systematic approach.* New York: Pergamon Press.

*BEUTLER, L. E. (1986). Systematic eclectic psychotherapy. In J. C. Norcross (Ed.), *Handbook of eclectic psychotherapy* (pp. 94–131). New York: Brunner/Mazel.

*BRABECK, M. M., & WELFEL, E. R. (1985). Counseling theory: Understanding the trend toward eclecticism from a developmental perspective. *Journal of Counseling and Development, 63,* 343–348.

*BRAMMER, L., SHOSTROM, E., & ABREGO, P. J. (1989). *Therapeutic psychology: Fundamentals of counseling and psychotherapy* (5th ed.). Englewood Cliffs, NJ: Prentice-Hall.

COHEN, L. H., SARGENT, M. M., & SECHREST, L. B. (1986). Use of psychotherapy research by practicing psychotherapists. *American Psychologist, 41,* 198–206.

CORSINI, R. J. (Ed.). (1981). *Handbook of innovative psychotherapies.* New York: Wiley.

DRYDEN, W. (1986). Eclectic psychotherapies: A critique of leading approaches. In J. C. Norcross (Ed.), *Handbook of eclectic psychotherapy* (pp. 353–375). New York: Brunner/Mazel.

EYSENCK, H. J. (1966). *The effects of psychotherapy.* New York: International Science Press.

*GARFIELD, S. L. (1980). *Psychotherapy: An eclectic approach.* New York: Wiley.

*GARFIELD, S. L. (1986). An eclectic psychotherapy. In J. C. Norcross (Ed.), *Handbook of eclectic psychotherapy* (pp. 132–162). New York: Brunner/Mazel.

* Books and articles marked with an asterisk are suggested for further study.

GARFIELD, S. L. (1987). Ethical issues in research on psychotherapy. *Counseling and Values, 31,* 115–125.

*GARFIELD, S. L., & KURTZ, R. (1977). A study of eclectic views. *Journal of Consulting and Clinical Psychology, 45,* 78–83.

GARFIELD, S. L., PRAGER, R. A., & BERGIN, A. E. (1971). Evaluation of outcome in psychotherapy. *Journal of Consulting and Clinical Psychology, 37,* 307–313.

GENDLIN, E. T. (1986). What comes after traditional psychotherapy research? *American Psychologist, 41,* 131–136.

*GOLDFRIED, M. R., & NEWMAN, C. (1986). Psychotherapy integration: An historical perspective. In J. C. Norcross (Ed.), *Handbook of eclectic psychotherapy* (pp 25–61). New York: Brunner/Mazel.

*GOLDFRIED, M. R., & SAFRAN, J. D. (1986). Future directions in psychotherapy integration. In J. C. Norcross (Ed.), *Handbook of eclectic psychotherapy* (pp. 463–483). New York: Brunner/Mazel.

HART, J. T. (1983). *Modern eclectic therapy: A functional orientation to counseling and psychotherapy.* New York: Plenum.

HART, J. T. (1986). Functional eclectic therapy. In J. C. Norcross (Ed.), *Handbook of eclectic psychotherapy* (pp. 201–225). New York: Brunner/Mazel.

HERINK, R. (Ed.). (1980). *The psychotherapy handbook.* New York: New American Library.

*HERLIHY, B., & GOLDEN, L. (1990). *Ethical standards casebook* (4th ed.). Alexandria, VA: American Association for Counseling and Development.

IMBER, S. D., GLANZ, L. M., ELKIN, I., SOTSKY, S. M., BOYER, J. L., & LEBER, W. R. (1986). Ethical issues in psychotherapy research. *American Psychologist, 41,* 137–146.

LAING, R. D. (1967). *The politics of experience.* New York: Pantheon.

LAMBERT, M. J. (1986). Implications of psychotherapy outcome research for eclectic psychotherapy. In J. C. Norcross (Ed.), *Handbook of eclectic psychotherapy* (pp. 436–462). New York: Brunner/Mazel.

*LAZARUS, A. A. (1986). Multimodal therapy. In J. C. Norcross (Ed.), *Handbook of eclectic psychotherapy* (pp. 65–93). New York: Brunner/Mazel.

*LAZARUS, A. A. (1989). *The practice of multimodal therapy.* Baltimore: Johns Hopkins University Press.

LUBORSKY, L., SINGER, B., & LUBORSKY, L. (1975). Comparative studies of psychotherapies. *Archives of General Psychiatry, 32,* 995–1008.

MELTZOFF, J., & KORNREICH, M. (1970). *Research in psychotherapy.* New York: Atherton.

MESSER, S. B. (1986). Eclecticism in psychotherapy: Underlying assumptions, problems, and trade-offs. In J. C. Norcross (Ed.) *Handbook of eclectic psychotherapy* (pp. 379–397). New York: Brunner/Mazel.

*MILLER, W. R. (1988). Including clients' spiritual perspectives in cognitive-behavior therapy. In W. R. Miller & J. E. Martin (Eds.), *Behavior therapy and religion: Integrating spiritual and behavioral approaches to change* (pp. 43–55). Newbury Park, CA: Sage Publications.

*MILLER, W. R., & MARTIN, J. E. (1988). *Behavior therapy and religion: Integrating spiritual and behavioral approaches to change.* Newbury Park, CA: Sage Publications.

MORROW-BRADLEY, C., & ELLIOTT, R. (1986). Utilization of psychotherapy research by practicing psychotherapists. *American Psychologist, 41,* 188–197.

*MURRAY, E. J. (1986). Possibilities and promises of eclecticism. In J. C. Norcross (Ed.), *Handbook of eclectic psychotherapy* (pp. 398–415). New York: Brunner/Mazel.

*NORCROSS, J. C. (1986a). Eclectic psychotherapy: An introduction and overview. In J. C. Norcross (Ed.), *Handbook of eclectic psychotherapy* (pp. 3–24). New York: Brunner/Mazel.

*NORCROSS, J. C. (Ed.). (1986b). *Handbook of eclectic psychotherapy.* New York: Brunner/Mazel.

*NORCROSS, J. C. (Ed.). (1987). *Casebook of eclectic psychotherapy.* New York: Brunner/Mazel.

*NORCROSS, J. C., & PROCHASKA, J. O. (1988). A study of eclectic (and integrative) views revisited. *Professional Psychology: Research and Practice, 19,* 170–174.

*PATTERSON, C. H. (1986). *Theories of counseling and psychotherapy* (4th ed.). New York: Harper & Row.

PAUL, G. L. (1967). Outcome research in psychotherapy. *Journal of Consulting Psychology, 31,* 109–188.

PECK, M. S. (1978). *The road less traveled: A new psychology of love, traditional values and spiritual growth.* New York: Simon & Schuster (Touchstone).

*PROCHASKA, J. O., & DICLEMENTE, C. C. (1986). The transtheoretical approach. In J. C. Norcross (Ed.), *Handbook of eclectic psychotherapy* (pp. 163–200). New York: Brunner/Mazel.

*ROBERTSON, M. H. (1986). Training eclectic psychotherapists. In J. C. Norcross (Ed.), *Handbook of eclectic psychotherapy* (pp. 416–435). New York: Brunner/Mazel.

RYCHLAK, J. F. (1985). Eclecticism in psychological theorizing: Good and bad. *Journal of Counseling and Development, 63,* 351–353.

*SMITH, D. (1982). Trends in counseling and psychotherapy. *American Psychologist, 37,* 802–809.

STANLEY, B., SIEBER, J. E., & MELTON, G. B. (1987). Empirical studies of ethical issues in research. *American Psychologist, 42,* 735–741.

STILES, W. B., SHAPIRO, D. A., & ELLIOTT, R. (1986). Are all psychotherapies equivalent? *American Psychologist, 41,* 165–180.

STRUPP, H. H. (1986). Psychotherapy: Research, practice, and public policy (How to avoid dead ends). *American Psychologist, 41,* 120–130.

STRUPP, H. H., HADLEY, S. W., & GOMES-SCHWARTZ, B. (1977). *Psychotherapy for better or worse: The problem of negative effects.* New York: Aronson.

SUE, D. W. (1981). *Counseling the culturally different: Theory and practice.* New York: Wiley.

TORREY, E. F. (1974). *The death of psychiatry.* Radnor, PA: Chilton.

VANDENBOS, G. R. (1986). Psychotherapy research: A special issue. *American Psychologist, 41,* 111–112.

*YOUNG, M. E., FELLER, F., & WITMER, J. M. (1989). *Eclecticism: New foundation for recasting the counseling profession.* Unpublished manuscript available from Mark Young, Graduate Programs in Counseling and Therapy, Stetson University, P.O. Box 8365, DeLand, FL 32720.

ZOOK, A., II, & WALTON, J. M. (1989). Theoretical orientations and work settings of clinical and counseling psychologists: A current perspective. *Professional Psychology: Research and Practice, 20,* 23–31.

NAME INDEX

SUBJECT INDEX

PHOTO CREDITS

This page constitutes an extension of the copyright page.

To the owner of this book:

I hope that you have enjoyed *Theory and Practice of Counseling and Psychotherapy*, Fourth Edition. I would like to know as much about your experiences with this book as possible. Only through your comments and those of others can I learn how to improve it for future readers.

School _____ Instructor's name _____

1. What I like *most* about this book is _____

_____

_____

2. What I like *least* about this book is _____

_____

_____

3. My specific suggestions for improving the book are _____

_____

_____

4. Did your instructor require or recommend that you use the manual that accompanies this textbook or *Case Approach to Counseling and Psychotherapy?*

_____

5. My general reaction to this book is _____

_____

_____

6. In what course did you use this book? _____

_____

7. In the space below or in a separate letter, please let me know what other comments about the book you would like to make. I welcome your suggestions!

Your name: _____ Date: _____

May Brooks/Cole quote you, either in promotion for *Theory and Practice of Counseling and Psychotherapy* or in future publishing ventures?

Yes: _____ No: _____

Sincerely,

Gerald Corey